Stalin and the Struggle for Supr

This is a major new study of the successor states that emerged in the wake of the collapse of the great Russian, Habsburg, Iranian, Ottoman and Qing empires and of the expansionist powers who renewed their struggle over the Eurasian borderlands through to the end of the Second World War. Surveying the great power rivalry between the Soviet Union, Nazi Germany and Imperial Japan for control over the Western and Far Eastern boundaries of Eurasia, Alfred J. Rieber provides a new framework for understanding the evolution of Soviet policy from the Revolution through to the beginning of the Cold War. Paying particular attention to the Soviet Union, the book charts how these powers adopted similar methods to the old ruling elites to expand and consolidate their conquests, ranging from colonization and deportation to forced assimilation, but applied them with a force that far surpassed the practices of their imperial predecessors.

ALFRED J. RIEBER is University Professor Emeritus at the Central European University, Budapest, and Professor Emeritus at the University of Pennsylvania.

Stalin and the Struggle for Supremacy in Eurasia

Alfred J. Rieber

 CAMBRIDGE
UNIVERSITY PRESS

CAMBRIDGE
UNIVERSITY PRESS

University Printing House, Cambridge CB2 8BS, United Kingdom

Cambridge University Press is part of the University of Cambridge.

It furthers the University's mission by disseminating knowledge in the pursuit of education, learning and research at the highest international levels of excellence.

www.cambridge.org
Information on this title: www.cambridge.org/9781107426443

First published 2015

Printed in the United States of America by Sheridan Books, Inc.

A catalogue record for this publication is available from the British Library

Library of Congress Cataloguing in Publication data
Rieber, Alfred J.
Stalin and the Struggle for Supremacy in Eurasia / Alfred J. Rieber (Central European University, Budapest, Hungary).
    pages   cm
Includes index.
ISBN 978-1-107-07449-1 (hardback) – ISBN 978-1-107-42644-3 (paperback)
1. Soviet Union – Foreign relations – Eurasia.   2. Eurasia – Foreign relations –
Soviet Union.   3. Borderlands – Eurasia – History.   4. Borderlands – Soviet
Union – History.   5. Stalin, Joseph, 1879–1953 – Political and social views.
6. Soviet Union – Politics and government – 1936–1953.   7. Hegemony – Soviet
Union – History.   8. Nation-building – Soviet Union – History.   I. Rieber, Alfred
J. Struggle for the Eurasian borderlands.   II. Title.
DS33.4.S65R43   2015
327.470509′041 – dc23   2015012672

ISBN 978-1-107-07449-1 Hardback
ISBN 978-1-107-42644-3 Paperback

To Marsha – Encore

Contents

List of maps		*page* viii
Acknowledgments		ix
List of abbreviations		xi
	Introduction	1
1	Stalin, man of the borderlands	9
2	Borderlands in Civil War and Intervention	43
3	The borderland thesis: the west	90
4	The borderland thesis: the east	126
5	Stalin in command	152
6	Borderlands on the eve	200
7	Civil wars in the borderlands	243
8	War aims: the outer perimeter	283
9	War aims: the inner perimeter	322
10	Friendly governments: the outer perimeter	356
	Conclusion: A transient hegemony	404
	Index	409

Maps

2.1 Russo-Japanese spheres, 1907–18   *page* 81
2.2 The Far Eastern Republic 1920–22 and the Kurile Islands   87
3.1 Poland, 1921–39   118
4.1 Xinjiang   142
4.2 Outer Mongolia and Tuva   147
5.1 Hungary, 1918–44   190
6.1 Poland, 1939–41, "The Fourth Partition"   203
6.2 Interwar Romania   216
6.3 Trans Caspian borderlands, 1917–40   219
6.4 Inner Asian borderlands, 1930s   228
9.1 Postwar Poland   343
9.2 Finland, 1940–44   353
10.1 Iran, 1941–6   382

Acknowledgments

The research for this book was supported by two Senior IREX Grants and several short-term grants in the 1990s and early years of the twenty-first century. A number of Russian scholars were of great assistance not only in pointing me in the right directions but also for engaging me in exchange of views. Most of all I am grateful to T. V. Volokitina, G. P. Murashko and A. F. Noskova of the Institut Slavianovedenie of the Russian Academy of Science. I appreciated, too, assistance from the staff of the former Archive of the All-Union Communist Party, renamed Rossiiskii tsentr khraneniia i izucheniia dokumentov noveishei istoriia (RTsKhIDNI), and subsequently again renamed Rossiiskii gosudarstvennyi arkhiv sotsial'no-politicheskoi istorii (RGASPI), which is the reference I have used. Additional archival material was made available to me in the Gosudarstvennyi arkhiv Rossiiskoi Federatsii (GARF). I was able to obtain more limited but still useful access to files in the Foreign Ministry archive, Arkhiv vneshnei politiki Rossiiskoi Federatsii. Ministerstvo Inostrannykh Del (AVP RF). As anyone who has worked in Russian archives knows, even in the best of times, the help of individual often anonymous archivists often makes the difference between frustration and fast, efficient service. I can only thank as a group those who displayed a thorough professionalism on my behalf.

For financial support during the period of writing this book, I am indebted to the National Council for Soviet and East European Research and the Central European University Foundation. Over the past decade, I was fortunate in being able to test my ideas in classes, colloquia and conferences at the Central European University where the diverse student body and faculty drawn from many countries of the former Soviet bloc provided a stimulating and challenging atmosphere. My doctoral students have been a particular source of inspiration; several of them have been cited in the present work.

Once more I am grateful to Michael Watson of Cambridge University Press for his faith in the book as a sequel to *The Struggle for the Eurasian*

Borderlands. Two anonymous reviewers for the Press helped me reshape and greatly improve the original draft.

Reflecting back on sixty years of immersion in the history of Russia, I realize more than ever the debt I owe to my teachers, Philip E. Mosely and Geroid T. Robinson at the Russian (now Harriman) Institute at Columbia, for setting an example of high standards of scholarship.

My thanks to Marsha Siefert for her always sound advice and valuable critical insights relating to the book and for her tolerance in living with the presence of Stalin's ghost for far too long. Beyond this, perhaps even she does not fully realize how our shared intellectual and emotional life has contributed in so many subtle ways to the way I think and write.

Abbreviations

AVP RF	Arkhiv Vneshnei Politiki Rossiiskoi Federatsii (Foreign Policy Archive of the Russian Federation)
DGFP	Documents on German Foreign Policy
DVP	Dokumenty Vneshnei politiki SSSR (Documents of the Foreign Policy of the USSR), Ministry of Foreign Affairs of the USSR
FRUS	Foreign Relations of the United States, US Department of State
GARF	Gosudarstvennyi Arkhiv Rossiiskoi Federatsii (State Archive of the Russian Federation)
RGASPI	Rossiiskii Gosudarstvennyi Arkhiv Sotsial'no-Politicheskoi Istorii (Russian State Archive of Social and Political History
USNA	United States National Archive, Department of State

Introduction

Conceived as a sequel to The *Struggle for the Eurasian Borderlands,* this book radically shifts the focus away from a comparison of the centuries-old competition among multicultural conquest empires for hegemony in Eurasia to the Soviet Union, the central player in the renewal of that contest in the first half of the twentieth century. Many of the issues remain the same, but the cast of characters has changed. The Soviet Union was heir to much of the territory of the Russian Empire and many of its problems, both foreign and domestic, flowed from that hard-won inheritance. But its response was radically different. Its new leaders were engaged in transforming its foreign policy as part of rebuilding a multinational state. From the outset they were obliged to enter into complex and often contradictory relations with a ring of smaller and weaker successor states, constituting the new borderlands, which had replaced the rival empires all along their frontiers. In many cases these borderland states were allies or clients of the major powers and perceived by the Soviet government as hostile or threatening.

In the first decade of Soviet rule, the leaders sought to fashion a foreign policy that privileged stability by establishing normal diplomatic relations within the postwar capitalist state system while nurturing the cause of socialist revolution. But darker clouds were already gathering. By the early 1930s, they were forced to confront a more direct and formidable challenge to their policy from the rising power of Nazi Germany and a militarist Japan. The imperialist designs of the two flank powers focused initially on exercising control over the successor states all along the Soviet frontiers, although their aspirations, at least in theory, like those of the Soviet Union, also extended beyond these territories. This book, then, is a study of how the Soviet leaders, primarily Stalin, who dominated policy-making during this period, sought to combine the twin processes of transforming the state and its relations with the external world within the context of a renewed struggle over the borderlands.

The Soviet state emerged from the wreckage of the Russian Empire much weakened and diminished. The war against the Central Powers, revolution and Civil War, and foreign intervention had stripped the old empire of its western borderlands. At one point in March 1918, the Treaty of Brest-Litovsk had reduced its territorial space in the west to its pre-Petrine borders, with the exception of St. Petersburg, renamed Petrograd and soon to become Leningrad. As one of the successor states of the Russian Empire, Soviet Russia had only partially recovered territories lost during the Civil War and Intervention. It had been forced to concede the loss of the former Kingdom of Poland, the Baltic Provinces (Estonia, Latvia and Lithuania), Bessarabia and the provinces of Kars and Ardahan in the Caucasus. In the Far East during the nadir of Soviet power during the Civil War, all the Inner Asian borderlands had fallen under virtual Japanese domination. Much of the Trans Caspian borderlands (Central Asia) had broken away and Russian influence in Iran and along the Afghan border was contested. The loss of Russian influence in the Chinese borderlands of Xinjiang, Mongolia and Manchuria and the creation, if only briefly, of an autonomous Far Eastern Republic in Eastern Siberia reversed two centuries of territorial expansion and political penetration.

Although the main rivals of the Russian Empire in the west and southwest, the German Kaiserreich, the Austro-Hungarian Empire and the Ottoman Empire, had also collapsed in defeat, the neighboring successor states of Soviet Russia in Eastern Europe, Poland and Romania, were hostile and supported by France, which sought to reconstitute its traditional policy of barrier states (*barrière de l'est*) in the new form of a *cordon sanitaire* against Bolshevism. Relations with the new Turkish Republic, heir to the Ottoman Empire, were exceptional. Diplomatic relations were established on the basis of dividing the Armenian borderland.

The Soviet Union had also recovered some of its influence in Trans Caspia, not only in the reconquest of the former colony of Turkestan and the khanates but also in restoring its influence in Iran where a treaty gave it the right to intervene if its perceived interests were threatened by a foreign power. In Inner Asia the major threat from Japan had receded, if only temporarily. A weak Chinese central government was, however, unable to restore its influence in its borderlands, with mixed results for Soviet influence. With Bolshevik assistance Outer Mongolia had secured its autonomy from China, while warlords in Xinjiang and Manchuria had wrested their autonomy from China by maneuvering among the Russians, Chinese and Japanese.

To survive at all, the Bolshevik leadership appeared to renounce for the time being their world revolutionary aspirations. After an initial internal debate and several abortive revolutions in Hungary, Germany and Bulgaria, they entered into negotiations to establish trade or diplomatic relations with their new neighbors and the major capitalist powers. But leaders of the outside world were not deceived; to them it was, as Kipling had put it earlier, "the truce of the bear." In fact, by 1921 the Bolshevik leaders had reached a crucial decision to domesticate their foreign policy. And they had begun to construct a state system on that basis. It was in theory, and to a degree in practice, a federal structure that allowed for expansion through the incorporation of new soviet republics. This was the state system that Stalin had done much with Lenin to construct. Over time, Stalin would gradually stand on its head Lenin's initial design of the relationship between the state and revolution; the revolution abroad would become increasingly dependent upon the strength of the Soviet Union rather than the success of socialism in Russia being dependent on the spread of revolution in the advanced capitalist West.

In constructing a new foreign policy, the leadership of the Soviet state and the Communist Party faced in more aggravated form a set of persistent factors with which their predecessors had grappled. What I have called persistent factors constitute a dynamic interplay among geography, demography and culture in the long-term process of state-building in Eurasia. These factors are not fixed or immutable. That is to say, they are not permanent. Rather, they evolve over time both in their separate and distinctive character and in their mutual interaction. Stated in another way, they evolve in the course of an evolutionary historical process, creating conditions that cannot easily be altered by the action of statesmen; even under great external pressures or internal upheavals they resist significant change. The existence of persistent factors sets limitations on the range of policy choices but does not determine a particular course of action. Different leaders will pursue different styles in conducting foreign policy, but they ignore only at their peril the restraints placed upon them by the persistent factors. Concrete examples will help to reduce this concept from the realm of abstraction to the arena of practical politics. But first, one more caveat. Because of their deep embeddedness in a country's history, they affect the formation of both domestic and foreign policy, so that the two aspects of statecraft cannot, and in this study will not, be separated.

In Russian and Soviet history four persistent factors have shaped the making of foreign policy together with implications for domestic policy. They are a multinational social structure; porous or permeable frontiers; cultural alienation; and relative economic backwardness.[1] Taken

---

[1] For the impact of persistent factors on imperial Russian foreign policy, see Alfred J. Rieber, "Persistent Factors in Russian Foreign Policy: An Interpretive Essay," in Hugh Ragsdale (ed.), *Imperial Russian Foreign Policy* (Washington and Cambridge: Woodrow

together they constitute a unique combination that distinguishes Russian and Soviet foreign policy from that of any other great power. Each requires a brief explanation. The multinational demography of the Soviet Union resembled to a large extent that of the Russian Empire, despite the loss of Finnish, Polish, Ukrainian, Moldovan and Armenian populations on the periphery. What made it so distinctive was first the number of nationalities, second the pattern of their concentration and dispersal, and third the lack of a clear-cut ethnographic line dividing the same national groups on either side of the Soviet frontier. Depending on how they were identified in the Soviet Union – and Stalin himself was inconsistent on this issue – there were between sixty and over a hundred nationalities representing all the world's great religions: Orthodox, Latin and Protestant Christianity, Islam, Judaism, Buddhism as well as numerous sectarians and animists. The peoples of the Soviet Union also spoke an enormous variety of languages, although Russian was the lingua franca of the ruling and local elites and the educated public. But the erratic imperial policies of assimilation had not eliminated strong regional identities where clusters of nationalities retained their distinctive cultural ethos and spoke their own languages in day-to-day exchanges. The nationalities were highly concentrated on the periphery of the state; but Russians and Ukrainians also had been widely dispersed throughout the country by a lengthy process of colonization over the centuries. As Stalin was quick to realize, the Russian settlers, mainly workers and minor officials, could form the iron framework around which a multinational state could be erected. But the problem remained, as it had persisted over time, of how to reconcile the dominant cultural and political position of the Russians with the aspirations of the nationalities for some form of cultural or political autonomy.

The Soviet Union had inherited the task from the Russian Empire of protecting and securing the longest and most turbulent frontier of any state in Eurasia. As a result of conquest, migration, colonization and resettlement over the previous several hundred years, the frontiers from the Baltic to the Sea of Japan had frequently shifted, becoming over time porous and permeable. These large-scale population movements

Wilson Center and Cambridge University Press, 1993), pp. 315–59. I have slightly altered some of the terminology. "Multicultural" has given way to "multinational" in order to reflect the evolution of ethnic groups into nationalities. "Cultural alienation" replaces "cultural marginality" which was criticized for implying inferiority: this had not been my intention. For the application of persistent factors to the Soviet period, see my essay, "How Persistent are Persistent Factors?" in Robert Legvold (ed.), *Russian Foreign Policy in the 21st Century and the Shadow of the Past* (New York: Columbia University Press, 2007), pp. 205–78.

contributed to creating borderlands on the peripheries of empires inhabited by very mixed and floating populations in which no one group held a majority; they were quite literally shatter zones. These shatter zones differed, for example, from mixed frontier societies in Western Europe by virtue of the large number of different religious and linguistic groups concentrated within them and the frequent shifts in the demographic equation.[2] Over long periods of time, these borderlands had been contested by competing imperial states, the Russian, Habsburg, Ottoman, Iranian and Chinese empires leaving a residue of competing historical claims. By contrast, similar territorial conflicts in Western Europe and elsewhere involved only two competing external powers and with few exceptions were limited to brief periods of time (e.g. Alsace actively only from 1870 to 1945).

The postwar settlement had drawn arbitrary lines of demarcation all along the Soviet frontiers, leaving the same nationalities facing one another across state boundaries. Many of these groups had participated in the Civil War and their loyalty remained doubtful in the eyes of the Bolshevik leaders. Stalin above all perceived the condition of divided nationalities as a two-edged sword: a potential threat of intervention and an opportunity for expansion. And he well knew the history of subversion and rebellion in the borderlands which he absorbed from the history of his native Georgia and which he had witnessed in 1905 and again during the Civil War. Finally, the existence of the mixed populations on the frontier also facilitated smuggling, illegal immigration and the penetration of ideas from abroad considered subversive by the Soviet government. Under Stalin measures were taken to intensify border surveillance and increase border guards. But porous frontiers also worked in reverse by allowing Soviet agents and propaganda to infiltrate the outer world. For Stalin the problem remained how to seal off the Soviet frontiers from external penetration, but also to transcend them through the medium of foreign Communist parties whose actions he sought to orchestrate from Moscow.

If the number, variety and location of the nationalities along the lengthy porous frontiers posed enormous questions of security, as they always had for the Russian Empire, then the cultural alienation of Russia from the rest of the world perceived by foreign observers and even some Russians

[2] Frontier societies in Western Europe were in the twentieth century almost everywhere bi-national; for example, German and French in Alsace-Lorraine; German and Danish in Schleswig; French and Italian in Savoy; Italian and Croatian in Istria; German and Polish in Silesia and Pomerania. In the Inner Asian borderlands the mix was generally between Chinese and Manchu or Chinese and Mongol, although in Xinjiang the frontier was complex enough to deserve the term "shatter zone."

delayed the entry of the Russian Empire into the European state system and its cultural world. Two centuries of Mongol rule, the acceptance of Christianity from Byzantium rather than Rome, and the sheer physical distance from the centers of European civilization have often been given as the reasons Russia did not participate, or only belatedly and partially, in the Renaissance, Reformation and early stages of the Scientific Revolution. From the time of Ivan IV (the Terrible) until Peter the Great Russia's rulers had tried unsuccessfully to gain European recognition as full-fledged members of the Christian Commonwealth. The conquest of the Muslim khanates of Kazan and Astrakhan and expansion into Siberia seemed to draw the Russians deeper into Asia, away from Europe. Throughout the sixteenth and seventeenth centuries Muscovy, as it was then known, was omitted from the registers of Christian states and the celebrated peace plans for Europe, like those of William Penn. Peter the Great and Catherine the Great expended great efforts to demonstrate that Russia, then a self-proclaimed empire, was part of Europe politically and culturally. But neither they nor their successors were successful in convincing large segments of European opinion, or even some of their own subjects like the slavophiles, who preferred to regard Russia as a distinct, indeed unique, entity. The long and unresolved debate among foreign observers and pre-revolutionary Russian intellectuals and officials, not to speak of Orthodox churchmen and religious sectarians, over whether the empire (or some part of it) belonged to Europe or not was revived and given a startling reverse spin under Bolshevik rule.

In 1917 it was the Bolsheviks who proclaimed their ideological separation from the rest of the world, but this time as a state and society building socialism – the most advanced form of European civilization. Stalin envisaged himself as a supreme modernizer, yet he could take pleasure from time to time in boasting that he was an Asiatic! Paradoxes of cultural identity multiplied. The early proclamations of world revolution were taken at face value by the rest of the world, including substantial elements of the old social democratic parties who split off to form Communist parties, and under the aegis of the Soviet Union to join the Third International or Comintern. How could the Bolsheviks reconcile their claims for both uniqueness and universality?

The persistent factor of economic backwardness proved the most difficult to tackle, as it had under the tsarist regime, because its resolution was deeply entangled in the nexus of foreign and domestic policy. To be sure definitions of economic backwardness depend upon the object of comparison, the standards of measurement and the perceptions of observers. In the case of Russia, the object of comparison was always "the West" and remained so in the Soviet Union. The standards of measurement were often subjective, but the advent of more accurate statistics in the late nineteenth century reenforced the impression that Russia still lagged behind the most industrialized countries in most categories. From the earliest period in its history the development of the economy was restricted by unfavorable climatic and geographic factors: short growing seasons, poor soil, extreme temperatures, a land-locked location, widely dispersed if abundant natural resources and the existence of a bonded, communally organized peasantry that was only beginning to undergo a transformation along the lines of individually owned landed proprietors when the revolution overtook the process. The expansion of the state in the eighteenth and nineteenth centuries eased some of these problems; the rich Black Earth region of Ukraine was annexed in the late eighteenth century, and colonization began by the end of the nineteenth century to populate most of the lands formerly occupied by nomads. But their exploitation was often hampered by the means employed to acquire them. Long and costly wars were necessary to conquer the Eurasian borderlands. These required the imposition of heavy burdens on the tax-paying population and the service nobility, raising the question of the extent to which Russia was a militarized state.

In the nineteenth century as the Industrial Revolution took hold in Western Europe, Russia fell further behind in military technology and railroad construction. It lost three out of four wars over the borderlands in the last century of the empire (the Crimean War, the Russo-Japanese War and the First World War, defeating only the Ottoman Empire in 1877–8). Russia's industrialization was slowed by the lack of investment capital, the social conservatism of its merchant class, an inadequate transportation system and the continued attachment of most of the peasantry to the land up to the 1880s. Economic backwardness never translated into dependency on the West as it did in other declining empires in the Middle East and Asia. But foreign loans, technology transfer and patterns of trade exposed Russia to pressure from abroad, and influenced the formation of its alliances. During the First World War Russia's needs for loans obliged the government to make concessions to foreigners that encroached upon its sovereignty.

The war and the Civil War led to massive population displacement and losses, de-urbanization and in the countryside a reversal of the process of individual landownership, leaving Bolshevik Russia relatively more backward in relationship to Western Europe than the tsarist government had been in the last decade of its existence. A key question shaping their foreign policy, as the Bolsheviks fully realized and debated, was whether to rely more heavily on developing commercial relations with the capitalist West, the acknowledged political antagonist, or to fall back on domestic resources. Stalin's decision was to come down on the side of greater autarchy. Surely one of his most important decisions, he carried it out under the shadow of war scares, which, genuine or not, linked industrialization to the requirements of foreign policy.

Persistent factors shape the contours of the problems. But individual policy-makers devise their own solutions. Stalin responded as a Marxist man of the borderlands. This book argues that Stalin's *Weltanschauung* was shaped by two powerful existential and intellectual influences. The first was his early life experiences growing up in the Georgian cultural milieu precariously surviving under the pressure of russification within the shatter zone of the South Caucasus. The second was his evolution as a professional Marxist revolutionary also shaped by the socioeconomic peculiarities of an underdeveloped borderland. Both these elements must be considered in seeking to come to terms with the much disputed problem of the role of ideology in Stalin's policy-making. In addressing the interconnected problems of state-building and foreign policy, he forged a tripartite ideology incorporating his perception of the nationalities problem in the borderlands, his endorsement of Russian political hegemony in the Soviet Union and his interpretation of revolutionary Marxism. He was not always consistent in balancing these elements. His synthesis may have lacked philosophical sophistication. But he was both flexible and uncompromising in manipulating it to reach the pinnacle of power in the party, state and international Communist movement. This interpretation would be incomplete, however, without injecting into the analysis a strong dose of Stalin's arbitrary, violent and ruthless personality traits. His actions threatened at times to undermine the edifice he was striving to construct; he was responsible for the death of millions, including not only of those who stood in his way but also those who sought to participate in the same endeavors.

1   Stalin, man of the borderlands

Soviet policy toward the borderlands was largely the work of Lenin and Stalin. But it was Stalin, a product of that milieu, who completed the structure in his own image.[1] He was raised, educated and initiated as a Marxist revolutionary in the South Caucasus, a borderland of the Russian Empire.[2] At the time of his birth in 1878, the region had become a crossroads, intersecting the movement of people and ideas from Western Europe, Russia and Trans Caspia. In his youth Iosif or "Soso" Dzhugashvili filtered elements of all these currents into a revolutionary ideology of his own making and tested it in its unique kaleidoscopic social and ethnic setting.

In his youth, the circulation of European and Russian books in translation, students from imperial universities to the region and the migrations of seasonal workers from Iran helped to spread radical political ideas among the small Armenian, Georgian and later Azerbaizhan intelligentsia. The economic life of the region was also undergoing significant changes. Burgeoning pockets of industrialization formed around the oil industry in Baku, textiles and leather manufacturing in Tiflis (Tbilisi) and Batumi, and mining in Kutais. A small proletariat was emerging in a multicultural environment. Dzhugashvili's first experiences as a revolutionary agitator were played out in three of these cities: Baku, Tiflis and Batumi where he encountered the complexities of class and ethnic strife. Already as a seminary student in Tiflis, the young Soso, like many of his contemporaries, identified himself with several strands of this borderland

---

[1] An argument can be made that Lenin too was a man of the borderlands, having been born of mixed ethnic background, raised in the old frontier town of Simbirsk and educated at Kazan University where Tatar, Chuvash and Russian cultures intermixed. Cf. Robert Service, *Lenin: A Biography* (London: Macmillan, 2000), pp. 16–18, 28–9, 67.

[2] Born under the name Iosif Vissarionovich Dzhugashvili, he was called by the diminutive Soso well into manhood. His most famous pseudonym was "Koba," a youthful nickname taken from the bandit hero of a Georgian novel and still used by his comrades in the 1930s. He only adopted the name Stalin in 1912 when writing his first article for *Pravda*. For the complex process of his naming, see Alfred J. Rieber, "Stalin: Man of the Borderlands," *American Historical Review* 5 (December, 2001), pp. 1677–83.

culture. Woven together, they helped to shape his beliefs, attitudes and politics. In the process he constructed an identity that combined native Georgian, borrowed Russian and invented proletarian components.

While many of his contemporaries in the revolutionary movement forged their careers and spent their lives in the South Caucasus, Stalin, as he began to call himself in 1912, projected himself onto the all-Russian stage, bringing with him as he rose to power trusted comrades from his early days as a labor organizer and propagandist. Along the way he propagandized a vision of the state that mirrored his presentation of self as a representative of three interlocking identifications: an ethno-cultural region (Georgia) as a territorial unit, Great Russia as the center of political power, and the proletariat as the dominant class.[3] Out of this amalgam he fashioned a foreign as well as a domestic policy which, once in power, he continued to test by trial and error in the great contest against the burgeoning threat of Nazi Germany and Imperial Japan, the flank powers that challenged Soviet interests in the Eurasian borderlands.

As a revolutionary and statesman, Stalin embodied a particular historical type of man of the borderlands. Unlike a Napoleon or a Hitler, also born into the peripheral cultures of great national powers, he did not attempt to efface all traces of his cultural origins or even to identify himself wholly with his adopted land, at least until quite late in his career. Even then the character traits shaped in part by the dominant culture of his formative period remained embedded in his mental universe. His attitudes toward relations between the Great Russian center and the nationalities of the periphery and between the Soviet state and the outside world reveal a set of deep and unresolved ambiguities. Georgian culture was not only the source of his mother tongue but also of images, reference points and patterns of behavior that marked his public as well as his private life. Yet he could be harsh in his criticism of the backwardness, provincialism and arrogance of the Georgians.[4]

Russia was his second, adopted culture, not only for the spare, functional usage of its language, but for its rich literary heritage. It was also the transmitter of conspiratorial, revolutionary Marxism that appealed to his lower-class origins, his intellectual pretensions, and, in its "hard" Leninist form, his authoritarian personality. Russia became for him the locus and fulcrum of power. Still, the attraction of full assimilation had its

---

[3] *Ibid.*, pp. 1651–91. Cf. Erik van Ree, "The Stalinist Self: The Case of Ioseb Jugashvili (1898–1907)," *Kritika* 11:2 (2010), pp. 257–82.

[4] Svetlana Allilueva, *Dvadtsat' pisem k drugu* (New York: Harper and Row, 1967), pp. 56–7. Cf. Robert C. Tucker, *Stalin as Revolutionary, 1879–1929: A Study in History and Personality* (New York: Norton, 1973), pp. 432–3, who interprets this evidence to conclude that Stalin had substituted a Great Russian for a Georgian identity.

limits. Russia had shielded Christian Georgia from the depredations of the Muslim Ottomans and the Iranians and permitted its cultural revival. Yet by the end of the nineteenth century tsarist policies of russification had antagonized Georgian intellectuals and students, including the young Soso Dzhugashvili. In his early years "Great Russian chauvinism" was not just a polemical phrase in Stalin's political vocabulary. Of the three worlds that shaped Stalin's political personality – Georgia, Marxism and Russia – the culture of the borderlands has been underestimated in the formation of his mature world view.

Unlike any of the other top Bolshevik leaders, Dzhugashvili grew up in a non-Russian cultural milieu and lived there for most of the first thirty years of his life, except for brief periods in exile mainly in Siberia – a different kind of periphery. Until late in 1907 the young Dzhugashvili/Stalin was still writing all his major articles and pamphlets in Georgian. The first volume of his collected works dating from 1901 includes twenty items in Georgian and only six in Russian, four of which were collective editorials in Russian-language periodicals and two very brief reports at the Stockholm Congress in 1906. He continued to write in Georgian until he moved his activities to Baku where, of course, his audience changed as well, and he began to publish in Russian.[5] For the following three years he published his articles only in the local press, in journals like *Bakinskii Proletariat* and *Gudok* ("The Whistle"). His first publication outside the South Caucasus came in February 1910 when his "Letter from the Caucasus" appeared in the Bolshevik organ *Sotsial Demokrat*. Two years elapsed before he contributed another piece for an all-Russian audience, in the form of a pamphlet "For the Party" written in Russian and circulated by the Bolshevik Central Committee throughout Russia. Shortly afterwards, he began to write regularly for the central Bolshevik organs in St. Petersburg.[6] This marked the end of his active participation in the provincial press of the South Caucasus but not his abiding interest in the region.

During the years before the revolution of 1917, Stalin participated in all-Russian politics from afar, as a provincial. To be sure he joined in the crucial debate between Mensheviks and Bolsheviks, but from a regional perspective. Moreover, he had little personal knowledge of Russia. It has frequently been noted that Dzhugashvili only briefly visited Europe three times in the period before the revolution. What is less frequently stressed is how little time he spent in Russia, at least as a free man. He spent

---

[5] I. V. Stalin, *Sochineniia*, 13 vols. (Moscow: Gospolitiizdat, 1946–52) vol. I, pp. 10–37; vol. II, pp. 1–40, 408.
[6] *Ibid.*, vol. II, pp. 416–20.

two years in Siberian exile from 1902 to 1904; six months in 1908–9 in various prisons and exile in North Russia; then a year from the fall of 1910 to the fall 1911 in prison and exile in North Russia; several months in prison in St. Petersburg after being at large for two days in the city followed by two months in exile in the north; a few days in Moscow and St. Petersburg in April 1912 were again followed by exile for a month in Siberia and an escape to St. Petersburg where he spent a year, his longest consecutive period of residence in Russia until he left for Krakow and Vienna in December 1912; and finally four years in Siberian exile beginning early in 1913 and ending with the outbreak of the February revolution. All in all, until Stalin was thirty-eight years of age he spent no more than a year and a few months in Russia at liberty: that is, outside prison and exile in the remote parts of the north and Siberia.[7]

The other future Bolshevik leaders had their primary identification with Russian language and culture and secondarily with other European languages. Those among the most prominent leaders whose ethnic origins were not Russian but Jewish, Ukrainian or Polish, were almost without exception wholly russified and internationalist in outlook. To be sure there was a large number of Bolsheviks at the secondary level who felt strong attachments to their ethnic origins, particularly Georgians, Armenians and Tatars. But their participation in Soviet politics was largely limited to the nationalities question narrowly defined. None played a leading role in the formation of foreign policy either in the Narkomindel or the Comintern, to say nothing of the Politburo. This unique dimension of Stalin's political personality explains why, for him alone among the Bolshevik leaders, the center–periphery relationship was the foundation for building the new multinational state and defending it against the outside world.

South Caucasus as a frontier

There were four features of the South Caucasus frontier society that played a significant role in shaping Dzhugashvili's sense of himself which he incorporated into his political thinking. Elements of all four may be found in other borderlands of the Russian Empire but not in the same form or interactive combination. They were: (1) kaleidoscopic patterns of population settlement and displacement constituting a cluster of "shatter zones" where numerous ethno-religious groups intermingled within changing administrative and political boundaries; (2) lengthy

---

[7] Tucker, *Stalin as Revolutionary*, remains the best guide to his years in exile.

traditions of rebellion, conspiracies and protest movements by the indigenous population against foreign and domestic enemies, combining social, ethno-religious and later nationalist components; (3) multiple channels of external cultural and intellectual currents that permeated the region and interacted with local cultures; and (4) complex interactions among craftsmen, workers, peasants and intelligentsia of different ethnic groups, some still rooted in highly traditional societies, who were entering revolutionary movements during a period of rapid industrial growth.

Of the thirteen administrative units comprising the South Caucasus *krai* at the end of the century, Tiflis Province where Dzhugashvili was born and educated contained the largest concentration of Georgians. In 1886, when he was seven years old, they officially numbered 366,041 but even the designation "Georgian" was open to question. While it was used in common parlance by Russians and others in the region, the Georgians called themselves Kartveli. This term derived from a family of languages that included peoples who were officially designated by other names such as *Mingreltsy* (Mingrelians), *Svanety* (Svanetians), *Adzhartsy* and others. Most of these peoples lived in the neighboring Kutais Province. The Georgian total could be increased by 20,000 in Tiflis if the smaller groups of Kartveli speakers (*Tushini, Pshavi* and *Khevsury*) are included. But even with this addition the Georgians did not constitute a majority or even a plurality in Tiflis Province. They were heavily outnumbered by Tatars (683,415), which was itself an imprecise ethnic term employed by officials until the early 1890s and used afterwards in popular speech to designate all Muslims. Although the Armenian population was only 193,610 they outnumbered the Georgians in the provincial capital of Tiflis.[8]

The second feature of the frontier society was a history of resistance and rebellion against foreign domination. After Russia's annexation of Georgia in 1801, integration had not proceeded smoothly. The Georgian nobility, similar to the Polish *szlachta*, demonstrated it had not renounced its tradition of resistance to foreign control. Up until 1845 when Prince M. S. Vorontsov became viceroy of the Caucasus, part of the Georgian nobility was highly disaffected. They participated in four rebellions and a major conspiracy in 1832 that resembled the Decembrist uprising. At the same time, beginning in 1804, there was a series of uprisings by mountain peoples and peasants which peaked on the eve and the morrow of the

[8] Prince V. I. Masal'skii, "Kavkazskii krai," in F. A. Brokgaus and I. A. Efron (eds.), *Entsiklopedicheskii Slovar'* (St. Petersburg: I. A. Efron, 1894), vol. XXVI, pp. 836–7; these statistics were compiled before the 1897 census; Vsevolod Miller, "Kavkazskie iazyki," *ibid.*, p. 814; D. Anuchin, "Rossiia v etnograficheskom otnoshenii," *ibid.* (1899), vol. LIV, p. 144.

emancipation of the serfs and broke out again in the 1870s. In 1865 an urban riot ripped through Tiflis. Political (that is, anti-Russian) and economic grievances were often mixed, a portent of things to come at the end of the nineteenth and beginning of the twentieth century.[9] The spirit of resistance was a major theme in Georgian folklore and the romantic revival in literature in the mid-nineteenth century that so deeply affected the young Soso Dzhugashvili.

The cult of violence in the South Caucasus permeated the whole range of social relations from the traditional tribal societies to urban youth. At one extreme, the masculine code of the warrior and the blood feud prevailed within the tribal regions to the north of Georgia.[10] At the other extreme, the incidents of urban and rural violence during the revolution of 1905 and its aftermath were more numerous in the Caucasus than elsewhere in the empire. During the revolution of 1905–7, according to a recent estimate, 3,611 high-ranking officials and government employees were killed by terrorists and 9,000 wounded. After January 1, 1907, according to official figures of the Ministry of the Interior, 3,060 terrorist acts were carried out in the province of Tiflis alone. Over half of these were bank robberies and holdups. The total number of casualties reported was 1,732 dead and 1,253 wounded.[11] Dzhugashvili participated in these exploits, although even now the details are obscure and contested.

The Georgian national revival was shaped in large measure by the peculiar class structure of the Georgians, which was a product of Russian administrative policies, patterns of settlement and the uneven distribution of industry. According to the census of 1897, the Georgian population was stratified along radically different lines than the other three major regional ethnic groups – Russian, Armenian and Azerbaizhani (Tatar).

---

[9] For the rebellions and conspiracies, see Stephen F. Jones, "Russian Imperial Administration and the Georgian Nobility: The Georgian Conspiracy," *Slavonic and East European Review* 65:1 (1987), pp. 53–76; Ronald Grigor Suny, *The Making of the Georgian Nation*, 2nd edn (Bloomington: Indiana University Press, 1994), pp. 71–2, 82–5, 119–20, 166–7; and I. G. Antelava, "Obostrenie klassovoi bor'by, razvitie i rasprostranenie antikrepostnicheskoi ideologii nakanune otmeni krepostnogo prava," in M. D. Lordkhipanidze and D. L. Mushelishvili (eds.), *Ocherki istorii Gruzii v vosmi tomakh* (Tbilisi: Met's'niereba, 1988–90), vol. V, pp. 170–83, 217–24.

[10] M. O. Kosven *et al.* (eds.), *Narody Kavkaza* (Moscow: Akademiia nauk SSSR, 1960), vol. I, pp. 297–304; Sh. Inal-ipa, *Abkhazy, Istoriko-etnograficheskie ocherki* (Sukhumi: Alashara, 1960), pp. 276–8; I. L. Babich, *Pravovaia kultura Adygov (Istoriia i sovremennost')*, avtoreferat (dissertation abstract) (Moscow, 2000), pp. 13–14, note 21. I am grateful to the author for bringing this source to my attention.

[11] Anna Geifman, *Thou Shalt Not Kill: Revolutionary Terrorism in Russia 1894–1917* (Princeton University Press, 1995), pp. 34–5. The majority of assassinations were carried out by the Armenian Dashnaktsutiun Party, while the Marxists planned most of the expropriations.

For one thing it was more highly polarized between nobles and clergy at one end and peasants at the other. The Georgian "big bourgeoisie" was less than half the size of the Russian or the Armenian, though more than double that of the Azerbaizhani bourgeoisie. The other Georgian urban groups, which included workers, were smaller than the Armenian and Azerbaizhani by a factor of two and a half to three and by a factor of seven in the case of Russians.[12] Moreover, the Georgian nobility was deeply split. A small number of large landowning families who had entered Russian civil and military service, accepted an imperial role and held aloof from the majority whose strong opposition to pressure from St. Petersburg to emancipate their serfs was for many the first step on the road to political resistance.

The growth of a Georgian national opposition to Russian rule was a multilayered process which may be broken down into four constituent elements.[13] First, most of the early nationalists drawn from the nobility were ambivalent in their attitude toward Russia and the Russians who were both their liberators and protectors from the Muslim Turks and Iranians but also their oppressors as representatives of the hegemonic colonial power. Later in the 1870s and 80s, a variation of this ambivalent stance cropped up among Georgian revolutionaries, mainly non-nobles who were inspired by Russian populism. They sought to join the national liberation of Georgia with the social liberation of the peasantry. Second, the Georgian nationalists confronted not one but a number of "others" in their construction of a national identity. Besides the Russians and the local Muslim population there were above all the Armenians, who began rapidly to replace the Georgians as the dominant economic and political group in the Georgians' ancient capital of Tiflis.

---

[12] Adapted from Bakshi Ishkhanian, *Narodnosti Kavkaza. Sostav naseleniia, professional'naia gruppirovka i obshchestvennoe razsloenie narodnostei, statistichesko-ekonomicheskoe izsledovanie* (Petrograd: Popov, 1916), p. 103.

Nationality	Nobles	Clergy	Merchants	Urban dwellers	Peasants
Russian	54,000	11,000	12,000	358,000	1,735,000
Armenian	14,000	12,000	12,000	123,000	878,000
Georgian	85,000	29,000	5,000	48,000	1,180,000
Azeri	49,000	700	1,700	139,000	1,512,000

Figures rounded off to nearest thousand. Nobles include hereditary and personal; merchants include honorary citizens; urban dwellers include petty bourgeoisie and workers.

[13] The best guides to the complexities of the process are Suny, *The Making of the Georgian Nation*, ch. 6, and Stephen F. Jones, *Socialism in Georgian Colors: The European Road to Social Democracy, 1883–1917* (Cambridge University Press, 2005).

Third, when Marxism began to penetrate the South Caucasus there was a strong tendency among the new brand of revolutionaries to replicate the earlier pattern of linking ethnic identity with class consciousness. Marxist groups and parties formed along national or federalist socialist lines. That is to say, they attempted to combine the nationalist radicalism of the disenchanted nobles with the social radicalism of the workers and peasantry. This tendency was on the rise even before the revolution of 1905, but the intense communal strife that broke out in the Caucasus during the revolution intensified the process. The national-socialist orientation became the hallmark of the three leading revolutionary parties in the region: the Georgian Mensheviks, the Armenian Revolutionary Federation (Dashnaktsutiun) and the Himmat (Endeavor) Party of the Muslim Tatars (Azerbaizhani). It was precisely against this nationalistic characteristic of the Caucasian revolutionary movements that the mature Stalin reacted most forcibly.

During the second half of the nineteenth century, life in the countryside in South Caucasus took a different course than in the rest of the empire due in large part to the peculiar modalities of the peasant emancipation and the growth of specialized crafts and manufacturing industries. Agrarian reform in the three provinces inhabited by Azerbaizhani brought little change into the traditional life of either the peasants, mainly settled on state lands, or the landowning beys and agas, most of whom lived at the level of their peasant neighbors.[14] While the countryside remained relatively stable, the big cities, particularly Baku, with its burgeoning oil industry, became centers of a large-scale in-migration by Russians from the north and seasonal workers from the Iranian province of Azerbaizhan across the frontier to the southeast.[15]

In Georgia the emancipation had a highly disruptive effect on the social structure and economic activities of both the nobility and the peasantry.[16] The nobles were forced to sell off most of their properties in the decades

[14] Ts. P. Agaian, *Krest'ianskaia reforma v Azerbaizhane v 1870 godu* (Baku: Akademiia nauk Azerbaizhanskoi SSR, 1956), and A. S. Sumbatzade, *Sel'skoe khozaistvo Azerbaizhana v XIX veke* (Baku: Akademiia nauk Azerbaizhanskoi SSR, 1958), pp. 151–4.

[15] On Iranian migration, see Audrey Alstadt, "Muslim Workers and the Labor Movement in Pre-War Baku," in S. M. Akural, *Turkic Culture: Continuity and Change* (Bloomington: Indiana University Press, 1987), pp. 83–91, and Cosroe Chaqueri, *The Soviet Socialist Republic of Iran, 1920–21: The Birth of the Trauma* (Pittsburgh University Press, 1994), pp. 24–6.

[16] The standard work on the emancipation is S. L. Avaliani, *Krest'ianskii vopros v Zakavkaz'e*, 2 vols. (Odessa: Avaliani Publ., 1912–14). But see also P. A. Zaionchkovskii, *Otmena krepostnogo prava v Rossii*, 2nd edn (Moscow: Moskovskoe uchebno-pedagicheskoe obshchestvo, 1960), and the lucid summary in Suny, *The Making of the Georgian Nation*, ch. 5.

following emancipation and then were often blocked from finding alternative careers in the bureaucracy or commercial enterprises by Russian and Armenian competitors who had been long entrenched in these positions. The revival of russification policies by the tsarist authorities in the 1880s added insult to injury. Already emotionally stirred by the Georgian romantic revival of mid-century, a number of the young déclassé nobles were increasingly vulnerable to revolutionary doctrines that combined national opposition to Russia with socialist opposition to capitalism. For reasons once again peculiar to Georgia they found their main mass support not from the small Georgian working class but from the peasantry.

The disaffection of the peasantry in Georgia heavily depended on local conditions. Nowhere was peasant resistance more pronounced than in Western Georgia, in particular the former Kingdom of Guria, renamed in 1840 the Ozurgeti district of Kutaisi Province.[17] By the turn of the twentieth century, the district contained all the ingredients of an explosive social situation: a mass of small landholding peasants under severe economic pressures from changing market conditions but relatively well educated and aware of external events; a tradition of peasant revolts by a culturally homogeneous population; and potential political leaders drawn from a group of youthful social democrats belonging to a European educated, déclassé local nobility and including many of the future leaders of Georgian Menshevism and the independent Georgian Democratic Republic: Noe Zhordania, Sylvester Jibladze, Noe Khomeriki, Isidor Ramishvili. The result was what S. F. Jones has called the prototype of "the peasant based national-liberationist movements" of the twentieth century.[18] As such it represented for Stalin all he despised and sought to destroy during his subsequent political career. Throughout his life, he carried with him the conviction, or suspicion, that any revolutionary movement based upon the peasantry, no matter how loudly it proclaimed its loyalty to international communism, that is to the Soviet Union (such as Tito's Yugoslavia and Mao's China), was fundamentally unreliable and vulnerable to the temptations of national communism.[19] The reasons for this were deeply embedded in his early exposure to the complexities of political protest in Georgia.

[17] The following is based on S. F. Jones, "Marxism and Peasant Revolt in the Russian Empire: The Case of the Gurian Republic," *Slavic and East European Review* 67:3 (1989), pp. 403–34.
[18] *Ibid.*, p. 434.
[19] This is not to deny that Stalin accepted Lenin's view of the poor and middle peasantry as allies in the struggle against tsarism or to ignore Soso's youthful flirtation with Populism in his student years in Georgia. Alfred J. Rieber, "Stalin as Georgian: The Formative Years," in Sarah Davies and James Harris (eds.), *Stalin: A New History* (Cambridge University Press, 2005), pp. 33–4.

The third characteristic of the South Caucasus as a frontier society was the multiple channels of communication that transferred ideas into the region and then exported them in altered form. In the second half of the nineteenth century, access to European thought increased, mainly through the Russian filter. The encounter and interaction with indigenous traditions produced a variety of cultural hybrids. Later, an influx of pan-Islamic and pan-Turkic ideas offered alternative forms of allegiance and identity to the Muslim population. The most powerful currents coming from Russia penetrated local ecclesiastical schools like the ones Stalin attended or else were conveyed into the region by small numbers of Georgian students who studied in imperial universities, mainly St. Petersburg. A second narrower channel led to institutions of higher learning in Central Europe (in the Kingdom of Poland) and then on to the larger field of Europe as a whole. Among those who imbibed their Marxism at the University of Warsaw were Noe Zhordania, subsequently the leader of the Georgian Mensheviks, and Pilipe Makharadze, a leading figure in the Georgian Bolshevik organization.

Dzhugashvili's Marxism came directly from Russia. The importation of Russian literature both in the original and in translation and Russian translations of European works of literature, history and politics fed these currents and left an indelible imprint on Stalin. In many cases Russian literary forms intermingled with the rich traditions of Georgian literature. Both enjoyed a heritage of Greco-Roman legends and their own versions of knightly tales and romantic heroism. Major Russian writers from Pushkin and Lermontov to Marlinskii and Tolstoy idealized aspects of Caucasian life, although they displayed an ambiguous attitude toward Georgians.[20] Thus, the resentment felt by so many Georgian nobles and intellectuals toward the administrative and bureaucratic insensitivities of Russian officials and clerics, shared by the young Soso Dzhugashvili, was mitigated by an admiration of Russian high culture.

Although Marxism found its way to the South Caucasus mainly through channels from Russia, the local social and economic conditions in Georgia shaped its contours in fundamental ways. Caucasian Marxists boldly confronted the question of overcoming ethnic difference in forging a revolutionary movement.[21] They adhered more closely than their Russian counterparts to a belief in the peasantry as a revolutionary force; the program of the Georgian Mensheviks in particular embraced this

---

[20] Cf. Susan Layton, "Eros and Empire in Russian Literature about Georgia," *Slavic Review* (Summer, 1992), pp. 195–213. See also Katya Hokanson, "Literary Imperialism, Narodnost' and Pushkin's Invention of the Caucasus," *Russian Review* 53:3 (1994), pp. 336–52.

[21] Sh. Davitashvili, *Narodnicheskoe dvizhenie v Gruzii* (Tbilisi: Federatsiia, 1933), p. 32.

view, compelling the Bolsheviks, Stalin among them, to compete with their rivals on this issue.[22] The social democratic appeal to the peasantry was one of the reasons why the Socialist Revolutionary Party never came close to gaining the support in the South Caucasus that it enjoyed in the Russian countryside. The early Georgian Marxists also took a different view of the role of the worker in the revolutionary movement than their counterparts in Central Russia by stressing the importance of spontaneity and the social equality of workers and intelligentsia in the movement, a position that created both problems and opportunities for Stalin.

Industrialization occurred in cities where widely divergent social groups, ranging from the tribal to the urbanized, rubbed shoulders with an equally variegated number of ethno-religious groups, further complicating ethnic relations and social identification. For Stalin the most important social consequences arose from the multicultural profile of the working class and the peculiar relationship of the working class to the intellectuals. In the South Caucasus, workers mixed easily with one another, especially where Russian was a lingua franca, whereas the nobles, merchants and clerics of different nationalities led separate lives. Consequently, social democracy in the Caucasus was from the outset a multicultural political movement unlike any other in the empire.[23] Relations between workers and intellectuals also exhibited regional nuances. The working class in Georgia, and to varying degrees throughout the borderlands, had grown from two major sources: the old craft structure and modern industry – oil, railroad construction and mining.[24] The influx of unskilled and semi-literate Azerbaizhani from the countryside and Iranian Azerbaizhan, raised formidable obstacles for labor organizers but offered an opportunity to men like Stalin who saw personal advantages in organizing politically unformed workers of low status.

In Georgia and elsewhere in the South Caucasus the older radicalism of the crafts (mainly Georgian) combined with the newer workers' (mainly Russian) consciousness to generate a strike movement that

---

[22] Jones, "Marxism and Peasant Revolt."

[23] G. A. Galoian, *Rossiia i narody Zakavkaz'e. Ocherki politicheskoi istorii ikh vzaimo otnoshenii s drevnikh vremen do pobedy Velikoi Oktiabr'skoi Sotsialistichskoi Revolutsii* (Moscow: Mysl', 1976), pp. 357–64; Ronald Grigor Suny, *Looking Toward Ararat: Armenia in Modern History* (Bloomington: Indiana University Press, 1993), pp. 90–2, 260.

[24] For the school of *remesleniki*, see Prince V. Masal'skii, "Tiflis," in *Entsiklopedicheskii Slovar'* (1901), vol. LXV, p. 268; for populist contacts with them Davitashvili, *Narodnicheskoe dvizhenie*, pp. 60–5, 79; for revolutionary populist influence on the earliest strike movements, E. V. Khoshtaria, *Ocherki sotsial'no-ekonomicheskoi istorii Gruzii: promyshlennost', goroda, rabochii klass (XIX–nachala XX v.)* (Tbilisi: Met's'nierba, 1974), pp. 204–8.

erupted simultaneously with that in St. Petersburg. It began in 1878 at the Zeitser Factory in Tiflis. After a pause of four years, a strike broke out at the Nobel plant in Batumi and in 1890 there was a major strike of railroad workers in Tiflis. A smaller work stoppage occurred at the Mantashev factory in Batumi in 1892. In a rising crescendo in 1894 and 1895 a series of large strikes of the workers in Tiflis tobacco factories attracted regional attention. According to participants, these strikes were all "spontaneous" without an organizational center or the guidance of a political party.[25] But this did not mean that all workers lacked a political consciousness.

In the 1870s and 80s in the main cities of the South Caucasus, Tiflis in particular, a social stratum of "worker–craftsmen" began to make contact with the young generation of populist intellectuals. Most of the craftsmen had attended the urban craft schools (*remeslennoe uchilishche*) where they had an opportunity to meet students from other institutions and to encounter the floating population of exiles and immigrants from Russia. The populist students from rural Georgia found them, rather than factory workers, to match their internalized image of "the toiler." The craftsmen produced their own writers like Iosif Davitashvili, the famous self-taught poet of the people. As early as the late 1870s, they formed their own mutual aid society in Tiflis, and in 1889 published an illegal handwritten journal which appeared for ten years under various names.[26] According to a report of a police agent in 1900, "there does not exist a single factory, plant or workshop that does not have its secret circles, the leaders of which are in constant contact with one another, and which gather in general meetings (*skhodki*)." According to the same report, the intelligentsia had not yet penetrated these circles but were taking "the first steps" to draw closer to them.[27] This was the setting for Dzhugashvili's debut as a conspiratorial agitator within the working class.

The rapid spread of Marxist ideas among the factory workers in Georgia was attributed by Pilipe Makharadze to the absence of any strong competition from other ideologies: "among us the Marxist orientation did not have to struggle with any other kind of tendency for hegemony

---

[25] F. Makharadze, *Ocherki revoliutsionnogo dvizheniia v Zakavkaz'e* (Tiflis: Gosizdat. Gruzii, 1927), pp. 47–51.

[26] *Ibid.*, pp. 62–3.

[27] The agent also noted that the formation of circles occurred "independently of nationality from Russians, Georgians and Armenians united by the general goals of the proletariat," TsGAOR, f. DPDD, op. 1898, ed. kh. 5, ch. 52, ll. 23–4, cited in G. A. Galoian, *Rabochee dvizhenie i natsional'nyi vopros v Zakavkaz'e, 1900–1922* (Erevan: Aistan, 1969), p. 11.

among the working class as took place in other countries," by which he meant trade unionism or economism inspired by a "bourgeois world view."[28] This was also true to a large extent in Russia as well. But in Georgia there was no "naive monarchism" among the workers and no experiments with police socialism that had disoriented the working class in Russia. With the decline of populism or rather its co-optation, Marxism had the ground all to itself.

Growing up in Gori

Dzhugashvili's home town of Gori was a microcosm of the South Caucasus frontier. To the north of Georgia stretched the tribal regions of the Abkhazians, Svanetians and Ossetians, societies still deeply rooted in a feudal–patriarchal way of life and closely related to the Georgians by family ties, a common language and customs. The southern boundary of the Ossetian settlements was a scant 30 kilometers from Gori, whereas Tiflis was 73 kilometers away.[29] Gori itself had a mixed population of Georgians, Armenians and Russians. The town was poised as it were between two very different worlds of the patriarchal, tribal and the urban, early industrial. The blending of cultures was also reflected in the social structure, architecture and urban grids of the three main cities – Tiflis, Batumi and Baku – that formed the triangle of Dzhugashvili's early revolutionary activity.[30] In each case contemporary accounts employ terms typical of the colonial discourse in describing the "European" and "Asian" sections of the cities.[31] Stalin bore the stigma of this discourse throughout

---

[28] F. Makharadze, *K tridtsatletniiu sushchestvovaniia Tifliskoi organizatsii. Podgotovlenyi period, 1870–1890: Materialy* (Tiflis: Sovetskii Kavkaz, 1925), p. 29.

[29] Many students from Ossetian schools came to study in Gori and Tiflis. M. M. Gapringashvili, "Gruzinskaia kul'tura v XIX v.," in N. Berdzenishvili *et al.* (eds.), *Istoriia Gruzii*, 5 vols. (Tbilisi: Gos-izd. Gruzinskoi SSR, 1946–54), vol. V, p. 548.

[30] Population statistics drawn from the census of 1897 give the following breakdown on the basis of language. Batumi: Georgian – 39.4 percent; Russians – 25 percent; Armenian – 21 percent; Greek – 9 percent; Turko-Tatar – 7.5 percent; with less than 1 percent of Jews, Poles, and Persians. Tsentral'nyi statisticheskii komitet Ministerstva vnutrennykh del, in *Pervaia vseobshchaia perepis' naseleniia Rossiiskoi imperii*, 79 vols. (St. Petersburg, 1903–5), vol. LXVI, pp. 146–9. Baku: Turko-Tatar – 36 percent; Russian – 34.8 percent; Armenian – 17 percent; Persian – 3 percent; German – 2.2 percent; Jews – 1 percent; Tatskii – 1 percent; Georgian – 0.09 percent. *Ibid.*, vol. LXI, pp. 154–5. Tiflis: Armenian – 38.1 percent; Georgian – 26.3 percent; Russian – 24.8 percent; Poles – 3.4 percent; Persians – 3.2 percent; Tatars – 1.7 percent; English, Germans and Swedes – 1.2 percent; Jews – 1.1 percent; a scattering of French, Italians, Lezginy, Ossetians and Greeks. *Ibid.*, vol. LXV, p. 267.

[31] See, for example, K. N. Bagilev, *Putevoditel' po Tiflisu* (Tiflis, 1896), pp. 26–9, and especially Vasilii Sidorov, *Po Rossii. Kavkaz. Putevye zametki i vpechatleniia* (St. Petersburg: M. Akinfiev and I. Leontiev, 1897), pp. 142–5, 163, 270, 274, 276, 595–6, 598, 605

his early career although on several occasions later on he sought to turn the epithet of "Asiatic" to his advantage.[32]

When Iosif Dzhugashvili was born, in either 1878 or 1879, Gori was by no means an insignificant or obscure town.[33] Its history reproduced in miniature the characteristics of the frontier society of which it was a part. Gori was first mentioned by Georgian chronicles in the seventh century as a location on the main caravan route of the South Caucasus. Like most inhabited places in Georgia, it suffered from many invasions and conquests, most notably by Timur in the fourteenth century, the Turks in the sixteenth century and the Iranians in the seventeenth century. But it also had its moment of glory as the capital of Kartelia before another Iranian conquest, by Nadir Shah in the eighteenth century and a period of harsh exploitation led to a revolt and the reestablishment of Georgian control under Irakli II. From that time until unification with Russia in 1801 it was a center of feudal conspiracies by local princes plotting against the Georgian kings.

History lingered on in the shape of the dominant man-made feature of the town, the fortress (*Goris-tsikhe*) with its thick and high crenellated walls and the legends attached to it. The fortress image subsequently occupied a prominent place in the mature Stalin's imagery. In the center of the court there was a large depression, possibly an ancient burial mound, and not far away a strangely shaped spherical yellow stone. Popular fantasy attributed to it a special meaning and linked it to the mythical figure of Amiran, the local Prometheus. It had been his sword which he hurled into the ground before he was chained to a cliff in the Caucasus. In a customary rite still practiced at the end of the nineteenth century, the local blacksmiths went to their workshops at midnight on Maundy Thursday and hammered their anvils as a sign that the chains binding Amiran still held him firmly. Otherwise the hero would break loose and avenge himself on those who had forged his bonds.[34] These and other

for vivid descriptions of the mixed Asiatic and European character of Tiflis, Baku and Batum. There were similar descriptions of Stalin's home town of Gori, *ibid.*, pp. 460–77, and in Al. Azhavakhov, "Gorod Gori," in *Sbornik materialov dlia opisaniia mestnosti i plemen Kavkaza* (Tiflis, 1883).

[32] See note 1.

[33] The exact date of Stalin's birth has long been disputed due to a confusion for which he is responsible. For the most recent analysis based on archival sources, see Miklos Kun, *Stalin: An Unknown Portrait* (Budapest: CEU Press, 2003), pp. 8–10.

[34] RGASPI, f. 71, op. 10, ed. kh. 273, l. 15 (based on contemporary sources). There were many local tales of Amiran as a liberator and other heroes who came from the people and "by strength or by guile" overcame their oppressors. *Ibid.*, l. 44. Another suggestive tradition associated with the fortress was the legend of the commander who in a time of danger gave refuge to the inhabitants of the quarter outside the walls, locked the gate himself and kept the key. To this day the inhabitants living in places visible from

tales of treachery, revenge and embattlement were the stuff of Soso's childhood.[35]

Gori Province had a reputation for being rebellious as well as a center of conspiracies. Throughout almost the entire nineteenth century, the peasantry, especially in the region of Ossetia, repeatedly rose against their landlords. The liberation of the serfs in 1864 did nothing to improve their lot. On the contrary, it reduced most of them to landless laborers or smallholders eking out a living on wretched parcels of land burdened with heavy taxes and exposed to the arbitrary violence of local officials.[36] On Sundays, they saddled their emaciated water buffaloes, loaded their carts with fruit, vegetables and cheese, and dragged their produce to the closed market sheds in Gori where they were often forced to sell for a pittance; or else they were cheated by sharp traders who took advantage of their desperate need for cash. Spontaneous peasant outbreaks increased after the liberation, although they remained localized and sporadic until the revolution of 1905.[37]

The peasants also suffered from the depredations of bandits, a persistent problem in the countryside. In the post-liberation period, the bandits began to come down from the mountains in the northern part of Gori Province and raided the big estates of Machabeli and Eristavi as well as peasant villages. The rural police offered little assistance, claiming the peasants "were bandits themselves and their accomplices."[38] Some bandits achieved brief notoriety, but their fame was overshadowed by popular avengers who hunted down bandits or protected villagers without extracting any payment from them.[39] The heroic and romantic tales that absorbed Georgian youth like Soso Dzhugashvili had their real equivalents in living memory. Subsequently, the role of the bandit became equivocal in Stalin's mind: as a revolutionary and "expropriator" he identified with it, but once in power he used it to stigmatize popular resistance to his rule.[40]

---

the walls have not forgotten the danger. However, the post of commandant was always given to the most trusted of the king's servitors. *Ibid.*, l. 16.

[35] For additional insights into the role of folkloric images in Stalin's writing, see Mikhail Vaiskopf, *Pisatel' Stalin* (Moscow: Novoe literaturnoe obozrenie, 2001), and the discussion in Rieber, "Stalin," pp. 1658–62.

[36] S. V. Machabeli, "Ekonomicheskii byt krest'ian Goriiskogo uezda, Tifliskoi gubernii," in *Materialy dlia izuchenii ekonomicheskogo byta gosudarstvennikh krest'ian Zakavkazskogo kraia* (Tiflis, 1887), vol. VI, p. 201.

[37] RGASPI, f. 71, op. 10, ed. kh. 273, l. 79.

[38] Sofrom Mgaloblishvili, *Vospominaniia o moei zhizni. Nezabyvaemye vstrechi* (Tbilisi: Merani, 1974), pp. 35–6.

[39] *Ibid.*, pp. 37–9.

[40] Compare his revolutionary pseudonym Koba, adopted from the avenging bandit hero of the Georgian writer Aleksandr Qasbegi (Kazbek), with the rhetoric used to identify

Gori lost some of its commercial importance when the Poti–Tiflis rail-road bypassed it in 1871, but it recovered as a center for transshipping grain and oats. By the time Stalin was born, its population had passed the 10,000 mark. A railroad spur later further improved its communications with the outside world. But the physical appearance of the town had changed little, with its narrow, crooked and dirty streets, its great market and the ruined fortresses recalling its past glories. The social structure of Gori remained highly traditional, not to say feudal. The local merchants and landowners had made common cause with the Russian bureau-crats in order to retain their dominant position. The town craftsmen, of whom Stalin's father was one, were hard-working but conserved their old-fashioned methods.[41]

In the 1860s, the Georgian national revival and greater cultural inter-action with Russia turned Gori into an important cultural center and a hot bed of political activity. The key to its renaissance was the connec-tion with Tiflis and especially the relationship between the Gori parish school and the Tiflis Seminary. A generation before Dzhugashvili was to follow this route to enlightenment, the top students from Gori went on to Tiflis, which served as a transmitter of fresh and bold ideas from Russia. They returned home as *Kulturträgers*. During Soso's years as a schoolboy in Gori and a seminarist in Tiflis, he began to construct the tripartite political persona, Georgian–Russian–proletarian, that became the foundation of his ideology of state-building.

His life in the Tiflis Seminary exposed him for the first time to the humiliation of russification and the blandishments of Marxism. By the time he arrived at the seminary, the relatively liberal atmosphere of the 1870s had given way to a harshly repressive regime. According to the anonymous memoirs of a former student published in 1907, the fac-ulty were "despots, capricious egotists who only had in mind their own prospects," which were to acquire a bishop's miter. Mainly Russians, they openly displayed their contempt for Georgians and their language. By 1900 there were only fifty Georgians out of 300 students. By 1905 there were no Georgians left.[42] In such an atmosphere it is hardly sur-prising that the long-established student circles for self-education turned more and more to radical politics.

kulaks in the 1930s and members of the Ukrainian Revolutionary Army (UPA) in the 1940s as bandits. For the psychological significance of Koba, see Tucker, *Stalin as Revolutionary*, pp. 79–82, and Philip Pomper, *Lenin, Trotsky and Stalin: The Intelligentsia in Power* (New York: Columbia University Press, 1990), pp. 158–63.

[41] Mgaloblishvili, *Vospominaniia*, pp. 11, 14.

[42] RGASPI, f. 71, op. 10, ed. kh. 73, ll. 153–4.

Before Stalin had enrolled, the Tiflis Seminary already had a reputation as a center of anti-governmental activity. Inspired by the spread of populist literature, the students repeatedly challenged the administration. Between 1874 and 1878 eighty-three of the recalcitrants were expelled. By the early 1880s, a new generation of Georgian populists coming from the lower strata of the population replaced the nobles and princes who had founded the movement. Resistance to the government's repressive policies after the assassination of the tsar in 1881 accelerated the transition from populism to Marxism and also took more violent forms. Close to the People's Will in Russia, they turned their attention more to students and worker–craftsmen than to peasants. In 1882 a group of seminarists formed a populist revolutionary circle around Gola Chitadze that included several future leaders of Georgian social democracy like Isidor Ramishvili and Noe Zhordania (subsequently Stalin's great rivals in the Menshevik wing of the Georgian party), Pilipe Makharadze and Mikha Tskhakaia the future Bolsheviks.

During the late 1880s, a few seminary students began to read Marxist literature, in particular the early essays of Plekhanov. For some, like Makharadze and Zhordania, the final stage in the transition to Marxism came only after they had left Tiflis in 1891 to continue their studies in Warsaw. From there they corresponded with their comrades in Tiflis, Silvester Dzhibladze and Egnati Ninoshvili, sending them illegal Marxist literature. When in 1894 Ninoshvili died prematurely, his friend, who had suffered expulsion with him, Silvester Dzhibladze, delivered a famous funeral oration at his grave site that for the first time publicly invoked Marxism as the revolutionary wave of the future. The appeal for a new direction met an enthusiastic response among the mourners and inspired the radical intellectual Grigori Tsereteli to call them *mesame-dasi*, the third generation, which the Georgian Marxists then adopted as their name.[43]

To be sure, there were disagreements among the early recorders of these events about how many of the group were "real Marxists" and how many were "under the strong influence of Marxist ideology."[44] The differences that later emerged between Mensheviks and Bolsheviks were

---

[43] Noe Zhordania, *Moia zhizn'* (Stanford: Hoover Institution Press, 1968), pp. 11–15; Makharadze, *K tridtsatiletniiu*, pp. 4–5, 14–17, 40–2. The memoirs of both Zhordania and Makharadze are replete with disparaging remarks about each other, but their accounts agree on the general nature of the transition from populism to Marxism among the Tiflis seminarians.

[44] The first position was held by Makharadze, *K tridtsatiletiiu*, p. 43, and the second by S. T. Arkomed, *Rabochee dvizhenie i sotsial-demokratiia na Kavkaze* (Geneva: Chaulmontet, 1910), pp. 145–51. That the former was a Bolshevik and the latter a Menshevik goes far toward explaining the difference between them.

not clearly drawn at this time. Moreover, the youthful seminarists had very little direct contact with the emerging workers' movement. During these same years from the late 1870s to the early 90s, a parallel and independent movement of worker activism in the form of strikes and secret discussion groups spread rapidly throughout the South Caucasus. Dzhugashvili cautiously and gradually adopted a Marxist outlook and began to associate with workers' study circles, a milieu he found more congenial to his plebian background than the discussion groups of the intelligentsia.

In 1900 Dzhugashvili's initiation into Marxism proceeded more rapidly with the arrival of a group of Russian social democratic exiles who injected fresh energy into the workers' movement in Tiflis and Baku. They arrived shortly after the workers had organized the first large-scale May Day demonstration with the participation of the Tiflis committee.[45] Among the newcomers was the veteran social democratic activist, Mikhail Kalinin, the future Soviet leader. His later efforts to diminish his own contribution to the development of a Leninist spirit among the Tiflis workers in favor of Stalin's role ring hollow in light of the contemporary attention paid to him by the police.[46]

The arrival of the Russian exiles coincided with a rapid growth of the strike movement that caused serious concern among the police. It was probably during this period, in the late summer or fall of 1901, that the Tiflis committee was taken over by the more radical elements in *mesame-dasi* supported by the Russian exiles who advocated joining the Russian Social Democratic Labor Party.[47] This was also the moment when Soso Dzhugashvili was co-opted to the committee, most likely in order to strengthen the radical group. For the first time police reports mention the name Dzhugashvili as an agitator, but note that "he conducts himself in a highly cautious manner."[48] Caution was still his watchword when at

---

[45] Stalin may have spoken at the demonstration but this is mentioned only by later memoir apologists. Vladimir Kaminskii and I. Vereschchagin, "Detstvo i iunost' vozhdia: dokumenty, zapiski, rasskazy," *Molodaia Gvardiia* 12 (1939), p. 93.

[46] The gendarmes described Kalinin as one of the "outstanding propagandists of antigovernmental ideas" who had a wide circle of acquaintances among like-minded thinkers and as a important revolutionary who maintained relations "with the leading representatives of the revolutionary party in many cities of Russia." G. Glebov, "M.I. Kalinin v 1900–1901 v Tiflise," *Zariia Vostoka* 46 (February 25, 1940), p. 3. No such "encomiums" for Stalin!

[47] A leaflet announcing this affiliation came as an unpleasant surprise to Noe Zhordania, one of the leaders of the moderates, who was in prison at the time and not in a position to challenge the decision. Zhordania, *Moia zhizn'*, pp. 33–4.

[48] Arkomed, *Rabochee dvizhenie*, pp. 39–40, 47–51; Galoian, *Rabochee dvizhenie*, pp. 10–12; Glebov, "M.I. Kalinin," pp. 247–8.

the end of 1901 he arrived in Batumi on a mission from the reconstituted Tiflis committee.

From Batumi to Baku

For Dzhugashvili, Batumi was the first opportunity to step out of the shadows of better-known and more active comrades and define himself more clearly against his enemies in the social democratic movement. Similar to Tiflis in many ways, Batumi bore even more clearly the stamp of a frontier town. An ancient urban site, it only passed under Russian sovereignty in 1878. Located twelve miles from the Turkish border but linked to Tiflis by rail, its population was highly mixed ethnically, as was the small working class concentrated in the late booming oil industry. The surrounding countryside was inhabited mainly by Georgians (Gurievtsy), Laz and Kurds.

When Dzhugashvili arrived there was no social democratic organization in Batumi. But there was an active Sunday school propaganda program run by two early adherents to *mesame-dasi*, Nikolai Chkheidze (known as "Karlo" in honor of Marx) and Isidor Ramashvili, both close associates of Zhordania and future Georgian Menshevik leaders. There were also small illegal circles of workers where social democratic propaganda circulated.[49] The future Mensheviks insisted that the increase in strike activity in Batumi in 1902 was spontaneous, though directed toward political goals by social democratic propagandists who were on the ground before Dzhugashvili's arrival. Subsequently, the mature Stalin claimed to have been the instigator of the strike and ridiculed his rivals as legal Marxists.[50] Thus he sought to portray himself as an advocate of conscious leadership over the idea of worker spontaneity even before the fateful split between Mensheviks and Bolsheviks had occurred over this issue.[51]

Although Dzhugashvili had been born, raised and educated in an ethnically mixed environment, he did not fully grasp the revolutionary and counter-revolutionary implications of communal strife until the eve of the revolution of 1905. The years between 1903 and 1919 were filled

---

[49] As early as 1897 the social democratic circles in Batumi had organized a partial translation of *The Communist Manifesto* into Georgian and hectographed 100 copies. L. E. Gorgiladze, "Rasprostranenie marksizma," in Lordkhipanidze and Mushelishvili, *Ocherki istorii Gruzii*, vol. V, p. 472.

[50] RGASPI, f. 71, op. 10, ed. kh. 73, ll, 327–38. Stalin was repaid in kind by Ramishvili, who stated "We have not sanctioned his activities and he conducts these in a self-willed way (*samovol'no*)." *Ibid.*, l, 351.

[51] For the background to this ideological split, see Leopold Haimson, *The Russian Marxists and the Origins of Bolshevism*(Cambridge, MA: Harvard University Press, 1955).

with communal riots, pogroms and two major revolutionary outbreaks. But tensions were already building in Soso's youth between the Armenian and Tatar communities and there was growing resentment between the Georgian and Armenian communities, especially in Tiflis. The sources of conflict stemmed from the economic development of the region, the boom in the oil industry, the spread of market relations and related changes in migratory patterns that brought growing numbers of Georgians into Tiflis and waves of illegal migrants from Iran into the Baku oil fields. The dangerous mixture of class antagonism superimposed upon older ethnic and religious rivalries exploded during the 1905 revolution. In Baku the fighting turned into a Tatar–Armenian war which spread to other cities, including Tiflis where it was only brought under control by a Georgian workers' militia, and to the countryside, especially in Nagorno-Karabakh.[52] That ethnic tensions and outbreaks of communal violence tended to split the revolutionary parties, including the social democrats, along national lines severely weakened the revolutionary movement in Stalin's eyes.

From the first stirrings of working-class consciousness in the South Caucasus, the more politically advanced workers tended to group themselves on the basis of their ethnic identity. Georgian, Armenian, Russian and Azerbaizhani workers maintained separate circles. The Georgian workers were more closely tied to their home villages to which they could return in the slack season. The Armenian and Russian workers were mainly permanent migrants with no ties to the countryside. The Muslim workers, largely unskilled, were divided between the local Azerbaizhani who retained close links to their villages and the migrants from across the Iranian frontier who were often seasonal and lived without their families in slums cut off socially from their southern compatriots. Ethnic separatism was reinforced by employment practices and distinctions in crafts and skills. Most workers were hired by their own countrymen. The Russians tended to be much more highly skilled than the others, with the Muslim workers occupying the lowest rung of the ladder.[53]

Socialist intellectuals also tended to identify themselves and their potential mass support with their ethnic origins. Perhaps nowhere else in the Russian Empire outside the South Caucasus were the emerging revolutionary parties so deeply marked by the tension between internationalist and nationalist aspirations. There were two major reasons for the competing identities. First, as we have seen, capitalist relations developed

---

[52] Tadeusz Swietochowski, *Russia and Azerbaizhan: A Borderland in Transition* (New York: Columbia University Press, 1995), pp. 36–42.
[53] Suny, *The Making of the Georgian Nation*, pp. 160–1, Swietochowski, *Russia and Azerbaizhan*, pp. 21–2.

unevenly within the populations of the main ethnic groups – Georgians, Armenians and Azerbaizhani – producing quite different levels of social consciousness among all classes in the three societies. Second, as we have also seen, there were equally pronounced differences among the three groups with regard to historic memories, territorial unity and political experience – all important indicators of national awareness. Consequently, the mixture of socialist and nationalist feelings among intellectuals tended to be highly volatile, and attempts to reconcile the two elements through various formulas became a trademark of the emerging revolutionary organizations. Among those attempts, Stalin's, like others', can only be understood within the context of the political controversies of that period. Roughly speaking, there was a hierarchy of political consciousness and action that distinguished the three groups. The Azerbaizhani were the slowest to break out of their traditional religious communities. Both the Armenian and Georgian intellectuals began more or less simultaneously their struggle to combine socialist and nationalist elements into a revolutionary ideology. But they ended up achieving a quite different balance of the two.

An Azerbaizhan socialist movement emerged against a complex cultural background made up of modern political movements – Islamism, pan-Turkism or just plain Turkism – that reflected the age-old rivalry of Iran and Turkey in the region. In addition there were Azerbaizhani liberals drawn from the merchant and industrial groups who also preceded the socialists on the political stage.[54] But, as in other regions of the Russian Empire, socialist groups among the Muslims made their appearance on the political scene at approximately the same time as the liberals, outflanking them on the left.[55] In Baku in the early years of the twentieth century, they found a fertile ground for their activities. One third of the oil workers and more than a quarter of the workers in the copper smelting industry, students in the secondary schools, as well as some students in the Russian *lycées*, were Turkic (Azeri) speakers. Migrant workers from Iran, numbering an estimated 100,000 by 1890, constituted half the number of Muslim workers in Baku. They formed a potential reservoir of recruits for social democracy, not only in Baku but across the border in Iran.[56]

---

[54] Firouzeh Mostashari, *On the Religious Frontier: Tsarist Russia and Islam in the Caucasus* (London: I. B. Tauris, 2006).

[55] For much of the following, see Tadeusz Swietochowski, "The Himmat Party: Socialism and the National Question in Russian Azerbaijan, 1904–1921," *Cahiers du Monde russe et soviétique* 19:1–2 (1978), pp. 119–25, and Audrey Alstadt, *The Azerbaijani Turks: Power and Identity under Russian Rule* (Stanford University Press, 1992), pp. 43–8.

[56] N. K. Belova, "Ot otkhodnichestva iz severo-zapadnogo Irana v kontse XIX nachale XX veka," *Voprosy istorii* 10 (1956), pp. 113, 117.

By 1904 a handful of Azerbaizhani radicals in the Baku organization of Russian Social Democracy founded a separate political group, Himmat (Endeavor), with their own newspaper of the same name. Because its program was vaguely socialist with strong nationalist overtones, it rapidly picked up mass support among both local and immigrant Muslim workers after the outbreak of revolution in Russia in January 1905. For the same reasons its relationship with the social democratic organizations of Baku was ambivalent. According to M. E. Rasulzade, one of its leaders and subsequently a participant in the Iranian "constitutional revolution" of 1906–11, Himmat was more often associated with the Bolsheviks in Baku than the Mensheviks. The contacts with "Koba," as Stalin was known to him, and his public support for the Bolsheviks gave rise to an incident which illustrates once again the youthful Dzhugashvili's sensitivity to language questions. In the ongoing debate among the social democrats about tactics, Andrei Vyshinskii, representing the Menshevik point of view, sneered at Rasulzade's ungrammatical Russian, whereupon Koba responded drily, "I don't think that if you gave a speech in Turkic you would do any better."[57] Dzhugashvili was also quick to ingratiate himself with Himmet. In 1907 he played a prominent role in a commission to organize a mass commemorative funeral for one of the leaders of Himmet martyred during a strike. At his gravesite, Dzhugashvili spoke of his close friend as a hero of socialist labor, seeking once again to establish a firm link between proletarian and national consciousness. But he soon learned the dangers of associating himself too closely with an ardent Muslim nationalist party.[58]

Himmet was important to Dzhugashvili in several ways. First, after his return from Siberian exile in 1907, he and his Bolshevik colleagues sought allies among the radical national parties in their rivalry with the dominant Menshevik organization in Baku for control over the workers' movement. They were motivated by three important tactical considerations. First, working with Himmet and other groups would facilitate their recruitment among the large number of unskilled and illiterate Muslim oil workers as a means of counter-balancing Menshevik influence among the mainly Russian skilled workers. Second, they calculated, rightly, that their agitation for militant strikes would elicit a more favorable response among the most highly exploited section of the workers who had very

---

[57] M. E. Rasulzade, "Vospominaniia o I. V. Staline," *Vostochnyi Ekspress* 1 (1993), p. 43.

[58] Michael G. Smith, "The Russian Revolution as a National Revolution: Tragic Deaths and Rituals of Remembrance in Muslim Azerbaijan (1907–1920)," *Jarhbücher für Geschichte Osteuropas* 49:3 (2000), pp. 370–3. Smith also points out the symbolic importance for the Bolsheviks (and I would stress for Stalin) of the cult of the dead.

little to lose in a confrontation with the owners and authorities.[59] Third, they recognized, as Dzhugashvili repeatedly pointed out, beginning with the outbreak of sectarian violence in February 1905, that national differences which had deeply split and weakened the workers in Baku were easily manipulated by the tsarist officials in order to drown the revolution in fratricidal warfare.[60]

The second reason for Dzhugashvili's interest in Himmet was as a conduit of revolutionary activity outside the southern frontiers of the Russian Empire – but not with an aim of establishing socialism. For example, in 1908 the Young Turk revolution broke out, evoking a sympathetic response among Muslims in Baku. Dzhugashvili encouraged the Himmet leader Rasulzade to contribute a political analysis to the legal Bolshevik newspaper *Gudok*. He then overcame the opposition of the titular editor to publish it on the grounds that praise for the bourgeois revolution in the Ottoman Empire contradicted the Bolshevik line of warring against the bourgeoisie in Russia. In his conversations with Rasulzade in 1920, Stalin justified his stand by stating "what we consider reactionary in Russia is progressive in Turkey."[61] Dzhugashvili also perceived the importance of maintaining good relations with Azerbaizhani Turks who were involved in radical politics in Iran. In 1906 one of the most respected Azerbaizhani Turkish intellectuals, Nariman Narimanov, a member of both Himmet and the Russian Social Democratic Labor Party, established a branch organization (*Ejtima-i-Amiyyun*, meaning Social Democracy) with overlapping leadership in order to mobilize and integrate the large number of politically disoriented immigrant Iranian Azerbaizhani workers in Baku. He smuggled arms, ammunition and propaganda across the border into Iran. As the counter-revolutionary pressures mounted in both Russia and Iran from 1907–8, the Azerbaizhani from Baku and their Bolshevik allies crisscrossed the frontier, escaping repression at home and bringing aid to the embattled Iranian revolutionaries in Tabriz.[62] These contacts

---

[59] My conclusions are based on the description of Bolshevik activities at this time by the Menshevik L. A. Rin (Iuri Larin), *O soveshchanii neftepromyshlennosti* (Baku, 1907), and Z. G. Orzhonikidze, *Put' bol'shevika: Stranitsy iz zhizni G. K. Ordzhonikidze* (Moscow: Gos-izd. politicheskoi literatury, 1956), pp. 61–2. See also Ronald Grigor Suny, "A Journeyman for the Revolution: Stalin and the Labor Movement in Baku, June 1907–May 1908," *Soviet Studies* 3 (1971), pp. 373–94.

[60] Stalin, *Sochineniia*, vol. I, pp. 84–5, 189.   [61] Rasulzade, "Vospominaniia," p. 43.

[62] Among them were one of the founders of the Communist Party of Iran, Bala Efendiev, one of the founders of Soviet Azerbaizhan and Stalin's comrade, 'Sergo' Ordzhonikidze, and the right-wing Himmetist (Menshevik), Ibrahim Abilov, who later became the ambassador of independent Soviet Azerbaizhan to Turkey. Swietochowski, *Russia and Azerbaizhan*, pp. 46–8; Ordzhonikidze, *Put' bolshevika*, pp. 82–5; and for his correspondence with Lenin on the possibility of organizing a social democratic group in Iran,

established for the first time a political link between the two Azerbaizhan borderlands based on the migrant population that would serve Stalin's purposes in Iran over the next four decades.

However, Dzhugashvili soon discovered that the establishment of a social democratic, to say nothing of a Bolshevik, organization in Iran was fraught with difficulties that did not exist in Baku. It turned out that Ejtima-i-Amiyyun was social democratic in name only. Because it kept changing its name during the Iranian revolution, it created confusion among contemporaries and subsequent historians about its true nature, which was radical democratic. During the years of the Iranian revolution, 1908–11, other groups also and with more justification calling themselves social democratic, sprang up in Tabriz, Resht and Teheran, each one based on a distinct ethnic identity, that is a "Persian Social Democratic Party," an Armenian social democratic party (Hnchak), and the Tabriz social democrats who were Azerbaizhani Turks. The Bolshevik group in Baku was concerned over these divisions, as they had been in the South Caucasus, and dispatched Dzhugashvili's subsequent close friend, Sergo Ordzhonikidze, to straighten things out. In March 1910 Ordzhonikidze reported that he had established links among the real social democratic parties, of which Ejtima-i-Amiyyun was not one. But it turned out that even the real social democrats had serious reservations about the possibility of creating a truly constitutional regime in Iran, to say nothing of a socialist government.[63] No wonder Stalin had strong reservations about attempting to sovietize Iran a decade later. And how much had happened to change his mind by 1946?

Whatever reservations Dzhugashvili may have had about the Bolshevik credentials of leaders among the Azerbaizhani revolutionary leadership, he recognized the importance of gathering them under the umbrella of the centralized Bolshevik fraction in order to defuse the potentially explosive ethnic rivalries among both workers and intelligentsia of different nationalities in the borderlands. But there were limits to his tolerance of their aspirations. After Narimanov had proven his Bolshevik credentials in the 1917 revolution in Baku, he joined the Azerbaizhani Communist Party, but soon found himself in disagreement with Stalin over the disposition

Sergo Ordzhonikidze, *Izbrannye stat'i i rechi, 1918–1937 gg.* (Leningrad: Izd. Polit-Lit., 1945), pp. 1–2.

[63] A. U. Martirosov, "Novye materialy o sotsial-demokraticheskom dvizhenii v Irane v 1905–1911 godakh," *Narody Azii i Afriki* 2 (1973), pp. 116–22. S. Enders Wimbush has argued that the Bolsheviks explicitly opposed a role for the Azerbaizhani as the advance guard of the revolution in Iran, fearing they would be infected by nationalism. "Divided Azerbaizhan: Nation Building, Assimilation and Mobilization between Three States," in William O. McCagg and Brian Silver (eds.), *Soviet Asian Ethnic Frontiers* (New York: Pergamon Press, 1979), pp. 67–8.

of the much disputed, multiethnic enclave of Nagorno-Karabakh. Stalin and Orzhonikidze favored assigning the region to Armenia against the strong opposition of Narimanov and other Azerbaizhani Communists. A compromise was arranged. The region was given autonomous status within the Azerbaizhan Republic which hardly satisfied the Azerbaizhani. As Narimanov became a vocal advocate of Azerbaizhani national culture, Stalin tried to sideline him by appointing him to the Central Executive Committee of the All-Union Communist Party in Moscow. But in the early 1920s he continued to complain about the suppression of Muslim rights and the over-representation of Armenians in the Azerbaizhan Party. He died before Stalin launched his attacks on Muslim Communists, sparing him vilification as a national deviationist.[64]

In the 1890s Marxism in Armenia owed its revival to the influx of Russian workers and the return of Armenian and Georgian students from the West including Stalin's future rival, Noe Zhordania, and one of his early associates, Pilipe Makharadze. For almost a decade there were signs that the intellectuals and workers of different nationalities not only in Armenia but elsewhere in the South Caucasus were willing to subordinate national differences to socialist unity. In 1898 the process reached its climax in the big Tiflis railroad strike when workers rejected any national differences among themselves and in the formation of the Russian Social Democratic Labor Party, which over the next few years incorporated local organizations of Armenian and Georgian socialists. But there was always a strong undercurrent of national rivalries. Following the Bolshevik–Menshevik split they rose to the surface. Armenians who had felt themselves outsiders in the Georgian-dominated regional organization joined the Bolsheviks, including Stalin's later associates in Baku, Stepan Shaumian and Suren Spandarian, while the greater part of the Georgian socialists supported the Mensheviks.

The drift toward nationalism of one faction of Armenian socialists was the occasion for one of Dzhugashvili's earliest polemics. Written in September 1904, his essay denounced the errors of "federalist-social democracy." Following Lenin's lead he equated the Armenian social democrats, who claimed to be "the sole defenders of the interests of the Armenian proletariat," with the Bund, which claimed the same monopoly over the organization of Jewish workers in the Pale. He accused the Armenians of national deviation without yet using the term itself, an

---

[64] Alstadt, The *Azerbaizhani Turks*, pp. 114–25; Stephen Blank, "Bolshevik Organizational Development in Early Soviet Transcaucasia: Autonomy versus Centralization, 1918–1924," in Ronald Grigor Suny (ed.), *Transcaucasia, Nationalism and Social Change: Essays in the History of Armenia, Azerbaizhan and Georgia* (Ann Arbor: University of Michigan Press, 1983), pp. 333–4.

accusation that he would revive again and again throughout his entire life. By asserting that "the Armenian proletariat will be the native son of its race (*plemeni*)," he wrote, they identified themselves first and foremost with the whole of Armenian society including the "blood-sucking Armenian bourgeoisie" and only secondarily with their class interests.[65] Stalin's uncompromising opposition to the classic form of federalism ultimately led him in 1923 to defy Lenin with whom he thought he had achieved a perfect agreement on this issue.

In Georgia the social democrats also evolved rapidly into a separate party, although they had initially accepted the program of the Russian Social Democratic Labor Party. They had even supported Lenin against the exclusivist claim of the Jewish Bund to represent the Jewish workers. Shortly after the initial Bolshevik–Menshevik split at the Second Congress of the All-Russian Social Democratic Labor Party (RSDLP) in 1903, one of the founders, and the emerging leader of Georgian social democracy, Noe Zhordania, led the overwhelming majority of Georgia socialists into the Menshevik camp. Two factors proved decisive in the outcome: the strong elective tradition among Georgian workers that emphasized local autonomy and the equally strong regional–ethnic identity of the workers and intellectuals that reinforced the desire for a more decentralized organization.

A borderland thesis

During the revolution of 1905 Dzhugashvili distilled his experience into an analysis that combined class and ethnic conflict in what might be called his "borderland thesis." At the Fourth Congress of the RSDLP, he denounced the Georgian Mensheviks as representatives of regions on the periphery of the imperial core lands (with the exception of South Russia) as "centers of small-scale production." Like the Jewish Bund in the western provinces and the peasant organizations of the Ukrainian Social Democratic Union (*Spilka*), he argued, they were engaged in "the tactics of backward towns," while the Bolsheviks represented "the advanced towns, the industrial centers" where revolution and class consciousness were primary. Lest his audience miss the point, he added that the Bolsheviks counted more workers among their delegates to the Congress (by implication including himself) and more Russians than the

---

[65] Stalin, *Sochineniia*, vol. I, pp. 37–40. For Lenin's attack on the Armenian social democrats, see Institut Marksizma-Leninizma pri TsK KPSS, *Leninskii sbornik*, 40 vols. (Moscow: Gos-izd, 1924), vol. V, p. 493.

majority of Menshevik delegates who were intellectuals, Jews and Georgians.[66] Over the following years he refined his "borderland thesis" into a nationality policy upon which to construct his vision of a multicultural class-based state.

During the Georgian phase of Dzhugashvili's political development, he plunged into two major intra-party controversies that wracked the Russian and European social democrats before 1914. They concerned the relative importance in both ideological and organizational terms of the two most powerful forms of social and political identity in early twentieth-century Europe: ethnic nationalism and proletarian internationalism. The first question was the right of national self-determination and the second was the right to represent workers of ethnic minorities. The slogan of national self-determination was formulated by Georgii Plekhanov for the First Congress of the RSDLP at Minsk in 1898, when the party adopted the defining term *rossiiskaia* (that untranslatable word which means all the people within the multinational empire) rather than *russkaia*, and passed a resolution stating simply "the right of self-determination for all nations."[67] A few years earlier Lenin had already addressed the question in similar terms, and he eagerly endorsed Plekhanov's draft of article 7 of the new party statutes. He never wavered from that position although he found it necessary to develop its ramifications under changing circumstances.[68]

The second question on the exclusive right of social democrats from the national minorities to organize and represent their proletarian brethren became the most fiercely debated and divisive in the history of the movement. First raised by the Bund at the Second Congress in 1903, it reappeared again and again in intra-party debates in one form or another. It soon became entangled with the complexities of the right to self-determination, its socioeconomic prerequisites, its cultural dimensions and its political form.

The debates within Russian social democracy were not conducted in isolation. The nationality question remained a lively one among social democrats in the German and Austrian multinational empires. Reflecting those interests, the Second International at the London Congress in 1896 had declared "in favor of the full autonomy of all nationalities"

---

[66] Stalin, *Sochineniia*, vol. II, pp. 32–3, 49–51.

[67] *Manifest Rossiiskoi Sotsialdemokraticheskoi Rabochei Partii* (Geneva: G. A. Kuklina, 1903), p. 5.

[68] See Mary Holdsworth, "Lenin and the Nationalities Question," in Leonard Schapiro and Peter Reddaway (eds.), *Lenin, the Man, the Theorist, the Leader: A Reappraisal* (New York: Praeger, 1967), pp. 267–8, and Iu. I. Semenov, "Iz istorii teoreticheskoi razrabotki V. I. Leninym natsional'nogo voprosa," *Narody Azii i Afriki* 4 (1966), p. 106.

without mentioning the right to national self-determination.[69] But in Central Europe as in Russia, pious resolutions settled nothing. Over the following decade, the polemics on the national question revolved around three major tendencies, although even here caution must be exercised in defining them because the leading proponents often shifted their position on one or another aspect. First was the so-called orthodox position held by Karl Kautsky, the powerful theorist of German social democracy, who had worked out the most comprehensive and sophisticated analysis of the dialectical relationship between capitalism and nationalism that served as the foundation for his justification of national self-determination.[70] His influence upon both Lenin's and Stalin's thinking about the national question was profound.

Second, the Austro-Marxists occupied a closely related position. Wrestling with the peculiar problems of the Habsburg borderlands, they had emphasized the cultural and psychological dimensions of nationalism and proposed solutions that would involve a variety of forms of national–cultural autonomy.[71] Third, Rosa Luxemburg represented the extreme internationalist wing of European social democracy. She reserved the right of self-determination exclusively and at all times for the working class, arguing that self-determination outside a strict class framework was an abstract idea. She posed the tough question that none of her comrades then or anyone else since has satisfactorily answered: who has the authority to speak for the nation?[72] Although Lenin believed that Luxemburg failed to recognize the emotional power of national feelings and thus ignored the need to offer the right to self-determination, he admired her intellectual position. Immediately after the publication of her work on the national question he wrote her a cordial letter, expressed

---

[69] *International Socialist Workers and Trade Union Congress* (London, 1896), p. 31. E. H. Carr checked the German version, *Verhandlungen und Bestachlusse des Internationalen Arbeiter- und Gewerkschafts-Kongresses zu* (London, 1897), p. 18, which translates "self-determination" as *Selbstbestimmungsrecht*, which Lenin translated into Russian as *samoopredelenie*. V. I. Lenin, *Sochineniia*, 30 vols., 3rd edn (Leningrad: Partizdat TsK VKP(b), 1936–7), vol. XVII, p. 455.

[70] Michael Forman, *Nationalism and the International Labor Movement: The Idea of the Nation in Socialist and Anarchist Theory* (University Park, PA: Pennsylvania State University Press, 1998), pp. 89–90.

[71] Tom Bottomore and Patrick Goode, *Austro-Marxism* (Oxford University Press, 1978), especially the Introduction; Forman, *Nationalism*, pp. 98–110; Robert A. Kann, *The Multinational Empire: Nationalism and National Reform in the Habsburg Monarchy, 1848–1918*, 2 vols. (New York: Columbia University Press, 1983 [1950]), especially vol. I: *Empire and Reform*, ch. 20 (although the turgid prose is difficult to follow), and *Die Österreichische Sozialdemokratie in Spiegel ihrer Programme* (Vienna: Dr. Karl Renner Institut, 1971), pp. 26–30.

[72] Rosa Luxemburg, *The National Question: Selected Writings* (New York: Monthly Review Press, 1976), pp. 140–3.

his admiration and sent her an example of his own work. Stalin by contrast had nothing good to say about Luxemburg either then or later.[73] The theoretical dimensions of the debate among Central European Marxists were far more highly developed by 1912 than among their Russian counterparts, and Russian social democrats tended to line up with one or other of these tendencies, or else, as in the exceptional cases of Lenin and Stalin, individuals selected what was required in patching together an eclectic theory of their own.

In 1912 compelling circumstances convinced Lenin of the urgency of constructing a fully developed theoretical position and a practical program on the nationalities question. The tendency to adopt socialism to nationalism, never far below the surface in social democracy on the periphery of the Russian Empire, had reemerged in what was for Lenin an ominous form. In August a number of anti-Bolshevik social democrats accepted Trotsky's invitation to meet in Vienna in order to counter Lenin's conspiratorial attempt to take over the party organization at the rump Prague Conference earlier that year. They discussed the need for a decentralized structure of the party which would meet the demands of the comrades from the borderlands. Prominent among their number were Georgian Mensheviks and Latvian social democrats, although the Poles stayed away. Lenin, who had already at Prague denounced national autonomy within the party as "a federation of the worst kind," now perceived the August Bloc as a systematic attempt to impose the Austro-Marxist theory of national cultural autonomy on Russian social democracy.[74]

With characteristic single-mindedness, Lenin immersed himself in the nationalities question, furiously writing articles and rounding up allies for a verbal onslaught against his opponents. By one count he wrote no less than thirty articles on the subject between 1912 and 1914.[75] It would be more accurate to describe most of these articles as touching upon the national question. Nonetheless, his interest was intense and

[73] Lenin, "O prave natsii na samoopredelenii," in *Sochineniia*, vol. XVII, pp. 427–40, for his lengthy polemic with her and *ibid.*, vol. XXVII, pp. 196–205, for his characterization of her. Cf. Stalin, *Sochineniia*, vol. I, pp. 57–61, when he simply lumped her together with Plekhanov, Axelrod and Zasulich as opponents of Lenin and, in 1931, when in *Bolshevik* he fiercely refuted the notion of A. G. Slutsky, a Soviet historian of Marxism, that Luxemburg had understood better than Lenin the dangers of Kautsky's centrism in 1911. *Ibid.*, 84–102.

[74] Lenin, "Bolnye voprosy nashei partii: liquidatorskii i natsional'ny voprosy" (November, 1912), in *Sochineniia*, vol. XVI, pp. 195–200, originally published in Polish, and "Tezisy po national'nomu voprosu," *ibid.*, pp. 507–13.

[75] Semenov, "Iz istorii," p. 107.

sharply focused. Simultaneously, he was busily urging some of his closest associates to help him recruit comrades of different ethnic origin
or else themselves to write specialized studies on the question. These
included Osip Piatnitskii, "Lenin's man Friday," Inessa Armand, and
Stepan Shaumian, Lenin's favorite among the Armenians.[76] Stalin was
only one of several Bolsheviks who responded to the call, although he
was the first. His work originally entitled "The Nationality Question and
Social Democracy" appeared in 1913 in three installments of the Bolshevik party journal *Prosveshchenie*, Among the others were Shaumian
himself, O. N. Loly (Stepaniuka), a Ukrainian and P. I. Stuchka (Veter-
ana), the Latvian legal specialist and later Commissar of Justice. Lenin
greeted all their contributions with enthusiasm, even writing the preface
to Stuchka's piece "The National Question and the Latvian Proletariat,"
although, as in the case of Shaumian, he may have disagreed with certain
points in the argumentation.[77] In Lenin's published works his specific
references to Stalin's work were rare but unequivocally favorable.[78] For
this reason Lenin disagreed with Alexander Troyanovskii that Stalin's
piece ought to be published in the unofficial "discussion" section of the
journal.[79]

Lenin's praise, taken together with some scraps of additional evidence, has been interpreted by most Soviet and some Western scholars to mean that Lenin guided, instructed or even edited Stalin's
work on the national question.[80] One problem with this version is the

---

[76] *Ibid.*, pp. 114–16.

[77] *Ibid.*, pp. 116–17. For example, he reproached Shaumian humorously but severely for
his failure to attack Great Russian chauvinism with sufficient zeal. But see Bertram
Wolfe, *Three Who Made a Revolution* (New York: Dial Press, 1948), pp. 583–7, for a
detailed description of Lenin's warm personal feelings for Shaumian.

[78] See, for example, Lenin, "O natsional'noe programme R.S-D.L.P.," in *Sochineniia*,
vol. XVII, p. 116.

[79] Widely reproduced, first by Stalin himself and by many Western historians. See, for
example, Tucker, *Stalin as Revolutionary*, p. 156. For the full passage, see Lenin, *Sochineniia*, vol. XVII, pp. 11–13 (October, 1913).

[80] Among the scholars who credit Lenin with having instructed or otherwise shaped
Stalin's ideas are: E. H. Carr, *The Bolshevik Revolution, 1917–1923*, 3 vols. (New York,
Macmillan, 1953), vol. I, p. 420, who states "external and internal evidence shows it
[Stalin's work] to have been written under Lenin's inspiration," but Carr does not say
what that evidence was; Boris Souvarine, *Stalin: A Critical Survey of Bolshevism* (London:
Secker and Warburg, 1940); and Isaac Deutscher, *Stalin: A Political Biography* (New
York: Oxford University Press, 1949), p. 117; Wolfe, *Three Who Made a Revolution*, pp.
578–88, where he states among other things that Lenin "sent for Stalin in 1913, initiated
him into the basic differences between the Austrian and Russian Marxist views and sent
him from Cracow to Vienna 'to gather all the Austrian materials,'" p. 581. Soviet historians, even after both stages of de-Stalinization at the Twentieth and Twenty-Second
Congress continued to present Lenin's and Stalin's views on the national question as
virtually interchangeable, e.g. A. S. Bogdasarov, *Razrabotka V. I. Leninym natsional'nogo*

unreliability of its sources, all of whom have dubious credentials: Trotsky, who was eager to prove that Stalin never had an original idea in his head; Krupskaya, whose memoirs were written at the height of the Stalinist terror; and Stalin himself, who enjoyed fostering the myth of himself as Lenin's comrade in arms and in thought.[81] Even those who reject this idea have with several exceptions ignored or played down the real differences between the two men that existed before the revolution and which were to break out into open conflict in 1922–3.[82] The two exceptions are Richard Pipes and Iu. I. Semenov, both of whom maintain that it was "in the main a work of Stalin" (Pipes) but also and importantly that there were significant differences between their views on the concept of the nation and on the right to self-determination.[83] Still, neither author is able to explain away Lenin's favorable response to Stalin's work. If Lenin had nothing but praise for Stalin why did he continue to urge his closest associate in Georgia, Shaumian, to assist him by sending books, reports and statistics on the nationalities in the Caucasus? Why did he find it necessary to write Shaumian after the publication of Stalin's work: "Do not forget also to *seek out* (*iskat'*) Caucasian comrades who can write articles on the national question in the Caucasus." Later Lenin renewed his plea: "A popular brochure on the national question is very much needed. Write it!"[84] What was Stalin's piece if not a popular brochure? And if Stalin's piece was theoretical rather than popular, then why did Lenin find it necessary to publish his own major theoretical contribution in which he failed to mention Stalin or his work and rejected out of hand

voprosa v gody novogo revoliutsionnogo pod"ema (Moscow: Vyshaia partinaia shkola pri TsK KPSS, 1956), pp. 34–9; T. Iu. Burmistrova, *Razrabotka V. I. Leninym programmy bol'shevistskoi partii po natsional'nomu voprosu (1910–1914): materially k 5. tome po kursu 'Istoriia KPSS'* (Moscow: Vyshaia shkola, 1962), pp. 34–9.

[81] Leon Trotsky, *Stalin: An Appraisal of the Man and his Influence* (New York: Stein and Day, 1967), pp. 156–8; Nadezhda Krupskaya, *Memoirs of Lenin* (London: Lawrence and Wishart, 1970). At the Twelfth Congress, Stalin referred to Lenin as "my teacher" on the nationalities question. Stalin, *Sochineniia*, vol. V, p. 266; Milovan Djilas, *Conversations with Stalin* (New York: Harcourt Brace, 1962), p. 157; and Tucker's interpretive explanation, *Stalin As Revolutionary*, p. 155.

[82] Tucker, *Stalin as Revolutionary*, p. 156, states that "Marxism and the National Question (sic) was basically Stalin's and the collaboration that underlay it seems to have been mutually beneficial." Cf. I. V. Stalin, *Works*, ed. Robert J. McNeal (Stanford, CA: Hoover Institution Press, 1967), pp. 43–4.

[83] Richard Pipes, *The Formation of the Soviet Union*, rev. edn (Cambridge, MA: Harvard University Press, 1970), pp. 40–1, and Semenov, "Iz istorii," pp. 116–17. Neither author, however, makes explicit the connection between these differences in interpretation in 1912–13 and the conflict over constitution-making in 1923. Cf. Pipes, *The Formation of the Soviet Union*, p. 291, in which he tacitly accepts Stalin's exposure in the 1923 debates of "inconsistencies" in Lenin's views as an accurate representation of Lenin's earlier statements.

[84] Lenin, "Pis'mo C. G. Shaumian," in *Sochineniia*, vol. XVII, p. 91.

several of Stalin's ideas without naming him?[85] The answers may lie in a more careful textual analysis of what Stalin wrote and what Lenin found objectionable in it as well as his view of the purposes to which that work might be most effectively put.

Stalin's *Marxism and the National and Colonial Question* turned out to be more than a refutation of Austro-Marxism and similar tendencies among the Jewish and Caucasian factions of the Russian party. He proposed two policy recommendations. The first was an unqualified endorsement of the right of self-determination for those nations that "in Russia may find it necessary to raise and settle the question of its independence." Second, he rejected what he mistakenly called the Austro-Marxist idea of national cultural autonomy, which would promote stronger national than class bonds as, for example, had emerged in Moravia in the Habsburg Monarchy between Jewish workers and the Jewish bourgeoisie. He countered with a proposal for "regional autonomy for such crystallized units as Poland, Lithuania, Ukraine, the Caucasus, etc." This would offer the advantage of basing politics on "a definite population inhabiting a definite territory." Stalin saw this as a way of breaking down national divisions and opening the way for class divisions. To be sure, Stalin's unspoken frame of reference was the Russian Empire where every borderland was a kaleidoscope of nationalities dotted with pockets of extreme socio-cultural fragmentation – "shatter zones." Only a party based on class could overcome the dangerous tendency of revolutionary movements to splinter along ethnic lines, which Stalin had observed in the Caucasus in 1905. In 1913 Stalin was writing in the context of what he called "the current situation." For him this meant the prospect of a bourgeois democratic revolution.[86] However, his analysis foreshadowed the nationality policy he would propose, defend and finally impose upon the party in the post-revolutionary era.

From Lenin's perspective there were several problems with Stalin's contribution.[87] Not only did it fall short of being a serious theoretical work, but it revealed substantial differences with his own thinking. Stalin had written that the right to self-determination meant the right of a nation to run its own internal affairs on the basis of autonomy within a federal structure. Lenin rejected this formula, insisting that the right to self-determination meant first and foremost the right to a separate state existence.[88] Lenin also opposed the idea that a nation could be

---

[85] Lenin, "O prave natsii," in *Sochineniia*, vol. XVII, pp. 427–74.
[86] Stalin, *Sochineniia*, vol. II, pp. 292–302.
[87] For these differences see Semenov, "Iz istorii," and Tucker, *Stalin as Revolutionary*, pp. 150–7.
[88] Lenin, *Sochineniia*, vol. XXV, p. 259; vol. XXVII, p. 255; vol. XXX, p. 19.

defined in an abstract way, as Stalin had done by listing its main features, without considering its historical progression. He also pointed out that it was a mistake to state that the Austrian Social Democrats had embraced the principle of cultural–national autonomy; in fact they had rejected it. Nevertheless, Lenin found Stalin's work useful as a blunt weapon against the Bund and Georgian "liquidators" who under the banner of national autonomy constituted the main threat to a unified highly centralized party organization.[89]

Stalin put into practice his theoretical perspectives during his service as Commissar of Nationalities and his activities as a commissar in the Civil War. He maintained his belief that the revolution and building a new state within the former tsarist empire could only be successful if the Bolsheviks could maintain the proper balance among territorial, ethnic and class relations. In his eyes this fine calibration required a degree of control over the revolutionary process that also placed him in a category of his own among the Bolshevik leaders. What had attracted Stalin to Lenin's writing in the first place was the criticism of spontaneity in the socialist movement. In his characteristically crude interpretation of Lenin, he embraced the idea that "the leaders give a program and the principles underlying the program . . . to the masses."[90] He then unfailingly applied it to the organization of revolutions, first in Russia, then in the borderlands, and finally beyond in the outer world. For Stalin the role of mass movements in revolutions appeared unpredictable at best and more often downright unreliable.

From the moment of his arrival in Petrograd in March 1917 until the Bolshevik seizure of power Stalin often found himself at sea in the tumult of events. He was never a tribune of the people. He played no role in the great spontaneous demonstrations of the July Days or even directly in the military preparations for the seizure of power itself. Leading up to October, at several critical points he took an equivocal position on the prospects of taking power.[91] Yet his administrative talents and hard work earned him respect from his comrades. Otherwise it is not possible to explain how in October he received the third-highest number of votes

---

[89] *Ibid.*, vol. XIV, p. 317; vol. XVII, p. 116.   [90] Stalin, *Sochineniia*, vol. I, p. 57.
[91] Stalin's biographers mostly follow the judgments of Trotsky and the Menshevik memoirist of the revolution, N. N. Sukhanov, who coined the phrase "a grey blur" to describe Stalin in October. See Tucker, *Stalin as Revolutionary*, pp. 163–80; Dmitrii Volkogonov, *Triumf i tragediia. I. V. Stalin: Politicheskii portret* (Moscow: Agenstva pechati Novosti, 1989), ch. 1. The most extreme denigration of Stalin's role is Robert Slusser, *Stalin in October: The Man Who Missed the Revolution* (Baltimore, MD: Johns Hopkins University Press, 1987). Cf. Service, *Stalin: A Biography*, pp. 143–6, who attributes a more active if behind-the-scenes role to Stalin.

behind Lenin and Trotsky in electing a new seven-man Political Bureau of the Central Committee.

As regards the spread of revolution, Stalin was openly skeptical about its chances in Europe. In April 1917 he was already claiming that "the base of our revolution is broader than in Western Europe." He insisted that "it is necessary to give up the outworn idea that Europe alone can show us the way."[92] After October, during the debate on the negotiations with the Central Powers that preceded the separate peace of Brest-Litovsk, Stalin made clear his differences over the possibility of revolution in Europe not only with Bukharin and Trotsky but also with Lenin. Stalin denounced Trotsky's position of "no war, no peace" as no position at all. "There is no revolutionary movement in the West," he went on; "nothing existed, only a potential, and we cannot count on a potential." Lenin, who was determined to make peace with Stalin, felt obliged "to disagree on some points with his fellow thinkers [including Stalin]; of course a mass movement does exist in the West but the revolution has not yet started there."[93] Stalin remained ever skeptical of the "potential" of mass revolutionary movements to generate a concerted seizure of power without at least the support of the first and foremost socialist state.

[92] Cited in Tucker, *Stalin as Revolutionary*, pp. 174–5.
[93] *The Bolsheviks and the October Revolution: Minutes of the Central Committee of the Russian Social-Democratic Labour Party (Bolsheviks). August 1917–February 1918* (London: Pluto Press, 1974), pp. 177–8.

2   Borderlands in Civil War and Intervention

Stalin's higher education in foreign policy took place during the Civil War when the line between state-building and revolution became blurred. To defend and if possible expand the territorial base of the revolution, to ward off the intervention of foreign powers, to create an international revolutionary movement and to improvise the rudiments of state power were, for the Bolsheviks, all parts of the same process. Yet individual leaders invested their energies and passions in different aspects of it. As a member of the Politburo, Stalin was naturally involved in major foreign policy decisions, but his main field of action was as a member of the Revolutionary War Council and Commissar of Nationalities. Initially, he took no active part in the Commissariats of Foreign Affairs and the Comintern – the two political centers of diplomacy and revolutionary action outside the old tsarist frontiers. Stalin did not appear at a Comintern Congress until 1924.

During the Civil War, Stalin learned to trust only those forces over which he could exercise direct personal control: that is, the party organizations and the army units under his command. Lenin and Trotsky also valued disciplined political and military organizations but, unlike Stalin, who relied on them exclusively for his success, Lenin and Trotsky did not discount the importance of coordinating the activities of the Red Army and the Russian Communist Party with local and republic party organizations.

After four years of Civil War and Intervention, Stalin concluded that the Soviet nationalities policy (that is, his policy) was the key to "a fundamental improvement of relations between Turkey, Persia, Afghanistan, India and other neighboring eastern states with Russia which formerly was considered a bugbear of these countries." Indeed, "without a systematic working out within the Russian Socialist Federated Soviet Republic of the aforementioned nationalities policy in the course of four years of the existence of Soviet power this fundamental change in the attitude of neighboring countries to Russia would be unimaginable."[1]

---

[1] Stalin, *Sochineniia*, vol. V, p. 116.

After the October revolution, when the territory controlled by the Bolsheviks shrank to the old Muscovite core, the recurrent problem of incorporating the former tsarist borderlands emerged again in acute form. Stalin, together with Lenin, was committed in theory to national self-determination, subject to conditions that would sustain and advance the revolution, a policy based upon the class interests of the proletariat. Yet even the most precise theoretical formulation could not have anticipated the complex conditions in which they had to be applied. In the chaos of the Civil War, a multiplicity of governments rose and fell. Some were openly counter-revolutionary. Others, in Ukraine, Georgia, Armenia, Belorussia and Turkestan, claimed to be "Soviet" and declared their independence. The new republics were not, however, ethnically homogeneous. In many areas, Ukraine, Turkestan and North Caucasus, for example, pockets of ethnic Russians, descendants of migrants and colonists, were left outside the authority of Moscow. For the most part, they constituted the working-class elements of the breakaway states, and they were opposed to the non-Russian nationalist elements that controlled the new governments. Thus, the advocates of the principles of self-determination and international class solidarity were at odds with one another.

If Stalin's theory of the state was rooted in his pre-revolutionary experience, his experience in the Civil War confirmed its practical value. Soon after his appointment as head of the Commissariat of Nationalities (*Narkomnats*), he used his authority to lay the foundations for the future Soviet state.[2] What Stalin appeared to have in mind was a commissariat serving as a nursery for breeding local Communist parties among the nationalities of the old empire. But he had to tread cautiously, for his views were not generally accepted within the party, and he was not strong enough to impose them even within his own commissariat. By November 1918 there were eighteen national sections (originally also called commissariats) in the People's Commissariat of Nationalities including most of the largest groups within the old tsarist empire like the Tatar, Polish, Belorussian, Armenian and Latvian peoples. But the addition of sections for peoples who had never been part of the empire, like Czechs and Iranians, introduced a decidedly international flavor to the commissariat.[3]

At the same time, the Central Committee of the Communist Party undertook a separate organization of non-Russian groups who shared

<hr>

[2] I concur with Jeremy Smith, "Stalin as Commissar of Nationality Affairs, 1918–1933," in Sarah Davies and James Harris (eds.), *Stalin: A New History* (Cambridge University Press, 2005), p. 46, that "Stalin's experience as Commissar profoundly affected his later attitude to non-Russian nationalities."

[3] Carr, *The Bolshevik Revolution, 1917–1923*, vol. I, pp. 277–85 for the structure.

sympathies with the new regime into a Federation of Foreign Communists. The western or European sections of this federation had a short and uneventful life. They were constituted from German, Habsburg and Ottoman prisoners of war who were rapidly absorbed into Comintern organizations in 1919. The Asian members formed their own Communist Organization of Peoples of the East divided into ten sections, representing diverse nationalities both inside and outside the old empire: Arabs, Iranians, Turks, Tatars, Kirghiz and other peoples. Its Central Bureau was headed by Stalin himself. This put him in command of both the state and party organizations dealing with the nationalities of the tsarist empire and of peoples lying beyond the old frontiers in the Eurasian borderlands of neighboring Asian countries.

From the beginning, it was clear that the two organizations over which Stalin presided were split along ideological lines between a Western (European) and an Eastern (Asian) orientation. In the *Narkomnats* the Latvian, Estonian, Lithuanian and Polish sections were run by supporters of the extreme internationalist position who opposed any concessions to the principle of nationality within the revolutionary movement. Stalin's deputy, Stanislaus Pestkowski, a Pole, went so far as to denounce the Leninist theory of national self-determination as "disastrous for the revolution and contrary to the principles of Marxism."[4] Stalin's differences with the leftist, Luxemburg tendency among the national Communist parties of the western borderlands emerged soon after the meeting in late October 1918 of a Conference of Communist Organizations of the Occupied Territories. The object of the conference was to coordinate Communist activities in Poland, Lithuania, Latvia, Estonia, Belorussia, Ukraine and Finland in the face of the imminent withdrawal of the German Army. Against the prevailing views of the conference to abolish frontiers and fuse the borderlands with the Russian republic, Stalin vigorously seconded Lenin's insistence on setting up provisional Soviet governments in the spirit of self-determination.[5]

At the opposite end of the spectrum, stood Stalin's other deputy and later his successor as the head of the Central Bureau of the Communist Organizations of the Peoples of the East (Musbiuro), Mirza Said Sultan-Galiev, who took an extreme autonomist position, favoring a loose federation of Soviet republics. For a while he and his Muslim associates even

---

[4] S. S. Pestkovskii, "Vospominaniia o rabote v Narkomnatse," *Proletarskaia revoliutsiia* 6 (1930), pp. 101, 124–31.

[5] Stalin personally edited out of the manifesto proclaiming a Lithuanian Soviet Republic all references to the internationalist line. James D. White, "National Communism and World Revolution: The Political Consequences of German Military Withdrawal from the Baltic Area in 1918–19," *Europe–Asia Studies* 46:8 (1994), pp. 1362–4.

agitated for a Muslim Red Army to overthrow Western imperialism in Asia, which they regarded as the main arena for world revolution.[6]

These widely divergent views within the state and party apparatus over a nationalities policy reflected the bewildering variety of cultural and economic differences prevailing in the borderlands. The more industrialized western territories, with their history of secular politics and trade union activity, contrasted sharply with the much less urbanized, predominantly agricultural and often semi-nomadic societies of the Caucasian, Trans Caspian and Inner Asian borderlands where the major unifying element was traditional Islamic culture. Lenin had perceived the potential for social conflict in this deep cleavage and strove to resolve it through his federalist scheme. In principle, Stalin accepted Lenin's program, but in practice he played by different rules.

Documents published in the post-Soviet period make it possible to penetrate deeper into the subterranean levels of Stalin's extraordinarily devious nationality policy. On one level he manipulated the internationalists against the autonomists in order to neutralize both. Simultaneously, he promoted his own plans for constructing a centralized state while paying lip service to Lenin's latter-day design for a genuine federation. On another level, he maneuvered to counter-balance the European orientation of Soviet foreign policy embodied in his arch rival, Trotsky, with an Eastern orientation which he perceived as a way of enhancing Soviet Russia's role in the international revolutionary movement. In characteristic fashion, Stalin reasoned that Russia might dominate the Asian Communists, but never the European. In the crucible of Russia's Time of Troubles, Stalin tested and refined the tactics that he would subsequently employ in his Second World War foreign policy with particularly striking results in the East European and Asian borderlands.

At first glance Stalin's behavior as Commissar of Nationalities appears hesitant, confused and even contradictory. There was, no doubt, some reality behind the appearance, for he was feeling his way through a political tangle. But as his record in dealing with different nationalities is compared, a remarkably consistent pattern emerges out of these contradictions. A policy begins to surface. It was devious, unprincipled, possible even consciously cynical, but it was a policy nonetheless.[7]

---

[6] M. A. Persits, "Vostochnye internatsionalisty v Rossii i nekotorye voprosy natsional'no-osvobozhditaľnogo dvizheniia (1918–iiul' 1920)," in *Komintern i vostok* (Moscow: Glav. red. vostochnoe literatury, 1969), pp. 90–2.

[7] M. A. Persits, "V. I. Lenin o levosektantskikh oshibakh pervykh kommunistov vostoka (1918–iul' 1920)," *Narody Azii i Afriki* 2 (1970), pp. 56–69; see also Stephen Blank, "Soviet Politics and the Iranian Revolution," *Cahiers du Monde russe et soviétique* 21:2 (1980), pp. 173–94.

During the Civil War, Stalin took an active role in three main areas in regulating relations between peoples of the borderlands and the center: Ukraine, the South Caucasus and the Muslim populations of the Volga region and Inner Asia. On occasion he exercised his authority in these areas as Commissar of Nationalities. But there were risks in doing this. The newly created organization was a hot bed of factionalism; as its chief he would be saddled with sole responsibility for its mistakes. Just as often he preferred to invoke his authority as a member of more powerful collective bodies like the Politburo or the Military Revolutionary Council, and his most important pronouncements were published in the party organ, *Pravda* and not in the organ of his commissariat, *Zhizn' national'nosti*. Moreover, throughout 1919 and early 1920 Stalin was frequently at the front and absent from the commissariat in Moscow where things were allowed pretty much to take their own course until his return. Several years after the end of the Civil War in 1923, when he was engaged in a political fight with the national opposition which included some of his colleagues in the commissariat, he bluntly reminded them that "the *Narkomnats* is a propaganda commissariat and does not have any administrative rights."[8] This was, at the very least, highly disingenuous. But if not an accurate description it was intended to convey an unmistakable message. Stalin had no intention ever of becoming a prisoner of the nationalities; he would always aspire to be their warden.

Stalin's disputes with the Ukrainian, Georgian and Muslim Bolsheviks reached a climax simultaneously. In the western borderlands Stalin had less room to maneuver than in the east. For one thing, Lenin and Trotsky were more directly involved in political and military operations. For another, although Stalin insinuated himself into various party and state organs dealing with Ukraine, he lacked reliable clients in the faction-ridden Ukrainian Communist Party. Finally, time and again internecine warfare, the breakdown of social relations and the collapse of political authority in Ukraine threatened to plunge the region into total chaos. It was a highly risky business for Stalin or anyone else to conduct a personalized policy for fear of making a disastrous mistake.

Ukraine

A brief description of the Civil War in Ukraine cannot do justice to the confusion and violence that produced nine different governments in

---

[8] "Iz istorii obrazovaniia SSSR," *Izvestiia TsK KPSS* 4 (315) (April, 1991), p. 170. These are hitherto unpublished stenographic records of the discussion sections of the Twelfth Party Congress on the nationality question.

the short span of three years. More than anywhere else in the former Russian Empire, the situation reproduced the Time of Troubles in the seventeenth century.[9] Throughout, Stalin showed little confidence in the abilities of the Ukrainian Bolsheviks to carry out their own revolution. When events proved that they had to rely on armed Russian workers from the outside, Stalin concluded that there was no justification for an independent Soviet republic in Ukraine. "Those who cannot take power do not deserve to hold it," became a Stalinist maxim.

In dealing with the question of Ukrainian autonomy, Stalin's position does not appear consistent, yet a carful reconstruction, admittedly with some of the pieces still missing, reveals his distinctive approach to the borderlands. In an interview for *Pravda* in late November but only published on December 7, 1917, he gave his first public statement on relations between the new Soviet government and the Ukrainian Central Rada. The Rada had been initially formed after the fall of tsarism in March and gradually evolved as the de facto government of an autonomous Ukraine. Stalin reiterated party policy as defined at the April Conference on self-determination through direct referendum or a national constituent assembly. There was room for a broad agreement with the Rada, he declared, and called for a meeting between its representatives and the Bolshevik government. He even went so far as to assert that the autonomy of Ukraine should be complete, "unrestricted by commissars from above." In peacetime there would be no objection to Ukrainian soldiers being stationed in Ukraine. But he was concerned about the reluctance of the Rada to summon a congress of workers, soldiers and peasants. He also expressed his reservations over the Rada's extension of its authority over more and more provinces outside the traditional boundaries of Ukraine.[10]

Within a few weeks Stalin sharpened his voice to reflect a rapidly changing situation in Ukraine. In his view three problems had erupted to threaten good relations. First the secretary-general of the Rada, Simeon Petliura, soon to be the *bête noire* of the Bolsheviks, had ordered the withdrawal of all Ukrainian military personnel from the front, creating widespread confusion and undercutting peace negotiations with the Central Powers. Fortunately, Stalin noted, the Ukrainian soldiers refused for the time being to obey. The second problem was the decree of the Rada disarming the soviets in Ukraine and the attempts to carry out

---

[9] John S. Reshetar, *The Ukrainian Revolution, 1917–1920: A Study in Nationalism* (Princeton University Press, 1952); Peter Kenez, *Civil War in South Russia, 1918: The First Year of the Volunteer Army* (Berkeley: University of California Press, 1976).

[10] RGASPI, f. 71, op. 10, ed. kh. 315, ll. 16–21. The article was not included in Stalin's *Sochineniia*.

this order in Kiev, Odessa and Kharkov; these were the centers of soviet and Bolshevik strength. Even more ominous, in the smaller towns the soviets were being disbanded, yet they were the only defense against the counter-revolutionary forces gathering in the south around the White leaders, General Lavr Kornilov and Ataman Aleksei Kaledin. The third related problem was the open intervention of the troops of the Rada against Bolshevik revolutionary detachments moving across Ukrainian territory in order to engage Kaledin's Cossacks. Stalin warned darkly that the blockade would end and fraternal relations would be reestablished between Ukrainian and Russian soldiers, or else it would not, in which case the Rada will "identify with the enemies of the people." Stalin now insisted that self-determination could not serve as a cloak for counter-revolution.[11]

The Rada refused to accept the conditions set by the Soviet government as he outlined them. The Bolsheviks then launched an attack against the Rada, using predominantly Russian troops, and occupied Kiev. Under their protection a congress of Soviets was held in Kharkov, proclaiming the first Soviet government of Ukraine. But the Ukrainian Bolsheviks were divided and the government had little authority, which remained in the hands of the Red Army command. The Bolshevik leaders in Petrograd were not unified on a clear course of action to take and differed on which faction to support.[12] Lenin sent his warm congratulations, but Stalin wired scornfully: "Enough playing at a government and a republic. It is time to drop the game; enough is enough." A prominent Ukrainian Bolshevik in the government, Mykola Skyrpnik, immediately shot back a protest: "Declarations like that of Comrade Stalin would destroy the Soviet regime in Ukraine."[13] The stark contrast between the two men's reactions illustrate their deep-seated differences over the issue of self-determination, which would erupt into a full-fledged dispute at the Eighth Congress in March 1919 during the discussions over a new party program, and even more explosively in the debate over the new constitution on the eve of Lenin's death.

In early 1918, the confusing internal situation was further complicated by negotiations at Brest-Litovsk where the Germans and Austrians were

---

[11] Stalin, *Sochineniia*, vol. IV, pp. 31–40. In talks with the left wing of the Cossack Military District, Stalin denied the Soviet expeditions were directed against the Cossacks, but only sought to defend the workers of Rostov na Donu against attack by Kaledin. *Ibid.*, vol. II, pp. 64–5.

[12] See the discussion in Pipes, *The Formation of the Soviet Union*, pp. 132–3.

[13] Roy Medvedev, *Let History Judge* (New York: Knopf, 1971), p. 16, quoting from an anonymous manuscript. By no means an advocate of national separatism, Skrypnik nevertheless continued to battle Stalin's high-handed treatment of the Ukrainian Communists until he took his own life in 1933.

pressing for an independent Ukraine which they could dominate, while the Ottoman Turks advocated a buffer state to protect them against a Russian revival. For Stalin the negotiations created enormous difficulties. It will be recalled that in January 1918 he had supported Lenin's position, although his reasoning had differed from Lenin's, on the necessity of accepting the harsh German peace terms against Trotsky's formula of "no war no peace." For him there was no mass basis for a revolutionary movement in the West on which the fledgling Soviet Republic could count if the war with Germany continued. He held out, however, for more negotiations, even to the point of accepting the surrender of Petrograd, "which would not amount to a full surrender or to the rotting away of the Revolution." When the Germans finally lost patience and issued an ultimatum, Stalin appeared to waver. At the meeting of the Central Committee on February 23 to consider the ultimatum, he proposed that "We could refrain from signing but open peace negotiations." Lenin rebuked him sharply: "Stalin is wrong when he says we could refrain from signing. Those terms have to be signed. If you do not sign them, you will sign the Soviet regime's death warrant in three weeks."[14] Stalin ended up voting, as he had always done, with Lenin, but in retrospect it is clear that he was imagining a different course of action in the borderlands.

A fortnight after the signing of Brest-Litovsk on March 3, which recognized an independent Ukraine, Stalin struck out in an unexpected direction. Having signed a separate treaty with Ukraine, the German High Command ordered its troops to enter the country in order to collect desperately needed food supplies for their hungry homeland. They swept aside the Soviet forces and briefly reestablished the Rada. Stalin reacted by denouncing the occupation as "a new shameful yoke which is no way better that the old Tatar yoke – such is the idea of the attack from the West." If there were to be a war with the Austro-German imperialists, it would not be initiated by the Bolsheviks; still less would it develop out of a revolutionary upsurge in the West. It would come," he declared, "over resistance to the Central Power's occupation of the borderlands," and then it would not be a revolutionary war but "a liberating *fatherland* (*otechestvennaia*) war of the workers and peasants in Ukraine which will have every chance of counting on all out support from Soviet Russia as a whole."[15] Stalin appeared to be moving away from Lenin again and toward a leftist position. However, instead of issuing a renewed appeal for

---

[14] *Protokoly tsentral'nogo komiteta RSDRP(b) avgust 1917–fevral' 1918* (Moscow: Gosizdat. politicheskoi literatury, 1958), pp. 200–2, 211–13.

[15] *Izvestiia*, March 14, 1918, reprinted in Stalin, *Sochineniia*, vol. IV, p. 47, italics in original. Stalin first used this formulation of a "fatherland war" in his memo to the secretariat of the Ukrainian Soviet Republic on February 24, 1918. *Ibid.*, pp. 42–3.

world revolution, he was appealing to a territorial concept, the defense of the borderlands.

Appointed acting head of the Bolshevik team negotiating for peace with the independent Ukraine after Brest-Litovsk, Stalin continued to resist Lenin's insistence on a rapid end to hostilities. On May 2, 1918, Stalin wired Lenin that events suggested that "a peace conference will no longer be possible." By this time the German Army had overthrown the Rada, arrested its ministers and disarmed a number of Ukrainian regiments. According to Stalin, a group of bourgeois landowners had then formed, under German auspices, a new government called the Hetmanate, with its echoes of the Cossack past, headed by Hetman Pavlo Skoropads'kyi, a former tsarist officer and commandant of the Free Cossack detachments. Stalin's subsequent analysis clearly illuminates the linkage he had forged between the threat of foreign intervention and the inherent weakness of the borderlands to defend themselves. He expressed his concerns in terms strongly reminiscent of nineteenth-century tsarist proconsuls of the borderlands, substituting the Germans for the English as the imperialists. "The Germans have occupied Feodosia and Ukrainian units were withdrawn from Simferopol to the north beyond Perekop," he wrote. "This means that the Germans wish to keep Crimea for themselves in order to throw a bridge across the Straits of Kerch, pushing on to Persia and Mesopotamia [and] along the Black Sea railroad line to Transcaucasus, through Kars and beyond."[16] Despite his opposition, negotiations with Ukraine dragged on until the collapse of the Central Powers in November 1918, when once again the question of who would control Ukraine broke to the surface.

Defeat in the West and the armistice of November 1918 forced the Germans to withdraw and abandon their puppet, Skoropads'kiy. Various Ukrainian nationalist groups, including former members of the Rada like Petliura, then formed a Directory and proclaimed an independent and sovereign state in opposition to both the Whites and Reds. The Bolshevik leaders were united in their aim of opposing the nationalists and reimposing Soviet power in the region but continued to disagree over the means and timing.

Throughout the summer and fall of 1918, Stalin fought a fierce administrative battle with Trotsky over the control of military operations in the southern and western borderlands from Galicia to the Crimea. Stalin denounced Trotsky in harsh language for supporting bourgeois military specialists in positions of command. He recalled Trotsky's late

[16] RGASPI, f. 71, op. 10, ed. kh. 287, l. 242. Stalin to Lenin, May 2, 1918.

adherence to the party, his equivocation at Brest-Litovsk and other errors, concluding, "if he is not reined in, he will spoil the entire army."[17]

At the operational level, Stalin exploited his position on the Military Revolutionary Council of the Russian republic to get himself appointed, in November 1918, to a small Ukrainian Revolutionary Council, which was to organize the reconquest of Ukraine. Although he was soon recalled to Moscow, he continued to exploit his connections in order to compete with Trotsky for control of the army leadership in Ukraine. When Lenin finally authorized an invasion of Ukraine, Stalin's rivalry with Trotsky escalated. They clashed over the military leadership in Ukraine with Stalin supporting Voroshilov, for whom Trotsky had only contempt, against Trotsky's supporters Grigorii Piatakov and V. A. Antonov-Ovseenko.[18] Grigorii Piatakov, a Russian born in Ukraine had taken an extreme internationalist position even before the revolution, when he opposed Lenin and by association Stalin too, on the need to reach an accommodation with Ukrainian nationalism.[19] Still, Stalin was not prepared to lose Ukraine whatever the Bolshevik commitment to self-determination. Stalin had been willing to back Piatakov's surreptitious preparations for the invasion, but he wanted the operation brought under his control.[20] Stalin's action is consistent with his distrust of the abilities of local non-Russian Bolsheviks, in this case Ukrainians, to carry out their own revolution, a view he maintained consistently, as for example in Georgia in 1921, and later in Eastern Europe in the closing days of the Civil War.

Stalin recognized that the defeat of the Central Powers opened up a new phase in the struggle over the borderlands. The victory of the Entente, he wrote, merely substituted one form of imperialist intervention for another which was also linked to local "nationalist appendages." As the imperialism of the Central Powers was dying, "the Anglo-French imperialists were gathering their forces in readiness to descend on the

---

[17] A. B. Kvashonin et al. (eds.), Bol'shevistskoe rukovodstvo perepiska. 1912–1927 (Moscow: Rosspen, 1996), Stalin to Lenin, October 3, 1918, doc. 22, pp. 52–3. See also Stalin, Minin and Voroshilov to Sverdlov, October 5, 1918, doc. 23, p. 54.

[18] Ibid. Trotsky to Antonov-Ovseenko, Lenin and Sverdlov, January 7, 1919, doc. 41, pp. 76–7. See also Jurij Borys, The Russian Communist Party and the Sovietization of Ukraine (Westport, CT: Hyperion Press, 1980, reprint of 1960 Stockholm edition), pp. 204–10.

[19] Pipes, The Formation of the Soviet Union, pp. 47 and 68.

[20] Kvashonin et al., Bol'shevistskoe rukovodstvo, Trotsky to Antonov-Ovseenko, Lenin and Sverdlov, January 7, 1918, doc. 41, pp. 76–7; and Piatakov to Lenin, Trotsky, Sverdlov and Stalin, January 20, 1918, doc. 42, pp. 77–9. In February the Bolshevik Central Committee arranged a compromise, replacing Piatakov as head of the Soviet Ukrainian government with Khristian Rakovski and appointing supporters of both Stalin and Trotsky to the commissariats.

Crimea in order to occupy Ukraine."[21] It was therefore imperative, he informed the Central Committee of the Ukrainian Communist Party, to reach agreements with the soldiers' soviets forming within the German Army of occupation to facilitate their withdrawal in order to avoid clashes. The main antagonist in the west was now the Polish legions which had already occupied Brest. German forces which had not formed soviets should be assured that "Russia did not want to spill a drop of German blood and would with pleasure permit their return to their homeland."[22]

With the German withdrawal, Lenin remained skeptical of the zealous efforts of the Russian Bolsheviks in Ukraine to overthrow the nationalist government in Kiev. He had thrown his weight behind a diplomatic compromise with the nationalists negotiated in October 1918 by the Bulgarian-born Khristian Rakovski and the Ukrainian-born Dmitrii Manuilskii, which was supported by the right wing of the Ukrainian Bolsheviks. He had been angered by the unauthorized march on Kiev by Piatakov's forces, surreptitiously backed by Stalin. Yet even after Piatakov was replaced as the chairman of the Ukrainian Soviet government by Rakovski, the advance continued. In February Kiev fell to the Red Army. Lenin's instructions to Rakovski had stressed the need to reach an accommodation with the peasantry and the Ukrainian-speaking intelligentsia. But Rakovski did not restrain the left wing of the Ukrainian Communist Party. Hasty measures of collectivization and discrimination against the use of Ukrainian language alienated much of the population. Within eight months the Whites drove out the Ukrainian Soviet government and plunged the region into renewed civil strife.[23]

The civil war in Ukraine soon became entangled with the reconstitution of Poland. The collapse of the Central Powers had invalidated the treaties of Brest-Litovsk and reopened the question of setting boundaries from the Baltic littoral to the Pontic steppe. Two fledgling powers, Bolshevik Russia and republican Poland, old antagonists in new guises, were the prime antagonists in an immensely complex political and military struggle. Neither side was fully united or consistent in defining its aims or conducting diplomacy and military operations. Also involved were nationalist elements within the populations of Lithuania, Latvia and Ukraine and more indirectly the White armies of Russia and the

[21] RGASPI, f. 71, op. 10, ed. kh. 294, l. 30.
[22] *Ibid.*, ll. 48–48b. He warned the overly zealous Piatakov that he should proceed along these lines without issuing ultimatums to the German troops. *Ibid.*, l. 50.
[23] The most detailed treatment of Rakovski's "reign" is now Francis Conte, *Christian Rakovski, 1873–1941: A Political Biography* (Boulder, CO: East European Monographs, 1989).

representatives of the Entente powers sitting in Paris.[24] On the Polish side, the old antagonists Dmowski and Piłsudski continued to offer different programs for a resurrected Polish state in the east. Dmowski and his followers favored a nationalist solution which meant in effect an expansion to include territories exhibiting predominantly Polish characteristics rather vaguely defined but including Wilno (Vilnius) with a minority Polish population. Piłsudski sought to recreate a federation of Polish, Lithuanian and Ukrainian lands along the lines of the pre-partition Commonwealth, "a union of all nations and peoples who live between us and Russia proper."[25]

In February 1919 Piłsudski sought to take advantage of the main involvement of the Red and White armies on the Ukrainian, Caucasian and Siberian fronts to launch a major offensive in Western Belorussia and West Ukraine. Having occupied Vilnius, the Poles issued appeals for federation addressed in Piłsudski's words to "the inhabitants of the former Grand Duchy of Lithuania," promising them "the possibility of resolving internal, national and religious problems on their own without any kind of coercion or pressure from Poland."[26] But the advance of the Polish army met resistance from local Belorussians, touching off reprisals and pogroms. By the summer Polish troops had occupied Eastern Galicia.

In the meantime, Moscow sought for the first, but not the last time, to reach an agreement by negotiation. The Soviet leaders accepted the Polish preconditions that the Red Army would not be used to support revolution in Poland; that no Polish Soviet government would be created; and that the border would be decided on the basis of self-determination.[27] On again, off again negotiations over the following eight months failed to reach a firm settlement. In December the Entente leaders in Paris agreed to establish an ethnographic boundary, the Curzon Line, to stabilize the situation. They began the delivery of arms and military supplies to Poland.[28] Deeply engaged against Denikin's volunteer army in the south, the Soviet government repeatedly offered to negotiate a fixed

[24] For an analysis favoring the Poles, see Piotr S. Wandycz, *Soviet–Polish Relations, 1917–1921* (Cambridge, MA: Harvard University Press, 1969); for the Russian perspective, see M. I. Mel'tiukhov, *Sovetsko-Polskie voiny. Voenno-politicheskoe protivostoianie, 1918–1939* (Moscow: Veche, 2001), pp. 1–105.

[25] Wandycz, *Soviet–Polish Relations*, pp. 118–22.

[26] I. V. Mikhutina, "Nekotorye problemy istorii pol'sko-sovetskoi voiny 1919–1920," in R. P. Grishina (ed.), *Versal' i novaia vostochnaia Evropa* (Moscow: Institut slavianovedeniia, 1996), p. 173.

[27] Ministerstvo inostrannykh del SSSR, *Dokumenty vneshnei politiki SSSR* (DVP), 27 vols. (Moscow: Izd. politicheskoi literatury, 1957–77), vol. II, doc. 70, pp. 105–6.

[28] A. Ia. Manusevich, "Trudnyi put' k Rizhkomu mirnomu dogovoru 1921," *Novaia i noveishaia istoriia* 1 (1991), p. 32.

boundary based on national self-determination and a permanent peace settlement.[29]

Piłsudski had larger ambitions. In his instructions to the commander of the Volhynian front in March 1920, he stated:

At the present time the Polish government intends to support the national Ukrainian movement in order to create an independent Ukrainian government and in this way significantly weaken Russia, deprive it of its richest agricultural and natural resource borderland (*okrain*). The guiding idea of the creation of an independent Ukraine is the creation of *a barrier between Poland and Russia* and to bring Ukraine under Polish influence and guarantee in this way the expansion of Poland economically (by creating a market for itself) and politically.[30]

His plans came closer to realization when Petliura, desperate for support, signed an agreement granting Volhynia to Poland, thereby virtually reestablishing Poland's boundary of 1771 in Ukraine.

Soviet leaders were equally divided and even less certain about their aims, changing positions as circumstances dictated. Lenin proved to be the most volatile of all. Initially, he was willing to accept the Entente proposal of December 1919 drafted by Lord Curzon to delimit a Polish–Soviet frontier along strictly ethnic lines. This would have assigned what the Poles called the *kresy*, that is Western Belorussia and Western Ukraine (Galicia) to Soviet Russia. But when the Red Army counter-offensive in July 1920 appeared to open the possibility of carrying the revolution to Warsaw and establishing a bridge to the west, he threw caution to the winds. His enthusiasm carried the majority of the Politburo. The Comintern fell into line. "The situation in the Comintern is splendid," wrote Lenin. "Zinoviev, Bukharin and I, too, think that revolution in Italy should be spurred on immediately . . . To this end Hungary should be sovietized, and perhaps Czekhia [sic] and Romania."[31]

Stalin's position appeared to be particularly convoluted. But his actions add up to more than a series of improvisations. He skillfully managed to establish links between three fronts that ran through the borderlands from Galicia to the South Caucasus and into Trans Caspia, often operating through his political allies whom he supported in factional struggles. The center of his concern was the southwestern front, where he was a member of the Revolutionary Soviet, facing the White Army of General

---

[29] DVP, vol. II, docs. 226, 230, 250, 261, pp. 331–3, 355–7, 386–7 and 399–400.
[30] Mikhutina, "Nekotorye problemy," p. 165. Italics in original.
[31] Trotsky appeared to have been inconsistent, appealing for the destruction of Piłsudski and the sovietization of Poland and then in May agreeing with Chicherin that "the sovietization on the bayonets of Moscow would be adventurous and in danger of over-reach." *Ibid.*, pp. 166, 168. See also L. D. Trotskii, *Kak vooruzhilas' revoliutsiia*, 3 vols. in 5 (Moscow: Vyshii voennyi revoliutsionnyi sovet, 1923–1925), vol. I, pp. 394, 418.

Wrangel in the Crimea. As a member of the Revolutionary Soviet of the western front facing the Poles, he could count on his close ally, Kliment Voroshilov, the commander of the front and founder of the famous First Cavalry Army, commanded by another ally Semeon Budenny. In the South Caucasus two of his allies, Sergo Orzhonikidze and Sergei Kirov, were the dominant members of the Kavbiuro.

During the Red Army's counter-offensive, Stalin was optimistic that both Wrangel and the Poles could be beaten. In order to gain Lenin's support for his two-pronged strategy, he took the extraordinary step of endorsing in almost the same words Lenin's call for "an uprising (*vostanie*) in Italy and in the not yet firmly established governments of Hungary and Czekhia [Romania must be crushed]."[32] Still, he adopted a more cautious attitude than his colleagues in the Politburo toward Curzon's proposal to mediate between the Bolsheviks and the Poles. He argued for stalling in order to gain time, while rejecting the mediation with Wrangel who was, he wrote Lenin, "*a Russian general with whom Russia itself will establish a modus operandi as it will arrange its internal affairs independently (samostoiatel'no)*".[33] Ignoring his advice, the majority of the Politburo voted to reject Curzon's offer and to continue the offensive. Once the Poles agreed to an armistice to take effect on July 30, Stalin pressed Voroshilov and Budenny to advance as fast as possible in the few days before the armistice took hold. His primary objective was to occupy Lvov.[34] Earlier that year Stalin had favored giving Galicia independence to prevent it from falling into the hands of the Poles. But once Curzon had drawn a new line including Galicia in Ukraine, Stalin had changed his mind.[35] At the same time, Stalin upbraided "Moscow," meaning Trotsky and the commander in chief of the Red Army, S. S. Kamenev, for failing to support the campaign against Wrangel.[36]

As the Red Army under M. N. Tukhachevskii drove on Warsaw, the debate on the disposition of forces took an unexpected turn in the Politburo. Lev Kamenev seized on the British proposal to mediate as an

[32] Kvashonin *et al.*, *Bol'shevistskoe rukovodstvo*, Stalin to Lenin, July 24, 1920, doc. 91, p. 91.

[33] *Ibid.*, Stalin to Lenin, July 13, 1920, doc. 86, pp. 142–3, italics in original. The Politburo decided to reject Curzon's offer and continue the offensive in Poland. *Ibid.*, note 5, p. 143.

[34] *Ibid.*, Stalin to Voroshilov July 22, 1920, and Stalin to Voroshilov and Budenny, July 23, 1920, docs. 89 and 90, pp. 146–7.

[35] I. V. Mikhutina, *Pol'sko-Sovetskaia voina, 1919–1920 gg* (Moscow: RAN, Institut sla-vianovedeniia i balkanistiki, 1994), pp. 182–3.

[36] Kvashonin *et al.*, *Bol'shevistskoe rukovodstvo*, Stalin to Trotsky, July 26, 1920, doc. 92, p. 149; Stalin to Lenin, July 29, 1920, pp. 150–1; and Stalin to Lenin, July 31, 1920, pp. 151–2. In these telegrams Stalin fiercely resisted Trotsky's attempt to create a separate Crimean front.

invitation to propose a strategic change in the disposition of the Soviet forces. In a memo on July 13 he noted: "what is especially important in view of the unexpected declaration of Curzon on Eastern Galicia together with Lvov, is that our forces should without fail (*obiazatel'no*) march into Galicia and occupy Lvov . . . Special attention should be paid to the occupation of Galicia which Curzon has declared Russian in advance."[37]

At this point, Stalin revealed his opposition to carrying the revolution outside the boundaries of what he considered the ethnic limits of Ukraine, as defined, coincidentally by Lord Curzon! In two articles in *Pravda*, he derided the "march on Warsaw" as "boastful" and "not corresponding to the interests of the Soviet government."[38] In the postwar recriminations over who had lost the battle for Warsaw, Stalin could claim with some justification that the capture of Lvov had been raised from a subsidiary objective to one equal to that of Warsaw.[39] In any case, from his point of view wresting all of Ukraine from the Poles was more expedient politically and more feasible militarily than the prospect of spreading revolution to Poland. Stalin remained true to his aim of a unified Ukraine (and Belorussia) as an essential part of state-building. In his pact with Hitler in 1939 and his wartime negotiations with Churchill and Roosevelt, he maintained this position, at one point firmly rejecting Roosevelt's plea to concede Lvov to the Poles.[40]

During the Civil War Stalin's skepticism about the ability of independent governments in the borderlands to defend themselves seemed justified. But he would push the logic of his position to an extreme in the crisis over Georgia. This became the decisive conflict over Soviet nationality policy, leading to Stalin's open break with Lenin and his victory over the national opposition.

It was not by chance that Stalin chose to challenge Lenin over the South Caucasus: this was the borderland that he had long regarded as

[37] Mikhutina, "Nekotorye problemy," p. 169, quoting archival source.
[38] Stalin, *Sochineniia*, vol. IV, pp. 333 and 339.
[39] In the hotly debated meetings of the Ninth Conference of the Party, Lenin and Trotsky sharply criticized Stalin for his overly optimistic view on the chances of taking Lvov and his refusal to reorient the movement of the First Cavalry Army north to support Tukhachevskii's left flank. Stalin justified himself by blaming the military errors of the army command and demanding an investigation. When Lenin refused, Stalin shot back, "This is why I demanded in the Central Committee the appointment of a commission which would clarify the reasons for the catastrophe [and] would guarantee us from new disasters. C[omrade] Lenin evidently wishes to care for the military command, but I think it is necessary to care for the cause." Kvashonin *et al.*, *Bol'shevistkoe rukovodstvo*, doc. 103 and note 2, pp. 160–2.
[40] How could he, Stalin, be less Soviet than Curzon? he asked. O. A. Rzheshevskii, *Stalin i Cherchill'. Vstrechi. Besedy. Diskussii. Dokumenty, kommentarii, 1941–1945* (Moscow: Nauka, 2004), doc. 177, p. 507. See below, Chapter 8.

his private preserve. The crisis built slowly and reached a climax only in the very last months of Lenin's life. It illustrates not only Stalin's methods for spreading Soviet power into the region, particularly his native Georgia. More fundamentally the outcome foreshadows Stalin's plans for the future structure of the Soviet Union. It also sheds light on Stalin's concept of state relations with the external world that became the basis of Soviet foreign policy.

The crisis began in 1920 when Lenin submitted to his colleagues, including Stalin, a draft of his thesis for the Second Comintern Congress on the national and colonial question. In his comments Stalin contemptuously dismissed Lenin's carefully drawn distinction between the relations of the Russian Soviet Republic with other independent Soviet republics in Ukraine, Latvia and Hungary and those with the autonomous republics within its own borders like the Bashkir and Tatar. In Stalin's words the difference "either does not exist at all, or is so small as to equal zero."[41] As events were to prove this was not a minor quarrel over definitional terms, even though at the time Lenin brushed aside Stalin's crude dismissal of his views without making an issue of it.

South Caucasus

With the defeat of the Whites in the south and the withdrawal of British and French interventionist forces in the winter of 1919–20, Moscow was in a position for the first time since the disintegration of the empire to deal directly with the three South Caucasian republics of Georgia, Armenia and Azerbaizhan.[42] There was no disagreement among the party leadership over the need to reestablish Russia's traditional power in an area of great economic and strategic significance. Once again, it was a question over the best way to accomplish this. Chicherin, Lenin and Stalin represented three nodal points on a wide tactical spectrum.

Chicherin, cautious as ever and sensitive to international complications, favored a gradualist approach whereby Russia would make treaty arrangements with the South Caucasian republics as if they were foreign countries. His plan was to enmesh them in a network of diplomatic, military and economic agreements that would transform them into dependencies of Soviet Russia. Lenin permitted Chicherin to spin his diplomatic web, partly in order to mask his own interventionist policy and

---

[41] Lenin, *Sochineniia*, vol. XXV, p. 624. See also a full translation and discussion in Smith, "Stalin as Commissar," pp. 51–4.

[42] Alex Marshall, *The Caucasus under Soviet Rule* (London: Routledge, 2010), ch. 4 is now the most comprehensive account.

partly to provide a fallback position in case it failed. He clearly preferred a combination of political and military action to install Soviet power in the region. But, as was his custom in such matters, he urged caution, circumspection and sensitivity to local conditions, especially with respect to Georgia. Stalin was determined to secure control over the regional party and army commands. He warned the republics that they had no choice but to join the Union. When they hesitated, he orchestrated armed intervention from the outside with scant respect for the local interests of either nationalists or Communists. His forward policy in the South Caucasus came in 1920–22 at the peak of his enthusiasm for an Eastern policy. His activities and even more those of his supporters threatened to embroil the Soviet state in conflicts with Turkey and Iran on the periphery of traditional Russian power.

In a highly complex and volatile political atmosphere where the Bolshevik leaders at the center and at the local level were often working at cross-purposes, Stalin followed his own course. Once again it is difficult to follow the twists and turns of his tactical adjustments. Even on his home grounds, he found himself occasionally outmaneuvered. For example, in 1919 he was forced to give up temporarily his insistence upon maintaining a South Caucasian Federation that would check the independent aspirations of local nationalists in Azerbaizhan, Armenia and Georgia. He lost this round to the young Anastas Mikoian, a russified Armenian born in Georgia and educated in an Armenian seminary in Tiflis, who had wide experience in the party organization in Baku and elsewhere. Lifting a page from Stalin's book, Mikoian grasped the political advantage of promoting separation as the most effective way of stealing the thunder of the nationalist opposition.[43]

Stalin was indirectly or directly involved in the three stages of Soviet advance in the region: the reconquest of North Caucasus, the absorption of the South Caucasian republics, and the redefinition of borders with Turkey and Iran. In early 1920, the Red Army moved into the strife-ridden mountain districts of North Caucasus. Political authority was in the hands of Stalin's close associate, Sergo Ordzhonikidze, formerly a medical orderly and a russified Georgian. Ordzhonikidze was head of the

---

[43] Stephen Blank, "Bolshevik Organizational Development in Early Soviet South Caucasus: Autonomy versus Centralization, 1918–1924," in Ronald Grigor Suny (ed.), *South Caucasus, Nationalism and Social Change: Essays in the History of Armenia, Azerbaizhan and Georgia*, rev. edn (Ann Arbor: University of Michigan Press, 1996), pp. 316–18. Stalin dismissed out of hand Mikoian's view that Azerbaizhan was in certain respects on a higher level than some Russian provinces; this was mistaking Baku for Azerbaizhan, he said. Stalin, *Sochineniia*, vol. V, p. 47. Cf. Anastas Mikoian, *Tak Bylo: Razmyshleniia o minuvshem* (Moscow: Vagris, 1999), pp. 150–3, who does not mention this incident.

North Caucasus Revolutionary Committee. His deputy, Sergei Kirov, was a Russian who settled in the Caucasus as a refugee from the police and became a Bolshevik organizer in Vladikavkaz. Stalin endorsed their repression of the small Cossack uprising with the assistance of the local Muslim mountain peoples, adding that if "things had been handled that well in Turkestan there would not be tens of thousands of Basmachi." The resettlement of the Terek Cossacks and the distribution of their lands to the Chechens had, in his view, contributed to the stabilization of the North Caucasus. Stalin favored the unification of the mountain peoples in a single autonomous Mountain Republic and the separation of Dagestan into a separate republic. He organized a "general toiling people's congress" in order to consolidate these achievements and "clear the atmosphere" in the North Caucasus.[44]

The way was then open to regain control of the rich oil sources in Baku. This meant in effect overthrowing the independent republic of Azerbaizhan which had survived both Turkish and British occupation. The central organs of the Russian Communist Party with Lenin in charge were still sending orders. But operational command was once again entrusted to Ordzhonikidze and Kirov, as the chairman and deputy respectively of the newly created Caucasian Bureau (Kavbiuro), which enjoyed wide discretionary powers throughout the region. They planned, and in April 1920 carried out, a military invasion of Azerbaizhan in coordination with a local coup by the loyal but small group of Azerbaizhan Communists. Meanwhile, Chicherin had continued to engage Azerbaizhan in diplomatic exchanges ostensibly aimed at forming an alliance against the White forces of General Denikin.

At the same time, Soviet diplomacy had responded favorably to the initiatives of the Turkish nationalist government of Mustafa Kemal "Ataturk" to settle their longstanding rivalry in the region. Kemal renounced pan-Turkic aspirations and abandoned his Azerbaizhan coreligionists. In return, the Bolsheviks agreed to partition Armenia. Within the year the independent Armenian Republic had collapsed in the face of a Turkish invasion from the southwest and Soviet pressure in the northeast. The situation here was particularly confused. There was virtually no proletariat in Armenia where the population was overwhelmingly agrarian. The handful of local Communists were young and undisciplined. In November 1920 Stalin gave orders to Ordzhonikidze to launch an invasion by the Red Army, and Lenin concurred. Stalin's main

---

[44] RGASPI, f. 71, op. 10, ed. kh. 316, ll. 11–12 and 24, Stalin to Lenin, October 26 and 30, 1920. In a revealing addendum Stalin strongly reproached the local Cheka for its demoralizing attempts to control leading party figures in the Kavbiuro including Ordzhonikidze.

concern was that a Turkish subjugation of Armenia would establish a common border with Azerbaizhan and threaten Soviet control of Baku.[45] Meanwhile, Chicherin was busy negotiating with the tottering Armenian nationalist government and Kemal in Ankara in order to avoid a clash with the Turks and secure the best common frontier. In this case, the political advantages were on the side of the Turks. The Bolsheviks gave up the provinces of Kars and Ardahan annexed by the Russian Empire after the Russo-Turkish War of 1877–8. Stalin ended up endorsing the demands of the Turkish negotiators which left a substantial part of the Armenian population under Turkish rule.[46]

The settlement created a frontier zone similar to those established at almost the same time in the west where parts of the Belorussian, Ukrainian and other ethnic populations of the old tsarist borderlands were allotted to Poland, Czechoslovakia and Romania. At the first politically favorable opportunity, Stalin sought to revise these frontiers, imposed by military necessity, in accord with his territorial concept of the state. His negotiations with Hitler in 1939 on the western frontiers, with Roosevelt and Churchill in 1944–5 on the same frontiers, and then his unilateral, postwar demands on Turkey for the "return" of the predominantly Armenian provinces of Kars and Ardahan were all of a piece.

The conquest of Azerbaizhan set the stage for intervention in Iran where the Russian revolution had stimulated a strong anti-imperialist reaction. By 1919 separatist movements threatened to break the country apart. In the northern provinces transient Azerbaizhani workers returning from the Baku oil fields, together with Russian soldiers from Iran's Cossack Guard, formed the basis for a populist, anti-Western separatist movement under the leadership of Kuchuk Khan. In Soviet Russia, Muslim Bolsheviks beat the drums for spreading revolution to the east. But, characteristically, they disagreed over who should direct the operation and whether it should be conducted under the banner of a class war or a national, anti-imperialist movement.

The split within the Soviet leadership over Iran was more predictable. Throughout 1920, Chicherin and his Deputy Commissar for Middle Eastern Affairs, the newly anointed Azerbaizhani Communist Nariman Narimanov, favored taking an anti-British line but warned against premature socialist adventures in Iran.[47] Meanwhile, Lenin was engaging the Asian Communists in a great debate at the Second Comintern

[45] RGASPI, f. 71, op. 10, ed. kh. 316, l. 45, Stalin to Lenin, November 16, 1920.
[46] Richard Hovannisian, "Caucasian Armenia between Imperial and Soviet Rule: The Interlude of National Independence," in Suny, *South Caucasus*, pp. 282–3.
[47] Chicherin was furious that Ordzhonikidze was recruiting Iranians for what he called an adventurist policy that would jeopardize Moscow's diplomatic relations with Teheran. Chicherin to Molotov, July 21, 1921, *Izvestiia TsK KPSS* 4 (303) (April, 1990), p. 167.

Congress in August 1920, where he argued for national liberation but against socialist revolutions in the east. Other Soviet leaders like Grigorii Zinoviev made wild statements about carrying a Holy War (jihad) into the colonial world. Stalin's position remained the most complex of all.

While Stalin was marshalling his forces to take control of the North and South Caucasus, he was increasingly alarmed over independent actions by radical Muslim Bolsheviks. Of particular concern were the Iranian émigrés living in Baku who in 1919 had formed a separate Adalat (Justice Party). Among its leaders were the Iranian-born Armenian Bolshevik Sultanzade (Mikhailian), who was entrenched in the Comintern *apparat* as head of the special section in charge of propaganda in the east, and Ja'far Javadzade (Pishevari), who was to play a key role in 1946 in the Soviet–Iranian conflict over the autonomy of Azerbaizhan. Sultanzade and his colleagues in Adalat were active in recruiting Iranian émigré workers in Turkestan and the South Caucasus to form an Iranian army.[48] But Stalin opposed their independent existence and insisted on their fusion with the Azerbaizhani Bolsheviks into a united Azerbaizhan Communist Party, "a name carrying more territorial than national connotations."[49] In May 1920 the Soviet Volga–Caspian fleet landed on the northern shore of Iran, occupying Resht and Enzeli in order to dismantle Denikin's Caspian flotilla. Following Trotsky's and Lenin's instructions to evacuate as soon as their assignment had been carried out, they did so in June leaving local authority in the hands of the radical nationalists led by Kuchuk Khan. But even Ordzhonikidze, and behind him Stalin, who was pushing for the sovietization of the South Caucasus, admitted that "there is not and cannot be any talk of a Soviet government in Iran."[50]

Stalin rapidly became disenchanted with events in Iran. Shortly after the Soviet landings and the proclamation by Kuchuk Khan of a Persian Soviet Republic, Sultanzade and his associates began to push for radical social and cultural policies. This alienated the local Muslim supporters of Kuchuk Khan, who found himself sidelined. Both Kirov and Ordzhonikidze reported that the local situation had gotten out of hand. There was a growing danger of international complications as well. When, in June, the radicals organized and took control of the First Congress of the Iranian Communist Party, Stalin moved against them. He supported

[48] Cosroe Chaqueri, "Sultanzade: The Forgotten Revolutionary Theoretician of Iran: A Biographical Sketch," *Iranian Studies* 27:2–3 (1984), pp. 215–17; V. N. Plastun, "Iranski trudiashchiesiia v grazhdanskoi voine v Rossii," *Narody Azii i Afriki* 2 (1972), pp. 57–8.
[49] Tadeusz Swietochowski, *Russia and Azerbaizhan: A Borderland in Transition* (New York: Columbia University Press, 1995), p. 90.
[50] Richard K. Debos, *Survival and Consolidation: The Foreign Policy of Soviet Russia, 1918–1921* (Montreal: McGill-Queens University Press, 1992), p. 187.

a minority faction and later, in September, "deposed" the leadership.[51] Reporting to Lenin, Stalin explained that Kuchuk Khan had been in correspondence with the Shah's government, and having learned that the Bolsheviks knew about this, fled into the forest. Without indicating his own role in replacing Sultanzade and his supporters, Stalin insisted that "in Persia only a bourgeois revolution is possible, relying on the middle class and with the slogan: 'drive the English out of Persia.'" Their program should call for the formation of a united republican government, now fragmented into separate khanates, the summoning of the Majlis [parliament] with universal suffrage and the formation of a national army "where above all the soviets should entrench themselves" and improve the position of the peasantry.[52]

Stalin urged a policy of retaining control over Resht and Enzeli until the evacuation of North Iran by the British. He argued that the British were not strong and most Iranians wanted them out of the country. Only an agreement with the Shah's government would protect "our rich fishing industry and millions of tons of rice supplies from the English and deprive them of a base which undoubtedly would threaten the entire Baku region from the south."[53] When necessary, Stalin was prepared to disown his over-zealous allies. When Chicherin protested vigorously that the "Baku comrades (Kirov and Ordzhonikidze) were forming special brigades of Iranian Communists to pursue an adventurist policy across the frontier in violation of treaties signed with Teheran, Lenin and the Politburo supported the cautious policy of the Soviet ambassador, F. A. Rotshtein." Stalin's reaction was: "perhaps Rotshtein is right that the adventurists have acted without authorization (vtorglis)."[54]

An important insight into Stalin's thinking about Iran and revolution abroad comes from his conversations with Rasulzade in 1920, when he argued that he had opposed the zealous local Communists in Baku who wanted to use the uprising in Ghilan across the border to carry out a sovietization of all Iran. This would have been a mistake, said Stalin, because communism or socialism "did not suit Iran." Rasulzade objected that the same could be said about Turkistan, but it had been incorporated

---

[51] Chaqueri, "Sultanzade," p. 217, and S. L. Agaev and V. N. Plastun, "Razrabotka programmy i taktiki kompartii Irana," *Narody Azii i Afriki* 3 (1976), pp. 32–3, 36–7. From his position in the Comintern, Sultanzade continued to dispute Stalin's usurpation of his functions. Stalin later used him to attack Bukharin's thesis at the Sixth Congress and then in the late 1930s had him arrested and executed. Chaqueri, "Sultanzade," pp. 224–5.

[52] RGASPI, f. 71, op. 10, ed. kh. 315, l. 44. Stalin to Lenin, November 16, 1920.

[53] *Ibid.*, l, 55. Stalin to Chicherin with copy to Lenin, November 7, 1920.

[54] Iu. N. Amiatovym *et al.* (eds.), *Lenin. Neizvestnye dokumenty, 1881–1922* (Moscow: Rosspen, 1999), docs. 313, 317, 334, pp. 458, 467, 484.

into the Soviet Union. Stalin thought for a moment and then answered: "However you may look at it, in Turkistan there is an intelligentsia that has finished Russian schools."[55] In defining the Soviet Union as Stalin thought it should be, was he not reflecting on his own experience as a man of the borderlands whose exposure to Russian culture had been crucial in his intellectual formation and revolutionary consciousness?

Stalin had now freed his hands to deal directly with Georgia where his differences with Lenin over the nationalities question were thrown into bold relief. Stalin had his own personal reasons for desiring an overthrow of the Georgian Menshevik government run by his old adversaries from the revolutionary underground. But here too, strategic interests were prominent in his reasoning. Once again the defense of Baku with its essential oil provided him with a justification. For him Georgia represented the third side of the triple threat to the oil fields, the first being from Iran, the second from Armenia. The territory east of Tiflis was wide open for an attack from Georgia by the Entente which, he argued, once it had reached Elizavetpol, could organize an Azerbaizhani bourgeois government, taking the Red forces in Azerbaizhan in the rear. "While the bourgeois government of Georgia exists, this threat is the most dangerous of all."[56]

The story of the Soviet conquest of Georgia has been told often and well.[57] Stalin's role in overthrowing the Georgian Menshevik Republic is well documented and unambiguous. In early 1921 he supported his colleague Ordzhonikidze's urgent request for permission to invade Georgia while Trotsky counseled delay and Lenin hesitated until his hand was forced by local initiatives. Stalin made certain that the Red Army units in the area were placed under the direct command of the Kavbiuro, headed by Ordzhonikidze, and independent of Trotsky's authority. When the troops were sent into action it was without the knowledge of the commander in chief of the Red Army, General Sergei Kamenev. A final Stalinist touch: even after he won Politburo approval for his interventionist actions, he did not inform the local Georgian Communist Party despite the fact that as a strong indigenous organization it would have been his most reliable ally if he had intended to encourage a broadly based uprising from below. It soon became obvious that this is precisely what he did not intend.

[55] Rasulzade, "Vospominaniia," pp. 43, 46, 49.
[56] RGASPI, f. 71, op. 10, ed. kh. 315, l. 45, Stalin to Lenin, November 16, 1920.
[57] See, for example, Pipes, *The Formation of the Soviet Union*, pp. 234–41, 266–82; Suny, *The Making of the Georgian Nation*, pp. 209–23, and especially Moshe Lewin, *Lenin's Last Struggle* (New York: Pantheon, 1968).

From the beginning of the campaign, Stalin and his associates simply ignored Lenin's preferences for extensive concessions to the vanquished Mensheviks. "I ask you," Lenin wrote to Ordzhonikidze, "to remember that the internal and international situation of Georgia demands from the Georgian Communists not the application of the Russian pattern, but the skillful and flexible creation of a distinctive tactic based on the greatest compliance with all kinds of petty bourgeois elements."[58] But Stalin and Ordzhonikidze, acting through the Kavbiuro, paid no heed to the sensitivities of the local Communists in the South Caucasus, and not only the Georgians. The Stalinists ran roughshod over the treaties which Lenin and Chicherin had negotiated with the three republics. At the Tenth Party Congress in 1921, Stalin accused Chicherin of making too much of "national self-determination . . . an empty slogan exploited by the imperialists" which "we disposed of two years ago." Calling this formulation "too diffuse" Stalin reminded the Foreign Commissar that it had been replaced by the new slogan, "the right of people to national separation." It was plain enough from the context that Stalin was not playing with words. Self-determination had been interpreted by local Communists as their right to represent the proletarian interests of their republics as the basis for real autonomy within a Soviet federation. National separation, as Stalin noted, was "more suitable for the former colonies." In other words it was not applicable to republics within the Soviet Union but only to anti-imperialist movements in the colonial world.[59]

Stalin took his revenge on the local parties in Armenia, Azerbaizhan and Georgia once all three republics had been incorporated into the Soviet Union. Operating out of the Kavbiuro, he and Ordzhonikidze bullied them into restoring the South Caucasus Federation and deprived them of the last shred of their nominal rights as independent republics. Subsequently, at the Twelfth Party Congress he justified his policy with an extraordinary argument for a Marxist. He declared that the South Caucasus Federation served the vital function of preventing the ten (sic!) nationalities of the region from killing one another. It also deprived Georgia of its privileged economic and geographical position in the Caucasus and restrained the Georgians from removing the Armenians from Tiflis, where they formed the majority, in order to create a genuine national capital.[60] He had already made it clear than in his view all the 65 million non-Russian nationalities among the Soviet republics lagged behind

[58] The full text of the letter is in Suny, *The Making of the Georgian Nation*, p. 211.
[59] *Desiatyi s"ezd RKP(b), mart 1921 goda: Stenograficheskii otchet* (Moscow: Gosizdat. politicheskoi literatury, 1960), p. 185.
[60] *Dvenadtsatyi s"ezd RKP(b), 17–23 aprelia 1923 goda: Stenograficheskii otchet* (Moscow: Gosizdat. politicheskoi literatury, 1923), pp. 488–9. A few months earlier Stalin warned

Russia "in the sense of statehood."[61] In other words, a reconstitution of the former empire along Soviet lines would serve similar purposes. It would eliminate communal warfare in the borderlands and reconcile the competing interests of ethnic groups who were incapable of creating their own nation state. These were not necessarily unworthy aims. Nor were they incompatible with the inclinations of the Bolshevik leadership. The difference was that Stalin's methods appeared to others, including finally Lenin, as too impatient, intolerant, coercive and self-aggrandizing.

In the shadows of Stalin's brusque interventions in the affairs of local Communists stood his larger design for the transformation of the loose federation of republics that had emerged from the Civil War into a unitary state with a federal facade. It must be recalled at this point that the first Soviet constitution of 1918 had left open the question of the final structure of the state: whether or not it would be a federation and if so what kind.[62] Earlier and more consistently than Lenin, Trotsky or Bukharin, Stalin outlined a theory of statehood in which he sought to give institutional form to his three principles of territory, nationality and class. As we have seen, his pre-revolutionary work on the nationalities question had already revealed his attachment to the idea that territory was the indispensable basis for national identity even as class identity transcended physical boundaries. It was Stalin's self-appointed task to reconcile these principles. His solution for a multinational state system like the Russian Empire was not the triumph of the class over the national principle but their fusion in the administrative framework of "regional autonomy of the borderlands" (*oblastnaia avtonomiia okrain*): that is, the territorialization of cultural and linguistic principles.[63]

At the end of the Civil War in October 1920, Stalin published in *Pravda* a comprehensive review of his nationality policy that aimed at illustrating how these principles would be carried out in the new Soviet state. In many ways it foreshadowed the policy of *korenezatsiia* (nativization or indigenization) that he zealously implemented in the 1920s. He built his argument around three concepts. First he envisioned a hierarchy of territorial units. These ranged from the "narrow administrative autonomy" of the Volga Germans, the Chuvash and the Karelians, to "the broader political autonomy" of the Bashkirs, Volga Tatars and Kirghiz, to the more highly developed form of Ukraine and Turkestan and the territory regulated

---

the Armenians that only the Soviet Union could save them from "physical extermination" by resolving "the age-old conflicts between the Armenians and the surrounding Muslim countries." Stalin, *Sochineniia*, vol. IV, pp. 413–14.
[61] *Desiatyi s"ezd, marta 1921*, p. 212.
[62] Carr, *The Bolshevik Revolution*, vol. I, p. 137, for details.
[63] Stalin, *Sochineniia*, vol. II, pp. 361–7.

by treaty such as Azerbaizhan. At the same time, he admitted that the administrative division of the Soviet state was not yet complete. Second, he insisted on close ties between the center and borderlands requiring the elimination of the isolation, patriarchal backwardness and distrust of the center that prevailed in the borderlands. Third, he promoted local national schools, theater and other cultural resources to raise the cultural level of the borderlands; and fourth, he demanded the staffing in so far as possible of all the party and soviet organizations, judicial, administrative, and economic, with local people who knew the language, customs and traditions of the population. Even the small number of indigenous intelligentsia and the even smaller number of local Communists, he insisted, should not delay the process of enlightening the masses; here he drew a parallel with the former tsarist army officers who had joined the Red Army.

Finally, Stalin reproached those comrades who had adopted a tactless attitude toward sovietization by promoting "heroic efforts" to introduce "pure communism." He drew examples from the failure to understand that the consolidation of living space in Azerbaizhan violated the Muslim beliefs in the sacredness of the hearth, or that the head-on clash with the religious prejudices of the Muslims in Dagestan should be replaced by indirect, more careful means. Significantly, he ended his paean to gradualism and sensitivity to national traditions with the reminder that the strengthening of ties between Central Russia and the borderlands "would smash to smithereens all and every intrigue of the Entente."[64]

There were already hints that the "liberalism" of Stalin's nationality policy was opportunistically related not only to the threat of foreign intervention still hanging over the country but also more fundamentally to the construction of a powerful state. Here was an early indication of his view that the fusion of the center and the borderlands would be the result not of a spontaneous joining together but of action by the center. As early as the Third Congress of Soviets in January 1918, he had made it clear that "the roots of all conflicts between the periphery and Central Russia lie in the question of power."[65] Stalin went on to demonstrate that socialist revolution in the Russian Empire had produced a situation in which a more advanced center, that is a territorial core possessing a proletarian class structure, was bound to dominate a backward periphery. Stalin revealed the other side of the coin of *korenizatsiia* when he expanded on the idea that the periphery was not only economically backward, compared to the Russian core, but also culturally underdeveloped. In particular, "the

[64] *Ibid.*, vol. IV, pp. 351–63.   [65] *Ibid.*, vol. IV, p. 31.

people of the East," as he called them, lacked the homogeneity of the central provinces. They were barely emerging from the Middle Ages, or else had only just entered the stage of capitalism.[66] At the constitutional debates during the Twelfth Congress in 1923, when Stalin was hard-pressed by his critics, he was even more bluntly explicit. He expanded upon his earlier delimitation of the center and the periphery along territorial–class lines. The center was a proletarian region, the periphery was peasant.[67]

This crude and distorted image of the center–periphery relationship enabled Stalin to draw some "theoretical" conclusions. Socioeconomic backwardness on the periphery gave the local bourgeois nationalists their opportunity to demand separation from the center, weakening the Soviet power. And this in turn created "a zone of foreign intervention and occupation" that further threatened the socialist center.[68] In practical terms, Stalin proposed to secure the territorial integrity and external security of the state by winning over the nationalities on the periphery. He offered them a form of association with the center, which he dubbed "socialist federalism." That is, it would be national in form and socialist in content.

In sum, there were two essential parts to Stalin's program of socialist federalism. First, he offered the nationalities control over their local affairs, including administration, justice and education conducted in their native language. There would be "no state language," he assured them. Second, he argued that the Russian Federation would protect them from foreign domination and the loss of those autonomous rights that would be guaranteed by a Soviet center.[69]

For Bukharin's and Trotsky's concept of the mutual interdependence of Russia and world revolution, Stalin substituted the mutual interdependence of Russia and its borderlands. In 1920 he wrote, "Central Russia, the hearth of world revolution cannot hold out long without the assistance of the border regions which abound in raw materials, fuels and foodstuffs. The border regions of Russia, in their turn, are inevitably doomed to imperialist bondage without the political, military or organizational support of the more developed Central Russia."[70] Stalin even went so far as to argue that the unity of center and periphery provided the two "constant conditions" that guaranteed the success and future

[66] *Ibid.*, vol. IV, pp. 74–5, 236–7.   [67] *Dvenadtsatyi s"ezd, aprelia 1923*, pp. 479, 650.
[68] Stalin, *Sochineniia*, vol. IV, pp. 162, 237, 372.
[69] *Ibid.*, vol. IV, pp. 70, 74, 166, 226–7, 237, 356, 358.
[70] *Ibid.*, vol. IV, p. 351; see also *ibid.*, vol. V, p. 22; "The federation of soviet republics is based on a community of military and economic affairs."

development of the revolution: that is, Russia's "vast and boundless land" and its autarkic resource base.[71]

Even as Stalin shaped the South Caucasus Federation in order to enhance his own power, he drafted a plan for a new constitution that would incorporate the various Soviet republics into the Russian Soviet Federated Socialist Republic. This meant reducing the status and rights of the Ukrainian, Belorussian, South Caucasian and Turkestan republics, which enjoyed various forms of treaty relations with the Russian republic, to the level of the autonomous republics, like the Bashkir and Tatar, which were already part of the RSFSR. Stalin ingenuously defended this plan by invoking the principle of equality of nationalities.

This so-called "autonomization plan" touched off a violent reaction among the anti-Stalinist Georgian Communists, who protested against the loss of sovereign rights. In the ensuing controversy Lenin, now seriously ill but still politically active, belatedly realized that Stalin's and Ordzhonikidze's treatment of the South Caucasian republics was more than a local squabble. He diagnosed it as a more serious disease which had spread with ominous swiftness throughout the party organs. He called it by its true name – "Great Russian chauvinism." He feared its contaminating effects on Soviet Russia's international struggle against imperialism. How could the Communists preach national liberation in the East if they treated their own minorities contemptuously and unequally? Lenin offered an alternative plan. The Russian Federation, Ukraine, Belorussia and the South Caucasian Federation would "together and equally" enter "a new union, a new federation" in which they would all retain their autonomy. Already terminally ill, Lenin was determined, nevertheless, to force an open confrontation with Stalin over the nature of the state.[72]

Stalin advanced several arguments in defense of the "autonomization" plan. As usual it is important to discriminate between the rhetorical flights and the substantive issues. Disingenuously, he invoked the principle of the equality of nationalities and the dangers of increasing Great Russian chauvinism. But he also argued from the rostrum of the Tenth Congress in December 1922, and even more forcefully behind the closed doors of the Politburo, that Lenin's proposal would lead to a fragmentation of the center. It would force the creation of an ethnic Russian republic and the separation of the eight autonomous republics that were already part of the RSFSR. Moreover, he declared, "such republics as Bashkiria,

---

[71] *Ibid.*, vol. IV, pp. 375–6, where Stalin contrasted the great advantage of a large state like Russia in organizing a strategic retreat with the limitations for maneuver of a small state like Hungary as a factor in determining the outcome of their respective civil wars.

[72] Lewin, *Lenin's Last Struggle*, pp. 47–54, 145–50.

Kirghizia, the Tatar Republic and Crimea will risk losing their capitals (that are Russian cities) and in any case will be obliged once again to carve out their territories (*perekroit' svoi territorii*) which will still further prolong the organizational reconstruction of the country."[73] To the end of his life Stalin remained irrevocably opposed to the creation of a separate ethnic Russian republic or a separate Russian Communist Party. The issue surfaced again in the mid-1920s when he refuted the proposals of Kalinin and Voroshilov to create a Russian Communist Party, and again, more ominously, in 1948 during the Leningrad Affair when similar proposals made by the Leningrad organization led to their destruction.

In addition to Stalin's "autonomization plan" there were two other points of conflict with Lenin on the nationalities question: the establishment of a bicameral legislature with an upper house based on representation of the republics, and the extent of the rights and representation of the republics in the central commissariats. Stalin gave in on the first two, which he regarded as formal concessions. Let the union republics proclaim their equality with the Russian republic; let there be a second house in the Soviet legislature, just so long as their precise rights and functions were not defined. At a later time, when Stalin's growing control over the party and state bureaucracy was stronger, he could fill the empty institutional vessels with his own content.

With Lenin incapacitated, Stalin pushed through his version of their compromise at the Twelfth Party Congress in April 1923. It was the last time a party congress seriously debated the relationship between the center and the borderlands. His main opponents were made up almost exclusively of the national opposition, mainly Ukrainians, Georgians and Tatars. They were not unified and their arguments were diffuse. Stalin's earlier concessions to Lenin enabled him, ironically, to strengthen his pose as the centrist, poised between the Scylla of excessive centralization tainted with Great Russian chauvinism and the Charybdis of fragmentation of authority in the face of capitalist encirclement. In his characteristically manipulative style, he also played the western against the eastern nationalities: "If we allow the smallest mistake in our relations with the small region of the Kalmyks, who are linked to Tibet and China, this would have a much worse effect on our work than a mistake in relations with Ukraine."[74] Even though the national opposition was able to

---

[73] *Izvestiia TsK KPSS* 9 (1989), 208; *Nashe Otechestvo: Opyt politicheskoi istorii* (Moscow: Terra, 1991), vol. II, p. 155; Stalin, *Sochineniia*, vol. V, p. 152.

[74] Stalin, *Sochineniia*, vol. V, p. 278. For a good summary of the Twelfth Congress debates, see Pipes, *The Formation of the Soviet Union*, pp. 290–3, and for greater emphasis on the "national opposition," Borys, *The Russian Communist Party*, pp. 331–5.

invoke Lenin's name, it was a crippled and absent Lenin whose conversion to their cause was belated and not fully understood by the rest of the Bolshevik leadership. Stalin's proposals were accepted all along the line.

Stalin's victory in the struggle over the constitution had significant implications for the conduct of foreign policy as well. Yet, aside from Lenin, one of the few leading Bolsheviks who appeared to realize just how significant was Khristian Rakovski, a repentant centralist. Recently published documents make clear that he foresaw how "the formal abolition of the independent republics will be the source of difficulties abroad as well as inside the federation. It will lessen the revolutionary-liberation role of proletarian Russia." But for others the domestication of Soviet foreign policy had already proceeded too far for them to turn back. Chicherin was, for once, wholly in favor of Stalin's "autonomization plan" and was one of the instigators of the plan for unifying under his authority the commissariats of foreign affairs of the union republics.[75] To be sure, Bukharin feebly defended the Georgians, but Stalin easily brushed him aside, mocking his sudden change of heart on the question of self-determination.[76]

Muslim borderlands

It is no easy matter to follow Stalin through the labyrinth of his dealing with the Muslim peoples. Initially, he appeared to champion local autonomist movements as a means of spreading Bolshevik power. Yet his actions often had the effect of frustrating or weakening his most ardent supporters. So, although Stalin originally granted the Bashkir nationalists unconditional autonomy, he worked behind the scenes with local Communist Party members to erode the foundations of that autonomy. He sided alternately with the Bashkirs, who demanded their own autonomous state, and the Tatars, who demanded a Volga–Ural republic which would have absorbed about a third of the Bashkir population. In Kazakhstan, at a crucial moment in a three-way struggle among the local population over the precise form of autonomy for the region, he intervened brusquely to impose his own solution rather than working out a compromise. At the head of the Revolutionary Committee he appointed to resolve the dispute stood none other than his deputy in *Narkomnats*, Petskovski, who was, as we have seen, a sworn opponent of autonomy

---

[75] *Dvenadtsatyi s"ezd, aprelia 1923*, pp. 172–3, 180, note 4.
[76] *Ibid.*, pp. 613–15, 650–1.

in any form. Only later, after the essential decisions had been taken, did Stalin permit a popular Kazakh leader to join the committee.[77]

In the meantime, Stalin was posing as a champion of all Asian peoples in their struggle against imperialism. As early as November 1917 he and Lenin launched an appeal to the Muslims of Russia and the East to support the revolution in Russia. They assured the Muslims of the former empire that their "beliefs, customs, national and cultural convictions are declared to be free and inviolable." They denounced all the secret treaties which had partitioned the Muslim states and ended in a call to arms: "Take power in your own countries – Comrades, brothers – we wait for your support."[78] Stalin pursued this line over the next few years. In November 1918, with the slogan, "Do not forget the East," he advocated a shift in party policy toward the Asian borderlands as "the most reliable rear area" and "inexhaustible reserve" of the revolution.[79] That same month, he took the lead in convening the First All-Russian Congress of Communist Organizations of the Eastern Peoples. His pronouncements began to urge equal status for revolutions in Europe and Asia, extolling "Muslim Communists" as the best bridge-builders between the two.[80] In the same spirit he promoted the career of the Tatar Bolshevik, Sultan-Galiev, in the state and party apparatus. As late as 1920 Stalin appointed his protégé to the three-man Executive of *Narkomnats* and made him co-editor of the commissariat's official organ. By that time Sultan-Galiev was well known as the outspoken champion of a large autonomous Tatar-Bashkir state and the prophet of a forward policy in Asia under the red and green banner of Marx and Mohammed.

Sultan-Galiev's flamboyant style led to clashes with party leaders of the dominant Western orientation. In 1919 at the first Comintern Congress Trotsky's draft manifesto reaffirmed the orthodox view that the liberation of the colonies was possible only in conjuncture with the social revolution of the metropolitan working class. The same year, at the Eighth Congress of the Russian Communist Party, pan-Islamism had been denounced in no uncertain terms. Despite these stern warnings Sultan-Galiev persisted in broadcasting his views, though his powerful protector, Stalin, now fell strangely silent. The Tatar leader even risked crossing swords with Lenin at the Second Congress of the Communist Organizations of Eastern Peoples at the end of 1919, when he won a compromise resolution which

[77] Persits, "V. I. Lenin o levosektantskikh oshibakh pervykh kommunistov vostoka," pp. 56–9; Stephen Blank, *The Sorcerer as Apprentice: Stalin as Commissar of Nationalities, 1917–1924* (Westport, CT: Greenwood Press, 1994), pp. 24–9, 144–50.
[78] RGASPI, f. 71, op. 10, ed. kh. 287, 9–12.   [79] Stalin, *Sochineniia*, vol. IV, p. 171.
[80] *Ibid.*, vol. IV, pp. 230–1, 236, 394–8.

gave equal billing to national liberation movements in the East and social revolution in the West.[81]

Sultan-Galiev immediately followed up his victory by proposing that Stalin be appointed Commissar of Foreign Affairs for the East and be entrusted "with the leadership of all internal and external policies of Soviet power in the East."[82] It is difficult to imagine that Sultan-Galiev had not consulted beforehand with his chief about the propriety of this extraordinary proposal. In any case, he and his associates must have shared full confidence in Stalin's sympathy with their twin goals of Muslim national autonomy within the Soviet state and Muslim leadership of the revolution in the East. There could be no mistake, moreover, that their proposal constituted a direct challenge to Lenin's leadership of the party and the state. Its acceptance would have recognized Stalin as a kind of "emperor of the East" allowing him to overshadow Trotsky and stand as Lenin's equal.

From Stalin's point of view there was a greater danger that radical Muslim Communists were taking over his revolutionary rhetoric on the East, driving it to its logical activist conclusions and escaping from his direct control. Coincident with events in Iran, Sultan-Galiev was agitating for a similar radical revolutionary course, albeit under his leadership and based in Turkestan. At the peak of his influence, having succeeded Stalin at the head of the Musbiuro, Sultan-Galiev sought to have his organization placed in charge of a Muslim Red Army to liberate the peoples of the East.[83] Meanwhile, at the Second Comintern Congress in 1921, leading Asian Communists had challenged Lenin's thesis on the colonial question. They argued that they suffered from a double exploitation, first of their country as a whole by the foreign imperialists, and second of the toiling masses by the national bourgeoisie tied to the imperialists. Consequently, it was possible and necessary for the toiling masses to carry out a revolution that liberated them from both the imperialists and their nationalist bourgeois allies: in other words transform an anti-imperialist into a socialist revolution. Along with the more famous challenge to Lenin by the Indian Communist M. N. Roy, Sultanzade developed a similar position from the rostrum of the congress.[84]

Stalin took no part in the Comintern debate on the national and colonial question, but it placed him in a delicate position. It was important

---

[81] Alexandre Bennigsen and Chantal Lemercier-Quelquejay, *Les mouvements nationaux chez les Musulmans de Russie: Le Sultangalievisme au Tatarstan* (Paris: Mouton, 1960).

[82] Persits, "Vostochnye," p. 92.

[83] Blank, "Soviet Politics and the Iranian Revolution," pp. 173–94.

[84] *Vtoroi Kongress Kominterna, 19 iiulia–6 avgusta 1920* (Kharkov: Izdat. 'Proletarii', 1929), pp. 172–3.

for him to maintain his credentials as champion of the Eastern peoples. But he was determined to keep control of their revolutionary activities and to subordinate them to the imperatives of building the Soviet state. Even as he directed the final stages in the Soviet conquest of the South Caucasus, he moved to assert his authority over the independent-minded Muslim Communists within his reach.

Contrary to the hopes of the Muslim Bolsheviks, Stalin was moving farther away from their views of autonomy and toward a more centralized state. As the Civil War wound down, Stalin saw a greater need to rein in the centrifugal forces on the still undefined frontiers. His restless clients had to be brought into line. In early 1921 he accused the Musbuiro headed by Sultan-Galiev of "unsatisfactory work," stripped it of its administrative authority and reduced it in name and function to an agitation and propaganda bureau. He reproached the Turkic Communists for "national deviation" and told them that henceforth their central bureau would confine itself to "the struggle with nationalist survivals and measures of strengthening communism *theoretically* in the east of our country."[85]

At the Tenth Party Congress in 1921 Sultan-Galiev openly clashed with his former mentor over Stalin's proposals to include in the central state organs representatives from the independent republics, like Georgia, but not from the autonomous republics like the Tatar–Volga or Turkestan. Stalin had made it clear that from his perspective the Turkic people had not passed through the stage of capitalism, had virtually no industrial proletariat and would require a special effort to pass from "primitive forms of economy" to socialism by skipping the stage of capitalism.[86] Sultan-Galiev blithely dismissed these Marxist categories. Turkestan's larger population, greater territorial extent and strategic location entitled it, in theory, to "independence," he insisted; thus it occupied in reality "a much more favorable position than Georgia" in its relations with the center. Besides, he added, there should be "no prodigal sons" and all republics should be treated the same way. Stalin turned on his erstwhile disciple, as only he could, accusing him of "slandering the party" and proposing "still-born, reactionary ideas."[87]

---

[85] Stalin, *Sochineniia*, vol. V, pp. 2–3, emphasis added, 402.

[86] *Desiatyi s"ezd*, p. 185. Stalin argued further that 65 million non-Russian nationalities lagged behind Russia in the sense of nationhood. He divided them into three groups: the Turkic peoples, the most backward nomadic pastoral tribes, and places like Azerbaizhan, which, having rejected Mikoian's claim for equality, required special methods to bring them into a Soviet economy. *Ibid.*, p. 212.

[87] "O tak nazyvaemoi 'Sultan-Galievskoi contrrevoliutsionnoe organizatsii,'" *Izvestiia TsK KPSS* 10 (309) (October, 1990), pp. 76–7, from previously unpublished archival material.

By the Twelfth Congress in 1923, soon after Stalin became General Secretary of the All-Union Communist Party, storm signals of "nationalist deviation" among Bolsheviks went up all along the periphery from Ukraine and South Caucasus to Central Asia. Even more ominous tensions were rising within the inner party circles over the outbreak of disturbances in the borderlands where the official end of the Civil War had not brought peace and stability. From 1921 to 1923 almost everywhere along the southern periphery uprisings and guerrilla fighting against Soviet power continued, albeit at a low level.[88] The toughest nodes of resistance were in the North Caucasus, where the Chechen uprising of 1920 was just winding down, and Central Asia, where the widespread Basmachi revolt drew support from sanctuaries across the Afghan frontier.[89] The Basmachi revolt, in particular, represented for Stalin the most dangerous scenario: national Bolsheviks plus an internal sectarian war plus foreign intervention.

More troublesome for Stalin were Lenin's belated but no less heartfelt expressions of support for some of their views. It appeared then that Trotsky held the balance. His rivalry with Stalin intensified during the Civil War but only reached a critical point during Lenin's break with Stalin over the nationality question. In the view of many historians, his refusal to deliver the *coup de grâce* to Stalin at the Twelfth Congress has always been regarded as a mistake and a puzzle. It was only in the 1990s when long-repressed documents came to light that it became clearer why Trotsky acted as he did.[90]

Trotsky's position at the Twelfth Congress has always appeared convoluted at best. As we have seen, Lenin had entrusted him with a letter and documents in order to defend the sick leader's views on the nationality question at the congress. Yet, Trotsky, the archives now reveal, begged off citing his own illness. Then he did not return the documents, as Lenin had asked him to. Instead, he worked out a compromise with Stalin before the discussion sections of the congress even met. Throughout the congress Trotsky did not once refer to Lenin's letter,

---

[88] Blank, The Sorcerer as Apprentice, chs. 5–11.

[89] Requisitioning by the Bolsheviks had sparked a Chechen uprising in 1920 which was put down the following year by the Red Army and loyal mountain peoples. Marie Bennigsen Broxup, "The Last Ghazawat: The 1920–21 Uprising," in Abdurahman Avtorkhanov and Marie Brenningsen Broxup (eds.), *The North Caucasus Barrier: The Russian Advance to the Muslim World* (London: Hurst and Co., 1992), pp. 116–31; William S. Ritter, "The Final Phase in the Liquidation of the Anti-Soviet Resistance in Tadzhikistan: Ibrahim Bek and the Basmachi, 1924–31," *Soviet Studies* 37:4 (1985), pp. 484–7.

[90] *Tainy natsional'noi politiki TsK RKP. Chetvertoe soveshchanie TsK RKP s otvetsvennymi rabotnikami natsional'nykh respublik i oblastei v g. Moskve 9–12 iiunia 1923. Stenographicheskii otchet* (Moscow: Insan, 1992) with an introduction by Bulat Sultanbekov.

leaving Rakovski alone to defend Lenin's position and take the brunt of Stalin's assault. Rather Trotsky placed his faith in the Red Army as the most concrete and effective method of resolving the national question. Privately, he proposed a compromise. Stalin accepted an amendment to his theses declaring that "one of the most important tasks of the party is the education of the Red Army in the spirit of brotherhood and merciless resistance to chauvinistic attitudes." Stalin then went one better than Trotsky by advocating that initial steps be taken to create national units in the army as the prelude to withdrawing essentially Russian units from the republics. But, he warned, to do this prematurely would invite external intervention; Turks would enter Georgia and half-Ukrainian, half-Polish bands would enter Ukraine.[91] Once again Stalin accepted a formal compromise while invoking the dangers of a foreign threat which might require postponement or revision of the point conceded.

What had not been clear until the revelations of post-communism is that Trotsky then pursued with great vigor his campaign to commit Stalin to a moderate policy on the nationalities of the Muslim borderlands. In the preliminaries to the critical debates at the Twelfth Congress, Trotsky had resisted the attempts of Sultan-Galiev to recruit him for the cause of greater national autonomy in the name of Lenin against Stalin. Instead, during the debates at the Fourth Party Conference immediately following the Twelfth Congress, Trotsky declared that he had joined with his Politburo comrades in regarding the compromising letters of Sultan-Galiev as proof that his evolution to a nationalist position "went beyond the limits where an illicit fractional struggle turned into direct state treason." He declared himself less interested in the legal question than how Sultan-Galiev arrived at this position, which was a political question. First, he explained, the party had not been able under the conditions of war communism to relieve substantially the oppressed condition of the nationalities which had long existed under tsarism. Second, in the party milieu where Sultan-Galiev operated, he had not encountered any opposition to his views; by focusing exclusively on the evils of Great Russian chauvinism, his associates had failed to consider the dangers of local nationalism. Without excusing Sultan-Galiev in any way, Trotsky nonetheless reserved his strongest criticism for the "leftists" at

---

[91] *Dvenadtsatyi s"ezd, aprelia 1923*, pp. 167–8, 172, 175; See also *Izvestiia TsK KPSS* 9 (1990), pp. 147–9, for Trotsky's letter. Trotsky in turn accepted Stalin's amendment to his amendment largely because "the nationalization of the army," as he called it, fully accorded with his ideas of forming regional-based militia to replace the regular army.

the conference, both Tatars and centralizers like Valerian Kuibyshev and
Dmitri Manuilskii who were known to be close to Stalin. He lambasted
Manuilskii for having declared that the nationality resolutions of the
Twelfth Congress would fail if they were not carried out "by the hands of
Great Russians." He reminded them that this could only lead to ignoring
the peasant masses who would then be won over by enemies like the Basmachi. It was up to the party to work with both the rightists and leftists
until the most advanced elements of the Communists–nationalists were
in command at the local level. Raising the political and cultural level of
the local cadres was the only means to strengthen the socialist enterprise
without offending national sensibilities.[92]

For Trotsky the Sultan-Galiev affair had several important lessons to
teach. First, that the party should be purged of nationalist elements
which went beyond the limits he had defined as giving aid and comfort
to the Basmachi. He urged, however, that these purges should be carried
out slowly and selectively. Second, in the financial sphere it was vital to
strike a balance between maintaining central planning and encouraging
local initiative that might require concessions at the expense of the plan.
Rigid adherence to centralization could only play into the hands of the
Basmachi.

As a general consequence of the debate over Sultan-Galiev, Trotsky
defended his amendments to the resolution of the Twelfth Congress on
nationalities against the opposition of Manuilskii but with the approval of
Kuibyshev and Stalin by stressing two points. First, for Trotsky the key
to overcoming the backwardness of the peoples of the borderlands was
to educate the younger generation. Rejecting as too mechanical the simple formula "being determines consciousness," Trotsky argued that the
process of creating the material conditions for the rise of an indigenous
proletariat through industrialization would be too slow; it was necessary
to jump stages (again!). Second, Trotsky warned that only the party could
succeed in raising the consciousness of the lower strata of the population (*nizy*). Unlike Europe, where the proletariat had developed its class
actions and institutions over many years, the peoples of Bashkiria and
Kirgizia (Kazakhstan) had practically no political life, and communism
was only a word. Those who joined with the Bolsheviks still retained
elements of conservatism. That is why, Trotsky concluded, a steady and
slow process of educating them within the party was preferable to excluding them at the first opportunity. That is why, too, comrades from the
center should avoid at all costs any sign of condescension in working

[92] *Dvenadtsatyi s"ezd, aprelia 1923*, pp. 73–80.

with the more backward comrades and never invoke the authority of the center in taking decisions.[93] While Trotsky continued to hammer away at Manuilskii, he did not criticize Stalin or use the occasion to flourish Lenin's letter. The reasons should now be clear.

Trotsky was genuinely concerned about the nationalist tendencies of indigenous party activists in the borderlands. By using Lenin's letter to exercise pressure on Stalin, he believed he had forced Stalin to identify Great Russian chauvinism as the main threat to unity within the party. Trotsky had no desire to defend Sultan-Galiev or the Georgians. Instead he wanted Stalin to go on record that the center would not impose its will by fiat on the borderlands, but rather follow a gradual course. By this time he should have learned that Stalin had no difficulty in switching positions for tactical reasons and that resolutions alone could not bind him.

Stalin, angered by Sultan-Galiev's renewed criticisms of Great Russian chauvinism at the meetings of the discussion sections preceding the Twelfth Congress, moved to exclude him from the party, strip him of his party positions and turn his case over to the secret police (GPU) for investigation.[94] The discovery of two conspiratorial letters from Sultan-Galiev linking him to the Basmachi enabled Stalin to persuade his Politburo colleagues to have Sultan-Galiev arrested. It was a sign of Stalin's investment in the case that Sultan-Galiev was the first prominent party member to suffer arrest for political reasons. From the rostrum of the Congress, Stalin attacked his fallen client and his supporters for having formed "an illegal organization" to undermine the confidence of the nationalities in the revolutionary [read Russian] proletariat, to seek "an alliance with openly counter-revolutionary forces" and to spread the organization beyond the boundaries of the Soviet state.[95]

Stalin's campaign to turn the activities of Sultan-Galiev into a more generalized ideological deviation called "sultangalievism" produced one of the most extensive intra-party debates over the nationality question. The arrest had raised larger questions in the central organs of the party on the implementation of the resolutions taken at the Twelfth Congress, and the decision was taken to call a special and secret party conference in June 1923 with representatives of the leading officials of the national republics

[93] *Tainy natsional'noi politiki*, pp. 245–53. These two interventions dispel the long-held belief that Trotsky did not speak at the conference and made no attempt to implement Lenin's instructions, albeit in his own way.

[94] The official order came from the Partkollegiia of the Central Control Commission headed by Stalin's creature, Valerian Kuibyshev, "O tak nazyvaemoi," p. 77.

[95] Stalin, *Sochineniia*, vol. V, pp. 301–12.

and regions.[96] The debates revealed the deep splits in the party over nationalities policy. It was more pronounced among the nationalities of the borderlands themselves, the Tatars, Ukrainians and Georgians, than among the central party leaders. Both Stalin and Trotsky were committed to the idea of maintaining party unity in the face of a potential split between the radical internationalists ("the left") and the radical national autonomists ("the right").

Because of Lenin's letter Stalin found himself on the defensive. He was forced to admit that he had defended Sultan-Galiev in the past, but excused himself on the grounds that intellectuals sympathetic to the revolution in the eastern borderlands were extremely rare. Stalin conceded he had even protected Akhmed-Zaki Akhmetovich Validov, one of the founders of the Bashkir Republic and president of its Military-Revolutionary Committee before he broke with the Bolsheviks and participated in the Basmachi revolts from 1920 to 1923. But this too he explained as a necessary temporary measure to keep other Tatar leaders loyal to the revolution. Subsequently, he had warned Sultan-Galiev that his contacts with extreme nationalists were dangerous, but to no avail. More accusatory than Trotsky, Stalin denounced his former protégé as having crossed the line "from the Communist camp to the camp of the Basmachi. From that moment he ceased to exist for the party." Nonetheless, after reviewing the sins of the "right" and "left" on the nationality question, Stalin acknowledged that if the leftists practiced a policy of "stratification" (*rassloenie*), which he defined as transplanting Russian forms into specific national conditions, then this could only separate the party from the local peasantry: "Of the two dangers, the left danger may turn out to be the greater danger of the dangers." Stalin concluded, rather surprisingly, that having recanted Sultan-Galiev could be freed; it was enough to exclude him from the party.[97]

What proved to be only the first act of the Sultan-Galiev drama demonstrated that Stalin's colleagues were not yet prepared to accept his interpretation of national deviation as tantamount to treason. He was not yet master of the Soviet Union. The GPU turned up evidence to corroborate many of Stalin's accusations – the creation of an illegal group, serious deviation from the party and state nationalities policies in the East, and even attempts to create "powerful, autonomous (*samostoiatel'nyi*) eastern states uniting all existing eastern governments on the territory of the USSR and eastern countries on our borders." But it categorized as

[96] Bulat Sultanbekov, *Pervaia zhertva genseka. M. Sultan-Galiev. Sud'ba, liudi, vremia* (Kazan: Tatarskoe kn. izd., 1991).

[97] *Tainy natsional'noe politiki*, pp. 81–5.

"dubious" reports by certain agents on the alleged plans of Sultan-Galiev "to establish ties with Turkish, Persian and Afghan embassies in Moscow or to provide support for the Basmachis." The head of the GPU, V. R. Menzhinskii, saw no further need to detain Sultan-Galiev. The Politburo concurred. For five years Stalin bided his time while he repeatedly blocked Sultan-Galiev's appeals for reinstatement into the party.[98] When he struck again he was de facto ruler of the Soviet Union and his denunciation of "sultangalievism" was part of a larger strategy of combining a campaign for intensification of the class struggle on the domestic front with an all-out attack on the bourgeois nationalist front, and the evocation of a war scare on the international front.

Inner Asian borderlands

Although Stalin was not directly involved in the struggle over the Inner Asian borderlands during the Civil War and Intervention, the Japanese threat to the Bolsheviks' reconstruction of Russian power in the region left a profound mark on him. As early as 1912 the Kwantung Army had drafted political plans for separating Mongolia as well as Manchuria from China as a bulwark against Russia.[99] It actively set them in motion during the First World War and the Russian Civil War when it became apparent that the Chinese showed signs of renewing their interest in Mongolia and the Russians were forced to withdraw their troops from the borderlands. Former officers of the Kwantung garrison sought to take advantage of the Bolshevik Revolution to detach the Maritime Provinces from the new Soviet republic and demilitarize all of Eastern Siberia. During the four-year campaign against the Red Army over 240,000 Japanese troops were involved at one time or another in the Intervention.[100]

In the renewed struggle over the Mongolian borderland following the Russian revolution, Japan undertook an ambitious if badly organized campaign to create a large, unified autonomous Mongolia under its protection in order to forestall Chinese efforts to reestablish their control over the region. In a Foreign Ministry memo of December 1918, the Chinese rehearsed their time-honored policy of treating with the borderlands:

---

[98] "O tak nazyvaemoi," p. 80.

[99] Chihiro Hosoya, "The Military and the Foreign Policy of Prewar Japan," *Hitotsubashi Journal of Law and Politics* 7 (July, 1974), p. 5.

[100] Japanese soldiers and politicians were not, however, in agreement on the scale of the Intervention or whether or not to work with the United States. S. S. Paskov, V. V. Sovasteev and A. G. Chernykh, "Iaponskaia interventsiia na sovetskom Dal'nem Vostoke i proval (1918–1922) po iaponskim publikatskiiami," *Narody Azii i Afriki* 6 (1977), pp. 21–35.

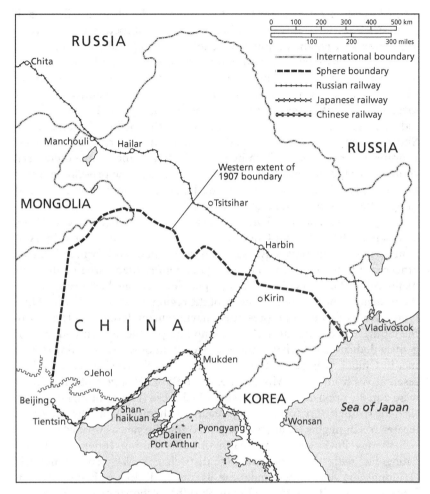

Map 2.1 Russo-Japanese spheres, 1907–18

if we can take advantage of this opportunity [the weakness of Russia] and apply ourselves to (improving) our links with the Mongolian government, we can (thereby) demonstrate the sincerity of our government in 'beckoning and leading by the hand' and 'cherishing the distant.' When the Mongolian government realizes that it cannot fully rely on the strength of the Russians, perhaps they will move into our sphere.[101]

---

[101] Cited in Thomas E. Ewing, *Between the Hammer and the Anvil? Chinese and Russian Policies in Outer Mongolia* (Bloomington: Indiana University Press, 1980), p. 117.

The Mongolian government found itself facing the classical dilemma of a Eurasian borderland squeezed between three competing powers, Russia, China and Japan. Its initial reaction was to appeal to China as the least dangerous threat to its autonomy. Chinese troops had already begun to arrive in March 1918, increasing in size to their maximum number within a year. The Chinese proposed a new treaty which aimed "to eliminate Russian influence on the Buddhist lamas opposed taking such a radical step." The Chinese then blundered badly. Beijing dispatched Xu Shucheng, an overbearing official, to head a newly created Northwest Frontier Defense Force which he exploited to assume virtual dictatorial control over the province. His brutal rule alienated the pro-Chinese faction and played into the hands of the Japanese, who also mismanaged things; the Russians reaped the benefits.

The Japanese countered the Chinese advance in February 1919 by convoking a Pan-Mongol Conference in Chita officially hosted by Ataman Grigorii Semenov, a Russian-Buryat Mongol and former Cossack officer in the tsarist army. The delegates represented three of the four major cultural centers of the Mongol people, each one harboring resentments against the dominant powers of the region, Russia and China. Only Outer Mongolia was not represented, having surrendered its autonomy to the Chinese. The Buryat Mongols, who had produced their own intelligentsia dedicated to resisting the encroachment of Russian colonists, had met in Chita a year before to urge expulsion of all Russian settlers. Representatives from Inner Mongolia and the Barga Mongols of Manchuria were equally opposed to the pressure of Chinese (Han) population resettlement in their territories. They regarded themselves as the only true legates of Chingghis Khan, and regarded the Buryats as upstarts.

Semenov envisaged a pan-Mongol state uniting Inner and Outer Mongolia with Mongol-speaking districts of Western Manchuria (Hulungbuir) and Tibet. Japanese agents had already been active in Urga on his behalf, urging the Living Buddha to cooperate with Semenov. Under Japanese protection, Semenov established himself in Chita, where he continued to work for a pan-Mongol state, initially clashing on this issue with Admiral Kolchak whose authority he defied. When they worked out a compromise, Semenov was left in command of all Cossack forces in the Far East. In June 1919 the Japanese funded a joint Mongol–White Russian expeditionary force to invade Mongolia, but the Mongols mutinied and the plan collapsed.[102] Once the Japanese failed

---

[102] Jamie Bisher, *White Terror: Cossack Warlords of the Trans-Siberian* (New York: Routledge, 2005), pp. 104–40, 174–80 and 188–91; see also David Footman, "Ataman Semenov," in *St. Antony's Papers on Soviet Affairs* (Oxford: St. Antony's College, 1955).

to obtain a place for the Mongols at the Paris Peace Conference, their support for a pan-Mongol movement withered, only to be revived again in the 1930s with more limited aims. They still clung to their hopes for a Siberian buffer and a dominant role in Manchuria. But the drama in Mongolia was not yet over.

With China's policy in Mongolia discredited and in disarray, and Japan's main interest directed elsewhere, the field was open for a restoration of Russian influence, first by the Whites in a failed campaign and then by the Reds in a successful intervention. Under the leadership of Baron Ungern-Sternberg, a half-Magyar, half-Russian Buddhist mystic and lieutenant of Semenov, a motley group of Russian, Mongolian, Buryat and Japanese soldiers invaded Outer Mongolia in February 1921, after an abortive raid the previous year, with the aim of establishing a Buddhist Empire, including Mongolia and Tibet. He drove out the Chinese and occupied Urga. He set up a puppet government with the Living Buddha as the titular head but himself as the real ruler, and unleashed a reign of terror. Local Chinese authorities in Mongolia appealed for aid from the Soviet government. Initially hesitant, Chicherin offered military assistance to drive out Ungern, but was rebuffed in Beijing. Determined to keep the Russians out, the Chinese failed to expel Ungern who began to move toward the Russian frontier.

Meanwhile, Comintern representatives in Urga were busy recruiting Mongolian radical nationalists in Urga. In November 1920 two clandestine groups met on Soviet territory and proclaimed a Mongolian Provisional People's Revolutionary Government headed by Sukhe Bator, a leader of the first group. He had been trained in the Mongolian Army by tsarist officers during the early years of autonomy and had learned Russian. After his death in 1923 he was succeeded by the leader of the second group, Khorloogin Choibalsan. The two men organized the pro-Soviet partisans' units that helped to liberate Urga from Ungern-Sternberg, who was tried and executed by the Red forces.[103] With Soviet assistance, the Mongol leaders reestablished the autonomy of Outer Mongolia, turning it paradoxically, into "the first Soviet satellite," in the words of Owen

Ewing, *Between the Hammer and Anvil?*, pp. 120–6, is skeptical about the plan and minimizes Japanese participation. John A. White, *The Siberian Intervention* (Princeton University Press, 1950), pp. 202–20, gives more credibility to the Japanese efforts. See also Owen Lattimore, "The Geographical Factor in Mongol History," in Lattimore, *Studies in Frontier History: Collected Papers, 1928–1958* (New York: Oxford University Press, 1962), pp. 241–58, and "The Outer Mongolian Horizon," *ibid.*, p. 260.

[103] Willard Sunderland, *The Baron's Cloak: A History of the Russian Empire in War and Revolution* (Oxford University Press, 2014), for a vivid portrayal of Ungern as a man of the borderlands.

Lattimore. A more underdeveloped, quasi-feudal, semi-nomadic society could hardly be imagined.[104]

Japan's four-year intervention in Russia's Siberian borderlands was a more ambitious enterprise than their experiment with pan-Mongolism. Unlike its Western allies, Japan opposed the restoration of a strong, centralized Russian state with full control over Siberia. It declined the Allied proposal to reestablish an eastern front against the Central Powers. It was determined to restrict the Russians to Siberia and "to prevent them at all costs from advancing into Northern Manchuria."[105] It sought to pursue its own aim of creating a vast autonomous region in Trans-Baikal Siberia behind the facade of Allied unity in order to avoid being isolated diplomatically. Toward that end it promoted the creation of a Russian army with a Cossack nucleus as the basis for a new government and engaged the services of a number of military adventurers who served as its agents and intermediaries with the local population.

In chaotic conditions following the Bolshevik seizure of power, adventurers like Semenov, Captain Ivan Kalmykov, General Pavel Ivanov-Rinov and others put themselves at the head of Cossack frontiersmen of the Ussuri and Amur hosts and recruited from the indigenous Buryat, Kalmyk and Chinese populations in order to repress local Bolshevik partisans, overthrow the representatives of the moderate socialists, like the Soviet Revolutionaries (SRs), and counter Chinese troops sent into Manchuria.[106] Like other Cossack hosts in the Russian Empire, those of the Ussuri and Amur regions held fast to their old traditions and retained a separate identity from the rest of the population. They were a professional military caste, owing the state nineteen years of service as soldiers and enjoying special tax privileges even after the introduction of universal

[104] Owen Lattimore, "Mongolia's Place in the World," in Lattimore, *Studies in Frontier History*, pp. 270–95, and Gerard M. Friters, *Outer Mongolia and its International Position* (Baltimore, MD: Johns Hopkins University Press, 1949), with Lattimore's "Introduction" in *Studies*.

[105] Chihiro Hosoya, "Japanese Documents on the Siberian Intervention, 1917–1922, part 1: November 1917–January 1919," *Hitotsubashi Journal of Law and Politics* 1 (April, 1960), pp. 46, 47, 48. Chief of Staff Uehara to Otani Supreme Commander of the Maritime Territory Expeditionary Force, April 10, 1918, and Plan of the Japanese General Staff HDQ to build up and guide a Russian Army in Far Eastern Russia, August 31, 1918.

[106] For good brief biographies of the adventurers, see White, *The Siberian Intervention*, pp. 196–9; for information on local recruits and Chinese forces, see James Morley, *The Japanese Thrust into Siberia* (New York: Columbia University Press, 1957), pp. 69, 110, 115, 181. Richard Ullman, *Intervention and the War* (Princeton University Press, 1961), for the British view of the high-handed Japanese behavior. The standard work on American policy remains Betty Unterberger, *America's Siberian Expedition: A Study of National Policy* (Durham, NC: Duke University Press, 1956).

military service for the rest of the population. Officially, they had been formed late in the history of the empire, the Amur in the 1860s and the Ussuri in 1882. But this amounted to little more than a change of name and location. They were drawn from the Trans-Baikal Cossacks who were themselves the descendants of the Siberian Cossacks of Ermak's time. On the eve of the World War I the entire Asian Cossack population numbered about 675,000 and they held an enormous quantity of land: 170,000 square kilometers, equivalent to half the size of Prussia. By and large the size of their individual plots was two to three times as large as that of the local peasants. And it was prime land as well. The Amur and Ussuri Cossacks held so much land, in fact, that much of it lay idle. This was due in part to the Cossacks' preference for the traditional pursuits of cattle-raising, hunting and fishing at the expense of agriculture.[107] Their anti-Bolshevik credentials were impeccable. But like their counterparts in the Don and Terek regions they could only be won over by the Intervention if they were assured of real autonomy. Kolchak did not offer it, and the Japanese appeared to be more interested in exploiting the economy of Eastern Siberia than in granting real autonomy to the Cossacks. For these reasons Semenov and his ilk could never mobilize more than a few thousand armed men from this potential reservoir in order to detach the borderlands from the Russian core.

In November 1918 the Japanese were willing to extend aid to the newly created White government of Admiral Kolchak at Omsk, and to restrain Semenov just so long as his government "understands the good intentions of Japan and are unbiased toward it." But they had by no means given up the idea of fostering "autonomous Russian institutions" under "the command of local forces."[108] The cabinet in Tokyo made it clear that they expected Admiral Kolchak to accept the autonomy of Siberia, restrict Russian forces in the region, abandon Russian interests in Outer Mongolia and abolish restrictions on foreign investment in a Japanese version of the "open door."[109] As Kolchak's power began to crumble under the pressure of the Red Army in the late summer of 1919, the Japanese began to consider the prospects for creating a buffer

[107] *Aziatskaia Rossiia*, 2 vols. (Cambridge: Oriental Research Partners, 1974 [St. Petersburg, 1914]), vol. I, pp. 369, 383–7.

[108] Hosoya, "Japanese Documents," pp. 49, 51. Prime Minister Ochida to Consul-General Sato at Omsk, December 5, 1918; War Minister Tanaka to Otani, December 12, 1918; M. I. Svetachev, *Imperialisticheskaia interventsiia v Sibiri i na Dal'nem Vostoke (1918–1922)* (Novosibirsk: Izd-vo "Nauka," Sibirskoe otdelenie, 1983), p. 116.

[109] Hosoya, "Japanese Documents," pp. 52–3. Cabinet meeting decisions, January 26, 1919.

state under Semenov that would extend from Irkutsk to Vladivostok. They were willing to entertain proposals for a coalition with the SRs and moderate socialists, but in all the internecine squabbles among the anti-Bolshevik Russian factions the Japanese defended Semenov. When the Western powers decided to terminate the Intervention in February 1920, the Japanese actually increased their expeditionary force in support of Semenov's claim to have formed an independent Cossack government for the entire Trans-Baikal region.[110]

When it became clear that Semenov lacked sufficient support within the population, they agreed to accept the compromise worked out between the Soviet government and the SR–Menshevik coalition in April 1920 to create a Far Eastern Republic as a buffer state and to begin to withdraw from most of the Trans-Baikal region. But they refused to evacuate the Maritime Provinces in light of "the geographic ties of the [Japanese] empire with Siberia." Taking advantage of a massacre of a Japanese garrison at Nikolaevsk, they landed fresh forces at Vladivostok and Northern Sakhalin. Eager to exploit the oil resources of Northern Sakhalin, the Japanese continued their occupation until 1925. They undertook a building program on the island and briefly pursued a policy of cultural assimilation. After the Japanese recognition of the Soviet Union in 1925, and the withdraw of Japanese troops from the northern half of the island, the production of oil remained in the hands of a Japanese company until 1944.[111] Disputes between Moscow and Tokyo over fisheries in the coastal waters of Sakhalin and the Amur Delta constituted a major sore point in their relations throughout the 1930s and up to 1945.

From 1919 to 1922 the Japanese sought to maintain the Far Eastern Republic composed of the Maritime Provinces and Sakhalin and ruled by a succession of right-wing Russian non-entities. At the same time, they continued to support Semenov in his madcap exploits, raiding across the borders of the Far Eastern Republic and seeking aid from anti-Bolshevik Chinese forces in Manchuria under the warlord Zhang Zuolin, the "Old Marshal."[112] Harried by Washington, unable to find a firm and reliable political base in the region and increasingly disheartened by the cost of the Intervention, a new Japanese government committed to a policy

---

[110] Svetachev, *Imperialisticheskaia*, pp. 179–80, 185–8, 200–4.

[111] Hara Teruyuki, "Japan Moves North: The Japanese Occupation of Northern Sakhalin (1920s)," in Stephen Kotkin and David Wolff (eds.), *Rediscovering Russia in Asia: Siberia and the Russian Far East* (Armonk: M. E. Sharpe, 1995), pp. 55–68.

[112] The best guide to these complex maneuvers is Svetachev, *Imperialisticheskaia*, pp. 223–67.

Map 2.2 The Far Eastern Republic 1920–22 and the Kurile Islands

of cooperation with the Western powers authorized the evacuation of all their positions on the Siberian mainland. Yet even in October 1922 during the last days of their occupation, the Japanese refused to surrender the city of Vladivostok with its huge quantities of arms until the Western consuls negotiated a settlement with the revolutionary army of the Far Eastern Republic.[113] They left behind a devastated economy and bitter memories of a prolonged and often brutal occupation regime. Stalin's war aims in the Far East in 1945 were largely shaped by this early struggle with the Japanese over the borderlands of Inner Asia.

Conclusion

Stalin's experience during the revolutionary year of 1917, the Civil War and the Intervention convinced him that the revolution could only succeed if it brought about a fusion of the Russian core with the borderlands in a strong centralized state that allowed territorial cultural autonomy regulated by a unified party. He made it clear that the center and the periphery were mutually dependent upon one another. The center was more highly industrialized and hence possessed a stronger proletarian base and a higher level of socialist consciousness; the periphery contained the raw materials that could enable the state to survive isolation and capitalist encirclement if revolution failed outside its borders. But the periphery also posed a potential threat by virtue of its relative economic backwardness and class structure. As a result, it had been, in Stalin's view, particularly vulnerable to foreign intervention which found natural allies in the national bourgeoisie and capitalist elements of the borderlands. This alliance had succeeded in detaching Finland, the Baltic Provinces, the former Kingdom of Poland with Western Belorussia and Western Ukraine (the *kresy* as the Poles called it) and briefly also Georgia, Armenia, Trans Caspia and the Maritime Provinces from the body politic of the old empire. He recognized that Bolshevik military weakness had enabled this to happen. But that local Communists had permitted this to happen diminished them in Stalin's eyes.[114] His dismissive attitude toward the parties of the Comintern and his terrible purges of the Polish and other parties in the late 1930s, as well as his deal with Hitler in 1939, which gave him a free hand in reversing these setbacks by substituting

[113] *Ibid.*, p. 284.
[114] See, for example, his attack on the Finnish social democrats for "indecision and incomprehensible cowardice" in failing to take power. Stalin, *Sochineniia*, vol. IV, pp. 23–4, and his frequent allusions to the separation of Georgia, Armenia, Poland and Finland from Russia as vassals of the Entente. *Ibid.*, vol. IV, pp. 352–3, 377 and vol. V, p. 17.

the Red Army for local Communist insurrections, must be understood in this light. As Stalin gained more power in the 1920s and early 30s, he maintained and in some cases strengthened the links between his nationality policy in the borderlands and Soviet foreign policy, the subject of the next two chapters.

3   The borderland thesis: the west

The rise and consolidation of Soviet power inaugurated a new era in Russia's relations with the borderlands. The Bolsheviks came to power in the Great Russian heartland. But the leadership assumed that their revolution would not be isolated there or even confined to the territory of the old tsarist empire. They expected it to break out elsewhere in Europe, particularly in the advanced industrial states and spread rapidly to the rest of the globe. Instead, what happened in the decade after the revolution was a series of civil wars in the periphery of tsarist Russia and disconnected revolutionary outbreaks and national liberation movements in Central Europe – Germany twice, in 1918 and 1924, Hungary in 1919, Bulgaria in 1924 – and China in 1927.[1]

All the Bolshevik leaders beginning with Lenin sought to resolve the dilemma by domesticating foreign policy. That is, without abandoning the rhetoric or the long-term goal of world revolution, they gave precedence to strengthening the institutions of the Soviet Union and centralizing state power by restricting autonomy in the borderlands and controlling the activities of foreign Communist parties in the Comintern. Stalin gradually accelerated this trend. By the mid-1930s his campaign to suffuse Soviet institutions and ideology with a Great Russian coloring suggests that the process of domestication was giving way to nationalizing the state.

Stalin lifted domestication to a new level. His victory in the constitutional struggle had marked a major stage in weaving his borderland thesis into the conduct of both domestic and foreign policy. His concept of the state had severely weakened if not wholly eliminated the political challenge of the national opposition led by representatives of the

---

[1] The rich and archive-driven revisionist literature which presents a more complex view of Soviet foreign policy in the 1920s than during the Cold War virtually ignores the connection between state-building in the borderland and Soviet relations with the external world. Cf. the survey of literature in Jon Jacobson, "Essay and Reflection: On the History of Soviet Foreign Relations in the 1920s," *International History Review* 17 (May, 1996), pp. 336–57.

borderlands. He now shifted his attention to defeating his ideological and personal enemies among the top party leadership by employing his borderland thesis in order to reformulate the relationship between the newly constructed Soviet state and the world revolution. At the same time, he moved to take under his control the main instruments of foreign policy, the army, the Foreign Commissariat and Comintern, all bastions of his rivals' influence and power. Finally, he did not neglect to finish off the remnants of the national opposition within the party and to refine his nationalities policy in ways that would further consolidate the political domination of the center over the periphery while preserving, partly in real and partly in bogus terms, the multicultural character of the state.

Stalin skillfully masked the subordination of foreign policy and the international Communist movement to his domestic struggle for power. There were good political reasons for this. To have rejected outright the mission of world revolution would have been to cut his ties with the Leninist legacy, and seriously compromised his claims to be Lenin's heir and successor. It would also have undermined the legitimacy of the Soviet state, which, by virtue of its multicultural constitutional structure, proclaimed its internationalist outlook and appeal. It would have needlessly sacrificed the support of foreign Communist parties which had already proved an important asset in opposing foreign intervention during the Civil War and, under the right circumstances, promised to be useful in the future by spreading Soviet influence abroad and possibly even extending Soviet state power in border regions outside the state frontiers. And what could he have put in its place? A naked personal dictatorship? He was not ready for this; neither was the party or the country. A national socialist regime? The next question here is, which nation? If Russian, then he and many of his close supporters would not themselves have qualified for leadership. To have opted for any of the traditional solutions to a monopoly of power would have meant handing his rivals in the party a blunt instrument with which to beat him down. The myth had to be kept alive and not just through false images and manipulated symbols, at least not so long as he had not fully carried out his domination over the party and state.

Beyond these instrumentalist factors, there is the complex and controversial question of whether Stalin, or any leader of what Robert C. Tucker has called "a mass movement regime" in the twentieth century, could have detached himself from the mental universe, the experiential influences and the ideological discourse which shaped his very being.[2]

---

[2] Robert C. Tucker, *The Lenin Anthology* (New York: Norton, 1973). The phrase has not caught on but seems to me to suggest elements of these new mass political phenomena that are lacking in other models like totalitarian, dictatorship or authoritarianism.

In the witches' brew of Stalin's personality there were the now all-too-familiar ingredients of pathological suspicion, vengefulness, cunning and cruelty. But as all his biographers have concluded, he possessed a strong streak of pragmatism and a profound understanding of power and how to use it, often in the most brutal fashion. He was also committed to building a powerful state, although it was not clear to him how this could be accomplished in a backward agrarian society drained by years of war and revolution. When he decided on the radical course of rapid industrialization based on a collectivized agriculture, he reinstituted Civil War, but under conditions where the opposition was virtually helpless to stem the juggernaut he commanded. Yet none of these elements were necessarily incompatible with the tripartite construction and presentation of himself as a revolutionary leader combining multiculturalism (his Georgian origins), political centralization (his identification with Great Russia) and the class struggle (his Bolshevik credentials), all of which he manipulated to shape an explanation and a transformation of the external world. It should not be forgotten that his description of reality and his utopian vision, like those of other leaders of mass movement regimes, was not only accepted by members of his party and a broad segment of the population under his control but also admired by a large number of Communist Party members and fellow travelers outside his fearsome reach.

For Stalin, domesticating foreign policy meant strongly emphasizing the territorial aspects of Soviet relations with its immediate neighbors: that is, the Eurasian borderlands. In the course of the five-year period of his struggle for power between 1925 and 1930, he generally avoided getting deeply involved in Soviet foreign policy. When he did, the results were not usually auspicious. But he was gradually forced to confront serious problems that the Soviet leadership had inherited from the Civil War, Intervention and domestic compromise with the peasantry, that is the New Economic Policy (NEP). At the most general policy level, he faced the need to reconcile the potentially conflicting goals of building a new, indeed unique form of state power, carrying out a socioeconomic revolution from above, and maintaining control over the international Communist movement. Stalin's response can best be illustrated by focusing on three political "campaigns" which are often treated separately but when examined together reveal a close interrelationship. The first campaign was Stalin's ideological conflict with his rivals, mainly Trotsky and Zinoviev, over the question of building socialism in one country; the second was the manipulation of a "war scare" connected to both the struggle for power and the introduction of the First Five-Year Plan; and the third was the renewed attack on the national Communist opposition within the Soviet Union, initially on Sultan-Galiev, but rapidly engulfing

Ukrainians like Skrypnik and the Georgians. At the same time Stalin undertook a reorganization of the institutions of Soviet foreign policy aimed at greater professionalization to deal on equal terms with what he regarded as the dangerous and hostile external world.

Three campaigns

Stalin's declaration in 1925 that it was possible to build socialism in one country was undoubtedly designed more for domestic than foreign consumption. Yet its implications for foreign policy and especially for relations with the borderlands were profound and lasting. Stalin's formulation was not altogether new and hardly startling. It has often been argued that Lenin and Bukharin had already prepared the theoretical groundwork. But Stalin too had long been moving toward the idea from a different direction. During the debates preceding the Brest-Litovsk negotiations, he was already skeptical about a revolution in the West. At the end of the Civil War he openly ridiculed earlier predictions that the revolution would break out first in an advanced capitalist country and then that the revolution in Russia could not survive without support "of a more profound and serious revolutionary explosion in the West." Instead, events had proven, he wrote, that "the socialist revolution can not only begin in a backward capitalist country, but can be crowned with success, make progress and serve as an example for the developed countries." In contrast to the counter-revolutionary "reserves" of the Entente – the White armies and partisans in the rear of the Red Army, the bourgeois governments of the border states, Poland, Romania, Armenia and Georgia, the Second Socialist International and the colonies – Stalin enumerated a set of Soviet "reserves" and historical conditions that enabled it to survive as "an oasis of socialism surrounded by hostile capitalist governments." The historical conditions were, first, Russia's vast spatial expanse, enabling it "to hold out for a long time, retreating into the depths of the country in case of a lack of success, in order to gather its strength and rebound on the offensive" (whereas, he suggested, a small country like Hungary lacked the room to maneuver and had succumbed to the enemies of the revolution). Second, "also a constant feature" in his eyes, was Russia's enormous productive resources, above all grain and fuel, that distinguished it from countries like Italy which had to import both. The new factors were the Red Army, the revolutionary movement in the West, which prevented a direct military intervention in Russia, and ferment in the colonial world.[3] Although Stalin stopped short of fixing a schedule for building socialism in one country, he had sketched

---

[3] Stalin, *Sochineniia*, vol. IV, pp. 374–81.

its main outlines. Five years later the internal political situation had changed sufficiently to take the next step.

In 1925 Stalin's aim was to expropriate the idea of socialism in one country, to set his personal stamp upon it and to set it in direct opposition to Trotsky's "permanent revolution." In order to accomplish this he had to engage in the kind of intellectual sleight of hand at which he was becoming a master. As with "national self-determination" and "federalism" he grossly oversimplified a complex idea borrowed from Lenin, among others. He then proceeded to perform the same surgery on the ideas of his opponents, first Trotsky and then Zinoviev. They found themselves forced to explain views that they never or no longer held while Stalin demanded that they either acknowledge or denounce them. Besides his bag of rhetorical tricks, Stalin could count upon a growing mood of domesticity within the party – a readiness to interpret socialism in one country as a turning away from the dangers of international complications without surrendering the banner of world revolution.

In conducting his ideological campaign of 1924–6, Stalin made three important statements about Soviet foreign policy. First, he asserted that, contrary to Trotsky, Soviet Russia would, in the course of building socialism, be "transformed into a base for the further unfolding of the world revolution, into a lever for the further disintegration of imperialism."[4] Second, in giving priority to strengthening the Soviet state at the expense, if necessary, of promoting world revolution, he would impose upon foreign Communist parties the primary obligation of defending the Soviet Union rather than advancing their own revolutionary prospects. Third, Stalin insisted that although the Soviet Union could build socialism with its own resources, it could not secure "a full guarantee against intervention and consequently against the restoration of the bourgeois order without the victory of revolution in at least a number of countries."[5]

In developing these ideas Stalin characteristically relegated his party rivals to the extreme poles of the political spectrum on the critical relationship between state policy and world revolution. He misconstrued Zinoviev's concern over the peasant question as "having transformed Leninism from an international proletarian doctrine into a product of specifically Russian conditions." He then distorted Trotsky's position by accusing him of believing that the dictatorship of the proletariat in one country "could not 'hold out in the face of a conservative Europe.'"[6] He caricatured Zinoviev as some kind of national Bolshevik and Trotsky as

---

[4] *Ibid.*, vol. VI, p. 399.   [5] *Ibid.*, vol. VIII, p. 263.
[6] *Ibid.*, vol. VIII, p. 14, quotation on 173.

a wild-eyed internationalist. This left Stalin free to occupy a fictitious center that he modestly admitted sharing with Lenin.

In fact, Stalin's formula marked in two ways a radical departure from Lenin, who after the revolution had repeatedly stated that the victory of socialism depended on "a socialist revolution in one or several *advanced* countries."[7] First, Stalin shifted priorities in his analysis from unleashing world revolution to defending the Soviet Union against foreign intervention. Second, he dropped from Lenin's formula the crucial modifier "advanced." Instead he substituted his own territorial criteria of "one or several countries" for Lenin's classical Marxist socioeconomic prerequisite.

Stalin's reformulation of socialism in one country was made in response to withering attacks from his main rivals, Zinoviev and Trotsky. Even though they were forced to tone down some of their harsh statements for publication, they raised serious objections that had a telling effect on Stalin. Zinoviev's criticism of Stalin's petty bourgeois inclinations and Trotsky's exposure of the disastrous economic consequences of autarky forced Stalin to backpedal.[8] At the Fifteenth Party Congress in November 1926, he scarcely mentioned his doctrine by name, but he sought to defend himself against accusations that socialism in one country meant the abandonment of the revolutionary mission. Expanding on the idea that socialism could not be finally achieved in one country until there had been revolutions in "at least several other countries," Stalin now insisted that "in order to win conclusively, we must bring it about that the present capitalist encirclement is replaced by a socialist encirclement, that the proletariat is victorious in at least several more countries. Only then can our victory be considered final."[9] The political implications of Stalin's formula were stunning.

If Stalin literally meant what he said, and his attitude toward revolutionary movements tends to confirm that he did, then he was asserting that the creation and security of a socialist state in the USSR depended

---

[7] Lenin, *Sochineniia*, vol. XXVII, p. 151; vol. XXXII, pp. 214–15; vol. XXXIII, p. 206. Emphasis added.

[8] S. V. Tsakunov, "NEP: evoliutsiia rezhima i rozhdenie natsional-bol'shevizma," in Iu. N. Afanas'ev (ed.), *Sovetskoe obshchestvo: vozniknovenie, razvitie, istoricheskii final* (Moscow: Rossiiskii gosudarstvennyi gumanitarnyi universitet, 1997), pp. 101–4, 108–10. As Stalin's editing of his speeches for publication show, he was still waffling on the idea of industrialization, not wishing to break with Bukharin, his erstwhile ally against the left, but unable to dismiss the idea without renouncing socialism in one country. *Ibid.*, p. 112.

[9] Stalin, *Sochineniia*, vol. VIII, p. 263. The importance of this statement was brought to my attention by Robert C. Tucker, *Stalin in Power: The Revolution from Above, 1928–1941* (New York: Norton, 1990), p. 46, although we draw somewhat different conclusions from it.

on carrying out revolutions in a belt of overwhelmingly agrarian, economically backward territories adjacent to the Soviet frontier. It meant
that the primary object of Soviet foreign policy was not to spread revolution to the highly developed capitalist states of Europe and North
America. Nor could the Soviet Union count on spontaneous revolutions
of the working class breaking out in the advanced countries. As early
as the debate on a separate peace with the Central Powers, Stalin had
dismissed such illusions, and he never changed his mind.

Second, "socialist encirclement" – the protective belt of buffer states
around the Soviet Union – would serve some of the same purposes as
the first line of defense formed by the national soviet republics on the
periphery of the Great Russian center. The first and foremost of these, as
Stalin made clear in the same speech, would be to increase the difficulty
and diminish the likelihood of foreign intervention, his chief obsession
in foreign policy. He warned, however, that "capitalists do not sleep";
they will not relax their efforts "to weaken the international position
of our republic and create the prerequisites for intervention. Therefore,
one cannot dismiss out of hand attempts at intervention or deny the
possibility of a restoration of the old order in our country linked to these
attempts."[10]

Third, as early as July 1928 Stalin concluded that at least several states
within the second protective belt would follow their own revolutionary
path to socialism. They belonged to what he called a second type of social
formation, the first being advanced capitalist countries and the third the
colonial world characterized by weak development of capitalism, strong
feudal survivals and a specific agrarian problem. Stalin explicitly referred
to "Poland, Romania etc." as belonging to this type; the "etc." offered
many tantalizing possibilities. In cases of this second type of revolution
the petty bourgeoisie, especially the peasantry, would "speak with its own
strong voice." Taking this into account, a victorious revolution leading
to the establishment of a dictatorship of the proletariat "can and probably will demand," according to Stalin, "some intermediate stages in
the form, let us say, of a dictatorship of the proletariat and peasantry."
To be sure, he added, Russia also belonged to the second type, but its
"proletarian dictatorship was established as the result of a more or less
rapid transformation (*pererastenie*) of the bourgeois democratic revolution to the socialist revolution." Stalin's careful choice of terms made
it clear that the path of revolution in neighboring countries would be
different: "There are no grounds for doubt that Poland and Romania
belong to that number of countries that will have to pass through several

[10] Stalin, *Sochineniia*, vol. VIII, p. 264.

more or less rapid intermediate stages on the road to the dictatorship of the proletariat."[11]

At the same time, Stalin extended this analysis to the highly complex revolutionary situation in China. He sought to make a distinction between the right wing of the Kuomintang led by Chiang Kai-shek in Nanking, which was leaning toward militarism, and the left wing of the Kuomintang supported by the Communists in Wuhan, which he predicted would become transformed into "an organ of the revolutionary-democratic dictatorship of the proletariat and peasantry."[12] Here Stalin was resurrecting and playing with a formula that Lenin had invented in 1905 and then discarded.[13] Stalin's skepticism about a genuine proletarian revolution in China merely intensified as Mao Zedung won over the party to his peasant-based revolutionary policy. For Stalin, then, revolutions in neighboring states would have to pass through "several intermediate stages" on their road to socialism. He had already covered more than half the distance to the post-World War II idea of "popular democracy" that implicitly granted the possibility of different roads to socialism.

Finally, Stalin responded to the accusations by Zinoviev and Trotsky that he had abandoned proletarian internationalism by assigning a new role – one is tempted to say a bit part – to the proletariat of the advanced capitalist countries. Stalin repeatedly argued that their main function was to prevent their governments from launching once again a unified Intervention against the Soviet Union.[14] To expect otherwise was to bask in illusions: "That the workers of capitalist countries cannot now support

[11] *Ibid.*, vol. XI, pp. 155–6. These pages include an extraordinary admission by Stalin that in 1917 the SRs and the Mensheviks became "the dominant strength in the country" because they had been able to organize the masses of the petty bourgeoisie. He implies, at least to this reader, that this situation forced the Bolsheviks to hasten the revolutionary process in order to break the control of the SRs and Mensheviks over the peasantry. Did this hastening, this "growing over" of the revolution, plunge the country into Civil War and lead to Intervention? Would it not have been possible then to avoid both Civil War and Intervention by proceeding through intermediate stages that would forge alliances with the petty bourgeoisie before they could be organized against the proletariat? Were these considerations uppermost in Stalin's mind in 1944–6? These are questions deserving detailed treatment in subsequent scholarship.

[12] *Ibid.*, vol. IX, p. 226.

[13] Lenin had developed this idea in 1905 when he believed that the only way in Russia to overthrow the autocracy and pass to a democratic republic was through a fighting alliance between the proletariat and the peasantry who shared a "union of interests." Lenin, *Sochineniia*, vol. VIII, pp. 84–5.

[14] For example, at the Fourteenth Party Congress, where he also cast further doubt on the primary revolutionary role of the Western proletariat by diagnosing "the main disease of the working class of the West" as a fear that it could not survive without the bourgeoisie. Stalin, *Sochineniia*, vol. VII, p. 285; see also, vol. VIII, pp. 160–4, 184 and vol. XI, pp. 25–6, 148.

our revolution by a revolution against their capitalists is for the time being a fact."[15] To extend the metaphor of the defensive glacis, the Western proletariat would constitute in Stalin's scheme a third line of outworks aimed at disrupting a concentration of enemy forces, as the buffer states would deprive them of a forward base of operations. What this amounted to was the mentality of a besieged fortress, or "camp" as Stalin preferred to call it.

As Stalin elaborated his mental map of defensive zones he also began to construct physical barriers against external penetration and internal flight. The evolution of Soviet frontier policy demonstrates that the besieged camp was not wholly a product of Stalin's state of mind. Following the revolution, a lively two-way traffic opened up across the borders of the new Soviet republic. But over the next ten years the emigration and immigration policies of the Soviet Union moved away from controlled exchange under the umbrella of internationalism to rigid controls that amounted to a virtual cessation of movement in or out of the country. Although Stalin put the final touches to sealing off Soviet borders, the process had already begun much earlier.[16] In 1921 the first restrictions on immigration were imposed for economic, not ideological reasons, in order to prevent the further influx of poor farmers, mainly from the United States. Other restrictions followed. Re-immigration of those who had left the country during the revolution and the Civil War was permitted up to 1927, when Stalin prohibited all immigration. Emigration by contrast was closed down relatively quickly. Once the prisoners of war, refugees and hostages returned to their own countries in the early 1920s, even travel abroad was highly restricted. Legal sanctions against the movement of peoples across Soviet frontiers were accompanied, as early as May 1918, by the creation of a special frontier guard. Five years later the guard was ideologically reinforced by the addition of political sections. In the course of the 1930s, Stalin carried the closed frontier policy and suspicion of foreigners to pathological extremes.[17] But the Civil War mentality, encapsulated in the phrase "capitalist encirclement," persisted even during the relaxation of international tension in the 1920s.

[15] *Ibid.*, vol. VIII, p. 264.
[16] This section is based on the work of Yuri Felshtinsky, "The Legal Foundations of the Immigration and Emigration Policy of the USSR, 1917–27," *Soviet Studies* 33:3 (1982), pp. 327–48, and Iuri Fel'shtinskii, *K istorii nashei zakrytosti: Zakonodatel'nye osnovy sovetskoi immigratsionnoi i emigratsionoi politiki* (Moscow: Terra, 1991).
[17] I. I. Petrov, "Zabota partii ob ukreplenii pogranichnykh voisk (1939–1941 gg.)," *Voprosy istorii KPSS*, no. 5 (1968). As E. H. Carr pointed out, from the very beginnings of the NEP Stalin's suspicion of foreign contacts extended to trade and cultural relations and provided another point of dispute between him and Chicherin. Carr, *The Bolshevik Revolution*, vol. III, pp. 349–50.

Stalin did not invent it, although he exploited and manipulated it to a frenzied climax.

One problem facing Trotsky, Zinoviev and the joint opposition was that they could not attack the central tenet of Stalin's argument because they had already accepted so many of the assumptions on which it was based: the creation and consolidation of the revolution in a backward, agrarian state with a centralized bureaucracy, regular army and secret police; the subordination of the nationalities on the periphery to the Great Russian heartland; and the "bolshevization" of the Communist International and its constituent parties. In a word, they had endorsed in principle and in practice the ideas and institutions dictated by the process of domestication.

In the two main foreign policy debates on the nationality question and the role of world revolution, most of the top Bolshevik leaders except for Lenin and Stalin had paid little attention to the former. For the most part they regarded it as something similar to the women's question: it would be solved by the coming of socialism. In any case, it was for them a secondary matter. This was a serious mistake on their part, which cost them dearly. At crucial points in the early 1920s, they missed opportunities to form an alliance with the national opposition to Stalin in the borderlands. Instead, they focused their attention almost exclusively on the relationship between the Soviet state and world revolution. This led, in turn, to a political struggle for influence within foreign Communist parties and control of the Comintern apparatus. Unfortunately for them, they had already acquiesced in the domestication, that is the bolshevization, of the Third International. Thus they missed a second opportunity to win allies, this time within the international Communist movement, in order to resist Stalin who had already brought the All-Union Communist Party under his control.

Another problem, just as important for them, was that their audience had changed. As Trotsky was the first to point out, the party had undergone a striking social transformation in less than a decade after October. His word for it was "degeneration," and many historians have followed his analysis. The problem is too large and complex to consider here except to stress that, without discounting for a moment Stalin's skill and success in controlling appointments, packing bureaucracies and outmaneuvering his opponents, his socialism in one country resonated among broad strata within the party and in the country at large.[18] It appealed to

---

[18] For the challenge to the argument that Stalin's rise to power can be attributed to his power over appointments – that is, packing the party bureaucracy – see James Harris, "Stalin as General Secretary: The Appointments Process and the Nature of Stalin's

Bolshevik pride in having won the Civil War and repelled foreign intervention; it attracted a wide range of social types who had been excluded
from any real political participation under the old regime and were now
summoned to staff the institutions of a state endowed with the unique
mission of building a wholly new society mainly by their own determination and talents; it appealed to an embryonic but growing sense of
Soviet patriotism that transcended the old religious, ethnic limitations;
and in the periphery during the 1920s it was still consistent with Stalin's
nationality policy of cultural autonomy. Stalin was able to harness many
of these sentiments to his invocation of the war scare and the threat of
foreign intervention, his drive for collectivization and industrialization,
even as it passed over into its frenzied and irrational phase, and finally
the search for internal enemies to explain his own failures.

Stalin's second campaign to place foreign relations at the service of
his domestic goals was the manipulation of the "war scare" as a means
of undermining his domestic opponents and serving to justify his policies of mobilizing the country on his own terms. As James Harris and
Silvio Pons have demonstrated, Stalin was a victim of his own personal
fears and delusions about capitalist encirclement embedded in Marxist-
Leninist theories of imperialism, which made him particularly susceptible
to intelligence reports on the gathering of anti-Soviet coalitions throughout the interwar period. Moreover, during these years, there was sufficient
evidence of hostile intent on the part of Britain, France, Japan and the
Soviet Union's neighbors to render a degree of plausibility to the dangers
of war. In each of the four cases when the war scares assumed major proportions, in 1927–8 in the West, 1927–32 in the East, and more generally
in 1934–5 and 1938–41, Stalin's reactions had profound consequences
for his domestic policies.[19]

In May 1927 two setbacks in foreign policy stirred the last organized
effort of the left opposition to challenge his growing power. The first was
the break in diplomatic relations with Great Britain following a clumsy
effort by Moscow to support the British trade unions in their General
Strike; the second was the virtual destruction of the Chinese Communist Party at the hands of Chiang Kai-shek, in which Stalin played an
ignominious part. In May 1927 eighty-three leading oppositionists sent
a letter to the Politburo attacking the government's foreign and domestic
policies. In July Stalin's response appeared in *Pravda*. "It can scarcely be

Power," in Sarah Davies and James Harris (eds.), *Stalin: A New History* (Cambridge
University Press, 2005), p. 82.
[19] James Harris, "Encircled by Enemies: Stalin's Perceptions of the Capitalist World,
1918–1941," *Journal of Strategic Studies* 30:3 (2007), pp. 513–45, and Silvio Pons,
Stalin and the Inevitable War, 1936–1941 (London: Frank Cass, 2002).

doubted," he began, "that the basic question of our day is the question of the threat of a new imperialist war. The issue is not one of some kind of vague and ill-defined 'danger' of a new war. The issue concerns a real and immediate threat of a new war in general, and a war against the USSR in particular." He not only blamed the opposition for the China fiasco but he raised questions about their loyalty to the country at a time of external danger. "What can be said about this same opposition that finds it appropriate on the occasion of the threat of war to increase their attacks on the party? Is it possible that the opposition is against the victory of the USSR in the coming battles with imperialism, against the development of the defensive capabilities of the Soviet Union, against the strengthening of our rear?"[20]

The party quickly adopted a series of resolutions followed by a vast propaganda campaign aimed at arousing the country to fever pitch. The period of breathing space was over. The bourgeois states, despite their differences, were forming a united capitalist front, adopting a more and more hostile position toward the USSR.[21] The war scare campaign may have been unfounded or exaggerated, but it achieved its political purposes. Both the opposition and the Stalinists had their own reasons for trumping one another's war cards. But they became victims of their own propaganda. Throughout the summer of 1927 independent observers reported on the panicky mood in Moscow spreading among the upper reaches of the Soviet leadership.[22]

As the intra-party struggle intensified in the summer of 1927, Stalin hastily retreated from his direst warnings and concentrated his efforts on exploiting the war scare in order to discredit the opposition. Already in August he drew a sharp distinction between his and Bukharin's view of the inevitability of war, a standard but abstract Marxist formula about the nature of capitalism that had no timetable attached, and a much more specific prediction by Zinoviev and Kamenev on the imminent possibility of war.[23] He then exploited Trotsky's tactical blunder in affirming the right to conduct a "defeatist" policy during time of war based on the model of Georges Clemenceau in 1917. In a letter to Dzerzhinskii, Trotsky outlined how Clemenceau's relentless demands "to sweep away the rubbish" of the French government while the enemy was 80 kilometers

[20] Stalin, *Sochineniia*, vol. IX, pp. 322, 330, 333–7.
[21] *Kommunisticheskaia partiia sovetskogo soiuza v rezoliutsiakh i resheniiakh s"ezdov, konferentsii i plenumov TsK.*, 8th edn (Moscow: Nauka), vol. IV, pp. 175, 258, 369.
[22] E. H. Carr, *Foundations of a Planned Economy, 1926–1929*, 3 vols. (New York: Macmillan, 1971–8), vol. III, pp. 1, 7–10. Carr takes the view that the scare was groundless in fact but not artificially worked up.
[23] Stalin, *Sochineniia*, vol. X, pp. 47–8, 199–200.

from Paris could not be considered class treason but a legitimate struggle against petty bourgeois flabbiness and indecisiveness.

The implication for Soviet Russia of Trotsky's defeatism was clear, and Stalin made the most of it. "In order to 'sweep away' such a majority [in the USSR] it will be necessary to start a civil war in the party. And there it is. Trotsky thinks of opening a civil war in the party at the moment when the enemy stands 80 kilometers from the Kremlin": at a time when the "danger of war turns into a threat of war." Stalin plodded on shamelessly juggling words: what was needed was "iron discipline in our party," a suppression of the splitters and disorganizers in the international movement. As the debates intensified, Stalin returned again and again to the refrain that it was impossible to defend the USSR while the opposition practiced its policies of factionalism and criticism, even fomenting the creation of separate parties.[24]

As the pace of industrialization and collectivization mounted and the errors and confusion of Stalin's hasty policies threatened chaos, he resorted for the first time to staging show trials. His aim was to provide the Soviet public with tangible evidence that there was a direct connection between domestic conspiracies and foreign intervention. During the spring and summer 1928, in the first of many fabricated cases, a group of fifty-three engineers in the coal-mining district of Shakhty were charged with wrecking activities orchestrated by foreign intelligence services. Stalin's personal participation in fabricating the evidence is well documented. But only a recently published document concerning the so-called Industrial Party case makes clear just how important it was for Stalin to link domestic conspiracies with the threat of foreign intervention. In late 1929 a large group of industrial managers and specialists were arrested on charges of wrecking, among them the talented Professor L. K. Ramzin. Stalin personally took charge of instructing the head of the OGPU, V. R. Menzhinskii, on the desired outcome of the interrogation of Ramzin. "In my opinion the most interesting in his testimony is the question of intervention" which, Stalin insisted, should become the main theme of further investigations and the trial itself. He was determined to link it to a group of émigré capitalists "who represent the most powerful socioeconomic group of all the groups existing in the USSR and emigration, the most powerful in terms of their ties to the French and English governments."

---

[24] *Ibid.*, pp. 53–4, 59, 81–2, 86–7. It would be tedious to trace Stalin's verbal manipulation of "dangers" and "threats" over the next few months and it has already been scrupulously done in N. V. Zagladin, *Istoriia uspekhov i neudach sovetskoi diplomatii (Politologicheskii aspekt)* (Moscow: Mezhdunarodnye otnosheniia, 1990), pp. 84–6, an impressive product of that brief period in Russian historiography before the ultra-nationalist trend took over.

The "principal interest" for Stalin was the timing of intervention. Was it not possible, he wondered, to find good excuses to predict its postponement since neither Poland nor Romania would be ready to move until 1931 or even 1932? Here as elsewhere he prompted Menzhinskii on the best means to elicit from Ramzin and others the answers that best suited his own purposes.

If the testimony of Ramzin is confirmed and firmly set by the other accused, then this will be a serious success for the OGPU since we can supply the information to sections of the Communist International and workers of all countries and conduct broad campaigns against the interventionists and succeed in paralyzing and undermining efforts at intervention over the next one to two years which is of no small importance for us. Understood?[25]

The implications were clear. By 1932 the First Five-Year Plan would have been fulfilled. By exposing the threat of intervention in the near future, Stalin could find another excuse to spur the pace of industrialization and bind ever closer the foreign Communist parties, all the while keeping alive the myth of foreign-inspired sabotage and wrecking.

For Stalin declarations about the inevitability of war, occasionally mixed with more frightening assertions about the danger or threat of war, did not necessarily mean that war was imminent. In the late 1920s it was more of a weapon to be used against internal enemies and a rationalization of the pressing need to industrialize the country.[26] This should be kept in mind when analyzing his famous speech, years later in February 1946, about the inevitability of war as long as capitalism survives.

Despite all talk of war in Moscow, the evidence for a concerted Western offensive against the Soviet Union was rather thin, the rupture of relations with Great Britain being exhibit A for the prosecution. Admittedly, throughout the 1920s the relations of the USSR with its western neighbors had its ups and downs, and Soviet leaders remained extremely

---

[25] "I. V. Stalin, Pis'ma," in V. S. Lel'chuk (ed.), *Sovetskoe obshchestvo: Vozniknovenie, razvitie, istoricheskii final*, 2 vols. (Moscow: Rossiiskii gosudarstvennyi gumanitarnyi universitet, 1997), vol. I, p. 427. In mentioning the alleged leaders of the émigré community, Stalin was unaware that several had already died.

[26] In the discussion of the draft of the Five-Year Plan at the Sixteenth Party Conference in April 1929, Iosif Unshlikht, about to become deputy chair for military industry of the Higher Council for the National Economy, proposed a series of recommendations to strengthen the military aspects of the plan, including the perfection of substitutions for rare raw materials along the lines of German war production in World War I, increased tempos for the production of military items, maximum coordination of military and civil production, improving technological and scientific innovation and attracting foreign technical assistance. The final resolution of the plan included a general recommendation for strengthening the military capabilities of the country. *Shestnadtsataia konferentsiia BKP(b), aprel' 1929 goda* (Moscow: Gosizdat. politicheskoi literatury, 1962), pp. 240–7 and 625. It was only in the second Five-Year Plan that a major increase in spending for military items was authorized.

sensitive to any sudden changes in the international barometer. An abundance of anti-Soviet feeling existed among the leadership of countries like Finland, Poland and Romania. However, Soviet diplomacy under the skillful management of Chicherin worked hard to reduce tension and not without success.

In his report to the Fourteenth Party Congress in December 1925 (published only in 1991), the Soviet Foreign Commissar outlined with great clarity the main objectives of Soviet policy: to expose "the phony character of British pacifism," and "to develop better relations with countries that are a direct threat to our security like Poland, the key to any attack on us, and to block the formation of any coalition for intervention against us." For him the major obstacle to success had not been the threat of a Western bloc. There was evidence of German disillusionment with Locarno and a growing antagonism between the United States and Great Britain, which, he urged, the Soviet Union should do its utmost to deepen. The main problem had been the "disconnection (*razobshchennost'*) between Soviet diplomacy on the one hand and the Communist parties on the other."[27] Chicherin claimed, rather overly optimistically as it turned out, that he had been able to eliminate this "harmful disconnection" in the West by reaching a complete consensus with the French and German Communist Party leaders which in the East "had long since been achieved." Chicherin was supremely confident that in the East Soviet support for the national movements in Turkey, Iran, Afghanistan and China was the only possible policy, leaving aside ideological considerations and "even if we stand solely on the grounds of a national foreign policy." His review of the world situation led him to a sanguine conclusion: "we see that there is no cause for panic, but that this general turn, this striving for agreement with us shows that our position with respect to the West is growing stronger and in the East the struggle against imperialism is taking giant strides forward."[28]

Chicherin was appalled by the war scare psychosis. Convalescing in Germany in 1927, he repeatedly wrote to Stalin and Rykov protesting against anti-German provocations by Bukharin and others which were undermining his policy of keeping the West divided, especially Germany from Britain. Upon his return to Moscow he attempted to disabuse his

[27] Just the year before, Chicherin had warned of the incompatible Soviet policies in the East and the West. "We cannot act in the East independently of how we act in the West." DVP, vol. VII, *prilozhenie* [appendix], p. 608.
[28] "Rech' narodnogo komissara inostrannikh del SSSR G. V. Chicherina na XIV s"ezd VKP(b)," *Kentavr* (October–December, 1991), pp. 121–4. Chicherin's analysis contains a number of suggestive parallels with the views of the imperialist rivalry school of Soviet analysts in the period immediately after World War II.

colleagues of the imminent danger of war. He was told that no one really believed in it, "but we have to use these rumors against Trotsky."[29]

What Chicherin could not say was that Soviet foreign policy carried the additional burden of Stalin's arbitrary interventions prompted by his domestic concerns. In the 1920s, Soviet diplomacy was most successful establishing good relations with Latvia and Lithuania. In 1926 and 1927 treaties of non-aggression and neutrality were signed with both countries in addition to a trade pact with Latvia. Negotiations to improve Soviet–Polish relations, highlighted by Chicherin's official visit to Warsaw in 1925, were brusquely interrupted two years later by the assassination of the Soviet ambassador. Stalin reacted in characteristic fashion by exploiting a crisis in foreign policy in order to destroy domestic opponents. He blamed the incident on agents of the British government who sought to provoke the Soviet Union into a war with Poland but then ordered the execution of "twenty terrorists and instigators [of war] from the ranks of Russian princes and nobles."[30] After a few months, Soviet–Polish negotiations on a non-aggression pact resumed, although they did not succeed for a variety of reasons. But in early 1929 relations between the Soviet Union and all its neighbors to the west appeared to improve with their signing of the Moscow protocol of the Kellogg–Briand Pact renouncing war as an instrument of national policy. Such gestures proved to be illusory.

Poland and Ukraine

At that very moment, the struggle flared up in the borderlands of the Pontic steppe (Ukraine) and Inner Asia (Manchuria), intensifying fears in Moscow of an imminent outbreak of war. As in the past, domestic and foreign policies became inextricably intertwined. In the western borderlands three issues sat at the center of the rising conflict: the competing nationalities policies of the Soviet Union and Poland, the domestic power struggle in both countries, and collectivization on the Soviet side of the frontier. From the late 1920s to 1931 when Stalin launched his "second revolution" of collectivization, industrialization and centralization, resistance intensified among the national minorities and the peasantry, assuming in the case of the latter mass proportions verging on a civil war.[31]

[29] Andrei Gromyko, "Diplomat leninskoi shkoly: k 90-letiiu so dnia rozhdeniia G. V. Chicherina," *Izvestiia*, December 4, 1962.
[30] Stalin, *Sochineniia*, vol. IX, p. 330. The official protest to Warsaw was more restrained.
[31] Andrea Graziosi, *The Great Peasant War: Bolsheviks and Peasants, 1918–1933* (Cambridge, MA: Harvard University Press, 1997). For purges among the nationalities, see

Although by this time Stalin had defeated his main rivals in the party leadership, most of them were still party members. To him they represented a potential center of opposition. As tensions mounted in the countryside and among the nationalities, former supporters showed signs of wavering as well. Reports by the security organ of particularly high levels of peasant resistance in the porous frontier districts of Ukraine, along with denunciations of Ukrainian nationalists, posed serious security problems and raised the specter of foreign subversion and/or intervention by the Poles and Romanians. Conspiracies were uncovered or invented lumping together kulaks, Ukrainian nationalists and foreign agents. Stalin used these to identify resistance to collectivization with a "nationalist deviation" and a "right opposition." He also sought to link the domestic resistance to an external threat from Poland as the front man for an anti-Soviet coalition of capitalist governments and European social democratic parties. His accusations became increasingly improbable and his methods more brutal. But in the overheated atmosphere of an armed camp surrounded by predatory enemies and penetrated by foreign agents, there was little incentive or political will to oppose him.

What gave verisimilitude to the entire scenario was the long and very real competition between the Soviet Union and Poland over the western borderlands. It may even have convinced Stalin, who had vivid personal memories of its most recent episode in the Soviet–Polish War of 1920, that the domestic crisis he had unleashed with collectivization was deeply linked to this struggle. In any case he sought to control and manipulate the connection. His aim was to discredit the remnants of domestic opposition to his rule by the peasantry in the countryside, the "Trotskyists" and the "nationalist deviation" within the party. Looking beyond (or was it behind Poland?) he wove another thread entangling the domestic opposition in a wider external network by conjuring up an anti-Soviet coalition of bourgeois governments and European social democratic parties. Stalin had spun a sturdy web. To pull out the separate strands is necessary for clarity of analysis. But it also, of necessity, diminishes the complexity of the whole. The simple chronology of events, his marches and countermarches, attacks, feints and probes, provides ample evidence of a kind of mad orchestration of these interwoven themes.[32]

To take these up one by one: Stalin's decision to launch collectivization in a sudden, unplanned and violent manner raised the struggle over

B. Nahaylo and V. Swoboda, *The Soviet Disunion: A History of the Nationalities Problem in the USSR* (New York: The Free Press, 1990).

[32] For the most recent analysis of Stalin's tactics of "zig-zigs" that has long been in the historiography, see David Priestland, *Stalinism and the Politics of Mobilization: Ideas, Power and Terror in Inter-War Russia* (Oxford University Press, 2007).

the borderlands to a new level. The beginning of collectivization corresponded to a shift in Stalin's evolving views on the nationality question which show up in three areas: the definition of nation and the nature of language, the historic relations between Russia and the nationalities, and the fate of national minority rights. The first Soviet constitution and the administrative division of the country into ethno-territorial blocs was a clear recognition of the multinational character of the Soviet Union. The drawing of internal boundaries was, with some exceptions, the product of serious scholarly research by ethnographers, geographers and economists faced with the formidable task of creating some kind of system out of the patchwork of nationalities speaking 146 different languages (according to the census of 1897). They were guided by the creation of a hierarchical structure, starting at the top with nation and moving down to nationality (*narodnost'*), national groups, ethnographic groups, and tribes, that implied a development from lower to higher forms of national identity and awareness. But the gradations had no firm theoretical foundation; nor did Stalin ever provide one.

On several occasions between 1913 and 1949 Stalin changed both his definition and his enumeration of nationalities within the Soviet Union. The question of how to identify nationalities was not limited to Stalin. Ethnographers too grappled with it. The 1920 census listed fifty-five nationalities; at the height of *korenizatsiia* in 1926 the number was inflated to a peak of 190. At the Eighth Party Congress in November 1936, Stalin suggested there might be "about sixty nations." In the same speech he noted that the Soviet Union was making the transition to socialism. The census-takers did not grasp the ideological implications of this statement in revising their count for the 1937 census to 106. It was a serious mistake.[33] What Stalin was signaling by his reduced number was that under his aegis progress had been made toward reducing the number of backward nations through assimilation to more advanced or master nations, just as the exploiting classes were being eliminated through collectivization and industrialization. In the 1930s it finally became clear that he equated nationality with the official recognition of a national state language within an officially circumscribed territorial unit. In practice this meant two things. First, that Stalin would determine who did and who did not constitute a nationality. Second, that the level of development of a literature written in the national language would serve him as a rough indicator of national identity. In line with the second point,

---

[33] Francine Hirsch, *Empire of Nations: Ethnographic Knowledge and the Making of the Soviet Union* (Ithaca, NY: Cornell University Press, 2005), pp. 284, 327–30.

in 1925 Stalin rehabilitated the slogan of a national culture that he had previously identified as a dangerous symptom of nationalism.[34]

Stalin's readiness to recognize the legitimacy of national cultures can only be understood in relation to the views that he was expressing at the very same time on socialism in one country. The building of socialism meant that all the national cultures would assume as their primary task not the defense of national peculiarities but instead the expression in different languages of a proletarian experience that was common to all the nationalities. From this emerged the notorious slogan "national in form, socialist in content." But there was another dimension to this connection. At the height of the frenzy of collectivization and industrialization Stalin reassured the nationalities that this drawing closer (*sblizhenie*) of nations would not lead to a full fusion (*sliianie*) of nations until the victory of the world revolution. Only then would "national languages inevitably fuse into one common language which, of course, would not be either Great Russian, German but something new." Any notion that the future language of socialism in the USSR would be Great Russian he disparaged as "Great Russian chauvinism."[35]

Nevertheless, as the clouds of war gathered in the late 1930s, Stalin grew increasingly concerned about the need to strengthen the place of the Russian language in the educational system. A decree of 1938 drafted by a committee headed by Andrei Zhdanov and approved by Stalin decreed the introduction of obligatory Russian-language training in the non-Russian Soviet schools. He cited the necessity of a common language in a multicultural society for the advanced training of cadres and "the requirements of defense." In its final version, the proponents of a radical policy of russification of non-Russian schools were rebuffed by Stalin, who warned that attempts to convert Russian from a subject of study to the language of instruction were "harmful."[36] At the end of his life, he reiterated his consistent attachment to the idea that Great Russian chauvinism was in the final analysis the equivalent of linguistic

---

[34] A. I. Vdovin, "Natsional'naia politika, 30-x godov (ob istoricheskikh korniakh krizisa mezhnatsional'nykh otnoshenii v SSSR)," *Vestnik Moskovskogo universiteta*, series 8, *Istoriia* 4 (1992), pp. 21–2.

[35] *Shestnadtsatyi s"ezd VKP(b), 5 noiabriia–5 dekabriia 1932 g.* (Moscow: Gosizdat. politicheskoi literatury, 1951), p. 290. In 1929 Stalin expanded his analysis on the fusion of languages during the final stage of the worldwide dictatorship of the proletariat but he did not publish it until 1949. See Vdovin, "Natsional'naia politika," vol. IV, p. 22; Yuri Slezkin, "The USSR as a Communal Apartment, or How a Socialist State Promoted Ethnic Particularism," *Slavic Review* 53 (Summer, 1994), pp. 414–52.

[36] Peter A. Blitstein, "Nation-Building or Russification? Obligatory Russian Instruction in the Soviet Non-Russian Schools, 1938–1953," in Ronald Grigor Suny and Terry Martin (eds.), *A State of Nations: Empire and Nation-Making in the Age of Lenin and Stalin* (Oxford University Press, 2001), p. 258.

"russification."[37] This line of thought ran parallel to his pronouncements on the gradual elimination of classes, a process which would only be fulfilled under full communism.

The establishment of national minority rights and their termination was another indicator that Stalin intended to shape his nationalities policy as the third pillar supporting his construction of socialism in one country along with collectivization and industrialization. As early as 1920 the Soviet government created administrative units down to the lowest level for national minorities within union republics, autonomous republics and regions. In May 1925 legislation introduced proportional representation for national minorities in all electoral organs of the USSR and, depending on the size of their populations, even permitted separate local soviets, schools and courts employing the indigenous language. In order to coordinate their activities republic conferences on work among the national minorities met in the late 1920s and early 30s; for example three times (1926, 1928 and 1933) in the RFSFR. The object was not only to protect small nationalities within the larger national republics and regions but also Russians and Georgians living in national areas where as representatives of the "master" nations they were likely to encounter considerable antipathy.[38] Soviet officials involved in these policies referred to them as "indigenization" (*korenizatsiia*), but Stalin never used the term, preferring to speak of "nationalization" or the "protection of national cultures."

Up until 1930 Stalin generally supported indigenization and personally intervened on numerous occasions to defend the national minorities against what he continued to call Great Russian chauvinism.[39] His careful monitoring of the policy reflected in large measure the real concerns he nourished since his early days as a revolutionary over the importance of recognizing cultural differences in welding together a broadly based movement, then forging an All-Union Communist Party and constructing a constitutional framework to rule a multicultural society. In addition, he reiterated his earlier view on the connection between reducing national conflict in the borderlands and defending and expanding the Soviet frontiers. Domestically, he actively pursued two aims: first, drawing frontiers between the Soviet republics and, second, securing appointments for the

[37] See Stalin's 1950 treatise "Concerning Marxism in Linguistics," in Stalin, *Works*, vol. III, pp. 114–48.

[38] Terry Martin, *The Affirmative Action Empire: Nations and Nationalism in the Soviet Union, 1923–1939* (Ithaca, NY: Cornell University Press, 2001); Gerhard Simon, *Nationalism and Policy toward the Nationalities in the Soviet Union: From Totalitarian Dictatorship to Post-Stalinist Society* (Boulder, CO: Westview Press, 1991).

[39] Martin, *Affirmative Action Empire*, pp. 144–5, 157, 230–1, 241–2, 246.

titular nationalities (those identified with the name of the republic or region) in prominent positions in the party and government apparatus.[40]

Stalin's nationality policy, and in particular the drawing of internal frontiers within the Soviet Union, was also closely related to foreign policy aims. Throughout the 1920s the Soviet government had been toying with the idea of transferring territories from the Central Agricultural Region and even the Kuban to the Ukrainian Soviet Republic with the aim of strengthening links between the periphery and the center. The decision to transfer large areas of territory from the RSFSR to the Belorussian Union Republic in 1924 was an extension of Stalin's insistence on creating a Belorussian republic in the first place, although the level of national consciousness among the population was known to be relatively underdeveloped compared to other ethnic groups along the western periphery. The justification was that it would serve as a buffer to check Ukrainian and Polish nationalism within the Soviet Union and promote revolution among the Belorussians and Poles across the frontier.[41] Similarly, the Politburo ordered a Moldavian Autonomous Republic to be carved out of Ukrainian territory, "above all for political considerations," and defined its frontier "not at the Dniester but at the Prut," in order to include Bessarabia which had been annexed by Romania in 1918.[42] As late as 1929 there was still evidence of the advantages of passing national minority legislation on the populations of the frontier zones. For example, the former Deputy Commissar for Nationalities under Stalin, Professor S. Dimanshtein, took note of the fact that "we are interested in the self-contained development of [our] Kurds who have many co-nationals almost across the border from them." An brief attempt was even made to establish a Kurdish national region in the Armenian republic.[43]

Parallel to internal indigenization, the early Soviet leaders promoted through the Comintern the transfer of the idea across the frontier into Poland. At the Second Congress of the Polish Communist Party in 1923, the decision was taken to merge three provincial Communist organizations in the northeast *kresy* into a West Belorussian Party and to incorporate the Communist Party of Eastern Galicia, formed during the Civil War and renamed the Communist Party of West Ukraine, as autonomous

---

[40] *Ibid.*, pp. 31 and 37.
[41] Hirsch, *Empire of Nations*, pp. 149–55. Stalin's close associate Abel Enukidze was the main figure in guiding this redistribution, mixing ethnographic, historical and economic arguments as they suited the purpose.
[42] Viktor Stepaniuk, *Gosudarstvennost' moldavskogo naroda. Istoricheskie, politicheskie i pravovye aspekty* (Kishinev: "Tipografia Centrală," 2006), pp. 308–9.
[43] Vdovin, "Natsional'naia politika," pp. 33–7. In the late 1930s the entire faculty of the National Minorities University in Moscow, including Professor Dimanshtein, was arrested.

units within the structure of the Polish Communist Party. The congress also mounted a renewed attack on Rosa Luxemburg's views on the nationality question by affirming the right of West Belorussia and West Ukraine to separate from Poland and fuse with Soviet Belorussia and Soviet Ukraine.[44] These parties rapidly found themselves in a delicate and later fatally compromising position between Ukrainian Communists like Skrypnik and the Polish Communists, both of whom were inclined to defend their own national Communist interests.[45]

At the same time, Ukrainian Communists redefined the "piedmont concept", and, as popularized by Skrypnik, they began in the early 1920s to introduce it into their propaganda war with Poland. In the pre-revolutionary years, Habsburg Galicia had been called the piedmont of Ukrainian unification; in the new version the Ukrainian SSR would embody this concept. In 1924 a Comintern resolution called for the Ukrainian territories in Poland, Czechoslovakia and Romania to be incorporated into the Ukrainian SSR.[46] Stalin subsequently dropped the word piedmont, as smacking of Ukrainian nationalism. But he did not abandon the idea of bringing all Ukrainians under Soviet rule, an aim he came close to achieving after World War II.

Within the Soviet Union the policy of indigenization showed signs of strain from the outset. The cracks began to widen throughout the 1920s as reports and letters from the periphery arrived in the center complaining about either reverse discrimination or the persistence of Great Russian or "great power chauvinism," as the local nationalities preferred to call it. These reports implicated a wide range of underground activities by Armenian Dashnaks, Azerbaizhani Mussavetists, Zionists, Chechen separatists, Pan-Turks, Pan-Islamicists, and Belorussian and Ukrainian national democrats.[47] The liberal attitude toward *korenizatsiia* began to dry up, drawing Stalin's attention in particular to the Ukrainian and Muslim areas.

---

[44] "Za pravil'noe osveshchenie istorii kompartii zapadnoi Belorussiasii," *Kommunist* 8 (May, 1964), p. 70; "Za pravil'noe osveshchenie istorii kommunisticheskoi partii Zapadnoi Ukrainy," *Kommunist* 10 (1963), pp. 40–1. To further complicate matters, the West Belorussian Party absorbed the Belorussian Revolutionary Organization, an illegal party formed in 1922 by elements of the left wing of the Belorussian Socialist Revolutionaries (SRs) which had some influence among the local intelligentsia and peasantry. "Za pravil'noe istorii kompartii zapadnoi Belorussiasii," p. 70. But their presence subsequently exposed the party to charges of nationalism.

[45] E. H. Carr, *The Twilight of the Comintern, 1930–1935* (New York: Pantheon, 1982), p. 268.

[46] Martin, *Affirmative Action Empire*, pp. 9, 225–7.

[47] These complaints provide the bulk of the documentation in L. S. Gatagova *et al.* (eds.), *TsK RKP(b)–VKP(b) i natsional'nii vopros* (Moscow: Rosspen, 2005) vol. I, especially docs. 242, 243, 245, 258, pp. 667–71, 673–5, 716–18.

The intra-party debate over indigenization in Ukraine began to reveal serious consequences for Soviet policy in the borderlands and its relations with Poland. In April 1926 Stalin granted a long interview to O. Ia. Shumskyi, the Commissar of Enlightenment of Ukraine, in response to Shumskyi's complaints over the sluggish pace of ukrainianization and the rough organizational methods of Kaganovich in the republic. At first Stalin was willing to concede that there was some truth in what Shumskyi said; but there was more error. Stalin made two forceful points: first, ukrainianization could not be imposed from above on the Russian proletariat in the republic; and, second, the weakness of the Ukrainian Communist cadres had enabled the indigenous intelligentsia to pursue an anti-Russian and anti-Leninist course. He singled out the pernicious effects of appeals by a well-known Communist journalist who called for "the immediate de-russification of the proletariat" in Ukraine and denied that Russian literary models contained any appeals for Communist parties and the working class in Europe. On the contrary, Stalin insisted, Communists and workers worldwide looked with sympathy to Moscow as "the citadel of the international revolutionary movement." But he admitted he was still willing to take a balanced view of things. Perhaps Kaganovich had been overly bossy (*pereadministrativnyi*), but he could learn to be more flexible. But Shumskyi too had to be brought along, given more party work; there was a need to strengthen Ukrainian cadres and pay special attention to educating Ukrainian youth. And it was important, Stalin added, not to persecute former members of the Ukrainian Socialist Revolutionary Party (Borobitsy) who later joined the Communists partly to atone for their past. "We have to forget that they committed sins at one time, we have no sinless people."[48] Within a year, his temper changed dramatically; his tolerance had withered away.

In 1927 problems with grain procurement were beginning to show signs of a prolonged crisis. At the same time the war scare was generating disturbing reports from the OGPU on the reliability of the population in the western borderlands. They emphasized the "defeatist mood" of the Polish population of the Soviet Ukraine and the western region (*krai*). According to local agents "the well-to-do and part of the poor population connected with relatives in Poland are impatiently waiting the advance (*vystuplenie*) of Poland and cherish hopes for the achievement of 'the great

[48] "Pis'mo I. V. Stalina sekretariu TsK KP(b) Ukrainu L. M. Kaganovichu i drugim chlenam Politbiuro TsK KP(b)U o besede s narkom prosveshcheniia Ukrainy A. Ia. Shumskim," *ibid.*, vol. I, doc. 154, pp. 382–5. Kaganovich followed this up by reaching a temporary accommodation with Shumskyi. *Ibid.*, doc. 160, pp. 402–4. The Borobisty ("Fighters") were members of the Ukrainian Socialist Revolutionary Fighters Party founded in 1918 by the Left SRs.

power ideas' of Poland."[49] In July 1928 during an increasingly tense intra-party debate over the grain procurement crisis, Stalin ominously invoked the danger of conducting a two-front war against the Poles and the peasantry. Only if the Soviet power could secure a six-month reserve of grain would they be able to bring the peasants to their senses and dispel their illusions by strengthening the defenses of the country.[50]

At the same time, the OGPU was reporting on the international contacts of the Belorussian nationalist intelligentsia. Returning émigrés were recruiting from abroad former Socialist Revolutionary members of the Belorussian People's Republic of 1920 who in turn maintained their foreign ties. Nationalists were described as being particularly active among peasants and students. Anti-Soviet views had reportedly infected the Institute of Belorussian Culture which "more or less openly expresses anti-Semitic and polonophile tendencies." To promote its ends, police agents noted, the nationalist movement was exploiting the "domestic and foreign difficulties of the Soviet Union."[51] Sounded in May 1928, this ominous note presumably referred to the grain procurement crisis and the gathering clouds of war.

The potential threat from Poland had been gradually building momentum since Marshal Piłsudski's coup in 1926. Piłsudski lost no time in announcing his new program, which radically reversed the policy of his predecessors aimed at the assimilation of minorities in Poland. Unlike him, his great rivals Dmowski and the National Democrats had accepted the terms of the Treaty of Riga. For him it was merely an armed truce. In the early 1920s, the National Democrats had pursued a vigorous policy of polonization of the national minorities, treating the Ukrainian and Jewish population of Ukraine as ethnic raw material. They sought to deprive the Ukrainians in Eastern Galicia of all the rights and privileges they had enjoyed under Habsburg rule. The government had discriminated against Ukrainians in higher education and state offices, had introduced an equal form of bilingualism which gave an advantage to Polish, persecuted the Orthodox Church in Volhynia and – probably most resented of all – had embarked on a systematic colonization of the *kresy*. Polish veterans and border guards were settled on the former large estates, creating what

---

[49] O. N. Ken and A. I. Rupasov, *Politbiuro TsK BKP(b) i otnoshenimi sosednimi gosudarstvami (konets 1920–1930-x gg.) Problemy. Dokumenty. Opyt kommentariia* (St. Petersburg: Evropeiskii dom, 2000), p. 484, citing Russian archives.

[50] V. Danilov *et al.* (eds.), *Tragediia sovetskoi derevni: Kollektivizatsiia i raskulachivanie: dokumenty i materially, 1927–1939*, 3 vols. (Moscow: Rosspen, 1999), vol. I, p. 327.

[51] "Doklad OGPU v TsK VKP(b) o politicheskikh nastroeniiakh v srede Belorussiaskoi intelligentsii," in Gatagova *et al.*, *TsK RKP(b)–VKP(b) i natsional'nyi vopros*, vol. I, doc. 209, pp. 567–70.

one historian has called "something analogous to Russian Cossacks." Official Polish propaganda cast aspersions on Ukrainian culture.[52] The policy backfired.

Resistance to polonization came from the extremes of left and right. A number of Ukrainian Communist groups in Poland coalesced into the Communist Party of West Ukraine, which fell under the influence of the Communist Party of Ukraine across the frontier rather than the Polish Communist Party to which it was officially subordinated. At the same time, a militant Ukrainian nationalist movement emerged in the mid-1920s, leading in 1929 to the formation of the Organization of the Ukrainian Nationalists (OUN). Its initial program was fascist. During World War II the OUN was to mount an armed resistance fighting all comers – the occupying German Army, the underground Polish Home Army, and the liberating Soviet forces – in order to forge an independent Ukraine.

Piłsudski sought to reverse the failed policy of his rivals by reviving his neo-Jagiellonian design to win over the minorities by reconfiguring the Polish state along federalist lines. In Volhynia his agents introduced an experiment which combined the traditional tolerant policies of the Polish–Lithuanian Commonwealth toward the Jews with modern concepts of national cultural autonomy for the Ukrainians. Unofficially, he conspired to turn the province into a springboard for subverting Communist rule across the border and undermining the Soviet Union. These activities, the so-called Prometheus plan, resembled a mirror image of Soviet ukrainianization and subversive Communist activities aimed at disrupting Polish rule in their eastern marches. Subsequently, both sides engaged in a shadowy war of espionage.[53]

For Stalin the decisive turn in the conflict over ukrainianization came when the Communist Party of Western Ukraine came out in defense of Shumskyi. This provoked a violent response from the Ukrainian Politburo dominated by Kaganovich who returned to the attack with a vengeance. It accused Shumskyi and his supporters of fostering an "orientation toward Europe and away from Moscow [which] is a first class legal cover for the propagation of a bourgeois restoration in Ukraine

[52] Janusz Radziejowski, *The Communist Party of Western Ukraine, 1919–1929* (Edmonton: Canadian Institute of Ukrainian Studies, 1983), pp. 4–7, quotation on p. 6; Werner Benecke, *Die Ostgebiete der Zweiten Polnischen Republik* (Cologne: Böhlau, 1999), pp. 123–33.
[53] Timothy Snyder, *Sketches from a Secret War: A Polish Artist's Mission to Liberate Soviet Ukraine* (New Haven, CT: Yale University Press, 2005). See also Étienne Copeaux, "Le mouvement Prométhéen," *Cahiers d'études sur la Méditerranée orientale et le monde turco-iranien* 16 (1993), pp. 1–36, and T. M. Simonova, "Prometeizm vo vneshnei politike Pol'shi 1919–1924 gg.," *Novaia i noveishaia istoriia* 4 (2002), pp. 47–64.

and its separation from the Soviet Union." In addition, they had committed two major sins. First, they had sold out to Piłsudski, who was
mobilizing the masses of West Ukraine in the war he was waging "against
Moscow for the attachment of Ukraine to European culture." Second,
they were responsible for disorganizing the masses in the face of Polish
fascism backed up by foreign imperialism.[54] When the West Ukrainian
Party attempted to defend itself to the Comintern, the Ukrainian Central Committee accused the wayward Communists of aiding and abet-
ting "an armed intervention against the Soviet Union in general and the
Soviet Ukraine in particular." Within the year Shumskyi and his associates recanted. His career was over, although he was only arrested and
shot in 1933.[55]

The controversy over "shumskyism" was symptomatic of a growing crisis among Communists involved in Ukrainian affairs. The Communist
Party of West Ukraine was itself divided over the question of ukrainianization. But the instability of its internal politics must also be attributed
to the intermittent intervention of other Communist parties, its official superior the Polish Communist Party, and the Communist Party of
Ukraine, the All-Union Communist Party of the Soviet Union and finally
representatives of the Comintern. In 1927–8 the Communist Party of
West Ukraine was exposed to withering criticism by Lazar Kaganovich
who in his capacity as First Secretary of the Communist Party of Ukraine
accused the entire Central Committee of nationalism and treason. He
expressed doubts over which side it would fight in the event of war.
A member of the Ukrainian Party Politburo, Vlas Chubar, shocked by
the disruptive effect of these accusations on the party, complained that:
"Mutual confidence and contact between us has been broken, so that no
one trusts anyone else. Questions have been decided without the knowledge of the [Ukrainian] politburo. I find this state of affairs oppressive."[56]
The situation was a microcosm of the factional politics characteristic
of a multicultural borderland people recently wracked by civil war and
struggling to assert their own identity while caught in the middle of an
intense rivalry between Poland and the Soviet Union, two powers striving
to impose their own version of a political solution on a long-contested

---

[54] "Rezoliutsiia TsK KP(b) Ukrainy 'O natsionalisticheskom uklone t. Shuskogo," *TsK
RKP(b)–VKP(b) i natsional'nyi vopros*, vol. I, doc. 193, pp. 486–93, quotation on
p. 493.
[55] "Rezoliutsiia TsK KP(b) Ukrainy o pozitsii kompartii Zapadnoi Ukrainy v natsional'nom voprose," *ibid.*, doc. 194, pp. 493–6, quotation on p. 495; Martin, *Affirmative Action Empire*, pp. 214–16.
[56] "Za pravil'noe osveshchenie istorii kompartii zapadnoi Ukrainy," *Kommunist* 10 (1963),
pp. 44–5.

borderland. By January 1928 the Communist Party of West Ukraine was hopelessly split. The Communist Party of Poland suspended the leadership and condemned it for "Ukrainian deviation" at a time when ukrainianization in the Soviet Ukraine had reached a high point.

The majority faction of the West Ukrainian Communist Party, denounced from all sides, met in a final conference to define its position. Their resolutions defending "shumskyism" lashed out at the policies of both the Polish and the Ukrainian Communist parties. They accused the Polish Communists of nationalist deviation for supporting autonomy of the *kresy* rather than their incorporation into the Soviet Belorussian and Ukrainian Republics and for failing to denounce national deviations in the Belorussian Workers' and Peasants' Assembly (Hramada). They also condemned the Czechoslovak Communist Party for its slogan of autonomy for the Transcarpathian Ukraine and, for good measure, the Romanian Party as well, for neglecting work in Bukovina. Turning their guns against the Ukrainian Communist Party, they blasted the "bureaucratic deformation of the process of ukrainianization" under the slogan "If we don't carry out ukrainianization, Piłsudski will." Attacking Great Russian chauvinism, they focused on the refusal to ukrainianize the working class, which diminished the significance of Ukraine in the Soviet system and limited its rights to the sphere of national cultural autonomy and finally drove out the "best representatives of the Soviet Ukraine, especially O. Shumskyi."[57] But theirs was a voice in the wilderness. By the end of the year the party was severely weakened. But its shrinking membership fought on and the party underwent something a revival when Warsaw abandoned Piłsudski's Volhynia project in the mid-1930s.[58] The entire episode demonstrated that the struggle over the borderlands between Poland and the Soviet Union was not simply between the two states but also just as fiercely between Communists on both sides of the frontier and within Polish domestic politics.

In the early months of 1930, the growing resistance to collectivization in the Ukrainian countryside fuelled fears of Polish intervention and intensified the struggle between the Communists. The OGPU reported confused rumors were being spread about the return of "land-lord bondage," and appeals were being made to spare Ukraine from "the yoke of communism" mixed with hopes for a coming war of Poland and Romania against the USSR – a Christian crusade of the world against communism. Overall a gloomy note prevailed: "a forecast of an apocalypse hung over the Ukrainian village." In February "mass disturbances

[57] Radziejowski, *The Communist Party of Western Ukraine*, pp. 154–6.
[58] Snyder, *Sketches*, pp. 138–44.

and in some places armed uprisings of peasants" had broken out in all eleven districts of the frontier zone from Belorussia to the Autonomous Republic of Moldavia. Agitators were calling for an uprising in the name of the Union for the Liberation of Ukraine, although the organization had presumably been broken up and its leaders placed on trial just a month earlier.[59] The Politburo reacted as if the threat of war with Poland and Romania was imminent by retreating from its policy of repression. Its dramatic shift illustrated once again how its domestic policy was powerfully influenced by events in the struggle over the borderlands.

In March 1930 the high powered Rykov–Iagoda Commission recommended a series of harsh measures to deal with the disturbances in the Polish settlements in the Belorussian and Ukrainian frontier districts. But almost immediately the Politburo found it necessary to reduce the numbers of proposed deportations, limit them to the most rebellious district and to give greater prominence to political work.[60] This was largely in response to fresh information on the lack of technical means to organize large-scale deportations and the evidence of a sharp increase in Polish espionage and heightened tension on the Polish and Romanian frontiers. The new measures appeared to reduce the number of disorders. But the Soviet leadership continued to take seriously the external threat. A commission chaired by Stalin assigned fresh resources to strengthening the defenses of the western frontier.[61] For the moment the internal situation had stabilized. But only for the moment.

During the harvest in mid-August 1932, Stalin lashed out at his party and police subordinates in Ukraine for failing to check widespread counter-revolutionary elements. "We might lose Ukraine," he wrote Kaganovich. The Ukrainian party, he stormed, sheltered "more than a few (yes, more than a few!) rotten elements conscious or not of Petliuraists and finally agents of Piłsudski." If things became worse, he predicted, they would open a front within the party. He demanded the replacement of leading officials like Kosior and Chubar and more vigorous political intervention of the party "above all in the frontier [underlined twice by Stalin] regions." In conclusion, he repeated: "We cannot lose Ukraine."[62]

---

[59] Ken and Rupasov, *Politbiuro*, pp. 511–12. Synder, *Sketches*, pp. 55–6, casts doubt on the existence of the organization except as a fabrication of the OGPU. Was this then a case of reality imitating theater?

[60] V. N. Khaustov *et al.* (eds.), *Lubianka: Stalin i VCheka-GPU-OGPU-NKVD, ianvar' 1922–dekabr' 1936* (Moscow: Rosspen, 2003), doc. 227, pp. 235–6.

[61] Ken and Rupasov, *Politbiuro*, pp. 508–20, includes the text of two Politburo resolutions, "O pol'skikh seleniiakh po pogranichnykh oblastiakh" and "Ob Ukraine i Belorussiasii," dated February 25 and March 11, 1930.

[62] Stalin to Kaganovich, August 11, 1932, in *Stalin i Kaganovich: Perepiska. 1931–1936 gg.* (Moscow: Rosspen, 2001), doc. 248, pp. 273–4.

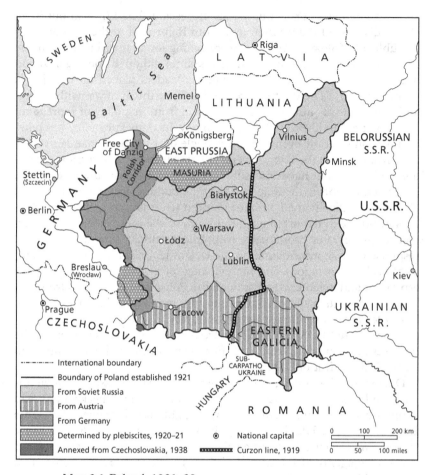

Map 3.1 Poland, 1921–39

Ukraine was not lost, but millions of Ukrainians were. The relentless pressure to collectivize created famine conditions that decimated the peasantry. The misery and death of millions of Ukrainians from starvation, and disease associated with it, reduced the mass of the peasantry to a condition of passivity rather than sparking rebellion. These tragic events, plus Moscow's successful diplomatic campaign, sharply reduced the danger of Polish intervention which had peaked in 1930.

Simultaneously, pressure was building against the main Ukrainian critic of Great Russian chauvinism and champion of Ukrainian cultural development, Mykola Skrypnik. His relations with Stalin had been uneasy ever since the Twelfth Congress, when he had indirectly criticized Stalin for having failed to implement the nationality policy which Lenin and Stalin himself had defined, by exposing the discrepancy between theory and practice.[63] By 1929 attacks on Great Russian chauvinism were no longer in high fashion. As early as 1926 Stalin had warned, in a letter to Kaganovich and other members of the Politburo of the Ukrainian Communist Party, that the movement "in Ukraine for Ukrainian culture and society ... led at every step by the non-Communist intelligentsia can take on in places the character of a struggle ... against Moscow in general, against Russians in general, against Russian culture and its highest expression – Leninism."[64] Despite such warnings Skrypnik shifted his attention more and more to promoting Ukrainian culture. As Ukrainian Commissar of Education, he took the lead in implementing indigenization by making the use of Ukrainian compulsory in higher education, introducing a Ukrainian orthography and promoting policies to ukrainianize the Russian working class of the republic.

Reflecting Stalin's fears, the cultural indigenization of Ukraine had scored notable successes by the end of the 1920s. Ukrainian had become the dominant language of the republic's administration, not only in the countryside but in the cities. The foundation of republican army units and the teaching of Ukrainian in regimental schools, where the language predominated, further advanced the national agenda. The drum beat of criticism from Moscow reached a peak in 1933 when Skrypnik's policies were attacked as challenging the idea of a single road to socialism, denying the primacy of All-Union interests and isolating the Ukrainian proletariat from Russian culture. In the face of Moscow's growing criticism, Skrypnik increasingly appealed to Lenin's and Stalin's authority in order to justify his policies, revealing, in retrospect, an almost pathetic desperation.[65] Interpreting Stalin's writings as a way of defending policies that Stalin no longer favored was a risky business. Citing Lenin to offset

---

[63] *Dvenadtsatyi s"ezd rossiiskoi kommunisticheskoi partii(b). Stenograficheskii otchet, 17–24 aprelia, 1923 goda* (Moscow: Izd. politicheskoi literatury, 1968), pp. 572–4. Skrypnik's intervention was preceded by that of Sultan-Galiev who, citing Trotsky and Lenin, made essentially the same point. *Ibid.*, pp. 567–8.

[64] Cited in M. Ia. Geller, "Soiuz nerushimyi," in Iu. N. Afanas'ev (ed.), *Sovetskoe obshchestvo: vozniknovenie, razvitie, istoricheskii final* (Moscow: Rossiiskii gosud. gumanitarnyi universitet, 1997), vol. I, p. 200, ellipses in original.

[65] Mykola Skrypnik, *Statti i promovy z nat'sional'nogo pytannia*, compiled by Ivan Koshelivets (Munich: Suchastnist, 1974), pp. 66–8, 140, 221, 229, 250; Bohdan Krawchenko, *Social Change and National Consciousness in Twentieth Century Ukraine* (Basingstoke: Macmillan, 1987), pp. 110–11, 131. Skrypnik may have been misled by the celebration of Lenin's views on nationalities at the Sixteenth Party Congress and other, albeit ambiguous, signs that Stalin was willing to grant more space to cultural manifestations of national differences. For these see Vdovin, "Natsional'naia politika," pp. 22–3, 27.

Stalin's policies could be fatal. As collectivization moved into high gear Skrypnik and Chubar sought to resist the absurdly high grain delivery quotas set by the center that were inducing famine conditions in Ukraine. Skrypnik's protests were unjustly characterized as evidence of nationalist deviation.[66] At the beginning of 1933 Stalin dispatched a secretary of the Central Committee, P. P. Postyshev, to Ukraine with extraordinary powers. Shortly thereafter Postyshev accused Skrypnik of having "delivered the policy of Ukraine into the hands of Petliuraists, Makhnovites and other nationalist elements."[67] Battered by several years of harassment and denunciations, Skrypnik committed suicide in July 1933.

Meanwhile, Stalin was giving greater credence to the connection between resistance to collectivization in the borderlands and national deviation. In 1931 and 1932 he personally took charge of the relentless and brutal mass campaign for collecting grain.[68] Angered by the shortfall in deliveries, he issued an order on December 14, 1932 demanding complete fulfillment within a month of the plan for procuring grain and sunflower seeds. He denounced the party organizations of Ukraine, the western oblasts and the North Caucasus for their "extremely poor work and lack of revolutionary vigilance" in the face of "counter-revolutionary elements – kulaks, former officers, followers of Petliura, supporters of the Kuban Rada [Cossacks]." He accused the local organizations of not acting in the cultural interests of the population but allowing "non-Bolshevik ukrainianization in almost half the regions of the North Caucasus." He ordered the deportation of all the elements in Poltava and villages of the North Caucasus except for those really loyal to the Soviet power and their replacement by kolkhoznik-Red Army veterans working on small plots in poor areas. Naming names, he ordered the arrest of district secretaries and their imprisonment from five to ten years. He warned the Ukrainian party organization "to avoid mechanical ukrainianization" and to eliminate all bourgeois nationalist elements from its ranks. In the North Caucasus, especially the Kuban area, all Ukrainian-language periodicals were to be replaced by Russian and by the fall all schools were to be taught in the Russian language.[69] Additional orders were sent to the

---

[66] The Politburo resisted the attempts of the Ukrainian Central Committee, "including Skrypnik" to reduce the levels of grain collection in July 1932. Molotov and Kaganovich to Stalin, June 6, 1932, *Stalin i Kaganovich*, doc. 186, p. 219.

[67] Krawchenko, *Social Change*, p. 136.

[68] R. W. Davies, "Stalin as Economic Policy-Maker: Soviet Agriculture, 1931–1936," in Sarah Davies and James Harris (eds.), *Stalin: A New History* (Cambridge University Press, 2005), pp. 130–4, confirms on the basis of archives Stalin's intense involvement in the grain procurement crisis.

[69] "Postanovlenie Politbiuro TsK BKP(b) 'O khlebozagotovkakh na Ukraine, Severnom Kavkaze i v Zapadnoi oblasti,'" in *TsK RKP(b)–VKP(b) Natsional'nyi vopros*, vol. I, doc. 252, pp. 696–7.

local party organizations in Kazakhstan, Central Asia and the Far East to transform all Ukrainian-language periodicals into Russian.[70]

As the policy of indigenization crumbled under a combination of internal and external pressures, it was becoming increasingly clear to the Soviet leaders that the piedmont principle, which had been intended to attract elements of the nationalities outside the Soviet borders, was being appropriated by Germany and Japan to exercise a centrifugal pull on the Soviet borderlands.[71]

In the national republics and autonomous republics of the USSR, the decimation of party cadres was no greater than in the RFSFR, yet there was one essential difference. Most of the victims in the non-Russian republics were condemned for nationalist deviation; none was so condemned in the Russian republic. Quite the contrary; along with the retreat from the high point of indigenization, Stalin launched a strong revival of Russian patriotism, beginning with the recasting of Russian history and spreading rapidly to other sectors of cultural and intellectual life.[72] As a result, in the words of Soviet historian Roy Medvedev, "by destroying tens of thousands of good Communists among the minority nationalities, the charge of nationalism helped to revive many nationalistic moods and prejudices."[73] These were, it should be added, never very far below the surface.

The purges were in one sense merely a continuation, albeit in radically intensified form, of the prolonged struggle between the Great Russian center and the periphery over cultural issues. Statistics tell only part of the story, but even by themselves they are eloquent. In the 1920s there was a steady rise in the percentage of native Communists in all the republics, except the Volga German ASSR, especially in Ukraine, Belorussia and the Crimean Tatar ASSR. After the mid-1930s when the purges cut deeply into their membership, the percentages declined in most of them. In the Central Asian republics the drop was from 5 percent in Kazakhstan to 15 percent in the Kirghiz Republic. Only in Ukraine was no decline recorded, although the pace of indigenization slowed and the earlier steady increase in numbers of Ukrainians in the Communist Party of the Soviet Union (CPSU) ceased altogether.[74]

---

[70] *Ibid.*, vol. I, p. 698, note 8.

[71] Martin, *Affirmative Action Empire*, pp. 8–9, 317, 312–18, 351.

[72] Lowell Tillett, *The Great Friendship: Soviet Historians on the Non-Russian Nationalities* (Chapel Hill: University of North Carolina Press, 1969), and David Brandenberger, *National Bolshevism: Stalinist Mass Culture and the Formation of Modern Russian National Identity* (Cambridge, MA: Harvard University Press, 2002).

[73] Roy Medvedev, *Let History Judge: The Origins and Consequences of Stalinism*, revised and expanded edn (New York: Columbia University Press, 1989), p. 207.

[74] T. C. Rigby, *Communist Party Membership in the USSR, 1917–1967* (Princeton University Press, 1968), pp. 369, 371, 373.

At the end of 1934, the year of ominous signs for Stalin, the Politburo introduced a new regime for the western borderlands. Terry Martin has argued that this was the prelude to a shift in Soviet policy to large-scale ethnic cleansing. The new regulations created a "forbidden border zone" of varying depth "into which no one could enter without special NKVD permission."[75]

Even before this, the security organs detected a potentially dangerous link between the resistance to collectivization in Ukraine and Belorussia and Polish intervention. As a precaution, in 1930 the Politburo ordered a vigorous campaign against deviations from the party line in the frontier districts of the two republics and a series of operations to strengthen border security. The arrest and deportation of kulak elements was to be carried out with great speed but quietly (*bez shuma*), avoiding any indication of a mass deportation.[76] The campaign gradually gained momentum, but up until 1936 the security organs were still more involved with internal actions. By the end of 1936 approximately half the German and Polish inhabitants in the border districts had been deported. At the same time similar policies were applied to the Finnish, Estonian and Latvian populations of the Leningrad border region.[77]

The attacks on national deviation elsewhere in the Soviet Union were, for the time being, more restrained. In the Transcaucasian Federation, for example, a number of prominent cultural figures were criticized or removed from their positions. But none of Stalin's opponents from the days of the Twelfth Congress were harmed.[78] The real drive toward greater russification only began later during the Second Five-Year Plan. Meanwhile, Stalin was refining his ideas on the nationality question in order to find the right formula that would strike a balance between recognizing the cultural differences in a multicultural state and centralizing the state apparatus to an ever greater degree. Meanwhile, he postponed a decisive strike against the last remnants of national deviation until the completion of the First Five-Year Plan could consolidate the power of the center vis-à-vis the periphery. The major thrust of the Second Five-Year Plan was to spread industrialization into the republics and thereby diminish if not eliminate the wide socioeconomic disparity that Stalin had deplored in the early 1920s.

---

[75] Martin, *Affirmative Action Empire*, pp. 329–32; Gerhard Simon, *Nationalism and Policy Toward the Nationalities in the Soviet Union* (Boulder, CO: Westview Press, 1991), pp. 60–2.
[76] Khaustov *et al.*, *Lubianka*, no. 227, pp. 235–6. See also no. 537, p. 682 for Postyshev's report on the frontier districts of Kiev region.
[77] Martin, *Affirmative Action Empire*, pp. 332–3.
[78] Suny, *The Making of the Georgian Nation*, pp. 258, 264–6.

Stalin's fears that external enemies would take advantage of the domestic turmoil prompted him to take a more active role in the formation of foreign policy. In November 1930 he expressed concern that the entire western frontier was vulnerable. The Poles, he wrote, were "in all probability" creating a Baltic bloc "with a view to launching a war versus the USSR." But for the moment his resources were stretched to breaking point. All he could propose was to increase the number of infantry divisions, to be paid for by boosting the sale of vodka.[79] He decided diplomacy was the best course of action to avoid the possibility of Polish intervention during the chaos of collectivization. He pressed for a treaty of non-aggression between the USSR and Poland. Here he ran into strong objections from the newly appointed Commissar of Foreign Affairs, Maksim Litvinov. Arguing from a different perspective, Litvinov insisted that negotiations with Poland would weaken the more important ties with Germany, complicate relations with France and increase the prestige of Piłsudski at a time when he remained committed to a federative policy aimed at detaching Soviet Belorussia and Ukraine with the support of France and the neutrality of Germany. Stalin saw things differently.[80]

Following the Japanese invasion and occupation of Manchuria, Stalin brushed aside Litvinov's objections to negotiate a treaty of non-aggression with Poland and pressed for similar agreements with all the adjacent states on his western frontier. From November 1931 to November 1932 Soviet diplomats concluded a series of pacts with Finland, Estonia, Latvia, Lithuania and Poland. A non-aggression pact with Romania followed in 1933. This set the stage for a major shift in Soviet policy toward its western neighbors following the coming to power of the Nazis in Germany. Soviet diplomacy exploited the serious fears among the Little Entente to negotiate a series of regional pacts defining aggression. According to the London Protocol of 1933, the participants pledged themselves to non-intervention in one another's internal affairs, a standard ploy of Soviet diplomacy that did not cover the activities of the Comintern. A formula was also devised to avoid contentious border disputes in the region. The signatories pledged themselves to recognize the territory of a state as that under its "actual (*fakticheskii*) administration."[81] The London Protocol of 1933 not only incorporated Stalin's territorial concept of guaranteeing the external security of the Soviet borderlands, but also established

---

[79] Khaustov et al., *Lubianka*, p. 435, letter dated November 1, 1930.
[80] Stalin was angry that Litvinov and his deputy Karakhan had disrupted promising negotiations with Poland in what he called a "gross mistake" (*grubuiu oshibku*). Stalin to Kaganovich, September 7, 1931 in *Stalin i Kaganovich*, doc. 48, p. 89.
[81] *Ibid.*, p. 102.

for the first time the idea of a common East European bloc against the dangers of German imperialism.

For a brief moment it appeared as though the Soviet Union would succeed in turning Poland from a potential enemy into a partner in resisting German expansion. Moscow was even prepared to join Warsaw in a joint declaration concerning "the inviolability and full economic and political independence of new political formations separated from the body of the former Russian Empire" – that is, the Baltic States. But the Poles were unwilling to entrust their hard-fought independence to either of its age-old enemies. Their foreign policy sought to balance the Soviet Union and Germany in order to avoid serving as the advance guard of either against the other. When Poland signed a non-aggression pact with Nazi Germany and Germany quit the League of Nations, Stalin and his associates recognized that a policy of collective security would have to go beyond regional agreements.

At the same time, Stalin concluded that it was necessary to shake up his own foreign policy establishment. He had been concerned over personal and policy differences among officials within the Foreign Commissariat and between them and representatives of the two union republics over policy toward Poland. Characteristically, he sought to resolve these by administrative measures. His first moves were to deprive the representatives of the union republics from participating in the formation of foreign policy. He had long been worried about the effect of their excessive "anti-polonism." In 1933 and 1934 he sidelined the last representatives of the historic type of *polpred* (ambassador), the "proletarian foreign politicians", men like Karl Radek, Lev Karakhan and Vladimir Antonov-Ovseenko. He then redesigned the collegial structure of the Foreign Commissariat by introducing the principle of the single head (*edinonachalie*). The Foreign Commissar, Maksim Litvinov, was given full authority within the Foreign Commissariat over the "*conduct*" of foreign policy.[82] At Stalin's urging, a Diplomatic Academy was established in 1934 in order to supply the commissariat with professionally trained specialists. These were all further steps in the direction of domesticating Soviet foreign policy and preparing for negotiations with France for a pact of alliance. If the main aim was to professionalize and centralize the making of foreign policy, Stalin also recognized the need to recognize the differences between regions, especially between the West and the East. In 1931 he had already created a special four-man commission in the Politburo of himself, Molotov, Kaganovich and Ordzhonikidze,

---

[82] "O Pol'she," April 20, 1931, and commentary, Ken and Rupasov, *Politbiuro*, p. 548.

which assumed broad powers over the formation of foreign policy. Initially, this commission took on a regional complexion dealing principally with the western neighbors, Finland, Estonia, Latvia, Lithuania, Romania, and indirectly with Poland, Turkey, France and Germany. But it soon broadened its purview. A separate commission of the Politburo was created to deal with Manchuria and later another with Mongolia.[83]

By the mid-1930s, then, Stalin had inaugurated a series of shifts in his borderland policies in the west. As the dangers of Hitler's rise to power gradually dawned on him, he accelerated the retreat from indigenization in the name of greater centralization and control over the republican Communist parties. Purges of alleged national deviationists, especially in Ukraine, even preceded the Great Terror. Then the assassination of Kirov in 1934 launched Stalin on a vast purge seeking to link the domestic opposition to foreign espionage. He also began to take measures to secure Soviet borders by undertaking the first steps in the deportation of suspected nationalities in the frontier provinces. At the same time, he sought to reduce tensions with countries on the western periphery of the Soviet Union and moved to strengthen diplomatic and political ties with the Western democracies, especially France. What will become clearer in the following chapters is the fundamental contradiction in Stalin's preparations for the war he was certain would come.

[83] "Voprosy NKID," November 22, 1931, and commentary, *ibid.*, pp. 562–3.

4   The borderland thesis: the east

The renewed campaign against the national opposition among Muslims in the second half of the 1920s was yet another skein of plots that Stalin wove entangling internal enemies and foreign governments. He was increasingly concerned by the persistence of a Muslim "religious movement" based on the schools and the economic influence of the mullahs. But he was still cautious about launching a massive anti-religious campaign against Islam.[1] In secret, however, in December 1927 Sultan-Galiev was arrested for the second time. Further arrests and a widespread purge of Tatar Bolsheviks followed. This time there was to be no thought of leniency. Genrikh Yagoda was put in charge of cooking up a case. Sultan-Galiev and his associates were falsely accused and condemned for forming a "counter-revolutionary program . . . that included the formation of a Turanian government"; this was not just a "federation with statist tendencies" as had been alleged in 1923, but implied the greater crime of aspiring to foster the dissolution of the Soviet Union.[2] After a long struggle against Crimean Tatar nationalists, "a party within a party" with a national program of "the Crimea for the Crimean Tatars," the president of the Crimean Central Executive Committee, Veli Ibragimov, was arrested in January 1928 and then shot.

Ethnic tensions caused by indigenization and social conflict aroused by collectivization proved an explosive mixture throughout the South Caucasus. In October 1931, the OGPU reported a serious rise in cross-border banditry linked to resistance to collectivization, fed by rumors of the collapse of Soviet power and supported by the Iranian government.[3] The

---

[1] *TsK RKP(b)–VKP(b) i natsional'nyi vopros*, vol. I, docs. 196, 197, 198, 204, pp. 499–521.
[2] After suffering years of imprisonment and torture, Sultan-Galiev was secretly re-tried in December 1939 and shot, despite the admission by NKVD interrogators that they had extracted his confession of contacts with foreign agents and Trotskyite groups by torture. "O tak nazyvaemoi," pp. 80–6.
[3] "Iz spravki Sekretno-politicheskogo otdela OGPU o politicheskom polozhenii v pogranichnikh s Persiei raionakh Azerbaizhana," *TsK RKP(b)–VKP(b) i natsional'nyi vopros*, vol. I, doc. 243, pp. 670 1.

general political situation in the Caucasian Federation of Azerbaizhan, Georgia and Armenia was especially troublesome. Union party officials ignored or discriminated against the interests of local minorities. In the summer of 1931 several thousand "Turkic" families resettled across the frontier with Turkey. Most serious of all, a massive armed uprising broke out in the Nakhchevan Autonomous Republic caused by violent "excesses" in the drive to collectivize. Among the participants were poor peasants, workers and party and Komsomol members.[4] The organizers of an uprising in Abkhaziia demanded that local Islamic traditions and economic activities be respected and not identified with kulaks.[5] In 1931 the leading party organs of the federation were still pressing ahead vigorously in their efforts to carry out the principles of indigenization despite the obstacles, which they freely admitted.[6] It would be unfair to emphasize resistance without acknowledging that the campaign to eliminate illiteracy and to bring large numbers of local elites into state and party administrative posts was winning converts to the Soviet cause. It was an accepted convention in party and police documents to emphasize shortcomings and the need to raise standards in the fight against chauvinism whatever its source. But there is also no question that the collectivization placed an ultimately unbearable weight on the entire policy and contributed to its abandonment.

Simultaneously with the crisis in Ukraine and Belorussia, the Soviet position along the volatile Afghan frontier deteriorated. Throughout the 1920s Soviet forces had continued to fight the Basmachi rebels. By the end of the decade, they appeared to have finally eliminated the problem on their side of the frontier. During the same period Moscow had encouraged the reformist ideas of King Amanullah. It provided subsidies and established a direct air link with Kabul. But in November 1929 a civil war in Afghanistan brought to power Nadir Shah, former commander in chief of the Afghan Army, who had capitalized on conservative opposition to Amanullah. The British, who had been wary of Soviet penetration, took advantage of the new government's tardy consolidation of power in the tribal areas of the northern provinces to encourage a revival

---

[4] "Iz dokladnoi zapiski otvetstvennogo instruktorov TsK A. A. Frenkelia v TsK VKP(b) o Zakavkazskoi partorganizatsii Ts KP(b) Azerbaizhana i TsK P(b) Gruzii," *ibid.*, vol. I, doc. 244, pp. 671–3, and "Iz spravki Sekretno-politicheskogo otdela OGPU v TsK VKP(b) o peregibakh i aktivizatsii antisovetskikih elementov v Zakavkaze," *ibid.*, vol. I, doc. 245, pp. 673–5.

[5] "Iz dokladnoi zapiski otvetstvennogo instruktora TsK VKP(b) G. A. Kozlova sekretariam TsK VKP(b) I. V. Stalinu, L. M. Kaganovichu i P. P. Postyshevu o volneniiakh v Abkhazii," *ibid.*, vol. I, doc. 246, pp. 675–80.

[6] "Iz dokladnoi zapiski Zakavkazskogo kraioma v TsK VKP(b) o rabote i sostoianii Zakavkazskoi partinoi organizatsii," *ibid.*, vol. I, doc. 247, pp. 680–4.

of Basmachi activity. Cross-border raids coincided with reports from the OGPU of widespread resistance to collectivization in the South Caucasus and along the Soviet–Afghan border. Local Soviet forces struck back. In "hot pursuit" of the Basmachi rebels, they entered Afghanistan, shocking Afghan opinion. Two years later the leader of the Basmachi, Ibrahim Beg, was chased back across the Soviet frontier, captured and executed. But the Soviet Union had lost its dominant influence in Kabul.[7] The Soviet leaders were fully aware that national tensions in Trans Caspia added another element to an already potentially explosive mix.

On the eve of the Afghan crisis the OGPU warned ominously that the Uzbek intelligentsia was "developing tendencies toward emancipation from Moscow, tendencies toward pan-Uzbek aspirations (national chauvinism), expressed in indifference to the interests of the national minorities, strivings to establish hegemony in Uzbekistan of only Uzbeks, etc."[8] Their hostility was reportedly directed not only against Russian colonists and officials in their republic but also toward Tadjiks whom they sought to assimilate. This had merely intensified a Tadjik national reaction.[9] Tadjiks bombarded Moscow with complaints and petitions, requesting that their status as an autonomous soviet republic within the Uzbek SSR be raised to the level of a union republic. The commission named to review the question was headed by Iakov Peters, a high-ranking official in the Eastern Department of the OGPU who was in close communication with Stalin throughout the deliberations. The creation of a Tadjik ASSR in 1924 had already contributed to breaking up the embryonic pan-Turkic movement that had united many Tadjiks and Uzbeks. Moscow's decision to create a Tadjik Union Republic, formally announced in December 1929, can logically be seen as another step in an effort to stabilize the borderland with Afghanistan, first by further weakening the pan-Turkic ties between the Tadjiks and Uzbeks, and second by placating the Tadjiks whose territory continued to be the site of fierce clashes with the Basmachi cross-border fighters.[10] In this case, as in Ukraine and Belorussia, the Soviet leadership struggled to disentangle the three typically

---

[7] Jonathan Haslam, *Soviet Foreign Policy, 1930–33: The Impact of the Depression* (London: Macmillan, 1983), pp. 32–3; Louis Dupree, *Afghanistan* (Princeton University Press, 1980), pp. 451, 458–61.

[8] "Doklad OGPU v TsK VKP(b) o politicheskikh nastroeniiakh v Uzbekistane," in *TsK RKP(b) – BKP(b) i natsional'nyi vopros*, vol. I, doc. 211, p. 574.

[9] *Ibid.*, vol. I, doc. 211, pp. 579–83.

[10] Francine Hirsch, *Empire of Nations: Ethnographic Knowledge and the Making of the Soviet Union* (Ithaca, NY: Cornell University Press, 2005), pp. 174–86. However, the author concentrates her attention on the ethnographic basis of the disputes over delimiting the frontiers between the Uzbek and newly formed Tadjik union republics while underestimating the international implications of the decision to create a new union republic.

interrelated problems of a borderland – social conflict, national resistance and foreign intervention.

Although the Soviet frontier with Afghanistan was porous and unsettled, it was not directly threatened by the penetration of the Germans and the Japanese. It was an altogether different situation in the borderlands of Xinjiang, Mongolia and Manchuria. Beginning in the early 1930s the Japanese began an active campaign to bring Manchuria and Inner Mongolia under their control and even to extend their influence into Xinjiang.[11] The Soviet Union also had to contend with the revival of claims by the Kuomintang to forge a united China, which meant the restoration of the power of a centralized state over the Inner Asian borderlands. More muted but similar in its aims, the Chinese Communist Party also sought to become the dominant force in reuniting China under the banner of Marxism-Leninism. Stalin's policy then was to encourage resistance to Japanese imperialism by both the Kuomintang and the Communists, while at the same time increasing Soviet influence through a combination of political and economic penetration. He often resorted to a double game, encouraging aspirations for autonomy or independence by regional leaders as a means of exacting concessions to Soviet interests by the Japanese and above all the Chinese.

Manchuria

In Manchuria Soviet interests were directly challenged, first by the Chinese and then more powerfully by the Japanese. In the summer of 1929 the forces of the Manchurian warlord Marshal Zhang Zuolin backed by the Chinese Nationalist government of Chiang Kai-shek closed down Soviet enterprises seized the telephone and telegraph lines of the Chinese Eastern Railroad (CER), dissolved Soviet trade unions and expelled fifty-five officials. Justifying their actions, the Chinese accused the personnel of the CER of spreading Communist propaganda. Clashes occurred between the railroad personnel and Chinese officials, leading to a full-scale undeclared war and a break in diplomatic relations between the

---

[11] The Japanese even flirted with the idea of creating an anti-Communist Islamic "citadel" stretching from Manchuria to Turkistan. Selçuk Esenbel, "Japan's Global Claim to Asia and the World of Islam: Trans-National Nationalism and World Power, 1900-1945,"*American Historical Review* 109:4 (2004), pp. 1154–62. The Japanese made even more feeble efforts to stir up trouble for Moscow in Georgia. Hiroaki Kuromiya and Georges Mamoulia, "Anti-Russian and Anti-Soviet Subversion: The Caucasian-Japanese Nexus," *Europe-Asia Studies* 61:6 (2009), especially pp. 1422–6. The main effect appears to have been merely to feed Stalin's suspicions about the potential disloyalty of the nationalities in the borderlands.

Soviet Union and China.[12] Stalin was incensed by the violation of the extra-territorial rights granted to the USSR by the treaty of 1924. More importantly, if tolerated it would have eliminated Russia's longstanding preeminence in Northern Manchuria and jeopardized the entire Soviet strategic position in the Far East. Stalin lost patience. In October he wrote an extraordinary letter to Molotov outlining in detail a rather hare-brained scheme for unleashing an "insurrectionary revolutionary movement in Manchuria." He suggested organizing, supplying and introducing into Manchuria Chinese troops who would "occupy Harbin and, gathering strength, depose Zhang Zuolin (sic!) and establish a revolutionary power (destroy the landlords, win over the peasants, create Soviets in the towns and countryside)."[13] After a heated debate at the highest level, a more conventional approach prevailed. In November the Red Army, supported by aircraft, staged a military incursion that routed the Chinese and led to a restoration of Soviet rights on the CER.[14] Alarmed, the Japanese Kwantung Army interpreted the Soviet move as the first step in incorporating Manchuria into the Soviet sphere and turning it into a base for the Chinese Communists to move south. For them the question then arose, who would get there first?

In the 1920s and 30s Japan intensified its activities in the borderlands while expanding the horizons of its foreign policy. As imperial ambitions grew, divisions deepened among the policy-makers over the means to achieve them. During the 1920s, tensions increased between the army command and the Foreign Ministry. Despite the failure of the Siberian intervention, the army remained committed to the acquisition of territory in the borderlands in order to protect the home islands from the spread of Bolshevism even if this meant going it alone. In these years the first discussions were held on the creation of a Co-Prosperity Sphere linking China and Japan against the West. The Foreign Ministry preferred to keep Japan within an international treaty system as the best means of guaranteeing its security. It sought to shift the emphasis from strategic concerns to informal economic arrangements as the basis for Japanese imperialism. By the 1930s Japanese imperialism operated in two worlds. Military expansion into Manchuria and North China ran parallel to Japanese diplomatic activity in an international system based on treaty rights, trade and investment throughout East Asia. Both outlooks

---

[12] The incident is most fully described in Peter S. H. Tang, *Russian Policy in Manchuria and Outer Mongolia, 1911–1931* (Durham, NC: Duke University Press, 1959), pp. 194–208.

[13] Stalin, "Pis'ma," vol. I, pp. 428–9. The letter is dated October 7, 1929. Stalin was apparently unaware that Zhang had been assassinated a year earlier and had been succeeded by his son, Zhang Xueliang.

[14] Tang, *Russian and Soviet Policy in Manchuria*, pp. 208–34, 242–59.

envisaged a special relationship with China but differed over its form.[15] The contradictions in the system proved irreconcilable. The fascination of the army with the borderlands proved irresistible.

While moderate Japanese governments pursued the path of negotiations within the international treaty system, the militant elements in Manchuria and the home islands grew increasingly restless. Even before 1931 the army had become virtually a "Manchurian institution, a justification for its growth."[16] Japanese evacuation of the southern Maritime Provinces, the shift to a civilian administration in Kwantung over the objections of the army and the ascendency of the moderates in Tokyo fed feelings of frustration among Kwantung army officers, some of whom occupied important positions in the national government. The stage was set for an open confrontation between the military and civil authorities over policies in the borderlands.

The army found allies for its Manchurian policy in the patriotic press and among business circles. It was a simple matter to portray the region as the El Dorado of North Asia. Long before the military occupation in 1931, the Japanese pursued a policy of economic development in what was still a rough and ready frontier region. The extension and integration of the railroad network and the credit system facilitated the growth of a big export market in soy beans. The Japanese also imported large quantities of raw materials including coal and iron ore that the home islands lacked. Partly as a result of Japanese efficiency and enterprise, the Manchurian economy, based on the silver standard, was the most stable in East Asia outside Japan itself. The Japanese-run Southern Manchurian Railroad was enormously profitable and did not appreciably suffer from the world economic crash in 1929. Japanese immigration, while not massive, attracted the ambitious and the entrepreneurial. By 1930, 230,000 Japanese lived in Manchuria. Imperial policy enabled Japanese settlers to acquire a large proportion of Manchurian land under cultivation, dislodging Chinese and Korean peasants and exploiting their labor power. Japanese officials and publicists who had served in the province were intoxicated by the sense of space, the opportunities for economic growth

---

[15] W. G. Beasley, *Japanese Imperialism, 1894–1945* (Oxford: Clarendon Press, 1987), represents an intermediate position between the earlier interpretations of Akira Iriye, *After Imperialism: The Search for a New Order in the Far East, 1921–1931* (Cambridge, MA: Harvard University Press, 1965), which emphasizes the oscillation between the moderate and extremist elements in Japanese domestic politics, and Gavan McCormack, *Chang Tso-lin in Northeast China, 1911–192: China, Japan and the Manchurian Idea* (Stanford University Press, 1977), who sees greater continuity in the commitment to overt interventionism in Manchuria by all factions in Japanese politics.

[16] Yoshihisa Tak Matsusaka, *The Making of Japanese Manchuria, 1904–1932* (Cambridge, MA: Harvard University Asia Center, 2001), p. 407.

and a belief in their civilizing mission. The foundations for the industrialization of Manchuria were laid long before its "undefined and indeterminate political status" had been resolved in 1931.[17]

Manchuria became the centerpiece of a vast campaign by public officials and intellectuals to justify and rationalize Japan's role in the world. Its three most fully developed themes were economic autarchy, a civilizing or redemptive mission and historical destiny. Manchuria's abundant natural resources were portrayed as the guarantee that Japan could withstand economic pressure from outside powers and enable the country to prepare for any future protracted war. A new generation of Japanese "reform bureaucrats" first launched schemes in Manchuria, subsequently embraced in Tokyo, to introduce technocratic solutions to economic problems, stressing the business-oriented, managerial approach and linking this to imperial expansion.[18] After 1931, the idea of autarchy became interlaced with pan-Asian sentiments linking cooperation between the new state of Manchukuo and China in an alliance under Japanese leadership against the domination of the white race. Disillusioned by the failure to obtain a commitment of the great powers to the idea of "racial equality" at the Paris Peace Conference, Japanese politicians and military increasingly reshaped the idea along pan-Asian lines. They used it to justify expansion into the borderlands. Even before Manchuria was occupied, it was portrayed by such varied sources as the Japanese-run Manchurian Youth League and army officers, who were later to play a role in the Manchurian incident, as a "racial paradise" where all Asians – Japanese, Chinese, Manchus, Mongolians and Koreans – could be treated equally. The thrust of this propaganda was anti-Western. In the 1940s the notion of pan-Asian racial harmony adorned the ideology of the Greater East Asian Co-Prosperity Sphere.[19]

The establishment of Manchukuo as a state, fictional as it may have been, rather than a colonial possession in the Western model, aimed at strengthening that policy. Japanese propagandists denied that Manchuria had been an integral part of China, claiming that sinicization was a

[17] Alvin D. Coox, *Nomonhan: Japan against Russia, 1939* (Stanford University Press, 1985), pp. 1–4, 11–12, 20–3; Raymond H. Myers, *The Japanese Economic Development of Manchuria, 1932–1945* (New York: Garland, 1982 [1959]), pp. 27–8, *passim*; Louise Young, *Japan's Total Empire: Manchuria and the Culture of Wartime Imperialism* (Berkeley: University of California Press, 1998), especially part 4 on "social imperialism."

[18] Janis Mimura, *Planning the Empire: Reform Bureaucrats and the Japanese Wartime State* (Ithaca, NY: Cornell University Press, 2011), especially chs. 2 and 3. The author calls their program "techno-fascism" as an alternative to making Japan a Communist state. *Ibid.*, p. 5.

[19] Naoko Shimazu, *Japan, Race and Equality: The Racial Equality Proposal of 1919* (London and New York: Routledge, 1998), pp. 178–9.

recent phenomenon, and that the region had its own distinctive historical development. Through the agency of sectarian and redemptive societies under Japanese patronage, the idea was propagated that Japan had a duty to spread its unique civilization, blending the Asian spiritual culture with Western technology. Manchukuo would be the laboratory for its implementation and a model for the rest of Asia to adopt.[20] If these utopian concepts had their roots in the period before 1931, so did the opposition to them.

In the interwar period there were three major threats to Japanese interests in Manchuria. The first came from the surge of colonization from China and the sharp increase in anti-Japanese sentiment among the new settlers; the second came from mounting political opposition to Japan's special status by the Kuomintang in Central China and its warlord allies in Manchuria; and the third came from disaffected elements in the province including bandits, private armies, secret societies and Mongol bannermen. In the 1920s the Chinese republican government took an even more active role than its imperial Qing predecessor in encouraging colonization of Manchuria as the most effective means of checking Japanese efforts to detach the region. The traditional seasonal agricultural migration mainly from Shantung Province increasingly gave way to permanent settlement. During "the years of spectacular migration" from 1926 to 1928, more than half of the million immigrants preferred to settle on the land rather than return to famine and unstable social conditions in Central China. The large landowner agencies also took advantage of government policies and the railroad system to recruit settlers. But these "refugee colonists," consisting mainly of single men, proved to be an unstable social group. Some of the pioneer settlers found opium cultivation an easy source of profit. A peculiar form of social banditry emerged in the form of armed gangs who "protected" virtually autonomous opium villages from the importunate demands of officials and tax collectors.[21] The Japanese militarists and nationalists were appalled by the flood of colonists from China that threatened to engulf the much smaller Japanese settlements, and by the growth of banditry that confirmed their worse suspicions about the disorderly character of Chinese administration. They identified the sinicization of Manchuria with a rise in Communist influence seeping in across the border from

[20] Prasenjit Duara, *Sovereignty and Authenticity: Manchukuo and the East Asian Modern* (Lanham, MD: Rowman & Littlefield, 2003), especially pp. 41–65, 103–20. See also Herbert P. Bix, *Hirohito and the Making of Modern Japan* (New York: HarperCollins, 2000), pp. 263–76.
[21] Owen Lattimore, "Chinese Colonization," in *Studies in Frontier History: Collected Papers, 1928–1958* (New York: Oxford University Press, 1962), pp. 313–23.

the north, abetted by Soviet officials enjoying extraterritorial rights along the Chinese Eastern Railroad. Finally, they were alarmed by the new nationalistic policies of the Kuomintang toward China's borderlands.

The second threat took the form of strong regional resistance to the Japanese by the warlord Zhang Zuolin, the "Old Marshal." Zhang was a typical product of Chinese borderland politics. He rose to prominence as an early opponent of the Chinese revolution and the Kuomintang policy of unifying the country. He ran the three northeastern provinces from Beijing with the help of a loosely organized clientele network or clique that was makeshift and non-ideological – in other words, as a warlord. But unlike other warlords he was able to exploit his unusual intermediate position among three powers: a weak Chinese central government, a Soviet Russia in temporary eclipse in the region, and an influential but not yet dominant Japan. He had blocked Japanese plans to create an independent "Manchuria–Mongolia" during World War I and then resisted their efforts to involve him in joint enterprises. He maintained his precarious independence by repressing anti-Japanese demonstrations in the region. Without appearing to act as Tokyo's agent, he ensured the safety and security of Japanese residents and investments against bandits and bolshevism. He laid plans to use his geographic and economic base in the northeastern periphery as a springboard to achieve hegemony over all China.[22]

The tension between Zhang Zuolin and the Japanese in the northeast revolved around his efforts to get them to support his drive to unify China under his rule and their efforts to turn him into a reliable collaborator for their detachment of the borderlands. The Kuomintang were willing up to a point to back him against the Japanese in Manchuria, but less enthusiastic about his ambitions south of the Great Wall.[23] The Soviet Union accepted the status quo so long as they were assured of real control of the Chinese Eastern Railroad under the facade of joint management, and Zhang was unwilling to challenge them directly on this issue.[24]

By 1927 the Japanese were deeply divided over their attitude toward Zhang. The government in Tokyo had briefly nourished hopes that they could reach an accommodation with him. The architect of the policy of cooperation with him was Matsuoka Yōsuke, a former diplomat, director and virtual chief executive officer of the Southern Manchurian Railroad who viewed Manchuria as the key to success in the struggle against the Anglo-Saxon world. "The day when Japan must retreat from

[22] McCormack, *Chang Tso-lin*, pp. 9–10, 33–6, 42–5.   [23] *Ibid.*, pp. 53–7.

[24] Alan S. Whiting, *Soviet Policies in China, 1917–1924* (New York: Columbia University Press, 1954).

Manchuria," he wrote, "is the day when the Yamato nation relinquishes its right to exist."[25] Subsequently, Matsuoka became Foreign Minister who negotiated the Treaty of Neutrality with the Soviet Union in 1941. He and others soon discovered that Zhang was not an easy man to control.

Following a large-scale internal review of the government's position in Manchuria and Mongolia, the Japanese drafted a new Manchurian policy. In consultation with its representatives in China and its advisors to Zhang, Tokyo concluded that it should expand its privileges by constructing six new railroads, taking over the management of the northern Manchurian forests, and surrendering extraterritoriality in exchange for the right of Japanese colonists to settle in the interior. The main point of the moderates in Japan was to get the Old Marshal to abandon his pretentions to become Chiang Kai-shek's rival as Chinese head of state and confine his ambitions to Manchuria where he could "establish special relations with Japan to settle Manchurian problems according to Japanese wishes." In sum, the moderate course set by the Japanese government was "to consider Manchuria a special area, separated from China proper and to settle all issues with Marshall Zhang Zuolin, the actual ruler of Manchuria."[26]

The Kwantung Army was no longer willing as they had been in the past to come to Zhang's assistance when he was threatened by internal opposition. Open rebellion by secret societies like the Big Sword and rival military cliques destabilized the northeast. The Kuomintang drove Zhang out of Central China in their revitalized Northern March under Chiang Kai-shek. Finally, even Tokyo gave up on him and forced him to accept an ultimatum to withdraw all his forces from North China to the northeast. The Kwantung Army occupied the key railroad junctions and planned to foment a local rising in order to justify their takeover and then they organized the Old Marshal's assassination.[27] Unexpectedly, his successor the "Young Marshal," Zhang Xueliang, moved even closer to the Kuomintang camp, exposing the weakness of the moderates in Japan and giving the Kwantung Army extremists an excuse to settle the Manchurian problem by force of arms.

The third threat came from a revitalization of the Kuomintang under Chiang Kai-shek and his campaign to unify all China including

[25] Matsusaka, *The Making of Japanese Manchuria*, p. 283.
[26] Pao-chin Chu, "From the Paris Peace Conference to the Manchurian Incident: The Beginnings of China's Diplomacy of Resistance against Japan," in Alvin D. Coox and H. Conroy (eds.), *China and Japan: Search for Balance since World War I* (Santa Barbara: ABC-Clio Inc., 1978), p. 74.
[27] McCormack, *Chang Tso-lin*, pp. 188, 203–8, 228–34, 246–8.

Manchuria. For a short period after the Chinese revolution, the Kuomintang had adopted a federative outlook toward the five races: Han Chinese, Manchus, Mongols, Tibetans and Muslims. But it soon abandoned this position, partly in reaction to the Japanese policy of fostering regional autonomy in order to increase its own control over Manchuria and Mongolia. Seeking to reestablish Chinese sovereignty over all its borderlands, the Kuomintang also denounced all unequal treaties, which clearly threatened the Japanese position in Manchuria. By 1927 the Northern Expedition of the Kuomintang to unify China had reached Shantung Province, where a clash with Japanese troops brought the two countries to the verge of war. In this tense atmosphere Sino-Japanese competition for influence over powerful local princes and warlords of the borderlands reached a critical point.

In its campaign to roll back Japanese influence in Manchuria, the Nationalist government in Nanking undertook a campaign to tie the province closer to China. In early 1931 it planned to cooperate with Zhang Xueliang in order to construct a new transportation and telecommunications system that threatened to undermine the dominant position of the Japanese-controlled Southern Manchurian Railroad, and develop its own port at Hulutao as a competitor with Dairen. It refused to renew Japanese mining and timbering concessions and limited the sale or lease of land to foreigners. Almost all Japanese enterprises in the region were beginning to feel the effects of the world economic depression. According to Akira Iriye, this provided "the immediate context" for the intervention of the Kwantung Army.[28]

The army officers were increasingly restive under the "weak and effeminate" rule of the parties at home that sought to reduce the size of the armed forces. They envisaged a Manchurian adventure as a means of renovating and revitalizing Japanese political life. A groundswell of popular support for their aggressive policy mounted under the impact of the world economic depression on Japan which affected most severely the classes from which the army officers were drawn: the shopkeepers, small business men, farmers and workers. The conquest of Manchuria took on the aura of a panacea for all Japan's domestic problems.[29]

In 1931, the Kwantung Army took advantage of an incident between their troops and Chinese border guards to launch a full-scale invasion and occupation of Manchuria. Stalin's initial response was again

[28] Akira Iriye, "Japanese Aggression and China's International Position, 1931–1949," in *The Cambridge History of China*, 14 vols. (Cambridge University Press, 1978–83), vol. XIII: *Republican China, 1911–1949*, pp. 496–7.
[29] Sadako N. Ogata, *Defiance in Manchuria: The Making of Japanese Foreign Policy, 1931–1932* (Berkeley: University of California Press, 1964).

cautious. The Japanese occupation of Manchuria caught the Soviet leadership off balance. But Stalin quickly recovered, affirming Soviet interests but refraining from unilateral action. In his eyes the Japanese intervention was part of a larger conspiracy by the imperialist powers to widen their spheres of influence in China. The United States was no exception. Stalin excluded any idea of Soviet intervention; even a diplomatic initiative was out of the question. That could only play into the hands of the imperialists by uniting them.[30] But he fully recognized the new danger on his eastern flank. In a letter to Voroshilov he noted that "It is possible that this winter Japan will not try to touch the USSR. But next year it could make such an attempt."[31] There is no direct evidence that links the Manchurian incident with the negotiation of pacts with the Soviet Union's five western neighbors with whom negotiations had been underway for some time. Nonetheless, the danger from Japan must have speeded up the conclusion of these pacts. In fact, the initial Soviet response to the Japanese occupation was to take a conciliatory line, and even propose a non-aggression pact with Poland.[32]

In an even more far-reaching concession, the Soviet Union began negotiations for the sale to Japan of the Chinese Eastern Railroad. Recognizing that the line was vulnerable to Japanese provocations, Stalin agreed to give up what both the imperial and early Soviet governments had considered the main instrument of their influence in the Manchurian borderland. The threat of war was real. The Japanese government and press were openly discussing the question of war with the Soviet Union and the seizure of the Maritime Provinces and the entire Far Eastern region. Japan was increasing its military forces on the Soviet frontier and improving access routes.[33] In an effort to avoid appearing pusillanimous,

---

[30] Stalin to Kaganovich and Molotov, September 23 [1931] in *Stalin i Kaganovich*, doc. 75, p. 116. In a rare insight into Stalin's use of the press, his letter gives specific instructions on the different tones to be used by *Pravda* and *Izvestiia* in their treatment of the incident; *Izvestiia*, as the government organ, was to take "a moderate and extra cautious tone in contrast to *Pravda*'s being allowed to abuse the Japanese freely."

[31] Letter of Stalin to Voroshilov, November 27, 1931, full text in Kyosuke Terayma, "Soviet Policies toward Mongolia after the Manchurian Incident, 1931–34," in Tadashi Yoshida and Hiroki Oka (eds.), *Facets of Transformation of Northeast Asian Countries* (Sendai, Japan: Center for Northeast Asian Studies, 1998), pp. 38–9. But toward Japan Stalin remained cautious, agreeing with his colleagues in the special commission, Molotov and Kaganovich, that the Soviet Union would not engage in any negotiations with Chinese Nationalists or Communists directed against Japan. Molotov and Kaganovich to Stalin, July 17, 1932 and Stalin's reply in *Stalin i Kaganovich*, doc. 200 and note 3, p. 228. Tangling with the Kwantung Army was not the same as fighting Chinese border guards.

[32] Haslam, *Soviet Foreign Policy*, ch. 7 and pp. 93–4.

[33] DVP, vol. XVI (1933), *prilozhenie* [appendix], p. 795.

Stalin insisted on reproaching Japan in advance for taking any action in violation of existing agreements on the status of the railroad.[34] Stalin's preferred tactic was "to bring pressure on Japan [by using] the perspective of a rapprochement of the USSR with Nanking and America in order to force it to speed up the conclusion of a pact [of non-aggression] with the USSR."[35] No doubt the recognition of the USSR by the United States in 1933 emboldened Stalin to take a firmer stand in Soviet relations with the Japanese. But, as we shall see, he was soon forced to come to terms with them.

Meanwhile, the new Chinese Communist leadership under Li Li-san had taken the bit and run with the Comintern slogan of a new revolutionary upsurge. What must have created the greatest stir in Moscow, however, were the provisions in the third part of the insurrectionary plan unfurled by Li Li-san at the meeting of the Politburo of the Chinese Communist Party in August 1930. According to the Communist leader, the organization of uprisings in the central provinces would be coordinated with actions in Manchuria: "The uprising in Manchuria will be the prologue for an international war since Manchuria is under the yoke of Japanese imperialism. It will not only be a clash with Zhang Zuolin but a struggle under the pressure of Japanese imperialism; simultaneously Japan will conduct a furious attack on the USSR." Li made it clear that the role of the Communists in the coming war was "to lead the international proletariat in the decisive struggle with imperialism."[36] He then stirred Mongolia into the cauldron:

After the success of the risings in China, Mongolia should immediately come forth with a political declaration uniting itself with the soviet power in China, recognizing that Mongolia is one of the republics joining the Chinese Union of Soviet Socialist Republics, and following that to raise a large army and advance into the north [i.e. China]. Secondly, it is necessary to gather hundreds of thousands of Chinese workers in Siberia, quickly arm them to prepare them for war with Japanese imperialism, that is so that they could pass through Mongolia, join the risings in China and attack the enemy.[37]

---

[34] Kaganovich to Stalin, September 13, 1933, in *Stalin i Kaganovich*, doc. 337, pp. 342–3, and September 18, 1933, doc. 349, p. 349. For the negotiations, see Jonathan Haslam, *The Soviet Union and the Threat from the East, 1933–1941: Moscow, Tokyo and the Prelude to the Pacific War* (London: Macmillan, 1992).

[35] Stalin to Molotov, Kaganovich, Voroshilov and Ordzhonikidze, June 18, 1932, in *Stalin i Kaganovich*, doc. 158, p. 200.

[36] A. M. Grigor'ev, "Komintern i revoliutstionnoe dvizhenie v Kitai pod lozungom sovetov (1928–1930)," in *Komintern i vostok. Bor'ba za leninskuiu strategiiu i taktiku v natsional'no-osvobozhditel'nom dvizhenii* (Moscow: Glav. red. Vostochnoi literatury, 1969), p. 331.

[37] *Ibid.*

The Comintern did not specifically address Li Li-san's madcap plans for the borderlands when they denounced the entire revolutionary strategy. But the danger to the Soviet position could not have gone unnoticed. In fact, it was exacerbated by the simultaneous claim on the borderlands by the Chinese Nationalists.

Xinjiang

Xinjiang was another example of what Owen Lattimore has called Chinese "secondary imperialism," which reached a high point in 1929. By this term he meant the attempt by the Kuomintang to bring under its control the warlords of the borderlands from Manchuria through Inner Mongolia into Xinjiang. Colonization was one means; another was to win over the local governors and attach them to the Nationalist cause. In Xinjiang these efforts collapsed in a tax revolt and an intervention by Muslim rebels from Gansu which spilled over the provincial border as it had done in the past. For the following five years, the province was plunged into an extremely complex civil war of the borderland type which James Millward has called "the deluge."[38] In attempting to sort out the complex cross-currents of this conflict, scholars have differed over the relative importance of ethnic, religious, socioeconomic and regional factors. It seems clear that the first three elements interacted differently in three subregions of the province. Muslim Uighurs in the center, constituted the majority of the population; the mixed Uighur, Kazakh and Kirghiz inhabitants of the Tarim Basin in the south were most receptive to Muslim penetration and the idea of separatism; the Ili-Zhungarian region in the north was divided between Uighurs who had come under the influence of Russia in the nineteenth century and Hui (Tungan) agriculturalists – Chinese converts to Islam resettled by and loyal to the Qing and used by the Chinese to garrison the oases of the Tarim where they were resented.[39] In the early stages of the revolts White Russians, armed

[38] James Millward, *Eurasian Crossroads: A History of Xinjiang* (New York: Columbia University Press, 2007), pp. 188–201.

[39] Owen Lattimore, *Pivot of Asia: Sinkiang and the Inner Asian Frontiers of China and Russia* (Boston: Little, Brown, 1950), and Allan Whiting and General Sheng Shih-ts'ai, *Sinkiang: Pawn or Pivot?* (East Lansing: Michigan State University Press, 1958), place greatest emphasis on the clash between Kazakhs and Uighurs and between nomads and agriculturalists, while Andrew D. W. Forbes, *Warlords and Muslims in Chinese Central Asia: A Political History of Republican Sinkiang, 1911–1949* (Cambridge University Press, 1986), argues that three regions, Uighuristan, Zhungaria and the Tarim Basin, displayed distinctive features linked to different historical developments. More recently, James A. Millward and Nabijan Tursun, "Political History and Strategies of Control," in S. Frederick Starr (ed.), *Xinjiang. China's Muslim Borderland* (Armonk, NY: M. E.

by the local Chinese population entered the fray, joined later by Chinese troops driven out of Manchuria by the Japanese in 1931. The Turkic Islamic rebels in the south (Tarim Basin) were the spiritual successors to the nineteenth-century Islamic Emirate of Ya'qub Beg. They were hostile to the pro-Chinese and very anti-Soviet. They were reacting to the imperial Russian past, to the suppression of the Basmachi and to the devastating impact of collectivization in Central Asia.[40] They established a short-lived Turkish-Islamic Republic of Eastern Turkestan, lasting from 1934 to 1935.

Combined Muslim forces might have seized control of the entire province in 1933. But they were split between the Tunguns and the Turkic peoples of the Tarim. The decisive blow was struck by the intervention of Soviet forces invited by Sheng Shicai, a Chinese general from Manchuria who became governor of the province. The revival of traditional Russian interest in Xinjiang under the Soviet banner was due to concern over border security, disruption of trade and Japanese pan-Turkic and pan-Islamic propaganda. The Soviet Union publically accused the Muslim forces from Gansu of being under Japanese influence and the Muslims of the Turkish-Islamic Republic of being under British influence, although there is little evidence to support these contentions.[41] However, a large proportion of the rebels were Kazakh refugees from the Soviet Union. They were fleeing the devastating effects on their culture of the combined effects of sedentarization, collectivization and secularization. In their great migration the Kazakhs suffered enormously, losing 80 percent of their herds and being decimated by a famine comparable to that in Ukraine. Over 40,000 left for Turkmenistan where they helped revive the Basmachi revolt. Thousands more trekked to China, but only a quarter survived this death march. The survivors, supported by their brethren in Xinjiang, launched guerrilla attacks from the cross-border sanctuaries.[42]

Soviet commercial interests had also increased after the completion of the Turkistan–Siberian (Turksib) railroad in 1924 had created the shortest route for the export–import trade of the province. Becoming the major trading partner of Xinjiang, virtually turned the province into an economic dependency. By the end of 1933 the Soviet forces, OGPU troops numbering about 7,000 with planes and tanks, together with Sheng's

---

Sharpe, 2004), p. 75, have further refined the complex origins and composition of the rebellious forces.

[40] Forbes, *Warlords*, pp. 115–21.

[41] Whiting and Sheng Shih-ts'ai, *Sinkiang*, pp. 16, 35–6; Millward, *Eurasian Crossroads*, pp. 198–9.

[42] Martha Brill Olcott, *The Kazakhs* (Stanford University Press, 1987), pp. 179–86.

troops, had repressed the Gansu-based rebellion and exploited differences between the Turkic- and Chinese-speaking leaders to undermine the Republic of East Turkestan.[43]

Stalin took a personal interest in strengthening the Soviet position in Xinjiang. In September 1935 he decided, after a meeting with the Soviet consul in Urumchi, G. A. Apresov, to grant Sheng a loan of 2 million rubles over several years in order to organize his army and help develop the oil resources close to the Soviet frontier. He placed all the agents of the OGPU in Xinjiang under Apresov as the sole authority of the Soviet government. Following the traditional tactics of Russians on the Inner Asian frontier, Soviet officials played both sides of the rebellion. They lured a leading Muslim rebel, General Ma Zhongying, and with his help other leaders of the rebel "36th division" to the Soviet Union in order to liquidate resistance to Sheng's regime. At the same time, they proposed to open trade relations with the rebel forces even before the conclusion of peace.[44]

Assuming full powers with Soviet support, Sheng carried out a policy resembling that being applied across the Soviet border. He recognized fourteen ethnic categories instead of the 'five races of China' identified by the Kuomintang, and adopted Stalin's policy of indigenization.[45] In the south he appointed prominent Uighurs to administrative posts but also promoted secular policies that offended traditional Muslim sensibilities. The reaction was not long in coming in the form of flight and revolt, a familiar sequence in the struggle over the borderlands. About 600,000 Turkic- and Iranian-speaking Muslims fled over the Afghan border in the first half of the 1930s. In the spring of 1937 a new rebellion flared in both the southwest and among Kazakhs in the Altai region of the north who had sought refuge from the collectivization of their herds in Kazakhstan in the early 1930s. Local uprisings broke out elsewhere among the Kirghiz. The Gansu Muslims returned in force. Once again Sheng appealed for Soviet aid which proved decisive in defeating the rebels. Isolated from the Chinese Nationalist center at Nanking and heavily dependent on the Soviet forces, he then carried out a severe purge of Uighur and Muslim intellectuals and political leaders. Finding himself without adequate

---

[43] Lattimore, *Pivot of Asia*, pp. 198–9; other authorities are less specific about the Soviet intervention. See, for example, Forbes, *Warlords*, pp. 168–70.

[44] Kaganovich, Molotov and Mikoian to Stalin, October 1, 1935, in *Stalin i Kaganovich*, doc. 699, pp. 594–5; *Ocherki istorii Rossiiskoi vneshnei razvedki*, 5 vols. (Moscow: Mezhdunarodnye otnosheniia, 1993), vol. III: *1933–1941*, pp. 216–18. The fate of Ma Zhongying in the Soviet Union remains unknown. Millward, *Eurasian Crossroads*, p. 200.

[45] Millward and Tursun, "Political History," p. 80.

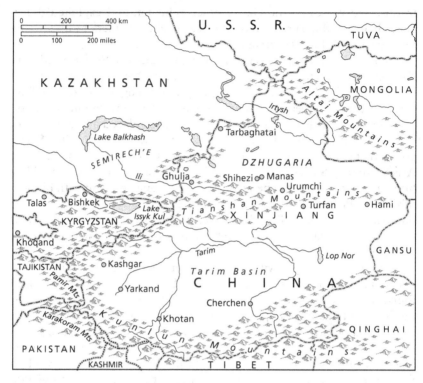

Map 4.1 Xinjiang

administrators, he requested aid from the Chinese Communists in Yenan,
who sent dozens of cadres including Mao Zedong's brother to staff government agencies and keep the communications route open to the Soviet
Union.[46]

In 1938 Sheng travelled to Moscow to meet Stalin. The Soviet leader
advised Sheng to form an army from the 400,000 Chinese living in
Xinjiang. He and Molotov were interested in the economic resources of
Xinjiang. Sheng requested permission secretly to join the Communist
Party of the Soviet Union. Stalin hesitated only briefly before agreeing.[47]
When Sheng returned to Urumchi, he actively pursued a policy of turning
the economy over to Soviet specialists, who had begun drilling for oil in
the mid-1930s. Much of the Soviet exploitation of mineral resources

[46] Millward, *Eurasian Crossroads*, pp. 209–10.
[47] A. M. Ledovskii, *SSSR i Stalin v sud'bakh Kitaia. Dokumenty i svidetel'stva uchastnika
      sobytii, 1937–1952* (Moscow: Pamiatniki istoricheskoi mysli, 1999), pp. 190–1, frag-
      ments of the stenographic report of their conversation.

remains obscure. But in 1940 Sheng signed the so-called "Tin Mines" Agreement with Moscow, which was far more than the name implied. It granted "privileges in Sinkiang so extensive as to constitute a state within a state."[48] A regiment of NKVD troops was stationed at Hami in order to defend against a possible Japanese invasion Sheng was turning the province into a virtual satellite of the USSR similar to that of the Mongolian People's Republic.

Mongolia and Tuva

In the aftermath of the Russian Civil War, Bolshevik support for revolutionary elements in Mongolia had been decisive in the coming to power of the Mongolian People's Revolutionary Party. The revolutionaries were led by Choibalsan, who had learned his Russian in a secondary school in Irkutsk before the revolution, and Sukhebator who had been trained by Russian officers in the new-style army units following the Chinese Revolution of 1911. The rank and file represented a cross-section of ethnic groups and social classes with about half Mongols from the eastern more revolutionary part of the country where contact with the outside world through trade had eroded the old feudal ties.[49]

During the Civil War renegade White officers seized power in Outer Mongolia and threatened to use it as a base against Soviet power in Siberia. In June 1921 Red Army units entered Outer Mongolia. Together with Mongolian partisans led by Sukhebator and Choibalsang, they scattered the White forces and entered Urga (later named Ulan Bator), where they enthroned the Bogdo Khan as constitutional monarch. The Soviet government, including Stalin, then insisted on returning to the position of its tsarist predecessor as an intermediary between the Mongols and China in negotiating autonomy for Mongolia under Chinese sovereignty. Beijing was adamantly opposed. The Soviet representative in Beijing, Adolph Ioffe, attempted to persuade the Politburo that its policy was counter-productive. "Mongolia was the most vulnerable spot in our Chinese policy and the only trump in the hands of the imperialists against us." The Soviet Union, he advised, should negotiate directly with Beijing.[50]

Once Ioffe's position was finally accepted in Moscow, new negotiations led by Lev Karakhan abandoned the earlier policy. In exchange, the Soviet Union obtained concessions from China, restoring its

---

[48] Whiting and Sheng Shih-ts'ai, *Sinkiang*, pp. 66–7; the full text of this extraordinary agreement in *ibid.*, pp. 280–6. See also Forbes, *Warlords*, pp. 144–52.

[49] Owen Lattimore, *Nomads and Commissars: Mongolia Revisited* (New York: Oxford University Press, 1962), pp. 78–89.

[50] S. G. Luzianin, *Rossiia-Mongolia-Kitai v pervoi polovine XX v.* (Moscow: Institute of the Far East, 2000), pp. 112–14, quotation on p. 114.

pre-revolutionary position on the Chinese Eastern Railroad. In Mongolia the Soviet representatives warned the Mongol leaders to tone down their anti-Chinese rhetoric and accept their autonomous status under Chinese sovereignty, dashing their hopes for immediate independence. The top Mongol officials split along three lines. One group reacted violently, denouncing the Soviet–Chinese agreements as a betrayal. A second group led by the president of the Revolutionary Military Council, El'bekdorzhi Rinchino, a Buryat Mongol, argued the Comintern line for accepting association with China as the best tactic to promote world revolution. The premier, B. Tserendorzh, opted for an intermediate position, declaring that an armed struggle with China would be hopeless. When, after the death of the Bogdo Khan in 1924, the Mongol revolutionaries proclaimed a Mongolian People's Republic, they drafted a constitution with the assistance of Russian Comintern representatives that adopted a Soviet form of government. Its provisions also reduced Chinese sovereignty to a formal legality and oriented foreign policy along a Comintern/Soviet line that envisaged a unity of all Mongol peoples including those of Buratiia, Tuva and Inner Mongolia.[51]

With the outbreak of the second phase of the Chinese revolution in 1925–7, discussions took place in Moscow and Ulan Bator over the possibilities of unifying the Mongol peoples. Three variants emerged: (1) incorporating a unified Mongolia into the USSR; (2) joining a unified Mongolia with a revolutionary Chinese federation; (3) retaining "two Mongolias" – Outer under the aegis of the Comintern and Inner under a Kuomintang and Chinese Communist coalition. But the split between the Kuomintang and the Communists in 1927 doomed all these plans and the Soviet government was forced to settle for an Outer Mongolia reduced in size, leaving many Mongols outside its borders.

The Bolsheviks rapidly followed up their collaboration with the indigenous revolutionaries against marauding Chinese bands and Cossacks by constructing an organizational base to influence the course of the revolution in Mongolia. In 1923 the Buryat Mongol autonomous region was raised to the level of an autonomous republic in order to demonstrate the progressive character of Soviet nationality policy.[52] A number of government and Comintern departments and bureaux were created to advise

---

[51] *Ibid.*, p. 120.

[52] Buryats numbered only 153 of the 1,326 members of the local party organization. Boris Chichlo, "Histoire de la formation des territoires autonomes chez les peuples turco-mongol de Sibérie," *Cahiers du Monde russe et soviétique* 28:3–4 (1987), p. 370. Very few members of the local Communist Party spoke Buryat and there was no tradition of Buryat Mongols serving in the tsarist army. The local leaders proposed correcting both those shortcomings. "Iz dokladoi zapiski M. P. Selifimova v Organizatsionno-instruktorskii otdel TsK RKP(b) o rezul'tatakh obsledovaniia partorganizatsii Buryat-Mongol'skoi ASSR," in *TsK RKP(b) i natsional'nyi vopros*, vol. I, doc. 69, pp. 167–8.

and assist the new regime in Ulan Bator but, as was so often the case in the early years of Soviet foreign policy, the overlapping jurisdictions created confusion and led to cross-purposes. The Mongol–Tibetan Department of the Oriental Political Bureau, staffed partly by Soviet Buryat Mongols, lent support to the Mongolian People's Party. The Comintern inherited many of the functions and personnel of this unit. But its representatives disagreed over whether Inner Mongolia should be considered part of the Chinese revolution, an extension of the Outer Mongolian revolution or an autonomous movement.[53]

As in the western borderlands, Ukraine in particular, so in the Inner Asian borderlands, Mongolia in particular, Soviet policy wavered between indigenization and repression of bourgeois nationalism. The important difference was that Moscow sought to unify all Ukrainians under its banner while they opposed the idea of pan-Mongolism, which, according to Robert Ruppen, "represented the desires of leading Mongols of both Outer and Inner Mongolia and of many prominent Buryats as well."[54] Instead, they continued the tsarist policy of separating their constituent elements: Buryats, Khalka (northern), Inner (southern) and western Mongols.

Throughout most of the twenties the Buryat Mongols enjoyed the status of high favor in Moscow's policies in the eastern borderlands. The All-Union Communist University of the Toilers of the East (named after Stalin) prepared as one of its main aims cadres for foreign parties of the East with a separate sector and special courses for Outer Mongolia and Tuva. Of the graduates representing fifty-four nationalities, there were twenty-eight Buryats, third in number after the Armenians and Tatars.[55] From the founding moment of the Mongol revolution in 1921, Buryats from across the Soviet frontier had guided the revolutionaries – men like El'bekdorzhi Rinchino, a powerful figure in the Ulan Bator government from 1921 to 1925. The Buryats had played a similar role in pre-revolutionary times when they brought the revolutionary ideas of Russian populists into Mongolia. But Rinchino and his fellow Buryats favored close relations between the Inner Mongols and their brethren to the north. In the complex maneuvering among various factions for control over the Inner Mongolian movement, the Buryats lost ground. The decision was made in Moscow to consolidate an Inner

---

[53] Christopher Atwood, "A. I. Oshirov (c. 1901–1931): A Buryat Agent in Inner Mongolia," in Atwood, *Young Mongols and Vigilantes in Inner Mongolia's Interregnum Decades, 1911–1931*, 2 vols. (Leiden and Boston: Brill, 2002), vol. II, pp. 44–90.

[54] Robert A. Rupen, *Mongols of the 20th Century*, 2 vols. (Bloomington: Indiana University Press, 1964), vol. I, pp. 186–9, quotation on p. 186.

[55] "Ob organizatsii tsentral'nykh kursov partrabotnikov natsional'nykh raionov," December 11, 1930, in *TsK RKP(b) i natsional'nyi vopros*, vol. I, doc. 236, pp. 650–2.

Mongolian Party and then in 1930 to place it under the authority of the Chinese Communist Party. From 1928 to 1931 most of the Buryats were denounced as bourgeois nationalists for their support of Mongol unity and recalled to the Soviet Union where Rinchino was executed in 1937.[56]

By this time other signs appeared that the Soviet leaders were determined to counter-balance their support for indigenization at home and Mongol unity abroad. Beginning in the mid-1920s, Russian colonists were systematically being settled in regions where the Mongols were a significant population, reducing the Buryats in their titular republic from 60 percent to 40 percent (1926–31) and the Kalmyks from 66 percent to 54 percent (1924–39). From 1926 to 1931, 15,000 Russians settled in the quasi-independent republic of Tanu Tuva.[57]

A quintessential borderland, Tanu Tuva was inhabited mainly by reindeer breeders and forest hunters. It had been part of the Chinese Empire since the Yuan dynasty. Then it was conquered by the Dzhungars, but restored to China by the Manchus. The Tuvans remained a fractious people, rising in rebellion several times before breaking away from the Qing in 1912. The local elites petitioned the tsar for incorporation into the Russian Empire. In 1914 their request was granted in the form of a protectorate under the name of the Urzhankhaiskii region. During the Civil War it became a battleground where the Red Army fought and defeated Kolchak's forces, Chinese and Mongol bands.

Throughout the 1920s the Soviet government and the Siberian Bureau of the party remained undecided about the final status of Tuva. In 1921 the Tuvinskii Popular Revolutionary Party, Bolshevik in form, proclaimed the Republic of Tanu Tuva. According to its constitution it was independent in domestic affairs but under the aegis of the RSFSR in foreign affairs. The Mongolian People's Republic continued to assert its claims on the region until 1925, when the Soviet Union recognized Tuva's full independence as the Tuvinskii People's Republic. This also proved a temporary solution. The Russian population enjoyed complete autonomy until they had completed the sovietization of their communities. In 1939 and 1940 the Tuvan authorities twice requested incorporation into the Soviet Union and were twice denied, ostensibly because the international situation was not favorable. By this time Tuva was linked by a highway to the nearby Trans-Siberian Railroad and economically tied to the Soviet Union. In August 1944 an extraordinary

[56] Rupen, *Mongols*, vol. I, pp. 234–40; Atwood, "Oshirov," pp. 56, 57, 60, 61, 84–6.
[57] Rupen, *Mongols*, vol. I, pp. 244–5.

Map 4.2 Outer Mongolia and Tuva

session of the National Assembly, with Soviet and Mongol representatives in attendance, issued another appeal to join the USSR, this time successfully. The secretary of the Popular Revolutionary Party of Tuva, Salčak Toka, explained the delay in tactical terms. Time was required to defeat the "Japanophile tendency" (that is pan-Mongolism) in the government and to quench the thirst of the masses for independence after centuries of submission to China. Little noticed and less commented upon at the time, the prolonged process of the incorporation of Tuva was an instructive example of Stalin's delayed-action incorporation of a borderland.[58]

---

[58] Chichlo, "Histoire de la formation des territoires autonomes," pp. 380–3; M. Kh. Mannai-ool, "Tuvinskaia Avtonomnaia Sovetskaia Respublika," *Bol'shaia Sovetskaia Entsiklopediia*, 3rd edn (Moscow: Sovetskaia entsiklopediia, 1970), vol. XXVI, p. 284.

The Mongolian People's Republic may have been the first Soviet satellite, but serious trouble was brewing there in the spring of 1932. A large-scale uprising encompassing much of the country prompted the Soviet Politburo to criticize the Mongol leadership for "blindly copying the policy of the Soviet power in the USSR" by rushing precipitously into collectivization and the abolition of private trade. Stalin took a personal hand in the affair, ordering a purge of leftist elements in the Mongol Central Committee, amnesty for the rebels and the adoption of a new political course. With a characteristic flourish, he instructed the leadership to blame the rising on Chinese agents and Japanese imperialists. He advised against sending in Soviet troops to bring the situation under control except as a last resort, and then only to employ Buryat Mongol detachments on a temporary basis.[59] Stalin discounted the panicky reports of the Soviet resident, insisting that any Soviet intervention could only inflame relations with Japan and lead to a "united front of Japan, China and Mongolia (sic!) against the USSR," which the world press would paint as the aggressor.[60]

Two points stand out in Stalin's analysis. First, his willingness to order a retreat on a leftist course of collectivization in Mongolia came at a time when he was pressing for just such a course in the Soviet Union. Second, his reluctance to send in troops contrasted with his decision to intervene in Xinjiang the previous year. Clearly, nothing would deter him from his radical course in domestic policy, and geo-cultural considerations made a difference in his policy toward the borderlands. Ever since the Manchurian incident, he had become very cautious in taking risks in areas close to Japanese interests.

The constant threat of conflict with Japan over the Inner Asian borderlands intensified the debate already under way in Moscow over military preparedness even before the rise to power of Hitler in Germany. The Soviet Union was not prepared in 1929 or 1930 to fight a war, let alone a war on two fronts. A rapid buildup of Soviet military strength in the face of threats to the external security and internal stability of the borderlands had encountered serious structural problems. The aim of the First Five-Year Plan was to lay down a heavy industrial base upon which a modern arms industry could be constructed. Yet, neither of the two variants of the plan submitted to the Fifteenth Congress in 1927 made any provision for substantial expansion of the military. Direct military spending

---

[59] Stalin to Kaganovich, June 4, 1932, in *Stalin i Kaganovich*, doc. 93, pp. 136–7.
[60] Stalin to Molotov, Voroshilov and Kaganovich, June 10, 1932, *ibid.*, doc. 116, pp. 157–8. That he took the situation very seriously may be judged by his order to remove all documents from Mongolia testifying to the activity of Soviet representatives in the country.

actually decreased from 1928 to 1929. At the time of the Manchurian crisis, the First Five-Year Plan was already in full swing. Capital allocations had been made, industrial enterprises were under construction and financial resources were strained to breaking point. Economic difficulties with the West after 1929 disappointed Soviet planners. Their calculations had been based on estimated revenue from dumping raw material abroad to make up for falling agricultural prices. This triggered Western economic retaliation. The import of foreign technology could only be paid for in hard currency, which was in short supply, or grain exports, which depended upon the success of collectivization, a dubious proposition in the early 1930s.[61] Rearmament would have to wait.

Moreover, Stalin was wary of efforts by the military to shift scarce resources to armaments. He had always harbored a suspicion of the motives of professional military men. He reacted sharply to the pressure from Marshal Tukhachevskii to undertake a massive rearmament program in the wake of the border clashes between the Red Army and Chinese forces. The Soviet leader denounced the proposals as leading to "red militarism." "It was incomprehensible," he stated, "that a Marxist could have such unrealistic ideas – to adopt such a project would mean to militarize the whole country and this was worse than wrecking."[62] Although there was a common feeling that something had to be done to strengthen defense, a debate, only fragments of which are available, suggest that none of the leaders including Stalin had a clear idea of how to reconcile competing priorities.[63] Even Stalin's famous speech on overcoming backwardness in February 1931 did not include any specific recommendations for improving the military sector, but rather appealed to patriotism and revolutionary enthusiasm as a way of increasing the tempo of industrialization.[64]

The dramatic increase in the tempo of military preparations in the spring of 1931 can only be attributed to growing tensions with Japan

---

[61] Manfred von Boetticher, *Industrialisierungspolitik und Verteitungskonzeption der UdSSR 1926–1939: Herausbildung d. Stalinismus u. "äussere Bedrohung"* (Dusseldorf: Drost, 1979), pp. 198 ff, 207, 295.

[62] G. Isserson, "Zapiski sovremennika o M. N. Tukhachevskom," *Voenno-Istoricheskii zhurnal* 4 (1963), p. 67.

[63] R. W. Davies, *The Soviet Economy in Turmoil, 1929–1930* (Houndmills: Macmillan, 1989), pp. 446–55.

[64] R. W. Davies, *Crisis and Progress in the Soviet Economy, 1931–1933* (London: Palgrave, 1996), pp. 15–17. Characteristically, Stalin demonstrated at the same time an ambivalent attitude toward bourgeois specialists who were necessary for introducing the new technology for armaments but represented for him a class enemy and a potential source of foreign espionage.

over Manchuria and unresolved problems with Poland. In September the Japanese invasion of Manchuria sparked another surge in military investment. Tukhachevskii was back in favor. He and other military leaders sought to introduce radical changes in the basic military doctrine of the USSR that had preoccupied them since 1926.[65] Stalin continued to take an ambivalent attitude toward these innovations.[66] But military forces in the Far East were greatly strengthened. The military budget for 1932 measured in current prices increased by about 120 percent.[67] Although expenditures were reduced the following year, the most striking improvement was in the sophistication of weaponry based on advanced technology that was considered even by Western estimates to rival those of other great powers.[68]

Stalin's policy of territorializing the revolution, the heart of which was the doctrine of socialism in one country, or what I have called the borderland thesis, did not go unchallenged within the higher echelons of the party. Although the leadership had agreed on a degree of domesticating the revolution, to the point of reducing the Comintern to an arm of Soviet foreign policy and signing international treaties with capitalist states, sharp disagreement arose over strategies of state-building and the promotion of revolution abroad. Beyond these differences, personal rivalries loomed large as the Leninist epigone battled to claim his legacy as the dominant figure in guiding the country to its completion of the socialist revolution. In this intra-party struggle Stalin and his borderland thesis had emerged triumphant by 1929.

Conclusion

The threat of war that Stalin first invoked in 1927 had became more real and pressing. Three powerful factors built this momentum. The

---

[65] Ibid., pp. 270–4, 296–7. For the development of the new strategic thinking that reversed Soviet attitudes on a defensive war, see below, pp. 244–5.

[66] Stalin's suspicion of the activities of Vasili Bliukher, commander of the Special Far Eastern Army date from this time. Bliukher was the hero of the border clashes with the Chinese in 1929. But his proposals to make the Soviet Far Eastern borderlands a special economic region to support the defense of the region did not meet with favor in Moscow. Haslam, Soviet Foreign Policy, p. 72; John Erikson, The Soviet High Command: A Military-Political History, 1918–1941 (Boulder, CO: St. Martins, 1962), pp. 240–6. For rumors that Bliukher even opposed the harsh tempos of collectivization see Mark von Hagen, Soldiers in the Proletarian Dictatorship: The Red Army and the Soviet Socialist State, 1917–1930 (Ithaca, NY: Cornell University Press, 1990), p. 320.

[67] The investment plans proved overly ambitious and they were scaled back the following year. But these were results again of structural limitations not policy. Davies, Crisis and Progress, pp. 164, 166–7, 174, 310.

[68] Ibid., pp. 432–4 and 475–6.

ideological foundations were a constant. That war was inevitable as long as capitalism survived was a mainstay of Marxist-Leninist ideology. The idea was briefly muted during World War II, but Stalin never abandoned it. If the inevitability of war was a constant, the Japanese occupation of Manchuria in 1931 and the coming to power of the Nazis in Germany signaled a revival of aggressive policies by the flank powers directed toward the Eurasian borderlands. The new threats were fueled not only by territorial aspirations, but also by ideologies combining anti-communism with radical plans to transform the societies all along the western and far eastern borderlands. At the same time, Stalin's hasty and costly drive to industrialize and collectivize the USSR had aroused opposition within the party, and more violently in the countryside, especially in Ukraine and Kazakhstan where resistance and flight across the porous frontiers created additional security problems. Although the opposition had been defeated and scattered and the countryside subdued, Stalin remained obsessed with finding or fabricating links between domestic and foreign enemies in the borderlands. In responding to the new situation, Stalin had two choices, not unlike his predecessors in the imperial government. One was to reach an accommodation with the most powerful states on the Soviet flanks by agreeing on spheres of influence. This course of action would require negotiating from a position of strength which he was still in the process of constructing. The other was to find external allies to divert or block the aggressive moves of the flank powers. As it turned out, Stalin did not commit himself wholly to one or the other policy, but rather oscillated between them, relying on his political instincts to calculate the exact balance of forces at play, but hampered by his tendency to suspect that the motives and aims of his interlocutors were as devious and manipulative as his own.

5   Stalin in command

Despite the war clouds gathering over the borderlands, Stalin long remained uncertain about the best means to oppose them. To be sure, he adhered steadily to his domestic course of building a great socialist power by creating a modern army, intensifying administrative centralization, forging cultural integration through socialist realism and furthering internal colonization through deportation and forced resettlement. Over the same period his consistent aims in foreign policy were to keep external conflict (in Spain and China) as far distant from the Soviet borders as possible and to prevent the Soviet Union from being isolated. By 1941 he had failed in the first aim and narrowly escaped failure in the second.

By leaving open the question of which foreign powers would most fully recognize the interests of the Soviet Union, Stalin permitted two groups within the Soviet ruling elite to advance their own agendas. He could afford to allow this once the opposition had been disgraced or exiled, although he had to exercise care that discussion did not spill over into factionalism. There could be no appearance of a new "opposition." Both groups adhered to the standard Soviet practice of promoting a division within the capitalist camp in order to prevent a united coalition forming against the USSR. But they differed over the choice of powers with whom to associate and the form of that association.[1]

---

[1] Jonathan Haslam, "Litvinov, Stalin and the Road Not Taken," in Gabriel Gorodetsky (ed.), *Soviet Foreign Policy, 1917–1991* (London: Frank Cass, 1994), pp. 55–64. Teddy J. Uldrichs, "Soviet Security Policy in the 1930s," *ibid.*, pp. 65–73, accepts the idea of an ongoing debate over foreign policy, but adds that "it also seems impossible, given what we know of Stalin's style of governing, that Litvinov and Molotov could have operated two entirely contradictory foreign policy lines at the same time." *Ibid.*, p. 73. Sabine Dullin, *Men of Influence: Stalin's Diplomats in Europe, 1930–1939* (Edinburgh University Press, 2008), is the most extensive treatment of Litvinov and the Litvinovtsy which explains the complex "strictly professional" relationship between Litvinov and Stalin and recognizes the importance of Litvinov's diplomatic style while maintaining that they shared fundamental goals in foreign policy.

Two tactics

Litvinov and his supporters in the Foreign Commissariat sought actively to engage the Western liberal democracies in a policy of collective security against fascism under the slogan of the indivisibility of peace. His opponents, V. M. Molotov and A. A. Zhdanov, favored a more passive policy verging on diplomatic autarchy until in 1939 they supported a closer association with Germany and Japan that did not, however, commit the Soviet Union to forming a military alliance with them. Molotov and Zhdanov had the advantage of occupying a much higher standing in the party. Litvinov was not even a member of the Central Committee when he officially presented his program to the government.

Litvinov was an old Bolshevik, but he had spent most of his revolutionary career abroad, mainly in England. He had learned English well, though he always spoke it with a heavy accent. He had married an English writer, his *"bourzhuika"* as he affectionately referred to her. Throughout his life he retained a cultural preference for England and things English, or at least European. Even in Moscow he enjoyed best the company of those who shared his tastes.[2] From the very moment of his appointment as Soviet representative to Britain on the morrow of the revolution, he doggedly pursued a policy of resolving conflicts with the capitalist world. A supreme realist, with no illusions about the imminent demise of capitalism, he once told Louis Fisher that "the prospects for world revolution disappeared on November 11, 1918."[3] As Chicherin's deputy in the Foreign Commissariat, Litvinov did not always agree with his chief, though the extent of their disagreements is still a matter of dispute. In general Litvinov was a strong believer in tying the Soviet Union to the international community by a dense web of treaties, conventions and protocols. He was a great supporter of disarmament, beginning with the abortive conference of 1922 with the Soviet Union's western neighbors. Later he favored signing the Kellogg–Briand Pact outlawing war. Chicherin was either skeptical or openly opposed to these agreements. Litvinov also saw little advantage in stirring up anti-colonial revolts at the expense of relations with Western Europe. He believed that it was possible to reach an accommodation with Britain over Afghanistan and "the east in

[2] Among his regular bridge partners were the distinguished physicist Peter Kapitsa, who had lived and worked for years in Cambridge, England, and Evgenyi Varga, the Hungarian economist, a former member of the Hungarian Soviet government in 1919 and a member of Stalin's secretariat. His wife Ivy was a reluctant fourth. Interview with Ivy Litvinov, Moscow, March, 1966.

[3] Louis Fischer, *Men and Politics: An Autobiography* (New York: Duell, Sloan and Pearce, 1941), p. 127.

general," but his view was not shared by the government. Litvinov had no sympathy for Trotsky's or Bukharin's more radical views and was drawn to Stalin's more cautious foreign policy. But he did not always share Stalin's more narrowly territorial concerns. For example, he was willing to recognize Romanian sovereignty over Bessarabia as a means of establishing good relations, but Stalin in this case supported Chicherin in keeping the question open in the form of an irredenta, the Soviet "Alsace on the Dnieper."[4] When Chicherin finally retired, Litvinov succeeded him and began to press for a major shift in Soviet foreign policy.

In Litvinov's opening gambit at the Central Executive Committee of the USSR in late December 1933, he made it clear from the outset that he considered Germany and Japan the most serious threats to peace. He singled out the recognition of the USSR by the United States as the greatest success of Soviet foreign policy. This set the tone for the remainder of his analysis. He reviewed the rise of "bourgeois pacifism" offering the evidence of the Kellogg–Briand Pact, the recent Soviet non-aggression pacts with France and Poland. By treating this phenomenon seriously he implicitly discounted previous warnings on the "threat" or "danger" of war from those countries. He then divided the capitalist powers into three groups, giving special emphasis to those who were interested in what he called, not for the last time, "the indivisibility of peace." Finally, he argued that anti-communism based on the class struggle was no longer the main motivation of the capitalist powers; it had receded to become a long-term goal. The main danger now lay with that aggressive group of powers who aimed at naked revision of international agreements and "the seizure of land."[5] Consciously or not Litvinov had, by raising the territorial question, touched a receptive chord in Stalin.

A few months later at the Seventeenth Party Congress, Stalin appeared to endorse some of the main lines of Litvinov's approach. On the first day he reviewed the Soviets' efforts to establish normal relations with their neighbors and especially to achieve a rapprochement with France and Poland. He contrasted this with the change in German foreign policy which, significantly, he did not identify with fascism, but rather with a revival of the old spirit of the Kaiserreich in the borderlands. This would mean aspiring to occupy Ukraine and moving against Leningrad, "turning the Baltic states into a staging ground for such a campaign." Second to the rapprochement with France and Poland he singled out the establishment of diplomatic relations with the United States as having "the

---

[4] *Ibid.*, pp. 128–35; Z. Sheinis, *Maksim Maksimovich Litvinov: Revoliutsioner, Diplomat, Chelovek* (Moscow: Izd. politicheskoi literatury, 1989), pp. 184–6, 218, 235.
[5] DVP, vol. XVI (1933), *prilozhenie* [appendix], pp. 778–82.

most serious significance in the entire system of international relations."
He deplored British policy of seeking to apply pressure by means of a
trade embargo. But he saved his choicest barbs for Japan. As with the
German threat to the western borderlands, he denounced the Japanese
militarists who threatened to launch a war and seize the Soviet Maritime Provinces.[6] In his long political report to the congress he struck a
more ambiguous note.

Stalin denounced the fomenters of war in an oblique fashion. When
war came, as it surely must, it would be, he predicted, "an imperialist
war," which he blamed on "extreme nationalism" without identifying
its chief offenders. He outlined four scenarios for war without indicating
which was the more likely to occur: (1) a war organized against one of the
great powers as a way of destroying it and at the same time exploiting its
resources in order to alleviate the economic crisis of capitalism; (2) a war
against an inferior military power with extensive markets that could then
be expropriated; (3) a war of a self-proclaimed "superior race" against
an alleged "inferior race"; and (4) finally a war against the USSR to
dismember and partition it. In every one of these cases he suggested war
would lead to the very opposite effect to that intended by the aggressor.
In the event of intervention against the USSR the result would be a war
against the bourgeoisie on two fronts, internal and external, leading to
"revolutions in a number of countries in Europe and Asia and to the
destruction of the bourgeois-landlord governments in those countries."
Significantly, Stalin stopped short of predicting what kind of regimes
would emerge from those revolutions, an omission which should be kept
in mind when considering his policies in the borderlands during and
after the Second World War. Just as significantly, he did not name a
power or group of powers that would be most likely to start any of these
aggressive wars. Stalin concluded with a veiled warning that seems to
have been ignored by contemporary statesmen and historians: "If the
interests of the USSR demand having closer relations to one or another
country which is not interested in violating peace, we will do so without
hesitation."[7]

Thus, on the eve of the momentous shift in Soviet foreign policy toward
collective security and Comintern policy toward a united front against
fascism, Stalin avoided making a final judgment as to which of the imperialist powers was the most dangerous. His analysis inclined toward the
view that Nazi Germany and Japan were the greater potential threat to

---

[6] *Semidesiatyi s"ezd VKP. 26 ianvaria–10 fevralia 1934: Stenograficheskii otchet* (Moscow:
Partizdat, 1934), pp. 13–14.
[7] *Ibid.*, p. 303.

peace in two out of the four cases, while he remained non-committal in the other two. He could hardly be accused of issuing a clarion call to collective action against fascism. He was loath to embrace the passionate anti-fascist rhetoric of the defeated opposition, whether coming from Trotsky or Bukharin. To do so would be to admit that they had been more prescient than the *vozhd*, something he could not afford or tolerate. Yet to continue to view all capitalist powers as equally aggressive would fly in the face of the Japanese occupation of Manchuria, a traditional contested borderland and staging ground only a decade earlier for their Siberian intervention. Nor could he ignore Hitler's repeated demands for *Lebensraum* in the western borderlands of the Soviet Union, territories that the Germans had already attempted to absorb and colonize under Ludendorff's military utopia (*Oberost*), little more than a decade earlier.[8]

As early as 1922 Hitler had made the conquest of Russia the cornerstone of his continental foreign policy, pursued with single-minded determination without sacrificing tactical flexibility.[9] The Eastern Slavs, but above all the Russians, were the object of intense and hostile propaganda throughout the 1930s that permeated all the institutions of German life – the SS, the army, schools, universities, popular literature and the Evangelical church. The emphasis was on the chaos and barbarism of the east.[10] *Lebensraum* was for Hitler the embodiment of the *völkisch* ideal. But it also represented in his view an economic necessity. Expansion to the east was not just a way to save the peasantry and find work for the unemployed and homesteads for the veterans of the armed forces. It was also a means of securing the raw materials that would endow Germany with an autarkic resource base impervious to the kind of blockade that had helped bring Germany to its knees in 1918.[11]

Despite these warning signs, Stalin's suspicions of the British and French also dated from the years of their intervention in the

---

[8] Ludendorff's plans aimed at a complete transformation of the region by mapping its topography and ethnologies, creating multilingual dictionaries, cataloguing its art-historical treasures, imposing social hygiene to cleanse the population in a literal sense, rebuilding its railroads, improving its roads and bridges and regulating movement along them – all to be accomplished in the German spirit. Vejas G. Liulevicius, *War Land on the Eastern Front: Culture, National Identity and German Occupation in World War I* (Cambridge University Press, 2000), ch. 1.

[9] Andreas Hillgruber, *Germany and the Two World Wars* (Cambridge, MA: Harvard University Press, 1981), pp. 47–51.

[10] Hans-Erich Volkmann (ed.), *Das Russlandbild im dritten Reich* (Cologne: Böhlau, 1994).

[11] Rolf-Dieter Müller, "Das 'Unternehmen Barbarossa' als wirtschaftliche Raubkrieg," in Gerd R. Ueberschär and Wolfram Wetke (eds.), *"Unternehmen Barbarossa." Der deutsche Überfall auf die Sowjetunion 1941: Berichte, Analysen, Dokumente* (Paderborn: Schöningh, 1984), pp. 173–94, and Ian Kershaw, *Hitler, 1936–45: Nemesis* (London: Penguin, 2000), pp. 412–15.

borderlands during the Civil War. His response was vintage Stalinism. He met uncertainty with ambiguity. He staked out the middle ground without indicating the direction in which he might move. Events would dictate. As he thought he had exhausted all the possible combinations that might lead to war, he armed himself against accusations of having misled the country. The point was not to commit himself prematurely to a course of action that he would later regret, or that might be used against him by whatever internal enemies might emerge in a moment of political confusion and uncertainty. Clearly, Litvinov was not to be allowed a clear field of action. Whatever Stalin's hopes that his multiple scenarios would insulate him retrospectively from accusations of being wrong, they were dashed when none of them turned out to be correct.

A discussion over foreign policy occupied an unusually prominent place in the Seventeenth Party Congress. There a formidable lineup cast doubts on Litvinov's analysis, in part no doubt because of Bukharin's passionate denunciation of fascism and call for action. Manuilskii discounted the special danger of fascism, upholding the line of the Sixth Comintern Congress. Lozovskii, the head of the Profintern, went so far as to greet the Nazi repression of the German Social Democrats as a boon for the Comintern and the Profintern, leaving the way clear for the Communists to organize the workers and boasting that fascism could never establish a foothold in the working class.[12]

As the champion of collective security, Litvinov's major achievements were to bring the Soviet Union into the League of Nations, obtain recognition by the United States and erect a system of defensive alliances with Czechoslovakia and France.[13] As long as his diplomacy strengthened the international position of the Soviet Union, Stalin supported and rewarded him. At the same time, Stalin's silence on the theoretical implications of collective security for capitalist encirclement and imperialist wars was disturbing to those who sought a more clear-cut sign that Soviet foreign policy had taken a decisive turn. To be sure, Stalin also endorsed local initiatives by Communist parties in Czechoslovakia and France which broke with the discredited policy of lumping together

---

[12] *Semidesiatyi s"ezd VKP*, pp. 307, 313 (Manuilskii), 347–8 (Lozovskii). Voroshilov chimed in by predicting that any attack on the Soviet Union would end up with the Red Army suffering only small losses in fighting on foreign soil. *Ibid.*, p. 97.

[13] The standard survey of Soviet diplomacy in these years is Jonathan Haslam, *The Soviet Union and the Struggle for Collective Security in Europe, 1933–39* (London: Macmillan, 1984). For the Soviet relationship to the French alliance system, see Piotr S. Wandycz, *The Twilight of French Eastern Alliances, 1926–1936: French–Czechoslovak–Polish Relations from Locarno to the Remilitarization of the Rhineland* (Princeton University Press, 1988), pp. 11–12, 51, 207–10, 294–6, 359–60, 400–1, 428; For Litvinov's role, Dullin, *Men of Influence*, especially ch. 3.

social democrats and fascists. They took the initiative in advancing a new form of united front from above and below that became known as the popular front. But here too Stalin let others take the lead. He allowed the Seventh Comintern Congress in 1935 to embrace the movement, yet he did not greet the delegates with a formal speech; he did not even appear at the congress. His enthusiasm for the proceedings was not overwhelming. "The Comintern Congress wasn't so bad," he wrote Molotov. "It will be even more interesting after the reports from Dimitrov and Ercoli [Togliatti]. The delegates made a good impression."[14]

Stalin's curiously detached view of collective security and the popular front annoyed Litvinov. In a secret memorandum to Stalin he complained bitterly that the Soviet press had taken "some kind of Tolstoyan view – non-resistance to evil" in the face of a massive Nazi anti-Soviet propaganda campaign. He considered the Soviet position "incorrect"; it merely encouraged further insults. He proposed a "systematic counter-campaign against German fascism."[15] But his plea fell on deaf ears. Despite the shift to collective security, Stalin made no new doctrinal pronouncement to justify what was surely the most dramatic change in Soviet relations with the capitalist world since 1921. Nor did he revise in print his definition of fascism as the terrorist wing of capitalism.

Litvinov's most powerful rival in foreign relations, V. M. Molotov, a long-time associate and supporter of Stalin, had little practical experience in diplomacy, although he had been active in Comintern affairs. While Stalin got on well with Litvinov, Molotov never trusted his predecessor as Foreign Commissar. Years later he recalled that Litvinov was a good diplomat, "but in spirit he occupied a different position, rather opportunistic, sympathized a great deal with Trotsky, Zinoviev, and Kamenev and, of course, he could not enjoy our full confidence."[16] As premier Molotov had on at least one occasion gone behind Litvinov's back in

---

[14] Stalin to Molotov, August 5, 1935, in Lars T. Lih, Oleg V. Naumov and Oleg V. Khlevniuk (eds.), *Stalin's Letters to Molotov* (New Haven, CT: Yale University Press, 1995), doc. 82, p. 237.

[15] Memorandum of Litvinov to Stalin, December 3, 1935, in *Izvestiia TsK KPSS* 2 (February, 1990), p. 212. Unknown to Litvinov, Stalin was at the same time (March 29, 1935) toning down Marshal Tukhachevskii's strong anti-Nazi polemics by editing his draft article for *Pravda* so as to eliminate a bellicose challenge to Germany. "Rukopis' stat'i M. N. Tukhachevskogo 'Voennye plany Gitlera s pravkoi I. V. Stalina," *ibid.*, 1 (January, 1990), p. 169.

[16] *Sto sorok besed s Molotovym. Iz dnevnika F. Chueva* (Moscow: TERRA, 1991), p. 98. The date of the diary entry is October 4, 1985. There is no evidence to support this accusation by Molotov. But he was certainly correct in stating that "Litvinov survived only by chance." *Ibid.*, p. 97.

trying to work out a deal with the Americans over debt settlement.[17] In 1936 Molotov publicly confirmed that there were two foreign policy groups within the party. One had adopted an attitude of "thorough going irreconcilability" between the Soviet Union and fascism in general and Nazi Germany in particular; the other, which was according to Molotov "the chief tendency," believed that "an improvement in Soviet–German relations was possible."[18]

Among the most influential members of the latter group was Andrei Zhdanov, who had gained his reputation as Kirov's successor in Leningrad and also enjoyed close personal relations with Stalin. Zhdanov, like Molotov, had no particular liking for the Western democracies or Litvinov's policy. As a candidate member of the Politburo and the chairman of the Foreign Affairs Commission of the Supreme Soviet, he began as early as 1936 to take a more independent line from that of the Foreign Commissariat. While Litvinov took pains to cultivate good relations with the Baltic States as part of the defensive glacis against German penetration, Zhdanov attempted to bully them by threatening to use the Red Army "if they do not mind their own business." At this time, officials in the Foreign Commissariat were still able to disown these inflammatory remarks.[19] Two years later it would not be so easy.

In 1935 Litvinov was initially successful in beating back attempts by Soviet representatives in the Commissariat of Trade and the Berlin embassy to develop better trade relations with Nazi Germany by accepting German credits. He opposed expanding relations with Germany on any level.[20] Only later did Litvinov learn that David Kandelaki, the head of the Soviet trade delegation in Berlin in 1935–7, as well as other trade representatives, were reporting directly to Molotov. They were part of a network that ran parallel to the traditional lines of diplomacy and

---

[17] US Department of State, *Foreign Relations of the United States: The Soviet Union, 1933–1939* (FRUS) (Washington, DC: Government Printing Office, 1952), pp. 579–80.

[18] Jane Degras (ed.), *Soviet Documents on Foreign Policy (1933–1941)*, 3 vols. (London: Oxford University Press,1953), vol. III, p. 184.

[19] Royal Institute of International Affairs, *Documents for 1936* (London: Oxford University Press, 1937), p. 408. See also Max Beloff, *The Foreign Policy of Soviet Russia*, 2 vols. (Oxford University Press, 1953), vol. II, pp. 78–9.

[20] Robert Tucker, *Stalin in Power: The Revolution from Above, 1928–1941* (New York: Norton, 1990), argues that the Soviet trade representative in Berlin, David Kandelaki, was carrying out negotiations without Litvinov's knowledge as part of his interpretation that Stalin already had a deal with Hitler in mind at this time. Dullin, *Men of Influence*, pp. 118–21, rejects this interpretation. By the end of the year Litvinov's objections were overturned; the Soviet need for foreign credits in developing the Second Five-Year Plan was too important.

worked at cross-purposes with it.[21] By this time Litvinov's disagreements with Stalin were beginning to strain relations between the two men. Sometime in 1936 Jacob Suritz, who was a witness, reported an ominous incident. Stalin approved of a proposal made by Litvinov and leaned over to place his hand on his Foreign Commissar's shoulder: "You see we can reach agreement." Litvinov removed Stalin's hand: "Not for long," he answered.[22]

A different kind of political split between sectarians and moderates was opening up in the internationalist Communist movement. At the Seventh Comintern Congress in August 1935 the leadership gave its official blessing to a broad coalition of social groups against fascism. They called for a vigorous promotion of both a united front – that is, unity of action of the Communists and social democrats at all levels from top to bottom – and a popular front – that is, a joint action with all anti-fascist republican elements outside the working class. The appeal represented the most radical shift in revolutionary tactics since the founding of the Comintern.[23]

Fresh from his heroic defense at the Reichstag Fire Trials in Berlin, the Bulgarian Communist, Georgi Dimitrov, gave the most flexible definition of the new policy. He reiterated that decisions on a wide range of questions, from Communist participation in coalition governments to relations with social democrats and bourgeois parties, would depend on actual circumstances. He singled out the sectarians within the Communist movement who had failed to perceive the threat of fascism

---

[21] John Erikson, *Soviet High Command: A Military–Political History, 1918–1941* (Boulder, CO: Westview, 1984), pp. 432–43 and 731 note 79, provided the first conclusive evidence by examining the German archives; Sheinis, *Litvinov*, pp. 360–1, adds details. There is no mention of Kandelaki's political mission in the published German documents, though his commercial contacts are fully recorded. *Documents on German Foreign Policy, 1918–1945* (DGFP) series C: *1933–1937*, 6 vols. (London: H. M. Stationery Office, 1957–83), vol. IV, pp. 28–9, 453–4, 783–4, 870–1, 967–72; vol. V, pp. 488–91, 571–3. The earliest revelations were disclosed by Walter Krivitsky in *Sotsialistichekii Vestnik*, March 31, 1938.

[22] Ilia Ehrenburg, *Postwar Years, 1945–1954* (Cleveland, OH: World Publishing, 1967), p. 278.

[23] Just how radical is still a matter of dispute. For a recent review of the conflicting interpretations, see Kevin McDermott and Jeremy Agnew, *The Comintern: A History of International Communism from Lenin to Stalin* (London: Macmillan, 1996), pp. 120–1. See also Kermit McKenzie, *Comintern and World Revolution, 1928–1943* (New York: Columbia University Press, 1964), for the most skeptical view. After signing the Nazi–Soviet Pact and ordering the invasion of Poland, Stalin justified his action to a group of associates: "Maintaining yesterday's position (the United Popular Front, the unity of the nation) today means slipping into the position of the bourgeoisie." Ivo Banac (ed.), *The Diary of Georgi Dimitrov, 1933–1949* (New Haven, CT: Yale University Press, 2003), entry for September 7, 1939, pp. 115–16.

in Germany and other countries for fear that the struggle for democratic rights would divert the workers from proletarian dictatorship. He mocked their pedantry, which reduced real social forces to arid formulas. Invoking Marx and Lenin, he denounced empty phrases and slogans such as "a revolutionary exit from crisis" without paying attention to conditions, class relations and the revolutionary maturity of the proletariat: "there can be no panacea suitable for all cases, all countries and all peoples," he concluded.[24] His initiative had the effect, if not the intention, of refuting the myth that the Bolshevik experience in 1917 was the only legitimate model for revolution. In this sense Dimitrov's intervention may be regarded as the embryo of postwar popular democracy.

Spain: an embryonic popular democracy?

The outbreak of the Spanish Civil War gave the Comintern's Popular Front movement its first chance to test the new policy in a revolutionary situation. The small Spanish Communist Party had been the first in Europe to join with the social democrats and republicans in an electoral alliance; together they won a majority of votes in the Cortes. The attempted coup by rightist army officers led by General Francisco Franco to overthrow the government created an unexpected opportunity for Stalin to deflect the threat of war from the western borderlands of the USSR to the farthest western reaches of Europe. Within a year the Japanese attack on China would reproduce the same opportunity in the Far East. In both cases Stalin was quick to act, leaving the Comintern and the local Communist parties the task of working out the relationship between the war against fascism and the revolution. But he remained keenly aware of the danger that either or both movements to defeat fascism could fall into the hands of Trotsky and his adherents. The link between events and possibilities in Spain and China rapidly became a major theme in Comintern propaganda.

Fresh evidence has come to light on how quickly Stalin recognized the need to support the Spanish republicans and acted more swiftly and decisively to support the republican government with arms than has hitherto been assumed. On September 6, 1936 he proposed "most urgently" (*pobystree*) sending fifty bombers, through Mexico as an intermediary, and twenty Soviet pilots directly to Spain to fly combat missions and

---

[24] *VII kongress Kominterna: sbornik dokumentov* (Moscow: Gosizdat, 1936), pp. 194 ff, and G. Dimitrov, *Selected Works*, 2 vols. (Sofia: Foreign Languages Press), vol. I, pp. 93–5, 97–9, 102–4. Sectarianism, he concluded, was no longer simply an "infantile disorder," as Lenin called it, "but a deeply rooted vice." *Ibid.*, p. 76.

to instruct Spanish pilots. In addition he urged the dispatch of 20,000 rifles, a thousand machine guns and 20 million cartridges. The shipment of even larger amounts of equipment began soon after.[25] By the end of the war the Soviet Union had dispatched sixty-eight shiploads of arms, the majority in the first year.[26]

In December the Soviet leaders sought to impress upon the Spaniards that their struggle should be viewed in its own peculiar social and historical context. Despite some similarities between the Spanish and Russian civil wars, the differences were significant enough to warrant a distinctive approach. In a letter from Stalin, Molotov and Voroshilov to the radical left-wing socialist President of the republic, Largo Caballero, the Soviet leaders emphasized that:

The Spanish revolution is following a path different in many respects from that which Russia had followed. This is due to different social historical and geographical conditions and to the different international situations which Russia had to face. It is quite possible that in Spain the parliamentary way will prove more appropriate towards the revolutionary development than was the case in Russia.

Just what the parliamentary way meant was left unspecified, as indeed it remained in the post-World War II discussions over the road to popular democracies. The Soviet leaders offered military advisors but they stressed the advising role. In the end over five hundred Soviet military personnel served in Spain, and many, especially the pilots, did more than advise. The "friendly advice" they did offer aimed at the best means to win over the peasantry, the petty bourgeoisie and middle-class elements, especially in order "to prevent the enemies of Spain from regarding it as a Communist republic and to forestall their intervention."[27]

---

[25] Stalin to Kaganovich, September 6, 1936, in *Stalin i Kaganovich*, doc. 801, p. 666; Stalin approved a decision not to inform Caballero until after the arrival of the arms. Kaganovich to Stalin, October 11, 1936, *ibid.*, doc. 853, p. 700, note 2. Iu. Rybalkin, "Moskva, Nastas'inskii, 13," *Rodina*, 9 (1996), p. 67, gives a figure for the first shipment of fifty tanks, thirty bombers and other arms. Stalin took this decision a month before the Soviet representative to the international committee on non-intervention declared that the failure to check the importation of arms to the rebels through Portugal would release the Soviet Union from the obligation to observe the embargo on arms to Spain. Stalin to Kaganovich and Molotov, October 11, 1936, in *Stalin i Kaganovich*, doc. 852, pp. 699–700.

[26] A. A. Grechko *et al.* (eds.) *Istoriia vtoroi mirovoi voiny, 1939–1945*, 4 vols. (Moscow: Voennoe izd-vo Ministerstva oborony SSSR, 1974), vol. II, p. 54. For a full discussion of Soviet military aid, the use of Soviet arms and lessons learned or misapplied, see Stanley Payne, *The Spanish Civil War, the Soviet Union and Communism* (New Haven, CT: Yale University Press, 2004), pp. 153–73, 308–10.

[27] An English translation of the original which appeared in *Guerra y Revolución en España*, 2 vols. (Moscow, 1971), vol. II, pp. 96–7 can be found in E. H. Carr, *The Comintern*

In Spain itself the situation was highly volatile. The Spanish Communists called for unity with the socialists along the lines of the Seventh Comintern Congress. But at the local level in both the cities and the countryside republican authority disintegrated. Power fell into the hands of local organizations, many of which demanded radical solutions to social questions. They seized land from big owners, attacked churches and demanded the nationalization of industry.[28]

The Spanish Communist leadership responded initially to the surge of social revolution from below by defending private property against the excesses of confiscation and collectivization. One of its most influential leaders, Dolores Ibárruri, "La Pasionaria," declared that this was only the bourgeois democratic stage of the revolution and called for the unity of all republicans around a moderate social program. In March 1937 the secretary-general of the Spanish Communist Party, José Diaz, reiterated the message of restraint: "we should not lose our heads . . . by trying to introduce experiments in 'libertarian communism' and 'socializations.'"[29] As the center of Spanish politics melted away, the republican middle classes, especially the petty bourgeoisie, rushed to join the Spanish Communists as the sole reliable bulwark of republicanism against the revolutionary actions of the anarchists and left-wing socialists.

After several months of indecision, the leadership of the Comintern took a firm stand against social revolution in Spain. Dimitrov once again boldly rejected the shop-worn formulas. He proclaimed that this was a fight for something new in politics, "a special state with a genuine people's democracy." He claimed to be bringing up to date Lenin's formula of 1905; this was to be "a special form of democratic dictatorship of the working class and peasantry" necessitated by the altogether unprecedented danger to democratic liberties posed by fascism. The collectivization of agriculture and the nationalization of industry could come at some subsequent time. So too the armed workers' militia reminiscent of the Red Guards in 1917 should be fused with regular units of the Republican Army. In other words, the Spanish Communists were urged to adopt positions that Lenin refused to endorse whether in 1905 or 1917. Under another name it resembled in fact the cautious stance of

---

and the Spanish Civil War (New York: Pantheon, 1984), pp. 86–7. Caballero's reply expressed doubts about the viability of a parliamentary outcome. *Ibid.*, p. 88.

[28] Burnett Bolloten, *The Spanish Revolution: The Left and the Struggle for Power During the Civil War* (Chapel Hill: University of North Carolina Press, 1979), pp. 54–6, 59–60; Mikhail Koltsov, *Ispanskii dnevnik*, 2nd edn (Moscow: Sovetskii pisatel', 1958).

[29] Quote in Bolloten, *The Spanish Revolution*, p. 220.

Stalin and Molotov in February 1917 and Zinov'ev and Kamenev on the eve of October.[30]

Dimitrov's declaration did not pass unchallenged in the Comintern or among the more militant elements in the Spanish Communist Party. The central question dividing both representatives of the Comintern and the Spanish Communists was whether the road to power led through the mobilization of the masses or through the penetration of the organs of government and the army. If they had looked to Stalin's writings for inspiration they would have found conflicting advice. Ever since the 1920s in China, Stalin had given prominence in his revolutionary strategy to the creation of a revolutionary army. Yet more recently, in the campaign preceding the adoption of the new Stalin constitution, he had emphasized the importance of "democracy." Wendy Goldman has argued that this campaign could serve many purposes. In the Soviet Union it became a means of breaking up family circles of oppositionists within the party and ensuring greater involvement of the masses in establishing and legitimizing the formal institutions of state power under the guidance of the Stalinist leadership.[31] In Spain, the Comintern representative and leader of the Communist Party, Palmiro Togliatti, reported that "democracy" was also a way of breaking up the power of the smaller anarchist parties and radical groups by submerging them in mass electoral politics supervised by a government strongly influenced by the Communist Party.

Togliatti was enlisted to correct the leftist errors. If anything, he was even more moderate than Dimitrov. He dubbed the struggle in Spain a "national revolutionary war" against foreign control by Germany and Italy on the one hand, and for the autonomy of the nationalities, that is the Basques and Catalans, on the other. He pointed out differences from Russia in 1917, insisting that the Spanish Communists were novices and the Spanish Socialist Party was far stronger than the Mensheviks had been in Russia. He insisted that a moderate social policy, which gave no hint of collectivization or large-scale nationalization, had a chance of winning over the middle classes.[32]

Togliatti's mission to Spain in July 1937 convinced him that the National Front government had lost touch with the masses. He urged the revival of the local committees of the Front created in the early days

---

[30] *Kommunisticheskii internatsional: Kratkii istoricheskii ocherk* (Moscow: Gos.izd politicheskoi literatury, 1969), pp. 439–40, and Carr, The Twilight of the Comintern, pp. 20–1.

[31] Wendy Goldman, *Terror and Democracy in the Age of Stalin: The Social Dynamics of Repression* (Cambridge University Press, 2007), pp. 127–30.

[32] Carr, *The Twilight of the Comintern*, p. 22, quotation p. 7. Palmiro Togliatti, *Opere*, 6 vols. (Rome: Editori riuniti, 1967–84), vol. IV (1977), pp. 139–54.

of the war and the revival of the Cortes, which hardly functioned at all. At the same time, he proposed that the status of the representatives of the Comintern ought to be fundamentally changed, allowing the Spanish Communist Party to carry on its own work independently. The Comintern Executive agreed with most of his proposals, but recommended putting an end to the economic chaos by taking over enterprises under the "uncontrolled power" of the anarchist trade unions and nationalizing them. It further recommended that peasants should be allowed to leave the "collective economies that had been forced upon them." Concurring with Togliatti, it advised the Spanish Communists to work with the leadership of the anarchist National Confederation of Labor (CNT) to isolate the militants who opposed unity of action but "not to force a fusion of parties with the socialists" in order to avoid the impression that they intended to swallow the Socialist Party. The Spanish Party accepted some of his recommendations, abandoning its campaign to push for fusion with the socialists.[33]

Initially, Togliatti worried that national elections might end up in an exchange of gunfire. But in September Stalin personally intervened, instructing the Spanish Communist Party to hold new elections. This came at the very time when Stalin was preparing the Soviet Union for elections to the Supreme Soviet. Although circumstances were very different in the Soviet Union and Spain, the chosen means of mobilizing the masses was similar. There can be little doubt that for Stalin promoting elections in Spain had the added advantages of appealing to the idea of unity of the left and of gaining support from the liberal democracies for the Spanish republic. The Spanish Communist leaders were unhappy about the prospect of competing at the ballot box with the socialists and anarchists, but they knuckled under to Moscow's pressure and complied. It was only due to the opposition of the socialists that the idea was quietly buried.[34]

The Spanish Communists continued to push the democratic line but put their own spin on it, emphasizing the link to unity without mentioning elections. As Diaz put it in February 1938: "It is not possible to

[33] M. T. Meshcheriakov, *Ispanskaia respublika i komintern: Natsional'no-revoliutsionnaia voina ispanskogo naroda i politika Kommunisticheskogo Internatsionala, 1936–1939 gg.* (Moscow: Mysl', 1981), pp. 115–25. The Spanish Communist Party resisted calls for national elections with the excuse that most of its membership consisted of soldiers and sailors who constitutionally were not allowed to vote. *Ibid.*, pp. 128–9.

[34] Alexander Dallin and F. I. Firsov (eds.), *Dimitrov and Stalin, 1934–1943: Letters from the Soviet Archives* (New Haven, CT: Yale University Press, 2000), p. 61; Ron Radosh, Mary Habeck and G. Sevastianov (eds.), *Spain Betrayed: The Soviet Union in the Spanish Civil War* (New Haven, CT: Yale University Press, 2001), pp. 375–81; Payne, *Spanish Civil War*, pp. 236–7.

separate democracy and unity . . . The enemies of unity are the enemies of democracy. Consultation with the people will not only further the strengthening of democracy but the strengthening of unity . . . Unity and democracy – this is the slogan of our party and all anti-fascists."[35]

By the spring of 1938 Diaz was prepared to go farther down the road to compromise. He reacted strongly to radicals within the party ranks who demanded a break with the middle-class elements in the coalition and the establishment of a purely workers' government. He believed that the front had to be broadened even more to fight against foreign intervention. He even went so far as to consider the possibility of ending the war which was bleeding Spain and turning it into a plaything of foreign governments. After conversations with Togliatti, he came out with a proposal to negotiate with Franco if the form of the Spanish government would be determined by a plebiscite with a guarantee of civil liberties. He was supported by Ibárruri. Togliatti and the second-ranking Comintern official in Spain, the Bulgarian Communist Boris Stepanov (Stoian Minev) helped draft a thirteen-point program which became the policy of the new government under Prime Minister Juan Negrin. At the same time, Diaz struggled to keep the coalition of the left intact.[36] But after Munich it came apart.

While the Spanish Communists preached restraint in social and economic policies, they increased their influence over the army. Early in the war they had pressed Caballero to establish a regular army in place of the militias that each party had created under its control. Their influence increased with the timely arrival of Soviet arms and the International Brigades, decisive factors in the defense of Madrid in November 1936. Soviet propagandists drew a parallel between Madrid and Petrograd in 1919 – both victories of a revolutionary army against the professional troops of the extreme right.[37] Two years later the Comintern would extend the parallel all the way to China, as we shall see, to embrace the defense of Wuhan against the Japanese Army.

Caballero's resistance to the Communist penetration of the army command had led to his fall and replacement by Juan Negrin, with Indalecio Prieto as War Minister. But Prieto also failed to curb the growing Communist influence in the armed forces. Under a barrage of Communist attacks, he was forced to resign. The creation of the second Negrin government in April 1938 represented the high point of the Communists' influence, despite the fact that they had only one cabinet minister in the

---

[35] M. T. Meshcheriakov, *Vsia zhizn' – bor'ba (O Xose Diase)* (Moscow: Politizdat, 1971), p. 159.
[36] *Ibid.*, p. 66.   [37] Payne, *The Spanish Civil War*, pp. 180–2.

first Negrin government and two in the second. Whether Negrin, a controversial figure, is regarded as a great patriot or a Communist stooge, his governments relied heavily on Communist and Comintern support especially in the armed forces. By September 1937 the army numbered 575,000 men, of whom 60 percent were members of the Spanish Communist Party. By the end of 1938 the Communists held most of the key positions in the Ministry of the Interior and key positions in the Ministry of Defense.[38]

The Republican Army enjoyed a brief resurgence in the summer of 1938, but then failed to follow up its tactical victories and lost momentum. The precise reasons for this turnabout are not clear. Reports to Moscow from Soviet officers and Comintern representatives give a mixed and often confusing picture. It is difficult to evaluate the conflicting claims of incompetence, treason and simple military error in this literature of denunciation.[39] The contribution of Soviet military advisors was also uneven.[40] For all the talk of treason on one side and interference by Soviet and Comintern agents on the other, the war was lost on the battlefield.

Historians have frequently pointed to the parallel between Communist tactics in Spain and those followed by the Communist parties of Eastern Europe in the period after World War II.[41] That there were similarities is undeniable. The argument can even be made, as it will be in subsequent chapters, that the concept of democracy of a new type, or popular democracy, was a model for postwar Communist parties, not only in Eastern Europe but elsewhere as well. But Stanley Payne has pointed out several important differences. First, the presence of the Red Army in Eastern Europe was crucial in the Communists' taking power;

[38] Bolloten, *The Spanish Revolution*, pp. 295–8, 325–32, 452–3; Payne, *The Spanish Civil War*, pp. 250–2, 260; Radosh et al., *Spain Betrayed*, pp. 369–70. Julián Casanova, *A Short History of the Spanish Civil War* (London: I. B. Tauris, 2013), pp. 122–5 and 181, rejects the view that Negrin was controlled by the Communists.

[39] Among the most detailed if not illuminating reports that have been published, those of Manfred Stern (Kleber) and Korol Sverchevsky (Karol Swierczewski) reveal the personal rivalries, suspicions, political intrigues and conspiracies, both real and imaginary, that characterized the inner history of the military operations. See Radosh et al., *Spain Betrayed*, "An Account by M. Fred [Stern] on work in Spain," December 14, 1937, doc. 60, pp. 295–368, and "Notes on the Situation in the International Units in Spain. Report by Colonel Com. Sverchevsky [Walter]," January 14, 1938, doc. 70, pp. 436–60.

[40] Payne, *Spanish Civil War*, pp. 166–72.

[41] This view is endorsed by such different authors as the Soviet historian Meshcheriakov, *Ispanskaia republika i kominterna*, p. 201; the strongly anti-Communist French historian François Furet, *The Passing of an Illusion: The Idea of Communism in the Twentieth Century* (University of Chicago Press, 1999), pp. 245–65, and the editors of *Spain Betrayed*, p. xxiii. Dimitrov himself seemed to confirm this when he wrote in March 1947 that "Spain was the first example of a people's democracy."

second, the Spanish socialists resisted Communist appeals to create a single workers' party, in contrast to Eastern Europe; third, the Spanish left, including it would appear the Communists, did not favor elections in the middle of the war, while elections were held under various constraints in Eastern Europe after the liberation; fourth, nationalization of the economy proceeded slowly and irregularly in Spain. In summary "the wartime Spanish Republic combined autonomous libertarian collectivization with a restored centralized state, increasing state control and a degree of nationalization ... Politically it remained a semi pluralist regime within a limited framework of law."[42]

Clearly, too, the internal politics of Spain were radically different from those in the East European state. Not the least of these differences were the existence before the war of a strong, legal Communist Party, autonomous movements in the Basque and Catalan regions and an anarchist movement unique to Spain. Clearly, too, the international context was different. To be sure, in both cases Stalin was anxious to avoid frightening the Western democracies by overtly promoting a social revolution. But in the Spanish case his tactics were designed to win support for the republican cause from France and Britain, while in Eastern Europe he sought to hold together the wartime alliance with Britain and the United States and possibly to prolong it into a period of postwar reconstruction.

In his secret postmortem report to the Comintern in 1940, Diaz attributed the failure of revolution in Spain to most of the same factors that Payne identified as representing the differences with Eastern Europe after the war with the clear intention of drawing lessons for the future that might well have influenced the ideological and political evolution of the Popular Front into the wartime United Front and postwar Popular Democracy. He pointed out three major problems. First there had been no unity of the anti-fascist states (Britain and France being at fault here) in overturning the phony policy of "non-intervention." Second, the left had been split, each party controlling its own trade unions and all the rest blocking the Communist call for a united workers' party. Third, the over-centralized and mechanical methods of governing by the coalition had alienated the national feelings of Catalonia and the Basque Province (by implication ignoring Stalin's nationality policy). Finally, the old state apparatus had not been destroyed, although it would have been premature to declare a dictatorship of the proletariat which would have reduced the social basis for a strong coalition. Diaz extolled

<hr/>

[42] Payne, *Spanish Civil War*, p. 305.

Negrin's thirteen-point program of radical democracy which had never been fully implemented.[43]

Many of the difficulties in evaluating what exactly was meant by the term "democracy of a new type" in the late 1930s stem from the uncertainties of its creators. There was not even agreement on what to call this new phenomenon. It was still in the process of formation both in theory and in practice. In fact, as will become clear in subsequent chapters, there was no clear-cut pattern for creating such a regime in Eastern Europe until 1949. Behind the rhetoric that separated a Togliatti from a Tito lurked a difference, which surfaced during World War II and again with the emergence of Eurocommunism, between choosing an insurrectionary or a parliamentary path to socialism. There was always the possibility of combining them or moving from one tactic to another. This seemed to be Stalin's preferred model, with himself as the final arbiter.

Inner Asian frontiers

In Inner Asia Stalin pursued his borderlands policy on two levels. In Inner Asia, he strengthened his control over Xinjiang and Outer Mongolia. In China he stepped up his military assistance to the Nationalist government of Chiang Kai-shek in order to keep the bulk of the Japanese Army engaged deeply in China as remote as possible from the Soviet frontiers. Through diplomatic channels and the Comintern, he pressed hard for the Nationalists and Communists to suspend their fighting and form a united front against the Japanese. Unlike his decision to reach an agreement with Nazi Germany in 1939 at the expense of the western borderlands, Stalin had no intention of partitioning China with Japan.

Following the Japanese attack, the Communists and Nationalists publicly buried their differences but not, as it turned out, very far below the surface. Chiang issued an order in July 1937 suspending all military operations against the Red Army. He concluded an agreement of cooperation with representatives of the Chinese Communist Party on mutually advantageous terms. The Communists agreed to incorporate the Red Army, officially renamed the Eighth Route Army, into the Nationalist forces but insisted on retaining a separate command structure. Within six months Communist guerrillas scattered south of the Yangtze were regrouped under the designation of the New Fourth Army. The Communists accepted Chiang's invitation to join the Kuomintang in forming

---

[43] RGASPI, f. 494, op. 10a, d. 2521, "Vooruzhennaia bor'ba ispanskogo naroda za svobodu i nezavisimost' Ispaniia" (Diaz to Manuilskii, January 1, 1940). See also Diaz's article in *Bol'shevik*, January, 1940.

a joint consultative commission which actually met several times in 1938 in order to discuss a common military strategy in Shansi Province. The Nationalist government revised the Extraordinary Law on Crimes against the Republic that had served as the legal basis for persecuting and arresting Communists. It recognized the legality of the Communist Party and over the following year released about 30,000 political prisoners.[44] The Soviet Union welcomed the burgeoning cooperation as a major victory in its political campaign to relieve pressure on its Inner Asian frontier.

On the eve of Chiang's announcement of the formation of the Eighth Route Army, Stalin extended a $50 million line of credit to the Nationalist government. This inaugurated a steady flow of advisors, volunteers and military supplies over the succeeding three years. In the first twelve months Soviet arms deliveries equipped twenty-four Nationalist divisions. The total cost of the supplies came to more than $173 million, not counting an additional $18 million for the support of Soviet advisors. Soviet engineers transported over the old caravan routes from Central Asia to Xinjiang over nine hundred planes, eighty-two tanks, over 600 tractors, 1,500 motor vehicles, 1,140 artillery pieces, thousands of machine guns and tens of thousands of rifles. At the height of the Soviet military aid in early 1939 there were over 3,600 military advisors in China and several hundred "volunteer pilots" flying combat missions against the Japanese.[45] The Soviet Union also sent technical specialists to increase Chinese oil production in the northwest frontier province of Gansu. In response to Chinese requests, the Soviet Union approved the establishment of direct flights between Alma Ata and Xami, but insisted that the Chinese forbid the flights of a German airline to Southern Xinjiang. An agreement was signed in September 1939 at about the same time that the Soviet and Chinese governments agreed to build an aviation factory in Urumchi to produce military aircraft for China.[46]

The policy of the united front took a dramatic turn in 1938 during the momentous battle between the Japanese and Chinese armies for Wuhan (Hankou). The parallel between Wuhan and Madrid was frequently invoked by Chinese Communist leaders in close touch

[44] M. F. Iur'ev et al. (eds.), *Kitai v period voiny protiv iaponskoi agressii (1937–1945)* (Moscow: Nauka, 1988), pp. 61–2.

[45] M. I. Sladkovskii, *Istoriia torgovo-ekonomicheskikh otnoshenii SSSR s Kitaem, 1917–1974* (Moscow: Akademiia nauk SSSR, Institut dalnego vostoka, 1977), p. 138 (based on the archives of the Soviet Foreign Trade Ministry); *Na kitaiskoi zemle: Vospominaniia sovetskikh dobrovol'tsev, 1925–1944 gg.,* 2nd edn (Moscow: Akademiia Nauk SSSR, Institut vostokovedeniia, 1977), pp. 175–6.

[46] DVP, vol. XXI (1938), docs. 184, 217; pp. 265, 310, note 169, p. 741; *ibid.*, vol. XXII, bk 2 (1939), note 66, pp. 527–8; note 290, pp. 639–40.

with Moscow, like Wang Ming, Soviet propagandists and even Western left-wing publications.[47] In the three-city urban sprawl that was Wuhan, Communist, left-wing Kuomintang and local regional militarists maintained a precarious balance. Following Moscow, the Chinese Communists on the ground still clung to the idea of an urban revolution under the umbrella of a united front. Chou En-lai drafted a seven-point document outlining a strategy that envisioned a mobilization and arming of the working class side by side with regular units of the Communist and Kuomintang forces and an inventory of resources including factories to be organized for defense. The objectives were to check the Japanese advance and to bring the Chinese workers back into the center of the revolutionary movement from which they had been absent ever since the disasters ten years before. A successful defense of Wuhan would prove Mao Zedong wrong; the proletariat would recapture its rightful place from the peasants as the vanguard of revolution.[48]

Stalin committed everything he could spare. On the eve of the battle he authorized a $50 million credit for the Kuomintang, the second loan within a year. The first squadron of Soviet "volunteer" pilots arrived just in time to challenge the Japanese for air superiority over Wuhan. During the four-month siege, they shot down over ninety Japanese aircraft while losing only sixteen of their own. On the ground the first group of Soviet military advisors, including several future generals in the Red Army, urged Chiang Kai-shek to organize a more active defense, combining strong counter-attacks by massing Soviet T-26 tanks that had recently begun to arrive with vigorous partisan operations in the rear of the Japanese lines. But the Chinese generals lacked the training and audacity to carry out a complex operational plan. Chiang refused to commit the tanks.[49] He also disbanded the militias in the city. The battle of Wuhan, little known in the West, was one of the most costly of any fought during World War II. The forces of the united front lost over a million men killed and wounded. The Chinese officer corps was decimated; its

[47] John W. Garver, *Chinese–Soviet Relations, 1937–1945: The Diplomacy of Chinese Nationalism* (Oxford University Press, 1988), pp. 74–5; Stephen MacKinnon, "The Tragedy of Wuhan, 1938," *Modern Asian Studies* 30:4 (1996), pp. 931–43, gives a vivid picture of the unprecedented flowering of political diversity in Wuhan which spread to the arts, especially drama and music.

[48] A. Ia Kaliagin, *Po neznakomym dorogam: Zapiski voennogo sovetnika v Kitae*, 2nd edn (Moscow: Nauka, 1977), pp. 92ff, is a summary of Chou's program; Iur'ev *et al.*, Kitai, pp. 61–2.

[49] Kaliagin, *Po neznakomym dorogam*, p. 282; A. I. Cherepanov, *Zapiski voennogo sovetnika v Kitae, 1925–1927*, 2nd edn (Moscow: Nauka, 1976), pp. 203–4; *V nebe Kitaia, 1937–1940: Vospitaniia sovetskikh letchikov-dobrovol'tsev*, 2nd edn (Moscow: Nauka, 1986), pp. 8–9.

German-trained cadres suffered losses of 80 percent. The Chinese Army never again fought so well. But the Japanese too sustained their heaviest casualties of the war.[50] After the fall of Wuhan to the Japanese, Dimitrov linked the fate of China and Spain in a renewed appeal for a united front as the threat to China rapidly assumed ominous proportions.[51]

Following a string of victories, which deprived the government of its main rail lines and port cities, the Japanese created a puppet government headed by Wang Jingwei, a former leading figure in the Kuomintang. His political program included making peace with Japan and initiating a struggle against the Soviet Union and the Chinese Communists. Soviet representatives in China reported that continued resistance depended on increasing military aid and putting to rest fears that the Chinese Communists were seeking to overthrow the government with Soviet help.[52] In dealing with the Kuomintang, Soviet diplomats only rarely mentioned relations with the Chinese Communists, suggesting, for example, that cooperation with them could only strengthen the anti-Japanese front. But they were fully aware that once the war was over, Chiang would renew his efforts to annihilate the Communists including the Eighth Route Army.[53]

Chiang was constantly nervous about any sign of rapprochement between the Soviet Union and Japan. Moscow had to reassure him repeatedly, even dispatching a personal message from Stalin. Beginning in June 1938 Chiang began to suggest the possibility of a military alliance with the Soviet Union, at first to be secret and only later to be made public and extended into the postwar period.[54] As an incentive to bring the Soviet Union into the war with Japan, the Chinese leaders proposed that their joint armies would drive the Japanese out of Manchuria, reestablish Chinese sovereignty over the province but extend broad autonomy similar to that enjoyed by Canada or Ireland in the British Commonwealth.[55] Although Stalin did not respond at the time, he could hardly have forgotten the idea when negotiating with the Chinese in 1945 after Yalta. Meanwhile, at a time when the Western powers, including the United States, were reluctant to supply China with any war material for fear of offending Japan, the Soviet supplies were crucial in keeping the Nationalist armies

---

[50] MacKinnon, "The Tragedy," p. 933.
[51] G. Dimitrov, "Edinyi front mezhdunarodnogo proletariata i narodov protiv fashizma," *Bol'shevik* 21–2 (November 15, 1938), pp. 53, 55.
[52] DVP, vol. XXII, bk 1 (1939), doc. 300, p. 359; *ibid.*, bk 2, note 66, p. 528.
[53] *Ibid.*, bk 2 (1939), doc. 1, p. 10.
[54] *Ibid.*, vol. XII (1938), docs. 233, 322, 329, pp. 334, 465–8 and 475–7. *Ibid.*, vol. XXII, bk 2 (1939), docs. 548, and 760, pp. 33–4 and 270–1; notes 183 and 184, pp. 592–3.
[55] *Ibid.*, doc. 282, p. 412.

in the field, a fact that was recognized and generously acknowledged by Chiang and his representatives.[56] Almost immediately following the occupation of Manchuria, Japanese forces began testing Soviet frontier defenses. The number of unpublicized border incidents increased from 152 in the three-year period from 1931 and 1934 to 136 in 1935 and 203 in 1936. At the end of World War II the total number had reached 1,600 (sic!).[57] In 1938 after a year of fighting in China the Japanese government was convinced that "the resolution of the China incident is being prolonged because of the aid which the Soviet Union is sending to China." Its annual plan for 1938 included a large-scale operation aimed at Changkufeng (Lake Khasan), a strategic point where the frontiers of Manchuria, Korea and the Maritime Provinces meet.[58] For the first time the Japanese probe involved strategic-size military units, but their incursion was thrown back by powerful Soviet counter-attacks. Yet even then there were senior Japanese officers who favored breaking off the fighting in China in order to move the bulk of the Japanese mainland troops against the Soviet Union. Preparing for a second major clash with the Red Army, the army staff planners pushed for the completion of two railroads that would link central Manchuria and run parallel to the Manchurian–Outer Mongolian border.

In 1939 they launched another attack at Nomonhan (Khalki-gol) along the ill-defined frontier where the northern and southern Mongols had been contesting pasture land since the Qing dynasty. Both the Japanese and Soviet forces included Mongol auxiliaries. The large-scale engagement involving tanks and aircraft ended in a decisive victory for the numerically superior and better-equipped Soviet forces under the command of General Georgii Zhukov. The Japanese suffered from large-scale desertions by Mongols of the Khingan Cavalry Division, some of who went over to the Soviet side, while others formed small and short-lived partisan detachments. The Kwantung Army was forced to accept a ceasefire, which the Soviet leaders arranged to announce at the conclusion of negotiations in Moscow of the Nazi–Soviet non-aggression pact. Stunned by the news, the army staff who had been pressing the cabinet

[56] *Ibid.*, docs. 186, 192, pp. 268, 277–80, note 161, p. 739; *ibid.*, vol. XXII, bk 2 (1939), note 205, p. 601.

[57] Hata Ikuhiko, "The Japanese–Soviet Confrontation," in James W. Morley, *Deterrent Diplomacy: Japan, Germany and the USSR, 1935–1940* (New York: Columbia University Press, 1976), pp. 88, 133–4.

[58] A. S. Savin, "O podgotovke Iaponii k napadeniiu na SSSR: Iaponskie istoriki svidetel'stvuiut," *Voenno-Istoricheskii zhurnal* 7 (July, 1991), pp. 88–9, citing material from the 102-vol. *Official History of the War in Greater East Asia* (Tokyo, 1966–88), p. 89.

for an alliance with Germany against the Soviet Union had the ground cut out from under them. Indeed, the entire Japanese government was thrown into disarray.[59]

Over the previous four years the cabinet in Tokyo, under pressure from the army and a radical group of "renovationists" within the Foreign Ministry, had been gradually moving toward a policy of isolating the Soviet Union: "a kind of anti-Soviet encirclement" in the words of Japanese historian Ohata Tokushiro. The Anti-Comintern Pact of 1936 had been for them only the first step toward that goal. They aimed at nothing less than forcing a complete Soviet withdrawal from Outer Mongolia and Xinjiang, the establishment of a demilitarized zone in Eastern Siberia up to Lake Baikal, the dismantling of the defenses of Vladivostok, and ultimately the purchase of the Maritime Provinces from a debilitated Soviet Union. If these demands were not met, they urged immediate preparations for a war which, in the long run, they considered inevitable in any case.[60]

Elements in the Japanese defense establishment did not limit themselves to undermining Soviet influence in the Inner Asian borderlands. Throughout the interwar period Japanese military intelligence had developed close relations with their Finnish, Estonian and Polish counterparts.[61] By the late 1930s they had succeeded in recruiting agents among disaffected nationalists throughout the entire western as well as the Inner Asian borderlands of the Soviet Union. They actively cooperated with German intelligence in promoting the Promethean League with its leading representatives among the Lithuanian, Georgian and Crimean Tatars. Soviet intelligence reported on the training of small groups of armed units from among disaffected national groups in the Caucasian, Trans Caspian and Inner Asian borderlands to carry out sabotage and guerrilla warfare. Many of these groups were infiltrated by Soviet intelligence. Recent revelations on these activities make it clear that spy mania in the Soviet Union was not an invention of the secret police, whatever twisted use was made of uncovering foreign espionage in order to discredit and destroy Stalin's domestic political rivals.

[59] Alvin D. Coox, *Nomonhan: Japan against Russia, 1939* (Stanford University Press, 1985), pp. 895–900; Ikuhiko, "The Japanese–Soviet Confrontation," pp. 152–8, Savin, "O podgotovke," p. 90; S. D. Dylykov, *Demokraticheskoe dvizhenie mogol'skogo naroda v Kitae* (Moscow: Akademiia nauk, 1953), pp. 39–40.

[60] Ohata Tokushiro, "The Anti-Comintern Pact, 1935–1939," in Morley, *Deterrent Diplomacy*, pp. 18–21, 31, 36.

[61] The following is based on Jeffrey Burds, "The Soviet War against 'Fifth Columnists': The Case of Chechnya, 1942–4," *Journal of Contemporary History* 42:2 (2007), pp. 274–82.

Purges in the borderlands

Historians have reached a consensus that Stalin's fear of war was a dominant factor in unleashing the Great Terror of 1937–8.[62] Among the primary targets for liquidation were party organizations and ethnic groups located in the borderlands. In explaining to Georgi Dimitrov the reasons for the terror, Stalin reviewed a series of events in foreign policy going back to 1905, 1917, Brest-Litovsk and the Civil War but "particularly collectivization. Then is when weak elements in the party fell away, went underground," he explained. "Being powerless themselves, they linked up with our external enemies, the Germans, the Ukrainians, the Poles, Belorussians, and the Japanese in our Far East. They were waiting for a war."[63]

Soon after the second Moscow trial in the summer of 1937, a widespread purge consumed numerous foreign and non-Russian ethnic groups, particularly Germans and Poles. At the same time, leading cadres of the Polish, West Belorussian and West Ukrainian parties were decimated and the two latter parties were dissolved the following year.[64] Beginning in January 1938 at Stalin's behest, the police unleashed a new wave of mass repression against the so-called "national contingents," targeting a hitherto unprecedented range of ethnic groups – Latvians, Estonian, Finns, Greeks, Romanians, Bulgarians, Macedonians, Iranians, Afghans, and Chinese.[65] A year earlier, the Politburo had already ordered vast sweeps of "undesirables" from the border districts adjacent to Turkey, Iran and Afghanistan and the organization of special defensive zones. In Armenia and Azerbaizhan this translated into the deportation of small numbers of Kurds into the interior. A larger number of Soviet citizens of Iranian background, about 6,000, were suspected of espionage

---

[62] Hiroaki Kuromiya, "Accounting for the Great Terror," *Jahrbücher für Geschichte Osteuropas* 53:1 (2005), pp. 86–101 reviews the literature.

[63] Banac, *The Diary of Georgi Dimitrov*, entry for November 11, 1937, pp. 67–9. Following hard on the heels of the show trials of 1946–7, the *Short Course of the Communist Party of the Soviet Union* stressed the threat of foreign spies, terror and dismemberment. Wladislaw Hedeler, "Ezhov's Scenario for the Great Terror and the Falsified Record of the Third Moscow Show Trial," in Barry McLoughlin and Kevin McDermott (eds.), *Stalin's Terror: High Politics and Mass Repression in the Soviet Union* (New York: Palgrave Macmillan, 2003), p. 52. Oleg Khlevniuk has argued that mass operations in 1937 were connected to Stalin's reading of the role of the fifth column in republican Spain as a likely scenario for Russia in the event of war. O. Khlevniuk, "The Reasons for the Great Terror: The Foreign Policy Aspect," in Silvio Pons and Andrea Romano (eds.), *Russia in the Age of Wars, 1914–1945* (Milan: Feltrinelli, 2000), pp. 159–69.

[64] "Za pravil'noe osveshchenie istorii kompartii zapadoi Belorussiasii," *Kommunist* 8 (May, 1964), p. 78.

[65] Paul Hagenloh, *Stalin's Police: Public Order and Mass Repression, 1926–1941* (Baltimore, MD: Johns Hopkins University Press, 2009), pp. 277–81. To be sure, the police were not too discriminating in identifying ethnic groups caught up in their operational sweeps.

against the state by Stalin and his associates, and were deported from the South Caucasus to Kazakhstan. These deportations were motivated by considerations that linked ethnicity to frontier defense.[66]

The dual mania directed against foreign spies and domestic class enemies in the borderlands was not limited to the nationalities. In the early stages of the raids on the "national contingents," the head of the NKVD, Nikolai Ezhov, targeted hired workers and refugees from abroad who had entered the Soviet Union in recent years as "defectors." Following up Stalin's warnings to the party and military leaders in the first half of 1937, he ordered Ezhov to arrest and deport all Germans employed in defense industries. At first, the targets were German citizens, but the campaign rapidly engulfed Soviet citizens of German nationality or those who had some contact with Germans or Germany. The Poles and those who were in any way linked to Poland were next followed by numerous other nationalities.[67] The purge even struck the "Kharbintsy," approximately 25,000 ethnic Russians who had been repatriated in 1935 following the sale of the Chinese Eastern Railroad. They were suspected of harboring anti-Soviet sentiments dating back to the Civil War and collaborating with the Japanese.[68]

For the Soviet leadership the initial wave of deportations and purges in the western borderlands were insufficiently thorough. At least this was the message that A. A. Andreev relayed to Stalin in 1938 during his whirlwind tour of potential troublespots throughout the Soviet Union. In the frontier districts of Belorussia, he uncovered weak party structures and subversive elements among the Poles and families of purge victims. He recommended that these elements be deported farther into the interior. Although Party Secretary Ponomarenko received a passing grade, Andreev fingered the Belorussian Commissar of Education as "a traitor and probably a Polish spy" and the Commissar of Agriculture as a "suspicious character." He suggested the removal of many party secretaries in the frontier districts who were Poles or Latvians. He also pointed out weaknesses in the frontier defenses and proposed a series of measures to prevent cross-border movement.[69]

---

[66] N. F. Bugai and A. M. Gonov, *Kavkaz: Narody v eshelonakh (20–60e gody)* (Moscow: INSAN, 1998), pp. 103–7.

[67] Marc Jansen and Nikita Petrov, *Stalin's Loyal Executioner: People's Commissar Nikolai Ezhov, 1895–1940* (Stanford: Hoover Institution Press, 2002), pp. 93–8.

[68] Barry McLoughlin, "Mass Operations of the NKVD, 1937–38," in McLoughlin and McDermott, *Stalin's Terror*, p. 123. By the time the national operations were terminated in the fall of 1938 a total of about 350,000 people had been swept up, of whom 247,157 had been condemned to death. Jansen and Petrov, *Stalin's Loyal Executioner*, p. 99.

[69] *Sovetskoe rukovodstvo: Perepiska, 1928–1941* (Moscow: Rosspen, 1999), docs. 235, 236, pp. 393–5.

Ukraine was particularly hard hit by the purges because of its large party organization, the number of prominent Ukrainians in the central apparatus and the vigorous cultural life within the republic. Ukrainian resistance to the centralists did not come to an end with the adoption of the new Soviet constitution. Their leaders were joined now by Vlas Chubar who replaced Rakovskii as Chairman of the People's Commissars of Ukraine and who was soon to become a candidate member of the All-Union Politburo. They maintained a drumfire of criticism against administrative, budgetary and judicial procedures that deprived the republics of their rights. In several cases they were able to win points for a special Ukrainian status among the union republics.[70] At the same time, a muted struggle continued over the question of bringing the constitutions of the republics in line with the Soviet constitution. Five years of intermittent discussion preceded the adoption of a revised Ukrainian constitution. It retained the formula that Ukraine had entered the USSR as an "independent treaty state limited only in matters reserved to the USSR under its constitution." As E. H. Carr stated: "This was a stronger affirmation of formal independence and sovereignty than appeared in the constitution of any other Union republic."[71]

Even while Stalin retained many of the formal aspects of indigenization and some of its educational policies, he unleashed a violent campaign against the local cadres. In the terrible year 1937 the Ukrainian apparatus was destroyed several times over. Almost all the leading officials of the party and soviets of the republic were arrested and most of them were executed. Over 180,000 party members representing 37 percent of the total were repressed.[72] Old opponents of Stalin like Grin'ko, moderate defenders of Ukrainian rights like Vlas Chubar, and even loyalists like Postyshev who could not, however, conceal their distaste for Stalin's excessive demands for subordination, were swept away; their immediate successors perished as well. A group around Grin'ko was accused at the trial of Rights and Trotskyites of having organized a "National Fascist Organization" that plotted with foreign agents to detach Ukraine from the USSR. It was the only case in which the Ukrainian leaders were publically identified with nationalist deviation, but it was enough to taint the entire Ukrainian party which had allegedly failed to discover and

[70] Robert S. Sullivant, *Soviet Politics and the Ukraine. 1917–1957* (New York: Columbia University Press, 1962), pp. 82–3.

[71] E. H. Carr and R. W. Davies, *Foundations of a Planned Economy. 1926–1929*, 3 vols. (New York: Macmillan, 1971), vol. II, p. 195.

[72] I. D. Nazarenko, *Ocherki po istorii kommunisticheskoi partii Ukrainy* (Kiev: Izd. Institut istorii partii, 1964). See also Robert Conquest, *The Great Terror of the Thirties* (New York: Macmillan, 1968), pp. 251–9.

eradicate it. As if to confirm this identification of political opposition and culture, the purge of the leadership was accompanied by a campaign to moderate ukrainianization and introduce a dose of russification through the medium of language.[73] The combined assault on the Ukrainian party apparatus and the use of the Ukrainian language were the kind of gross political errors that, as Bukharin had warned, played into the hands of the real nationalist enemies of the Soviet Union.

On the eve of the war the purges of the Ukrainian Communists could only have benefited the number of Ukrainian nationalist organizations outside the Soviet Union. They were active in Ukrainian communities in Western Ukraine, in the Carpatho-Ukraine under Czech sovereignty, in the Bukovina under Romanian control and scattered in smaller émigré colonies in Germany and France. Of these the most militant and best organized was the Organization of Ukrainian Nationalists (OUN) whose main strength was in Western Ukraine. When Red Army forces occupied the area in 1939 as the Soviet share of the partition of Poland with Germany, the leadership discovered its supporters were bitterly divided and demoralized. They confronted a strong network of underground opponents of sovietization. After the German invasion in 1941 they became the core of an anti-Soviet resistance that fought a civil war within the larger war of the Great Powers over the fate of Ukraine.[74] In Belorussia the purges made an almost complete sweep of the party leadership; one half the membership lost their party cards. By 1937 there was no one left to work in the Central Committee in Minsk and replacements were chewed up within a year of their arrival.

Moscow's reaction to the perceived threat of Ukrainian cultural autonomy had traditionally sparked an opposite reaction on the Polish side of whatever territorial demarcation existed at the time, and vice versa. If ukrainianization had its counterpart in the Volhynian experiment, then the Soviet repression of nationalist deviation had its cross-border counterpart in the "revindications of souls." In December 1937 the Polish Defense Corps put into play its plans to encourage Ukrainians to convert from Orthodoxy to Roman Catholicism. The inspiration came from the military rather than the clergy. In the mix of incentives and coercion employed to restore "their true nationality" there were no harsh measures of arrests and deportation comparable to those taking place across the

---

[73] Paul Wexler, *Purism and Language: A Study in Modern Ukrainian and Belorussian Nationalism (1840–1967)* (Bloomington: Indiana University Press, 1974), pp. 158–65, records the attack on Ukrainian linguistic specialists as favoring dialecticism and archaisms in order to render the language different from Russian.

[74] John Armstrong, *Ukrainian Nationalism*, 2nd edn (New York: Columbia University Press, 1963), chs. 2 and 3.

Soviet border. But the aims were more radical. There were plans to pol-
onize the entire Ukrainian population of Volhynia by 1944.[75] The main
beneficiaries of the attempts of both Moscow and Warsaw to impose
their control over the fractious peoples of the Ukrainian borderlands
were the extreme nationalists, the OUN and the deviant Communists in
the remnants of the West Ukrainian Party.

The North Caucasus was, like Ukraine, a region that had suffered
enormously from collectivization, and was further disorganized and
demoralized by the purges. In Ossetia almost the entire Obkom bureau
was arrested and a large part of the small intelligentsia wiped out. The
Chechen-Ingush Autonomous Republic was decimated in two massive
waves of arrests that may have amounted to 3 percent of the population.
In the Kabardino-Balkarskii region the popular hero of the Civil War
and First Secretary of the Obkom, B. E. Kalmykov, was arrested and
executed. Because of the relatively small numbers of Old Bolsheviks and
party intelligentsia in these backward regions, the losses were probably
more damaging than in Ukraine where replacements could be found
more easily. In any case, the purges severely weakened local resistance
to the German invaders in 1942, contributed to widespread disaffection
and delayed the reestablishment of Soviet power in these areas after the
liberation.[76]

In the South Caucasian borderlands, Stalin took a personal interest
and played a direct role in the destruction of the old cadres. Knowing
Stalin and the region as he did, Beria presented Stalin with a picture that
he was ready to accept of close links between internal subversion and
the threat of external intervention assisted by old political enemies in
the emigration. The potential existed for exploiting widespread disaffection with Moscow, and Stalin was never one to underestimate potential
opposition, especially when he had been responsible for enlivening it.
In light of the older tradition of Menshevism in Georgia and the affair
of the Georgian Communists that brought Lenin's conflict with Stalin
into the open in 1922, Stalin had many old scores to settle. He had
appointed Beria as First Secretary in 1931 to carry out a more or less
continuous purge. During the Great Purge Trials some of the survivors
of these quarrels, like Budu Mdivani, an Old Bolshevik and a member
of the Caucasian Bureau from 1920 to 1921, were implicated with the

[75] Timothy Snyder, *Sketches from a Secret War: A Polish Artist's Mission to Liberate Soviet
Ukraine* (New Haven, CT: Yale University Press, 2005), pp. 162–7.
[76] M. S. Totoev, *Istoriia Severo-Osetinskoi ASSR* (Ordzhonikidze: Severo-Osetinskoe kni-
azhnoe izd., 1966), p. 247; B. E. Kalmykov, *Stat'i i rechi* (Nal'chik: Kabardino-
Balkarskoe knizhnoe izd., 1961); *Narody kavkazy*, 2 vols. (Moscow: AN SSSR, Institut
etnografii, 1960–2); Conquest, *The Great Terror*, p. 287.

leading oppositionists, Trotsky, Zinoviev and Bukharin, as well as being denounced as British agents. Massive replacements for the top posts of the Georgian Communist Party in 1937 suggest that virtually the entire leadership from the 1920s perished. But the executions were not limited to party members. Prominent writers, poets, dramatists and other intellectuals disappeared.[77]

During the period of the Nazi–Soviet Pact and tense relations with the Western powers, Beria reported on the creation in Istanbul of a branch of the Council of the Confederation of the Caucasus, an émigré organization formed in Paris in 1934, under the leadership of Noe Zhordania. Its members allegedly included Georgian Mensheviks, Muslim Musavatists and North Caucasus mountain peoples. (One of the latter, Sultan-Girei Klych, collaborated with the Germans in 1942 in an attempt to raise the Adigei and other tribes in revolt against the Soviet power.) After the fall of France the Paris group scattered. Together with remnants of the Prometheus group they found refuge in a number of European and Middle Eastern countries. These groups were allegedly connected to Trotskyite elements supported by the Turkish government.[78] Given the belief widespread among the Soviet leadership that Turkey, and possibly Iran, would join in an attack on the Soviet Union if German forces penetrated deeply enough into the North Caucasus, such reports could not but reinforce and intensify suspicions of nationalist deviations. To be sure, in 1942–3 the German Army fell short of its objectives in the region. Moreover, although there were German-sponsored anti-Soviet movements among the mountain peoples, to be treated in Chapter 8, the Germans bungled efforts to expand their contacts with Georgian émigrés, which dated back to the Georgian independence movement they had supported at Brest-Litovsk. But this could not have been foreseen in 1939–41.

Armenia, like Ukraine, was particularly singled out for having harbored a "right-Trotskyite national center." A year before a seesaw struggle over the review of party documents had revealed the resistance of some local party leaders to wholesale repression. Then Nersik Stepanian, one of the

[77] Conquest, *The Great Terror*, pp. 249–50; David M. Lang, "A Century of Russian Impact on Georgia," in Wayne Vucinich, *Russia and Asia* (Stanford University Press, 1972), pp. 238–9.
[78] *Nakanune 22 iiunia 1941 goda: dokumental'nye ocherki* (Moscow: Nauka, 2001), doc. 133, vol. I, bk 1, pp. 270–8. French intelligence interpreted the connection between Georgian émigrés and German espionage in Iran as a means of promoting internal disturbances in the Soviet Union in order to detach the oil region of Azerbaizhan, initially uniting it to Turkey, but then, as in 1918, joining it to a government which would give the Germans economic control. *Ibid.*, appendix, "Captured Material," doc. 5, pp. 333–4.

Armenian party leaders denounced Beria's book, *The History of the Bolshevik Organization in the Transcaucasus*, as a blatant falsification. Beria's published reply attacked the party leadership and demanded their physical elimination. This sealed their doom. Veteran Bolsheviks like S. N. Martikian, hero of the Baku Commune and president of the Sovnarkom in Armenia, and A. Khandzhian, the First Secretary of the Party, both of whom had received the Order of Lenin less than six months earlier, were executed. After ten months of massive repressions Stalin sent a letter to the bureau of the Armenian Central Committee expressing dissatisfaction that the leadership was protecting enemies of the people and that certain executions had been "premature with the aim of preventing the unmasking of the remaining enemies who remained at large." A wave of arrests followed, which destroyed most of the top leaders of the party, government, armed forces and cultural establishment in the republic. The purge reached down to the local level where one-third of the secretaries of primary organizations and of party organizers were eliminated. Even after 1938 the process continued.[79]

The Azerbaizhan Party organization suffered greater losses than any other republican organization except for Georgia. In Azerbaizhan Beria took charge, entrusting the purge to M. D. Bagirov, who had also entered the secret police during the Civil War. Bagirov wiped out the entire leadership of the party, government, local military commanders and much of the older generation of the Azerbaizhan intelligentsia. From 1937 to 1938 over 10,000 officials were removed and presumably shot. Bagirov also denounced as "politically suspect" the entire émigré colony of Iranian Azerbaizhan, which had fled to Soviet Azerbaizhan after the collapse of the Ghilan Republic in Northwest Iran. These purges had a pronounced effect on the Soviet position in Northern Iran during and after World War II.[80] During the period of tension with France and Britain following the Nazi–Soviet Pact, Beria's reports emphasized the threat to the oil industry of Azerbaizhan of émigré diversionists directed by the French and penetrating Soviet territory across the Turkish and Iranian frontiers. He urged a thorough purge of the enterprise Azneft, especially the distilling plants, and the recruiting of additional agents to combat sabotage.[81]

[79] Ts. P. Agaiana (ed.), *Ocherki istorii kommunisticheskoi partii Armenii* (Erevan: Alestan, 1967), pp. 365–6; *Aktivnye bortsy za Sovetskuiu vlast v Azerbaizhan* (Baku: Azerbaizhanskoe gosudarstvennoe izd., 1957).

[80] M. S. Iskanderov, *Ocherki istorii kommunisticheskoi partii Azerbaidahzan* (Baku: Azerbaizhanskoe gosudarstvennoe izd., 1963), pp. 540–3, with extensive lists of purged leaders; Medvedev, *Let History Judge*, p. 344.

[81] *Nakanune*, doc. 41, vol. I, bk 1, pp. 94–5.

In the five republics of Soviet Central Asia the purges had no direct effect on foreign policy except in so far as they played a role in the evolution of Soviet nationality policy during the war. The party organizations in Central Asia were small, and the arrests so sharply reduced their numbers that in certain districts of Tadzhikistan, for example, only one to four members were left alive. As was the case throughout the national republics, the top leadership of the party and local soviets was destroyed. The Old Bolsheviks, who were even rarer here than elsewhere, were among the first to go. For several months in the winter of 1937–8, the Central Committee of the Turkmen Party ceased to exist. Recruiting new party members virtually came to a halt in this period. In Uzbekistan the First Secretary Akmal Ikramov, a Bolshevik since 1918 and member of the All-Union Central Executive Committee, perished with most of the Uzbek leaders of the party, soviet, Komsomol and main army units. Ikramov and his chief rival in the Uzbek organization, Faisullah Khadzhaev, a Bolshevik since the revolution and chairman of the Republic Narkom, were implicated in the trial against Bukharin as the leaders of a nationalist plot to work for an independent local economy and ultimately the secession of Uzbekistan under British protection. Kazakhstan passed through the greatest ordeal. In the late 1930s all members and candidates of the Central Committee Bureau were executed, along with most of the Central Committee itself, almost all the secretaries of the gorkom and raikom organizations in addition to many rank-and-file Communists. The Kazakh intelligentsia lost many of its leading figures. This was accompanied by rigid centralization in the administration and economic life of the republic which retarded recovery from the terrible losses inflicted on agriculture, primarily the herds, by collectivization.[82] The Tadzhik frontier was particularly vulnerable to penetration from Afghanistan, Iran and Turkey by kulaks and Basmachi. Stalin's troubleshooter, Andreev, recommended the transfer of Tadzhik army units to the European part of the Union to remove them from

---

[82] S. B. Baishev, *Ocherki istorii kommunisticheskoi partii Kazakhstana* (Alma Ata: Kazakhskoe gosudarstvennoe izd. 1963), pp. 376–7; Shamurad Tashiliev, *Ocherki istorii kommunisticheskoi partii Turkmenistana* (Ashkabad: Turkmenistanskoe gosudarstvennoe izd., 1965), pp. 494–6; Abdy Kair Kazakhaev *et al.* (eds.), *Ocherki istorii kommunisticheskoi partii Kirgizii* (Frunze, Kirgizstan: 1966), pp. 284–9; E. V. Vasil'ev *et al.* (eds.), *Ocherki istorii kommunisticheskoi partii Tadzhikistana* (Dushanbe: Institut ta"rikhi partiia, 1964), pp. 177–9; E. Iu. Iusupov *et al.* (eds.), *Ocherki istorii kommunisticheskoi partii Uzbekistana* (Tashkent: Izd. Uzbekistan,1964), pp. 373–7; *Report of Court Proceedings: The Case of the Anti-Soviet 'Bloc of Rights and Trotskyites'* (Moscow: People's Commissariat of Justice of the USSR, 1938), pp. 217–25, 348; *Sovetskoe rukovodstvo*, docs. 216, 217, 218, 219, pp. 372–5.

subversive influences.[83] Despite the fact that Russians in these organizations were not spared, the removal of the national cadres who had been
the founders of the local parties and ardent supporters of the Bolsheviks in the Civil War, when their cause was not popular among many of
the local populations, created widespread and deep bitterness among the
republics, which only surfaced after the denunciation of the Stalin cult.
Stalin's indiscriminant assault on the national parties weakened Soviet
influence in all the borderlands on the eve of a war that would test and
strain the bonds of the "great friendship."

Another shift

By early 1939, Stalin was concerned that the united front in Europe
along with its diplomatic twin – collective security – was running into
the sand. After five years of collective security Stalin once again speaking
ex cathedra at the Eighteenth Congress in March 1939 warned that the
second imperialist war had already begun, that it would lead to a new
economic crisis and an even broader struggle for markets. His speech
was set against a background of frustration at Soviet foreign policy and
the Popular Front over the intervening period. In Europe Nazi Germany
had rearmed, devoured Austria and Czechoslovakia; the Spanish Civil
War had been lost to the fascists. The Japanese had advanced deeply
into North and Central China. Under pressure, the Soviet Union had
sold to Japan its rights to the Chinese Eastern Railroad. The Japanese
had repeatedly violated Soviet territory. The outer perimeter of Soviet
security appeared increasingly vulnerable. The only bright spots in Inner
Asia were the stronger ties forged with Xinjiang and Outer Mongolia
and Red Army victories over the Japanese in 1938 at Changkufeng, and
then again at Nomonhan in 1939. But in the West throughout the period
Moscow's official ally in collective security, France, had proven again
and again to be a weak reed. From Britain the gusts of appeasement were
strongly felt in Moscow. The Popular Front had lost ground everywhere.
The danger of Soviet isolation was growing even as the pressure mounted
on its western and eastern frontiers.

Stalin's pronouncements on foreign policy at the Eighteenth Congress
were terse and formulaic. They barely filled eighteen of the seventy-five
printed pages in his report. He rehearsed, without enthusiasm, Soviet
efforts to secure peace through collective security. The League of Nations
had been virtually useless, but "the Soviet Union considers that in such
dangerous times, even such a weak organization as the League should not

---

[83] *Sovetskoe rukovodstvo*, docs. 221, 222, 223, pp. 377–9.

be ignored." He enumerated the Soviet treaties with France, Czechoslovakia, the Mongolian People's Republic and China without comment or
distinction as to their importance, but concluded that collective security was "in disarray." He singled out Germany, Italy and Japan as the
aggressor states, but warned that the "non-aggressor states," as he called
the Western democracies, were playing a dangerous game. Although they
were much stronger than the fascist governments, they had retreated from
their position of strength to a position of non-intervention (in Spain and
China) in order "to save their own skins." But this could only lead to a
wider conflict, to a world war. "Not to prevent the aggressors from doing
their dirty work as in China or still better in the Soviet Union... means
to weaken both and then when they are sufficiently weak to enter the
field with fresh forces in 'the interests of peace' and dictate their terms."
As an example of the Western "policy of provocation," Stalin evoked a
recurrent Soviet nightmare – the attempt to detach the Soviet Ukraine.
He denounced the Western press for having created a furor over Nazi
intentions to use the Sub-Carpatho Ukraine, which they acquired with
the occupation of all of Czechoslovakia, as a magnet for Ukrainian separatists. Stalin ridiculed the notion: "Perhaps the Germans have the crazy
idea of dreaming of uniting the elephant (the Soviet Ukraine) to the billy
goat (Sub-Carpatho Ukraine) but we will find enough strait jackets for
these madmen in our country."[84]

Expressing his disillusionment with collective security, Stalin con-
densed the aims of Soviet foreign policy in a set of characteristically
Stalinist incantations.

We stand for peace and strengthening of all business-like ties with all countries;
we stand and will stand on this position as long as these countries maintain
similar relations with the Soviet Union and do not try to damage the interests
of our country. We stand for peaceful, close and neighborly relations with all
neighboring countries having common frontiers with the USSR; we stand and
will stand for this position so long as those countries do not try to damage,
directly or indirectly, the interests of the safety and inviolability of the frontiers
of the Soviet Union.

Repeating the refrain again and again of the "inviolability of Soviet frontiers" Stalin insisted, too, that the Soviet Union would observe the greatest caution and "not be drawn into a conflict by provocateurs of war
who are accustomed to bank the fires with the hands of other peoples." He offered assurances that the Soviet Union would continue to
support people who were already victims of aggression and fighting for

---

[84] Stalin, *Works*, vol. I (14), pp. 328–40.

their independence. This clearly pertained not only to China but to any country which resisted the advance of the Germans or the Japanese in the borderlands neighboring the Soviet Union.[85]

Stalin's report to the Eighteenth Congress signaled that the policy of collective security was now fair game, even though Litvinov himself was not, at least not yet. Litvinov had never given up on collective security, even though he bitterly condemned the ruling circles of the Western powers for their shortsightedness and anti-Soviet attitudes. He, Ivan Maiskii and Jacob Surits kept reminding one another that the Chamberlains and Bonnets were prepared to go to virtually any lengths in order to appease Hitler and to turn him against the Soviet Union. But even after Munich, Litvinov could still state: "I believe, however, that they will reach the point where the peoples of England and France would have to stop them, for there is no other way to organize the peace. England and France will certainly come out of this greatly weakened, but even then the potential forces of peace will be superior to the potential forces of aggression." Not surprisingly then, Litvinov chose to interpret the spirit of Stalin's speech as a continuation of the policy of collective security against aggression particularly by reaching an agreement with Great Britain. He only acknowledged in passing that "the Soviet Union more than any other country is perfectly capable of looking after the defense of its frontier while it does not reject cooperation with other countries."[86] Under his stewardship Soviet foreign policy was still defensive and based on negotiations aimed at mutual advantage for the contracting parties rather than ultimatums, as the Nazis and later in different hands the Soviet leadership would adopt. Clearly, Litvinov did not believe that contradictions might arise between general agreements against aggression and specific strategic guarantees of Soviet borders. Yet this is precisely what happened, and this became the source of his downfall.

The western borderlands

During March and April 1939 a series of threats to Soviet security erupted along the complex frontiers that had long been the contested zones of contact between a Russian state, whether imperial or Soviet, and the external world. After a twenty-year lull, the German–Soviet contest over the Baltic littoral was heating up again. Following Hitler's successful tactics in dismembering Czechoslovakia, he sought to bring pressure on the Polish and Lithuanian governments by exploiting the question of the *Volksdeutsche* in the key ports of Danzig and Kleipeda. If successful, his

---

[85] *Ibid.*, p. 343.   [86] DVP, vol. XII, bk 1 (1939), doc. 157, pp. 210–11.

campaign would gain him strategic footholds from which to pursue an even more aggressive policy in the Baltic.

The Poles always represented a difficult problem for Hitler. He hardly mentioned them in *Mein Kampf*. Soon after coming to power he began to explore the possibility of winning over Poland to his plans for expansion to the east. These were renewed from time to time throughout the 1930s. In January 1935 Herman Göring on a visit to Poland came close to proposing an anti-Russian alliance and a joint attack on the Soviet Union. He suggested a partition of the Soviet borderlands, with Ukraine going to Poland.[87] At the same time, the Germans exerted pressure on Poland by stirring up trouble in Danzig. The Free City had been created by Paris Peace Conference, along with a land corridor in order to give Poland access to the Baltic. It was a time bomb waiting to explode.[88] Ninety-five percent of the population was German. The port was administered by a joint German–Polish commission and governed by an elective legislative body. Tensions between Danzig and the Polish government existed before the Nazis won legislative elections in 1933, but they intensified over the following years. From 1936 the city became a separate administrative district (*Gau*) in the Nazi party system and the *Gauleiter* who virtually ruled there was appointed by Hitler. After the destruction of Czechoslovakia, Hitler opened a campaign to gain strategic footholds in the Baltic. The Germans were reluctant to press the Poles too hard for fear of driving it into the arms of Great Britain. But they conducted a war of nerves against them.[89]

In January 1939 Hitler and the German Foreign Minister, Ribbentrop, made their last effort to draw the Poles into the Anti-Comintern Pact. He assured them of support "in every way" in dealing with the Ukrainian question as long as they exhibited a "more pronounced anti-Russian position."[90] When the Poles declined to make any firm commitments,

---

[87] *Polish White Book*, cited in Bohan B. Budurowycz, *Polish–Soviet Relations, 1932–1939* (New York: Columbia University Press, 1963), p. 67. See also pp. 87, 97–8 and 133–7.

[88] For the question of Danzig see, in general, Anna M. Cienciala, *Poland and the Western Powers, 1938–1939* (London: Routledge and Kegan Paul, 1968).

[89] Ribbentrop repeated the oft-stated German slogan: "Danzig was German – had always been German and would always remain German." Beck responded with a historical discourse of his own and dismissed the possibility of "an Anschluss," declaring that he "could never prevail upon the people to accept it." *Documents on German Foreign Policy*, series D, vol. V, doc. 81, p. 106.

[90] *Ibid.*, doc. 120, pp. 159–61. Ribbentrop continued his hectoring of the Polish Foreign Minister Józef Beck, mixing threats and promises and reiterating Germany's willingness to cooperate with Poland over a "Greater Ukraine." Beck made no secret of "Polish aspirations directed toward the Soviet Ukraine and a connection with the Black Sea" (sic!), but was in no hurry because the Soviet Union in his view would disintegrate by itself one day. *Ibid.*, doc. 126, pp. 167–8.

Hitler stepped up the pressure. In March Germany again demanded a return of Danzig as "a free city in the framework of the German Reich." Hitler was now determined to intimidate the Poles, recover the frontier of 1914 and resettle the Polish population of these regions.[91] Despite the British unilateral guarantee to Poland at the end of March, Hitler tightened the screws on Poland, denouncing the German–Polish non-aggression pact on April 28, while at the same time offering to trade part of Slovakia for control of Danzig. Hitler was still willing to bide his time on incorporating Danzig. But his policy had in fact shifted from cooperation with Poland to planning for a fourth partition of Poland with the Soviet Union as a prelude to the next step of dismembering the Soviet Union.[92]

In March, Ribbentrop brought to a head the crisis over the port of Klaipeda, like Danzig also created by the Peace Conference to give Lithuania a viable deep-water port on the Baltic. In the previous months German agents in the Baltic republics had stepped up their efforts to organize the German minority, including former landowners and White Guard officers from the days of the Russian Civil War in a campaign to regain confiscated lands. The center of this activity was a society of former officers of the *Freikorps* of von der Goltz and Bermondt-Avalov with branches in Estonia and Latvia. According to Soviet diplomats the aim was to "turn these countries not only into an economic base and springboard of German fascism in a war against the Soviet Union but also into a colony of fascist Germany which in their time Hindenburg with the help of von der Goltz and Belmondt-Avalov attempted to establish."[93] Following the tactics used in the Sudetenland, Ribbentrop brought pressure on the Lithuanians to cease their attempts to "lithuanianize" the Germans in Klaipeda and to allow the free development of National Socialist ideas. The Lithuanian government met the main Nazi demand

---

[91] *Ibid.*, vol. VI, doc. 99, p. 125.

[92] In August 1939 Hitler told the League of Nations' High Commissioner in Danzig, the distinguished historian Carl J. Burckhardt, "Everything that I undertake is directed against Russia. If those in the West are too stupid and blind and too liberal to understand this, then I shall be forced to come to an understanding with the Russians to beat the West and then after its defeat, turn with all my concerted forces against the Soviet Union. I need Ukraine, so that no one will starve us out as they did in the last war." Carl Burckhardt, *Danziger Mission*, p. 348, as quoted in Klaus Hildebrand, *The Foreign Policy of the Third Reich* (Berkeley: University of California Press, 1973), p. 88.

[93] DVP, vol. XXII, pt 1 (1939), doc. 112, pp. 157–8. Potemkin instructed the Soviet representatives in the three republics to remind their governments of these historic events and the role of the Soviet Union in strengthening their independence and economic viability. Meanwhile, the economically important Jewish population of Klaipeda, under the shadow of growing anti-Semitism within the government, was selling out and leaving. *Ibid.*, doc. 97, p. 142.

to abolish its twelve-year-old martial law. By creating a new mass organization, the Cultural Union of Klaipeda, Germans signaled in effect the legalization of the Nazi Party in Lithuania. They went on to win the local elections and then exerted their political influence to bring about changes in the central Lithuanian government.[94] According to a high official in the Eastern Section of the German Foreign Ministry, the object of German pressure was to achieve the neutrality of the Baltic Republics which, in the event of war with the Soviet Union, would prove as important as the neutrality of Belgium and Holland on a western front. When followed up by non-aggression pacts with Germany, neutrality would block the automatic triggering of the mutual assistance treaties with the Soviet Union.[95]

The Nazi campaign of intimidation culminated with Ribbentrop's ultimatum on March 20, 1939 demanding the transfer of Klaipeda to Germany and threatening to occupy the rest of Lithuania in case of a refusal. The capitulation of the Lithuanians encouraged the more than 40,000 Germans throughout the country to mobilize politically. They joined forces with the supporters of Voldemar Augustinas to press for a German orientation of Lithuanian foreign policy.[96] Augustinas was the leader of an extreme right-wing organization first created by the German military command in 1917, and one of the organizers of the coup of 1926 which brought him to power first as premier and then as Foreign Minister. The German occupation rapidly turned the city into an armed camp.[97]

While the Lithuanians gave in, the Poles did not. Perhaps they recalled the remark of Frederick II (the Great) in 1772: "He who holds Danzig holds Poland."[98] Hitler had been willing to work with the Poles if they had been willing to cede Danzig, provide extra-territorial lines of communication across the Corridor and join the Anti-Comintern Pact, even though he was meeting opposition within his own Foreign Ministry, the military, and even strong currents of public opinion. According to social democratic exiles in 1939, "an action against Poland would be greeted by the overwhelming mass of the German people. The Poles are enormously hated among the masses for what they did at the end of the

---

[94] *Organy gosudarstvennoi bezopasnosti SSSR v Velikoi Otechestvennoi Voine. Sbornik Dokumentov*, 2 vols. *Nakanune (noiabr' 1938 g.–dekabr' 1940 g.)* (Moscow: A/O Kniga i biznes, 1995), doc. 2, vol. I, bk 1, pp. 9–12.

[95] V. G. Komplektov (ed.), *Polpredy soobshchaiut . . . Sbornik dokumentov ob otnosheniiakh SSSR s Latvei, Litvoi i Estonnei. Avgust 1939–avgust 1940 gg.* (Moscow: Mezhdunarodnye otnosheniia, 1990), p. 20.

[96] *Ibid.* See also Geoffrey Roberts, "Soviet Policy and the Baltic States, 1939–1940: A Reappraisal," *Diplomacy and Statecraft* 6:3 (1995), pp. 678–84.

[97] DVP, vol. XXII, pt 1 (1939), docs. 159 and 193, pp. 212–14 and 245–6.

[98] Quoted in Raymond Leslie Buell, *Poland, Key to Europe*, 3rd edn (New York: Alfred A. Knopf, 1939), p. 358.

war."[99] Once the Poles defied him, however, Hitler turned on them with fury. When Great Britain, followed by France, gave a unilateral guarantee to Poland in March, seeking to head off further Nazi aggression, he was forced to reconsider his options. Although he was not fully convinced that the Western allies were seriously committed to defending Poland, given their recent performance at Munich, he decided to take the precaution of settling with the Soviet Union as the best guarantee of avoiding a two-front war. This meant radically reversing his policy toward Poland and moving to destroy it.

That Hitler may already have been considering this possibility before the last Polish rejection of his proposals to cooperate is suggested by the post-Munich disposition of the Czechoslovak region of the Carpatho-Ukraine. It was a quintessential borderland with a mixed ethnic population, mainly illiterate and poor peasants living in scattered villages. Nonetheless, it possessed disproportionately great strategic and political significance.[100] Formerly part of the Hungarian Kingdom, it had been awarded to Czechoslovakia by the peace settlement and promised, but not granted, autonomy until the crisis of 1938. Hard on the heels of the German occupation of the Sudetenland, the Hungarian government presented its demands to Prague for the cession of the districts of Slovakia with Hungarian majorities and the Carpatho-Ukraine. Budapest then requested Germany, Italy and Poland to serve as arbiters in the negotiations. Germany vetoed Polish participation. In November 1938, in accord with Mussolini, Hitler awarded Hungary the southern districts of Slovakia and the southwestern districts of Carpatho-Ukraine, including the provincial capital of Uzhgorod. The autonomous Sub-Carpathian government shifted its capital to Khust and began to consolidate its administrative autonomy. The Germans made a few gestures toward supporting the government, touching off speculation in Western Europe

---

[99] Ian Kershaw. *Hitler: Hubris 1889–1936* (New York: W.W. Norton, 1999), pp. 441–2, and Kershaw, *Hitler: Nemesis*, pp. 43, 201 and 237. Woodruff, *The Ideological Origins*, pp. 21–8 and 83–111, calls these two aspects of *Lebensraum* "migrationist colonialism," deeply rooted in the nineteenth century, and "economic imperialism," a later development.

[100] Paul Robert Magocsi, *The Shaping of a National Identity: Subcarpathian Rus' 1848–1948* (Cambridge, MA: Harvard University Press, 1978), pp. 9–20. The census of 1930 recorded 63 percent Rusyns (speakers of various Ukrainian dialects whose identities were strongly shaped by other national groups in the region), 15.4 percent Magyars, 12.8 percent Jews, 2.9 percent Czechs, and less than 2 percent Germans and Slovaks, with a scattering of Romanians, Gypsies and Poles. *Ibid.*, p. 13. Cf. Albert S. Kotowski, "Ukraine Piedmont? Die Karpaterukraine an Vorabend des Zweiten Weltkrieges," *Jahrbücher für Geschichte Osteuropas* 49:1 (2001), pp. 67–95, who argues that the region was not a serious problem in European power politics, although he acknowledges that Germany's main aim was to manipulate the question in the diplomatic game against Poland, Hungary and the USSR.

Map 5.1 Hungary, 1918–44

that Hitler might use the province as a "piedmont" to create a unified Ukraine. At the same time, Ukrainian nationalists in Polish Galicia led by the Greek Catholic Metropolitan of Lvov, Andrii Sheptyts'kyi, who would later play an important role during Hitler's occupation of Ukraine in 1941–2, entertained great hopes for the Sub-Carpathian government as the first "Ukrainian" land to gain its freedom in Europe. Volunteers poured in from across the Polish frontier to join the Carpathian armed forces. Recalling memories of the First World War, they called themselves the Sich Riflemen. Pro-Ukrainian disorders broke out in Lvov. The Polish government, ruling over a minority of 6 million Ukrainians eager to gain their own autonomy, was not pleased, concerned that the autonomous Sub-Carpathian government would fall under German influence and "endanger Poland's strategic position."[101]

However, on March 14 Germany disclaimed any intention of acting against the Soviet Union in Ukraine and agreed to allow Hungary to annex the remainder of Carpatho-Ukraine (the Second Vienna Award). This gave Hungary and Poland a common frontier. Perhaps more

[101] The Poles favored and supported the Hungarian claims, which would establish a common frontier between Poland and Hungary, destroy a bridgehead for Soviet influence and be "the equivalent to the annihilation of Ukrainian nationality" in the region. DGFP, series D, vol. V, docs. 67, 76 and 81, pp. 90–1, 98–100 and 105–6.

importantly the award may have led Warsaw and Moscow to believe, mistakenly as it turned out, that Germany had given up its Ukrainian ambitions.[102] Thus did Hitler, like Stalin, advance through a smoke-screen of deception toward the conclusion of the Nazi–Soviet Pact.

Litvinov reacted to the German moves by unleashing a whirlwind of diplomatic activity that only ended the day of his dismissal on May 3. His aim was to conclude a pact of mutual aid and non-aggression with Great Britain and France and at the same time strengthen the security of Soviet borders through negotiation with neighboring states. The Soviet campaign, approved by Stalin but orchestrated by Litvinov and his closest associates, sought to gain three objectives in the negotiations with Finland, Estonia, Latvia and Lithuania: first, to strengthen collective security by forging closer economic and political ties with all the states in the Baltic littoral; second to prevent Germany from gaining a preponderant influence through a combination of internal subversion and external pressure; and, third, to improve the defenses of the approaches by sea to Leningrad.

In February the Soviet Union completed negotiations with Poland for a commercial treaty based on the most favorable nation clause. An attempt to duplicate this success with Finland failed in early March when the Finns refused to increase their imports of Soviet goods. On March 28 Litvinov sent identical notes to Estonia, Latvia and Lithuania warning that any agreement whether voluntary or concluded under external pressure, which diminished or limited their sovereignty and independence or led to the political or economic hegemony of a third state or the concession of exclusive rights and privileges within its territory or its ports would be viewed by the Soviet government as unacceptable, incompatible and even in violation of treaties and agreements regulating relations with the Soviet Union "with all the ensuing consequences."[103] These warning were buttressed by strong reminders of the fate of Czechoslovakia as a consequence of caving in to Hitler's demands for the protection of the *volksdeutsch* minority.[104]

At the same time, Litvinov also began the long, torturous process of negotiations with Finland to strengthen the Soviet strategic position in the Baltic which only ended with the outbreak of the Soviet–Finnish War. For Moscow, the first storm warnings came when the Finns rejected Litvinov's proposal to lease for thirty years four islands in the Gulf of

---

[102] DVP, vol. XII, pt 1 (1939), docs. 138, and 145, pp. 185 and 195. This was not the way Litvinov, who was more concerned with the creation of an independent Slovakia, chose to interpret it.
[103] *Ibid.*, doc. 180, p. 231.   [104] *Ibid.*, docs. 181, 182, pp. 232–3.

Finland, guarding the approaches to Leningrad.[105] Litvinov then appointed his close collaborator, Boris Shtein *polpred* in Rome, who had served for two years in Helsinki, to conduct negotiations over the exchange of territory that would give Finland large stretches of heavily forested areas in northern Soviet Karelia in return for the islands. These negotiations were further complicated by a previous request from Sweden and Finland to the League to militarize the Aaland Islands. Litvinov replied that this raised serious security issues for the Soviet Union. There was a danger that pro-German elements in Finland in cooperation with Germany could put pressure on the Finnish government to gain control over the islands once they were fortified in order to launch "some kind of adventure." The Soviet Union would require guarantees in the event of militarization that could only be obtained through an improvement of relations with Finland. But negotiations with Finland over the exchange of territory had reached an impasse. In a note to Stalin, Litvinov held out hopes for a change in the Finnish government after elections, and proposed a compromise formula for accepting the militarization of the Aaland Islands on condition of an iron-clad guarantee that the islands would not be put at the disposal of a third power under any circumstances.[106] But he had no time to follow up.

On the Danubian frontier the Soviet position was also eroding. On March 23 Romania concluded an agreement with Germany on strengthening their economic relations that closely tied Romania to the German economy. The country was obliged to develop its agricultural, timbering and wood-working enterprises to meet the demands of the German market and to create joint stock companies for the exploitation of Romanian oil, manganese, copper, bauxite and other mineral resources. In exchange, Germany was to supply Romania with arms, military equipment and machinery for military and mining industries; and to improve Romania's transportation and communication infrastructure. The method of accounting was to be based on the German financial policy of clearing. A secret protocol obliged the Romanian government to assist and encourage by all means possible the production and refining of oil. Additional economic agreements further expanded German commercial activities in Romania.[107] These also raised alarm signals in Moscow.

---

[105] *Ibid.*, doc. 119, p. 163 and *ibid.*, bk 2, note 65, p. 526. According to Litvinov, the Soviet Union had no intention of fortifying the islands, but merely using them as observation posts. The Finnish refusal was based on questions of sovereignty and the presence of a large Finnish population. Litvinov offered to help resettle them in Finland.

[106] *Ibid.*, doc. 239, pp. 297–9.

[107] *Ibid.*, doc. 173, pp. 226–7 and note 86, pp. 537–8; DGFP, series D, vol. VI, doc. 78, pp. 91–6.

In seeking to apply the principle of collective security specifically to a defense of the western borderlands, Litvinov responded to a French initiative by outlining the basis for a five- to ten-year mutual assistance pact between the Soviet Union, France and Great Britain. His draft obliged the three powers "to render all manner of assistance including that of a military nature to the East European governments situated between the Baltic and Black Seas and bordering on the USSR in case of aggression against these states." He insisted, however, that Britain's guarantee to Poland should be limited exclusively to aggression by Germany. The three powers were to recognize the necessity of negotiating a separate agreement with Turkey on mutual assistance.[108]

Neither Great Britain nor the states on the Soviet western borders – Finland, Estonia, Latvia, Poland and Romania – were ready to enter into an alliance that included the Soviet Union. Repeated efforts by the Soviet government in April and May 1939 to offer assistance to the Polish government in case of German aggression were turned down.[109] Two days after Litvinov's proposals the British cabinet discussed and rejected them and advised France to do the same.[110] The Soviet gambit not only failed but appeared to have backfired. Shortly after Litvinov's dismissal, the Estonians and Latvians signed non-aggression pacts with Germany. Sounding a new hostile note toward Moscow, the Estonian press warned of the dangers of accepting Soviet aid against German aggression as the prelude to the penetration of Bolshevism.[111]

After the Eighteenth Congress, the Foreign Commissar saw signs all around him that his influence was diminishing. Appointments were made to the commissariat without Litvinov's approval. He began to realize that not all Soviet ambassadors were reporting directly to him. Many of them were sending their dispatches to Molotov or meeting with Stalin and Molotov in the Kremlin. Stalin manipulated personal rivalries among Litvinov's associates. Molotov and Zhdanov were leading the public attack against collective security, linking it to the Commissariat of Foreign Affairs, though they still paid tribute to Litvinov. Litvinov drafted a letter of resignation He wrestled with his conscience and finally did not submit it. Maiskii, an eyewitness, reported the final personal confrontation with

---

[108] DVP, vol. 00, doc. 229, pp. 283–4.
[109] DVP, vol. XII, bk 1 (1939), docs. 293, 298, 306, pp. 352, 356–7, 367–8.
[110] According to the unpublished minutes of the Cabinet Committee on Foreign Policy, dominated by figures hostile to the Soviet Union, Poland and probably Romania would oppose such a pact and practically speaking the Soviet proposals "could only raise suspicions among our friends and strengthen the hostility of our enemies." The final decision of the cabinet was to keep the negotiations alive but secret. DVP, vol. XXII, bk 2, note 101, pp. 541–2. This attitude hardly changed throughout the Anglo-French–Soviet negotiations.
[111] DVP, vol. XXII, bk 1 (1939), doc. 291, p. 350.

Stalin and Molotov. While Stalin remained calm, "Molotov was violent, flew at Litvinov and accused him of all the mortal sins." A week later NKVD troops surrounded the commissariat. Molotov, Malenkov and Beria arrived and announced to Litvinov that he had been dismissed.[112] Stalin informed the top officials of the Foreign Commissariat that Litvinov had resigned as the result of "a serious conflict" between him and Molotov, "arising from a disloyal attitude of Litvinov toward the Council of People's Commissars."[113]

With the dismissal of Litvinov and his replacement by Molotov, Soviet policy shifted emphasis to a more exclusively territorial base to which collective security was held hostage. The shift had already been foreshadowed by a speech of Andrei Zhdanov, chair of the Commission for Foreign Affairs of the Supreme Soviet. Zhdanov claimed that the delegates should only be interested in the immediate neighbors of the Soviet Union whose borders divided peoples of the same nationality.[114] Yet the shift did not mean an absolute repudiation of collective security until the actual signature of the Nazi–Soviet Pact. Negotiations on a mutual assistance pact between the Soviet Union, Britain and France, based on Litvinov's original proposals in May, continued throughout the summer of 1939.

At the same time, Soviet diplomats were conducting on and off negotiations with Germany on a commercial-credit treaty. Historians have differed over the political significance of the Soviet–German contacts. Those relying mainly on the German documents give greater credence to the view that the Soviet leaders were strongly inclined to reach a political agreement as well. By and large, this interpretation reflects the position of the German ambassador, Schulenburg, who was actively working for a rapprochement with Moscow.[115] The publication of the Soviet documents on the events leading up to the pact reinforce the argument that Stalin and Molotov were not only keeping their options open but were more reluctant than is generally believed to reach an accord with Hitler. The initiative for concluding a pact clearly came from Ribbentrop. As late

[112] Sheinis, *Litvinov*, pp. 360–3, Dullin, *Men of Influence*, pp. 230–1.
[113] DVP, vol. XXII, bk 1 (1939), doc. 269, p. 327. But Beria was preparing a more sinister case against Litvinov and his associate Boris Stein when the outbreak of war saved them. Zinovii Sheinis, "Sud'ba diplomata: Shtrikhi k Portretu Borisa Shteina," in *Arkhivy raskryvaiut tainy... Mezhdunarodnye voprosy: sobytie i liudi* (Moscow: Izd polit. literatury, 1991), pp. 304–6.
[114] Dullin, *Men of Influence*, p. 236.
[115] Tucker, *Stalin in Power*, pp. 233–7 and 348–50; Gerhard Weinberg, *The Foreign Policy of Hitler's Germany*, 2 vols. (University of Chicago Press, 1980), vol. I: *Starting World War II, 1937–1939*, pp. 604–5; Alan Bullock, *Hitler and Stalin: Parallel Lives* (London: HarperCollins, 1991), p. 237.

as July 26 the Soviet chargé in Berlin, Georgii Astakov, restated Moscow's view that the commercial-credit negotiations with Germany did not in any way contradict the negotiations with Britain and France and ought not to be considered by the Germans as a form of competition.[116] On August 2 Ribbentrop informed Astakov, famously, that "on all problems relating to the territory between the Black and Baltic Seas, we can agree without difficulty." Ribbentrop expressed satisfaction that the national principle was growing stronger in the Soviet Union at the expense of the international, making it easier to establish good relations.[117]

Reporting to Molotov, Astakov reviewed the German initiatives. He concluded that the Germans wished to give the impression that they were ready to declare their disinterest in the fate of the Baltic states, except for Lithuania, Bessarabia, and "Russian Poland," while denying any aspirations in Ukraine. In exchange they would expect Soviet disinterest in the fate of Danzig, the former provinces of "German Poland" with some additional territory up to the Warta or even the Vistula Rivers, and, for purposes of discussion, Western Galicia. All this would depend, he added, on the failure of the Anglo-French–Soviet military–political negotiations. Astakov shrewdly concluded that the Germans' aim in the short run would be "to neutralize us in case of war with Poland," and that their long-term commitment to such arrangements could not be guaranteed.[118] In effect, he correctly anticipated the main territorial provisions of the Nazi–Soviet Pact and foresaw its brief life span.

As the German plans for war with Poland took concrete shape and the Anglo-French delegation in Moscow continued their negotiations, the Germans pressed harder for an agreement, proposing that Ribbentrop visit Moscow. But Molotov was not to be hurried. He wanted concrete proposals. When he got them he answered by berating the Nazi government for its consistent anti-Soviet position; he then declared that the Soviet policy of "peaceful co-existence of various political systems" and its lack of aggressive intentions toward Germany provided a basis for improving relations. But he did not respond directly to the German proposals on a joint guarantee of the Baltic states. He stated that the first step on that path would be the signing of the trade agreement and the second the conclusion of a non-aggression pact or a renewal of the 1926 neutrality agreement with a protocol dealing with other questions

[116] DVP, vol. XXII, bk 1 (1939), doc. 431, p. 549.
[117] Ibid., doc. 445, pp. 566–9; A week earlier an official of the economics section of the German Foreign Ministry had already set the tone for this conversation. Ibid., doc. 434, pp. 554–6.
[118] Ibid., doc. 455, pp. 585–7.

of foreign policy.[119] The Germans made it clear that the urgency with which they were pressing for an agreement meant an attack on Poland was imminent. According to Schulenburg, "Hitler was ready to take into account everything that the USSR desired." Stalin now held all the cards.

Meanwhile, the August negotiations with Britain and France on a mutual assistance pact had run into difficulties. Molotov insisted upon resolving two issues. First, he demanded a joint guarantee against German aggression, direct or indirect, in the Baltic states; second, he insisted on obtaining transit rights for the Red Army across Polish and Romanian frontiers in the event of German aggression. The assumptions underlying these demands were twofold. The Soviet leaders were fearful that Hitler might subvert or entice the Baltic states into opening the gates to the German Army without a war and that Poland and Romania might prefer to join Hitler if pressured or persuaded rather than fight Germany as a Soviet ally. Soviet intelligence was providing ample evidence to support these fears.

Information had been reaching Molotov and Stalin since May 1939 about increased German political activity in Lithuania, the rise of anti-Soviet sentiment in the Estonian press and the danger of a German attack through the Baltic states.[120] After Estonia signed a non-aggression pact with Germany, Molotov insisted that Estonia reconsider its position and place itself under Soviet protection: "Estonia could not count on anyone rendering her assistance against aggression and on a scale she might wish unless Estonia took the appropriate advanced steps."[121] But the Baltic states were paralyzed by the fear that a guarantee against aggression by the Soviet Union could be used to undermine their independence through a combination of internal subversion and the intervention by the Red Army. In addition, Lithuania was concerned that a Soviet guarantee would give an excuse to Poland to announce an analogous guarantee, seriously compromising Lithuania's relations with Germany.[122]

At the first meeting of the military negotiations in Moscow between France, Britain and the USSR, Marshal Voroshilov, the head of the Soviet delegation, restated the Soviet position: unless the Anglo-French obtained permission for Soviet forces to cross into the territory of Poland and Romania in the event of German aggression then "the whole present attempt to conclude a military convention is doomed to failure."[123] The

[119] Ibid., docs. 469, 470 and 474, pp. 609–11, 615–17.
[120] Ibid., docs. 291, 358, 375, 394, 414, pp. 350, 442, 478–82, 505–7, 529.
[121] Soviet Peace Efforts on the Eve of World War II (Moscow: Novosti Press, 1971), p. 363.
[122] DVP, vol. XXII, bk 1 (1939), doc. 429, pp. 545–6.
[123] Soviet Peace Efforts, p. 495. He was following the instructions given to him by Molotov and Stalin. DVP, vol. XXII, bk 1 (1939), doc. 453, p. 584. Marshall Shaposhnikov had

Soviet representatives also insisted that a military convention precede a political settlement, reflecting once again their suspicion that the British and the French were not serious about the alliance, but only using the negotiations to bring Hitler to the conference table over Poland the way they had over Czechoslovakia.[124] But this demand aroused Chamberlain's suspicions that acceding to the Soviet view would open the way for Soviet penetration into all Eastern Europe.[125] The French military representatives supported the Soviet position, concluding that it was strategically sound. But diplomatic efforts failed to shake the uncompromising opposition of Poland and Romania to granting transit rights for the Red Army.[126] The French stand was further weakened by the unwillingness of the British to join them in exerting pressure.[127] The Germans had no scruples about reaching a territorial settlement with the Soviet Union that would meet all Molotov's demands in the Baltic states, Poland and Romania.[128]

The Nazi–Soviet Pact abruptly, if only briefly, interrupted Stalin's policy of advancing Soviet aims in the western borderlands in accord with the West; after the German invasion in 1941 he immediately renewed these efforts with greater success. The main objectives of Soviet foreign policy

prepared a general outline of the number and disposition of the military forces of the Soviet Union, France and Britain in the event of war based on five situational variations of an attack on one of them or on Poland and Romania. Here, too, Shaposhnikov stressed that Soviet participation in any war against Germany was only possible if the Red Army was given free passage through Poland, Lithuania and Romania. *Ibid.*, doc. 447, pp. 573–8.

[124] Even Maiskii believed that the ruling elite in Britain, with Chamberlain in the forefront, favored a deal with Hitler. But he concluded in a burst of optimism. Inspired by a Marxian metaphor, he predicted that the subjective factor would be overcome by the objective interests of the Germans and the British, which were diametrically opposed. Then Chamberlain, in a supremely ironic twist of history, would be the builder of an Anglo-British bloc against Germany. There was only one hitch, he added, "The picture would change radically if and when in the order of the day the problem of a proletarian revolution would arise outside the borders of the USSR." *Ibid.*, doc. 452, pp. 582–3.

[125] Haslam, *The Soviet Union*, p. 224.

[126] Hugh Ragsdale, "The Soviet Position at Munich Reappraised: The Romanian Enigma," in Marsha Siefert (ed.), *Extending the Borders of Russian History* (Budapest: CEU Press, 2003), pp. 35–72, has established that at the time of Munich the Romanian Army favored facilitating the transfer of Red Army units through Romania to assist the Czechs, but King Carol vetoed the plan. By 1939 there was no longer any chance of Romanian concessions to Moscow.

[127] *Soviet Peace Efforts*, pp. 507, 546, 547–9.

[128] There are numerous treatments of the Nazi–Soviet negotiations leading to the pact. See especially Haslam, *The Soviet Union*, ch. 10; Gabriel Gorodtetsky, "The Impact of the Ribbentrop–Molotov Pact on the Course of Soviet Foreign Policy," *Cahiers du Monde russe et soviétique* 31 (1990), pp. 27–42; M. I. Semiriaga, *Tainy stalinskoi diplomatii 1939–1941* (Moscow: Vyshaia shkola, 1992); and Geoffrey Roberts, *Stalin's Wars: From World War to Cold War, 1939–1953* (New Haven, CT: Yale University Press, 2006), ch. 2.

from August 1939 to June 1941 consisted in increasing Soviet influence and then imposing control over the borderlands all along the periphery. It soon became all too clear that the Soviet Union had no more intention of joining Germany, Japan and Italy in a great anti-British coalition than it had of joining Britain and France in a great anti-German coalition.

The secret protocol of the Nazi–Soviet Pact that defined respective spheres of influence in Eastern Europe was brief and dangerously vague. Provisions were made for the partition of Poland. But the dividing line was more precise in the Baltic – the northern boundary of Lithuania – as opposed to the Black Sea area. The Soviet side expressed its interest in Bessarabia and the German side merely announced its "complete political disinterestedness in these areas" of southeastern Europe.[129] Over the next ten months, the Soviet Union moved rapidly to incorporate most of the areas in its sphere into the USSR, and then to increase its demands. The Germans were annoyed at first and then alarmed.

The Nazi invasion of Poland cast the first small shadow over the implementation of the pact. On the second day the German Foreign Minister Ribbentrop urged the Soviet Union to move "at the proper time" to occupy its sphere, admitting that: "this would be a relief to us."[130] A few days later his request became "urgent." But the Soviet leaders were not to be hurried. They also wanted a legitimate excuse. Stalin expressed contradictory views on his motivations for occupying the borderlands assigned to the Soviet Union by the pact with Hitler. In the privacy of his office, he told Dimitrov, Zhdanov, Manuilskii and Molotov that the situation offered an opportunity to advance the revolution. "The annihilation of [Poland] would mean one less bourgeois fascist state to contend with. What harm would result from the rout of Poland if we were to extend the socialist system to new territories and populations?"[131] Were these his genuine convictions concealed behind subsequent public statements that stressed the theme of national unification of Ukrainians and Belorussians? Or, more in line with the interpretation of Stalin as a man of the borderlands, was this not further evidence that Stalin's concept of the state combined the idea of socialism in one country with unification of its national components?

In negotiating a public statement with the Germans justifying Soviet intervention in Poland, Molotov's first draft declared that Poland was falling apart and it was necessary for the Soviet Union to come to the aid

---

[129] Raymond J. Sontag and James S. Beddie (eds.), *Nazi–Soviet Relations, 1939–1941: Documents from the Archives of the German Foreign Office* (Washington, DC: Department of State, 1948), p. 78.

[130] *Ibid.*, pp. 86, 90.

[131] Banac, *The Diary of Georgi Dimitrov*, entry for September 7, 1939, pp. 115–16.

of the Ukrainians and Belorussians "threatened" by the Germans.[132] The Germans were appalled. After some wrangling the two parties agreed on a joint communiqué that omitted the offending word: "In view of the internal incapacity of the Polish State and of the dissention of the population living in its former territory," the two powers invoked the necessity of bringing about "a new order by the creation of natural frontiers and viable economic organizations."[133]

Although the Nazi–Soviet Pact shocked the West and many in the Communist world, the apparent reversal of fronts may be interpreted as a continuation of Stalin's borderland thesis, especially when taken together with the Treaty of Neutrality with Japan which would follow. As Stalin and Molotov repeatedly pointed out to the German and Japanese ambassadors in Moscow, their new-found relations secured their rear and enabled them to turn the full force of their expansion to the west and south respectively. What they did not say was that this strategy also deflected the Germans and Japanese from expanding further in the borderlands adjacent to the Soviet Union. Like Stalin's policy in Spain and China in the mid-1930s, his aim was to keep the flank powers engaged far distant from the Soviet frontiers. At the same time, he carried out deportations and purges in the Soviet republics which to his suspicious mind could only strengthen the defense of the frontiers. In the short term his strategy worked well; too well in the west as it turned out, because France was defeated quickly and Hitler could once again turn east, his primary destination. It worked better in the case of Japan, as we shall see. It enabled the militarists to turn away from the Manchurian–Mongolian borderlands, where the Red Army had given them a sound thrashing, to the south. There they could expect to benefit from the German defeat of the colonial powers, France and the Netherlands, and challenge the weakened British and the United States. Questions remained. How much time could Stalin win? How could he continue to rely on the demoralized Communist parties faced with German occupation? How could he hold together the deeply divided anti-Japanese forces in China and continue his support for their struggle against Japan?

---

[132] This feeble justification was powerfully refuted by post-Soviet Russian historians. See, for example, N. S. Lebedeva, "Chetvertyi razdel Pol'shi i katynskaia tragediia," in Iu N. Afanas'ev (ed.), *Drugaia voina, 1939–1945* (Moscow: Rossiiskii gosudarstvennyi gumanitarnyi universitet, 1996), pp. 248–50.

[133] Sontag and Beddie, *Nazi–Soviet Relations*, pp. 91, 100.

6   Borderlands on the eve

In the brief hiatus between the Nazi–Soviet Pact and the German invasion of the Soviet Union, Stalin scrambled to consolidate his hold over his recently acquired borderlands and to advance additional demands for strong points along the periphery of the USSR.[1] Contrary to his intentions, the consequences were disastrous. His brutal treatment of the populations in the newly acquired borderlands provoked hostility to Soviet power and increased social instability. His utter lack of sensitivity to the reaction of the powers, both Axis and Western, brought him to the brink of war with France and Britain over Finland and possibly even accelerated the Nazi attack. It was very much the style of a Commissar of Nationalities. Subjugating and integrating the borderlands was for him the best guarantee of state security. The opinion of the outer world counted for very little.

If Stalin had long been preparing an accommodation with Hitler, his actions after August 1939 gave no evidence of having used the time well. Plans for the partition of Poland had been drawn up hastily. Stalin quickly had second thoughts about incorporating large numbers of Poles into the Soviet sphere. The agreement over Poland had to be renegotiated almost at once. Stalin's advance into the other territories in his sphere was marked by confusion, haste and enormous errors of judgment. He had not even taken the trouble to prepare the ground politically. On the contrary, he had made his task of absorbing the borderlands more difficult for himself. In the case of the Baltic states, Western Belorussia and Western Ukraine he had only recently decimated the ranks of local Communist parties. In the case of Finland he improvised a political solution that proved to be a complete fiasco.

---

[1] The most detailed analysis of this disputed period is Gabriel Gorodetsky, *Grand Delusion: Stalin and the German Invasion of Russia* (New Haven, CT: Yale University Press, 1999). My interpretation accepts his view that Stalin lacked a "blueprint," but seeks to modify his statement that "Soviet policy remained essentially one of Realpolitik" (p. 7) by introducing the ideological and cultural dimensions of Stalin's borderland thesis.

The Baltic and Danubian frontiers

Shortly after the collapse of Poland, Stalin belatedly decided that it would be preferable to turn over all of the heavily ethnic Polish provinces to Hitler's tender mercies in exchange for Lithuania. The original demarcation of spheres had divided Warsaw in half. The revised German–Soviet Boundary Treaty of September 28, 1939 brought the Soviet frontier back to the Bug River. It left in Soviet hands the prewar districts of Eastern Poland where the Poles were in a distinct minority, constituting about a third of the population.[2] For centuries the area had been a frontier zone where Poles and Russians had contended for political and cultural hegemony while the local population had displayed wavering loyalties.

Belorussians, Ukrainians, Jews and "locals" whose national consciousness was so underdeveloped that they used no other term to identify themselves took advantage of the collapse of Polish authority to take revenge on their most recent oppressors. Polish army units retreating from the Germans were ambushed by Ukrainian bands. The Ukrainians also turned against the Jewish population which began to arm in self-defense. The embattled Polish settlers in the *kresy* formed a Civil Guard to protect themselves. Before the Red Army arrived on the scene, incipient civil war had broken out. Initially, the Jews extended the most enthusiastic welcome to the Soviet troops. They had suffered from Polish anti-Semitism; Ukrainian marauders offered no relief and stories of Nazi atrocities in occupied Polish territory began to filter in. The Ukrainians and Poles had the most to lose. By the end of 1939 about 30,000 Ukrainians sought refuge in the Nazi-run General Government while another 10,000 were repatriated to the West by German intelligence units who falsified their "racial" origin.[3] Among those left behind, the Ukrainian nationalist organization OUN exchanged gunfire with Red Army units but then directed its members to infiltrate the local government organizations that the Soviet authorities were beginning to form.

---

[2] DGFP, series D, vol. VIII, docs 90, 104, 109, 131, pp. 92, 105, 109, 130; *Pravda*, September 28, 1939.

[3] Jan T. Gross, *Revolution from Abroad: The Soviet Conquest of Poland, Western Ukraine and Western Belorussia* (Princeton University Press, 1988), ch. 1. Wiktor Sukiennicki, "The Establishment of the Soviet Regime in Eastern Poland in 1939," *Journal of Central European Affairs* 23 (1963), pp. 191–218. B. M. Babii, *Vozz'ednannya zakhidnoe Ukraini z Ukrains'koiu RSR* (Kiev: Vid-vo AN URSR, 1954), p. 63. As late as the end of 1940 the Soviet representatives on the mixed commission to determine the nationality of those claiming German origin complained about the falsification of documents. Ministerstvo inostrannykh del rossiiskoi federatsii, *Dokumenty vneshnei politiki 1940–22 iiuniu 1941* (DVP) (Moscow: Mezhdunarodnye otnosheniia, 1995), vol. XXX, bk 1, doc. 466, p. 713.

The Soviet forces turned the disorders to their advantage before clamping down. Officers encouraged attacks on the class enemy, mainly Polish "pany," but also middle-class Jews. Very primitive tactics were employed to recruit village committees and local officials to take over the administration. Cadres from the Soviet Ukraine and Belorussia hastily organized elections, first to "Popular" (*Narodnyi*) Assemblies and then in a plebiscite to join the appropriate Soviet Republic.[4] Police units began to round up suspects. There were summary executions. Within a few months the first of four waves of deportations was under way. The total number of former Polish citizens moved or voluntarily recruited for labor in the Soviet Union ranges from Vyshinskii's figure of just fewer than 388,000 to the Polish government-in-exile's estimate of 1.25 million. Over half of those deported were ethnically Poles; about 30 percent were Jews. The deportations were carried out in a brutal manner and many perished on the road to the east. Altogether the brief Soviet occupation of Eastern Poland may have caused the death of 300,000 civilians. The harsh Soviet occupation policies destroyed much of the original sympathy with which the Jewish and Belorussian populations had greeted the Red Army. Large numbers of Jews elected to return to their homes in Nazi-occupied Polish territories rather than remain under Soviet rule.[5] So much for the myth of Jewish–Soviet connivance.

With the occupation of the *kresy* by the Red Army, Stalin seized the opportunity to seek revenge for the defeats in the Soviet–Polish War in which he had been directly involved, and to destroy Polish influence once and for all in the long-contested western borderlands. Polish armed resistance to the invading Red Army was limited to the northeast of the country; in the southeast Polish forces crossed into Romania to be interned. Most of the Polish army, about 190,000 men, surrendered to the Red Army. The officers were separated out and placed in three major camps under wretched conditions. At first the Soviet authorities attempted to exploit them as forced labor and to win converts to the Communist cause. But the police infiltrators and informants were soon reporting almost universal anti-Soviet sentiments and uncovering secret organizations printing their own newspapers.[6]

As early as January 1940, preparations were made under Beria's direction to liquidate the prisoners. The timing of the massacre remains

[4] *Documents on Polish–Soviet Relations, 1939–1945*, 2 vols. (London: Heinemann, 1961), vol. I, pp. 67–70 and note 67, p. 572.
[5] Gross, *Revolution from Abroad*, p. 206; Nicholas Vakar, *Byelorussia: The Making of a Nation* (Cambridge, MA: Harvard University Press, 1956), pp. 164–5, 168–9.
[6] R. G. Pikoia *et al.* (eds.), *Katyn: Plenniki neob'iavlennoi voiny. Dokumenty, materialy* (Moscow: Mezhdunarodnyi fund "Demokratiia," 1997), doc. 183, pp. 330–6.

Map 6.1 Poland, 1939–41, "The Fourth Partition"

obscure, but circumstantial evidence points to a coordination of the mass shootings of the prisoners with Action AB of the SS.[7] Beria's letter of early March to Stalin proposing to shoot the prisoners in the three camps and jails of Western Ukraine and Western Belorussia divided the inmates in typical NKVD bureaucratic fashion into social subcategories – officers by rank, frontier guards, police, spies, former big property owners and deserters – accusing them all of conducting counter-revolutionary, anti-Soviet activity in the camps and anticipating freedom in order to struggle actively against Soviet power. Stalin and other members of the Politburo signed off on the order.[8] At the same time, the Politburo issued an order "on the security of the western regions of the Ukrainian and Belorussian Soviet Republics." It stipulated that an 800 meter border zone be cleared of all inhabitants and their dwellings (with the exception of certain towns), and ordered within two months the deportation for a period of ten years the families of all repressed officers, police, former landowners and Polish officials numbering approximately 22–25,000 families. Those families considered the most dangerous were to be arrested. Their confiscated property was to be given to local Soviet organs for the resettlement of Red Army men and Soviet workers assigned to the region. Refugees from the war who wished to settle in the Soviet Union were forbidden to settle for five years within a 100 kilometer border zone. Refugees who expressed a desire to leave the Soviet Union for territory occupied by the Germans were to be deported to the northern parts of the Soviet Union.[9] The porous frontiers were sealed.

Soviet expansion in the Baltic borderlands raised fresh problems in dealing with the local population and placating the great powers. There were no serious minority problems in the three Baltic states or Finland. Neither the Russian minorities in Latvia and Estonia, 10.6 percent and 8.2 percent of the population respectively, nor the smaller Jewish minorities had suffered persecution, and both had enjoyed cultural and political rights until more authoritarian policies were introduced in the mid-1930s. Even so, there was no fertile ground here for the cultivation of ethnic tensions. Thus, the Soviet Union could not expect any strong sympathies from the minorities. Moreover, Stalin could not count on German assistance to destroy the sovereignty of the three Baltic republics. Quite the contrary: Ribbentrop had extracted a verbal promise from Stalin that the Soviet Union would not seek to alter the sociopolitical structure of the Baltic states. Not that Stalin's verbal promise counted for much. But

---

[7] *Ibid.*, p. 42, note 21.   [8] *Ibid.*, doc. 216, pp. 384–90 with facsimile.
[9] *Ibid.*, doc. 208, pp. 375–8.

insofar as he wished to keep the German alliance afloat he needed to consider the effects of open aggression.

Stalin decided to move cautiously in strengthening his strategic position in the Baltic littoral by demanding military bases from Estonia, Latvia, Lithuania and Finland at key points on the Baltic coast. The three small Baltic republics agreed, and Molotov piously promised to respect their sovereignty. Soviet diplomatic and military representatives in the three countries received confidential instructions not to interfere in domestic politics and to refrain from any activity that would fuel rumors of a future sovietization of the area. The entering Soviet troops behaved in an exemplary fashion, in striking contrast to the local Poles who unleashed pogroms in Vilnius when the Lithuanian and Soviet forces entered the city.[10] Stalin justified his cautious approach in a meeting with Zhdanov and Dimitrov on October 26 following the conclusion of treaties with Estonia on September 29, Latvia on October 5 that gave the Soviet Union naval and air bases, and a mutual assistance pact with Lithuania on October 10 that transferred Soviet-occupied Vilnius and the surrounding areas to Lithuania. His remarks in private deserve a full citation here:

During the first imperialist war the Bolsheviks overestimated the situation.
– *We got ahead of ourselves and made mistakes!*
– *That can be explained by the current conditions, but not justified.*
– *There must be no copying of the positions the Bolsheviks held then.*
– *We have learned a few things since then and gotten smarter!*
– It should be remembered that the current situation is different: At that time there were no Communists in power.
– *Now there is the Soviet Union!*

– We believe that in our pacts of mutual assistance we have the right form to allow us to bring a number of countries into the Soviet sphere of influence.
– *But for that we will have to maintain a consistent posture, strictly observing their internal regimes and independence.*
– *We are not going to seek their sovietization.*
– *The time will come when they will do that themselves!*[11]

In light of what followed in both the Baltic republics and the countries of Eastern Europe after 1945, this is a remarkable statement. It comes as close to repudiating Lenin as Stalin ever dared to go. His criticism of the Bolshevik revolutionary strategy in 1917 faintly echoes his stand

[10] Geoffrey Roberts, "Soviet Policy and the Baltic States, 1939–1940: A Reappraisal," *Diplomacy and Statecraft* 6:3 (1995), pp. 672–700; Alfred E. Senn, *Lithuania 1940: Revolution from Above* (Amsterdam and New York: Rodopi, 2007), pp. 55–67. This work is now the standard treatment of the Soviet takeover of Lithuania.
[11] Banac, *The Diary of Georgi Dimitrov*, p. 120. Italics in original.

in February 1917, when he and Molotov were editing *Pravda* and supporting the provisional government before Lenin returned to deliver his stunning April thesis on the necessity of taking power. The question remains: what changed his mind about the sovietization of the Baltic republics and does this shed light on a similar radical shift in his views in 1945–6?

"Current conditions," to borrow Stalin's words were what changed in November 1939 when Finland refused to grant bases. Stalin wasted little time in negotiating and late that month the Red Army launched its attack. The Soviet offensive bore all the marks of another improvisation. During the summer the Supreme Military Council of the Red Army had prepared an operational plan for a Finnish campaign. Their assumption was that the Finns might receive direct aid from Germany and/or Britain and France. They concluded that the fighting would be "far from easy, demanding several months of stubborn, hard fighting." They recommended the deployment of troops not only drawn from the Leningrad Military District but also from supplementary units.

Stalin rejected the plan of his military advisors. He blamed the Council for having exaggerated the military preparedness of the Finns and authorized the commander of the Leningrad Military District, General K. A. Meretskov, to draft a new plan using only troops from the Leningrad district. The plan ignored practical difficulties and dispersed the attacking forces. As soon as the Red Army went into action, the lack of adequate preparations for offensive operations became clear, inasmuch as all previous military planning had been based on a defensive strategy.[12] Moreover, the Soviet Commissar of Defense, Stalin's old comrade in arms, K. E. Voroshilov, still clung to many of the outmoded military concepts, reflecting his experience in the Civil War.

Stalin's political tactics were also rooted in the Civil War era. His plan was to set up an alternative Soviet government on Finnish soil, and use the military victories of the Red Army to spark a civil war that would topple the national government. But here too the ground was badly prepared. Stalin was forced to appoint a Soviet citizen, the veteran Comintern politician, Otto Kuusinen, to head a Karelian government at Terijaki. The secretary-general of the Finnish Communist Party, Arvo Tuominen, who had served in Stalin's secretariat, defected from the party, and from his

---

[12] "Akt o prieme narkomata oborony soiuza SSR tov. Timoshenko, S. K. ot Voroshilova, K. E. maia 8, 1940," *Izvestiia TsK KPSS* 13 (January, 1990), pp. 210–12. The analysis is by the former Soviet Deputy Defense Minister and Chief of the General Staff, M. Moiseev.

haven in Stockholm called upon the workers to defend their homeland. The appeals of the Terijaki government fell on deaf ears.

The Finnish Communist Party had a long tradition stretching back to the fierce civil war of 1918–19. But since 1930 it had been outlawed and had declined in numbers. Its major support had come from the workers of the south and west where sympathies still remained. But the workers and the party also harbored strong nationalist feelings, due partly to the homogeneous ethnic composition of the population and partly to membership, if only nominal, in the national Lutheran Church. The unprovoked external attack on a relatively prosperous country was almost universally resisted. The large potential for new recruits with deeper grievances in the depressed and backward areas of the north and east close to the Soviet frontiers could not be exploited by the Terijaki government because the Red Army failed to break through the Finnish lines in the early stages of the war. It was only after defeat in the more unpopular "Continuation War" of 1941–4 that these areas became fertile grounds for recruiting Communists.[13]

Finnish military and political resistance forced Stalin to compromise. He abandoned the Terijaki experiment and did not even press for the legalization of the Finnish Communist Party in the peace negotiations. He was content to acquire a series of strategic strong points: the entire Karelian isthmus with the city of Viborg (Viipuri); the western and northern shores of Lake Ladoga which provided a defensive glacis for Leningrad; part of the Rybachi and Sredni peninsulas together with the demilitarization of the Arctic coastline and transit rights across Petsamo which, in Molotov's words, ensured the safety of Murman and the Murmansk railroad; a thirty-year lease on the peninsula of Hangö where the Soviet Union began to construct a naval base; and some islands in the Gulf of Finland that protected the approaches by sea to Leningrad.[14]

Aside from strategic concerns, Stalin used the opportunity presented by the acquisition of territories inhabited by Finnish speakers to create the first of five new Soviet Socialist Republics that emerged from his territorial policies of 1939–41. Shortly after the peace treaty, the annexed territories were joined with the Karelian ASSR into a new Karelian–Finnish Union Republic. There was very little ethnic justification for such a move. The percentage of what is called a titular nationality, in this case Karelo-Finns, living in the republic was not only far smaller than in

---

[13] Erik Allardt, "Social Sources of Finnish Communism: Traditional and Emerging Radicalism," *International Journal of Comparative Sociology* 5:1 (1964), pp. 49–72.

[14] V. M. Molotov, *Soviet Peace Policy* (London: Lawrence and Wishart, 1941), p. 62; H. J. F. Procopé (ed.), *Finland Reveals her Secret Documents on Soviet Policy, March 1940–June 1941* (New York: Wilfred Funk, Inc., 1941), p. 1.

any other union republic but also was smaller than in any autonomous republic or even the majority of autonomous oblasts. The percentage of Russians living in the area was second only to that of the Russian Union Republic.[15]

"Current conditions" also changed his views on the future of the three Baltic republics. The absorption of the Baltic republics proceeded in several stages, though these were more the result of improvisation than planning. During the initial stage following the conclusion of the treaties of mutual assistance, the establishment of Soviet military bases had proceeded without friction despite the presence of about 90,000 Red Army men in the Baltic states. The arrangement lasted eight months. All three republics attempted to balance Soviet influence with Germany. They signed successive trade agreements that assured Germany of 70 percent of all Baltic exports. But they also bent over backwards to avoid antagonizing the Soviet government. They adopted a strict policy of neutrality toward the Soviet–Finnish War.

Nevertheless, the Soviet leadership opened the second phase of its incorporation of the Baltic republics in June 1940, allegedly concerned over the activities of the dormant Baltic Entente, the alliance that Estonia, Latvia and Lithuania had concluded in 1934. On June 14 Molotov informed the Soviet representatives in the three Baltic states that the treaties of mutual aid with the Soviet Union had failed to check the Entente from expanding its anti-Soviet aims by recruiting Lithuania into the pact and preparing to admit Finland as well. He accused the Entente of having held two conferences behind the back of the Soviet Union, of having secretly opposed its influence in the Baltic littoral and then of having organized all kinds of activities of an anti-Soviet character, including secret military talks which violated the mutual assistance treaties.[16] The following day Molotov issued twenty-four-hour ultimatums to the three republics. He demanded they accept an occupation by the Red Army and replace their governments with individuals acceptable to the Soviet

---

[15] The following figures are from data in 1959: titular nationality as a percentage of total population – 13.1 percent (the nearest union republic with such a low figure was the Kazakh with 30 percent and the nearest autonomous republic was the Abkhaz with 15.1 percent). Robert A. Lewis, "The Mixing of Russians and Soviet Nationalities and its Demographic Impact," in Edward Allworth (ed.), *Soviet Nationality Problems* (New York: Columbia University Press, 1971), pp. 146–9. By 1959 the Karelian–Finnish SSR had been reduced to an autonomous republic within the RSFSR but the size of the territory remained the same.

[16] V. P. Naumov (ed.), *1941 god*, 2 vols. (Moscow: Mezhdunarodnyi fund Demokratiia, 1998), vol. I, pp. 29–30, doc. 10. The public announcement by TASS included a demand for the arrest and trial of the Lithuanian Minister of the Interior and head of the political police. *Ibid.*, vol. I, p. 39, doc. 11.

Union. Can this abrupt reversal of Stalin's policy of the previous year be attributed solely, or even mainly, to the alleged anti-Soviet activities of the Baltic Entente? Or should the decision be placed in the context of what was happening on the western front where the French and British armies had been soundly defeated and France had asked for an armistice?

In his conversation with the German ambassador, Friedrich von der Schulenberg, on June 17, Molotov offered his congratulations on the German victory, remarking that Hitler and the German government "could hardly have expected such rapid successes" (nor, he might have added, could Stalin and the Soviet government!). Molotov felt compelled to explain to Schulenberg his justifications for the Soviet move. The main reason, Molotov stated, was to head off Anglo-French intrigues; this was hardly credible given the circumstances. Second, the Soviet Union did not wish problems with the Baltic states to spoil its relations with Germany, and there were elements in those countries who sought to do precisely that. The implication here was clear enough: pro-Germans within the Baltic governments looked to Germany for assistance in resisting Soviet domination. This had been one of Stalin's major concerns in negotiating with the British and French in the summer of 1939 over "indirect aggression." Unlike the Western allies, the Germans had been willing to leave the Baltic states to their fate. This was not 1919, and there was no British fleet in the Baltic.

Once the Baltic republics had accepted the Soviet demands, Stalin dispatched three high-powered plenipotentiaries; Zhdanov to Estonia, Vyshinskii to Latvia, and Dekanozov to Lithuania, in order to negotiate or dictate if necessary the formation of friendly governments. Within two months, under their supervision 25,000 "undesirable" citizens of the three states were deported to remote regions of the Soviet Union. These were still "selective deportations" aimed at removing the prewar elites.[17] Stalin's policy of class warfare with ominous overtones of ethnic cleansing imposed from above revived an old self-fulfilling prophecy of disloyalty in the western borderlands.

By the end of June "people's governments" had been installed in the three republics. Although pro-Soviet, they were composed mainly of non-party elements. They endeavored to preserve at least nominal

---

[17] V. M. Zemskov, "Prinuditelnye migratsii iz Pribaltiki v 1940–50kh godakh," *Otechestven-nyi arkhiv* 1 (1993), p. 4. For example, in Latvia the deportees included 380 former army officers of the tsarist and Latvian armies, 601 leaders of the judiciary and security organs, 2,329 active members of right-wing parties and "anti-Soviet organizations" and 1,240 landowners and high-up government officials. "Pod maskoi nezavisimosti (dokumeny o vooruzhennom natsionalisticheskom podpol'e v Latvii v 40–50kh gg.)," *Izvestiia TsK KPSS* 11 (1990), p. 115.

independence while adopting the Soviet model of administration.[18] This phase lasted less than a month. In mid-July the third phase began when Soviet plenipotentiaries ordered elections to people's assemblies under radically altered election laws and under the watchful eye of the Red Army. Communist candidates who had never received more than 5 percent of the vote were elected everywhere with 90 percent. The new parliaments immediately proclaimed their transformation into socialist Soviet republics and requested admission to the Soviet Union. Decrees on the nationalization of land and industrial properties rapidly followed. Massive reinforcements of Soviet troops poured into the republics.

Stalin might have preferred a more gradual process of absorption that would in the long run have given him fewer problems. But the German victories in the west came more rapidly than he expected. By absorbing the three Baltic republics, he had extended Leningrad's defensive glacis to the south. But the extreme haste with which the three stages were compressed within a period of ten months left a dangerous legacy. The local Communist parties, weakened by years of persecution and Stalin's purges, were in no position to consolidate the sovietization of the new republics.

Once the three republics had been annexed, it proved impossible to find any veteran Communists to head the new republican governments. Instead, fellow-travelling intellectuals were co-opted, like the writer Justas Poletskice in Lithuania, Professor A. Kirchenstein in Latvia and the poet and physician, Dr. Johannes Vares in Estonia. Vares was not a member of the Communist Party until he became Prime Minister and then President of Estonia in the summer of 1940.[19]

The Latvian Party was treated with particular brutality, although many of its members had played a key role in the Bolshevik Revolution and Civil War. Driven underground by the authoritarian government in 1934, its Central Committee was abolished by the Comintern and replaced by a Provisional Secretariat which was then also liquidated. In 1936 the Foreign Bureau of the Comintern Central Committee was wiped out.

---

[18] Senn, *Lithuania 1940*, p. 69, argues that "real power never actually passed into the hands of the people's government in Lithuania." The Foreign Minister, Vincas Krėvė-Mickevič, recalled that he attempted to slow down the incorporation of Lithuania by proposing to Molotov that the country be allowed the status of Mongolia, as a "people's republic," but that Molotov had rejected the argument, stating that "if Lithuania remained independent, Germany would surely take part of it and that the Lithuanians should have no fear of 'russification' in the Soviet state." *Ibid.*, p. 180.

[19] P. D. Grishenko and G. A. Gurin, *Bor'ba za Sovetskuiu pribaltiku v Velikoi Otechestvennoi voine, 1941–1945*, 2 vols. (Riga: Kiesma, 1966), vol. I, pp. 22–3. K. Tazva, "Poet-borets," in *Ob estonskoi literature: sbornik literaturno-kriticheskikh stat'ei* (Tallin: Estonskoe gosudarstvennoe izd. 1956).

Lenin's former colleague, the legal theorist, P. I. Stuchka, and the Old Bolshevik, Jan Lentsman, both of whom also occupied positions in the central organs, perished. A massive purge of party members followed, reducing the Riga party organization to a handful. There was a brief revival after the Seventh Comintern Congress encouraged rebuilding the organization with workers. But the purges continued. In 1940 there were only 1,000 party members. They were isolated from the Comintern Executive and unprepared to assist in the imposition of Soviet power which was mainly the work of the Red Army, NKVD and party cadres from the center.[20]

The Estonian Party was also crushed by the purges in 1937–8. A large number of Estonians had been living in the Soviet Union in the 1920s and 30s, including many of the Old Bolshevik leaders of the revolution in Estonia, veterans of the Civil War and rank-and-file workers. In the rising tide of suspicion against foreign connections, they were swamped by accusations of having links with "the bourgeois police of Estonia." Many were executed. Among the most prominent were Jan Anvelt and Hans Poqelman. Anvelt, a Bolshevik since 1907, was one of the founders of the first Bolshevik newspapers in Estonian, a leading figure in the short-lived Estonian Soviet government and a veteran of the Civil War. He had survived four years of illegal work in the underground before leading the rising of 1924. He finally emigrated to the Soviet Union where he served as commissar in the Zhukovskii Military Academy and as a high official in the Soviet Navy and the Comintern. His close colleague, Poqelman, a journalist and party veteran since 1905, had suffered arrest and exile before returning in 1917 to play an active role in the Civil War. Subsequently, he became a high official in the Comintern. With them perished the rest of the Estonian leaders. The Estonian Party was so badly crippled by the purges that the Central Committee ceased to exist in early 1938.[21]

The Lithuanian Party, numbering no more than 2,000 in 1937, lost its entire leadership in the purges and was a negligible factor in the Soviet incorporation of Lithuania into the Soviet Union. As in the case of Estonia, the absence of reliable Communist cadres required the assignment of Russians to command the Lithuanian army units incorporated into the Red Army.[22] The damage to the Communist cause of these baseless

[20] "Za pravil'noe osveshchenie istoriii kompartii Latvii," *Kommunist* 12 (1964), pp. 67–8; G. Zvimach, *Latyshskie revoliutsionnye deiateli*, 2 vols. (Riga: Latyshskoe gosudarstvennoe izd., 1966), vol. II, pp. 369–74, 378, 444.

[21] A. Pankseev, *Ocherki istorii kommunisticheskoi partii Estonii*, 3 vols. (Tallin: Parei Ajaloo Institut, 1961–70), vol. III, pp. 39–41.

[22] Grishenko and Gurin, *Bor'ba za sovetskuiu pribaltiku*, vol. I, p. 24.

killings was starkly revealed in January 1941 by A. A. Andreev, Stalin's Politburo emissary dispatched to survey the damage.

Andreev submitted a grim report. The Communist parties had emerged from the underground greatly weakened, he reported, numbering only 1,220 in Lithuania and 120 in Estonia. Since then these derisory numbers had barely increased: in Lithuania there were 2,321 members and 565 candidates; in Latvia 1,518 members and 1,125 candidates; in Estonia 1,064 members and 893 candidates. The Komsomols were doing better, but recruiting new party members faced huge problems. The large industrial plants that had provided some of the most dedicated worker cadres for the revolution and Civil War in 1917–20 had been broken up during the 1930s into smaller enterprises. Many of them no longer had any Communist workers. There was scarcely an organization outside the central administrative departments that was under Communist control. There were virtually no party members in the countryside. Some feeble efforts were made to redistribute land but there was no campaign for collectivization.[23]

The inescapable if unstated conclusion of Andreev's litany of complaints and criticism was that the local population remained profoundly anti-Soviet. Clearly, there was a limit beyond which outsiders appointed from Moscow could push sovietization without triggering internal disturbances that could not be welcome to Stalin at a moment of international crisis. The advance of the frontiers provided forward bases to meet a German attack, but the entire rear area was under only nominal Soviet control.

On the Danubian frontier, Stalin waited to cash in his Bessarabian chip until the fall of France eliminated Romania's great power ally in the West. King Carol was already convinced that Romania would have to rely on Germany to protect its territorial integrity in the face of Soviet pressure. German economic and political penetration of Romania was proceeding rapidly, when Molotov informed the German ambassador of the Soviet intention to occupy Bessarabia and Bukovina. The Germans tried to hedge on their earlier agreement on spheres of influence. Schulenburg complained that the sudden Soviet démarche would create "chaos in Romania," jeopardizing oil shipments to Germany. Molotov brusquely dismissed the objection. Schulenburg pleaded the necessity of a peaceful solution to the Bessarabian question. Molotov insisted on a rapid solution and if it was resisted, the Soviet Union would resort to force. Then the Germans objected that Bukovina had not been mentioned in the pact. Molotov countered that "Bukovina is the last missing part of a 'unified

[23] Sovetskoe rukovodstvo, pp. 420–37, doc. 250.

Ukraine' and for that reason the Soviet government must attach as much importance to solving this question simultaneously with the Bessarabian question." The following day, presumably after a conversation with Stalin, he informed the German ambassador that the Soviet government was limiting its demands to the northern part of Bukovina and the city of Czernowitz (Cernăuti).[24] This brought most of the Ukrainian population to Bukovina within the Soviet borders. Most significantly for Stalin they constituted, it may be recalled, the most highly educated and nationally conscious group of Ukrainians living outside the Soviet Union.

The settlement still left the Ukrainian population of the Sub-Carpatho Ukraine, formerly under Czech and subsequently under Hungarian domination, outside Soviet control. Truly "the last missing part of Ukraine," it was only annexed to the Soviet Union in 1944 when Stalin demanded it from a surprised Eduard Beneš. The line traced by Molotov also made provision for Soviet control of the direct rail connection from Bessarabia to L'viv (Lvov) via Czernowitz. The Soviet government agreed to repatriate the 100,000 *Volksdeutsche* as they had done in Volhynia following the partition of Poland, and in the Baltic states. Insistent upon absorbing all the Ukrainians for sound political reasons, Stalin was less finicky about adding non-Slavic peoples if the strategic situation demanded it. According to Romanian statistics, in 1930 Romanians were just over 56 percent of the population of Bessarabia; Russians and Ukrainians made up only 23 percent.[25]

Strategically, annexing Bessarabia made the Soviet Union a riparian state on the Danube.[26] The key southern districts bordering the Danube were added to the Ukrainian SSR. Molotov was quick to follow up the advantage by pressing later in the year for an entirely new international Danube authority limited to the riparian states. Molotov objected strenuously to the German proposal to include Italy.[27] In the meantime

[24] DVP, *1940–22 iiunia 1941*, vol. XXX, bk 1, docs. 217 and 225, pp. 364–6 and 374–6. The German version differs slightly in details. Cf. Sontag and Beddie, *Nazi–Soviet Relations*, pp. 158–62. For Romania's shift in policy, see Grigore Cafencu, *Prelude to the Russian Campaign from the Moscow Pact (August 21, 1939) to the Opening of Hostilities in Russia (June 22, 1941)* (London: F. Muller, 1945), pp. 288–97.

[25] Sabin Manuila (ed.), *Recensământul general al populaţiei româniei din 29 decemvrie 1930* (Bucharest: Institutul Central de Statistică, 1938), pp. 75–8. These figures seem reasonable when compared to Soviet data for 1959 which indicate that Moldavians (i.e. Romanians) constituted 65 percent of the population of the union republic and Russians accounted for 10.2 percent compared to 12.3 percent in 1930. Lewis, "The Mixing of Russians," p. 146.

[26] For the strategic advantage of the Soviet occupation of Bessarabia and Northern Bukovina, see Gorodetsky, *Grand Delusion*, pp. 30–3.

[27] DVP, *1940–22 iiunia 1941*, vol. XXX, bk 1, docs. 385, 386, 446, pp. 606, 607, 680.

the Soviet representatives on the joint Romanian–Soviet demarcation commission demanded a thalweg in the delta that gave them control of the principal channels. When the new international commission met in October, the Soviet representatives proposed virtually to hand over the administration of the lower reaches of the Danube, that is access to the Black Sea, to a joint Soviet–Romanian commission that they easily could have dominated. No action was taken because Germany and Italy opposed the scheme. But Stalin revived his proposals in 1948 under more favorable conditions and succeeded in eliminating all Western powers from the international commissions.[28]

Over the following five years Bessarabia and Bukovina suffered the terrible fate shared by all the borderlands of the western frontiers of the Soviet Union. Three military occupations were accompanied each time by massive looting, deportations, repatriations and executions, terrorizing the civilian population. The cycle began with a hurried exchange of notes culminating in the Soviet ultimatum of June 27 that gave the Romanian Army twenty-four hours to begin evacuation of the province. Haste was dictated, presumably, by the need to prevent not only the organization of resistance but also the removal of supplies, equipment and livestock. There were several armed clashes between the rapidly advancing Red Army and Romanian units loaded down with booty. Most of the large landowners and the business and professional classes fled with the Romanian Army. A few months later, as part of the Nazi–Soviet agreements, most of the German colonists were repatriated to the Reich, depriving the province of some of its most successful cultivators. The Soviet authorities began almost at once to organize the deportation of "social undesirables" as it had in the Western Ukraine and the Baltic states. Official Soviet statistics acknowledged that prior to the outbreak of war 300,000 inhabitants of the Moldavian republic "were evacuated to the interior of the USSR."[29] But there was a counter-flow of about 300,000 refugees from Romania, many Jewish, who claimed native residence in the province.[30]

---

[28] A good survey of the problem can be found in Beloff, *The Foreign Policy of Soviet Russia*, vol. II, pp. 323–4, 340–1. See also Nicholas Dima, *Bessarabia and Bukovina: The Soviet-Romanian Territorial Dispute* (Boulder, CO: East European Monographs, 1982), pp. 38–41.

[29] *Nazi–Soviet Relations*, p. 158; *Bol'shaia Sovetskaia Entsiklopediia*, 30 vols., 3rd edn (Moscow: Izd. Sovetskaia entsiklopediia, 1970–81), vol. XVI, pp. 429–30. General Nicolae Rădescu, *Forced Labor in Communist Romania* (New York: Commission of Inquiry into Forced Labor, 1949), pp. 45–6.

[30] A. M. Lazarev, *God 1940 Prodolzhenie sotsialisticheskoi revoliutsii v Bessarabii* (Kishinev: Katia Moldoveniaske, 1985), pp. 68–72, 83. A non-Soviet source estimated that 150,000

Sovietization of Bessarabia faced formidable obstacles despite widespread dissatisfaction with former Romanian rule. "This province was," in the words of Hugh Seton-Watson, "perhaps the most misgoverned in Europe."[31] Romanian officials had mismanaged and plundered the great natural wealth of the province. The peasantry received some land in the reforms of 1918 but were then completely neglected. The rural proletariat was among the poorest in Eastern Europe. Yet the local Communist Party was minuscule, numbering only 375 members. They were unequal to the task of mobilizing the demoralized and impoverished peasantry and rallying the intellectuals to the new regime. Over 5,000 party activists from the Soviet Union rushed in to assist them in organizing a local *druzhina* and village committees. As they fanned out across the province the Soviet government reversed its stand on the political future of Bessarabia. It announced that Bessarabia would not be folded into the Moldavian Autonomous Republic within the Ukrainian Union Republic and run by the Ukrainian apparatus as assumed by the Communist underground. Rather, it would form the nucleus of a new union republic of its own.[32] It was a shrewd move to offset any nationalist opposition that might form around the large Orthodox religious houses and petty commercial and manufacturing groups that constituted the main resistance to Soviet rule.

Nationalization of large- and middle-scale enterprises was carried out rapidly, but socialization of agriculture proceeded more cautiously. Economic policy was an accelerated and foreshortened NEP. Some small producers survived in the towns. In the countryside a large-scale redistribution of land based on the Bolshevik land decree of 1918 abolished the latifundia and large church holdings and also confiscated well-to-do peasant land above an established norm. Over 186,000 landless and poor peasants were the beneficiaries. Some of the most productive vineyards, orchards and cattle farms were not broken up but transformed into sovhozy. The agrarian reforms produced an anomalous situation; the left bank of the Dniester River had been thoroughly collectivized in the mid-1930s while the right bank kept its small-scale individual peasant economy. On the eve of war there were only 120 collective farms holding just over 4 percent of the peasant plough land in the entire Moldavian Republic.[33]

expatriates returned to Bessarabia in the first month of Soviet occupation. David Dallin, *Soviet Russia's Foreign Policy* (New Haven, CT: Yale University Press, 1952), p. 239.

[31] Hugh Seton-Watson, *Eastern Europe between the Wars, 1918–1941*, 3rd edn (New York: Harper and Row, 1967), p. 336 and 337–8 for a searing indictment of Romanian rule.

[32] Lazarev, *God 1940*, pp. 83, 88, 91, 95, 99, 114.   [33] *Ibid.*, pp. 161–2, 254.

Map 6.2 Interwar Romania

As a result of the brief period of Soviet rule there was probably more popular support for the new authorities than anywhere else in the newly acquired western borderlands. Dockers and workers in the canning factories from the working class and the mass of poor and landless peasants reaped immediate benefits. The sharp reversal of their fortunes after the reconquest by Romanian forces on the right flank of the German invasion in July 1941 could only have reinforced their preferences for Soviet power.

The rapid Soviet conquest and absorption of the borderlands created fresh problems with Berlin. From the beginning their new relationship had been fraught with tensions along the Baltic littoral and Danubian frontiers. The German government adhered strictly to the letter of the pact; it categorically refused all appeals for aid from Finland and the Baltic states and even advised the Romanian government to submit to the Soviet ultimatum. But it expressed concern that the precipitous Soviet actions threatened German economic interests in the Baltic states and Romania. Berlin took a series of counter-measures. First, the Soviet occupation of Lithuania, including a strip of territory assigned to Germany, triggered the German occupation of Memel, the abolition of the Free Port Zone, and the seizure of stores. Second, in reaction to the Soviet occupation of Bessarabia, in August 1940 Germany extended a unilateral guarantee of Romania's frontiers in order to secure its vital supplies of oil and grain. The Soviet Union protested both moves.[34]

The more serious case was Romania. Molotov objected in particular to the lack of consultation. He pointed out that the Soviet Union had neither verbally nor in writing renounced all further interest in Romania. On the contrary, it had expressed its intentions to reopen the question of Southern Bukovina and had anticipated German support.[35] While the Germans began to send direct military assistance to Romania and Finland, the Soviet Union put additional pressure on both governments to make concessions on the Danube and in the Gulf of Finland.[36] Added to these political frictions were difficulties over German–Soviet economic relations. German deliveries lagged. In response the Soviet Union canceled all long-range agreements, demanding priority for German goods that would help their armaments industry over an eight- to ten-month period. It was at this time, in September 1940, that Hitler began to make serious preparations for an attack upon the Soviet Union.[37]

Trans Caspian frontier

In Trans Caspia, along the long frontier with Iran, the Soviet Union's dormant rivalry with Germany flared up again. By the late 1920s the Soviet government showed increasing concern over the security problems along the porous frontier between Soviet and Iranian Azerbaizhan. Pressure was brought to bear on Iranian border crossers to accept Soviet citizenship or face expulsion from frontier zones. The local Communist leadership was displeased with the reaction of the local Iranian Communists. In 1935 Beria began a purge of all Caucasian Communists, including Iranians.[38] When it appeared that these domestic problems could be exploited by foreign powers, Stalin reacted forcefully.

[34] DVP, *1940–22 iiunia 1941*, vol. XXX, bk 1, docs. 334 and 367, pp. 540–1, 583–4.

[35] *Nazi–Soviet Relations*, pp. 178–80, 182, 185–6, 191–4.

[36] The Soviet Union repeatedly protested against the presence of German troops in Finland, but Hitler dismissed this as a secondary issue. DVP, vol. XXX, bk 2, part 1, *noiabria 1940–1 marta 1941 g.*, docs. 505, 510 and 511, pp. 54, 62, 66, 68.

[37] *Nazi–Soviet Relations*, pp. 199–201.

[38] Touraj Atabaki, "'Incommodious Hosts, Invidious Guests': The Life and Times of Iranian Revolutionaries in the Soviet Union 1921–39," in Stephanie Cronin, *Reformers and Revolutionaries in Modern Iran: New Perspectives on the Iranian Left* (London: Routledge Curzon, 2004), pp. 155–9.

In 1936 growing Nazi penetration of the northern provinces of Iran and Afghanistan began to ring alarm bells in Moscow. Hitler was building his Iranian policy on foundations already laid down during the Kaiserreich and Weimar periods. Before the Nazis took power, German economic experts had replaced the American mission of Arthur Millspaugh and had organized the National Bank of Persia. Another group gained control over the communications and air transport system of Iran. The Nazis broadened these contacts, extolling the Persians as an Aryan race and publishing a Persian-language newspaper that stressed the awakening of Persian nationalism.[39]

As soon as the Soviet Union caught wind of negotiations between Iran and Nazi Germany for oil concessions in the Caspian provinces, they warned that continued German exploration would be regarded as "an unfriendly act." The Soviet ambassador was convinced that the German penetration of Iran was the prelude to Iran's campaign "to sever large territories from the Soviet Union." Litvinov informed the Politburo that the Nazis were setting up an elaborate espionage network throughout Iran. This prompted Stalin to apply pressure to Teheran in the fall of 1936 by instituting a brief press campaign, recalling the Soviet ambassador and dispatching Soviet naval units to the South Caspian.

A major point of contention arose over the Iranian concession to Germany to construct docking facilities in the Caspian port of Pahlavi (Anzali). For two years Soviet diplomats conducted a campaign of mounting intensity against what the government officially interpreted as a violation of the agreement of 1927 regulating frontier issues and "the spirit of the treaty of 1921."[40] German economic penetration of the northern Iranian provinces, the Caspian ports and the opening of a direct air connection between Berlin and Kabul prompted Deputy Foreign Commissar Stomoniakov to cable the Soviet chargé d'affaires in Teheran: "Of course we must take every measure to prevent Germany from taking root (*vnedrenie*) in neighboring regions of Iran, especially on

---

[39] Miron Rezun, *The Iranian Crisis of 1941: The Actors, Britain, Germany and the Soviet Union* (Cologne and Vienna: Böhlau, 1982), pp. 9–16; S. L. Agaev, *Germanskii imperializm v Irane, Veimarskoi respublika, tretii reik* (Moscow: Nauka, 1969). For German intelligence activities, see Bernard Schulze-Holthur, *Daybreak in Iran: A Story of the German Intelligence Service*, trans. Merwyn Savill (London: Staples Press, 1954); and, for the earlier period, Christopher Sykes, *Wassmus, "The Persian Lawrence"* (London: Longmans Green and Co., 1936); for the Soviet reaction, see DVP, vol. XIX (1936), docs. 353, 368, 388, 395, pp. 555, 583–5, 616–18, 629, note 227, pp. 779–80.

[40] DVP, vol. XXI (1938), doc. 68, p. 117. The Soviet government repeatedly rejected Iranian reassurances that they were not in violation of these agreements and intended no harm to Soviet interests. *Ibid.*, doc. 116, 199, 226.

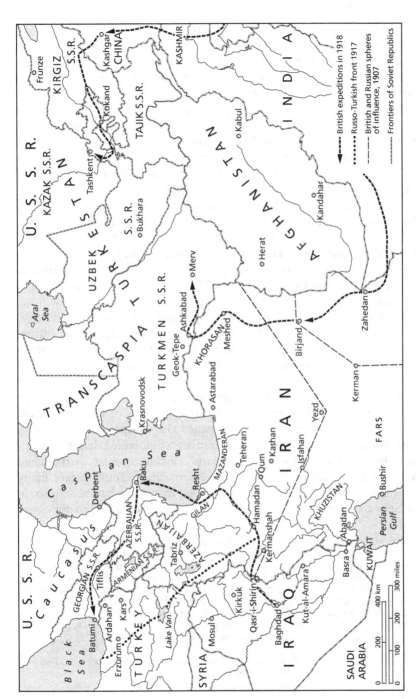

Map 6.3 Trans Caspian borderlands, 1917–40

the Caspian coast."[41] The evasive Iranian responses to Soviet protests infuriated Stomoniakov, who denounced them as "fools" for not under-standing Soviet dissatisfaction with German economic penetration.[42] Under Soviet pressure the Iranians finally yielded, agreeing to resolve the question of German construction of the docks in direct talks with Litvinov in Geneva. After prolonged negotiations, the Iranians agreed not to hire foreign experts from countries conducting hostile policies against the Soviet Union and to dismiss those already employed once they had completed their work.[43] Although the issue of the Caspian port was settled amicably, the Soviet Union continued to be alarmed by Nazi penetration of Iranian institutions.

As the Second World War approached, the war of nerves in Iran inten-sified. Estimates of the number of German technical advisors varied from 700 to several thousand, but there was no disagreement between Soviet and British intelligence about the key positions they occupied in Ira-nian communications and the army. Germany's share of Iranian foreign trade jumped from 14 percent in 1935–6 to over 45 percent in 1940–41. After the Iranian refusal in 1938 to renew the trade treaty with the Soviet Union the Soviet share dropped precipitously from 35 percent to less than 1 percent.[44] In 1939 there were disturbing signs of an official anti-Soviet campaign, culminating in a purge of pro-Soviet elements in the political as well as the cultural sphere. According to Soviet consular reports the Shah was rapidly drifting toward repressive, "quasi-fascist tendencies."[45] The Iranians kept pressing their claims for rectifications of the border; conflicts arose over the management of water resources along the Trans Caspian frontier. Litvinov was exasperated by the eva-sive Iranian negotiation tactics. The Iranians complained that the abrupt expulsion of 40,000 thousand "Iranians" (including many Armenians) from the Soviet frontier region with Azerbaizhan would create many domestic problems. The expellees included many who had been born in the Soviet Union, spoke no Iranian, and lacked the means to subsist in

[41] *Ibid.*, vol. XX (1937), docs. 367 and 384, pp. 549–50 and 569–72; quotation p. 571. Soviet diplomats in Kabul were extremely sensitive to signs of German and Japanese activities in Afghanistan, although these were far less extensive than in Iran. The problem of reaching a final delimitation of the Soviet–Afghan frontier on the Amu Darya dragged on until 1946. But relations were generally stable, although there was always a hint that a concerted failure to check German expansion might lead to a shift in policy. *Ibid.*, docs. 188, 195 and 196, pp. 240–2 and 247–8; *ibid.*, vol. XXI (1938), doc. 360, p. 511.

[42] *Ibid.*, vol. XX (1937), docs. 394 and 445, pp. 582–3, 670–1 and note 218, pp. 758–9.

[43] *Ibid.*, vol. XXI (1938), docs. 439, 461 and 493, pp. 606–7, 643 and 686–7; note 82, p. 717.

[44] B. Kh. Parvizpur, *Sovetsko-Iranskie otnosheniia v gody vtoroi mirovoi voiny (1939–1945)* (Tblisi: Met's'niereba, 1978), pp. 7–8, 10–11.

[45] DVP, vol. XXII, bk 1 (1939), docs. 50, 93, 226, pp. 70–1, 138–40, 279–80.

Iran. The Iranian ambassador requested a three-month delay to screen some of them. Litvinov drily "expressed doubt that the NKVD would agree to wait that long."[46] The Iranian tilt toward Germany prompted Stalin in early 1939 to order partial mobilization of the Red Army in frontier regions bordering Iran.

In the wake of the Nazi–Soviet Pact, Iranian–Soviet relations appeared to improve. The Iranian government expressed its great relief at the announcement. The concurrent negotiations with the British and French had caused a "great fear" of an Anglo-Russian agreement, a "nightmare" for Teheran, that would foreshadow a repetition of the 1907 partition. Despite the reassurances of the Soviet ambassador, the top officials in Iran could not in his view free themselves from anxieties that "the mere shadow of a Soviet–British entente raises."[47] A new commercial treaty was signed between Moscow and Teheran. But the appearance was deceptive. Its main function, as it turned out, was not to increase trade between the two signatories but rather to circumvent the British blockade and provide an alternative overland transit route for Iranian–German trade through Soviet territory. Moreover, a new threat to the Soviet position surfaced in the South Caucasus as relations deteriorated with the British and French who feared Nazi–Soviet collaboration in the Middle East as well as Eastern Europe. Anglo-French contingency plans to bomb Baku from Iranian bases were captured in 1940 and published by the Germans. Always sensitive to the protection of the oil fields, the Soviet government submitted a request for the use of air bases in Northern Iran, withdrawing it almost immediately as panic gave way to more sober estimates of the threat.[48]

The incident illustrates the difference between the situation in Eastern Europe, where Soviet demands for bases and/or territory from the small neighboring states was pursued with vigor, and the Middle East where such demands were tentative and quickly withdrawn. The original discussions leading to the Nazi–Soviet Pact did not divide Iran into spheres of influence. Subsequent attempts by Hitler to entice Stalin away from Eastern Europe and into Iran were a thinly veiled attempt to embroil the Soviet Union with the British in an area that was, unlike Eastern Europe, of vital national interest to Great Britain. Thus, the thrust of Soviet diplomacy toward Iran was to bring sufficient pressure on Teheran to prevent German domination of the country, but to avoid conflict with Great Britain. It was only Hitler's decision to attack the Soviet Union

---

[46] *Ibid.*, doc. 224, p. 278.   [47] *Ibid.*, doc. 505, pp. 661–3.
[48] Rezun, *The Iranian Crisis*, pp. 36–42.

that opened the way for a revival of Anglo-Soviet collaboration against German influence in Iran.

In the summer of 1941, both the Soviet Union and Britain shared a common concern that an impending coup in Iran would depose Riza Shah and bring openly pro-Nazis ministers to power. Yet neither wished to act alone. Both demanded the expulsion of all German nationals. But the Soviet note also revived a claim to exploit oil deposits in Northern Iran. The pro-German government stalled in hopes that Soviet resistance would collapse. The two allies then decided on a joint military occupation but agreed not to enter Teheran and to leave the Shah on the throne. The Soviet government justified its action by accusing Iran of allowing the German agents to turn the country into "an arena for the preparation of an attack on the Soviet Union," which enabled them to invoke Article 6 of the Treaty of 1921. Shortly after the Anglo-Soviet intervention, the Soviet government pressed the British to depose Riza Shah. He had been holding out for maintaining diplomatic relations with the Axis governments. Conversations between Maiskii and Eden suggest that sooner or later Moscow would have demanded the occupation of Teheran in order to consolidate the main road passing through the province of Semnan, the location of the Kevir-Kurian oil concession. At this point the idea of opening a supply route from the south was not of immediate concern to the Soviet Union. The prime objective was to secure the southern frontier from direct attack to reassert the primacy of Soviet economic, and by implication political, interests in the border provinces of Iran.[49]

Recalibrating the Nazi–Soviet Pact

With the Japanese wedged deeply in China and the Germans unable to subdue Britain, the Soviet leaders considered that they were in a favorable position to bargain hard and gain time. It was a serious miscalculation. The Germans were determined to make a final attempt to resolve their differences with the Soviet Union in agreement with the Japanese plan to create a four-power consortium to divide the world. For his part, Stalin wanted a clear idea of the long-range plans of the Germans, Italians and Japanese and how the Soviet Union would fit into those plans. On the eve of Molotov's visit to Berlin in November 1940, Stalin instructed him "to prepare a preliminary outline of the *spheres of influence of the USSR* in Europe and also in the Near and Middle East,"

[49] *Ibid.*, pp. 68–73, 78–80.

sounding out Germany and Italy without reaching any concrete agreements before Ribbentrop's planned visit to Moscow.[50] When Molotov
arrived, he refused to meet jointly with German, Japanese and Italian
representatives. He insisted that Moscow and Berlin had first to settle their relationship. Throughout the discussions between the Foreign
Commissar, Ribbentrop and Hitler, fundamental differences emerged.
Following Stalin's script, Molotov wanted specific answers; Hitler was
vaguely expansive. Molotov was particularly uneasy about the meaning
of the Japanese Co-Prosperity Sphere in Asia.[51] The Nazi leaders considered that the "decisive question was whether the Soviet Union was
prepared and in a position to cooperate with us in the great liquidation
of the British Empire." In this spirit they presented the draft of a general
political agreement among the four powers.[52]

In the course of the talks Molotov outlined Soviet "security interest"
along the periphery from Finland to Turkey. The Germans regarded the
list as a formidable and ultimately unacceptable list of demands. Molotov
hammered on the theme that the Germans were violating the 1939 pact
by sending troops into Finland and supporting, if only indirectly, "political demonstrations against the Soviet–Russian government." He dismissed Hitler's assertion that the exchange of Lithuania for the voevodina of Lublin had been an economic sacrifice for Germany. He expressed
concern over the future disposition of Poland. He objected to German
policy in Romania: "Germany was guaranteed the entire territory of
Romania and completely disregarded Russia's [sic] wishes with regard
to Southern Bukovina." Moving on to the Balkans, Molotov noted that
"for reasons of security the relations between Soviet Russia and other
Black Sea Powers were of great importance." He reiterated his com-
plaint that the German guarantee to Romania "was aimed against the
interests of Soviet Russia, 'if one might express oneself so bluntly.'" He
inquired whether Hitler would consider revoking the guarantee. When
this request was turned down on the spot, Molotov wondered what the
Germans would say "if Russia was given Bulgaria, that is, the independent country located closest to the Straits, a guarantee under exactly
the same conditions as Germany and Italy had given Romania." This
would help the Soviet Union to come to an agreement with Turkey over
the Straits. Hitler and Ribbentrop assured Molotov that they favored a
revision of the Montreux Convention that would give the Soviet Union

---

[50] DVP, vol. XXIII, bk 2, pt 1, *1 noiabria 1940 g.–1 marta 1941 g.*, doc. 491, pp. 30–1.
Stalin also gave specific instructions on all other issues taken up in the negotiations.
Ibid., pp. 30–2.
[51] *Ibid.*, p. 40.   [52] *Nazi–Soviet Relations*, pp. 225, 253.

sole rights to send warships through the Straits. But Molotov wanted an assurance "not only on paper but 'in reality.'" Hitler countered that Bulgaria unlike Romania had not requested a guarantee of its territory and admitted that Germany might be obliged to send troops into Bulgaria if the British attempted to seize bases in Greece. On no point was there a meeting of minds.[53]

The differences widened when the official Soviet reply to Ribbentrop's draft arrived in Berlin after Molotov's return to the Soviet Union. There were new Soviet demands. In addition to the immediate withdrawal of German troops from Finland and the conclusion of a "mutual assistance pact between the Soviet Union and Bulgaria which geographically is situated inside the security zone of the Black Sea boundaries of the Soviet Union," Stalin demanded "the establishment of a base for land and naval forces of the USSR within range of the Bosporus and Dardanelles by means of a long-term lease" from Turkey. In case of Turkish refusal to grant the base, Germany, Italy and the Soviet Union would agree to work out and carry through "the required military and diplomatic measures," in other words a possible joint armed intervention. The Soviet reply also avoided any mention of expansion in the direction of the Indian Ocean, as the German proposal had stipulated. Stalin had no desire to be a pawn in Hitler's campaign against Britain. Rather he wanted recognition that the "area south of Batum and Baku in the general direction of the Persian Gulf is recognized as the center of the aspirations of the Soviet Union." The statement, though intentionally vague in its geographic limits, did not make claims beyond the traditional Russian and Soviet sphere of influence in Northern Iran, as stated, for example, in the Anglo-Russian agreement of 1907 or later in the Anglo-Russian agreement of 1941, a position which he consistently maintained throughout the crisis of 1948. The final Soviet demand was for Japan to renounce its concessions for coal and oil in Northern Sakhalin.[54] The German government did not even bother to draft a reply. Acceptance of Stalin's proposals would have greatly strengthened the Soviet strategic position in the Baltic and Black Seas and undermined the German position in Romania without in any way weakening Britain. Within a month Hitler ordered the preparation of Operation Barbarossa.

Turkey and the Straits

In the meantime, Stalin sought to develop his own line of negotiations with the Turks, who found themselves in an increasingly uncomfortable

[53] *Ibid.*, pp. 237, 238, 245.   [54] *Ibid.*, pp. 258–9.

political situation, made doubly unsettling by the announcement of the Nazi–Soviet Pact. Up to that point the Turks had managed to maintain more or less equally good relations with Germany, Great Britain, France and the Soviet Union. Economically, Turkey was closely tied to Germany. By the end of 1937 more than three-quarters of Turkey's foreign trade was controlled by Germany through the discriminatory clearing agreements that exchanged Turkish raw materials, particularly chrome, for credits in Reichmarks. As international tensions grew, the Turks attempted to balance their dependency on Germany with trade agreements with Great Britain, but the two countries were not natural trading partners. On the eve of the war, Turkish diplomacy was guided by the brilliant diplomat, Numan Menemenciolğlo, who had learned his trade under the Ottomans, and like so many Ottoman diplomats had a French (Swiss) education. The aim was to have Turkey serve as the mediator between Britain and France on the one hand and the Soviet Union on the other, in order to ensure its security against Italian expansion in the Mediterranean and German expansion in the Balkans.[55] The challenge was to negotiate simultaneously with Britain and the Soviet Union, who distrusted one another, without antagonizing Germany. While negotiations with Britain and France neared completion in October 1939, the Turkish Foreign Minister, Şükrü Saraçoğlu, visited Moscow in hopes of completing the connection. There he encountered Stalin at his most intransigent.

On October 1, in one of his rare encounters with a foreign ambassador, Stalin devoted over five hours to the meeting during a period of rapid developments in Eastern Europe, demonstrating the great importance he attributed to relations with Turkey. Saraçoğlu had come to discuss the conclusion of a Turkish–Soviet Pact of Mutual Assistance. A month earlier Molotov had raised the question of reexamining Soviet–Turkish relations in light of the Soviet pact with Germany. He had reassured the Turks that a common language could be found if the object of mutual assistance would be to support one another in case of an attack on either power in the region of the Straits or the Balkans.[56] The Turkish draft incorporated Molotov's formula with the proviso that Turkey would not be obliged to fulfill its obligations if this led to a conflict with Britain and France.[57] In Moscow Molotov began the talks by asking pointedly against whom the projected Soviet–Turkish Pact would be directed: surely not Italy; even less so Bulgaria. What about Germany? Such a pact the Soviet Union could not conclude. The Turkish minister attempted to

[55] Selim Deringil, *Turkish Foreign Policy during the Second World War: 'An Active Neutrality'* (Cambridge University Press, 1989), especially pp. 41–58 and 71–92.
[56] DVP, vol. XXII, bk 1 (1939), doc. 527, p. 12.   [57] *Ibid.*, doc. 560, pp. 49–51.

reassure the Soviet leaders that his country's projected pacts with Britain and France excluded the possibility that they would be directed against the Soviet Union. But Stalin was not reassured. He advised Turkey not to sign a pact with Britain and France; it would not be to its benefit. Turkey would have to assume obligations with respect to Romania and Greece that were too onerous. And what of Bessarabia? "We do not intend to attack Romania," Stalin said, "but we will not give up Bessarabia again without a conflict." If Britain and France attacked the Soviet Union, then Turkey would not be obliged to assist us, Stalin continued. And we will not go to war with Germany. So what is the purpose of the pact? Saraçoğlu expressed his belief that Britain and France had learned their lesson and were now inclined to reach an agreement with the Soviet Union. A Soviet–Turkish Pact could eliminate the misunderstandings that had kept them apart and lead to further agreements to ensure the peace. Stalin was not convinced. The negotiations proved sterile.

Inner Asian frontiers

In questions relating to the Inner Asian borderlands Stalin and Molotov continued their policy of supporting China while holding a firm line in their dealings with Japan. The Soviet leadership was increasingly concerned over the split opening up between the Nationalists and the Communists that threatened civil war in China. In the fall of 1940, the Commissar of Defense, Timoshenko, made the point bluntly in his briefing of General Chuikov to head the Soviet military mission in China. Chuikov's instructions were to restrain Chiang's military activities against the Communists. But Timoshenko added that "the command of the Chinese Red Army was also inclined to turn its weapons against Chiang, failing to take into account the dangers that this poses for the entire Chinese people and their revolutionary achievements." Stalin reminded Chuikov that his decision to support the Nationalists rather than the Communists reflected the political necessities of the world situation. "Assistance to the Communists," he pointed out, "could be regarded as the export of revolution to a country with which we have diplomatic relations." In sending supplies to Chiang he was merely shoring up the strongest bulwark against Japanese aggression in the Far East. He believed that the position of the Chinese Communists was still not consolidated in the country. For Stalin it all came down to power relationships; "Chiang can easily join the Japanese against the Communists, the Communists cannot join the Japanese." He was concerned that the Communists still harbored illusions. "Some Chinese Communists are dizzy with the idea of an easy victory over the Japanese. It seems to them that if the Japanese defeat Chiang that the Communists could master the situation in the country and drive out the Japanese aggressors. They are badly mistaken." Stalin suspected that if Chiang sensed the danger of losing power or if the West refused to aid him, he would find a way to cooperate with the Japanese. This had to be prevented at all costs.[58]

The Soviet representatives in China were instructed to prevent an open break between the Chinese Communists and the Kuomintang. In January 1941 the Soviet ambassador, A. S. Paniushkin, informed Chiang that Kuomintang attacks on the Communists weakened the military effort against Japan and he warned that civil war would be ruinous for China. General Chuikov, newly arrived from Moscow, carried out Stalin's instructions with military bluntness; such attacks, he declared, could jeopardize the shipment of Soviet military supplies to the Nationalist government.[59]

By this time, however, direct Soviet influence over both contending parties in China had drastically declined. In the wake of the Nazi invasion of June 1941, Moscow recalled the Soviet pilots and most of the military advisors to assume the more urgent task of defending the homeland. The flow of supplies dwindled to a trickle. Soviet influence in Manchuria had already been dealt a severe blow in 1940 when the partisan moment there was virtually wiped out by the Kwantung Army's systematic anti-guerrilla campaign. The survivors, about a thousand men, crossed into Soviet territory where they regrouped and rearmed. They did not reenter the province until the Soviet invasion of 1945. Thus, in both frontier provinces the Soviet presence disappeared and direct access to China was cut off.

The Japanese leaders, shocked by the Nazi-Soviet Pact and sobered by the defeat at Nomonhan, sought to reach an accommodation with the Soviet Union that would strengthen their hand in China and free them to advance to the south. The first stumbling block was the delimitation of the disputed frontier between Manchuria (Manchukuo) and Outer Mongolia. Despite the existence of a joint boundary commission, Molotov took a personal hand in the negotiations, giving proof of his toughness in bargaining over the small details.[60]

Once the frontier issue had been cleared away, in July 1940 the Japanese proposed a neutrality pact. In conversations with Ambassador Tōgō,

[58] V. I. Chuikov, "*Missiia v Kitae.*" *Po dorogam Kitaia, 1937–1945: Vospominaniia* (Moscow: Glav. red. vostochnoi literatury, 1989), pp. 257–9.

[59] Kaliagin, Po neznakomym dorogam, p. 292; Chuikov, "*Missiia,*" pp. 264–6.

[60] DVP, vol. XXX, bk 1, *1 ianvaria–31 oktiabria 1940 g.*, docs. 158, 171, 177, 186, 189, pp. 280, 301, 310–11, 318–20, 322–4.

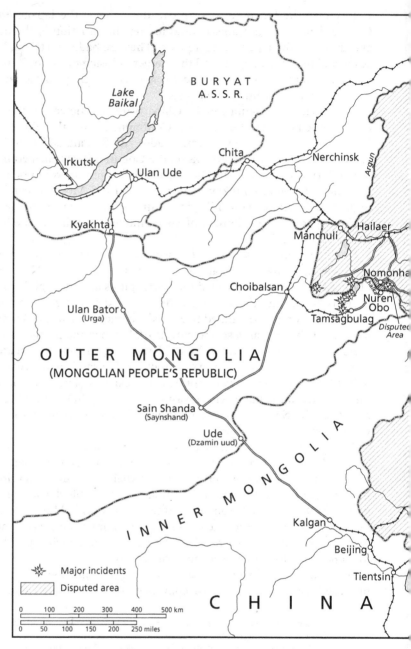

Map 6.4 Inner Asian borderlands, 1930s

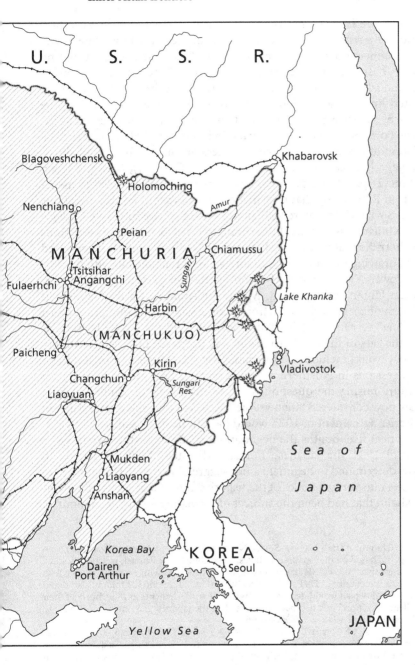

Molotov made it clear that Soviet interests in the Far East were limited and not territorial. He disclaimed any interest in China: "the Soviet
Union is concentrating on its own defense," he told Tōgō; "it had no
weapons to spare for other countries; in fact," he added, somewhat
disingenuously, "we cannot be concerned about other nations." What
interested him was a revision of the Portsmouth Treaty of 1905. "The
Japanese had committed serious violations, and as a result we cannot consider the Portsmouth Treaty to be valid in its entirety." He insisted on the
liquidation of Japanese oil and coal concessions in Northern Sakhalin.[61]

The negotiations took a different turn after Germany, Italy and Japan
signed the Tripartite Pact and Molotov returned from Berlin with assurances from Ribbentrop that the Japanese were eager to improve relations
with the Soviet Union by recognizing a Soviet sphere in Outer Mongolia and Xinjiang, as well as the termination of Japanese oil concessions
in Northern Sakhalin. But the Japanese, like the Germans, entertained
hopes of drawing the Soviet Union into a closer relationship with the Tripartite Powers. They proposed a non-aggression pact like that between
the Soviet Union and Germany. Molotov responded warily. He insisted
on tying the pact to serious territorial concessions, including the return
of the "lost" territories of Southern Sakhalin and the Kurile Islands, or
at least the sale of the northern group. He proposed instead a neutrality
treaty that would include a renunciation by the Japanese of their oil and
coal concessions in Northern Sakhalin with compensation. This would
not require raising the question of Outer Mongolia or Xinjiang which
Molotov now considered "inadvisable" (*netselesoobrazno*). Any revision of
the fisheries agreement of 1925 would have to be dealt with separately.[62]
Over the next five months the negotiations made no further progress.

In April 1941 the Japanese Foreign Minister Matsuoka arrived in
Moscow determined to negotiate a non-aggression treaty. His aim was to
resolve the outstanding issues of the fisheries and coal deposits on Northern Sakhalin that had been the subject of wrangling for eighteen months.

---

[61] Hosoya Chihiro, "The Japanese–Soviet Neutrality Pact," in Morley, *Deterrent Diplomacy*, p. 45, based on the Japanese archives. According to the Russian version, Molotov
only stated that "the USSR has its needs and is occupied with securing its needs in
defense of the country." DVP, vol. XXX, bk 1, doc. 242, p. 403. Molotov also noted
that a neutrality pact would deprive the "White Guard" elements in Manchuria of their
"privileged position" that had been supported by the Japanese, an obvious reference to
the Intervention of 1918–20. *Ibid.*, p. 406.

[62] DVP, vol. XXX, bk 2, part 1, *1 noiabria 1940 g–1 marta 1941 g*, doc. 533, pp. 111–12.
Molotov ironically dismissed Japanese suggestions to buy Northern Sakhalin and the
Maritime Provinces as "a joke." A neutrality treaty freed Japan's hands for action in
the south as the non-aggression pact with Germany had freed its hands for action in
the west. *Ibid.*, doc. 537, p. 118.

Molotov was adamant. He reiterated that the Soviet Union could not conceive of a non-aggression pact without the return of "the lost territories," that is, a return to the territorial status quo before the Russo-Japanese War of 1904–5. Given the fact that the Japanese would probably not consider the return of Southern Sakhalin and the Kurile Islands, he added, it was only "appropriate to negotiate a treaty of neutrality."[63] Stymied by Molotov's intransigence and completely unaware of Hitler's plan to invade the Soviet Union, Matsuoko accepted Stalin's compromise offer to sign a treaty of neutrality. In a separate declaration, the Soviet Union recognized the inviolability of Manchuria and the Japanese recognized the preeminent interest of the Soviet Union in Mongolia. A letter from Matsuoko to Molotov stated the desirability of an agreement on fisheries and on the liquidation of Japanese concessions in Northern Sakhalin. It was a triumph for the Soviet Union.

The Japanese expected, incorrectly, that the treaty would discourage China and that would improve Tokyo's bargaining position with the United States and Great Britain. But the Soviet Union continued to supply China with arms. The main advantage for the Soviet Union was that the treaty deepened the split among Japanese policy-makers on the eve of the German invasion. It did not eliminate the possibility of a two-pronged war, but it reduced its likelihood. Despite the military pressure of the German *Blitzkrieg* in the fall of 1941, Stalin refused to denude his eastern frontier. The Japanese reported a withdrawal of only 7 percent of the Soviet forces to the west; their offensive plans had anticipated a withdrawal of 80 percent. Even the Japanese attempt to extort further diplomatic concessions from the Soviet Union in the Far East proved fruitless. Stalin dismissed their proposals on the Sakhalin concessions and the cessation of aid to China.[64]

In surveying Stalin's borderland policies in the shadow of war, three stages stand out: first he displayed an extreme sensitivity and a strong reaction to any sign of growing influence or pressure by Germany and Japan on the Soviet frontiers in the Baltic littoral, Danubian frontier, Trans Caspia and Inner Asia. Second, he extended diplomatic support and where necessary military aid to governments like republican Spain and Nationalist China engaged in resisting and containing German and Japanese aggression at a far remove from the Soviet borders. At the same

---

[63] N. Slavinskii, *Pakt o neitraliteta mezhdu SSSR i Iaponiei. Diplomaticheskaia istoriia, 1941–1945* (Moscow: TOO Novina, 1995), pp. 70–96, for the stenographic record. Cf. Chihiro, "The Japanese–Soviet Neutrality Pact," pp. 62–3; and Bix, *Hirohito*, pp. 393–4, for summaries based on the Japanese record.

[64] Chihiro, "The Japanese–Soviet Neutrality Pact," pp. 76, 84, 91–3, 95–6, 103–4.

time, he endorsed the idea, which did not originate with him, of popular front movements, allowing Communist parties to join other "non-fascist" parties in coalitions to oppose German and Japanese expansion. Third, when this tactic failed, he sought to seek accommodation with Germany and Japan. This took two forms: first, advancing Soviet boundaries in the western borderlands and settling the boundary between Outer Mongolia and Manchuria; and, second, signing treaties of non-aggression with Germany and neutrality with Japan. During the two years before the outbreak of war, he and Molotov pursued a policy of strict, even legalistic, adherence to the treaties while seeking to avoid associating the Soviet Union with the long-range plans of either Germany or Japan. But Stalin left open the tantalizing possibility that this could change.

In his conversations with Matsuoka, Stalin reassured him that "as far as the Anglo-Saxons were concerned, the Russians had never been their friends and did not strongly wish to be their friends." He was now convinced that the negotiations with the Japanese were not a diplomatic game, as he had thought, but the serious basis for cooperation. Although Hitler had told Molotov that Germany did not need military assistance from other countries, that could change. "If the affairs of Japan and Germany took a turn for the worse then it would be possible to raise the issue of a quadripartite pact and of the cooperation of the Soviet Union on the big questions."[65] The hint was clear. If Germany and Japan found it necessary to secure the direct assistance of the Soviet Union, then they would be forced to meet Stalin's demands in the areas he and not they considered vital to Soviet interests. Judging from Stalin's negotiations with Germany and Japan in 1939 and 1941, these would include restoring the Russian position in the Far East before 1905 and recognizing Soviet hegemony in the Balkans and at the Straits. As it turned out he could not get what he wanted from Hitler and Matsuoka; later he got almost all of it from Churchill and Roosevelt.

Stalin's tactics in acquiring and in consolidating the western border-lands may have been hasty and improvised, but the broader lines of his policies were clear and consistent. The formation of five new Socialist Soviet Republics was intended to ease the process of integrating these lands into the body politic of the Soviet Union. From the time of the Civil War, it had been a cardinal principle of Stalin's borderland policy to establish union republics in the contested frontiers of the Russian Soviet republic. From his perspective, it represented an ideal balance between

---

[65] Slavinskii, *Pakt o neitraliteta*, p. 92. The author argues this meant that Stalin was ready to adhere to a four-pact alliance to divide the world, a fact concealed from the Soviet public for fifty years. *Ibid.*, p. 98.

political centralism and cultural devolution necessary for the preservation of a multinational state. He had remained true to the vision he outlined in the debates over the Soviet constitution in 1922. The territories he added in the period 1939–41 were strategically important, but politically exposed. There were historical precedents for Russian control over those areas, a point that Stalin and Molotov never hesitated to point out. But this was mainly a justification for international consumption. Granting union republic status to these territories extended to them certain cultural advantages, not to say rights. Stalin recognized the importance of acknowledging a nation's historical and cultural identity; the symbolic content of the institutional structure and the use of local languages evoked powerful emotional responses. They would be tolerated just so long as they did not stimulate political aspirations. His multinational solution may have been a far cry from local autonomy, to say nothing of a real federation, but it was the next best thing. It created important positions and opened bureaucratic careers that were normally denied to minority nationalities in large authoritarian multinational states. And it allowed those who took advantage to salve their nationalistic conscience. It created alternative channels to movements for national liberation. At the same time it enabled the central apparatus to exercise all real political and economic authority.

The key to success in assimilation – and it could perhaps never be a total success – was time: time to build new cadres of loyal local officials, to transform the culture from a nationalist to a Soviet content, to reach the young indigenous population by introducing them to Russian language and culture. But in 1939–40 time was a precious commodity. And Stalin was not a patient man. The hasty and often brutal means he employed to secure a territorial buffer undermined his drive for integration. For strategic purposes he compromised his own nationalities doctrine. By annexing part of Ingria and Bessarabia he created irredenta for Finland and Romania, turning them into revisionist states. Their right-wing politicians and military were emboldened to plan more ambitiously for an even Greater Finland and a Greater Romania at Soviet expense with the support of Germany. In the event of war, the loyalty of the Baltic populations was highly problematic. Instead of being reluctant allies of the Soviet Union in resisting German aggression that threatened their national independence, they became subversive elements in the rear of the Red Army.

Stalin's error was not in signing a non-aggression pact with Hitler. Given the history of Western appeasement and apparent attempts to turn Germany to the East, the pact was a logical precautionary step consonant with Soviet national security. In fact, Litvinov gave the most reasoned defense of the pact in a memo drafted in 1940 for Soviet radio, but never broadcast. He emphasized that although he had nothing to do with the negotiations, he would have signed it but acted differently. He restated his disappointment with the Western response to his policy of collective security. The reactionary elements in those countries had done everything in their power to turn Hitler to the East. "Under these conditions the choice facing the Soviet Union," he declared, "was either to accept for purposes of self-defense the proposal made by Germany to conclude an agreement on non-aggression and guarantee the Soviet Union a continuation of peace for a specific period which could be used by the Soviet government to better prepare its forces for possible attack by an aggressor; or to reject Germany's proposed pact of non-aggression and thereby allow the fomenters of war within the Western camp to drag the Soviet Union rapidly into an armed conflict with Germany in highly unfavorable conditions for the Soviet Union in conditions of its complete isolation." However, Litvinov took pains to separate himself from the Zhdanov–Molotov line. It was still necessary, he argued, to continue the negotiations with Britain and France.[66] In other words, the Nazi–Soviet Pact should have been used to strengthen the supporters of collective security in the West by demonstrating the danger to Britain and France of having to fight a one-front war against Germany. Litvinov had never given up on the policy of collective security. He believed that Soviet diplomacy could play a decisive role in resolving the fierce struggle dividing Western opinion by tipping the balance in favor of the advocates of collective security and against appeasement. Above all, he believed, the Soviet Union must remain part of the international system and avoid isolation. Stalin never fully understood the international system, and what he saw of it he distrusted. For him the best diplomacy was bilateral in form and vague in content. He preferred agreements that left him a great deal of room to maneuver. His favorite instruments were the army and obedient members of local Communist parties. For him the best form of security was territorial. The combination was, in his mind, irresistible.

In Trans Caspia the main objective of Stalin's policies was to oppose German and Japanese efforts to gain commercial and political influence by using technical experts and cultivating sympathetic politicians in the ruling elites. In neither case were local left-wing elements numerous or sufficiently well disciplined in the Bolshevik mold to create a united front. In Inner Asia, technical and military aid to Outer Mongolia and Xinjiang

---

[66] Sheinis, *Litvinov*, pp. 374–5. Molotov refused to approve the test for international broadcast and Litvinov was then dismissed from his post on the Radio Committee of the Foreign Commissariat.

steadily increased their dependence on the Soviet Union, providing a defensive glacis against a further Japanese advance to the west and maintaining the only overland route for supplying China with military aid. Stalin's attitude toward the Chinese Communists was ambivalent. He pressed them hard to accept the tactic of a united front, but was reluctant to supply them with any military aid that might antagonize Chiang and push him into an agreement with Japan. Stalin's representatives in Yenan were wary of Mao Zedong. They deplored his ideology of agrarian revolution and his hostility to a united front and they supported the returning students' faction in the Chinese Communist Party to offset his policies. Above all Stalin feared a civil war that would weaken resistance against Japan. He continued to regard Chiang as the only Chinese leader who could hold the country together.

On the eve of war, Soviet relations with foreign Communist parties underwent a radical change, foreshadowing the abolition of the Comintern in 1943. Stalin had never shown much respect for it. It was not a healthy organism. Its history had been marked by intense factionalism, periodic purges and rapid volte-faces. In 1929 the patient took a turn for the worse. The removal of Bukharin as its head changed the way in which decisions were reached. Stalin was determined to eliminate all traces of open disagreement and private dissention. In a series of spiteful measures, he signaled that the Comintern would no longer play a prominent role in international relations. He took personal control over the Comintern administration and created a special section of his secretariat to by-pass the established chain of command; no decisions were to be taken without his sanction.[67] A new wave of repression began as a purge of the "rights," that is the supporters of Bukharin, but rapidly degenerated into an orgy of personal denunciations that crossed ideological lines. For his own dark reasons, Stalin did not, however, turn over the Comintern to the "left" doctrinaires. A number of prominent "Bukharinites" including a few like Humbert-Droz who did not openly recant, were not suppressed but merely transferred. Stalin's stalwarts came down hard on the German, Czech and Polish parties. The Italian and Bulgarian parties enjoyed relative immunity because the Italian leadership had chosen exile in France rather than Moscow and Dimitrov was able to protect most if not all his countrymen.[68]

---

[67] Jules Humbert-Droz, "La crise de croissance de l'internationale communiste," in *Annali 1967* (Milan: Istituto Giangiacomo Feltrinelli, 1968), pp. 33–40, and throughout; Niels Erik Rosenfeldt, *Stalin's Secret Chancellery and the Comintern* (Copenhagen: C. A. Reitzels, 1966), pp. 49, 59, 62–3.

[68] Branko M. Lazich, "Stalin's Massacre of the Foreign Communist Leaders," in Milorad M. Drachkovitch and Branko M. Lazich (eds.), *The Comintern: Historical Highlights: Essays, Recollections, Documents* (Stanford University Press, 1966), pp. 167–9, 173.

Stalin had drawn the clumsy distinction between "the right" as a tendency not yet well-defined, which ought to be exposed and chastised, and "the right" as a group or faction which ought to be repressed. His agents in the Comintern defined "the right" in the German Communist Party as a faction and demanded its destruction by "organizational methods." The hammer fell next on the Czech rightists.[69] The Polish Communist Party was shaken to the core, foreshadowing its abolition seven years later. It was accused of having worked for the Polish secret police in their efforts to infiltrated the West Ukrainian Party and subvert the Ukrainian SSR. The savagery of these purges in the years before the Kirov assassination in 1934 may in part be attributed to Stalin's grave concern over the stability of Ukraine during the worst years of collectivization. But the wave of denunciations merely facilitated the infiltration of the Polish Communist Party by the Polish police; provocateurs then helped to cripple the party by denouncing its leaders.[70]

Increasingly feeble and dominated by sectarians ("the left"), the Polish Party showed little enthusiasm for the Popular Front. Dimitrov prodded them to get rid of their image as "Moscow's agents." He further urged them to build bridges to other parties and mass organizations and to select an authoritative and self-confident leadership.[71]

As we have seen, by 1937 Stalin had made explicit the link between the dangers of foreign aggression, the stability of the borderlands and internal subversion by the joint opposition. Simultaneously, he drew his web of intrigue and terror around the national parties in the Comintern. As early as 1936 the NKVD had already launched a campaign to uncover agents provocateurs in the enfeebled Polish Communist Party and to root out members of the Polish Military Organization in the USSR which by this time no longer existed except as a convenient fiction in the fertile imagination of police agents.[72]

---

[69] *La correspondance internationale*, January 9, 1929, no 2; March 13, 1929, no. 23; May 4, 1929, no. 37; May 8, 1929, no. 38; June 12, 1929, no. 49; X Plenum IKKI, *Mezhdunarodnoe polozhenie i zadachi Kommunisticheskogo internationala* (Moscow: Partizdat, 1929), speeches by Ulbricht, pp. 5–7; Kuusinen, pp. 16–20; and Manuilskii, pp. 62–4; Stalin, *Sochineniia*, vol. XI, pp. 306–9.

[70] F. I. Firsov and I. S. Iazhborovskaia, "Komintern i kommunisticheskaia partiia Pol'shi," *Voprosy istorii KPSS* 12 (December, 1988), pp. 41–3.

[71] "Novye dokumenty G. Dimitrova," *Voprosy istoriii KPSS* 8 (August, 1989), pp. 75–7.

[72] The Comintern Executive responded to the mounting pressure to exert greater vigilance by notifying Ezhov, the head of the NKVD, that the Polish Party was "the major supplier of spies and provocateurs in the USSR." It accused the party of every sin in the Stalinist book: left sectarianism, right nationalist deviation, factional struggles and links to Polish intelligence. William J. Chase, *Enemies within the Gates? The Comintern and Stalinist Repression, 1934–1939* (New Haven, CT: Yale University Press, 2001), pp. 116–19, 121–24, quotation on p. 116.

With the approval of the Politburo, Ezhov coordinated the so-called "Polish operation," the most devastating attack on a national group within the Soviet Union and on the largest Communist Party in Eastern Europe.[73] Within Poland the purge wiped out the remnants of the old majority which had been sympathetic to Bukharin and then eliminated the minority. Members of the Polish Politburo in exile in Paris were recalled to Moscow and arrested. Other Stalinist loyalists considered it their duty to return from Prague, Spain and Warsaw to defend themselves. They too perished. The entire leadership was engulfed, including the last member of the Polish Politburo who had endorsed the arrest of all his colleagues. Yet the operation was carried out in such secrecy that neither the Comintern Executives nor the rank and file of the Polish Party knew about them.[74] It was only a formality then when the Comintern Executive ordered the dissolution of the party. Reorganization was out of the question because "the central organs were in the hands of spies and provocateurs." Stalin approved, but characteristically noted that "the dissolution is two years late." The Comintern recommended that the party be entirely recreated by Polish members of the International Brigades fighting in Spain.[75]

Ezhov's scythe cut a wide swath in the Polish and Hungarian sections of the Comintern, reducing them to one man each. The Chinese and Bulgarian sections also lost almost all their members to the "conveyer." The German section was reduced by 70 percent. Among the Yugoslav party cadres in the Soviet Union at least 800 out of 900 were arrested and only forty of these survived the camps. Tito, rescued by Dimitrov, survived unchallenged at the top of the decimated party. The leaders of the Romanian Party in Moscow were almost all shot, including Marcel Pauker whose wife Ana survived, adopted Soviet citizenship and emerged after the war as a leader of the party.[76] The Iranian Communists who had fled to Moscow after the collapse of the Ghilan Republic in 1921 were already in trouble in 1932 and little was heard of them thereafter.[77]

---

[73] Nikita Petrov and Arsenii Roginskii, "The 'Polish Operation' of the NKVD, 1937–8," in McLoughlin and McDermott, *Stalin's Terror*, pp. 153–72.

[74] Firsov and Iazhborovskaia, "Komintern," pp. 48–51.

[75] Chase, *Enemies*, pp. 287–9. Formal dissolution was delayed by nine months, reflecting Stalin's wishes to avoid demoralizing all the other parties.

[76] Robert Levy, *Ana Pauker: The Rise and Fall of a Jewish Communist* (Berkeley: University of California Press, 2001), pp. 37, 53–4 and 63–4.

[77] Alfred Burmeister, *Dissolution and Aftermath of the Comintern: Experiences and Observations, 1937–1947*, Research Program on the USSR East European Fund, no. 77, pp. 1–2; Ivo Banac, *With Stalin Against Tito: Cominform Splits in Yugoslav Communism* (Ithaca, NY: Cornell University Press, 1988), pp. 67–8; Ghita Ionescu, *Communism in Romania* (London: Oxford University Press, 1964), pp. 43, 352, 355; Chaqueri, "Sultanzade,"

The purges struck hard at the elite Comintern schools in the Soviet Union. The Communist University for the National Minorities of the West which had enrolled about 600 students from the western Soviet borderlands in the period 1933–6 was dissolved. Most of the students were sent to Spain except for the Volga German contingent who were arrested. Some of the German graduates survived, however, and went on to occupy important posts in the German Democratic Republic after the war. The Communist University of the Toilers of the East suffered fewer losses, but the Chinese students appeared to have been singled out. The staff of the Lenin school for the upper ranks of the Comintern was decimated. The Comintern German-language newspaper was repeatedly purged, leaving only one person in charge by the end. When the paper was finally suspended, most of its readership joined the staff in the camps. The most fortunate Communists were those who had been imprisoned in their own countries, Hungary, Romania and Poland in particular, beyond the reach of the NKVD.[78]

The devastating effects of the Comintern purges on the national parties elicited a few desperate efforts by individual Communists to stem the bloody tide. Evgenii Varga wrote a personal letter to Stalin courageously arguing that the purges were leading to the demoralization of Communist cadres in fascist countries "who would have a prominent role to play in the forthcoming war!"[79] Although Dimitrov authorized most of the purges, he knew that they were decimating his organization. He tried to protect some of his colleagues but sacrificed others in what amounted to triage.[80] But he was unwilling to confront Stalin directly. The best he felt he could do was to point out that the arrests of former leaders of the parties in the independent states of Lithuania, Latvia and Estonia as well as Poland, "left sincere Communists in those countries disoriented and

---

pp. 3–2: 226, 234; Touraj Atabaki, "'Incommodious Hosts Invidious Guests': The Life and Times of Iranian Revolutionaries in the Soviet Union 1921–39," in Stephanie Cronin, *Reformers and Revolutionaries in Modern Iran: New Perspectives on the Iranian Left* (London: Routledge Curzon, 2004), pp. 155–9; Kevin McDermott and Jeremy Agnew, *The Comintern: A History of International Communism from Lenin to Stalin* (London: Macmillan, 1996), pp. 148–9.

[78] Burmeister, *Dissolution*, pp. 5–12.

[79] "Muzhestvo protiv bezzakoniia," *Problemy mira i sotsializma* 7 (1989), p. 91.

[80] F. I. Firsov, "Dimitrov, the Comintern and Stalinist Repression," in McLoughlin and McDermott, *Stalin's Terror*, pp. 75–7. There is some evidence he was not alone; others in the Comintern Executive, including Wilhelm Pieck, Vasil Kolarev and Mátyás Rákosi (himself probably rescued by Dimitrov), attempted to have the cases of their arrested colleagues reviewed. N. S. Lebedeva and M. M. Narinskii, "Komintern i vtoraia mirovaia voina, 1939–1941," in K. M. Anderson and A. O. Chubar'ian (eds.), *Komintern i vtoraia mirovaia voina*, 2 vols. (Moscow: Pamiatniki istoricheskoi mysli, 1994), vol. I, pt 1: *Do iiunia 1941 g.*, p. 53.

with no connection to the Comintern." He requested assistance from the Central Committee in selecting a few comrades from the All-Union Communist Party who spoke the native languages to help reconstruct the shattered parties.[81]

The wonder was that the international cadres were not utterly demoralized, that the parties did not simply wither away. To be sure, many party members in Eastern Europe and the Soviet Union had quite literally nowhere else to go. To attempt to escape from prison or evade arrest and flee would probably have meant falling into the hands of the Gestapo or foreign security agencies. In Spain and the rest of Western Europe, a more subtle power held them in place. They were unable to conceive of a political existence outside the party which defined their entire world view. The celebrated intellectuals who denounced "the God that failed" were exceptional both in their ability to rationalize their actions and to reconstruct their world view on a different basis.[82]

What may appear to be even more surprising than the behavior of the rank and file was Stalin's view of the condemned. During and even after the Great Patriotic War, some survivors of the camps were permitted to return to their homelands and even to occupy positions of real responsibility in the new "Popular Democracies." There were pressing practical reasons for these unofficial "amnesties" of former "spies and saboteurs." But beyond that Stalin could be sure that these men and women would be eager under all circumstances to prove their unconditional loyalty to instructions from Moscow.

The Nazi–Soviet Pact shook the tottering structure of the Comintern to its foundations, triggering prominent if not mass defections. The new Comintern line, dictated by Stalin, created an unforeseen problem when it undertook initially to condemn both the fascist and capitalist democratic governments of equal responsibility in the outbreak of an imperialist war. Although the leaders of the Communist parties generally endorsed the demise of collective security, too much had been invested in anti-fascism to give it up so easily. In France, Thorez led the parliamentary delegation of Communists in a summons "to fight against fascism and Nazism," greeting all Communist recruits in the army and voting for the war credits. The Belgian Party followed suit, while the British

---

[81] Dimitrov to Andreev, January 3, 1939 in Chase, *Enemies*, doc. 44, pp. 307–8.

[82] For the internal world of the Communists, see Annie Kriegel, *The French Communists: Profile of a People* (University of Chicago Press, 1972), especially part 2. For insights into the attitudes and rationalizations of sympathetic Western visitors to the Soviet Union in the Stalinist years, which have parallels with the behavior of embattled Communists, see Michael David-Fox, *Showcasing the Great Experiment* (New York: Oxford University Press, 2012).

Communist Party took a more ambivalent stand, advocating national unity against Germany but also a two-front war directed against the Chamberlain government. The German Communists found the new line particularly hard to swallow. Walter Ulbricht asserted that their first task ought to be the struggle for a people's republic: "This aim can only be achieved by means of a struggle for peace, for a popular revolution with the aim of overthrowing the fascist military criminals, eliminating the causes of war [and] the reign of capital."[83] Stalin rejected the idea of revolution and tolerated no deviations: "the division of capitalist countries between fascist and democratic has lost its former meaning," he declared. Once the Red Army invaded Poland, the Comintern Executive denounced Communists who had supported their countries and disavowed the formation of anti-fascist "national legions" made up of volunteers of "Communists and revolutionary elements" on the Spanish model. Beginning in late October 1939 the Soviet leaders, followed by the Comintern Executive, turned the full force of their propaganda against the British and French for continuing the war after the surrender of Poland.[84] But they did not abandon the idea of the popular front in China; instead they urged the Chinese Communists, and with even greater insistence, to maintain the anti-Japanese front in the face of deteriorating relations with the Kuomintang.

A subtle change began to seep into Comintern instructions after the fall of France. Stalin had to give up the illusion that a stalemate in the west would keep the bulk of German troops engaged far distant from the Soviet frontier. The French Communists were now urged to defend the material interests of the working class but also "to struggle against the foreign yoke for the real freedom and independence of France."[85] This had to be done legally, to be sure, and directed mainly against the government of Pétain. When the French Communists went too far in negotiating with the German occupation authorities, the Comintern sounded the alarm, instructing them to reject any form of collaboration and cautiously to exploit mass discontent against the occupiers. As German and Italian intervention in the Balkans proceeded, first in the Vienna arbitrations giving part of Romanian Transylvania to Hungary, then in the pressure on Bulgaria to join the Tripartite Pact, and finally in the invasion of Greece and Yugoslavia by Italian and German forces, the Comintern broadened its appeals to resist the aggressors.[86] The Soviet leadership

---

[83] Lebedeva and Narinskii, "Komintern," p. 15.   [84] *Ibid.*, pp. 8–14, 16–20.

[85] *Ibid.*, doc. 104, pp. 371–2. By early 1941, the Comintern Executive had taken up the position that de Gaulle, despite his anti-democratic views, "is playing objectively a progressive role" in weakening the occupier. *Ibid.*, doc. 140, p. 475.

[86] Chase, *Enemies*, pp. 39–44; docs. 142, 164, 166, pp. 482–4, 518, 519–20.

began to grasp the importance of drawing distinctions among the Communist parties and their goals. According to Stalin, *"World revolution as a single act is nonsense. It transpires at different times in different countries."*[87] Andrei Zhdanov picked up the theme a month later. During a discussion in the Central Committee Secretariat on the reestablishment of Comintern schools, he stressed the importance of studying one's own country. "We got off the track on the national question," he declared. Dimitrov chimed in: "A combination of pro[letarian] internationalism and the healthy national feelings of the given people. Our 'internationalists' have to be trained," he concluded.[88] Stalin was even more explicit when he told Dimitrov that different conditions demanded a reconstruction of the Comintern. "Today," he said in April 1941, "the national tasks of the various countries stand in the forefront. But the position of Com[munist] parties as sections of an international organization, subordinated to the Executive Committee of the KI [Communist International], is an obstacle." Brusquely dismissing the *"parochial* interests" of the Comintern Executive, he spelled out his new approach: "The membership of the Com[munist] parties within the Comintern in current conditions facilitates bourgeois persecution of them and the bourgeois plan to isolate them from the masses of their own countries, while it prevents the Communist parties from developing independently and resolving their own problems as *national* parties."[89] The Comintern Executive responded immediately. In a discussion among the "troika" of leaders, Dimitrov, Thorez and Togliatti, further progress was made toward "granting full independence to the individual Com[munist] parties, converting them into authentic national parties of Communists in their respective countries, guided by a Communist program, ready to resolve their own concrete problems, in accordance with the conditions in their countries, and themselves bearing responsibility for their decisions and actions."[90] In 1943 the Comintern was abolished in name only. It was restructured as the Section of International Information under the aegis of the Central Committee of the CPSU with most of the same personnel. Then in December 1945 it was renamed the Section of Foreign Policy with new functions to prepare cadres for relations with foreign Communist parties and workers' organizations.[91]

The timing and rationale, as well as the discussions involved in the preliminaries leading up to the restructuring of the Comintern after

---

[87] Banac, *The Diary of Georgi Dimitrov*, entry for January 21, 1940, p. 124, italics in original.
[88] *Ibid.*, entry for February 27, 1941, p. 137.
[89] *Ibid.*, entry for April 20, 1941, p. 156.   [90] *Ibid.*, entry of April 21, 1941, p. 156.
[91] G. M. Adibekov *et al.* (eds.), *Organizatsionnaia struktura Kominterna, 1919–1943* (Moscow: Rosspen, 1997), pp. 228–40.

its abolition, point in several directions. Stalin had long distrusted the organization for harboring all kinds of oppositionists. The difficulties of coordinating the activities of all the individual parties were magnified in the complex conditions of war. It was clear that Communist parties in countries under foreign occupation would have very different tasks than those which were still independent. It also suited Stalin, as will become even clearer in the chapters devoted to his war aims, to deal on a bilateral basis with each party. In this way he could intervene, when necessary, to adjust its policies to the specific needs of the Soviet Union. At the same time, by allowing a degree of freedom of action, he could discredit the leadership of an individual party for committing errors without invoking change in the "general line" which would affect all the parties. Finally, the prominence of the leaders of the two leading Communist parties in the West suggests that as in Spain, Stalin may already have concluded that the national traditions of France and Italy, with their history of representative institutions and more highly developed socioeconomic structures, might better suit them for a "parliamentary path" to socialism than the backward, agrarian states of Eastern Europe. This would be in accord with his earliest pronouncements on Romania and Poland and, as we shall see, with his views on France and Italy during and immediately after World War II.

Stalin's approach to foreign policy recalls the older Russian tradition of dealing with weaker but troublesome non-Russian peoples of the Eurasian borderlands. A recurrent strategy was to cultivate a small "Russian party" on the opposite side of the frontier. The aims were multiple and complex: first, to use them when convenient to stir up internal rebellions or disorders; second, to negotiate agreements which compromised the sovereignty of the local ruling elites; and, third, to take advantage of pressures from external powers to demand concessions and occupy strategic strong points along the frontier or even station armed forces inside a disputed territory. Originally designed to deal with steppe peoples, these tactics were also applied in modified form to foreign relations with powers along the western frontiers that shared indeterminate frontier zones with Russia – Sweden, Poland and the Ottoman Empire. Stalin, whose early experience in foreign policy replicated, *mutatis mutandis*, the conquest of the non-Russian periphery during the Civil War, had re-learned the value of these tactics. The only difference was the greater usefulness of local Communists as "the Russian party." With this reservation, Stalin may be called the last of the steppe politicians.

7   Civil wars in the borderlands

The German invasion of the Soviet Union ripped apart the fabric of Soviet society at its most vulnerable seam along the western and southwestern borderlands. In the case of the territories annexed in 1939–40 – the Baltic republics, Western Belorussia, Western Ukraine and Bessarabia – hostility toward the Soviet power, Russian carpetbaggers and Jewish and Polish minorities lay close to the surface. Bitter memories of forced deportations of indigenous political and cultural elites, anti-religious decrees and the beginnings of collectivization were recent and vivid.[1] The national Communist parties in the borderlands, decimated by the purges four or five years earlier, were in no position to help sustain Soviet power or organize resistance to the invasion, or later to the Nazi occupation authorities.

For a decade Stalin had preached the doctrine of capitalist encirclement and the threat of war. He had eliminated any challenge to his personal dictatorship and secured full control over decision-making in foreign policy. He had tamed the Comintern; the danger no longer existed that foreign Communist parties might drag the Soviet Union into an international conflict by engaging in revolutionary adventurism. He had undertaken a rapid industrialization of the country, laying the foundations for a modern armaments industry. These were extraordinary achievements. Yet the means he had chosen to obtain his ends threatened to undermine the security of the state that he strove to guarantee. In the tension-filled years leading up the outbreak of the conflict, he had severely reduced the capabilities of the architects of the Soviet security system. The purges had cut deeply into the ranks of the weapons designers, the officer corps and the diplomats.[2] Stalin remained obsessed

---

[1] V. S. Parsadanova, "Deportatsiia naseleniia iz zapadnoi Ukrainy i zapadnoi Belorussii v 1939–1941 gg," *Novaia i noveishaia istoriia* 2 (1989), pp. 26–44; N. S. Lebedeva, "The Deportation of the Polish Population to the USSR, 1939–41," in Alfred J. Rieber (ed.), *Forced Migration in Central and Eastern Europe, 1939–1950* (London: Frank Cass, 2000), pp. 28–45.

[2] For weapons designers, B. L. Vannikov, "Iz zapisok Narkoma Vooruzheniia," *Voenno-Istoricheskii Zhurnal* 2 (February, 1962), pp. 78–86; "Zapiski sovremenika o M. N.

with the security of the borderlands. But his suspicious nature was robbing him of the ability to assess the main source of danger or even to distinguish between imagined and real threats. This showed up most clearly in military planning and intelligence-gathering.

The planning of military operations was based on a faulty assumption which reflected the overweening importance that Stalin and his closest advisors attributed to Ukraine. After the Nazi–Soviet partition of Eastern Europe into spheres of influence, the operational plan was revised for the fifteenth time since 1924. A dispute over the main theater of operations had arisen between the Commissar of Defense, S. K. Timoshenko and Marshal B. M. Shaposhnikov, who argued, correctly as it turned out, that the main German attack would come on the northwestern front. Timoshenko, supported by his subordinates in the Commissariat and General Staff including Generals N. F. Vatutin and G. K. Zhukov, believed the main thrust would come in the southwest. They may have been influenced by the fact that they had all begun their service in the Kiev military district. Stalin supported their view, convinced that Hitler could not fight a prolonged war without the grain and iron ore of Ukraine.[3] Other strategic factors were also in play. Timoshenko pointed out that a Soviet counter-offensive along the southern front would cut Germany off from its important economic base (presumably Romanian oil) and influence the Balkan countries to come in on the Soviet side.[4]

On the basis of Stalin's repeated concern over the loyalty of the Ukrainians, it is also a fair assumption that he feared a deep penetration of the German Army into this volatile borderland would lead to serious political consequences. In this he was right. This explains in part the last draft

Tukhachevskom," *ibid.*, 4 (April, 1963), pp. 67–8; P. K. Oshchepov, *Zhizn' i mechta: zapiski inzhenera-izobratelia, instruktora i uchenego* (Moscow: Moskovskii rabochii, 1967); speeches by B. P. Beschev and N. M. Shvernik at the Twenty-Second Party Congress, *Current Digest of the Soviet Press* 14:2 (February 7, 1962), pp. 24–5, 14:5 (February 24, 1962), pp. 25–6; Roy Medvedev *Let History Judge* (New York: Knopf, 1971), pp. 228–30. For the officer corps, Roger Reece, "The Red Army and the Great Purges," in J. Arch Getty and Roberta T. Manning (eds.), *Stalinist Terror: New Perspectives* (Cambridge University Press, 1993), p. 213. In certain frontier districts like Kiev the replacement of top officers was extremely high, up to 100 percent of corps commanders and 96 percent of the divisional commanders. O. F. Suveninov, "Vsearmeiskaia tragediia," *Voenno- Istoricheskii zhurnal* 3 (March, 1989), pp. 47–8. For the diplomats, V. V. Sokolov, "Na postu zamestitelia Narkoma inostrannykh del SSSR (O zhizni i deiatel'nosti B.S. Stomoniakova"), *Mezhdunarodnaia zhizn'* 5 (1988), pp. 147–8; A. A. Roshchin, "V narkomindele nakanune voiny," *ibid.*, 4 (1988), pp. 122–3, and Sabine Dullin, *Men of Influence: Stalin's Diplomats in Europe* (Edinburgh University Press, 2008).
[3] Iu. A. Gorkov, *Kreml'. Stavka. Genshtab* (Tver: RIF LTD, 1995), pp. 55–6; M. Zakharov, *General'nyi Shtab predvoennyi gody* (Moscow: Voenizdat, 1989), pp. 219–20.
[4] V. P. Naumov *et al.* (eds.), *Rossiia XX veka: Dokumenty. 1941 god*, 2 vols. (Moscow: Mezhdunarodnyi fund Demokratiia, 1998), vol. I, doc. 134, p. 289.

revision of the operational plan which included a proposal to forestall a German offensive by "attacking the German Army at the moment when it would be at the stage of deployment and had not yet succeeded in organizing its battle front and coordinating the action of the different branches of its forces."[5] This assumed that the Red Army would have ample notification of a German offensive and would already be deployed to launch a preemptive attack. The draft was never approved by Stalin, although it has been interpreted as evidence that he was planning a preventive war.[6] All the revisions including the last ones were variations on Marshal Tukhachevskii's concept of an active defense followed by counter-attacks. The real problem was not the lack of a plan or the damaging assumption that the main direction of the invasion would come in the southwest. Rather it was the unforeseen breakdown in the organization of the operational defense which depended on a strongly fortified line facing the western frontier.

The construction of such a line required very large resources, and construction was slow. In January 1939 the NKVD had sharply criticized the condition of the fortified regions. This led Stalin to authorize the creation of Special Departments of the NKVD which were given extraordinary powers not only to investigate subversive activities in the Red Army and Navy but also to report on the military and moral shortcomings of the armed forces at every level. After the territorial expansion of the Soviet Union from 1939 to 1940 an attempt was made to move the fortifications to new positions further west. Construction work continued at a high tempo. But the NKVD continued its criticism of the army. New emplacements were not provided with large-caliber guns and half the pillboxes lacked artillery. Consequently, the decision was taken in the spring of 1941 to retain the old fortified regions as the basis for operational defense. On the eve of the war their restoration had not reached a level of combat preparedness.[7] The fortified regions were

---

[5] Gorkov, *Kreml'*, pp. 61–2.

[6] The idea of a preemptive strike was initiated by Victor Suvorov (a.k.a. Rezin), *Ice Breaker: Who Started the Second World War?* (London: Hamish Hamilton,1990), with a Russian edition in 1992. The book gave rise to an extensive debate in Russia. See *Mif 'Ledokhoda': nakanune voiny* (Moscow: 1995). For Western refutations of the central thesis, see Gabriel Gorodetsky, "Was Stalin Planning to Attack Hitler in June 1941?," *Journal of the Royal United Services Institute* 1341:3 (1986), pp. 19–30; David M. Glantz, *Stumbling Colossus: The Red Army on the Eve of World War* (Lawrence: University of Kansas Press, 1998), pp. 1–8; Teddy Uldricks, "The Icebreaker Controversy: Did Stalin Plan to Attack Hitler?," *Slavic Review* 58:3 (Fall, 1999), pp. 626–43; and John Erikson, "Barbarossa, June 1941: Who Attacked Whom?," *History Today* 51:7 (2001), pp. 11–17.

[7] *Organy gosudarstvennogo bezopastnosti SSSR v Velikoi Otechestvenoi Voine: Sbornik dokumentov.* 2 vols. (Moscow, A/O Kniga i biznes, 1995), vol. I, bk 1: *Nakanune (noiabr' 1938–dekabr' 1940)*, docs. 4 and 5, pp. 22–5, 26–8, 35.

woefully undermanned. The operational rear required reorganization in order to support the new lines of defense. But the underdeveloped transportation networks, especially roads, were inadequate to move food, fuel and munitions efficiently and rapidly to the front line units. When the German attacks struck the forward positions and broke through, their momentum could not be contained. Counter-attacks, frantically ordered by Stalin could not be organized and the entire southwest front collapsed. The buffer zone of the borderlands acquired by diplomacy turned out in military terms to be a trap.

In the field of intelligence, the very abundance of information tended to obscure rather than clarify Hitler's intentions, and Stalin reacted by suspecting the most reliable sources. Even after the massive arrests and executions of high-ranking officers, Stalin continued to show a profound distrust of the professional military leaders right up to the outbreak of war. He insisted that military intelligence be subordinated to the Commissariat of Defense rather than the General Staff. Even then, Marshal Timoshenko complained that he was not informed about all the intelligence-gathering operations. His deputy, F. I. Golikov, who headed the Main Intelligence Administration, reported directly to Stalin; he had close ties with Beria with whom he often presented joint reports. On the eve of the invasion Stalin appears to have relied heavily on Beria who was "filtering out" material on the threatening situation on the Soviet frontiers.[8]

In the months before the invasion, the Soviet leadership was bombarded with intelligence reports from agents in Germany and Japan warning of an impending attack.[9] The information was collected and analyzed by several Soviet intelligence organizations. But in line with Stalin's suspicion of "departmentalism," there was no central clearing house or even a systematic exchange of information within the intelligence community. Like most intelligence, the material that Stalin was reading contained raw – that is, unevaluated – data, some of it contradictory or mistaken in specifying the date of the attack. But there were other reasons why Stalin failed to credit the mass of accurate intelligence and was taken by surprise on June 22, 1941.

---

[8] Vladimir Lota, *Sekretnyi front General'nogo shtaba* (Moscow: Molodaia Gvardiia, 2005), pp. 36, 46–7, 60–8.

[9] Two large collections of documents contain intelligence reports: Naumov, *1941*, and *Organy gosudarstvennogo bezopasnosti*. The latter is the official publication of the Russian security services (FSB) which seeks to demonstrate that the intelligence was ample and accurate enough to predict the timing and scope of the attack but that the information was disregarded by Stalin and the supreme command.

David Holloway has identified three factors that diminished the value of Soviet intelligence. First, Stalin was suspicious of certain well-placed agents, such as Victor Sorge in Tokyo, who had access to secret documents in the German embassy; second, Soviet intelligence lacked an agent in the top ranks of the Nazi and Wehrmacht elite; and, third, the Germans had been successful in spreading dis-information which had already worked to defame Marshal Tukhachevskii, leading to his execution.[10]

These shortcomings were magnified by Stalin's erroneous assumptions about Hitler's strategic plans and intentions with respect to the Soviet Union. He believed that Hitler would not repeat the mistake of Imperial Germany in 1914 by fighting a two-front war. So long as Britain resisted, the Soviet Union had time to perfect its military preparations.[11] He also suspected that Britain, desperate to draw the Soviet Union into the war, was feeding him false information on the impending attack. He further assumed that Hitler would precede an attack by issuing an ultimatum demanding more economic concessions. Finally, he was led to understand that the German leadership was divided over the question of war with the Soviet Union and that it was imperative to avoid a provocation that would tip the balance in favor of the more aggressive military planners in Berlin.[12]

Under pressure from the Soviet High Command, Stalin reluctantly began to strengthen the frontier defenses on the eve of the German attack. Beginning on June 12, Timoshenko and Zhukov repeatedly urged Stalin to bring the front line forces up to full combat readiness. Stalin, fearing this would provoke Germany, only agreed to issue orders on the very eve of the German invasion. Timoshenko's independent initiative to mobilize the Kiev Military District was blocked by Beria who denounced the move to Stalin as fraught with dangerous consequences for Soviet–German relations. Beria lost no chance to undermine the professional cadres, and Stalin was always ready to lend a willing ear.[13] The mistakes in planning and the failure of intelligence led to a series of disasters.

---

[10] David Holloway, "Stalin and Intelligence: Two Cases," unpublished paper. I am grateful to Professor Holloway for sharing this with me.
[11] Stalin was not alone in holding this view. In his memoirs Marshal K. A. Meretskov noted that "we could not stay out of the war until 1943, of course ... but it was not inconceivable (*ne iskliucheno*) that we could stay out of war until 1942." *Na sluzhbe narodu*, 5th edn (Moscow: Izd. politicheskoi literatury, 1988), pp. 194–5.
[12] Holloway, "Stalin and Intelligence"; Gorodetsky, Grand *D*elusion, pp. 222–6; and Roberts, From World War to Cold War, pp. 64–70.
[13] G. K. Zhukov, "Iz nepublikovannykh vospominanii," *Kommunist* 14 (1988), pp. 97–9.

The initial defeats and retreat of the Red Army accompanied by mass defections, panic, surrender and flight appeared to presage the disintegration of the Soviet system. Stalin faced deeply disturbing political questions about the loyalty of the population. How extensive was the disaffection? What could be done to offset its potentially devastating effect on the conduct of the war? At a later stage, how could Soviet power be reestablished in the borderlands?

The outbreak of hostilities ignited for the third time within a generation the flammable tinder of civil war in the western Eurasian borderlands.[14] The term civil war is used here to encompass a great variety of conflicts which historians have variously called ethnic cleansing, deportation and forced resettlement, wars of national liberation, partisan or revolutionary warfare, resistance and collaboration, Shoah or Holocaust, and internal wars. Each of these has given rise to a vast literature and the concepts themselves have undergone refinements and permutations.[15] Admittedly, the conflicts in the Eurasian borderlands do not meet the classic attributes

---

[14] Alfred J. Rieber, "Civil Wars in the Soviet Union," *Kritika* 4:1 (2003), pp. 129–62, links the civil war of 1941–8 to earlier struggles over the Eurasian borderlands. The civil war in the Inner Asian borderlands did not directly involve the Soviet Union before its declaration of war against Japan in August 1945.

[15] Much of the early literature on the European resistance movements was devoted to the question of whether or not the resistance made a substantial contribution to the war effort. For two contrasting interpretations, see Henri Michel, *European Resistance Movements, 1939–1945* (Oxford University Press, 1960), and Walter Laqueur, *Guerrilla: A Historical and Critical Study* (London: Weidenfeld and Nicolson, 1977), ch. 5. The military value of the resistance has been virtually dismissed by John Keegan, *The Second World War* (New York: Penguin, 1990), pp. 483–96. Related debates have taken place over the real and mythic character of the resistance, the difficulties of making clear distinctions between resistance and collaboration, and the instrumental uses of these terms in the discourse of the Cold War and the post-Soviet nationalists. One of the earliest attempts to broaden and refine the patterns of behavior in occupied territories was Stanley Hoffmann, *Decline or Renewal: France Since the 1930s* (New York: Viking, 1974), pp. 26–44. An important distinction was made between collaboration in Western and Eastern Europe by John A. Armstrong, "Collaborationism in World War II: The Integral Nationalist Variant in Eastern Europe," *Journal of Modern History* 40:3 (1968), pp. 396–9. Since then further revisions have been introduced by Jan T. Gross, *Revolution from Abroad: The Soviet Conquest of Poland's Western Ukraine and Western Belorussia* (Princeton University Press, 1988), and Jacques Semelin, *Unarmed Against Hitler: Civilian Resistance in Europe, 1939–1943* (Westport, CT: Praeger, 1993). Russian historians have retained the strict definition of collaboration while acknowledging complex motivations. See, for example, Mikhail Ivanovich Semiriaga, *Kollaboratsionizm: Priroda, tipologiia i proiavleniia v gody Vtoroi Mirovoi Voiny* (Moscow: Rosspen, 2000). The controversy triggered by Hannah Arendt's *Eichmann in Jerusalem: A Report on the Banality of Evil*, rev. and enlarged edn (New York: Viking, 1965), over whether there was or was not a Jewish resistance produced a flood of books. Most useful here are Jack Nusan Porter, *Jewish Partisans: A Documentary of Jewish Resistance in the Soviet Union during World War II*, 2 vols. (Washington, DC: University Press of America, 1982), and Dov Levin, *Fighting Back: Lithuanian Jewry's Armed Resistance to the Nazis, 1941–1944*, trans. Moshe Kohn and Dina Cohen (New York: Holmes and Meier, 1985).

of the genre exemplified in the experience of the English, American, and Spanish civil wars. The conventional definition insists on engagements between two relatively evenly matched regular armies commanded by rival governments, each claiming legitimate authority over the same territory; in these cases, foreign intervention, where it existed, remained limited to supplying men and material, and did not lead to international war.

The crucial difference in the Soviet case was that its civil wars took place under a unique set of circumstances.[16] First, they were fought in the midst of a large-scale conventional war with the overwhelming preponderance of military power deployed by the two belligerents, each of which took a highly ambivalent if not openly hostile attitude toward irregular armed bands – even, on occasion, those operating behind the lines of its mortal enemy. Second, in their conduct of the war on the eastern front, both Nazi Germany and the Soviet Union, and in the Far East the Japanese, adopted radically transformative means and aims that deeply affected the demographic and social structures of the civil population under their control. Third, the clash of the great powers and the civil wars were both continuations, albeit on a more violent and destructive scale, of a long-term contest over the structure and boundaries of states contending for control of the borderlands. Fourth, Stalin perceived the conflict through the prism of a "civil war mentality," a legacy of previous episodes in the struggle over the borderlands that had already in the prewar period impelled him to exterminate most of the potential leadership of an internal opposition, especially in the national republics. As a result of these four factors, the civil wars in the Soviet borderlands were, as the plural implies, many-sided, uncoordinated and confused, often taking the form of minimal or everyday acts of resistance, with many incidents of participants switching sides, dropping out and reentering, and overshadowed by terrible reprisals on the part of the German occupation forces, the Soviet police and the "destruction battalions."

The transformative nature of the war

On the Nazi side the transformative character of the war was expressed in a set of four interrelated myths that underlay Hitler's war aims: the *völkisch* ideal, the fear of a "Slavic flood," *Lebensraum* and redemptive

---

[16] Parallel civil wars in Greece, Albania and Yugoslavia were fought within territories totally occupied by the Axis powers. The nearest parallel to the Soviet case was that of China. But even there the main bases of the Nationalist and Communist forces were outside the Japanese zone of occupation.

anti-Semitism.[17] From the opening volley of the war against Poland, Hitler was determined to exploit the civilian population, both Jews and Poles alike, as forced labor, to weaken them physically, strip them of their cultural identity and inundate them with waves of German colonists who would encounter no resistance from the enfeebled and de-nationalized local population.[18] In 1941 Hitler resurrected the bugbear of "Judeo-Bolshevism" by announcing that the Soviet Union was to be the object of a "war of annihilation." It was a slogan shared by large sections of the German military and economic elites. They too endorsed the necessity of killing off Soviet prisoners of war and selected groups of civilians in order to clear the way for the large-scale colonization of the East by German agricultural settlers.[19] This fitted well into Hitler's belief that the independent German farmer was the *völkisch* ideal, the main guarantor of the longevity of the Reich for a thousand years.[20] "My long term policy," he boasted in 1941, "aims at having eventually 100 million Germans

[17] Saul Friedländer, *Nazi Germany and the Jews: The Years of Persecution* (London: Weidenfeld and Nicolson, 1997); Woodruff D. Smith, *The Ideological Origins of Nazi Imperialism* (New York: Oxford University Press, 1986).

[18] Martin Broszat, *Nationalsozialistische Polenpolitik, 1939–1945* (Stuttgart: Deutsche, 1961); Robert L. Koehl, *RKFDV: German Resettlement and Population Policy, 1939–1945. A History of the Reich Commission for the Strengthening of Germandom* (Cambridge, MA: Harvard University Press, 1957). An excellent overview is John Connelly, "Nazis and Slavs: From Racial Theory to Racist Practice," *Central European History* 32:1 (1999), pp. 1–34, who stresses the role of resistance versus compliance as the major criterion in Hitler's treatment of different Slavs, although it seems to me that he underestimates Hitler's particularly hostile attitude toward the Russians as distinct from that of many of his subordinates.

[19] Hans-Adolf Jacobsen quotes the infamous statement, "The Bolshevik soldier has forfeited every claim to be treated as an honorable soldier and in keeping with the Geneva Convention." Jacobsen, "The Kommissarbefehl and Mass Execution of Soviet Russian Prisoners of War," in Helmut Krausnick *et al.* (eds.), *Anatomy of the SS State* (New York: Walker, 1968), p. 524. According to Jacobsen's figures, based on an OKW Prisoner of War Department report on the whereabouts of Red Army prisoners, dated May 1, 1944, the total taken was 5,165,381, out of whom 2 million died from "wastage," 280,000 perished in transit camps and 1,030,157 were shot while attempting to escape or while being transferred. But the total was probably closer to 4 million. *Ibid.*, p. 531. See also Christian Streit, *Keine Kameraden: Die Wehrmacht und die Sowjetischen Kriegsgefangenen, 1941–1945* (Stuttgart: Deutsche, 1978); Horst Boog *et al.* (eds.), *Das Deutsche Reich und der Zweite Weltkrieg, vol. IV: Der Angriff auf die Sowjetunion* (Stuttgart: Deutsche Verlags-Anstalt, 1983), especially the chapter by Jürgen Forster, "Das Unternehmen 'Barbarossa' als Eroberungs- and Verniehungs-Krieg," pp. 413–50; and Eberhard Jäckel, *Hitlers Herrschaft: Vollzug einer Weltanschauung* (Stuttgart: Deutsche, 1986). Winfried Baumgart, *Deutsche Ostpolitik: Von Brest Litowsk bis zum Ende des Ersten Weltkreises* (Vienna: Oldenburg, 1966), notes that during World War I the army command's order of priority for the distribution of food produced on Russian territory was: the Army of Occupation, the Russian population and the inhabitants of the Kaiserreich. In 1941 the needs of the Russian population were not taken into any account whatsoever.

[20] Karl Lange, "Der Terminus 'Lebensraum' in Hitlers Mein Kampf," *Vierteljahrschaft für Zeitgeschichte* 13 (1965), pp. 426–37.

settled in these territories." The morale of the common German soldier required the germanization of the conquered lands, which was, in Hitler's words, "a positive war aim."[21]

Once the invasion of the Soviet Union had begun, Nazi policies toward the Jews also underwent a transformation from persecution to extermination. Whatever the effects of confusion in the Nazi bureaucracy, Hitler's own tactical flexibility, the latitude given to subordinates on dealing with the Jewish question, and the practical difficulties involved, nonetheless the decision to murder the Jews was irrevocably taken after June 1941.[22] Indoctrinated by the regime's relentless propaganda and exposed to heavy casualties in a brutal campaign, the officers and men of the Wehrmacht often indiscriminately expanded the killing fields.[23] The combination of Hitler's genocidal racist policy against the Jews, his war of extermination against the Russians, the destruction of state institutions, the radical redrawing of boundaries and massive resettlements of populations all contributed to plunging the borderlands into a cauldron of destruction and bitter internecine warfare.[24]

In the early months of Barbarossa, according to one set of general instructions generated by the SS, Hitler was inclined to tolerate

[21] Norman Rich, *Hitler's War Aims* (New York: Norton, 1973–4), pp. 2, 326–32, and *Hitler's Table Talk, 1941–1944: His Private Confessions,* with an introduction by Hugh Trevor-Roper, 2nd edn (London: Weidenfeld and Nicolson, 1973), pp. 3–4, 17, 21–2, 33, 34–5, 37–9, 40, 42, 53, 55, 68, 92–3, repeat his references to exploitation and colonization of the East. Mark Mazower, *Hitler's Empire: Nazi Rule in Occupied Europe* (London: Allen Lane, 2008), ch. 7, places the ambitious resettlement plans for the East in a European context.

[22] Götz Aly, *"Final Solution": Nazi Population Policy and the Murder of the European Jews,* trans. Belinda Cooper and Allison Brown (London: Oxford University Press, 1999), p. 254, argues for a March 1941 date for when the decision to deport European Jews to the East was taken.

[23] Omer Bartov, *The Eastern Front, 1941–45: German Troops and the Barbarization of Warfare* (New York: St. Martin's, 1986); Bartov, *Hitler's Army: Soldiers, Nazis and War in the Third Reich* (New York: Oxford University Press, 1991); and Stephen G. Fritz, *Ostkrieg: Hitler's War of Extermination in the East* (Lexington: University Press of Kentucky, 2011), especially pp. 85–92. But compare Truman Anderson, "Incident at Baranivka: German Reprisals and the Soviet Partisan Movement in Ukraine, October–December 1941," *Journal of Modern History* 71:3 (1999), pp. 585–623, who cites Wehrmacht orders that "the Ukrainian population which sympathizes with the Germans is to be exempted from collective punishment."

[24] To be sure, Hitler's theory and practice of war in the East was often inconsistently applied and modified by the competing needs and conflicting viewpoints of his subordinates. The classic treatment remains Alexander Dallin, *German Rule in Russia, 1941–1945: A Study of Occupation Policies,* rev. 2nd edn (Boulder, CO: Westview Press, 1981). See also Timothy Mulligan, *The Politics of Illusion and Empire: German Occupation Policy in the Soviet Union, 1942–1943* (New York: Praeger, 1988), and Theo Schulte, *The German Army and Nazi Policies in Occupied Russia* (Oxford: Berg, 1989), and especially Fritz, *Ostkrieg.*

individual Ukrainians in administering the conquered territory at the communal and district level. In the higher administration, Ukrainians "worthy of confidence" could also be appointed on an individual basis as advisors without any political authority. But "the economic aim in the final analysis is the development of Ukraine as the breadbasket of Europe, and as the main repository of European industry which will be paid for by agriculture and raw materials." The population was to be treated benevolently as long as they cooperated in agricultural production. No restrictions would be placed on the use of the Ukrainian language. The Ukrainian Autocephalous Church was free to conduct ceremonies but "places of worship should not become objects of pilgrimage for political purposes."[25]

This view was shared by groups within the Nazi Party and army who also sought to encourage separatist movements similar to those fostered by the German High Command in 1915–18, or else to recruit anti-Stalinist Russians and other nationalities to the German side. The leading exponent of such measures was Alfred Rosenberg. Rosenberg had been the head of the Foreign Affairs Office (APA) of the Nazi Party which from the mid-1930s dabbled in plans to carve up the Soviet Union into its constituent historical parts, an aim already articulated by Hitler. The leading figures in the APA were *Volksdeutsche* from the Baltic and Pontic frontiers. Rosenberg's plans amounted to nothing less than a massive spatial reorganization of Eurasia. Greater Russia would be permanently weakened by the detachment of an expanded Belorussia, the Baltic states, Ukraine, an enlarged Don region, the Caucasus and Soviet Turkistan. The Baltic states would be attached to Germany in the course of one or two generations after the expulsion of the local intelligentsia, especially the Latvian. They would be replaced by German colonists. Greater Russia would be like the General Government in Poland, a dumping ground for undesirable populations. Rosenberg's plans for Ukraine included not only creating an economic base for Germany but also, and here is where he departed from other Nazi leaders including Hitler, in granting the Ukrainians a "sympathetic special treatment."[26] In January 1943 he summed up for Hitler the conclusions of a group of military representatives of the rear areas of the eastern front and organizations in charge of political and economic activities in the occupied territories. In their view it was necessary to offer extensive concessions to the local

---

[25] Wolodymyr Kosyk (ed.), *Das dritte Reich und die ukrainische Frage: Dokumente, 1934–1944* (Munich: Ukrainian Institute, 1983?), doc. 88, September 1941, p. 539.

[26] Alex J. Kay, *Exploitation, Resettlement, Mass Murder: Political and Economic Planning for German Occupation Policy in the Soviet Union, 1940–1941* (New York and Oxford: Berghahn, 2006), pp. 18–22, 73–84.

population in order to combat the partisan movement. In his "Eastern Declaration" Rosenberg proposed to Hitler to create national representations of different nationalities, form national armies as allies in the war against Bolshevism, abolish the Soviet economic system and restore private property. The only significant official effect of Rosenberg's memo was an instruction by Goebbels's ministry underlining the need to avoid in propaganda intended for the Russian population any discriminatory language or mention of German colonization. Instead the Russians were to be praised for their soldierly heroism and zeal for hard work as a prelude to recruiting them into ranks of the Wehrmacht and the labor force of the Reich. Distributed to the front, this line elicited a sympathetic response among several Army Group commanders including Field Marshal von Kleist and Field Marshal von Manstein as well as panzer divisional commanders.[27]

However, other top Nazis, beginning with Hitler himself, and including Heinrich Himmler and Erich Koch, a fanatical Nazi racist appointed by Hitler as Reichskommissar for Ukraine, had other plans. While Himmler dreamed of a vast program of deporting Ukrainians from the right bank of the Dnieper and resettling Germans, Hitler focused on eliminating non-Germans through famine and killing throughout the entire East. Koch busily undermined Rosenberg's plans almost from the moment he assumed office in September 1941. In organizing the murderous policy toward the Jews, Roma and other "undesirables," he brigaded German police and Ukrainian, Latvian, Lithuanian, Cossack and Central Asian units into the Order Police for the Reichskommissariat. The various overlapping administrative authorities often acted at cross-purposes, but with one goal in mind: the complete germanization of the East.[28]

Stalin's aims were no less transformative, if more veiled. The Soviet leader was not disposed like Hitler to engage in "table talk" or to announce to the world his next motives and plans, however vaguely defined. This is not to say that Stalin was more of a pragmatist; he was just more secretive. To a greater degree than Hitler his aims must be

---

[27] Dallin, *German Rule*, pp. 549–50, and A. V. Okorokov (ed.), *Materialy po istorii russkogo osvoboditel'nogo dvizheniia, 1941–1945 gg. (Stat'i, dokumenty, vospominaniia)*, 2 vols. (Moscow: Graal', 1997), vol. I, pp. 47–8.

[28] Dallin, *German Rule*, pp. 154–65; Karel C. Berkhoff, *Harvest of Despair: Life and Death in Ukraine under Nazi Rule* (Cambridge, MA: Belknap Press, 2004), pp. 35–47. The occupation regime in East Ukraine under Werhmacht control was more severe than in West Ukraine under Romanian occupation but less repressive than under Koch. All over Ukraine local differences depended on a number of complex factors including the activity of the partisans. Aleksandr Gogun, *Stalinskie kommandos: Ukrainskie partizanskie formirovaniia. Maloizuchennye stranitsy istoriii, 1941–1944* (Moscow: ZAO Tsentropoligraf, 2008), pp. 12–14, 15–19.

sought in his tactical moves, which were not always consistent or unambiguous. To foreign statesmen he gave the impression that the war was all about territory and security in the traditional sense of the word.[29] He enlarged on this theme at Teheran: "What was needed was the control of certain physical points within Germany, along German borders, or even farther away to insure that Germany would not be able to embark on another course of aggression."[30]

Stalin's strategic thinking reflected both a profound understanding of the persistent factors facing Russian leaders, stretching back to the Seven Years War in the eighteenth century and those most recently advanced by tsarist negotiators in 1915–16.[31] In the interwar period, the Soviet leadership reacted to perceived threats from the USSR's immediate neighbors, Poland and Romania, by reaffirming the need to restore territory lost after World War I. In acquiring these territories, strategic considerations were uppermost in the minds of the Soviet leadership. Ever since the mid-1920s, discussions in both the Politburo and the Revolutionary Military Council, as well as the operational plans of the General Staff, emphasized the strategic importance of these areas for both the Soviet Union and its prospective enemies, Poland and Romania:

Large-scale victories with large-scale political results are possible only south of Poles'e: for us, sovietization of Galicia and Bessarabia and a direct threat as a consequence of this to the capitals of both governments, and for our opponents the splitting off from the Soviet Union of the richest regions inside our country, the creation for the Poles of "Greater Poland" and for Romania of "Greater Romania," the loss for us of such important economic seaports as Odessa and Nikolaev and as a direct consequence of this a threat to our most important coal and railroad resources in the Donetsk and Krivoi Rog basins.[32]

---

[29] In his conversations with Anthony Eden in December 1942 Stalin stated: "I think that the whole war between us and Germany began because of these western frontiers of the USSR, including particularly the Baltic States. That is really what the whole war is about and what I would like to know is whether our ally, Great Britain, supports us regarding these western frontiers." Cited in Lubomyr Y. Luciuk and Bohdan S. Kordan (eds.), *Anglo-American Perspectives on the Ukrainian Question, 1938–1951: A Documentary Collection* (Kingston, Ontario: Limestone, 1987), p. 53.

[30] *Foreign Relations of the US, 1943: Conferences at Cairo and Teheran* (FRUS) (Washington, DC: US Government Printing Office, 1961), p. 532.

[31] An imperial conference of March 1756 was the first to spell out a policy of granting East Prussia to Poland while Russia acquired Courland and "frontier rectifications" to bring to an end "disorders" in Western Belorussia and Western Ukraine. *Sbornik imperatorskago russkago istoricheskago obshchestva*, 148 vols. (St. Petersburg, 1867–1916), vol. CXXXVI (1912), pp. 31–3. For similar but more ambitious goals during World War I, see *Russian Diplomacy and Eastern Europe, 1914–1917* (New York: King's Crown, 1963).

[32] Oleg N. Ken and Aleksandr I. Rupasov, *Politbiuro TsK VKP(b) i otnosheniia SSSR s zapadnymi sosednimi gosudarstvami (konets 1920–1930-kh gg.): Problemy. Dokumenty.*

But there was more to Stalin's war aims than acquiring territory, primary though that may have been. Stalin pursued his own transformative policy by organizing the extermination or forced resettlement of potentially dangerous classes. With the outbreak of war Stalin resorted to measures of arrests and deportation on a violently ascending scale in response to real or imagined opposition within the Soviet Union.[33] His repressive methods were rooted in his experiences in the Russian Civil War, the struggle against the kulaks and national deviationists, and during the incorporation of new territories. When in 1944 Soviet forces crossed the frontiers of 1940, he applied his radical population policies to Eastern Europe and Germany, leading to the expulsion of Germans from all territories east of the Oder–Neisse–Trieste line, the destruction of prewar social and political structures in the same region, and equally massive deportations and resettlement of both class and national "enemies." The radical and transformative aspect of Stalin's wartime policies, like those of Hitler, incited powerful reactions among the populations of the western borderlands and often led to unintended consequences in Central Europe, where the Soviet advance sparked or stoked civil wars outside the Soviet frontiers.[34]

Timothy Snyder has made the argument that the terrible human losses inflicted in equal measure by Nazi Germany and the Soviet Union on the peoples of the west Eurasian borderlands, or "bloodlands" as he calls them, reduces any differences in their transformative policies to insignificance.[35] If the verdict is based on body counts, discussion ends. What is missing is the difference between Hitler's and Stalin's policies and plans as they emerged during the war over the future shape of the borderlands. Hitler not only planned but pursued with murderous fury

Opyt kommentariia (St. Petersburg: Evropeiskii dom, 2000), pp. 495–6. At the same time, Soviet diplomacy aimed to prevent Poland from "using western Ukraine and western Belorussia as 'piedmonts' in the struggle against the Ukrainian and Belorussian Republics." *Ibid.*, p. 497.

[33] Andrei Bolianovskii, "Mezhdu natsianal'nymi ustremleniiami i kolonializmom Gitlera: Vostochnoevropeiskie formirovaniia i Voorezhenykh silakh Germanii v 1941–1945 gg," *Ab Imperio* 3 (2012), pp. 141–5.

[34] See the following articles in Rieber, *Forced Migration*: T. V. Volokitina, "The Polish-Czechoslovak Conflict over Teschen: The Problem of Resettling Poles and the Position of the USSR," pp. 46–63; Emilia Hrabovic, "The Catholic Church and Deportations of Ethnic Germans from the Czech Lands," pp. 64–82; G. P. Murashko, "The Fate of Hungarian Minorities in Slovakia after the Second World War: Resettlement and Re-Slovakization, Moscow's Position," pp. 83–95; and A. S. Noskova, "Migration of the Germans after the Second World War: Political and Psychological Aspects," pp. 96–114.

[35] Timothy Snyder, *Bloodlands: Europe between Hitler and Stalin* (New York: Basic Books, 2010).

the extermination not only of the Jews but also the Poles, and the subjugation of the Russian population to a state of slavery while colonizing the borderlands with millions of Germans. Stalin showed flashes of anti-Semitism, disliked the Poles and hated the Germans. Although he publically ignored the Holocaust, he employed Jews in the propaganda apparatus, the security services and weapons procurement. He treated the Poles brutally in 1939–40 but also allowed the bulk of their captured armed forces to leave the Soviet Union for the West, and he created his own Polish army. While depriving Poland of a third of its territory, he restored a Polish state, which was inconceivable to Hitler. He deported Soviet Germans to the East and then expelled millions of Germans from the borderlands as the Red Army advanced. But he had no plans to exterminate or enslave the Germans (whatever forced labor he inflicted on POWs after the war). He had no plans to colonize the borderlands with Russians. The borderlands would look a great deal differently had Hitler won the war in the East. To be sure, for the people on the ground these larger issues were less important than their day-to-day struggle to survive. This was one reason why the nature of the civil war in the Soviet Union was so complex.

Phases of the civil wars

Civil wars in the Soviet borderlands fall into three fairly distinctive phases, although there were important regional differences reflecting specific historical and ethno-confessional traditions. The common factors shaping each phase were the military situation, German occupation policies and Soviet counter-measures.[36] Phase one, from the outbreak of war until early 1942, bore the impress of the initial German victories. Phase two, which lasted until early 1944, was marked by dramatic changes in the fortunes of war: significant German advances in the south and the "wild flight" of the Red Army, succeeded by the German disaster at Stalingrad and, perhaps even more critically, the defeat at Kursk, followed

---

[36] John A. Armstrong, *Soviet Partisans in World War II* (Madison: University of Wisconsin Press, 1964), pp. 22–6, proposes a different set of three phases for the partisan movement, but also attributes his periodization to the military situation and German occupation policies. In a related analysis, but one confined solely to partisan and anti-partisan warfare, six factors have been singled out to encompass the complex nature of this aspect of the struggle behind the lines: "strategies of occupation, relations between front and rear, the driving forces behind policies of cooperation and co-option on the one hand and behind policies of coercion and terror on the other hand, and finally, the factors that shaped relations between partisans, occupiers and population on the ground." "Introduction," in Ben Shepherd and Juliette Pattinson (eds.), *War in a Twilight World* (New York: Palgrave Macmillan, 2010), pp. 6–7 and 19.

by a steady but costly Soviet advance without the great breakthroughs that had characterized the earlier German offensives. In Phase three the Soviet army "liberated" or "reoccupied" the western borderlands and advanced into Central Europe, bringing military victory but no immediate end to the civil wars within the Soviet Union or the threat of civil strife in the territories between the collapsing power of Nazi Germany and the expansion of Soviet power. These conflicts magnified the problems of the newly established governments friendly to the Soviet Union and complicated Stalin's relations with his Western allies.

The first phase

The beginning of Operation Barbarossa already signaled the opening phase of civil war in the Soviet borderlands. The German invasion provoked anti-Soviet groups to attack the retreating Red Army, launch pogroms against the Jewish population, and attempt to establish or reestablish national independence. The First Secretary of the Estonian party, Karl Siare, defected to the Germans and then betrayed several partisan units. Many groups were isolated and poorly armed; often ignored by the local population, they suffered heavy losses. Most were destroyed within six months. The Germans were willing to accept assistance in hunting down Communists, Jews and Red Army stragglers, but repressed all efforts to set up autonomous or independent governments. Forces loyal to the Soviet Union, including Red Army units and individuals cut off from the main body, Communists and members of the Komsomol sought to form partisan groups behind the German lines. The largest concentration of partisans was located in the Belorussian SSR and Russian provinces (*oblast*) of Smolensk and Orel. Much smaller groups emerged in the national borderlands, the Karelo-Finnish Republic, the Baltic republics, Ukraine and North Caucasus.[37]

Already in this early phase of the war Stalin launched his first preemptive strikes against categories of individuals suspected of anti-Soviet behavior. Shortly after the German attack reports began to reach Stalin of panic, desertion, unauthorized flight and defection.[38] He reacted on

---

[37] Grishenko and Gurin, *Bor'ba za sovetskuiu pribaltiku*, vol. II, pp. 191, 39–43, 291ff; A. S. Chaikovs'kyi, *Nevidoma viina: Partizans'kii rukh Ukraïni 1941–1944 rr., movoiu dokumentiv, ochyma istoryka* (Kiev: "Ukraina," 1994), pp. 16–25, 173–75; G. N. Sevost'ianov (ed.), *Voina i obshchestvo*, 2 vols. (Moscow: Nauka, 2004), vol. I, pp. 274–5; Ponomarenko and Voroshilov to Stalin, October 31, 1942, in *Vestnik arkhiva prezidenta Rossiiskoi federatsii, Voina 1941–1945* (Moscow: OAO, 2010) doc. 92, pp. 198–201.

[38] See, for example, "Polozhenie v raione g. El'nia: Iz pis'ma chlenov Shtaba oborony g. El'nia, Smolenskoi oblasti v Politbiuro TsK VKP(b)," *Izvestiia TsK KPSS* 7 (1990), pp. 94–5; "O nedostatkakh v organizatsii zheleznodorozhnykh perevozok:

July 9 by issuing an order, as president of the State Committee of Defense (GOKO), to the Moscow area destruction battalions that they liquidate enemy diversionists or parachutists. He assigned them, as the first of three major tasks, "the struggle with possible counter-revolutionary outbreaks."[39] In the same spirit, Lavrentii Beria's watchful NKVD frontier troops detained over 700,000 suspects during the first year of the war.[40] Conflicting evidence reached Stalin concerning the Soviet Germans. Eight thousand flocked to the militia and fought in defense of the Brest fortress, while others, according to reports from the army and party leadership of the southern front, sniped at retreating Soviet troops and welcomed the Wehrmacht with bread and salt. Angrily Stalin ordered Beria "to boot them out of there" (*vyselit' s treskom*). Within two months the deportation of between 438,000 and 446,000 Volga Germans was under way.[41] Throughout the first six months of 1941, Stalin continued to receive disquieting reports from the command of the frontier troops along the Turkish, Iranian and Afghan frontiers of increased military activity combined with "bandit" or "black partisan" border crossings and internal disturbances.[42] The fear that foreign intervention would also trigger massive internal opposition along this frontier continued to haunt him throughout the war.

In the newly annexed Baltic republics, the first phase began with a brief but fierce anti-Communist uprising in Lithuania, where national consciousness had developed rapidly in the interwar period. From around 100,000 to 125,000 men were involved, including at least one-half the

Donosenie zamestitelia nachal'nika 3 Upravleniia NKO SSSR F. Ia. Tutushkina V. M. Molotovu," *ibid.*, pp. 198–200; "O poteriakh VVS Severo-Zapadnogo fronta v pervye dni voiny: Donesenie zamestitelia nachal'nika 3 Upravleniia NKO SSSR F. Ia. Tutushkina I. V. Stalinu," *ibid.*, pp. 201–2; "Obstanovka na Severo-Zapadnom fronte: Donesenie chlena Voennogo Soveta Severo-Zapadnogo fronta V. N. Bogatkina nachal'niku Glavnogo upravleniia politicheskoi propagandy RKKA L. Z. Mekhlisu," *ibid.*, pp. 202–4; and "Ob ostavlenii Rigi: Dokladnaia zapiska TsK P(b) Latvii," *ibid.*, pp. 212–13.

39 "O meropriiatiiakh po bor'be s desantami i diversantami protivnika v Moskve i prilegaiushchikh raionakh: Postanovlenie Gosudarstvennogo Komiteta Oborony," *ibid.*, p. 205.

40 I. I. Petrov, "Iz istorii partiinogo rukovodstva pogranichnymi voiskami (1941–1945 gg.)," *Voprosy istorii KPSS* 1 (January, 1985), p. 36; A. V. Toptygin, *Neisvestnyi Beriia* (Moscow: Izd-vo "Olma-Press," 2002), pp. 439–40, presents official figures that the NKVD detained over 700,000 deserters and 72,000 draft-dodgers in the first six months of the war.

41 Nikolai F. Bugai, *L. Beriia – I. Stalinu: "Soglasno vashemu ukazaniiu"* (Moscow: AIRO-XX, 1995), pp. 36–9. The hunt was pursued into the ranks of the Red Army, and by 1945 a total of 33,625 Volga German veterans had been resettled, many having been sent to labor armies.

42 *Pogranichnye voiska SSSR v gody Velikoi Otechestvennoi Voiny: Sbornik dokumentov i materialov* (Moscow: Nauka, 1976), pp. 601–5.

Lithuanian military that had been absorbed into the Red Army in 1940. They seized control of the capital, Kaunas, and proclaimed a provisional government before the Germans arrived, dispersing and driving them underground. The local Communist parties, decimated by the purges four or five years earlier, were in no position to help organize resistance to the Nazi occupation.[43] The German invasion also touched off a massive pogrom. In the suburbs of Kaunas Lithuanian paramilitary nationalists slaughtered 2,300 Jews before the Einsatzgruppen arrived and began to recruit Lithuanians into their ranks. Many of the recruits were relatives of those who had been killed or deported by the Soviet authorities in 1940. By November 1941 the Germans and their Lithuanian helpers had exterminated 72 percent of all Lithuanian Jews. In 1942 small groups of survivors, mainly youths, formed resistance groups in the ghettos until it became clear that they were doomed unless their rebellions broke out into the forest. About 1,800 managed to join the partisans.[44]

In Latvia and Estonia during the initial phase of the civil wars, there was more support for the Soviet cause than in Lithuania, going back to the days of the Russian Civil War in 1918–20. Pro-Soviet militiamen in both countries covered the evacuation of 30,000 Estonians and 60,000 Latvians, engaging in fierce fights with local nationalists.[45] Revolts in Latvia and Estonia were smaller and less well organized. A premature attempt to seize Riga from the retreating Red Army was led by underground remnants of a prewar Latvian paramilitary organization. After the German arrival anywhere from 10,000–15,000 of them collaborated with the Wehrmacht in guarding communications and hunting down stragglers, escaped POWs and party cadres who had taken to the woods. In the late fall, the Arais detachment, many of whom had been trained

---

[43] Grishenko and Gurin, *Bor'ba za sovetskuiu pribaltiku,* vol. I, pp. 22–4, 112–14; K. Tazva, "Poet-borets," in *Ob estonskoi literature: Sbornik literaturno-kriticheskikh stat'ei* (Tallin: Estonskoe gosudarstvennoe izdatel'stvo, 1956); "Za pravil'noe osveshchenie istorii kompartii Latvii," *Kommunist* 12 (1964), pp. 67–8; G. Zuimach, *Latvishskie revoliutsionnye deiateli* (Riga: Latviiskoe gosudarstvennoe izdatel'stvo, 1958), pp. 87–93; *Ocherki istorii kommunisticheskoi partii Latvii,* 3 vols. (Riga: Latviiskoe gosudarstvennoe izdatel'stvo, 1966), vol. III, pp. 369–74, 378; *Ocherki istorii kommunisticheskoi partii Estonii,* 3 vols. (Tallin: Estonskoe gosudarstvennoe izdatel'stvo, 1970), pp. 39–41; Algirdas Martin Budreckis, *The Lithuanian National Revolt of 1941* (Boston: Lithuanian Encyclopedia Press, 1968); Vytas Stanley Vardis, *Lithuania under the Soviets: Portrait of a Nation, 1940–1965* (New York: Pager, 1965), pp. 69–71, 74–6.

[44] Martin Dean, *Collaboration in the Holocaust: Crimes of the Local Police in Belorussia and Ukraine, 1941–44* (London: Macmillan, 2000), pp. 43–5, 62–3; Levin, *Fighting Back,* p. 95.

[45] Alexander Statue, *The Soviet Counterinsurgency in the Western Borderlands* (Cambridge University Press, 2010), p. 54.

in Germany, massacred 27,000 Latvian Jews in the Rumbl'sk forest.[46] In Estonia anti-Soviet resistance also centered on prewar paramilitary groups. In the summer of 1941 they committed acts of sabotage in the rear of the Red Army, and attacked the hastily organized local Soviet People's Defense Units who were attempting to carry out a scorched-earth policy. In the northern districts they were reinforced by volunteers who returned from having fought on the Finnish side in the Winter War to proclaim a "partisan republic." But the Estonian nationalists who helped the Germans to occupy Tartu were disarmed when they requested the right to establish an Estonian Republic.[47] During the first year of war the Germans opposed the formation of any large military units by the Baltic peoples. But they allowed the Estonians to create a Home Guard (*Omakaitse*) which together with local police units assisted the Germans in hunting Jews and Red Army stragglers.[48]

In Belorussia there was evidence of the same pattern of hasty, panic-stricken retreats and the breakdown of local authority, but also of confused and contradictory reports on the reaction of the local population.[49] The Belorussian anti-Communist emigration provided leadership for the civil administration of the population and helped to recruit local police battalions (*Schutzmannschaft*) of 20,000 men which later became the nucleus for the Home Guard. There is abundant evidence that the local population participated in the denunciation of Jews and offered no objection to their expropriation and humiliation. This facilitated the escalation of the murderous policies of the German occupation authorities with the collaboration of the Belorussian auxiliary police and local administration. Without their assistance, for example, it would not have been possible to organize so swiftly the ghettoization of the Jewish population of Belorussia. As the evidence of mass killings became known, however,

---

[46] *Pogranichnye voiska*, pp. 565–67; "Iz istorii Velikoi Otechestvennoi Voiny: Ob ostavlenii Rigi," *Izvestiia TsK KPSS* 7 (July, 1990), p. 212; "Pod maskoi nezavisimosti," pp. 116–17.

[47] "O podpole v estonii," *Izvestiia TsK KPSS* 7 (1990), pp. 168–71, based on NKVD archival sources but without specific references; Grishenko and Gurin, *Bor'ba za sovetskuiu pribaltiku*, vol. II, pp. 239–47; Mart Laar, *War in the Woods: Estonia's Struggle for Survival, 1944–1956* (Washington, DC: Compass, 1992), pp. 12–14. The author was subsequently Prime Minister of independent Estonia.

[48] Seppo Myllyniemi, *Die Neuordnung der Baltischen Länder, 1941–1944: Zum nationalsozialistischen Besatzungspolitik* (Helsinki: Suomen Historiallinen Seura, 1973); Toivo U. Raun, *Estonia and the Estonians* (Stanford University Press, 1987), pp. 158–9.

[49] According to German field reports the local population greeted the invaders with bread and salt, but the local Communist Party representatives praised the Belorussian peasantry's high level of patriotism. For the German reports, see Nicholas Vakar, *Belorussia: The Making of a Nation* (Cambridge, MA: Harvard University Press, 1956), ch. 13; for the party reports, see "Polozhenie v raione El'nia," pp. 93–5, and "O razvitii partizanskogo dvizheniia," *Izvestiia TsK KPSS* 7 (1990), p. 210.

there was a growing sense of revulsion among the local population.[50] Later, in the second phase, the Home Guard was particularly effective in anti-partisan sweeps in the Smolensk area.[51] The mass of the Belorussian peasantry apparently resisted the blandishments of the collaborationist regime, but they did not immediately join the partisans in any numbers. Instead, in the wake of the German advance they began to dismantle the collective farms. For people without arms or military training this was the major form of everyday resistance or "warfare" against the Soviet system.[52]

By August 1942 the situation in the western borderlands seemed critical. The secretary of the Belorussian Communist Party, Panteleimon Ponomarenko, reported that the Germans were making every effort to recruit elements of the Soviet population "in order to draw the partisans into battle not with the Germans but with the formations of the local population, and to withdraw from battles with the partisans their own units to send to the front." These formations – he listed ten of them – were bombarded with propaganda displaying slogans like "For an Independent Ukraine," "Free Belorussia from forced russification, "Independent Latvia," "Crimea for the Tatars"; in the case of the Crimean Tatars, inter-ethnic rivalries were stirred over the use of resources. Ponomarenko urged efforts to counter these groups through propaganda and specially trained personnel.[53]

The civil wars in Ukraine were the most complex and savage of all, due to longstanding ethnic and religious splits and equally sharp ideological divergences rooted in the experience of the Ukrainian revolutionary war of 1918–20 and the fierce infighting among émigré groups in interwar Poland and elsewhere in Europe. The German invasion released a flock of historical ghosts from the older generation. Former tsarist officers,

---

[50] Leonid Rein, *The Kings and the Pawns: Collaboration in Byelorussia during World War II* (New York and Oxford: Berghahn Books, 2011), pp. 263–72. For the involvement of the local police in the murder of Jews, see also Dean, *Collaboration in the Holocaust*, pp. 38, 46, 60, 65 and *passim*.

[51] John Loftus, *The Belarus Secret: The Nazi Connection in America* (New York: Paragon House, 1989). Loftus was a member of the Office of Special Investigations of the Criminal Justice Department of the US Department of Justice. His account is based on the archives of the SS and interviews with members of Einsatzgruppe B. See also V. Kalush, *In the Service of the People of a Free Belorussia: Biographical Notes on Professor Radoslav Ostrowsky* (London: Abjednannie, 1964), written, according to Loftus, by Ostrovskii (Astroŭski), himself a veteran anti-Bolshevik revolutionary who had been a leader of the Belorussian Hramada under Polish rule.

[52] In February 1942 the local civil administration ordered the formal liquidation of the collectives. By this time many of the peasants were convinced that the Red Army would never return. Bernhard Chiari, *Alltag hinter der Front: Besatzung, Kollaboration und Widerstand in Weisrussland, 1941–1944* (Dusseldorf: Droste, 1998), p. 129.

[53] *Istochnik. Dokumenty russkoi istorii* (1995) 2 (15), pp. 120–2.

supporters of Hetman Pavlo Skoropads'kyi, and relics of Semon Petliura's army – figures all too familiar to Stalin – returned in the baggage trains of the Wehrmacht. During the first phase of the civil war in Ukraine four well-defined groups had established themselves.[54]

The Ukrainian Central Committee was the most consistently collaborationist. Formed in the General Government (former Polish districts of Western Galicia under German occupation), it promoted cultural activities to break the monopoly of Polish culture while quietly laying the political groundwork for a future Ukrainian state. After June 1941 the Germans allowed it to spread its activities into Eastern Galicia. Closely associated with it was the metropolitan of the Greek Catholic Church, Andrei Sheptyts'kyi, who had been active in promoting the mission of expanding his church throughout the USSR after the Soviet annexation of Galicia in 1939. Soviet efforts to disrupt his plans and break the power of the Greek Catholic Church had been hampered by the inability of the official Russian Orthodox Church, crippled by the Soviet anti-religious policies, from competing with the solid phalanx of Greek Catholic clergy.[55] When the Germans invaded, their propaganda appeared at first to encourage the revival of religious life in Ukraine. Deceived by this, Sheptyts'kyi wrote letters to both Hitler and the Vatican expressing his fervent support for the German Army. In his letter of September 23, 1941, congratulating Hitler on the taking of Kiev he wrote: "The business of liquidating and extirpating Bolshevism, which you as the Führer of the great German Reich have taken upon yourself as the goal in this campaign, has earned your excellency the gratitude of the entire Christian world." Similar sentiments were repeated on January 14, 1942.[56]

The Organization of Ukrainian Nationalists (OUN) was the most militant revolutionary group with strong fascist leanings. Formed in 1929 by veterans of the Ukrainian revolutionary war and a younger generation of anti-Polish activists, its main enemy in the interwar period was the Warsaw government. It was active throughout communities of the

---

[54] The standard survey continues to be John A. Armstrong, *Ukrainian Nationalism*, 3rd edn (Englewood, CO: Ukrainian Academic Press, 1990). But see also Orest Subtelny, *Ukraine: A History*, 2nd edn (Toronto University Press, 1994), especially ch. 23.

[55] Bohan Rostslav Bociurkiw, *The Ukrainian Greek Catholic Church and the Soviet State (1939–1950)* (Edmonton and Toronto: Canadian Institute of Ukrainian Studies Press, 1996), pp. 45–61.

[56] "Al'ians: OUN-SS," *Voenno-Istoricheskii zhurnal* 4 (1991), p. 62. For the letter to the Vatican in August 1941, see Hans Jacob Stehle, "Sheptyts'kyi and the German Regime," in Paul Robert Magocsi (ed.), *Morality and Reality: The Life and Times of Andrei Sheptyts'kyi* (Edmonton: Canadian Institute of Ukrainian Studies, 1989), p. 129. Actually, the Germans pursued a policy of divide and rule among various branches of Orthodoxy in Ukraine and the General Government. Berkhoff, *Harvest of Despair*, pp. 232–9.

Ukrainian "piedmont" in Volhynia, the Sub-Carpatho Ukraine region in Czechoslovakia, and the Bukovina in Romania. The NKVD tracked its contacts with the Gestapo and accused it of espionage within the Soviet Union. Moscow denounced it as a tool of Nazi Germany and in 1938 ordered the assassination of its leader Evhen Konovalets.[57] It was hardly surprising that at the end of the war Stalin insisted upon the incorporation of the "piedmont" territories into the Ukrainian Soviet Socialist Republic.

Even before the German invasion, OUN had split into two warring factions. One wing led by an old comrade in arms of Konovalets, Andrei Mel'nyk (OUN-M), initially clung to a germanophile position. The breakaway group under Stepan Bandera (OUN-B) was quickly disillusioned by Hitler's hostility to Ukrainian statehood and ended up opposing Germans as well as Poles and Communists. Initially, the clandestine OUN-B placed their hopes on a mass political movement. It clashed with the OUN-M for control over local administration, leading in September 1941 to a round of mutual assassinations. The Gestapo successfully destroyed the legal organizations of both groups.[58]

Late in 1941, the German security service (SD) reported on the basis of captured documents that OUN-B was planning to organize an underground state. Bandera's propaganda was reportedly having "a great effect on reducing the labor enthusiasm of the population and increasing general discontent." All German intelligence sources were in agreement that OUN-B represented the only serious threat to the German occupation stretching from Volyhia to the Crimea. OUN-M was reportedly losing ground. Skoropads'kyi appealed only to the older population who remembered the German occupation of 1918.[59] Despite widespread arrests of its members, the same sources reported that by August 1942 OUN-B had become increasingly active across the frontier in the General Government as well as Volyhia and East Ukraine.[60] By early 1942 OUN-B decided to bring under their control some of the armed bands that had formed spontaneously in reaction to brutal German occupation policies and the infiltration of Soviet partisans from the north.[61] This brought them into conflict with the fourth Ukrainian nationalist group.

---

[57] "OUN na sluzhbe fashizma, "*Voenno-Istoricheskii zhurnal* 5 (1991), 16.
[58] Volodymyr Kosyk, *Ukraïna i nimechchyna u Druhii svitovii viini* (Lvov: Ivan Franko University, 1993), pp. 122–3, 177.
[59] Kosyk, *Das dritte Reich*, docs. 101, 103, 110, 115, pp. 547, 548, 549, 554, 557.
[60] *Ibid.*, doc. 137, p. 576. There were even reports that the OUN-B had penetrated the Reich, presumably as the result of deportations. *Ibid.*, doc. 154, p. 591.
[61] Oleksandr Vovk, "Do pitannia postannia UPA pid provodom OUNSD," *Ukrains'kyi istoryk* 30 (1995), pp. 138, 141; Chaikovs'kyi, *Nevidoma viina*, pp. 222–3. I am grateful to Yaroslav Hrytsak for providing me with these sources.

The Ukrainian Insurgent Army (UPA) was originally formed by Taras Borovets (whose *nom de guerre* was Taras Bulba, whence the name *bul'bovtsy*), claiming to represent a democratic anti-Soviet strain linked to the tradition of Petliura. He volunteered to assist the Wehrmacht in wiping out pockets of Red Army men. He gathered a force of 3,000 men before the Germans attempted to disarm him. Taking to the woods, the *bul'bovtsy* followed the torturous path of so many fighters in these civil wars. They fought both Germans and Soviet partisans, then reached a truce with the Soviet partisans for mutual survival. German and Soviet agents competed in a deadly game to turn them.[62] By the spring of 1942 it had become clear that labels of collaborationism and resistance were not very useful in identifying group loyalties; they were to become even less so in the second phase when the situation became even more tangled.

Meanwhile despite Hitler's orders, the Wehrmacht, hurting for replacements, was recruiting among Ukrainians. By the end there were at least five Ukrainian military units formed on the basis of accords with the Germans: the Nationalist Military Detachments (VVN), the Brotherhoods of Ukrainian Nationalists (DUN), the Galician Division of the Waffen SS, the Ukrainian Liberation Army (UVV) and the Ukrainian National Army (UNA). Informed estimates put the total of Ukrainians who served as Osttruppen and Nazi auxiliary units at around 250,000.[63]

In the Ukrainian civil wars the Jewish population suffered the greatest losses, mainly in the first phase, although the slaughter continued until the return of the Red Army. Anti-Semitism in Ukraine had a long and checkered history dating back to the seventeenth century. During the Ukrainian revolutionary war of 1918–20 the popular image of the Jews as agents of Bolshevism was widespread. OUN-B embraced anti-Semitism at its Second Congress in Cracow in August 1941:

The Jews in the USSR constitute the most faithful support of the ruling Bolshevik regime, and the vanguard of Muscovite imperialism in Ukraine. The Muscovite Bolshevik government exploits the anti-Jewish sentiments of the Ukrainian masses to divert their attention from the true cause of their misfortune and to channel them in times of frustration into pogroms on Jews. The OUN combats

[62] "OUN na sluzhbe," p. 55.
[63] Peter J. Potichnyj, "Ukrainians in World War II: Military Formations. An Overview," in Yury Boshyk (ed.), *Ukraine During World War II: History and its Aftermath. A Symposium* (Edmonton: Canadian Institute of Ukrainian Studies, 1986), p. 62; Wolfdieter Bihl, "Ukrainians in the Armed Forces of the Reich: The 14th Waffen Grenadier Division of the SS," in Hans-Joachim Torke and John-Paul Himka (eds.), *German–Ukrainian Relations in Historical Perspective* (Edmonton: Canadian Institute of Ukrainian Studies, 1994), p. 141.

the Jews as the prop of the Muscovite Bolshevik regime and simultaneously it renders the masses conscious of the fact that the principal foe is Moscow.[64]

Two years later it omitted the resolution from its program and Jewish specialists were admitted to the ranks of the UPA. But by then there were few Jews left in Ukraine to reap the benefits; when the Soviet forces returned, the UPA executed its Jewish doctors.[65] Most Jewish historians argue that the destruction of the Jewish population of Ukraine, reduced from 870,000 to 17,000 could not have been accomplished without the aid of the local population, because the Germans lacked the manpower to reach all the communities that were annihilated, especially in the remote villages. They admit that there were cases of Ukrainians assisting hunted Jews but minimize their number. Ukrainian historians question the reliability of their colleagues' sources, maintaining that the Ukrainian auxiliaries were assigned mainly to duties as guards and that their two SS divisions were only formed in 1944–5, after the bulk of the Jewish population had been killed.[66] Individual cases have been and will continue to be cited on both sides of the question. But the condemnation of Jews by churchmen, nationalists and ordinary peasants, whatever their motives or numbers, revealed abiding social antagonisms that erupted into open violence under the pressures of this transformative war.

Along the southern borderlands the Don Cossacks and Crimean Tatars were among the most disaffected elements, although they too were divided, contributing recruits both to the Red Army and to the

[64] Resolution of the Second Congress, as quoted in Philip Friedman, *Roads to Extinction: Essays in the Holocaust* (New York: Conference on Jewish Social Studies, Jewish Publication Society of America, 1980), pp. 179–80 and 182–9.

[65] Shmuel Spector, *The Holocaust of Volhynian Jews, 1941–1944* (Jerusalem: Achva Press, 1990), p. 271.

[66] From the large often polemical literature, in addition to Friedman, *Roads,* and Spector, *Holocaust,* see, for example, Peter J. Potichnyj and Howard Aster (eds.), *Ukrainian–Jewish Relations in Historical Perspective* (Edmonton: Canadian Institute of Ukrainian Studies, 1990), especially the contribution of Aharon Weiss, "Jewish–Ukrainian Relations in Historical Perspective," pp. 409–20, and the comments by John-Paul Himka. For the role of the Ukrainian police in the deportation of Ukrainians to Germany see Berkhoff, *Harvest of Despair,* pp. 261–8. In his eagerness to prove that only the Germans bear the burden of guilt, Daniel J. Goldhagen, *Hitler's Willing Executioners: Ordinary Germans and the Holocaust* (New York: Alfred E. Knopf, 1996), pp. 223–30, 408–9, considers the Ukrainian police, when he considers them at all, as operating under different pressures than the Germans. For a more balanced picture, see Amir Weiner, *Making Sense of War: The Second World War and the Fate of the Bolshevik Revolution* (Princeton University Press, 2001), pp. 258–70, although the argument that few Jews also survived in Greece and France fails to take into account the ease with which the Germans could round up the highly concentrated urban Jewish population of these countries.

armed opposition. The fact that Hitler considered the Cossacks racially acceptable descendants of the Goths and the Tatars also facilitated their recruitment into the German forces. Early in the campaign individual Wehrmacht commanders accepted Cossack volunteers to be used as scouts or replacements in combat units. For this reason it is difficult to determine how many Cossacks defected. By July 1942 there were several company- or regimental-sized formations in action. According to the testimony of the general of the Osttruppen, there were 75,000 men in the so-called Eastern Battalions, including an unspecified number of Cossacks, but their major involvement only occurred in the second phase.[67]

The first exaggerated reports from partisan units in Crimea to Marshal Budennyi claiming that "the overwhelming majority of the Crimean Tatars in the mountain districts and adjacent areas are following the fascists" were retracted, but not before the damage was done in Moscow. The Germans brought with them Tatar émigrés representing the old Milli Farka Party of the Civil War days. In December 1941 they formed a Tatar National Committee led mainly by former landowners, dispossessed kulaks and sons of ulema. By February 1942 plans for the creation of a Tatar army were well under way. Nine thousand volunteers were immediately accepted, the men recalling "vivid memories of the comradeship in arms in the period 1917–1918." Soviet counter-measures were frustrated by the absence of Crimean Tatars in the underground party organizations and ineffective propaganda.[68]

By the end of the first phase, there were very few active supporters of the Soviet system behind the German lines. But the anti-Soviet groups were badly divided. Probably the smallest number were ideologically committed collaborators, volunteers in the local police and German military units. A slightly larger group had gone into hiding, disillusioned by the behavior of the Germans but unwilling to organize resistance against them. By far the largest number of individuals was either passive or willing to cooperate on a limited basis.

In February 1943 Stalin was already concerned about the potential for civil war in the borderlands. In a conversation with the ambassador of the Polish government-in-exile, Tadeus Romer, he commented that

---

[67] Samuel J. Newland, *Cossacks in the German Army, 1941–1945* (London: Frank Cass, 1991), p. 86; Iurii S. Tsurganov, *Neudavshiisia revansh: Belaia emigratsiia vo Vtoroi Mirovoi Voine* (Moscow: Intrada, 2001), pp. 124–6.

[68] "Krymsko-Tatarskie formirovaniia: Dokumenty tret'ego reikha svidetel'svuiut," *Voenno-Istoricheskii zhurnal* 3 (1991), p. 9; Edige Mustafa Kirimal, *Der nationale Kampf der Krimtürken mit besonderer Berücksichtigung der Jahre 1917–1918* (Emsdetten: Lechte, 1952), p. 305; Bugai, *L. Beriia – I. Stalinu*, pp. 146–8.

it would be good to establish contact between the Russian–Ukrainian and Polish partisans. "Up to this time," he said, "there have been only fights (*drachka*)." He urged the Poles to order their partisans "not to pick fights (*pikirovat'sia*) with Ukrainian partisans." At the same time, Stalin gave Romer some surprising advice about the activities of the Polish Home Army. He suggested that the Poles should refrain from large-scale disruption of the German rear, although this could create serious problems for the Germans because it would lead to reprisals and heavy losses among the cadres. Better to wait, he added, until the counter-attack of the Red Army would create conditions favorable to a general uprising by the Polish people.[69] While this may appear to run counter to Stalin's general views on the importance of armed risings in the rear of the German Army, other comments to Romer suggest that what Stalin had in mind at this moment was a closer coordination, leading to control of the Polish underground by Moscow.[70]

The second phase

A second phase began roughly after Stalingrad, when Germany lost the strategic initiative and suffered serious manpower shortages. Responding to the forced labor drafts, thousands of young men joined German-sponsored militia and military units, partly under pressure and partly in order to fight the partisans who began to appear in large numbers in 1943. Unnumbered others fled to the forests to join various bands or to seek protection from the partisans against German exploitation. During this phase the Soviet government sought to centralize and reorganize the operations and structure of the partisan units which during the first year of operations were split among numerous civil and military authorities.[71] Activities were better coordinated to disrupt German communications, launch reprisals against anti-Soviet units, and reassert a Soviet presence in the occupied territories through intimidation and terror. More ominously, Stalin, often prompted by Beria, reacted violently to signs of disaffection in the North Caucasus by ordering massive deportations of entire ethnic groups.

---

[69] "Stalin i Pol'sha. 1943–1944 gody. Iz rassekrechennykh dokumentov rossiiskikh arkhivov," introduction and commentary by A. F. Noskova, *Novaia i noveishaia istoriia* 3 (May–June, 2008), pp. 112–13.

[70] Subsequently, Stalin became disillusioned with the government-in-exile, but not with the idea of a large Polish armed force fighting on the side of the Red Army. In May 1944 he told Oscar Lange that the Poles were "good fighting material" and he hoped to increase the number in the Polish Army to a million men. *Ibid.*, p 125.

[71] Sevost'ianov, *Voina i obshestvo*, vol. II, p. 278.

In the Baltic republics Latvians and Estonians collaborated more fully with the Germans than the Lithuanians. After Stalingrad the Germans reversed their policy of forbidding the formation of large military units in the Baltic territories and issued mobilization orders. The Estonians responded by fielding six frontier regiments and forming the 20th SS Division. In addition, 5,000 Estonians left for Finland where they enlisted in the "Continuation War" against the Soviet Union. Russian and Estonian sources disagree on the degree to which participation in German-sponsored units was voluntary and also on their responsibility for civilian deaths in the republic.[72] For the first time the NKVD reported that Estonian émigrés were beginning to consider the possibility of a German defeat and the need to find alternative sources of outside support by making contact with British and American intelligence in Sweden and Finland.[73] Under German pressure, in 1943 representatives of Latvian local self-government endorsed the mobilization of four classes of youth that provided more than 30,000 men for two SS divisions, known collectively as the Latvian Legion. At the same time, according to NKVD documents, about 30,000 mainly working-class men were active in the Latvian underground in Riga and other cities, while 20,000 joined the partisans.[74]

In Belorussia the creation of a Central Council (Rada) at the end of 1943 was an act of desperation by the Nazi authorities working with the local nationalists. Less than a puppet government, its main function was to combat the increasingly active partisan movement at a time when the German front was under crushing pressure by the Red Army. The attempt to invoke the spirit of the First All-Belorussian Congress of 1917 as a forerunner of a re-born, independent Belarus was pure fantasy.[75]

By the end of 1943, too, large areas had become refuges for a variety of armed groups engaged in a multisided struggle that remains obscure in many details. There were bands of Red Army soldiers, some still holding out against the Germans, others virtual deserters; elements of the underground Polish Home Army (*Armja krajowa*) competed with

[72] Russian sources from the late Soviet period claim that a grand total of 50–60,000 Estonians fought on the German side and shared responsibility for the deaths of approximately 60,000 civilians, 64,000 Soviet POWs and about 250,000 Jews. "Podpol'e v Estonii," pp. 172–3. Grishenko and Gurin, *Bor'ba za sovetskuiu pribaltiku*, vol. II, pp. 239–47; Raun argues that the Estonians showed great reluctance to serve in German units and volunteered in small numbers. Laar claims that Soviet efforts to form partisan detachments in Estonia repeatedly failed due to the absence of support from the local population and the opposition of 15,000 "forest brothers." Raun, *Estonia and the Estonians*, p. 159; Laar, *War in the Woods*, pp. 11, 18–19.
[73] "Podpol'e v Estonii," p. 174.   [74] "Pod maskoi nezavisimosti," p. 118.
[75] Rein, *The Kings and the Pawns*, pp. 166–75.

Belorussians for positions in the local administration, or else hunted Jews. Still others bided their time until they could participate in Operation Burza (Tempest) to liberate towns in their borderlands (*kresy*) between the departure of the Germans and arrival of the Soviet forces. Jewish refugees and armed partisans, perhaps as many as 10–15,000 at their peak strength, fought for survival. But their number diminished as losses could not be replaced and the Soviet Partisan Command discouraged the creation of separate Jewish units for fear of antagonizing the local population.

Finally, nationalist Belorussian bands fought Soviet partisans or hid out in hope of emerging from the war as representatives of an independent country; a few like the Kaminsky Brigade degenerated into banditry.[76] Despite the increasingly chaotic situation, the Germans refused to grant the Belorussian civil administration any autonomy to mobilize the population "against the Bolsheviks."[77] The extreme splintering of the warring groups was due to the underlying ethnic conflicts and the inability of the Belorussian political leaders to overcome the low level of national consciousness among the peasantry, who remained passive until a concerted effort by the Soviet authorities stimulated a burgeoning partisan movement.

The driving force behind the organization of a mass partisan movement was Ponomarenko. In contrast to the pessimistic reports of Beria's men, he extolled the patriotic, spontaneous response of the Belorussian collective farmers. Both interpretations were self-serving. Ponomarenko proposed a separate administrative organ of "the partisan struggle," offered to take command of it and, apparently on his own authority, urged his party people to remain behind the rapidly advancing German lines in order to organize and lead the local partisan detachments.[78] Although the Central Committee publicly endorsed most of Ponomarenko's

---

[76] Vakar, *Belorussia*, pp. 195–6; Dean, *Collaboration*, pp. 142–4; Porter, *Jewish Partisans*, pp. 8–9, 11–12, 19; Alexander Dallin, "The Kaminsky Brigade: A Case Study of Soviet Disaffection," in Alexander and Janet Rabinowitch (eds.), *Revolution and Politics in Russia: Essays in Memory of B. I. Nikolaevsky* (Bloomington: Indiana University Press, 1972), pp. 243–80; Witalij Wilenchik, *Die Partisanbewegung in Weisrussland, 1941–1944* (Wiesbaden: Harrassowitz, 1984). In all cases, numbers are elusive. By contrast, the labor draft produced 100,000 volunteers for work or military service. Mulligan, *The Politics of Illusion*, p. 85.

[77] Jerzy Turonek, *Belarus' pad niametskai akupatsyiai* (Minsk: Belarus, 1993), pp. 98, 117, 176; Chiari, *Alltag hinter der Front*, pp. 114–28.

[78] As part of his personal appeal to Stalin, Ponomarenko also contrasted the "utter fearlessness" of the Slavic population with the urbanized Jews who "were seized by an animal fear." See the telegrams of Ponomarenko to Stalin July 2, 1941, and undated, but no later than July 12, 1941, in "O razvertyvanii partizanskogo dvizheniia," *Izvestiia TsK KPSS* 7 (1990), pp. 196, 210.

recommendations, a muted struggle within the party *apparat* seriously hampered the central organization of the partisan struggle. Long before the outbreak of war, preparations to wage partisan warfare on Soviet soil aroused Stalin's suspicions of defeatism and were disrupted in 1937 by the blood purges. Up until the spring of 1942 attempts to revive the project encountered resistance from several sources including Lev Mekhlis, the High Command, and more importantly from Beria. As part of his imperial bureaucratic design to expand the power of the NKVD under the guise of promoting the war effort, he insisted that "the organs of the NKVD should in the future carry out the organization of partisan detachments and diversionist groups."[79] Beria intended to wage the civil war on his own terms.

Stalin's decision in May 1942 to appoint Ponomarenko to head a Central Partisan Staff in Moscow with deputies from the NKVD and NKGB did not resolve the bureaucratic infighting or allay suspicions over the trustworthiness of units beyond the immediate reach of army and police.[80] For Beria the key to success of the partisans was to bring them under the control of the frontier troops. Their main purpose would be, as he stated in 1943 in his instructions to the chief of its Political Administration, the intensification of the struggle "against ideological diversionists."[81] For the army command specific sabotage missions directed against communications networks and carried out by well-organized units drawn from the regular army took precedence.[82] Foremost in Ponomarenko's program were political issues directed mainly at retaining the loyalty of the civilian population and combating both collaboration and nationalist agitation.[83] By June 1943 Ponomarenko was

[79] "Ob organizatsii bor'by v tylu germanskikh voisk," *Izvestiia TsK KPSS* 7 (1990), p. 217; "O sozdanii partizanskikh otriadov i diversionnykh grupp dlia deistvii v tylu protivnika," *ibid.*, 9 (1990), pp. 197–8; and I. G. Starinov, "Podryvniki na kommunikatsiiakh agressora," *Voprosy istorii* (1988), pp. 100–12, which are the important memoirs of a participant. Even before any diversionist activity was reported, the NKVD was already in the grip of a civil war mentality. The day after the German invasion the Moscow city and oblast administration of the NKVD issued instructions to its agents to "uncover the counter-revolutionary underground," although it was left to their vivid imagination as to who this might include. "Moskovskie chekisty v oborone stolitsy, 1941–1942," *Voenno-istoricheskii zhurnal* 1 (1991), p. 10.

[80] Leonid D. Grenkevich, *The Soviet Partisan Movement, 1941–1944: A Critical Historiographical Analysis* (London: Frank Cass, 1999), pp. 6–7, 84–6, 91–5; Starinov, "Podryvniki," pp. 108–11.

[81] Petrov, "Iz istorii partiinogo rukovodstva," pp. 38–9.

[82] Vsevolod Ivanovich Klochkov, *Deistviia partizan Ukrainy na zheleznodorozhnykh kommunikatsiiakh v tylu fashistskikh voisk, 1941–1944* (Kiev: Nauka, 1984).

[83] Panteleimon Kondratevich Ponomarenko, *Vsenarodnaia bor'ba v tylu nemetsko-fashistskikh zakhvatchikov, 1941–1944* (Moscow: Nauka, 1986), pp. 420–3, contains the full text.

able to report to Stalin with pride that there were 10,000 partisans in the forests of Bryansk. But even then there were problems of command and organization.[84]

In Ukraine the splintering effect of the second phase multiplied the fronts of the civil war and inaugurated the most murderous episode of ethnic cleansing. In the western and central regions the fighting among the rival nationalist groups intensified as German and Soviet agents penetrated their organizations.[85] The OUN-B clashed with the Borovets group, forcibly incorporated some of its units into their growing ranks, and usurped the name Ukrainian Insurgent Army.[86] Metropolitan Sheptyts'kyi, increasingly disillusioned by the Nazi "reign of terror," began to fear that the civil war was tearing Ukraine to pieces. The Germans, he wrote, were exposing the young to "terrible demoralization" by "recruiting them into police and militia units and misusing them for perverted purposes." In May 1943 he reported to the Vatican, "All of Volhynia and part of Galicia are full of bands which have a certain political character. Some are made up of Poles, others of Ukrainians, and others of Communists; others are truly bandits, people of all nationalities, Germans, Jews, and Ukrainians." After Stalingrad, on the initiative of the Germans, he agreed to endorse the formation of a volunteer SS Galician Division in the vain and naive hope that "if the German defeat continues and there is a period of anarchy and chaos we will be very happy to have a national army to maintain order and counteract the worst outrages until regular Soviet troops arrive."[87]

---

[84] Ponomarenko to Stalin, June 21, 1943, *Vestnik arkhiva presidenta, Voina,* doc. 110, pp. 263–5. Ponomarenko singled out the commander of the Bryansk detachments for condemnation.

[85] "OUN na sluzhbe," p. 55.

[86] Soviet sources citing the NKVD archives state that "on the basis of imprecise figures the northern and southern groups of the Ukrainian Insurgent Army (in November 1942?) are estimated at approximately 15,000." "OUN na sluzhbe," p. 50. Armstrong, *Ukrainian Nationalism,* p. 115, gives an estimate of 30–40,000. Ukrainian émigré sources give slightly more generous figures reaching as high as 45–50,000; but as Subtelny notes, "Compared to other underground movements in Nazi-occupied Europe, the UPA was unique in that it had practically no foreign support. Its growth and strength were, therefore, an indication of the very considerable popular support it enjoyed among Ukrainians." Subtelny, *Ukraine,* p. 474.

[87] Stehle, "Sheptyts'kyi," pp. 134–8. The response was overwhelming. Over 82,000 mobbed the recruiting offices, but only 13,000 were judged worthy of meeting the SS standards. Subtelny, *Ukraine,* pp. 472, 477. Controversial evidence suggests that the Germans used threats of reprisals to coerce individuals who sought to avoid service in the division. Yury Kyrychuk, *Narysy z istoriï ukraïns'koho natsyonalno-vyzvol'noho rukhu 40–50 rokiv XX stolitiia* (Lvov: Ivan Franko National University, 2000), p. 52. Although OUN-B opposed the idea, it may have attempted to infiltrate the division for its own purposes. Yaroslav Hrytsak, *Narys istoriï ukraïny: Formuvannia modernoï*

German intelligence sources confirmed Sheptyts'kyi's estimates of UPA strength, reporting that important parts of the Kiev and Zhitomir regions and the whole of Volhynia–Podolia were under UPA control. The Wehrmacht was suffering huge material losses to the Ukrainian resistance. They had lost control over one-third of the arable land, 17 percent of wheat production and massive numbers of livestock. Food deliveries to the front were under constant threat, requiring heavy military guard.[88]

While the fratricidal conflict among Ukrainians was taking place, a bloody ethnic war was breaking out in the mixed Ukrainian–Polish areas of Volhynia and Kholm. The killings began in the spring and summer of 1943, reaching a climax in the winter, when the UPA unleashed a massive assault to cleanse the area of the Polish population. Its aim was to forestall postwar Polish claims to the area. The Polish Home Army came to the defense of their countrymen and conducted their own reign of terror against the Ukrainian population west of the San River. Here was a case of neighbors turning against one another with rare ferocity.[89] It recalled in many ways the fierce Haidamak rebellions of the eighteenth century that became enshrined as myth in Ukrainian folklore.[90]

The German penetration into the Kuban also revived myths of Cossack liberties. As in the Crimea and the Don the Germans allowed the return of émigré veterans, thus establishing another historic connection with the Russian Civil War. In October 1942 the Germans organized a self-governing region with a population of 160,000 modeled on the prerevolutionary Cossack communes. They established a Junkers' Officer School, reintroduced the paraphernalia of the traditional Cossack regiments, and nourished high hopes for the formation of a Cossack Army of 75,000 men. Although their plans were doomed by the Stalingrad

ukraïnskoï natsiï XIX–XX stoletiia (Kiev: Heneza, 1996), p. 251. Thus were the lines between collaboration and resistance blurred.

[88] Kosyk, *Das dritte Reich*, docs. 176 and 179, pp. 609, 611.

[89] Timothy Snyder, "'To Resolve the Ukrainian Problem Once and For All': The Ethnic Cleansing of Ukrainians in Poland, 1943–1947," *Journal of Cold War Studies* 1:2 (2000), pp. 86–120, provides the comprehensive account. But see also Weiner, *Making Sense*, pp. 253–5. Polish sources estimate 60–80,000 men women, and children were slaughtered. Antoni B. Szczesniak and Wieslaw Szota, *Droga do nikad: Dzialalnosc Organizacji Ukrainskich Nacjonalistów i jej likwidacja w Polsce* (Warsaw: Wydawn. Ministerstwa Oborony Narodowej, 1973), p. 170. See "Al'ians: OUN-SS," pp. 57–8, for Soviet documentation.

[90] Jaroslav Pelenski, "The Haidamak Insurrections and the Old Regimes in Eastern Europe," in Jaroslaw Pelenski (ed.), *The American and European Revolutions, 1776–1848: Socio-Political and Ideological Aspects* (Iowa University Press, 1980), and Zenon E. Kohut, "Myths Old and New: The Haidamak Movement and the Koliivshchyna (1768) in Recent Historiography,"*Harvard Ukrainian Studies* 1:3 (1977), pp. 359–78.

defeat, about 14,000 Cossacks accompanied the retreating Germans to Belorussia, where their units fought Soviet partisans.[91]

In the North Caucasus security organs launched a preemptive strike against alleged potential opponents of the Soviet system.[92] The Kalmyks were the first people of the autonomous republics to suffer mass deportation, followed by the Chechens and the Ingush. Like most people of the region the Kalmyks suffered terribly from both the German occupation and the Soviet return, yet they supplied fighters to both sides: 20,000 men to the Red Army and 5,000 cavalry placed under German command. After Stalingrad the rapid reconquest of the region led to a muted contest between the advocates of reconstruction and rehabilitation (mainly party cadres) and the NKVD, which won out in the end. In October 1943 Stalin approved Beria's recommendation for deportation as a punishment for fighting against the Red Army and as "a means for regulating inter-ethnic conflict (*mezhdunatsional'nyi konflikt*)."[93]

In the Chechen–Ingush republic armed opposition to collectivization had never been fully repressed. From 1937 to 1939, eighty bands of more than a thousand men kept up the clandestine struggle, although most of these had been broken up on the eve of the war. The German attack stimulated the formation of new bands as well as a series of assassinations of party and NKVD personnel. On the other hand, the Chechens also produced their share of recruits for the Red Army. Moreover, by August 1943 local NKVD units were reporting that "for six months bandit activity was virtually paralyzed as a result of amnesty and arrests." But Beria ignored them, advancing plans to deport the entire population that were finalized in December and carried out in January and February 1944.[94]

Divided loyalties and civil strife also ripped apart the Karachaev and Cherkessy autonomous okrugs. The *karachaevtsy* sent a strong group of volunteers to the Red Army, but the arrival of the Germans led to the formation of the Karachaev National Committee and the dissolution of collective farms. In 1944 the NKVD reported fighting against twelve bands, supported by substantial elements among the population and the ulema. With the return of the Red Army the National Committee fled with the Germans and the bands were repressed. Nevertheless,

[91] Newland, *Cossacks*, pp. 61, 86; Tsurganov, *Neudavshiisia revansh*, pp. 127–42. According to the intelligence of a Russian émigré organization, even after Stalingrad, despite depressed living conditions in the Taganrog area, "the population was favorably disposed toward the anticommunist [Cossack] army." *Ibid.*, p. 129.

[92] A perceptive analysis of unrest and repression in the North Caucasus is Marshall, *The Caucasus under Soviet Rule*, pp. 244–52 and 255–71.

[93] Bugai, *L. Beriia – I. Stalinu*, pp. 69–70. Following the arrest of local bands 91,919 Kalmyks were deported and the autonomous republic was abolished.

[94] *Ibid.*, pp. 69–70, 101.

the Sovnarkom ordered the indiscriminant deportation of over 69,000 persons.[95]

A similar situation developed in the Kabardino–Balkarian Autonomous Republic, where the population was subjected to even greater conflicting pressures. Several thousand men rallied to the Red Army and at least 5,000 more were executed by the Germans. But several thousand more either joined a nationalist legion (as 600 of them did) and anti-Soviet bands, or deserted from the Red Army. Reporting to Stalin that in 1942–3 the NKVD had arrested over 1,700, including members of the Communist Party and Komsomol, Beria accused the nationalists of conspiring to unite Balkaria with Karachaev into a state under Turkish protection. Having played to Stalin's borderland complex, he then proposed to use the troops "freed" from the Chechen–Ingush operation to deport the entire population of Balkaria, concluding with his formulaic phrase, "I await your orders."[96] Stalin responded in predictable fashion.

In the Russian core the largest potential source of an army of Russians to fight Russians was the abortive Vlasov movement. Taken prisoner by the Germans in early 1942, Major-General Andrei Andreevich Vlasov represented himself as a Russian nationalist willing to organize an army of Soviet POWs as an independent ally of Germany in order to sweep away the Soviet regime. But in the end Hitler contemptuously brushed aside the proposals of Vlasov's supporters in the intelligence section of the German General Staff: "We will never build up a Russian army; that is a phantom of the first order," Hitler declared. Speculation continues to this day on how great a chance Vlasov had to create a large anti-Soviet army. His German handlers waxed enthusiastic over his one and only contact with the Soviet population in early 1943 during a speaking tour that took him to Riga, Pskov and the surrounding area. They also provide evidence that even as late as the fall of 1943, 2,000–3,000 POWs were volunteering for his movement every day and that the appearance of small Vlasov units at the front had a striking effect on the Red Army desertion rate. In late 1944, when hopes for a German victory were fading, Heinrich Himmler on his own responsibility acceded to their pleading and permitted the formation of the Committee for the Freedom

---

[95] *Ibid.*, pp. 56–61.

[96] *Gosudarstvennyi arkhiv Rossiiskoi Federatsii* (GARF) f. 9401, op. 2, d. 64, vol. II, pp. 162–7. The entire episode is analyzed in N. F. Bugai, *Kavkaz: Narody v eshelonakh (20–60 gody)* (Moscow: Insan, 1998), pp. 120–33, 153–73, which, on the basis of archives, demonstrates Beria's determination to use the breakdown of order in the North Caucasus in order to enhance his own power and discredit local bureaucracies, mainly party and Komsomol, not under his control.

of the People of Russia (KONR) and the recruitment of two divisions; Vlasov wanted ten.[97] But the gesture was too little, too late. In the end Vlasov and his Russian Liberation Movement were a negligible military factor and an ephemeral political phenomenon. But Vlasov gave rise to serious concern among the Soviet leaders. Initially they reacted to his proclamations with studied silence, but his tour of the northwest front forced their hand. They moved rapidly to condemn him and attempted to penetrate his organization with their agents.[98] If anything, the shadowy Vlasov movement merely confirmed Stalin's suspicions of anyone who survived behind the German lines and increased his fears of internal opposition.

By the end of the second phase – that is, at the height of the German advance – it is impossible even to give precise figures on how many of the 70 million people living behind the lines were involved in the civil wars. Recent estimates of active participants have not changed the earlier ones: about a million individuals were engaged on each side. But these numbers still tell us little because the motivations and the level and steadfastness of commitment were so radically different. Moreover, it is impossible to count the passively disloyal. There was a large and ill-defined "twilight zone," as Armstrong calls it, that expanded and contracted often in response to rumors or reports from the front. At times parts of the same village were controlled by different bands; a different village elder was often selected every day to avoid fatal accusations of collaboration with the Germans or cooperation with the partisans. The most widespread evidence of "leaving the Soviet system" was the massive de-collectivization, at least where the Germans permitted it. But there was no mass peasant uprising as there had been during the Civil War of 1918–20.[99]

---

[97] The standard work remains Catherine Andreyev, *Vlasov and the Russian Liberation Movement: Soviet Reality and Émigré Theories* (Cambridge University Press, 1987). The German case for Vlasov has been made by one of his handlers, Wilfried Strik-Strikfeldt, *Against Stalin and Hitler: Memoir of the Russian Liberation Movement, 1941–1945* (London: Macmillan, 1970). Access to Soviet archives has not substantially changed the picture except to disclose more details on the complex relationships between Vlasov and the émigrés. Tsurganov, *Neudavshiisia revansh*, chs. 7 and 8. In a cruel irony Vlasov was originally turned over to the Germans by Russian peasants. *Materialy po istorii Russkogo osvoboditel'nogo dvizheniia, 1941–1945 gg. Stat'i, dokumenty, vospominaniia* (Moscow: Graal, 1997), pp. 64–5.

[98] Alexander Dallin and Ralph S. Mavrogordato, "The Soviet Reaction to Vlasov," *World Politics* 8:3 (1956), pp. 307–22; Armstrong, *Soviet Partisans*, pp. 243–8.

[99] Armstrong, *Soviet Partisans*, pp. 312–17, 330; Semiriaga, *Kollaboratsionizm*, pp. 485–529; Hiroaki Kuromiya, *Freedom and Terror in the Donbas: A Ukrainian-Russian Borderland, 1870s–1990s* (Cambridge University Press, 1998), pp. 259–95. But compare Weiner, *Making Sense*, p. 305.

Still, the Soviet system in much of the occupied territory was in a shambles. On January 1, 1944, a Politburo decree signed by Stalin and Georgii Malenkov outlined the need to restore the shattered Soviet structure of the Belorussian republic:

Bearing in mind that in regions liberated from the German occupiers, the party, soviet and economic organs will have to be practically created anew and that a large number of new activists will have to be drawn into their work, the Belorussian state and party organizations are obliged to improve in every possible way the selection of cadres in Soviet and party organs, promoting people for work in these organs who are completely reliable and capable of restoring the economy that has been ruined by the German invaders and liquidating the consequences of the German occupation.[100]

As the Red Army advanced, the NKVD assumed a larger role in cleansing the liberated territories of enemies of the regime. By March 1943 according to a report to Stalin, 30,750 individuals had been arrested.[101] Without the war there could not have been civil war; but without the contradictions and brutality of the Germans the anti-Soviet forces would certainly have multiplied greatly. As it was, neither side succeeded in convincing the mass of the population in the borderlands that its victory would be in their best interests.

The third phase

During the third phase the advance of the Red Army changed the character of the civil wars in three ways. First, the anti-Communist bands in the pre-1939 territories of the USSR were either broken up or disintegrated of their own accord, and large-scale desertions of Osttruppen took place despite belated, desperate efforts by the Wehrmacht to recruit from the local population. Second, the nationalist bands dug more deeply into the congenial soil of their native strongholds in the Baltic republics and Western Ukraine, fighting in ever diminishing numbers until the war was long over. Third, Stalin and Beria extended their policy of massive deportations to the Crimea and the frontier zone with Turkey.

In Belorussia a three-way struggle opened up. The partisans, still starved of arms and equipment, nevertheless increased at an exponential rate. Shortages of manpower forced the Germans early in 1944 to create a

---

[100] Politburo Protocols, 1 January 1944, "O blizhaishchikh zadachakh Sovnarkoma BSSR i TsK P(b) Belorusii," *Rossiiskii gosudarstvennyi arkhiv sotsial'no-politicheskoi istorii* (RGASPI) f. 17, op. 3, d. 1049, ll. 236–8.

[101] Merkulov to Stalin, March 18, 1943, *Vestnik arkhiva presidenta, Voina,* doc. 102, pp. 224, with lists by regions pp. 225–32.

Weissruthenische Heimatwehr, which the local nationalists vainly envisaged as the nucleus of a Belorussian Army. Elements of the Polish Home Army became more active, unleashing terrorist tactics against Jews, partisans and Polish civilian "collaborators"; a few even entered into agreements with local German commanders to conduct joint operations against the Soviet partisans.[102] In the wake of the Red Army, NKVD units arrived. In the first half of 1945 they were arresting a monthly average of about 1,000 and killing about 100 "bandits" and other "anti-Soviet elements." Interrogations revealed a great variety of ethnic identities and political affiliations, ranging from former White officers to members of the Belorussian Communist Party.[103]

The retreat of the Wehrmacht from Estonia and Latvia forced the nationalist "collaborationist" organizations underground, where they joined other groups of "forest brothers" in forming a "resistance" to Soviet reoccupation. Some of their leaders – like Stalin, also "men of the borderlands" – assumed that they could win only with the help of foreign intervention. In Estonia the Union for Armed Struggle pinned its hopes for "liberation" on assistance from Britain or the United States. "in case of war" or "some kind of political upheaval." For ten years in dwindling numbers they fought on. According to the records of the Estonian émigrés and the Soviet security services the "forest brothers" killed a total of about 1,700 Soviet personnel from among the army, partisans, party, police and new Russian settlers, while losing about 1,500 of their own in dead and 8,000 taken prisoner.[104] In Latvia the "forest brothers" resembled their Estonian counterparts, but their service in the German Army made them hardened, experienced and well organized. As early as January 1945 Beria reported to Stalin that the security organs had

---

[102] Chiari, *Alltag hinter der Front,* pp. 160–1, 289–95. In December 1943 there were about 100,000 partisans in Belorussia, but according to Starinov, "Podryvniki," p. 109, only 60 percent were armed. By the end of the war there were 374,000, as the fence-sitters jumped to the Soviet side. N. I. Epoletov, "Iz opyta raboty kompartii Belorussii po razvitiiu partizanskogo dvizheniia (1941–1944)," *Voprosy istorii KPSS* 5 (May, 1987), pp. 106–8.

[103] "Osobaia papka Stalina," in GARF, f. 9401, op. 2, d. 92, 276–82, 289–90; d. 93, ll. 49–52. In early 1945 in the rear of the First Belorussian Front, for example, one monthly list of arrests included 31 Germans, 590 Lithuanians, 214 Poles, 47 Russians, and 19 Belorussians.

[104] Laar, *War in the Woods,* pp. 19–20, 61–2, 77–81, 176, and "Podpol'e v Estonii," p. 175, agree on these statistics based on NKVD and Estonian archives, although neither gives exact citations. Where they disagree is on the total number of "forest brothers." Estonian émigré sources claim 40,000 at their peak strength, while Russian military historians add 6,500 amnestied to the killed and captured for a total of 16,000. The discrepancy might be explained by the large number of "forest brothers" who simply dropped out of the fight or emigrated during the postwar decade.

arrested 5,223 men, the majority being "German sympathizers," including the head of the Latvian Lutheran Church. Over the following eight
years the Latvian groups carried out 3,000 killings, of whom 90 percent were Latvians. Although their largest units were broken up in 1946,
bands remained in the field until the early 1950s.[105]

Of the three Baltic peoples, the Lithuanians continued to display
the highest level of political consciousness and organization. An estimated 100,000 took part at one time or another in the struggle against
the restoration of Soviet power. Following the German withdrawal they
formed a United Resistance Movement that combined a political arm,
armed groups, and communications and supply networks. Already in
1944 Stalin was incensed by their activities, demanding an end to
"liberal attitudes" and calling for the strictest repressive measures.[106]
The NKVD needed little encouragement. From July 1944 to January
1945 they arrested 20,949 men. Beria's reports to Stalin increasingly
differentiated among the prisoners as if to deny any unified character
to the resistance and predetermine punishment according to categories
of the Soviet criminal code.[107] Stalin, determined to extirpate the root
causes, reverted to his 1940 policy of deportation (the official term was
resettlement) of the families of "bandits" to the east and of Poles from
Lithuania across the new Polish frontiers.[108]

There was a surprising upsurge of underground activity in Lithuania after the end of World War II. Beria raised the old bugbear of foreign intervention: although the Lithuanian Liberation Army had been
"partially destroyed," he reported, it "is counting on a new war of the
USSR against England and the US and is preparing for a rising in the rear
of the Red Army," when it was forced once again to retreat from Lithuanian soil. In December 1945 the Lithuanian underground formed a
National Council of Lithuania, but in April 1946 the NKVD seized most
of its members, who "all came from the Soviet institutions of the Lithuanian SSR."[109] Undaunted, the military bands formed their own organization, the Lithuanian Freedom Fighters' Movement, which was able to

[105] GARF, f. 9401, op. 2, d. 92, 2212–19, 2269; Boris Meissner, *Die Baltischen Nationen: Estland, Lettland, Litauen* (Cologne: Mockus, 1991), pp. 232–45; Semiriaga, *Kollaboratsionizm*, p. 528.
[106] Laar, *War in the Woods*, pp. 26–8.
[107] Beria's categories included intelligence and counter-intelligence agents of the enemy, their collaborators, participants in the nationalist, anti-Soviet Lithuanian or Polish underground, traitors to the fatherland, German henchmen (*stavniki*) and accomplices (*posobniki*), and, beginning in March 1945, bandits. The latter were associated with the Lithuanian Liberation Army, whose raids Beria enumerated in great detail. GARF, f. 9401, op. 2, d. 92, l. 96, 155–6, 389; d. 96, 5–7.
[108] *Ibid.*, d. 97, ll. 273–74, 332.   [109] *Ibid.*, d. 96, ll. 306, 310–14; d. 102, ll. 290–1.

maintain units of up to 800 men and to create serious difficulties for the re-sovietization of the republic.[110]

The third phase of the civil war in Western Ukraine was fought on a larger scale than anywhere else in the borderlands. As the Germans retreated, they continued to be harassed by large bands of the UPA which were estimated to have at least 80–100,000 fighters, and possibly as many as 400,000.[111] The UPA had become engaged in a three-front war against the Wehrmacht, the Polish Home Army and the Soviet partisans. In 1944 alone the UPA launched 800 attacks against the Soviet authorities, in one region of Galicia alone killing 1,500 party and Komsomol activists. At the same time the Soviet forces claimed to have destroyed thirty-six bands of 4,300 Ukrainian nationalists. As it advanced, the Red Army sought to mobilize all able-bodied men between eighteen and fifty in the region, but thousands slipped through the nets into the underground. The party dispatched over 30,000 workers and 3,500 specially trained agitprop personnel into Western Ukraine in an attempt to stabilize the political situation. But it had to admit that the persistence of wartime attitudes complicated their work. By the end of 1944, when Western Ukraine was cleared of Germans, the local party membership had barely reached 30 percent of the prewar figure.[112]

Reoccupation of Ukraine by the Red Army intensified the fighting as the UPA multiplied its attacks in all directions – against the newly arrived Soviet authorities, Polish civilians and the NKVD. Beria punctiliously tallied the score in his fortnightly reports to Stalin. In the first year of the liberation stage from February 1944 to February 1945 the NKVD killed 73,333 "bandits" and took 73,966 prisoners; in addition 53,383 "bandits" and military objectors had voluntarily surrendered.[113] As the war drew to a close, fighting shifted almost exclusively to Western Ukraine. There insurgent activity flared briefly, then steadily diminished. The losses on the Soviet side were increasingly civilians – chairmen of rural soviets, teachers, self-defense units. By June 1945 casualties had sharply declined, but the number of operations remained steady at about 700, suggesting that the large bands had been broken up.[114] Even so, in January 1946 the Soviet authorities still felt it necessary to deploy

[110] *Ibid.*, d. 102, ll. pp. 47–8, 291, 308. By the early 1950s the NKVD had penetrated and rendered useless underground links with foreign intelligence. Laar, *War in the Woods*, pp. 26–8.

[111] Kosyk, *Das dritte Reich*, doc. 192, p. 621. This latter figure seems inflated.

[112] Galina Georgievna Morekhina, *Partiinoe stroitel'stvo v period Velikoi Otechestvennoi Voiny Sovetskogo Soiuza, 1941–1945 gg.* (Moscow: Izd. politicheskoi literatury, 1986), pp. 121–3, 133.

[113] GARF, f. 9401, op. 2, d. 92, ll. 9–14, 248–53, 275; d. 93, ll. 247–51, 395.

[114] *Ibid.*, d. 96, ll. 13–18; d. 97, ll. 13–16, 346.

20,000 NKVD troops, 10,000 supply troops and 26,000 militia against the insurgents.[115]

Stalin's war against the nationalities on the southern borderlands reached its peak with the deportation of the Crimean Tatars, but its momentum continued with a different justification. Tens of thousands of Crimean Tatars preferred to retreat with the Germans than to remain under Soviet power. But small bands kept operating in the rear of the advancing Red Army. Once again the Soviet authorities reacted at cross-purposes. The local party cadres sought to improve relations with the remaining population, while the NKVD hatched other plans. In his most ambitious operation Beria got approval from the GOKO to carry out the deportation of 180,000 Crimean Tatars as "traitors to the motherland."[116]

Where even Beria could not cook up a case of conspiracy, he took a different line in justifying forced resettlements. Toward the end of the war he played on Stalin's fear of interethnic conflict in Georgia and of pan-Turkic agitation and Turkish influence in the frontier zones in order to propose a virtual ethnic cleansing of the Transcaucasian border districts. First it was the turn of 16,700 households of Turks, Kurds and Khemshily (Armenian Muslims) from five border districts and several villages of the Adzharian Autonomous Republic. This was followed by a massive deportation of 90–100,000 Meskhetian Turks (Islamicized Georgian peasants). None of these peoples had been occupied by the Germans or showed any signs of "bandit" activity.[117] But the wartime experience had intensified Stalin's fears over the potential defection of Soviet nationalities who shared a common frontier with the same or similar ethnic and religious groups.[118]

---

[115] *Ibid.*, d. 102, ll. 101–10, 116–18. The final blow to the insurgent cause was the agreement negotiated by Lazar Kaganovich (who had replaced Nikita Khrushchev as First Secretary of Ukraine) with Poland and Czechoslovakia for joint action in hunting down the remnants of the UPA. David Marples, *Stalinism in Ukraine in the 1940s* (New York: St. Martin's, 1992), p. 68.

[116] Bugai, *L. Beriia – I. Stalinu*, pp. 149–53, 159.

[117] Bugai, *Kavkaz*, pp. 211–17. Speculation that their removal signaled how seriously Stalin was contemplating military action at the end of 1944 now appears baseless. Instead, Stalin's "Special File" reveals his concern over reports on pan-Turkism and Turkish–German relations during the war. GARF, f. 9401, op. 2, d. 99, ll. 19–41 (on pan-Turkism); d. 100, ll. 108–244, 276–469 (translations of German documents on Turkey and Iran during the war); d. 102, ll. 110a–383 (translations of documents on German activities among the Turkic peoples).

[118] There were exceptions. For example, Stalin was talked out of deporting the Karelo-Finnish people in 1944 by the vigorous intervention of the secretary of the Karelian Republic Party, who argued that "there was no parallel with the Crimean Tatars." But then again, on this occasion Beria was not involved. S. G. Verigin, "O planakh likvidatsii Karelo-Finskoi SSR v avguste 1944 g," in Evgenii I. Klement'ev and Viktor

The re-sovietization of the western borderlands drew upon lessons learned from the Russian Civil War, collectivization and the absorption of new territories in 1939–40 but exhibited its own special features. The process was complex but may be summarized as six interrelated tactics.[119] The Soviet authorities pursued an agrarian policy that mixed more generous distribution of land and property to the peasants in the Baltic states than in the period 1939–40 and the application of a harsher class conflict throughout. The more radical attack on kulaks in the West Ukraine backfired, inciting many peasants to join the insurrectionary forces. Second, deportation was employed, but more selectively and less harshly than in prewar period. Third, periodic amnesties were declared which "crippled the resistance in every borderland region."[120] Fourth, the widespread use of locally recruited militias (destruction battalions) proved particularly active and effective in Western Ukraine in securing the countryside. Fifth, the NKVD employed imaginative tactics in infiltrating insurrectionary bands and in maintaining a wide informer network. Sixth, an end to persecution and a more tolerant policy toward the Russian Orthodox Church won over many adherents among the clergy and laity while the Greek Catholic (Uniat) Church was firmly repressed. Resovietization was successful in eliminating open resistance and imposing Soviet institutions on the recovered territories. But it left a residue of bitter memories that would, forty years later, help nourish the elements that brought about a dissolution of the Soviet Union.

Conclusion

The participants in the civil wars from 1941 to 1947 stood even less of a chance than their predecessors did in 1918–20 of overturning the political system or winning independence. They were not united by any ideology except for anti-communism. Their programs were nationalistic but otherwise vague and often authoritarian. They could not count on any external support. Ignored by the Western allies, they were either used as cannon fodder or exposed to terrible reprisals by the Germans. They were poorly armed and heavily outnumbered by the great armies that fought over and around them. They frequently turned their wrath against longstanding ethnic enemies, slaughtering the innocent. They had to contend with the patriotic response among the Soviet population,

N. Birin (eds.), *Karely, Finny: Problemy etnicheskoi istorii* (Moscow: Institut etnologii i antropologii RAN, 1992), pp. 18–22, 28.
[119] The following is based on Alexander Statiev, *The Soviet Counterinsurgency in the Western Borderlands* (Cambridge University Press, 2010).
[120] *Ibid.*, p. 201.

both spontaneous and artificially promoted, to what was perceived as a just war against an aggressor. There were also fears of reprisals. The slightest sign of disloyalty or disaffection touched off a savage Soviet overreaction, the result of Stalin's complex attitudes toward the borderlands from whence he sprang, and of his fears that the Anglo-Americans might seize the opportunity to replace the fading Germans as the new advocates of dismembering the USSR. These fears were largely fantasy. Unlike the government-in-exile after the Russian Civil War in 1920, the governments-in-exile of Estonia, Belorussian, Ukraine and Georgia after World War II were minor affairs with few adherents and no political influence; the exception was the Polish government-in-exile in London. But the core of their international support came from the diaspora in the West (Great Britain, France, the United States, West Germany and Canada) following the violent experiences of the second civil war of 1941–53. This was sufficient cause to attract the attention of Soviet intelligence services and could only have fed Stalin's suspicions of the potential disloyalty of the borderlands in the event of a new war.[121] Employing a small carrot and heavy stick, Stalin invested large resources in the re-sovietization of the borderlands. The process was barely complete at his death.

[121] The history of these shadow governments has not been written. Some, like the Estonian, were headed by former collaborators of the Nazis like Radaslaŭ Astroŭski; others, like the Georgian, by the venerable foe of Stalin, Noe Zhordania. But there were no assassinations organized by the NKVD of exiled leaders as there had been in the 1920s and 30s.

8 War aims: the outer perimeter

There is no evidence that Stalin had a master plan in mind for the political future of the borderlands in postwar Eurasia beyond the new Soviet frontier. If he had one, or even the elements of one, he did not share them with any of his colleagues in the leading organs of the party or military: in other words the individuals who would have to carry out such a plan. As more documentary evidence becomes available, it becomes clearer that throughout the war he had not made up his mind about a number of questions, including the pace and extent of the socioeconomic transformation of the postwar regimes within the states liberated by the Red Army; there is evidence that he changed his mind about some, such as the Soviet occupation zone in Germany. Although these conclusions are still debated, the following pages will attempt to demonstrate their validity.

Despite the absence of a master plan, Stalin's policies can be explained as an application of his borderland thesis within two distinctive but interconnected spatial dimensions or fields of operation. Let us call them the inner and outer perimeters. The inner perimeter refers to the territories lying within the operational sphere of the Red Army and the outer perimeter to the sphere of Anglo-American military operations. In both, the military commanders assumed special administrative powers during the liberation. There was no formal agreement on this delimitation, although Stalin referred at least once to such a separation of responsibilities. The boundary between them resembled a frontier zone; it was initially blurred and porous, even on occasion disputed. Stalin's tacit acceptance of this separation reflected his estimate of the Soviet needs arising from the German invasion and the threatening presence of a militarist and expansionist Japan. He responded by entering into an unprecedented military and political alliance with the leading democratic capitalist powers in order to win the war and obtain guarantees of Soviet security and stability in the postwar period. For Stalin a successful outcome of the war would involve an extension of the wartime alliance in order to prolong the flow of economic aid for the reconstruction of the shattered Soviet economy, prevent the rapid recovery of a strong Germany and Japan, and gain Allied acquiescence in Soviet hegemony over the Eurasian borderlands.

In return, as it were, he was willing to join a neo-Wilsonian international organization (albeit with the self-protection of the veto power), recognize implicitly the old imperial interests of Great Britain and the expanded imperial interests of the United States, and to counsel restraint to the leaders of the Communist parties in Western Europe, Greece, Iran and China, encouraging them to join in coalition governments dominated by pro-Western parties and assist vigorously in reconstructing their national economies. By having dissolved the Comintern and then dealing with the leaders of Communist parties on a bilateral basis, Stalin appeared to endorse the idea of separate roads to socialism.

The inherent contradictions and potential for conflict between Soviet aims in the outer and inner perimeters increased in the final stages of the war. The question facing Stalin was how to maintain the fragile wartime alliance while at the same time making certain to his own satisfaction (which set the bar very high) that Soviet hegemony in the inner perimeter would eliminate centers of political opposition real, potential or imagined. Balancing the requirements of his war aims in the outer and inner perimeters required the kind of finesse that had not been the hallmark of his personal rule. Yet the attempt was made.

As the next two chapters explore this attempt, it will become clear that the touchstones of his policies in the outer and inner perimeters in Europe would be Germany and Poland. Stalin's aims for each illustrate most vividly the complex set of connections linking aims and policies in the outer and inner perimeters. In Trans Caspia and Inner Asia, Iranian Azerbaizhan, Xinjiang and Manchuria played similar key roles in Stalin's policies.

Except for Stalin's views on territorial changes on the Soviet frontiers, his government never issued a public statement of its official war aims. Stalin signed off on the Atlantic Charter, the Yalta Declaration on the Liberated Territories and the United Nations Charter. But these were general statements of principles drafted in the main by others, vague in language and open to widely different interpretations. They cannot be accepted as representing Soviet war aims, although neither can they be dismissed completely as irrelevant to them. We are left with a broad field for speculation filled with interpretations ranging from stage one of a Soviet design for world domination to a search for national security in conventional great power terms. The ambiguity and controversy might have been eliminated or reduced had Litvinov remained or returned as

Foreign Commissar, as he himself has argued.[1] But this assumes either that his policy was fundamentally different from Stalin's, which is highly problematic to begin with, and even if true the differences would not have been tolerated by the Soviet leader in official negotiations with the West, or else that he could have presented the Soviet case in clear, comprehensive and compelling terms that Western diplomats would have understood.[2] But here too the unspoken assumption is that the Cold War was only a matter of lack of understanding on one or both sides rather than fundamental disagreements over interests.

As it was, neither Stalin nor Molotov was ready or perhaps willing to disclose fully and frankly their aspirations for the postwar world. Nor did Soviet diplomats make their task any easier. Inexperienced and truculent where they might have been conciliatory, eager to please the leadership rather than willing to report unpleasant facts, they were fully aware of the fate of their predecessors. Consequently, they were wary of appearing to be sympathetic to the West. They tended to exaggerate the extent of local support for the Soviet Union in the liberated territories in order to protect themselves from accusations of pessimism and defeatism and at the same time they inflated the threat from the West in order to avoid accusations that they lacked vigilance.

In assessing Stalin's war aims it should be kept in mind that his success and survival as a politician had depended upon his skill in adjusting his views to changing circumstances within a flexible ideological framework of his own devising. In making decisions, he took account of his estimate of the balance of strategic forces, partly defined in military but also partly in socioeconomic terms. Stalin's pragmatism was the pragmatism of a Marxist-Leninist tempered by his grasp of the historical foundations of Russia's status as a great power. For him the Red Army had always been a factor of critical importance in determining the political complexion of the borderlands, whether Ukraine in 1919, Georgia in 1921, the Baltic republics, West Ukraine or West Belorussia in 1939–40. And he restated his conviction in the oft-cited remark to Djilas that "everyone

---

[1] Vojtech Mastny, "The Cassandra in the Foreign Commissariat: Maxim Litvinov and the Cold War," *Foreign Affairs* 54 (1975–6), p. 370.

[2] Geoffrey Roberts, "Litvinov's Lost Peace, 1941–1946," *Journal of Cold War Studies* 4:2 (2002), pp. 23–53, gives a comprehensive analysis of Litvinov's vision of a postwar Europe based on the idea of a division of spheres of influence between Britain and the Soviet Union. As he points out, several historians have identified serious flaws: the assumption of the return of the United States to isolationism; an exaggeration of British power; and the instability of an intermediate neutral belt between the two power blocs. To these might be added the failure to consider the activities of local Communist parties, tacitly or actively supported by the Soviet Union, which went beyond what the Western powers were willing to accept as "influence."

imposes his own system as far as his army can reach."[3] But he also recognized that the army alone could not determine the future of the postwar states. Stalin's approach to the question of war aims was also shaped by his Marxist-Leninist outlook on the nature of war. He understood the importance of making the distinction between just and unjust wars, of periodically reassessing the balance of strategic and social forces in the theater of operations, and of perceiving war as the extension of politics by other means.[4] Having learned his lessons at the end of the Civil War in compromising with Piłsudski and Atatürk, Stalin showed a willingness in the latter stages of World War II to cut deals with anyone who would play the game with him, whether authoritarian nationalists like Chiang Kai-shek or democratic politicians like Beneš.

But it was in Stalin's nature too to cultivate an aura of impenetrability, to mask the fact that he had not made up his mind, or even under certain conditions, that he had but was reluctant for tactical reasons to show his hand. He could, of course, be brutally precise in giving orders; but he could also be terse or elliptical especially when dealing with a situation in flux, forcing his interlocutors to hazard their own interpretation and reserving the right, as it were, to interpret his own pronouncements depending upon changing circumstances. This passion for being secretive and cryptic immensely complicates the task of the historian pondering the evolution of his thinking.

Maintaining the coalition

In ranking the war aims of the Soviet Union in the outer perimeter, first place on Stalin's agenda would have to be the maintenance of the coalition with Great Britain and the United States, "In this war of liberation we shall not be alone," Stalin pointedly declared in his first public address after the invasion. Yet, his military alliance with Great Britain and the US lacked any ideological justification in Marxist-Leninist ideology. It went far beyond peaceful coexistence as defined by Lenin and it did not fit easily into the theory of imperialism with its prescribed tactic of exploiting imperialist rivalries. The "anti-Fascist", or "anti-Hitlerite" alliance as Moscow called it, evolved in a way that had no exact parallel in world diplomacy up to that time. It involved joint strategic planning, economic assistance and long-term political arrangements worked out by continuous negotiation often in the form of direct correspondence

---

[3] Milovan Djilas, *Conversations with Stalin* (New York: Harcourt, Brace and World, 1962), pp. 114–15.

[4] Raymond L. Garthoff, *How Russia Makes War* (London: Allen and Unwin, 1954) ch. 3; M. Leonov, "Lenin o voine i roli moral'nogo faktora v nei," *Agitator i propagandist Krasnoi Armii* 6 (March, 1945), pp. 19–32.

between the three heads of state and culminating in personal meetings at the summit conferences of Teheran, Yalta and Potsdam. The relationship was also unprecedented in the history of Soviet foreign relations. This is one reason, along with the fear of foreign contacts instilled by the years of terror, why it often worked badly at the intermediate and lower levels of the Soviet civil and military bureaucracies. That it worked at all was a function of Stalin's endorsement and the great advantages it offered the Soviet Union in its war for survival and its determination to fight to the finish.

Maintaining the coalition was the best guarantee of opening a second front, securing vital supplies of equipment and food through Lend-Lease, discouraging a separate peace by the West, negotiating mutually acceptable postwar territorial settlements, preventing the rapid recovery of Germany and Japan as aggressive powers, and obtaining postwar economic assistance for reconstruction. None of these aims was to be achieved without tough bargaining. Mutual suspicion was constantly breaking the surface. But during the war, even in its latter stages when serious differences over several of these issues were beginning to appear, Stalin reiterated in the strongest terms his favorable interpretation of the alliance. "What matters is not that there are differences, but that these differences do not transgress the bounds of what the interests of unity of the three great powers allow, and that in the long run they are resolved in accordance with the interests of that unity." This show of unity would reveal the bankruptcy of Hitler's propaganda aimed at sowing mutual distrust. But, he added, the alliance of the great powers is "founded not on casual, short-term considerations but on vital and lasting interest."[5] It appeared he was stating that interests trump ideology. But no one knew better than Stalin that ideology often defines interests.

Stalin regarded the opening of a second front as the touchstone of the alliance.[6] In his earliest wartime speeches, he deplored the absence of a second front; for example, attributing the success of the German summer offensive in 1942 to the fact that the Germans and their allies were able to concentrate their entire land forces on the eastern front. In Molotov's conversations with Eden in December 1941, and with Roosevelt and his advisors in May–June 1942, he expressed the view that a political commitment to a second front was essential. Churchill was loath to give it, but Roosevelt was not. In his exchanges with Molotov, Roosevelt in characteristic fashion made a number of extravagant remarks apparently

---

[5] J. V. Stalin, *The Great Patriotic War of the Soviet Union* (Moscow: International Publishers, 1945), p. 137.

[6] Roberts, *From World War to Cold War*, pp. 134–42, for a summary of this issue in 1942–3. See also I. N. Zemskov, *Diplomaticheskaia istoriia vtorogo fronta v Evrope* (Moscow: Izd. politicheskoi literatury, 1982).

288   War aims: the outer perimeter

aimed at reassuring the Soviet leaders of American goodwill. For example, he declared "it is possible that we shall have to live through another
Dunkirk and lose 100–120,000 men," but "it would ease the situation
and raise the spirit of the Red Army even higher." This was exactly the
sort of commitment Stalin welcomed. But Molotov soon discovered that
Churchill was appalled by the idea, regarding it as "folly" and adding,
"we shall not win the war by doing such stupid things."[7]

On Stalin's instructions the joint communiqué summarizing Molotov's
talks in Washington included the wording "a full understanding was
reached on the urgent task of creating a second front in Europe in 1942."
He was even willing to accept Roosevelt's proposal to reduce the tonnage
of Lend-Lease shipments so that the surplus shipping could be used
to open a second front. He appeared, then, to give more credence to
Roosevelt's bland assurances than did Molotov. Whatever his thinking
on that score, he believed that the wording of the communiqué on the
second front and military supplies "is imperative because it will bring
confusion to the ranks of Hitler and the neutral countries in the whole
of Europe."[8] Although Stalin made no mention of the advantage such a
political commitment might be in future negotiations with his allies, it is
clear from his subsequent statements and behavior that this too would
serve his purposes.

In Stalin's correspondence with Churchill and Roosevelt, he turned
angry and suspicious over the repeated postponement of the second
front more regularly and with greater passion than over any other issue
with the possible exception of the postwar Polish frontier. "The Germans
look on the threat from the West as a bluff," he stated, and the absence
of the second front "plays into the hands of our common enemies." He
wondered why the British could not send twenty to thirty divisions to
Russia as they had to France in 1914. He was dismayed by the news that
the cross-Channel invasion "previously postponed from 1942 until 1943
is now being put off again, this time until the spring of 1944." When
Churchill attempted to explain the difficulties, Stalin sharply reproached
him, declaring that it was not "just the disappointment of the Soviet government but the preservation of its confidence in its allies, a confidence
which is being subject to severe stress."[9]

[7] O. A. Rzheshevskii (ed.), *Vtoraia mirovaia voina; actual'nye problemy* (Moscow: Nauka, 1995), doc. 70, p. 177, and doc. 109, p. 274.
[8] *Ibid.*, doc. 94, p. 219, and commentary p. 221.
[9] Ministry of Foreign Affairs of the USSR, *Correspondence between the Chairman of the Council of Ministers of the U.S.S.R. and the Presidents of the U.S.A. and the Prime Ministers of Great Britain during the Great Patriotic War of 1941–1945*, 2 vols. (Moscow: Foreign Languages Publishing House, 1957), vol. I, pp. 21, 24, 56, 58–9, 95, 105–6, 132, 138.

For Stalin the second front meant a cross-Channel landing in France. While he welcomed the Allied military campaigns in the Mediterranean and Italy, he declared that this was not a second front, but only "something like a second front."[10] A few weeks later at the Teheran Conference he strongly supported Roosevelt's endorsement of a cross-Channel landing against Churchill's preference for pursuing a Mediterranean strategy. The idea that Stalin was guided by political considerations in seeking to prevent the Allies from landing in the Balkans or committing more forces to Italy misses the essential point. Given the topography and state of communications in the Mediterranean littoral, any Allied landing could be met and contained as it had been in Italy by a relatively small number of German troops, whereas a landing in Northern France would require a major German effort and draw off far larger forces from the eastern front. Moreover, once they broke out of their beachheads, the Allied forces would be operating in ideal tank country, as Hitler knew only too well. To stop an advance into the heart of Germany, the Wehrmacht would have to commit major panzer forces, in contrast to what would be required to fight another campaign in the mountainous Balkans.[11] For Stalin the main point was to defeat Germany as quickly as possible.

Linked to Stalin's hopes for a second front were his fears and suspicion that the Allies might negotiate a separate peace with Germany and its satellites. Throughout the war Soviet officials reacted strongly to Nazi propaganda, attempting to drive a wedge between the Soviet Union and the Anglo-Americans by reviving the hoary comparison between Russia's "oriental barbarism" and enlightened Western culture. Stalin welcomed Churchill's and Roosevelt's call for the unconditional surrender of Germany at the Casablanca Conference in 1943, even though he had not been consulted beforehand. Yet he was never fully convinced that they might not try to slip out of their public commitments with respect not only to Germany but to its satellites.

---

[10] J. V. Stalin, *On the Great Patriotic War of the Soviet Union* (London: Hutchinson, 1943), p. 103. Speech on the twenty-sixth anniversary of the October Revolution, November 6, 1943.

[11] Ministerstvo innostranykh del SSSR, *Sovetskii Soiuz na mezhdunarodnykh konferentsiiakh perioda Velikoi Otechestvennoi voiny 1941–1945 gg.; Tegeranskaia konferentsiia rukovoditelei trekh soiuznykh derzhav – SSSR, SShA i Velikobritanii (28 noiabria–1 dekabria 1943 g. Sbornik dokumentov* (Moscow: Izd. politicheskoi literatury, 1978), pp. 96–7. The view that Stalin determined Allied policy at Teheran does not stand up to close scrutiny. Cf. Keith Sainsbury, *The Turning Point: Roosevelt, Stalin, Churchill and Chiang Kai-shek 1943. The Moscow, Cairo and Teheran Conferences* (Oxford University Press, 1985). The Americans were already firmly committed to the idea and by this time had asserted their leadership in the Anglo-American alliance. For Churchill's strategy, D. Reynolds, *In Command of History: Churchill Fighting and Writing the Second World War* (New York: Random House, 2005).

Stalin never failed to point out that the Soviet Union was fighting against a European army. He counted fully one-quarter of the enemy as being composed of non-German formations, most of them drawn from Eastern Europe: twenty-two Romanian divisions, fourteen Finnish, thirteen Hungarian, ten Italian, one each from Slovakia and Spain, and smaller units of Croatian, Flemish and French volunteers.[12] He reacted strongly in the final stages of the war to any hints that the governments of Hitler's satellites intended to abandon Hitler by negotiating with the West. In 1944, when the Red Army approached their frontiers, Romania, Hungary and Bulgaria made their first overtures to the West, hoping to have British or American troops take part in their "liberation," flown in if only in token numbers. The Western allies promptly rejected such overtures. But Stalin interpreted the appeals themselves as confirmation of his suspicion that German propaganda was having a subversive effect on Allied unity. His own agitprop geared up to refute Goebbels's favorite theme that irreconcilable ideological differences would split asunder the Grand Alliance; Russia would be isolated and Germany, like Frederick the Great's Prussia, saved at the last moment in a replay of the "miracle of the house of Brandenburg" ending the Seven Years War. To Stalin attempts to play the West against the Soviet Union smacked of a fascist conspiracy and were rooted in some kind of "objective" conditions.[13]

Stalin's suspicions reached a climax in March 1945 over the so-called Berne incident, when German commanders in Northern Italy made a tentative approach to surrender to the Anglo-American forces. Stalin angrily accused his allies of negotiating "behind the back of the Soviet government which has been carrying on the main burden of the war against Germany." As a result, he asserted, the Germans had been able to shift several divisions to the East. He claimed to have information that Field Marshal Kesselring "has agreed to open the front and permit the Anglo-American troops to advance to the East and the Anglo-Americans have promised in return to ease the peace terms for the Germans."[14] This was not true.

But Stalin's suspicions were not unfounded in other cases. In the closing days of the war many German units along with Hungarian, Croat

---

[12] These were his figures for November 1942 when the German–Austrian divisions numbered 179. Stalin, *On the Great Patriotic War*, p. 63.

[13] V. L. Israelian, *Antigitlerovskaia koalitsiia, 1941–1945* (Moscow: Mezhdunarodnye otnosheniia, 1964), ch. 12; US Department of State, *Foreign Relations of the US* (FRUS) (Washington, DC: Government Printing House, 1943), vol. I, pp. 484–512. For Bulgaria and Hungary (1944), vol. III, pp. 301ff, 827. For Romania, A. Cretzianu, *A Lost Opportunity* (London: Cape, 1957).

[14] FRUS (1945), vol. III, pp. 731–46.

and Osthilfe troops facing the Red Army attempted to make their way west in order to surrender to the British and Americans. Most Western commanders abided by the terms of inter-Allied agreements and turned these desperate men back to the east. But their actions scarcely placated Stalin. He was even piqued by the arrangements for the final surrender ceremony at Rheims. He insisted upon a full-scale, formal repetition of the signing in Berlin in the presence of the victorious Soviet marshals in order to destroy the impression that the Germans preferred to surrender to the West.[15] Clearly he hoped to banish any lingering hopes of anti-Soviet elements that once the war was over they could count on Western support in a new contest over the future of Europe.

In coalition politics Lend-Lease was only second in importance to Stalin though it was no substitute for the absence of a second front. He had specific requirements. As we have seen, he requested tanks and planes from Britain. He instructed Molotov to obtain from Washington monthly deliveries of fifty B-25 bombers, 150 Boston-3 bombers and 3,000 trucks. An additional list of 8 million tons of supplies for the year beginning July 1, 1942 included mainly raw materials that would be used, Molotov explained, to build metallurgical plants and powers stations and furnish railroad equipment necessary not only for the pursuit of the war but for the home front.[16] Although the Lend-Lease convoys to the northern Soviet ports carried most of the supplies, the Iranian corridor became increasingly important. By 1943 the Americans had constructed a rail line through the British and Soviet occupation zones that opened another safer route.[17]

By the end of the war the United States had shipped 360,000 trucks, 43,000 jeeps, 2,000 locomotives, and 11,000 railroad cars, along with communication equipment, particularly radios. In addition, Lend-Lease supplied raw materials and foodstuffs, including canned goods that were vital to the troops defending Stalingrad. As Jacques Sapir has suggested, without these food shipments, "it is very probable that . . . average food consumption for the civilian population would have declined by a third." Moreover, Lend-Lease enabled the Soviet planners "to focus on arms production without having to fear a possible breakdown of the industrial

---

[15] Speech of May 9, 1945, in *Vneshnaia politika Sovetskogo Soiuza v Otvechestvennoi voiny: Dokumenty i materialy*, 3 vols. (Moscow: Gos. polit-literatury, 1944–7), vol. III, p. 44. As a result victory day was celebrated in the Soviet Union one day later than in the West.

[16] Rzheshevskii, *Vtoraia mirovaia voina*, doc. 77, pp. 198–9, doc. 78, p. 200.

[17] Thomas Ricks, "U.S. Military Missions to Iran, 1943–1978: The Politics of Economy of Military Assistance," *Iranian Studies* 12:3–4 (1979), p. 171; T. H. Vail Motter, *The Persian Corridor and Aid to Russia* (Washington, DC: Office of the Chief of Military History, Department of the Army, 1952), pp. 465–7.

apparatus."[18] Early on in the war, Stalin had already paid tribute publically to the financial and material aid from the United States and Great Britain.[19]

The significance of Lend-Lease went far beyond the demeaning statistical approach of postwar Soviet spokesmen like N. A. Voznesenkii.[20] Aside from the quantitative contribution of food and military equipment, aid enabled the Soviet leaders to shift the domestic allocation of resources by freeing resources for civilian use in both investment and consumption, mitigating the food crisis and replacing worn out capital stock. Moreover, the high technology of much aid contributed to the mobility and maneuverability of the Red Army, particularly in its great offensives after the battle of Kursk in 1943.[21] For all these reasons Stalin deeply resented any interruption of the deliveries. When the convoys to Murmansk were briefly suspended in July 1942 due to a high number of sinkings by U-boats, he accused his allies of an unwillingness to accept very high losses while "the Soviet Union is suffering far greater losses."[22]

Economic aims

Soviet interest in obtaining a long-term loan from the United States for reconstruction, as opposed to Lend-Lease, appeared relatively late in the war.[23] It reflected his understanding that the cost of war had increased the gap between the Soviet and the capitalist economies, intensifying the persistent problem of economic backwardness. Could the Soviet Union afford to return to a policy of autarchy? The first, unrealistic proposal came from Mikoian in December 1943 for a loan of one billion dollars at 0.5 percent interest, with repayment to begin sixteen years after receipt of the credit. The Soviet leaders were already aware of the American

---

[18] Jacques Sapir, "The Economics of War in the Soviet Union during World War II," in Ian Kershaw and Moshe Lewin (eds.), *Stalinism and Nazism: Dictatorships in Comparison* (Cambridge University Press, 1997), p. 233. The importance of American canned food at Stalingrad is mentioned several times in Konstantin Simonov's famous war novel *Days and Nights*.

[19] For example, in his speeches on the twenty-four anniversary of the October Revolution in November 1941 and May Day 1944; Stalin, *On the Great Patriotic War*, pp. 31, 124.

[20] Mark Harrison, *Accounting for War: Soviet Production, Employment, and the Defense Burden, 1940–1945* (Cambridge University Press 1996), pp. 133–6. Khrushchev later had some words of praise, but Mikoian, who should have known better, was more grudging in his acknowledgments. Nikita Khrushchev, *Memoirs* (Boston: Little, Brown, 1970), p. 199; Anastas Mikoian, *Tak bylo* (Moscow: Vagrius, 1999), pp. 408–13.

[21] Harrison, *Accounting for War*, pp. 140–6.

[22] Ministry of Foreign Affairs of the USSR, *Correspondence*, vol. I, doc. 57, p. 56.

[23] John Lewis Gaddis, *The United States and the Origins of the Cold War, 1941–1947* (New York: Columbia University Press, 1972), pp. 174–97, gives the full picture from the American side.

desire to open up the Soviet market to trade in order to help ease the transition from war to a peacetime economy. This fitted their ideological perceptions of a postwar capitalist crisis of overproduction. They soon also concluded, if they had not already taken note, that the slow response was due to the determination of the Americans to obtain political concessions in return for credits. But they also disagreed on the need and size of the loan.

According to Mikoian, he proposed to Stalin on the eve of the Yalta Conference that he should accept a negotiating figure of $2 billion at 3 percent interest. But Voznesenskii regarded this as unacceptable. Stalin's response was "If we are to get credits from the Americans, why $2 billion? That's too little. We should ask for 6 billion." Mikoian was appalled. They would never get it, he replied. But he advised Stalin to request the sum from Roosevelt at Yalta since relations with him were still good. But Stalin never raised the question there.[24] A year passed before Molotov revived and revised the Soviet proposal for a loan of $6 billion at an interest rate of 2.25 percent.[25] Once again the Unites States postponed action. By this time Soviet negotiators balked, briefly, at signing the Fourth Lend-Lease Protocol which, at the insistence of the US Congress, included a provision for reimbursement of Lend-Lease materials for use in postwar reconstruction, even though the US government offered a loan at 2.75 percent for thirty years to make the payments. In the interim Stalin had received the American businessman, Eric Johnston, who had waxed enthusiastic about the possibilities of postwar trade.[26] It was clear to the Soviet leader that different interests in the United States perceived a continuation of the coalition in different ways. He intervened personally, if unofficially, to attempt to persuade influential members of Congress to endorse the loan. In conversations with an American Congressional delegation in mid-September 1945, he restated the Soviet need for a low-interest, long-term $6 billion loan. He dismissed his prewar commitment to Soviet economic self-sufficiency. Justifying the size of the loan, he calculated that it would pay for 5 million tons of rails, 10,000 locomotives, 150,000 railroad cars and 40–50,000 machine tools. Clearly the order would be placed with American firms. In conclusion he struck an optimistic note: "the tie which has held us together no longer exists and we shall have to find a new basis for our close relations in the future.

---

[24] Mikoian, *Tak bylo*, pp. 493–4.
[25] A. N. Iakovlev *et al.* (eds.), *Sovetsko-amerikanskie otnosheniia, 1939–1945: Dokumenty* (Moscow: Materik, 2004), doc. 266, pp. 602–4. In submitting his memo to Harriman, Molotov inquired whether this was a favorable moment to raise the question and was assured it was.
[26] FRUS, *Europe* (1944), vol. IV, pp. 973–4.

That will not always be easy... [but] as Christ said 'seek and ye shall find.'"[27] The Americans were not convinced.

Stalin's hopes for a continuation of favorable economic relations with the United States in the postwar era were sustained by his diplomatic representatives in the US and theoreticians of the Institute of World Economics and World Politics. Reporting from Washington in July 1944, Ambassador Andrei Gromyko, a former economics professor at Moscow State University, gave a surprisingly optimistic prognosis of future Soviet–American relations. In discussing credits with him, various officials in the Roosevelt administration had named a figure of $5–6 billion or more over twenty to twenty-five years at 2.00–2.50 percent interest. (No doubt he had been talking with Henry Morgenthau who favored extending a loan of $10 billion to the Soviet Union.) Gromyko anticipated extensive technical aid, especially in the chemical and radio industry, and the exchange of information in the field of agriculture where American technical achievements had been striking. He too warned that there were anti-Soviet elements still at large especially in the Republican Party. But he was convinced that "conditions existed for the continued cooperation between the two countries in the post war period."[28]

For a time after the war Soviet economic specialists, encouraged by articles in the American press on the favorable attitude of the business community, anticipated a large increase in trade between the two countries.[29] As late as May 1946 the Soviet Union reiterated its willingness to negotiate a settlement of all economic questions with the United States including the extension of long-term credits, resolution of the Lend-Lease question and an agreement on trade and navigation.[30] But there was no response from the American side.

Stalin also needed his coalition partners to secure reparations payments, eliminate Germany's war-making capacity and weaken its industrial base. During the war he created a special commission on compensation for the losses inflicted on the Soviet Union by Hitlerite Germany and its allies (the Commission on Reparations) under the chairmanship of Ivan Maiskii, with representatives from different governmental departments. In his final report, Maiskii suggested that the figure of

[27] *Ibid.* (1945), vol. V, pp. 882–3; Gaddis, *The United States*, pp. 259–61.
[28] G. N. Sevastianov (ed.), *Sovetsko-amerikanskie otnosheniia, 1945–1948* (Moscow: Mezhdunarodnyi fond 'Demokratiia', 2004), doc. 244, pp. 539–54. Largely free of ideological cant, this is one of the most comprehensive and balanced estimates from a Soviet point of view of American politics.
[29] *Ibid.*, doc. 334, pp. 716–17.
[30] *Ibid.*, doc. 112, p. 229. Negotiations on Lend-Lease were renewed in 1947–8, 1951–2 and 1960. In 1972 an agreement was signed but never implemented.

$5 billion dollars which Molotov intended to submit to the European Advisory Commission as the Soviet share was too low. At Yalta, Stalin revised it to $10 billion and stubbornly held to that figure after Roosevelt made the mistake of accepting it as the basis for future negotiations. Overall, the principle guiding the work in the Maiskii commission was "to take from Germany and its allies everything that can be taken" while "allowing for the 'famine minimum.'" The total amount of goods and services to be extracted including forced labor and annual procurements from current production was $75 billion, of which the Soviet Union would receive 50–80 percent. In a separate memorandum Maiskii insisted that an annual quota of 5 million German workers should be sent to the USSR for compulsory service "in the form of something like labor armies [to]carry out tasks assigned to them under the command of the NKVD."[31] Soviet policy toward its coalition partners became mired in a deep contradiction between its short-term and long-term needs, its plans for economic recovery and its haphazard resort to expedient measures. Citing Stalin, Maiskii explained to Harriman in January 1945 that the Soviet Union would insist on not only the military but the industrial disarming of Germany. It was a question of security. As long as Germany had a powerful economic machine "no one could sleep peacefully." This meant the entire liquidation of Germany's military production and the larger part of its heavy industry.[32] Maiskii did not give Harriman details.

The Soviet leaders were impatient for the Reparations Commission established at Yalta to begin work. But they allowed Soviet officials on the occupied territory of their erstwhile enemies to confiscate everything they could in an uncoordinated, desperate effort to assist reconstruction at home. This was taking place not only in Germany, but in Hungary, Romania and Manchuria. When Allied representatives in Bucharest pointed out that Soviet policy was unnecessarily destroying the possibility of producing goods for reparations by crippling the local oil industry, a Soviet official responded: "My country needs every ounce of equipment of all kinds that we can get by any means." There was no intention of rebuilding plants in the Soviet Union but of obtaining spare parts.[33]

[31] Aleksei Filitov, "Problems of Post-war Construction in Soviet Foreign Policy Conceptions during World War II," in Francesca Gori and Silvio Pons (eds.), *The Soviet Union and Europe in the Cold War 1943–53* (New York and London: St. Martin's Press), pp. 6–7.
[32] Iakovlev *et al.*, *Sovetsko-amerikanskie otnosheniia, 1939–1945*, doc. 271, p. 617.
[33] Public Record Office, Foreign Office. 942/217/EIPS/120/105 and 108; Alfred J. Rieber, "The Crack in the Plaster: Crisis in Romania and the Origins of the Cold War," *Journal of Modern History* 76 (March, 2004), p. 74.

Appalled by the arbitrary stripping of German industry in the Soviet zone of occupation, the Americans were alarmed at the prospect of a complete collapse of the German economy. They were reluctant to press ahead on the question of reparations for fear that the Soviet demands would have a disastrous effect on their zones. In September 1946 the United States proposed that the removal of industrial equipment from the Soviet zone should be coordinated with removals from the western zones in the spirit of treating Germany as an economic whole. But the Soviet response refuted these proposals by citing chapter and verse of the Potsdam agreements which placed the authority for the removal of industrial equipment from the Soviet zone under the exclusive control of the Soviet occupation authorities, while establishing a joint four-power commission for removals from the western zones.[34] At the same time, President Truman held up extending a loan of $1 billion that he had been authorized in June 1945 to lend through the Export–Import Bank. These decisions had come on top of the sudden termination of Lend-Lease in May 1945, which caused Stalin to complain bitterly. It appeared to the Soviet leader that the Americans were using their economic weapons for political ends.

In his conversation with Secretary of State George C. Marshall in April 1947, Stalin made clear how economic relations lay at the center of a successful continuation of coalition politics. He noted that the extent of destruction by the invading armies was coming to light more visibly all the time. He insisted that a resolution of the question of Lend-Lease payments was linked to the extension of credits, but that ever since his conversations with Ambassador Harriman in January 1945 the US had persistently postponed action on the Soviet request for a loan of $3–6 billion, or more if possible. He argued that the Big Three agreement on the economic unity of Germany could not be achieved without political unity. The division of Germany could only lead to a revival of German chauvinism. That had been the result when Napoleon tried it, he stated. Reparations payments to the Soviet Union of $10 billion had been agreed upon by Roosevelt, Stettinius and Hopkins. But the Reparations Commission was no longer functioning. Soviet removal of German industrial equipment had only yielded $2 billion – "that's pennies (*groshi*)," he said. Reparations had to be paid out of current production, as agreed at Yalta, and that meant that Germany had to be treated as an economic unit.

---

[34] Sevastianov, *Sovetsko-amerikanskie otnosheniia, 1945–1948*, doc. 5, pp. 15–19. The Soviet government continued to protest over the failure of the Western governments, after six months of delays, to implement the decisions taken at Potsdam on supplying the USSR with advanced deliveries of industrial goods from their zones. *Ibid.*, doc. 76, pp. 170–1.

But Stalin pronounced himself to be an optimist. The negotiations at the Moscow Foreign Ministers Conference could resolve these questions by compromise. "It was only necessary to have patience and not to despair." But above all the Germans should not be allowed to play games with the coalition partners for their own advantage.[35]

Yet the discussion with Marshall also demonstrated from the American point of view that reaching agreements on economic issues was increasingly complicated by growing hostility toward the Soviet Union in the United States, stemming from political conflicts over Eastern Europe where Stalin was unwilling to jeopardize Soviet control which rested on shaky ground. His need for economic resources not only involved him in a contradictory policy toward the West, but also ran counter to his political requirements for security in the borderlands.

Germany

It was only through maintaining the coalition that Stalin could be assured of an active role in further weakening Germany, either by mutual agreement on dismemberment, joint control over key industrial areas like the Ruhr, or a political settlement that would postpone the reemergence of a strong, unified, nationalistic German government. But the Soviet leadership found it difficult to combine these aims into a single policy which they could present to their coalition partners. For example, their ambivalent attitude toward dismemberment illustrates both the inherent difficulties of a policy aimed at imposing a punitive peace on a powerful nation state and the contradiction between weakening Germany by breaking it up politically into its constituent parts and treating it as an economic whole as the best guarantee of a full payment of reparations.

The problem of dismemberment

At Teheran, Stalin had not yet made up his mind about dismemberment, although his comments suggest he was leaning in that direction. When Roosevelt proposed breaking up Germany into its constituent states, Stalin took the position that "Roosevelt's plan for dividing Germany into five or six states and two regions can be considered (*rassmotren*)." Later, when speaking to Churchill, he expressed doubts about its effectiveness in preventing the revival of Germany as a unified great power: "There are no measures which can eliminate the possibility of the unification of Germany." A year later, in his conversation with the Polish–American

---

[35] *Ibid.*, doc. 185, pp. 406–13.

economist Oscar Lange, Stalin noted that the extension of Polish territory to the west at the expense of Germany had been informally discussed
at Teheran where both he and Churchill had endorsed the idea in the
context of weakening Germany. He told Lange that he had supported
Roosevelt's position on dismemberment which was not quite the case.[36]
Stalin was still debating the question in his own mind. Clearly, the issue
of dismemberment was connected to other questions about the postwar
treatment of Germany. As on other issues where he had not yet committed himself he permitted and even encouraged discussion among his
subordinates.

Planning the Soviet war aims for Germany was carried out at several
levels within the government bureaucracy and party organs. Along with
the Reparations Commission, Stalin created two other commissions, the
Commission on Questions of the Peace Treaties and Postwar Construction chaired by Litvinov and the Commission on Armistice Problems
chaired by Voroshilov. The Litvinov Commission met from early 1942 to
the eve of the Yalta Conference. Its membership brought together some
of its chairman's old and trusted associates with high-ranking officials
of the post-Litvinov Foreign Commissariat and the Central Committee.
The shattered remnants of the Litvinovtsy who had survived the purges
of the 1930s were represented by Jacob Surits, the former ambassador to
France, and Boris Shtein, the former ambassador to Italy. Liaison with
Molotov in the Foreign Commissariat was supplied by S. A. Lozovskii,
the Deputy Commissar. The Comintern veteran, D. Z. Manuilskii served
as the link to the Department of Foreign Affairs of the Central Committee. Among the experts who provided a historical perspective, the most
active was Evgenii Tarle, the distinguished historian who had become one
of the leading figures in creating a new nationalist school of historiography to replace the defunct internationalist school of M. N. Pokrovskii.
Other historians also prepared special reports on areas of their special-
ization, like E. A. Adamov, the leading authority on the Turkish Straits.
In addition, the commission received memoranda written by Eastern
European Communist leaders.[37]

---

[36] *Tegeranskaia konferentsiia*, pp. 166–7; A. F. Noskova (preface and commentary), "Stalin
i Pol'sha, 1943–1944: Iz rassekrechennykh dokumentov rossiiskikh arkhivov," *Novaia i
noveishaia istoriia* 3 (May–June, 2008), p. 133.

[37] *Arkhiv vneshnei politiki. Ministerstvo inostrannykh del* (AVP RF), fond 0512, Komissiia
Litvinova, op. 2, p. 8, d. 4, protocol 5, 31. Filitov, "Problems," p. 4, with access to
different files in the same archive, notes that Litvinov originally proposed a much more
high-powered committee with leading figures in the party and government such as
Molotov, Zhdanov, Mikoian and others, as well as four commissions, including one on
the territorial status and state structure of the conquered and occupied countries to be
headed by Vyshinskii, with himself as deputy head. But this proposal was not adopted.

The Voroshilov Commission established on September 4, 1943 originally included a number of high-ranking army officers, diplomats and party members including the deputy chairman, Marshal B. M. Shaposhnikov, V. P. Potemkin, Ivan Maiskii, A. A. Igna'ev, M. P. Galaktinov, S. B. Krylov, S. T. Bazarov and later Admiral I. S. Isakov. Its membership was sharply reduced in June 1944 to four men, Voroshilov, Shaposhnikov, Bazarov and Isakov. A number of well-known historians were called in to serve as experts.[38] The records of the two commissions reveal frank, wide-ranging discussion with diverse points of view. The Litvinov Commission took a broad view of European affairs, touching upon territorial questions, power alignments and proposals for supranational organizations. It devoted a great deal of attention to France and Italy, as might have been suspected from its membership, as well as the smaller states of Eastern Europe. Standing in the shadows of all these questions was the future relationship with Great Britain. Up to the end of their deliberations, signaled by the Yalta Conference, the United States was a much more remote presence in the minds of the planners.

The instructions to the Litvinov Commission by the Foreign Commissariat provide an unusual and highly significant insight into the thinking of the top Soviet leadership. According to a statement by Litvinov in March 1944, "our commission, with the approval of the government [surely this means Stalin and Molotov], was to prepare its work ignoring the possibility of serious social upheavals (*pereverotov*) in Europe and taking its point of departure from the existing structures."[39] In other words, the planners were to operate on the assumption that there would not be any radical social transformations in Europe by the end of the war, although the possibility was not excluded. "Of course," Litvinov added with respect to the situation in France," if there is a change in the class structure then it will be a different story."[40] During the life of the commission there was no change in these instructions and, as the memoranda from members of local Communist parties residing in Moscow make clear, they had not devised any specific plans for transforming the social structures of the liberated countries of Eastern Europe.

The central issue for all three commissions was how to prevent the revival of Prussian militarism and a repetition of the disastrous course of German history following the Treaty of Versailles. The question of dismemberment proved one of the most troublesome. Stalin had already made it clear in his first conversations with Eden that Germany must surrender East Prussia. At Teheran he had demanded additional German

---

[38] AVP RF, fond Molotova, op. 6, p. 15, d. 150, ll. 2–4.
[39] *Ibid.*, f. 0512, Komissiia Litvinova op. 2, p. 8, d. 4, protocol 5, 31.   [40] *Ibid.*

territory for Poland up to the Oder. During his meetings with Churchill in October 1944 he insisted that Germany should be deprived of the possibility of revenge, one guarantee of which would be to reduce its heavy industry capacity to a minimum. In addition he specifically proposed that East Prussia and Silesia should be ceded to Poland except for the Königsberg region which he reserved for the Soviet Union. He agreed with Churchill that the French should share in the occupation of Germany but then, surprisingly, he suggested the possibility that the occupation of Germany might be shared with smaller Allied powers.[41] But he left open the final resolution of dismembering the rest of Germany. Instead he resorted to tactics familiar in such circumstance of seeking to elicit from others, in this case his Western allies, definite proposals against which to react. The problem was that they faced a similar quandary.[42] Stalin was getting no help from his advisors.

Opinion was divided in the Litvinov Commission as to whether dismemberment was the best means to weakened Germany. Litvinov endorsed the idea, although he recognized the political obstacles it would encounter. He argued that in theory Germany could be rendered harmless for many years by imposing disarmament and heavy reparations. But to be truly effective these measures required close and unified supervision by the Big Three. Unfortunately, there was no guarantee of such long-term cooperation and "the possibility of divergence among them raises the danger of a deliberate weakening of controls on the part of several powers and even of active encouragement of rearmament and reindustrialization of Germany." But to rearm and reindustrialize a dismembered Germany "was a matter of many, many decades."[43] Manuilskii worried that Litvinov had left Prussia too strong even in a dismembered Germany. He was less concerned about western and southern Germany under French and English influence than about a resurgent Prussia either acting with Poland against the USSR or else serving as a piedmont (sic!) for German unification.

His colleagues reminded him that Prussia stripped of Upper Silesia, East Prussia, the Rhenish and Westphalian regions and Schleswig would be a harmless agrarian society. Lozovskii was more worried about

[41] Rzheshevsky, *Stalin i Cherchill'*, p. 427. Cf. Winston S. Churchill, *The Second World War*, 6 vols. (Cambridge, MA: Houghton Mifflin, 1948), vol. VI, pp. 240–1, who states that Stalin proposed to detach the Saar and the Ruhr from Germany, but the Soviet record does not mention this.

[42] For the discussions between the Western allies, see Philip E. Mosely, "Dismemberment of Germany," *Foreign Affairs* 28:3 (1950), pp. 487–98, and Bruce Kuklick, *American Policy and the Division of Germany: The Clash with Russia over Reparations* (Ithaca, NY: Cornell University Press, 1972), pp. 28–32, 74–6.

[43] AVP RF, f. 0512 Komissiia Litvinova, op. 1, p. 7, d. 62, 27.

Germany's future economic power and stated his preference for "the agrarianization" of the entire country as the best means to weaken it for decades. Litvinov thought Lozovskii was knocking down an open door; disarmament and reparations would have "the same result," but politically "it was not possible to pose openly the question of depriving Germany of all its industry." Indicating that he was in touch with his old friend Maiskii, Litvinov reassured Lozovskii that the Rhenish West-phalian complex (the Ruhr) would serve as a guarantee for the payment of reparations and that "Germany would be left with nothing more than a subsistence level of industry."[44]

At Yalta, Molotov proposed the establishment of a Commission on Dismemberment and Stalin insisted on including a proviso for the dismemberment in the public protocol. Yet only a few months later, when German defeat was imminent, F. T. Gusev, his representative on the European Advisory Commission, explained that dismemberment was agreed upon "not as an obligatory plan but as a possible means of exerting pressure on Germany with the aim of rendering it harmless in the event other means proved inadequate."[45] At the moment of Germany's surrender, Stalin publicly abandoned the idea and with it the recommendations of both the Litvinov and Maiskii Commissions. In other words, the threat of dismemberment had served Stalin's purpose. It had dashed any German hopes of negotiating a last-minute separate peace with the West in hopes of salvaging national unity.[46]

To have continued with this policy could only have encouraged a permanent political division of Germany in which each separate state could easily fall dependent upon the resident occupying power. Such a situation could lead, in turn, to a revival of nationalist, anti-Communist forces outside Soviet control and agitation for reunification at the expense of Soviet interests. Stalin had already obtained strong assurances that Germany's capacity to revive had been severely weakened. In agreement with his Western allies, Germans had been expelled from East Prussia, Silesia and Pomerania – already a partial dismemberment; the division of Germany into zones of occupation without a timetable for evacuation gave the Soviet Union a strong bargaining position in the future organization of a German government; Germany was to be treated as an economic whole facilitating the extraction of reparations for the Soviet Union from

[44] *Ibid.*, ll. 23–6.
[45] "Iz materialov Evropeiskoi konsul'tativnoi kommissii," *Mezhdunarodnaia zhizn'* 5 (1955), p. 40.
[46] Mosely, "Dismemberment," pp. 492–8; Vojtech Mastny, *Russia's Road to the Cold War: Diplomacy, Warfare and the Politics of Communism, 1941–1945* (New York: Columbia University Press, 1979), p. 242.

the more heavily industrialized western zones. Stalin failed, however, to win approval for his idea of four-power control over the Ruhr.

Treating a defeated people

Beyond dismemberment there were questions of how to treat the conquered German population. Although Soviet propaganda harped on the theme of punishing the Germans, the Soviet leaders gave mixed signals. While Stalin ranted against the Germans to Beneš, Molotov appeared to take a more moderate line. In his surprisingly expansive conversation with the American businessman, Donald Nelson, in October 1943, Molotov was quoted as saying: "The Germans like any other people were not bad." They need to be guided on the right path, although he admitted that as long as the war continued the majority were bound to follow Hitler's lead. But once peace had been established and Hitlerism extinguished they could be taught the ways of cooperation with other people.[47] Similarly there was general agreement among the members of the Litvinov Commission that in order to secure the peace against the threat of a new war of conquest by the Germans in twenty or thirty years, "it was necessary not only to eliminate the Nazi regime from all aspects of German life, but also to take measures in agreement with the Western allies to reeducate the German people."[48] By April 1944 discussions in the Voroshilov Commission began to emphasize the importance of winning over the German population in a spirit of reconciliation rather than revenge.[49] This attitude foreshadowed a second major shift in official policy toward the Germans.

In Stalin's early speeches he had also made a distinction between Hitler and the German people in hopes of driving a wedge between them. Only when pressed to the wall did he resort to promoting a demonological portrait of all Germans. By 1942 Soviet propaganda had mounted a drum beat of hatred against Germans, maintained at a high level until almost the end of the war. But this campaign was directed mainly at the officers and men of the Red Army and civilians on the home front and under occupation. As soon as the tide of battle turned after Stalingrad, Stalin began once again to explore cautiously the idea of organizing a German domestic opposition along two potentially contradictory lines of approach: the traditional right embodied in the German officer corps

[47] Iakovlev et al., Sovetsko-amerikanskie otnosheniia, 1939–1945, doc. 179, pp. 387–93.
[48] AVP RF, fond Molotova, op. 6, p. 15, d. 150, 87–8; f. 0512. Komissiia Litvinova, op. 2, p. 8. d. 4, ll. 27–8.
[49] Ibid., fond Molotova, op. 6, p. 15, d. 150, 87–8.

and the radical left centered on the émigré German Communists in the
Soviet Union.

The creation in July 1943 of a National Committee for a Free Germany
may be interpreted as Stalin's first sketch of a "friendly" postwar government. Its membership and program bore the unmistakable stamp of a
National Front. The organizational work was painfully slow. But by early
1943, after the German defeat at Stalingrad, a number of Free German
Committees were established in the Soviet Union. Representatives of
these groups were then brought together to form a National Committee. Initially the membership was scraped together from German POWs,
officers and soldiers, left-wing émigrés and a small group of veteran
Communists, several of whom were to become high officials in the German Democratic Republic. The committee called for the constitutional
reconstruction of Germany along radical democratic lines, widespread
social reform stopping far short of full blown socialism, and punishment
for war criminals. Its rhetoric was strongly patriotic, evoking the spirit of
Taurrogen and General Yorck's declaration in the name of the German
people against submission to Napoleon and for a war of national liberation in alliance with the Russians. The committee even adopted a flag –
the black, red and white of Imperial Germany. That the committee had
direct access to a member of the Politburo, Alexander Shcherbatov, was
a measure of the importance Stalin attributed to it.[50]

The announcement of the creation of the National Committee surprised and dismayed the Western allies and many Communists. Stalin's
appeal for an anti-Hitlerite uprising in Germany appeared feeble as long
as the Wehrmacht maintained its strategic superiority. Despite Soviet
efforts to revive the domestic cadres of the German Communist Party,
there were no visible signs of a resistance movement within the Third
Reich that might have produced an alternative set of leaders in the
event of Hitler's defeat. Initially, the National Committee lacked credible leaders. Most of the senior officers in captivity remained suspicious
that the committee was merely a propaganda instrument of the Soviet
government; they were fearful that they would be treated as traitors if
the Hitler regime survived the war. But the German defeats at Stalingrad and Kursk yielded an impressive batch of high-ranking officers
who were willing to accept the prospect of defeat and to plan for the
future. The Soviet authorities sought to allay both suspicions and fears by

[50] Wolfgang Leonhard, *Child of the Revolution* (University of Chicago Press, 1967),
p. 294, and more generally ch. 6; Bodo Scheurig, *Free Germany*, 2nd edn (Middletown,
CT: Wesleyan University Press, 1970); N. Bernikov, "Natsional'nyi komitet svobodnoi
Germanii," *Voenno-Istoricheskii zhurnal* (July, 1963), pp. 111–12.

permitting them to organize separately as the Union of German Officers led by a few well-known figures like Field Marshal Edwin von Paulus and General Walter von Seidlitz, and then when their confidence and a modicum of trust were restored to merge them with the National Committee.

In September 1943 a joint declaration of the two groups called for an end to a hopeless war and the setting up of a German government enjoying the trust of the people. They began to distribute propaganda leaflets at the front and to broadcast over a Free German radio station.[51] This flurry of activity came soon after Italy dropped out of the war and Mussolini had been overthrown by an army coup led by Marshal Bagdolio, who, with the support of the army, formed a provisional government. Were not the Italian events suggestive in Stalin's mind of what might happen in Germany? If Bagdolio was an instrument of Anglo-American influence in Italy, might not Seidlitz or some other German general play the same role in undermining Hitler? Molotov and Stalin firmly denied that the two committees were anything but propaganda organs designed to weaken the moral of the Wehrmacht. But supervision of these organs was placed under the authority of the Commissariat of the Interior and the Central Committee, not the Commissariat of Foreign Affairs. And they were created in anticipation of a possible collapse of Germany at a time when relations with the United States and Great Britain over the second front were strained.[52]

There were a number of other reasons why a Free German National Committee could also serve Stalin's pursuit of war aims within the context of coalition politics. In the summer of 1943 the Grand Alliance had not yet arrived at a common policy for postwar Germany. The Big Three had yet to meet, although in June Churchill and Roosevelt were pressing Stalin for a summit conference. The two Western leaders were worried that Stalin might react to their recent postponement of a second front by exploring the possibilities of a separate peace. There were rumors that peace feelers had been exchanged between German and Soviet representatives in Stockholm; although unknown at the time, the initiatives all

---

[51] Bernikov, "Natsional'nyi komitet," pp. 113–14.

[52] G. P. Lynin and I. Laufer (eds.), *SSSR i germanskii vopros, 22 iiunia 1941 g.–8 maia 1945 g. Dokumenty iz arkhiva vneshnei politiki Rossiiskoi Federatsii* (Moscow: Mezhdunarodnye otnoshemniia, 1996), p. 18, and doc. 50, pp. 227–8. In October 1943 Stalin replied to Eden's inquiry: "The German committee is a propaganda organ . . . Of course, there are people in the German committee who dream of settling the fate of Germany. However, you have to remember that no government with any self-respect would deal with prisoners of war." AVP RF, f. 048, op. 52a, p. 458, d. 3, 17, quoted *ibid.*, p. 664, note 70.

came from the German side.[53] The Anglo-Americans hoped to scotch such negotiations by securing Stalin's endorsement of the principle of unconditional surrender. They succeeded at Teheran.

Immediately after the Teheran declaration on unconditional surrender the National Committee shifted its propaganda line, calling for a popular anti-fascist uprising in the rear of the Wehrmacht and encouraging desertions in the front line. The culmination of this campaign came in December 1944 with the Appeal of Fifty Generals to the People and Army.[54] After the Yalta Conference, when it became clear to Stalin that the unified National Committee had outlived its usefulness, he lopped off the traditional right, shunting aside the German officers but also giving up the idea of a popular uprising. The German people had not responded to the call to revolt and the Western press was raising questions of Soviet intentions to communize Germany. In light of the disappointing results, the top Soviet leadership informed the Central Committee of the CPSU that the Western attempt to portray Free Germany as an attempt to pave the way for the creation of "a Communist Germany" was simply untrue. It had merely been an attempt to undermine the fighting strength of the German population.[55]

In response to Stalin's request, the German Communists recommended the liquidation of the committee. Dimitrov then proposed to concentrate all political propaganda in the hands of the Political Administration of the Red Army and the creation of a provisional organ of administration for the liberated territory of Germany appointed by the Soviet High Command from anti-fascists. "At the head of them should be placed the most reliable and strongest workers (*rabotniki*) from among the German Communists." The circulation and format of publications of the Free German Committee should be reduced and distribution should be limited to POWs and not the German population.[56] But Free Germany and the Union of German Officers were only dissolved in November 1945 on Beria's recommendation. The late date suggests that these had not been designed solely to serve as organs of propaganda.[57]

[53] Ingeborg Fleischhauer, *Die Chance des Sonderfrieden: deutsch-sowjetische Geheimgesprache, 1941–1945* (Berlin: Siedler, 1984), and V. Sokolov and I. Fetisov, "Byl' i nebyl' o tainykh Sovetsko-germanskikh kontaktakh v Stogol'me v period voiny," *Mezhdunarodnaia zhizn'* (January, 1992), pp. 28–37.
[54] Leonhard, *Child of the Revolution*, pp. 322–5.   [55] RGASPI, f. 17, op. 128, d. 49, 18.
[56] Letter Dimitrov to Molotov and Malenkov, February 27, 1945, *ibid.*, d. 717, 135–6.
[57] Lynin and Laufer, *SSSR i Germanskii vopros*, p. 664, note 70; G. M. Adibekov *et al.* (eds.), *Organizatsionnaia struktura Kominterna, 1919–1943* (Moscow : Rosspen, 1997), p. 237.

Planning for the reconstruction of a postwar German civil administration also proceeded along parallel lines, reflecting once again the different priorities and perspectives of the three commissions and the shadow Comintern. In both the Voroshilov and Litvinov commissions a lively discussion took place without any reference to the activities of the German Communist Party. Beyond the obvious agreement that all vestiges of the Nazi regime should be eliminated from public life, the commissioners were uncertain who would take its place. Litvinov for one expressed the view that "it is difficult now to decide from which elements a new state authority can be created," while the old Comintern veteran Manuilskii could only produce the innocuous suggestion to follow "a humanistic line" in selecting cadres.[58]

The main concern of the Voroshilov Commission was to prevent a complete breakdown of the state administration. Maiskii, always the supreme realist, proposed restoring Weimar legal norms because without some kind of legal system it would be "impossible to organize normal life." Divergent views emerged over the extent of a purge of Nazi supporters in the state bureaucracy. In response to a suggestion that all Nazi officials down to the block leaders, 600,000 men, should be arrested, Voroshilov counseled his colleagues to avoid the mistakes of the Italian armistice which had been burdened by excessive detail. But Admiral Isakov countered that it was also necessary to avoid what had happened in Italy where only a few fascist leaders had been punished while the overwhelming majority of fascist officials remained at large. Maiskii supported Voroshilov by emphasizing the importance of establishing general principles and leaving the interpretation up to each occupying power. They compromised by accepting his recommendation with an amendment that mandated the arrest of all the leadership down to the *Gauleiter* level.[59]

Paradoxically, at the very time Stalin expressed his preference for dismemberment, Voroshilov criticized the British and American proposals in the European Advisory Commission for failing to mention the location and central organs of a German government. He worried that this indicated their lack of commitment to the idea of a unified Germany. He insisted, however, that the central organs should be "democratic" and under "the effective control" of the occupying powers. If there was a contradiction here, Voroshilov did not notice it. Instead he elaborated: "it is impossible to deny completely the participation of Germans in the creation of these organs, for it is impossible to govern 70 million people without help from the population." Yet, he repeated, the key to peace

[58] AVP RF, f. 0512 Komissiia Litvinova, op. 2, p. 8, d. 4, l. 28.   [59] *Ibid.*, ll. 111–12.

and stability in Central Europe was the cooperation of the Allies in the postwar period. This was the sole guarantee that the Germans "cannot for their own ends exploit differences among the Allies or even minor disputes that might arise in the course of the occupation. Precisely for this reasons," he concluded, "there ought to be a unified [Allied] consultative organ empowered to reach agreement on all important questions concerning the whole of Germany before these measures are announced to the German government for implementation." To this end Maiskii's suggestion was accepted that the three Allied supreme commanders meet periodically to resolve the most pressing issues.

Voroshilov took every occasion in the deliberations of the commission to emphasize the importance of unanimity among the Allies and the need to demonstrate to the Germans in the postwar period "the absence of any disagreements or tension" among the Big Three.[60] He recognized that disagreement might arise over specific economic issues, but his proposed solutions were always the same; the Allies should resolve them jointly without the participation of a German government in the discussions.[61] This idea ran like a leitmotif through much of the Soviet correspondence and official documentation that has come to light for the wartime period. Generally, too, this view was accompanied by an optimistic, if sometimes guarded, prognosis for the continuation of unity in the postwar period. But elsewhere in the Soviet hierarchy different plans were being hatched that, however much they may have been intended to fit within the framework of coalition politics, were potentially inimical and destructive of it.

Political action

During the closing months of 1944 the German Communists in Moscow under Dimitrov's guidance were working out plans along different lines for the immediate postwar administration of German territory liberated by the Red Army. Here too there were false starts and shifts in emphasis, illustrating the uncertainty of the Soviet leadership and Stalin himself about the means by which the general war aim of weakening Germany in the long term could best be achieved.

Discussions between Pieck and Dimitrov began in early 1944 and led to the creation of a Working Commission that drafted the action program of the Bloc of Militant Democrats in late 1944. They took their ideological inspiration from Pieck's address to party members in November 1944 highlighting Lenin's pamphlet, "Two Tactics of Social Democracy," in

---

[60] *Ibid.*, ll. 116–18.   [61] *Ibid.*, ll. 121, 142, 149.

which he stressed the need to complete the bourgeois democratic revolution in a way most advantageous to the proletariat.[62] The action program concentrated on socioeconomic changes, including nationalizing major war industries, utilities, mines, banks and monopolies, creating a large sector of state ownership; forming a large land fund from the expropriations of fascists and speculators; and unifying the trade unions into a single body.[63] It was similar to plans for the transformation of other territories liberated by the Red Army. Over the following few months, however, the program underwent moderating revisions. After Yalta, Pieck pronounced the action program obsolete. The new main aims were to restore order, restore a functioning economy and turn over available fallow land to the peasants. But even after Germany surrendered, as Ulbricht complained to Pieck in the summer of 1945, many comrades were still infatuated by the old idea of the 1930s of a Red Front and even "speak of Soviet power and the like."[64]

The plans for political action were unclear to the end of 1944. Was there to be a loose or formal coalition of anti-fascist groups? Revisions in the action program did not at first affect the idea of forming People's Committees to lay the foundation for the new order. But in April 1945 another shift took place with instructions to have administrative organs appointed from pre-1937 members of anti-fascist organizations – workers who resisted Hitler and intellectuals not tainted by Nazi ideology.[65] These various scenarios were abandoned. In the face of social chaos, urban destruction and depopulation, spontaneous anti-fascist committees (Antifas) sprang up in towns and cities. The Soviet commanders were grateful for their assistance in helping to carry out daily administrative tasks. But in May Soviet aircraft deposited on German soil three initiative groups composed of German Communists who had been living in exile in Moscow. They repudiated the committees as too heterogeneous and unpredictable and ordered them to disband. They immediately set about reconstituting the political life of the Soviet zone. Unlike the other occupying powers, the Soviet authorities did not form a military government, as Voroshilov had proposed. The initiative groups immediately began to reconstruct a multiparty system from the remnants of the prewar anti-Nazi Social Democrats, Catholic Center and National Liberals, renamed the Liberal Democratic Party.[66] In metaphorical terms the

---

[62] Gregory W. Sandford, *From Hitler to Ulbricht: The Communist Reconstruction of East Germany, 1945–1946* (Princeton University Press, 1983), pp. 13–14.

[63] Horst Laschitza, *Kämpferische Demokratie gegen Faschismus* (Berlin: Berlin Deutscher Militärverlag, 1969), pp. 82–92.

[64] Sandford, *From Hitler to Ulbricht*, p. 40.   [65] Laschitza, *Kämpferische*, pp. 93–8.

[66] Sandford, *From Hitler to Ulbricht*, pp. 23–8.

slogans of 1848 replaced those of 1813, on the one hand, and 1919, on the other. Germany had been defeated, but for Stalin the longer-term problem of how to shape a German policy within the context of coalition politics and at the same time promote the preeminent position of the German Communists remained unsolved. When the paradox of Soviet occupation economic policy – that is, a combination of restoring the economy and looting it – is added to the mix, the problem was most probably unsolvable.

In June 1945 Stalin declared to the German Communists gathered in Moscow to help set policy for the Red Army Political Directorate in the Soviet zone that it was necessary to "declare categorically that the path of imposing the Sov[iet] system on Germany is an incorrect one; an anti-fascist democratic parliamentary regime must be established."[67] In perfect accord with Stalin's statement, in August Marshal Zhukov clearly outlined the four major tasks facing the Soviet military administration in Germany. The first most pressing problem was to cover the Soviet war costs by extracting from Germany war booty, reparations payments (including the 15 percent from the western zones) and dismantled industrial plant as quickly as possible, "for we will not live permanently in Germany." The situation could change, he reminded his staff, and therefore speed was of the utmost importance. Second, he declared that the army of occupation henceforth had to depend wholly on local resources; it could no longer be a burden to the homeland: "Let the Germans support us," he said. Third, and related to point two, the homeland was to be freed not only from the expenses of maintaining the army of occupation but also from replenishing military stores – boots, soldiers' blouses, overcoats – and other supplies for the army of occupation. This would require drawing up an organizational plan for light industry and agriculture requiring the Germans to supply the labor and raw materials for the production of everything necessary "from soup to nuts (*ot igolki do korki*) for us." At the same time, he continued, every effort must be made to meet the minimal needs of the local population so that they will not suffer as the Soviet population had at their hands. These requirements were outlined, he declared, in the Potsdam agreements and must be observed.

As for political tasks, Zhukov placed the liquidation of fascism through the organization of the German people on the basis of the program of the electoral bloc of the four legal parties. To be sure, he added, the Komandatura should not have the same relations with all four: "we should support in every way and promote the *growth* [of the Communist Party] and an increase in their authority, while we should *support* the

[67] Banac, *The Diary of Georgi Dimitrov*, entry June 7, 1945, p. 372.

other parties with the aim of neutralizing *those elements of the population* which supported the two bourgeois-liberal parties, and guide their *activity* in that channel which is *necessary* for us." Although he condemned the program of the Christian Democrats as being tinged with fascism, he insisted that this did not mean excluding them from politics. But they should only be tolerated, while the Communists and Social Democrats were to be actively encouraged to increase their strength. The second political aim was to stamp out the German militarist tradition and prevent the revival of military organizations which had secretly flourished under the Weimar Republic. Third, Zhukov reminded his staff of Stalin's declaration that a German state and the German people would continue to exist. This meant that great responsibility rested on the army of occupation to promoted good relations with them. He then acknowledged that elements of the army and the reparations officials had been guilty of pillage, rape and all manner of illegal activities which could not be tolerated in the future. Zhukov insisted that he would be merciless in punishing those among the Soviet soldiers and officers guilty of criminal acts, resorting if necessary to executing the perpetrators by shooting. The NKVD had been instructed to carry out a thorough purge of these criminal elements. The fourth political question was to avoid any interference by the military field commanders in the life of the Germans. Their duty was to train the troops and maintain strict discipline. Relations with the population were to be the exclusive prerogative of the staff of the military administration.[68] Zhukov's instructions, which, to be sure, reflected Stalin's views, were designed specifically for Germany. But, as we shall see, their general outlines were remarkably similar, if some of the detail differed, to those issued for the treatment of Germany's allies, Austria, Finland, Hungary and Romania.

A year after the end of the war the contradictions in Soviet aims for postwar Germany came home to roost. In May 1946 Stalin made his last effort to reach a settlement with his Western allies on the future of Germany through negotiation. He personally dictated to Vyshinskii a directive for the Soviet delegation at the Paris meeting of the Council of Foreign Ministers. He began his nine-point instructions with a declaration that the Soviet Union opposed the dismemberment and agrarianization of Germany but insisted on full military and economic disarmament buttressed by four-power control over the Ruhr. He had no objection to the development of the peaceful production of iron, steel and finished goods within limits set by inter-Allied control and their export. He

---

[68] *Sovetskaia politika v otnoshenii Germanii, 1944–1954: Dokumenty* (Moscow: Rosspen, 2011), doc. 11, pp. 249–59, italics in original.

repeated his demand for reparations set at a minimum of $10 billion, to be met by current production from the Ruhr, as well as fixed assets as a means of preventing a revival of German aggression. Stating his agreement in principle on a peace treaty, he insisted on the preliminary formation of a united German government "sufficiently democratic to extirpate all vestiges of fascism in Germany and sufficiently responsible to fulfill all its obligations to the Allies including the delivery of reparation deliveries to the Allies." He raised no objections to the creation of a central German administration as a transition to the creation of a German government. He defined the three main purposes of the occupation forces to be: a guarantee of full disarmament, the democratization of a political regime and – once again the leitmotif – the delivery of reparations. "Until those tasks are fulfilled we consider absolutely necessary the presence of occupation troops in Germany and the maintenance of the zones of occupation." He considered the possibility of creating a federal state for Germany "the constituent parts of which could freely separate" as deserving attention, although from his perspective this was as dubious proposition. But if the German people decided in a nationwide plebiscite or in a plebiscite within separate German states to separate from Germany then "from our side, there would be no objection."[69] Thus, Stalin appeared to smuggle back into his plans for Germany the possibility of dismemberment. But he also left open the door if only a crack to extending his concept of the borderlands to the territories of the Soviet zone of occupation, where the Communist Party had secured a dominant position, if an all-German government proved to be less than friendly to the USSR and threatened to fall under Western influence.

Austria

Soviet plans for Austria during the war did not differ significantly from those for Germany proper. But the outcome of their implementation was strikingly different. This was due, first, to the paradoxical Soviet attitude toward Austria, shared by the United States and Britain. Together they agreed to treat Austria as both a victim and perpetrator of aggression, a country to be liberated but also punished, to restore its independent status but to continue to occupy it.[70] What confounded Stalin's aims was the

[69] Sevastianov, *Sovetsko-amerikanskie otnosheniia, 1945–1948*, doc. 111, pp. 227–8.

[70] Lynin and Laufer, *SSSR i germanskii vopros*, doc. 63, pp. 301–2, notes 96 and 97, pp. 671–2. The Czech government-in-exile was even more insistent on the restoration of Austria as a victim of pan-germanist expansionism. *Ibid.*, p. 302. See also Ministerstvo innostrannykh del, *Moskovskaia konferentsiia Ministerstrov inostrannykh del SSSR, SShA i Velikobritanii* (Moscow: Izd. politicheskoi literatury, 1984).

structure of Austrian society and politics which proved highly resistant to Communist infiltration. The country had no agrarian question and no ethnic minority whose grievances could be manipulated and exploited, having exterminated its Jewish population. Continuity of prewar politics was assured, especially by the revival of a strong and independent Social Democratic Party as well as the presence of a conservative People's Party (*Volkspartei*) and the lack of aggressive leadership among the Austrian Communists.[71] The Social Democrats had sunk deep roots in Austrian society in the last decades of the Habsburg Monarchy. Their nationality policy was the most enlightened among the prewar imperial multinational states. In the interwar period the left wing, forming its own Revolutionary Socialist Party, remained militant, enabling the party to resist the blandishment of the Communists, and the party as a whole fought to defend democracy in the mid-1930s. The Popular Front in Austria did not materialize, due in part to the suspicions of the regular Social Democrats and the Revolutionary Socialists, the former smarting from the Communist denunciations of them as social fascists and the latter proclaiming revolutionary principles in advance of the new Communist line.[72] Many of its leaders fled to the West after the Anschluss and were influenced by the more moderate views of the British Labour Party. They returned as pragmatists, willing to cooperate with the People's Party in order to avoid the mistakes of the 1930s, but also to accept a working arrangement with the Communists. They did not give up their basic program of nationalization and extension of social rights to the workers. The Communists anticipated a split between the Revolutionary Socialists, who had remained for the most part in Austria during the war, and the exiles, but they were consistently outmaneuvered.[73]

In its early stages, Soviet policy appeared to mirror its activities in Germany. Communist exiles in Moscow were flown in by the Red Army. The Soviet occupation forces encouraged the revival of other political parties, in contrast to the Western allies. The leaders of the Social Democrats and the People's Party recognized the need to work with the

---

[71] The Austrian Communist leaders were a moderate lot, and men like Ernst Fischer were sophisticated intellectuals who admired much in the Habsburg past, particularly the heroic figure of Eugene of Savoy. Harry Piotrowski, "The Soviet Union and the Renner Government of Austria, April–November 1945," *Central European History* 20:3–4 (1987), pp. 270–4.

[72] Martin Kitchen, "The Austrian Left and the Popular Front," in Helen Graham and Paul Preston (eds.), *The Popular Front in Europe* (New York: St. Martin's Press, 1987), pp. 50–5.

[73] Kurt Snell, *The Transformation of Austrian Socialism* (Albany: State University of New York Press, 1962), and Melanie A. Sully, *Continuity and Change in Austrian Socialism: The Eternal Quest for the Third Way* (Boulder, CO: East European Monographs, 1982).

Soviet occupation authorities. Therefore, they agreed to political parity with the Communists in forming mass organizations which the Communists sought to bring under their control. The Red Army discovered the veteran Social Democrat, Karl Renner, in retirement and brought him to the Soviet command in Vienna where he offered his services to establish a democratic government. According to Anastas Mikoian, Stalin's reaction was positive: "What!" he exclaimed," the old traitor is still alive. He is exactly the man we need." If Stalin expected Renner, an elderly respected figure with a strong anti-Nazi record, could be easily manipulated, he was grievously mistaken and grievously Stalin paid for it.

Renner assembled the various party leaders and parceled out the ministerial posts. The Communists demanded and received two ministerial portfolios, Interior and Education and Public Information. But Renner also assigned two under-secretaries in every ministry to members of the other parties. The Communists were delighted to have a person in each ministry who could veto the decision of a cabinet minister. But then again, this meant that the Social Democrats and the People's Party had a veto over the Communist Minister of the Interior. Renner's government promptly proclaimed a republic and passed two transitional constitutional laws that spared Austria the confusion that characterized other Eastern European governments. The Soviet Union recognized the government on April 27, even before it permitted Allied troops to occupy their zones in Vienna. Annoyed and suspicious of Soviet motives, Truman and Churchill refused to recognize the government until September.[74]

Apparently encouraged by the initial successes of his aims, Stalin assumed a benevolent attitude toward Austria. This may seem surprising in light of the fact that the Austrians had supplied thirty-five divisions to the Wehrmacht fighting on the eastern front. But as Stalin's similar attitude toward the Finns who had fought hard against him testifies, he was willing to subordinate the desire for revenge to his more pragmatic war aims. In May he responded to Renner's appeal for food by authorizing 1,800 tons of grain, meat, fats, sugar and coffee for Vienna.[75] At Potsdam he defended its government against British and American complaints. He proposed that the authority of the Renner government be extended to

---

[74] William Bader, *Austria Between East and West, 1945–1955* (Stanford University Press, 1966), pp. 8–9, 15–18, 22–7; Piotrowski, "The Soviet Union," pp. 252–5; Karl Renner, *Denkschrift über die Geschichte der Unabhängigkeitserklärung Österreichs und die Einzatzung der provisorischen Regierung der Republik* (Vienna: Österreichische Staatsdruckerei, 1945), pp. 9–21; Adolf Schärf, *Österreichs Erneuerung, 1945–1955: Das erste Jahrzehnt den zweiten Republik* (Vienna: Wiener Volksbuchhandlung, 1955).

[75] In his personal letter to Renner announcing the delivery, Stalin took the unusual step of greeting the Socialist leader as "Esteemed Comrade." Mikoian, *Tak bylo*, p. 482.

all of Austria. He renounced any reparations payments from Austria, but demanded that German assets in that country be confiscated and counted toward a payment of German reparations. He continued to insist on this point in the following years.[76] At the same time, he accepted Renner's proposal to broaden his government by including representatives from the western zones. This cleared the way for British and American recognition and the elections of November 1945, which were conducted freely and fairly. Why did Stalin permit free elections in Austria? He had no reason to cherish illusions about the outcome.

The reports of the Soviet representatives on the ground gave a realistic picture for once of the political situation in the country, including a pessimistic evaluation of the strength of the Communist Party. In early August 1945, Colonel Merkulov reported that in public Renner was taking "a confident and high-handed attitude toward the small and weak Communist Party," attributing their few successes to the presence of the Red Army. Renner was also confident that the long tradition of the Social Democratic Party passed from father to son would enable it to resist inroads by the Communists. Merkulov noted the existence of a radical wing of the People's Party, but acknowledged that most of its representatives were in the Vienna region. Their influence at the national level was only nominal, although the leadership joined with the Social Democrats in endorsing the socialization of the main branches of industry. Merkulov conceded that the three parties were cooperating with one another, but he criticized the Communists for taking "a particularly picayune attitude" on serious matters until the Soviet authorities nudged them to correct their course. He further admitted that the reputation of the Red Army had suffered from "acts of violence committed by individuals," and that efforts were being made to restore confidence in the Soviet authorities.

Another problem was the dismantling of factories which was resented by workers. The population as a whole, in Merkulov's view, did not consider themselves to blame for the war or Hitler's rise to power. He compared the successful cultural campaign of the Western powers with Soviet propaganda which he considered "in its infancy." The document strongly implies that in the Great Power competition for influence, the Soviet Union was simply outclassed.[77] It should not, then, have come as a surprise that the Communists fared badly in the election, although the

---

[76] *Sovetsko-amerikanskie otnosheniia 1945–1948*, docs. 175 and 191, pp. 382–4, 420.

[77] RGASPI, f. 17, op. 128, d. 749, 2–12, 17–18. Reports on the local situation remarked on the "long-term very strong position" of the Austrian social democrats "whose cadres in the period of the Hitlerite occupation remained largely intact." *Ibid.*, d. 49, 189ob.

magnitude of their defeat may well have been unexpected. The Communists won 5.4 percent of the vote and four seats in the parliament. Even more devastating, they lacked any strong regional concentration of electoral strength in the country.[78]

The election results marginalized the Communist Party in Austrian politics. The new government tossed it a bone by assigning it a makeshift Ministry of Power and Electricity, but abolished the system of undersecretaries. The new Social Democratic Minister of the Interior purged the *Staatspolizei* of the Communists who had been put in a controlling position by the Soviet occupation authorities. Over the next two years the Soviet Union demonstrated a greater interest in securing economic concessions than supporting the small and weak Communist Party. For Stalin the main proof of Austria's friendliness was to be measured by the creation of a joint stock company for the exploitation of oil, with the Soviet contribution in the form of the confiscated German assets.[79] As we shall see, Stalin was prepared to negotiate similar economic agreements with the Iranian and Chinese Nationalist governments even if this meant sacrificing the political prospects of the local Communists. In the case of Austria his policy paid off handsomely. Between 1947 and 1955 the Soviet Union received over 63 percent of the country's oil production.[80]

The Soviet leaders did not have a high regard for the Austrian Communist leadership. A key difference between them emerged in conversations between Andrei Zhdanov and the representative of the Austrian Party, Johann Koplenig, the party leader, and Fuhrnberg in February 1948. Zhdanov reproached them on two counts: first, for relying too heavily on the presence of the Soviet Army and assuming that the occupation regime would remain in place for a long time; and second for believing that the division of Austria was preferable to the creation of a unified and independent Austria. He advised them to follow the example of the German comrades in agitating for unification. The Austrian Communists must stand on their own feet, Zhdanov insisted, and the Soviet forces would support them if they propose to lighten the occupation regime. But the

[78] Bader, *Austria*, p. 42.
[79] *Ibid.*, pp. 69–74, 110–21. Soviet negotiators outsmarted themselves on this issue. In June 1946 they gave up their right as an occupying power to veto Austrian state legislation in return for granting the government the right to sign bilateral agreements with one of the occupying powers without obtaining permission from the others. This backfired later when Austria defended its decision to join the Marshall Plan against Soviet protests by citing the same right to sign bilateral agreements. *Ibid.*, pp. 62, 73.
[80] *Ibid.*, p. 121.

Austrians were not convinced. Koplenig pointed out that a unified Austria would mean economic dependence on the United States. Austria did not have the $200 million to buy back the German assets confiscated by the Soviet Union and would have to rely on the United States for aid. Zhdanov reminded the Austrians that to give up their demand for the $200 million in reparations would be a great concession. He repeated his advice to concentrate on building the party's internal strength: "reliance on the Soviet forces is wrong and the independence of the country cannot rest on foreign troops." Fuhrnberg replied that the Soviet policy had not been clear on this point but that the Yugoslavs had informed them that a divided Austria would be better. "That is radically incorrect advice," said Zhdanov.[81] The Soviet leader was giving similar advice to the Finnish Communists in assigning greater weight to local initiatives in advancing their objectives than to over-reliance upon Soviet intervention.

Korea

The third territory jointly occupied by the Soviet Union and the United States provides an even more convincing case for Stalin's determination to maintain the coalition into the postwar period. It is also another example of his uncertainty or hesitation in fashioning a consistent policy in the outer perimeter during the period of occupation. As the Red Army advanced down the Korean peninsula a broad social upheaval convulsed the country. The Japanese had stacked the flammable tinder; the presence of the Soviet forces ignited it and the Americans smothered it. Forty years of direct, harsh rule by a Japanese colonial regime had left the Korean economy in the hands of a small group of conservative aristocratic landowners allied to a central bureaucracy. The Japanese recruited Koreans to staff the lower levels of the bureaucracy and provide about half of the national police. The overwhelming majority of the population were tenant farmers. Local trade was in the hands of itinerant peddlers and small shopkeepers who could not be said to constitute a commercial middle class. The Japanese monopolized large-scale trade and controlled almost all the manufacturing. During the last fifteen years of their rule, the Japanese launched a mini industrial revolution under their direct control, imposing harsh working conditions. Below the surface of what appeared to be a well-regulated and placid society social ferment was bubbling up. This too was in reaction to Japanese policies.

The Japanese conquest of Manchuria and the economic depression of the 1930s spurred the emigration of thousands of Koreans seeking work

[81] RGASPI, f. 77, op. 3, d. 100, 10–15.

in Manchurian industrial enterprises. There Korean left-wing elements whose organizations at home had been broken up by the police found opportunities to form insurgent bands. Some made their way west to join the Communist Eighth Route Army. Periodically, the Kwantung army mounted large-scale "anti-bandit" campaigns against them, but by the end of the war there may have been as many as 160,000 guerrillas hiding in the heavily wooded mountainous areas of Manchuria.[82]

Although large numbers of Koreans living in the Russian Far East had supported the revolution, Stalin became suspicious of them when tensions with Japan increased in the mid-1930s. In 1937 he ordered the NKVD to carry out a long-planned mass deportation of the Korean population inhabiting the frontier districts. In the process, however, they rounded up almost all the Koreans in the Far Eastern region (*krai*), numbering at least 175,000, and packed them off to the Central Asian republics. About 8,000 Chinese were also snared by the NKVD nets. Widespread arrests took place among the Koreans accused of being Japanese spies. Especially hard hit were those who were associated with the army, secret police or defense industries.[83] Yet, at the very same time, the Soviet press was celebrating the growth of a major partisan movement in North Korea directed against an increasingly repressive and exploitative Japanese occupation regime. The partisans were reported to have made contact with their counterparts across the Manchurian frontier.[84]

The Red Army offensive into Korea released the pent-up forces of social revolution throughout the country, but the effects were far more pronounced in the more industrialized northern part of the country. Many landlords, collaborators and most of the Japanese officials fled to the south where the colonial regime remained in place until the arrival a month later of the Americans, who occupied the southern half of the country. A social as well as a military demarcation line rapidly came into being. This had not been the original intention of either the Soviet Union or the United States.

[82] This section has relied heavily on the classic work by Bruce Cumings, *The Origins of the Korean War*, 2 vols. (Princeton University Press, 1981), vol. I, chs. 1 and 2. See also George M. McCune, *Korea Today* (Cambridge, MA: Harvard University Press, 1950).

[83] Michael Gelb, "An Early Soviet Ethnic Deportation: The Far Eastern Koreans," *Russian Review* 54 (1995), pp. 389–92; Pavel Polian, *Ne po svoei vole... Istoriia i geografiia prinuditel'nykh migratsii v SSSR* (Moscow: Memorial, 2001), pp. 91–3; and Walter Kolarz, *The Peoples of the Soviet Far East* (London: George Philips and Son, 1954), pp. 32–8.

[84] V. Rappaport, "Partizanskoe dvizhenie v raionakh Severnoi Korei," *Tikhii okean* 12 (1937), pp. 161–74. According to the Japanese press, 13,000 partisans were operating in the northern frontier districts.

The Big Three had agreed at the Yalta Conference to a vague kind of joint trusteeship for Korea and entrusted the Soviet Union with the military occupation of the entire country. In May 1945 Stalin again assured Harry Hopkins that he favored a four-power trusteeship lasting for an indeterminate time, perhaps five to ten years, perhaps longer.[85] At the Potsdam Conference, the Korean question was referred to a meeting of the military advisors where the Americans informed the Soviet representatives that they had no plans to land troops in Korea.[86] Only on the eve of the Soviet invasion – quite literally at the last moment – the United States insisted on a share in the occupation. Surprisingly, Stalin raised no objection to establishing the thirty-eighth parallel as the zonal boundary, possibly because he saw this concession as a bargaining chip in claiming a share for the Soviet occupation of the Japanese home islands.[87] He had in fact ordered the preparation of a landing on the northern-most island of Kyushu. If that was his intent he played his cards badly.

With the Japanese defeat, the Koreans were caught up in a wave of euphoria. Whatever their political inclinations, they were intent on asserting their independence. People's committees sprang up spontaneously throughout the country. Student organizations replaced the hated police. In Pyongyang groups of nationalists and Communists formed a Committee for the Preparation of Korean Independence led by Cho Man-sik, a conservative nationalist willing to work with the left. Under the pressure of the Soviet occupation authorities, the Communists were granted parity with the nationalists on the committee. In retrospect this can be seen as the nucleus of the future government of North Korea, although there is no evidence to suggest that prior to February 1946 Stalin planned to create a separate regime in the North. On the contrary, his views were in flux, though not as inchoate as the Americans who had no policy at all.

Stalin's caution stemmed from two sources: the lack of a unified and disciplined Communist Party and the prospects for establishing an all-Korean government under joint Soviet–American tutelage that could evolve into a government friendly to the Soviet Union. The Red Army provided a benevolent cover for the Communists to rebuild their depleted and divided cadres. The long Japanese occupation had produced a Korean diaspora, scattering radicals from Shanghai to Irkutsk and Yenan to Hawaii. It was something of an anomaly to call all these groups "Communist" as the Japanese were inclined to do. From 1928 to

[85] FRUS, *The Conference of Berlin (The Potsdam Conference)*, vol. I, p. 47.

[86] *Ibid.*, vol. II, pp. 345–53.

[87] Robert M. Slusser, "Soviet Far Eastern Policy, 1945–50: Stalin's Goals in Korea," in Yonosuke Nagai and Akira Iriye (eds.), *The Origins of the Cold War in Asia* (University of Tokyo Press, 1977), pp. 123–46.

1945 former members of the Korean Communist Party were obliged to join a foreign Communist Party, either the Soviet, Chinese or Japanese, because no party organization, legal or illegal, had been able to survive the Japanese police repression of the 1920s. By 1945 these émigrés had coalesced into four loosely grouped factions: the guerrilla, the Yenan, the Siberian (sometimes called the Irkutsk or simply Soviet) and the domestic faction.[88]

The guerrilla faction drew its strength from the partisans who had fought the Japanese in Manchuria and escaped to the USSR in around 1940 where they were brigaded into a separate Red Army unit. They were uneducated and largely unknown outside their native villages. Among them was an obscure and somewhat mysterious figure who was known by the pseudonym, Kim Il-sung. He had participated in the anti-Japanese partisan movement with the Chinese Communists, and apparently spent some time in the Soviet Union, although there are many "dark spots" in his biography. In grooming him for a leadership role, the Red Army command no doubt counted on his need to rely on their support in as much as he was virtually unknown in Korea. Even with their help, he still commanded many fewer supporters than either the Yenan or the domestic faction.

The Yenan faction was composed of leftist intellectuals who had spent many years in exile with the Chinese Communists in Yenan. They had lost touch to a certain degree with Korean realities. Their program echoed Mao Zedong's New Democracy, with its emphasis on a broad social base and gradualist approach to nationalizing the means of production.[89] The faction also included Koreans who had fought with the Chinese Communists called the Korean Volunteer Army, operating in Southwest Manchuria and North China. When the war ended, the Soviet occupation authorities in Korea blocked their attempt to return home, disarmed them at the Manchurian–Korean border and sent them back across the Yalu River into China. The majority only returned to Korea in the late 1940s where they soon occupied key positions in the army. Some of their leaders managed to filter back home to the North through South Korea to form the New People's Party.

The Soviet faction was composed of émigrés from the Korean community in Soviet Central Asia. A hand-picked group of no more than

[88] I mainly follow A. N. Lankov, *Crisis in North Korea and the Failure of De-Stalinization, 1956* (University of Hawaii Press, Center for Korean Studies, 2007), pp. 12–17.

[89] Robert Scalapino and Chong-sik Lee, *Communism in North Korea* (Berkeley: University of California Press, 1972), pp. 138–9, 217–18, 334–7, and Koon Woo Nam, *North Korean Communist Leadership, 1945–1965* (Tuscaloosa: University of Alabama Press), pp. 43–8.

250 Soviet Koreans who were members of the All-Union Communist Party accompanied the Red Army in August 1945. They were invaluable to General Romanenko's political command in making contact with the Korean population. They were thoroughly russified, well educated and experienced in technical administrative matters. Although loyal and trustworthy in the eyes of the Soviet authorities, they lacked the credentials of those who had taken part in the partisan movement. That role was reserved for the young and dynamic but little known Kim Il-sung.[90]

The domestic Communists were mainly Korean intellectuals, veterans of the Comintern, a few educated in the Soviet Union and others in Japan. In the 1930s, they had instigated peasant disturbances and worker's strikes. But their efforts to resuscitate a Korean Communist Party were unsuccessful until the defeat of Japan. Under the mistaken impression that Korea would be allowed to determine its own fate, or else to forestall the imposition of an American military government (AMGOT), the domestic Communists constituted themselves as the Communist Party of Korea and joined with their old nationalist rivals to proclaim a Korean People's Republic in Seoul in the American zone. Their program for social change was more radical than that of their northern comrades, but still within the limits of a united democratic front. It was only in 1946 that the Soviet authorities constituted a separate North Korean Communist Party which merged with the new People's Party.

Despite the hostility of the American military government, the Korean Communist Party in the South grew rapidly. By the spring of 1946 it had enrolled 20,000 members, over four times the number who had rallied to Kim Il-sung's northern branch.[91] But the Political Administration of the Red Army was not impressed. The Communist Party of South Korea was described as lacking a clear program of action.[92] Moreover, the Soviet observers reported the existence of two factions within the party in the South divided over the issue of creating a united front.[93] Not subject to its control, the Soviet command refused to render the Communists in the South any aid as they sought to gain approval from

---

[90] Chong-sik Lee, "The Russian Faction in North Korea," *Asian Survey* 8:4 (1968), pp. 270–88; Dao-sook Sek, "A Preconceived Formula for Sovietization: North Korea," in Thomas T. Hammond (ed.), *The Anatomy of Communist Takeovers* (New Haven, CT: Yale University Press, 1975), pp. 477–81.

[91] Nam, *The North Korean Communist Leadership*, pp. 6–10, 71–2, and Scalapino and Lee, *Korean Communism*, pp. 238–50.

[92] RGASPI, f. 17, op. 128, d. 47, ll. 19–20, V. Sapozhnikov to Dimitrov, November 5, 1945.

[93] *Ibid.*, ll. 23–4, Korneev to Paniushkin.

the American command to legalize their activities.[94] The four factions had little in common with one another, having been forged by different experiences and influenced by different cultural models: "most of them were strangers to one another."[95]

Faced with this complex situation, Stalin gambled once again on reconciling two incompatible aims. He envisaged the trusteeship plan as a means of gaining time to build up a strong unified Korean Communist Party under his control. At the same time, he sought to cooperate with the Americans in order to avoid a confrontation This meant giving up, temporarily at least, extending support to the Communists in the South. When the trusteeship plan was accepted at the Foreign Ministers Conference in December 1945, it provided for the election of a provisional government to act during a five-year transitional period to independence. The Soviet representatives then bargained hard to obtain conditions for the elections which would have given the Communists a great advantage. These included a stipulation that only those parties that accepted the decision of the Moscow Conference on the trusteeship plan could participate. Initially, the Communists along with all the other Korean parties had vigorously rejected the trusteeship plan. Under Soviet pressure the Communists abandoned their opposition, while the right-wing parties in the South held firm. This was the same tactic Stalin had used to discredit the Polish government-in-exile when it refused to accept the Yalta agreement on the Polish frontiers. The American negotiators, however, would not accept the Soviet proposal and the strategy failed.[96] Korea, like Germany, would remain divided.

---

[94] Koon Woo Nam, *The North Korean Communist Leadership, 1945–1965: A Study in Factionalism and Political Consolidation* (University of Alabama Press, 1974).

[95] Lankov, *Crisis in North Korea*, p. 15.

[96] *Ibid.*, p. 17. For the final Soviet negotiating position see Sevastianov, *Sovetsko-amerikanskie otnosheniia, 1945–1948*, doc. 82, pp. 179–80.

9   War aims: the inner perimeter

As Stalin's thinking evolved during the war, his strategic aims in the inner perimeter gradually took shape along three converging lines. His first aim was to obtain military bases – "strong points," as he first called them at the Teheran Conference – on the periphery of the Soviet Union in Europe and Asia; the second aim was a demographic transformation by annexing territories along the frontiers of Finland, Poland, Czechoslovakia and Romania inhabited by nationalities similar to those in adjacent Soviet republics, and by expelling German-speaking populations from Eastern Europe; and the third aim was to promote the establishment of friendly governments on the borders of the Soviet Union. The meaning of friendly governments in the inner perimeter was not, at first, uniformly fixed in Stalin's thinking; it differed most in his attitude toward with European and Asian states. In general, however, friendly states would serve as political buffers and economic providers in rebuilding the Soviet economy.

Strong points and security in Europe

In the early months of the war, Stalin first outlined the territorial dimensions of his war aims in Europe during his negotiations with Anthony Eden on the conclusion of an Anglo-Soviet alliance. His territorial demands in the Middle Eastern and Far Eastern borderlands, while equally well defined, came later, when he began to plan for the war against Japan. His political aims for friendly governments throughout the Eurasian borderlands from Finland to Manchuria evolved more slowly and were subject to change throughout the war and postwar years, reflecting shifts in local conditions and the balance of forces as he perceived them.

In December 1941 Stalin held his first wartime meeting with a leader of his Western allies. He surprised Eden by insisting that the conclusion of a military alliance depended on Britain recognizing the security needs of the Soviet Union: "I think that the whole war between us and

Germany began because of these western frontiers of the USSR including particularly the Baltic States. That is really what the whole war is about and what I would like to know is whether our ally, Great Britain, supports us regarding these western frontiers."[1] He was asking Britain to recognize the territorial expansion of the USSR in the western borderlands that Hitler had endorsed in the pact of 1939. But there was more to come. Stalin further insisted that Finland cede additional territory for having violated the peace treaty of March 1940 by joining Germany in attacking the Soviet Union. In these same conversations, Stalin demonstrated some flexibility in adjusting the Soviet–Polish frontier on the basis of the Curzon Line, taking into account the distribution of the Polish population. He offered the possibility of exchanging Lvov (L'viv) for Belostok and Vilno (Vilnius). He envisaged maintaining Poland as a viable state by compensating it in the west at the expense of Germany. He required adjustments on the prewar Romanian frontier which would give the Soviet Union control over the three arms of the Danube estuary. Romania could be compensated with territory from Hungary inhabited mainly by Romanians. Germany would be broken up into smaller states; the northern part of East Prussia, including Königsberg would pass under Soviet control for twenty years while the southern part would go to Poland; Czechoslovakia would be enlarged with German territory. Yugoslavia would be restored to its prewar frontiers and awarded additional territory from Italy. The special interest of the Soviet Union in the borderlands outside these territorial concession was outlined in paragraph 12 of the Soviet draft, which read:

In resolving all future plans for the organization of Europe above all in the Eastern part of Europe, the role of the USSR shall be taken into consideration as that of a power waging a great war of liberation in the interests of all European states subjected to aggression and occupied at present by the troops of Hitlerite Germany, and being the major factor in the cause of safeguarding lasting peace in Europe and the prevention of new acts of aggression by Germany.[2]

With only slight modifications Stalin adhered to these war aims, except for the dismemberment of Germany, throughout the rest of the war. They represented a combination of strategic and ethnic considerations

---

[1] Lubomyr Luciuk and Bohdan S. Kordan, *Anglo-American Perspectives on the Ukrainian Question, 1938–1951: A Documentary Collection* (Kingston: Limestone Press, 1987), citing a transcript of the conversation of December 17, 1942 in the Public Record Office. An only slightly different wording appears in the official Soviet transcript of the meeting. O. A. Rzheshevskii (ed.), *Vtoraia mirovaia voina: actual'nye problemy* (Moscow: Nauka, 1995), doc. 7, p. 31. The English translation, *War and Diplomacy* (Amsterdam: Harwood Academic, 1996), is often awkward and not idiomatic.

[2] Rzheshevskii, *Vtoraia mirovaia voina*, doc. 5, pp. 22–4, citation on p. 23.

which in his borderland thesis were mutually reinforcing principles. In defending his demands to Eden, and subsequently to Churchill and Roosevelt, he frequently resorted to arguments based on persistent factors in Russian foreign policy. But the restoration of Russia's imperial frontiers was not an absolute principle for him – witness his plans for Poland. Characteristically, he juggled his strategic, ethnic and historical claims to suit individual cases.

Soviet claims against Finland were mainly strategic. The territorial provisions in the armistice terms of September 1944 were harsh but not unreasonable. Stalin and Molotov had softened the demands of Marshal Shaposhnikov in the Voroshilov Armistice Commission. Finland was required to meet three conditions: first, to accept the frontier of 1940, providing Leningrad with a defensive glacis in Karelia; second, to surrender Petsamo with its rich nickel deposits, depriving Finland of access to the Arctic Ocean; and, third, to grant a long-term lease on Porrkala-Ud, a bay lying 20 kilometers from Helsinki which the Soviet Union intended to convert into a naval base.[3] After the bitter experience of Finnish resistance in the Winter War, Stalin had clearly given up on reincorporating Finland into a Soviet multinational state or of imposing a Communist government on the Finns. Estonia, Latvia and Lithuania were also mainly of strategic importance, as the abortive Soviet negotiations with the British and French in 1939 and the pact with Nazi Germany illustrated. Having incorporated them into the Soviet Union, he was not about to set a precedent by giving them up, especially after they had provided an easy corridor for the Nazi invasion. Moreover, in his eyes the short-lived interwar independence of Estonia, Latvia and Lithuania had only been possible as the result of the Intervention in 1919 of the Germany Army and the British Navy.

The absorption of Western Belorussia and Western Ukraine served both strategic and ethnic ends. Stalin had no interest in swallowing the Poles; they had proven themselves to be as indigestible as the Finns. But he sought to put an end to the long historical struggle over control of the borderlands between Russians and Poles by bringing all or as many as possible of the Belorussians and Ukrainians into their respective soviet republics and ending once and for all the threat of a Ukrainian piedmont. But annexation was not sufficient; these regions had to be cleansed of their Polish inhabitants and cultural influences. Following the Soviet occupation of Eastern Poland in 1939 he ordered the

[3] Alfred J. Rieber, *Zhdanov in Finland: The Carl Beck Papers in Russian and East European Studies 1107* (Center for Russian and East European Studies, University of Pittsburgh, 1995), pp. 18–19.

deportation of Poles who inhabited the *kresy*, especially targeting the recent colonists implanted as part of Piłsudski's grand design. The same ethno-strategic considerations applied to his incorporation of Northern Bukovina with its mixed Jewish–Ukrainian population and key rail center of Chernovtsy (Czernowitz). Yet he held off, it would appear for political reasons, absorbing the last large group of Ukrainians in the Sub-Carpatho Ukraine district of the Czechoslovak Republic until late in the war. The frontier with Romania also reflected his strategic concerns. The recovery of Bessarabia in 1940 had enabled him to create the Moldavian Soviet Republic, virtually completing the process of forming an almost solid bloc of national republics on the historically vulnerable western frontier of Russia. This was important to Stalin and presumably to the party as well as a demonstration that Soviet policies had finally solved the problem of how to organize a multinational state in historically disputed territories inhabited by ethnically mixed populations. Almost all the territories Stalin claimed had been part of the Russian Empire except for Northern Bukovina and Western Galicia which had been long under Habsburg rule. In line with his definition of a nation, the populations of these territories historically had displayed a weakly developed consciousness. He could also argue that the populations of Volhynia under Polish rule and Bessarabia under Romanian rule had suffered discrimination and persecution on ethnic grounds – never mind that across the frontier the same populations had undergone equal or greater suffering from collectivization; but for Stalin "dekulakization" was a class conflict and hence historically justified.

In order to win British endorsement of his aims, Stalin invoked the principle of equivalence, a mainstay of his negotiating technique with his coalition partners throughout the war. He was willing to recognize what he believed to be the strategic equivalent for Britain in Western Europe of Soviet security requirements in Eastern Europe. He offered to support the establishment of British bases at Dunkirk, Boulogne and other points on the French coast as well as in Belgium and Holland. He further suggested that it would be expedient for Britain to sign military alliances with Belgium and the Netherlands as an additional guarantee of its own security and their independence. At the same meeting, he balanced this off nicely with a proposal to sign military alliances between the Soviet Union and Finland and Romania with the right to maintain military bases on their territory. In another chilling echo of the Nazi–Soviet Pact he proposed that all the provisions for guaranteeing frontiers and external military bases be included in a secret protocol.[4] In sum,

---

[4] Rzheshevskii, *Vtoraia mirovaia voina*, doc. 4, pp. 12–13.

Stalin had sketched the outlines of a new division of Europe into spheres of influence with a defensive glacis in the borderlands protecting the expanded territorial frontiers of the Soviet Union.

What Eden may have missed at the time was the unspoken underlying current of demographic politics in Stalin's territorial proposals. If carried out, his redesign of European frontiers would have changed the geo-cultural relationship between the Slavs and the non-Slavs, that is the Germans and their allies. In his sessions with Eden, Stalin did not explicitly raise this issue, but the implications were clear enough. The shift of Poland as far west as the Oder, the enlargement of Czechoslovakia at the expense of Germany, the loss by Finland of its frontier zones, and the incorporation into Yugoslavia of the Italian territories of Trieste, Fiume and islands in the Adriatic signaled both a reversal of a centuries-old movement to the east of the German people as colonists and conquerors and an advance of the Slavs toward the west.[5] It should be kept in mind that Stalin's proposals were made far in advance of any indication that the postwar governments of Poland, Czechoslovakia and Yugoslavia would be transformed into Communist regimes. To be sure, his territorial demands were intended to punish his enemies and reward his allies. But was there not something more to it than that? We need only recall Stalin's use of the Slavic theme in his wartime propaganda to be convinced of it.

Soviet wartime propaganda on Slavic solidarity was a screen behind which Stalin acted to bolster political relations with the Slavic people in the borderlands that had been for so long contested between the Russians and Germans, and at the same time to weaken alternative sources of cultural dependency, in particular the French. The most radical step in his campaign was to encourage the leaders of the Slavic states to expel the Germans bodily from Eastern Europe and repopulate the evacuated areas with Slavic settlers. Once again he invoked historical precedents for the reconstruction of the borderlands, although he had to reach back centuries. In his dealings with the Poles over their postwar frontiers, he revived the idea first proposed by the Russians during the Seven Years War, and restated in 1915, of expelling the Germans from East Prussia and annexing all or part of the province. As compensation for the Poles giving up the *kresy* he spoke of restoring the old Polish lands up to the Oder, thus reconstructing Poland as it had existed under the medieval

---

[5] *Ibid.*, p. 11. Stalin also suggested that Romania "should be somewhat expanded to the west at the expense of Hungary within the area where up to 1,500,000 Romanians now live." *Ibid.*, p. 13. It is not clear in the text, but it must be assumed from the numbers that Stalin was referring to a reversal of the Vienna Awards and the restoration of Transylvania to Romania.

Piast dynasty which, in his mind, was an anti-German Poland to replace the multinational Poland of the Jagellonian dynasty built at the expense of the Belorussians and Ukrainians, and repeatedly aspiring to a Dnieper frontier at the expense of the Russians.[6]

Very early in the war Soviet diplomats in London made it clear that their government supported the idea first raised by the Czech government-in-exile of expelling the German population from the Sudetenland. When Beneš came to Moscow in December 1943 he brought with him a memo-randum "On the Transfer of the Germans." Stalin made no objections to Beneš's radical formulation of an expulsion policy.[7] But he and Molotov were disappointed that Beneš did not wish to move the Czech borders further to the west, as they were encouraging the Poles to do. Stalin continued to give unequivocal support to Beneš's position despite the growing doubts of the Americans and British about the practical diffi-culties of such a massive operation; Beneš was, after all, referring to the expulsion of 2 million Germans.[8]

Stalin was equally supportive of the Czechoslovak determination to expel the Hungarian minority from Slovakia, especially the settlers who followed the Hungarian army of occupation in 1939. "We will not stop you," Stalin told the Czechoslovak minister in Moscow, Zdeněk Fier-linger, in June 1945. "Drive them out. Let them experience themselves what domination over others means." When Fierlinger asked for active Soviet assistance in deporting both Germans and Hungarians, Stalin replied, "But do our military really create obstacles?"[9]

By December 1944 as part of the ethnic cleansing of Germans from the borderlands, Stalin had already ordered the round-up of all able-bodied Germans from the ages of seventeen to forty-five for males and eighteen to thirty for females inhabiting territory liberated by the Red Army in Romania, Yugoslavia, Hungary, Bulgaria and Czechoslovakia, whether

---

[6] FRUS, *Conferences at Cairo and Teheran*, pp. 532, 604. Tony Sharp, "The Russian Annex-ation of the Konigsberg Area, 1941–1945," *Survey* 23:4 (1977–8), pp. 156–62; Stalin, *Works*, vol. II, pp. 184–6; D. Anishev, "Pol'skii narod na puti k svobode i nezavisimost'," *Bol'shevik* 13–14 (July, 1944), pp. 49–55, 61. Stalin was wrong about the territorial dimensions of the Piast dynasty.

[7] A. F. Noskova, "Migration of the Germans after the Second World War: Political and Psychological Aspects," in Rieber, *Forced Migration*, pp. 97–101.

[8] *Ibid.*, pp. 103–5.

[9] G. P. Murashko *et al.* (eds.), *Vostochnaia Evropa v dokumentakh rossiiskikh arkhivov, 1944–1953* (VE), 2 vols. (Moscow and Novosibirsk: Siberskii khronograf, 1997), vol. I, doc. 77, p. 232; G. P. Murashko, "The Fate of Hungarian Minorities in Slovakia after the Second World War: Resettlement and Re-Slovakization: Moscow's Position," in Rieber, *Forced Migration*, pp. 83–90. In some cases the Soviet military and even the NKVD complained to Moscow that the expulsions were being carried out by the local Czech and Slovak populations with great brutality.

citizens of Germany and Hungary or not. They were to be transported by railroad to the coal mines of the Donbas and the metallurgical plants of the south.[10] Possibly as many as a million German-speaking former citizens of Hungary, Romania, Yugoslavia and the Soviet Union were deported to labor camps in the Soviet Union.

Overall figures vary on the total number of Germans who fled, were expelled or deported from the west Eurasian borderlands. A figure of 13–15 million is approximately correct. About 7 million fled their ancestral lands in East Prussia, Brandenburg and Poznan, never to return. Large numbers perished in the mass exodus. The Czechs expelled 3 million Germans from the Sudetenland. About 100,000 Germans were expelled from the Polish *kresy* or deported to Central Asia. Approximately 500,000 *Volksdeutsche* who had lived for 200 years in Voevodina and other areas of Yugoslavia were driven out. Two hundred and sixty thousand Germans fled or were deported from Hungary and another 120,000 from Romania despite protests by the first postwar coalition governments.[11] It is not possible to tell how many of those who left their homes were refugees and how many deportees, how many were transferred through the direct action of the Soviet military and police and how many were driven out by the non-German local population. In any case Stalin bears a heavy responsibility for the exodus, not only due to his direct orders but also to the atmosphere of hatred and revenge spread by Soviet propaganda and agitation. But many Germans, especially but not exclusively the Nazi officials, share that responsibility for imposing brutal and murderous policies upon the conquered populations of the region that engendered these feelings without the encouragement of the Soviet authorities.

During the week of negotiations in Moscow in December 1941, Eden sought to resist the unrelenting and often fierce pressure from Stalin and Molotov to recognize the Soviet frontiers of 1941. His arguments that he had to consult with Churchill and the cabinet, the United States and

---

[10] T. V. Volokitina *et al.* (eds.), *Sovetskii faktor v vostochnoi Evrope, 1944–1953*, 2 vols. (Moscow, Rosspen, 1999), vol. I: *1944–1948 g*, doc. 27, pp. 116–17. On January 20, 1945 Beria reported that a total of 67,930 Germans had been interned in those countries. Regular reports were sent to Stalin on the deportations. *Ibid.*, doc. 33, p. 132.

[11] These estimates are taken from an early work by Joseph B. Schechtman, *Postwar Population Transfers in Europe, 1945–1955* (Philadelphia: University of Pennsylvania Press, 1962), pp. 94–5, 167, 170–3, 194–5, 209, 270, 273 and 282. A massive documentation of the exodus by a team of scholars was officially sponsored by the West German government: *Dokumentation der Vertreibung der Deutschen aus Ost-Mitteleuropa*, 5 vols. (Bonn: Federal Ministry for Expellees, n.d.), with a lengthy introduction, vol. I, pp. 1–160. See also Theodore Schieder, "Die Vertreibung des Deutschen aus dem Osten als wissenschaftliches Problem," *Vierteljahreshefte für Zeitgeschichte* 8 (1960), pp. 1–16.

the Dominions, and that the Soviet draft did not meet the standards of the Atlantic Charter, made no impression on his hosts. They repeatedly declared that if Great Britain did not recognize the Soviet frontiers there would be no treaty. They could not be budged. As a result a treaty was not concluded. Only a joint communiqué was issued.[12] Stalin had stated and defended his position when the military situation had reached one of its lowest points: the German Army was at the gates of Moscow. The conclusion was inescapable that in his mind frontiers were not a topic for negotiation.

Within six months Stalin had changed his mind about linking Britain's recognition of the 1941 frontiers to a treaty of alliance. In a sudden reversal he informed Molotov, who was in London stubbornly defending the entrenched Soviet position, to sign a treaty without a guarantee on frontiers. "We do not consider [the British draft treaty] an empty declaration" – a characteristic rap on the knuckles for an overly zealous subordinate? – "but regard it as an important document. It omits the question of the security of frontiers, but this is not a bad thing perhaps, for it gives us a free hand. The question of frontiers, or to be more exact, of guarantees for the security of our frontiers along one or another part of our country, will be decided by force."[13] Stalin's willingness to postpone for the time being his territorial demands was due, as we shall see, to other more pressing military concerns. But the issue was never far from his mind. He repeatedly returned to the question in his dealings with his allies, concentrating on the Polish frontier in his desire to enlist their support in bringing pressure on the Polish government-in-exile to accede to his demands.

By the time Molotov returned to London in the spring of 1942 to negotiate the final draft of the Anglo-Soviet Treaty of Alliance, the British had conceded on the incorporation of the Baltic republics and the territorial demands made on Finland. But Eden raised an additional complication over the right of individuals in the territories claimed by the Soviet Union to emigrate. Molotov explained that the Finns had already cleared out of the districts to be transferred to the USSR and there was no question of bringing them back. (In fact they had returned with the Finnish troops in 1941 and would again leave with them in 1944.) As for Poland, Molotov was willing to include in the treaty a provision for the right of national minorities in West Belorussia, West Ukraine and Lithuania – that is, the Poles – to emigrate. But the Lithuanians would not get permission to

---

[12] Volokitina et al., Sovetskii factor, vol. I, doc. 14, pp. 60–1.
[13] Ibid., doc. 38, p. 122. Molotov dutifully acknowledged that "the new treaty can have a positive influence. I failed to appreciate it at first." Ibid., doc. 47, p. 138.

emigrate. He also drew the line on Bessarabia. The province had been Russian territory for a hundred years, he declared; the inhabitants, he claimed, were not Romanian, but Moldavians.[14]

While Churchill had given in to Stalin on the Baltic states, Roosevelt held to the principles of the Atlantic Charter; he declined to recognize the Soviet absorption of Estonia, Latvia and Lithuania unless there was a plebiscite.[15] In general the Americans persistently opposed making any territorial settlements until after the war when the populations of disputed regions could vote, at least in theory, free of external restraints. In seeking approval of frontier changes from his allies, Stalin encountered the dilemma of reconciling Churchill's realpolitik with Roosevelt's neo-Wilsonian ideology. What did Roosevelt really mean by advancing his proposal to Molotov in 1942 of the Four Policemen? According to the Soviet record, Roosevelt suggested that Britain, the USSR, the United States and possibly China would be the only major powers allowed to maintain arms. "The aggressor countries and their accomplices – Germany, Japan, France, Italy, Romania in addition to Poland and Czechoslovakia – should be disarmed." He went on to state the "Churchill would have to accept this proposal if the USA and the USSR insisted on it." Stalin found the idea most congenial.[16] Yet he appeared to be bewildered by Roosevelt's offhand and evasive manner of dealing with serious questions and baffled by the behavior of American diplomats who were responsible for interpreting their leader's vague assurances; like Roosevelt they appeared to the Soviet leaders to be either quixotic or crafty. This confusion led to Yalta with its Declaration on Liberated Territories echoing the Atlantic Charter but contradicted by secret diplomacy over the disposition of Poland and Manchuria.

In the wartime conferences at Teheran and Yalta, Stalin elaborated on his borderland thesis, seeking to justify Soviet claims on strategic, ethnic and historicist grounds that would be familiar and acceptable to his allies. At Teheran he argued that "what was needed was the control of certain strong physical points either within Germany, along German borders or even farther away to insure that Germany would not be able to embark on another course of aggression." He favored applying the same

---

[14] *Ibid.*, doc. 31, p. 113.

[15] To the end of the war, Soviet officials bitterly denounced American diplomats in Sweden for encouraging and supporting émigrés fleeing the Baltic republics. RGASPI, f. 17, op. 128, d. 49, ll. 103–5 ob.

[16] Volokitina *et al.*, *Sovetskii factor*, doc. 68, p. 174 and doc. 82, p. 204. It is something of a mystery as to why Roosevelt included Poland and Czechoslovakia in this list but did not mention Hungary, which had declared war on the United States. But then Roosevelt's knowledge of Eastern Europe was not one of his strong points.

method to Japan, stating "that the islands in the vicinity of Japan should remain under strong [Allied] control to prevent Japan from embarking on a course of aggression." In Europe he returned to the principle of equivalence, suggesting that the British might wish, for example, to strengthen their hold on Gibraltar at Spain's expanse.[17] When Churchill accepted the idea in principle that Poland should be reconstituted between the Curzon Line and the Oder, with the inclusion of East Prussia, Stalin was quick to agree to the formula, with one reservation. He resurrected his claim for the northern part of East Prussia including Königsberg and Memel. "Russians do not have ice-free ports on the Baltic," he stated and besides, "these were ancient Slavic lands."[18] Stalin reiterated that the postwar Soviet frontier with Poland should be based on the nationality principle: "the Ukrainian lands should go to Ukraine and the Belorussian to Belorussia, that is, between us and Poland the frontier of 1939 should exist as fixed by the Soviet Constitution."[19]

At Yalta Stalin further developed the historical justification for his territorial demands. He pointed out that in the course of history Poland had served as a corridor for the invasion of Russia. Twice in thirty years the Germans had attacked through Poland. Although both Roosevelt and Churchill supported Stalin's territorial claims on Poland by accepting the Curzon Line as the basis for a settlement, the Soviet leader felt obliged to press his case more insistently. He brushed aside Roosevelt's suggestion that the Soviet Union might consider leaving Lvov (L'viv) and the surrounding oil fields in Polish hands as a gesture of goodwill.[20] But he was incensed by Churchill's dismissal of the Polish Committee of National Liberation as unrepresentative of the Polish people. Stalin insisted that the Curzon Line was the idea of Curzon and Clemenceau in 1919, based on the principle of ethnicity, and that the Russians had not been consulted. Lenin had rejected the line, and now the Soviet government was retreating from Lenin's position. "What do you want, that we be less Russian than Curzon and Clemenceau?" How could they, Stalin and Molotov, return to Moscow and justify

---

[17] FRUS, *Conferences at Cairo and Teheran*, pp. 552, 604. These comments of Stalin are not included in the Soviet transcript of the conference.

[18] *Tegeran, Ialta, Potsdam: Sbornik dokumentov* (Moscow: Mezhdunarodnye otnosheniia, 1967), p. 53. *Tegeranskaia konferentsia*, p. 167.

[19] *Tegeran, Ialta, Potsdam*, p. 50. A year before Yalta, in an extraordinary two-hour interview with the Polish–American priest, Father Stanislaw Orlemansky, Stalin sought to have his views on postwar Poland conveyed to the Polish–American community in order to gain their approval, or at least their neutrality, on the territorial changes he proposed. VE, vol. I, doc. 3, pp. 36–42.

[20] FRUS, *The Conferences at Malta and Yalta, 1945* (Washington, DC: US Printing Office, 1955), pp. 677–8. The Soviet record does not include details of Roosevelt's suggestion.

themselves to the Ukrainians?[21] Behind Stalin's words even deeper shadows loomed.

As far back as the Soviet–Polish War of 1920 Stalin had been directly involved in the struggle over the *kresy*. As Commissar of the First Cavalry Army he had been involved in the controversy over the main objective of the advance into Poland. For him, as we have seen, occupying Lvov was more important than taking Warsaw. Uniting all Ukrainians in a Soviet federation was preferable to a revolution in Warsaw, in which he had little confidence. Between the wars West Ukraine in Polish hands was a thorn in the side of Soviet Ukraine, and Polish colonization of the *kresy* aimed at changing its ethnic profile. Stalin's revenge in 1939 and 1940 was to deport tens of thousands of ethnic Poles, especially the colonizing frontier guards, reversing Piłsudski's colonizing policy. Most of the Polish officers shot by the NKVD in 1940 at Katyn came from the *kresy*. When the Red Army crossed the old Polish–Soviet frontier, clashes with units of the Home Army first broke out in these frontier zones.

Stalin's hopes were disappointed that the British and Americans might force the Polish government-in-exile to accept a radical reconstruction of Polish national territory by willingly surrendering the *kresy* in return for Silesia, Pomerania and the southern part of East Prussia. Although Roosevelt and Churchill at Yalta agreed to the Soviet position on the Soviet–Polish frontier, the Polish government-in-exile resisted the enormous pressure brought to bear on them by Churchill and Eden, thus greatly complicating negotiations over the composition of a provisional Polish government.

Rounding out the Soviet territorial war aims in the borderlands, the annexation of the Sub-Carpathian region is a unique and in many ways a puzzling case. It was never the subject of discussion among the Big Three, but rather the result of bilateral relations between the Soviet Union and the Czechoslovak government-in-exile. For the latter it came as a sudden and unwelcome surprise. Until the last few months of the war the Soviet Union appeared to be unequivocally committed to restoring the 1938 boundaries of Czechoslovakia. Moscow had never recognized the Munich Agreement whereas even Churchill was slow to denounce it. President Beneš was determined to secure Soviet friendship as the one sure guarantee of his country's territorial integrity after the war, and unlike Poland made every effort to achieve this goal. In the fall of 1939 Beneš repeatedly told the Soviet ambassador in Britain, Maiskii, that it was necessary

---

[21] *Tegeran, Ialta, Potsdam,* pp. 99–100; Maiskii gave a dramatic description of Stalin's anger. O. A. Rzheshevskii, *Stalin i Cherchill'. Vstrechi. Besedy. Diskussii: Dokumenty, kommentarii, 1941–1945* (Moscow: Nauka, 2004), doc. 177, p. 507.

for postwar Czechoslovakia to have a common border with the USSR, even going so far at one point as to suggest the possibility of a federative link with the Soviet Union. The common border could be achieved either by incorporating the "Carpathian Ukraine into Czechoslovakia or into the USSR." More fancifully, Beneš concluded that "if in the course of the war a socialist revolution broke out in Germany and a civil war ensued, and the West supported the counter revolution and the East the revolution, then Czechoslovakia would of course be on the side of the East."[22] His gamble for Stalin's approval appeared to have paid off. In December 1943 Stalin assured him that "Sub-Carpathian Russia [sic!] will be returned to Czechoslovakia and that settles it once and for all."[23] Less than a year later the situation had changed dramatically.

As the Soviet forces crossed the 1938 frontier between the Ukrainian SSR and the Sub-Carpathian region a series of events transpired, now heavily documented but leaving tantalizing gaps, that led to a declaration in November 1944 by the first congress of the local National Committees of Transcarpathian [*Zakarpatskaia*] Ukraine announcing its decision to unite with the Ukrainian Soviet Republic. The document summarized a number of historical injustices, including the lack of autonomy under the Czechoslovak Republic, the voluntary surrender of the region to the "Hungarian fascists," the desire to reunite the Ukrainian people and the heroic liberation by the Red Army as a justification for its decision. But it came as a surprise to the delegate of the Czechoslovak government-in-exile, F. Nemets, the Social Democrat Minister of Economic Reconstruction who was on the ground, and to Beneš in London. The Czech President had long been convinced that despite Soviet assurances the region would and should be ceded to the Ukrainian Republic in order to create a common frontier with the Soviet Union and strengthen Czech–Soviet ties. But he and his associates were disturbed by the methods used to bring this about and the implications for the future of the districts in Slovakia that were inhabited by Ukrainians. They were particularly

---

[22] DVP, vol. XXII, bk 2, *1 sentiabria–31 dekabria 1939 g.* (1992), doc. 802, pp. 326–7; see also doc. 625, p. 122.

[23] Vojtech Mastny (ed.), "The Beneš–Stalin–Molotov Conversations, December 1943: New Documents," *Jahrbücher für Geschichte Osteuropas* 20 (1972), pp. 376–90. (The term Sub-Carpathian Russia is a mistranslation of *Podkarpatskaia Rus'*, the official Czech designation of the region indicating that the local population were Ruthenian and not Ukrainian.) Similar assurances had been made throughout the war by Soviet diplomatic representatives in London and by Molotov himself. V. V. Mar'ina, *Zakarpatskaia ukraina (Podkarpatskaia Rus') v politike Benesha i Stalina (1939–1945): Dokumental'nyi ocherk* (Moscow: Novyi khronograf, 2003), pp. 34–8. The author uses published and unpublished documents from the Czech archives. These have been checked against the Russian language versions in VE, vol. I, where there are slight differences.

distressed by the arbitrary and unlawful recruiting of local men into the Red Army.[24]

The movement to secede was clearly the work of local Communists. Veterans of the Comintern, trained mainly in Moscow, they represented the only organized political group in the region that had been heavily Communist in the prewar period.[25] Their operations were facilitated by Soviet partisans, the NKVD and the commander of the Fourth Ukrainian Army, General I. E. Petrov. But it is not clear to what extent they were acting independently of Moscow within the wide latitude Stalin had permitted the local commanders engaged in military operations. Beneš for one believed that the Ukrainian Communists had acted without orders from Moscow and even against Stalin's wishes.[26] His main protest was directed against the drafting of Czechoslovak citizens into the Red Army. There is some evidence in favor of this explanation. First, the local National committees, reconstituting themselves as the National Soviet, delivered an ultimatum to the delegate, Nemets, to leave the region within three days, a demand totally at odds with Soviet policy with respect to the Czechoslovak government-in-exile. Second, the Czech Communists in London and Moscow were thrown into disarray, apparently knowing nothing about the activities of their comrades in the Sub-Carpathian region and unable to reconcile the decision to secede with the Soviet–Czechoslovak agreements on reconstituting the national territory, which they had heartily endorsed. But on the advice of Dimitrov they shifted their position and dispatched their own delegation to the region. Its report contained the extraordinary admission that the Transcarpathian Communist Party had already been separated from the Czech Communist Party and "had become independent" (*samostoiatel'naia*); "From the moment we became aware of the actual situation we also exercised no influence on the activities of the Transcarpathian comrades."[27]

Clearly the Czech Communists wished to avoid any responsibility for the loss of territory that would damage their nationalist, patriotic image. Finally, the commander of the Fourth Ukrainian Army, General Petrov, was relieved of his command in 1945, allegedly for the slow advance of the Soviet forces under his command. But his removal coincided with preparations for the arrival of Beneš, transiting through Moscow, in the liberated territory of Slovakia. Was this a signal that there would be no

---

[24] Mar'ina, *Zakarpatskaia ukraina*, pp. 37–8, docs. 29 and 31, pp. 216–17, 221–2.
[25] *Ibid.*, pp. 76–7.
[26] *Ibid.*, doc. 41, pp. 233–6, and F. Nemec and V. Moudry, *The Soviet Seizure of Sub-carpathian Ukraine* (Toronto: W. B. Anderson, 1955), doc. 50, pp. 291–2.
[27] Mar'ina, *Zakarpatskaia ukraina*, p. 100.

more "spontaneous" developments on Slovak territory?[28] On the other hand it is difficult to imagine that Stalin had not been informed of what was taking place. Had he given his tacit approval or was he waiting to see what the reaction of the Czechs would be to a loss of national territory?

As the situation threatened to get out of hand on the ground and in the international area, Beneš sought to limit the damage. Stalin was willing to provide a face-saving resolution. In January 1945 the Soviet leader wrote Beneš that he had no intention of unilaterally resolving the question of the Transcarpathian Ukraine. But the "Soviet government has not forbidden and could not forbid the population of the Transcarpathian Ukraine from expressing its national will." He reminded Beneš that the Czech leader had already stated his willingness to cede the region to the Soviet Union and that he, Stalin, had declined the offer. But he would not unilaterally violate agreements between the two countries. The issue had to be decided at the governmental level and only after the defeat of Germany.[29]

During the discussions in March 1945 between Beneš and the Soviet leaders, Molotov and Stalin made clear the political and strategic importance of the Sub-Carpathian region for the Soviet Union. Molotov reassured Beneš that the international frontier between Transcarpathian Ukraine to be ceded to the Soviet Union and Czechoslovakia would be identical to the internal border between the region and Slovakia. Beneš declared he understood the great strategic and political consequences of the new frontier. It would extend Soviet territory beyond the Carpathians creating a common border with Czechoslovakia, "which is very important for the security and peace of Central Europe." Here Beneš was undoubtedly referring to the damaging effect the absence of such a frontier in 1938 had on the international position of Czechoslovakia on the eve of the Munich Conference. Molotov agreed, pointing out that the cession of Transcarpathian Ukraine would also create a common frontier with Hungary. As a result that country would be forced to become "reconciled to its fate," meaning an end to its revanchist aspirations in the Danubian area.

Another political advantage for the Soviet Union in Molotov's eyes would be "the considerable enthusiasm (*voodushevlenie*) the transfer of

---

[28] *Ibid.*, pp. 123–4. Both the Czech and Slovak Communists were eager for different reasons to cede the region without further delay, while Beneš sought to postpone formal cession until after he had returned to Prague, the war was over and the Parliament could vote on the measure. Nemec and Moudry, *The Soviet Seizure*, pp. 140–5, 163, Mar'ina, *Zakarpatskaia ukraina*, p. 99, docs. 65, and 66, pp. 280 and 281.

[29] Mar'ina, *Zakarpatskaia ukraina*, doc. 61, p. 274,

the Transcarpathian Ukraine to the Soviet Union would arouse throughout the entire Ukraine."[30] It was a moment when the idea of reunification of the Ukrainian people was assuming greater propaganda value for
Moscow. The civil war in West Ukraine was in full swing and the advance
of the Red Army had forced the insurgent UPA to fall back into the
Carpathian foothills.[31] Thus, whatever the origins of the movement to
join the region to Soviet Ukraine, and they appear complex and perhaps
permanently obscure, the strategic advantages of obtaining this frontier
"strong point" at the confluence of three borderland frontiers fitted well
into Stalin's general war aims.[32]

Turkey and the Straits

Stalin's attempts to realize the historic aspirations of Russia to gain a
favorable regime at the Straits and possibly recover territory ceded to
Turkey in 1921 underwent one of the most radical transformations in
the course of the war.[33] In his discussions with Eden in December 1941,
he did not press his claims for preeminent influence in one region of the
borderlands where he had been so insistent in his dealings with Hitler:
that is, the Balkans, especially Bulgaria and the Straits. Fearful of the
Turks joining Hitler by attacking the South Caucasus, he was willing, he
told Eden, to promise them the Dodecanese for their neutrality.[34] How
real was the danger?

On the eve of the invasion of the Soviet Union, Turkey had signed a
Treaty of Friendship with Germany as part of its attempts to strengthen
Ankara's ties with the West that had begun with similar treaties with
Britain and France in 1939. The German ambassador in Istanbul
reported widespread sentiment for a Germany victory. But the Turkish
leadership was wary of repeating the disasters of World War I and
expressed no irredentist desires. Nevertheless, President Inonu extended
official toleration to the small group of pan-Turkish intellectuals. He
endorsed the visit to Berlin of Nuri Pasha, the brother of the famous

---

[30] *Ibid.*, doc. 67, p. 284. Beneš too recognized how important from "the strategic geographical point of view" the transfer would be. The Soviet version of these talks differs
in some details. Cf. VE, vol. I, doc. 55, pp. 183–7.

[31] See p. 279.

[32] Mar'ina, *Zakarpatskaia ukraina*, pp. 164–9, summarizes and carefully evaluates the gaps
in the documentary evidence. See also her examination of the differences in wording of
the Russian and Slovak texts of the final agreement of transfer, June 29, 1945., *ibid.*,
pp. 159–60.

[33] Geoffrey Roberts, "Moscow's Cold War on the Periphery: Soviet Policy in Greece, Iran,
and Turkey, 1943–8," *Journal of Contemporary History* 46:1 (2011), pp. 70–5.

[34] Rzheshevskii, *Stalin i Cherchill'*, p. 48.

Enver, who negotiated the formation of a separate division of Turkic and Muslim POWs in the Wehrmacht.[35] Inonu kept several pan-Turks in important government offices until 1944, when it became clear that the Soviet Union was winning the war. Then he ordered the arrest of all the leading figures. But Moscow remained suspicious that pan-Turkism would have become a live option for Turkey in the event of a German victory.[36]

During the German summer offensive of 1942, Stalin was eager to bring Turkey into the war in order to relieve pressure on his embattled armies. As allies, the Turks would have fought a Balkans campaign, and in the end it would have been their troops, leavened no doubt by the British, that liberated Bulgaria. Ironically, this strategy, rather than a breakthrough in Northern Italy or amphibious landings in the soft underbelly of Europe, would have given the Western powers the best chance of securing a foothold in the Balkans. But the British did not press the Turks. They accepted Ankara's excuses that it needed a large quantities of war material in order to fight the Germans – material the British were in no position to supply. In 1943 Stalin began to lose interest in the Turks, and by the summer of 1944, as the Red Army was poised to invade Bulgaria, the Soviet government let it be known that "Turkey's entry into the war would serve no useful purpose and was no longer desired."[37]

By this time Stalin had obtained, without even trying, assurances from Churchill, made first at Teheran, that "Russia must have access to warm waters" and that the Montreux Convention of 1924 should be revised in Russia's favor. Stalin was delighted to elaborate on the point by expanding Russia's need for warm-water ports to include those in Manchuria lost by Russia in 1905. Yet in his conversations with Churchill in October 1944, Stalin missed an opportunity to stake out his claim. Churchill pressed him to state what changes he wanted in the Montreux Convention. Stalin avoided a direct answer, stating only that "the Convention did not correspond to contemporary conditions and was pinpointed (*zaostrena*) against Russia." He had no desire to infringe Turkey's sovereignty, but "it was not possible that Turkey hold Soviet trade and shipping by the throat." Churchill counseled patience but assured Stalin that Britain fully endorsed the right of the Soviet Union to have free access

---

[35] S. Deringil, *Turkish Foreign Policy during the Second World War: An 'Active' Neutrality* (Cambridge University Press, 1989), pp. 130–1.

[36] Şaban Çaliş, "Pan Turkism and Europeanism: A Note on Turkey's 'pro-German Neutrality' during the Second World War," *Central Asian Studies* 161 (March, 1997), 103–14.

[37] FRUS, *Europe* (1944), vol. V, p. 898; Moscow made it clear even earlier that the Turks had waited too long. *Ibid.*, pp. 875–7, 893–5, 898.

through the Straits to the Mediterranean for its commercial shipping and warships. At Yalta the United States and Great Britain reiterated their endorsement of revision without being specific.[38] Stalin then overreached himself.

In a burst of self-confidence Stalin engaged the Turks in bilateral negotiations under the legitimizing cover of the Grand Alliance. A month after Yalta the Soviet Union denounced the Soviet–Turkish Treaty of Non-Aggression as being out of date. When the Turks hastened to mend their fences to the north, Molotov told them that the conditions for an alliance would have to include changes in the frontiers of Kars and Ardahan. These were unjust, he argued, having been drawn by the Turks in 1921 when the Soviet Union was weak. But these were still conditions and not demands.[39] At Potsdam, Molotov insisted that a new Straits regime to replace Montreux should be determined jointly by the USSR and Turkey as the two states chiefly concerned with commercial navigation and security in the Black Sea. This was too much for Churchill, who pointed out that the Turks would never accept bilateral negotiations on the Straits question. Molotov countered with historical precedents, citing the treaties of 1805 and 1833.[40] But for the British these agreements represented the most undesirable solution of the Straits question. It was at best a tactical blunder for Molotov to have brought them up.

The Soviet government then appeared to stand down from its extreme position. In its first formal note to the Turkish government on revision dated March 1946, it proposed that all the riparian states should draft a new international status for the Straits. It was a retreat in name only, for by this time Romania and Bulgaria, the only other riparian states, were firmly in Communist hands. But Molotov also insisted that in return for a treaty of mutual aid the Soviet Union required a modification of the 1921 frontier, in effect the cession of territory in the provinces of Kars and Ardahan along the 1914 frontier line, and a Soviet base in the Straits. Conditions for an alliance had become demands.[41]

In a characteristic borderlands operation, Stalin began even before the war was over to launch a campaign for the repatriation of Armenians from the diaspora, linking their return to the territorial demands by asserting their historic rights to Eastern Anatolia. Between 1946 and 1948 over 100,000 Armenians returned with exalted expectations to miserable conditions. Once again the nationalities policy backfired. Faced

---

[38] FRUS, *Conferences at Cairo and Teheran*, pp. 600–1. Rzheshevskii, *Stalin i Cherchill*, doc. 161, pp. 423–4; FRUS, *Europe* (1946), vol. VII, 1946, pp. 827–36.
[39] FRUS, *Europe* (1945), vol. II, pp. 256–7.   [40] *Ibid.*, pp. 1427–8.
[41] FRUS, *Europe* (1946), vol. VII, pp. 806–8, 840–1, 864, 874.

by a rising tide of Armenian nationalism, Soviet propaganda, evidently under the influence of Beria, shifted its demands for the return of Kars and Ardahan from the Armenian to the Georgian Republic.[42]

By this time, however, it was clear that the Soviet error of overinterpreting the Western approval of revising the Straits Convention was playing into the hands of the Turks. Resorting to their nineteenth-century tactics, they threw themselves on the mercy of the British, and then with more ominous implications for the Russians into the arms of the United States. The Americans, who had never been a party to any previous Straits conventions, including Montreux, suddenly materialized as the champion of the internationalization of the Straits and the defender of Turkish territorial integrity. President Truman sent a sharp note to Stalin and ordered the Seventh Fleet into the Eastern Mediterranean.[43] With this backing the Turks held firm. Russia's last grasp for the Straits fell short.

Strong points and security in Inner Asia

As early as December 1944 Stalin made it clear to Ambassador Harriman that he was prepared to enter the war against Japan, in return for which he required a virtual restoration of the hegemonic position the Russian Empire occupied in the Inner Asian borderlands, a historical comparison he delighted in making. At the Yalta Conference, Roosevelt and Churchill accepted his specific demands which were then incorporated into the final agreement.[44] In return for a promise to enter the war against Japan no later than three months after the termination of hostilities in Europe, the Soviet Union would receive the southern half of Sakhalin and the Kurile Islands (although it was not clear whether this included the entire chain, including the southernmost islands which had never been Russian). The northern and central group had great strategic significance, providing access to the Pacific for the Soviet Far East Fleet in the same way that bases in the Turkish Straits, if they had been acquired, would have given the Soviet Black Sea Fleet access to the Mediterranean. As Stalin publicly stated in his victory speech, the acquisition of Southern Sakhalin and the Kuriles was not only "the means to connect the Soviet Union with the

---

[42] Claire Mouradian, "L'immigration des Arméniens de la diaspora vers Arménie soviétique, 1946–1962," *Cahiers du Monde russe et soviétique* 20:1 (1979), pp. 79–86, and Mouradian, *L'Arménie, de Staline à Gorbatchev: histoire d'une république soviétique* (Paris: Éditions Ramsay, 1990), pp. 50–1.

[43] Daniel Yergin, *Shattered Peace: The Origins of the Cold War and the National Security State* (Boston: Houghton Mifflin, 1977), pp. 234–5, dates the origins of the containment policy to the American reaction and response.

[44] FRUS, *The Conferences at Malta and Yalta, 1945*, pp. 378–9 and 984.

[Pacific] ocean [but] as the base to defend the country from Japanese aggression."[45] Under exclusive Soviet control they constituted reliable "strong points." In addition, the Soviet Union would obtain a long-term lease on the naval base of Port Arthur; the port of Dairen was designated as a "free commercial port" with "preeminent" Soviet interests (a dangerously vague definition that the Soviet Union would subsequently interpret to mean the exclusive right of Soviet and Chinese armed forces to occupy the area); a Sino-Soviet condominium was to manage the Chinese Eastern and Southern Manchurian railroads; and recognition of the status quo in Outer Mongolia (which was de facto independent). Stalin pledged to respect Chinese sovereignty in Manchuria, to conclude a pact of friendship and alliance with China and to assist the nationalists in liberating China from the Japanese. The Soviet Union made no promises of aid to China in the postwar period. When the terms of the Yalta agreement became known in China several months later, there was widespread indignation. But recent evidence suggests that Chiang was fully apprised of "the deal" when it was made.[46]

Stalin gained most of what he wanted in the wrangling over the extent of Soviet control over the strong points in the Kuriles, Sakhalin and Manchuria, as well as securing the independence of Outer Mongolia and a recognition of Soviet mineral rights in Xinjiang. But in the absence of a deadline for the withdrawal of the Red Army from Manchuria, Stalin held an ace up his sleeve. He played it in the postwar period to seek further economic concessions for the Soviet Union in Manchuria, strengthening his hand in the Inner Asian borderlands.

Friendly countries in Eastern Europe

Poland

"Poland is a big deal (*bol'shoe delo*)!" Molotov scribbled in a note in January 1945, exhibiting a rare burst of emotion. "We do not know how governments are being organized in Belgium, France, Greece, and so forth. We are not asked and we do not even say which of these governments we like. We do not interfere, since this is the zone of the activities of the Anglo-am[erican] armies."[47] His comment followed the

---

[45] I. V. Stalin, *O Velikoi Otechestvennoi Voine Sovetskogo Soiuza* (Moscow: Gos-izd. politicheskoi literatury, 1946), pp. 180–3.

[46] Peter Kuh, "Die Risiken der Freundschaft: China und der Jalta-Mythos," *Bochumer Jahrbuch zur Ostasienforschung* (Bochum: Studienverlag Dr. N. Brockmayer, 1984), pp. 248–86.

[47] VE, vol. I, doc. 36, pp. 117–18, a handwritten note.

liberation of most of Poland by the Red Army and the announcement on December 31 of the recognition by the Soviet Union of the Polish Committee of National Liberation as the provisional government. The British and American governments refused to break relations with the Polish government-in-exile in London and Roosevelt requested that Stalin delay the recognition by a month. Stalin demurred, justifying his actions in terms familiar to the Western statesmen. The Red Army was bearing the brunt of the fighting for Poland's liberation; Poland bordered on the Soviet Union and the nature of its government was inseparable from Soviet security; the Polish National Committee recognized the need to preserve a tranquil rear area while the government-in-exile and the Home Army threatened civil war behind the front lines. He further pointed out that the resignation of Mikołajczek from the government-in-exile had deprived it of the last shreds of its legitimacy.[48]

Stalin's recognition of the Polish provisional government marked the end of a long search for a non-Communist government which would recognize the loss of the *kresy* and the acceptance of the Curzon Line as the Soviet–Polish frontier, thus meeting the major criteria for a definition of a "friendly" regime. In little over a month after the invasion of the Soviet Union, Stalin had exercised one of those sharp reversals of policy that was characteristic of his appraisal of changing circumstances by recognizing the Polish government-in-exile. Stalin consented to annul the Nazi–Soviet agreement on Polish territories, without, however, recognizing the prewar Polish frontiers; he endorsed the formation of a Polish Army on Soviet soil commanded by an appointee of the government-in-exile, though subordinated to the Soviet operational command; and he freed all Polish prisoners of war and deportees under the terms of an amnesty, as if they had been guilty of something. As a result the Polish embassy got the right to send embassy delegates all over the country in order to set up recruiting stations and assist Polish citizens. "To tolerate on their territory such activities of a foreign government," as one historian reminds us, "was unprecedented."[49]

Stalin's bid for Polish support initially met a sympathetic response from General Władysław Sikorski, the premier of the government-in-exile. A career officer and nobleman who had fought against Soviet Russia in the

---

[48] Ministry of Foreign Affairs of the USSR, *Correspondence*, vol. I, docs. 367 and 381, pp. 282–3, 289–92.

[49] Ito Takayuki, "The Genesis of the Cold War: Confrontation Over Poland 1941–1944," in Yonusuke Nagai and Akira Iriya, *The Origins of the Cold War in Asia* (New York: Columbia University Press, 1977), p. 158. The text of the agreement and a record of the negotiations are in *Documents on Polish Soviet Relations, 1939–1945*, 2 vols. (London: Heinemann, 1961–7), vol. I, pp. 117–42.

Civil War, he was nevertheless a partisan of reconciliation between the two countries. "I have never conducted, and have never agreed with the policy directed against Soviet Russia for twenty years," he told Stalin face to face in December 1941.[50] He had confidence that Germany would not defeat Russia and that the way back to Warsaw lay through Moscow.

Sikorski favored a radical reconstruction of Europe built around a European-wide agreement, reflecting his concern that Polish national interests would be discounted by the Anglo-Americans. In particular, he objected to the language of the Atlantic Charter. He perceived it to be an obstacle to Polish claims on German territory after the war. He was even more concerned about the language of the Anglo-Soviet Treaty of Alliance in 1942.[51] His plans included the formation of a Polish–Czech federation, not as a *cordon sanitaire* against the USSR but with its approval and military support as a means of ending Soviet isolation. He was the first statesman to advance the idea of Polish expansion to the west, to the Oder River, as a necessary means of destroying Germany as a great power. A staunch defender of the 1938 eastern frontier with the USSR, he nevertheless had doubts that Poland would ever be able to recover all its lost territories, and he was willing to negotiate with Stalin on the final delimitation. Within Poland itself he saw the need for greater democratization and an industrial policy. A prewar rival of Piłsudski, Sikorski believed in cooperation with all political elements in Poland except for the Communists.

Sikorski's government-in-exile was initially dominated by officers and prewar civil servants who had close ties to the authoritarian right. But he also created a liaison group called the Delegatura or representation of the government in order to keep contact with the political parties in the underground, which had organized themselves into a Political Consultative Assembly. The structure was similar to that of the Free French with its Delegation acting as a liaison between de Gaulle's government-in-exile and the National Council of the Resistance in Occupied France. But the Delegatura was more successful in creating a virtual underground state in Poland. There were two other striking differences. The Polish Communists were absent from the united resistance, and in Polish politics the extreme right was not collaborationist, as in France, but inside the

---

[50] *Documents on Polish–Soviet Relations*, vol. I, p. 231.
[51] Anthony B. Polonsky, "Polish Failure in Wartime London: Attempts to Forge a European Alliance, 1940–44," *International History Review* 7:4 (1985), pp. 576–91. These proposals and the Polish-inspired committee of foreign ministers of governments-in-exile aroused strong Soviet suspicions. *Ibid.*, p. 586.

Map 9.1 Postwar Poland

government. Clearly, Sikorski had a tougher row to hoe than General de Gaulle.[52]

The first conflict in Soviet–Polish relations came over the formation of the Polish Army. Sikorski was torn between the political need to leave a substantial force in the Soviet Union and the humane impulse to rescue as many Polish citizens, including a large number of children, from near starvation in Soviet camps. He ordered a partial evacuation but had the ground cut out from under him in an obscure intrigue that involved his own commander in the Soviet Union. General Władysław Anders took it upon himself to negotiate with the Soviet authorities a total evacuation in the summer of 1942 to British-occupied Southern Iran.[53] By this time Stalin had become disenchanted by the nationalistic and anti-Communist attitudes of the Polish officers in Russia and the disputes over the citizenship of the population in the territories annexed from Poland and incorporated into the USSR. He refused to countenance the additional recruiting of Polish forces in the Soviet Union, joking roughly with the Polish ambassador: "Should we form another Polish Army, it will hurry to leave for Iran or Iraq."[54] The Soviet government then closed down all the recruiting and welfare stations for the Poles, arrested some of the embassy delegates and began to exert pressure on the Czechs to renounce the idea of federating with the Poles.[55]

In the meantime, Stalin and Dimitrov began to reassemble the shattered ranks of the Polish Communists. This was done incrementally and secretly with each major advance in organization and visibility reflecting the deteriorating relationship with the Polish government-in-exile. In August 1941 Stalin instructed Dimitrov: "It would be better to create a workers' party of Poland with a Communist program. The Commun[ist] Party frightens off not only alien elements, but some of our own as well."[56] Two lines of action were pursued. A small "initiative group" of ten men was dropped into Poland to recreate a workers' party not formally linked with the Comintern.[57] In January they formally established

---

[52] Sarah M. Terry, *Poland's Place in Europe: General Sikorski and the Origins of the Oder–Neisse Line, 1939–1943* (Princeton University Press, 1983), pp. 3–6, 37–9, 46–7, 102–3; Keith Sword *et al.* (eds.), *The Formation of the Polish Community in Great Britain, 1939–1950* (London: School of Slavonic and East European Studies, 1989), p. 91.

[53] Terry, *Poland's Place*, pp. 222–44.

[54] *Documents on Polish–Soviet Relations*, vol. I, p. 493.

[55] *Ibid.*, vol. I, pp. 393–6; Moscow accused the Polish delegates of engaging in intelligence activities. *Ibid.*, vol. I, pp. 404–8, 411–13.

[56] Banac, *The Diary of Georgi Dimitrov*, entry August 27, 1941, p. 191.

[57] *Ibid.*, entries September 1, December 18, 1941, pp. 192, 206. Instructions to organize partisan detachments to disrupt the German communications system urged patient systematic work and caution in working with the Polish Socialist Party. *Ibid.*, entry

the Polish Workers Party (PPR), claiming within months a membership of 4,000 with 3,000 partisans organized into a People's Guard (*Gwardia Ludowa*). But the attempt to organize National Committees for the Struggle (*Narodowe Komitety Walki*) in order to lay the foundations for a National Front failed dismally. The local Communists were also unsuccessful in negotiating with representatives of the Delegatura and Home Army for a unified underground something like the French National Council of the Resistance, but more radical in aiming to replace the government-in-exile after liberation.[58]

A second line was laid down in the Soviet Union where a small number of former members of the Polish Communist Party and the left wing of the Polish Socialist Party formed a Union of Polish Patriots. At the very time Sikorski was in Moscow talking with Stalin, a group of pro-Soviet politicians assembled in Saratov under the leadership of Wanda Wasilewska, a writer and former member of the Polish Socialist Party. She had adopted Soviet citizenship, joined the CPSU, and in 1945 married the Deputy Commissar of Foreign Affairs of the Ukrainian SSR, O. Korneichuk. Wasilewska's record of her meetings with Stalin make it clear that the Soviet leader was unwilling for well over a year to allow a formal organization of Polish Communists in the Soviet Union.[59] On March 1, 1943, the Union of Polish Patriots was formed in Moscow with Wasilewska as chair. By this time the tenuous bonds of cooperation between the Soviet Union and the government-in-exile were badly frayed. The key issue was the Soviet insistence on the recognition of the plebiscite of November 1939 that approved the incorporation of West Belorussia and West Ukraine (*kresy* to the Poles) into the USSR, although friction had also developed between the Home Army and the People's Guard in Poland. Stalin was signaling that he was prepared to form an alternative government if the London Poles did not accept the loss of the *kresy*.

The break in relations was initiated by Moscow in April 1943 when the government-in-exile demanded an International Red Cross investigation of the massacre of more than 20,000 Polish officers taken prisoner by the Red Army in 1939. In rapid succession the Soviet Union announced the formation of a Polish Kościuszko Division made up of men who had not been evacuated to Iran and the convening of a congress of the Union of

---

July 17, 1942. Subsequently, one of the leaders, Marceli Nowotno, was murdered on suspicion of working with the Gestapo by two of his associates, who were then condemned by a party court and executed.

[58] Antony Polonsky and Bolesław Drukier, *The Beginnings of Communist Rule in Poland* (London: Routledge and Kegan Paul, 1980), pp. 6–7.

[59] *Wspomnienia Wandy Wasilewskiej (1939–1944)* (Warsaw: Archiwum Ruchu Robotniczego, 1982), vol. VII.

Polish Patriots. The congress pledged friendship with the Soviet Union and finessed the problem of the *kresy* by declaring "Our eastern frontier must be a bridge and not an obstacle between Poland and her eastern neighbors" (sic!) while demanding the "return" of East Prussia, Silesia and the mouth of the Vistula (i.e. Danzig).[60]

But all was not well within the Polish Communist camp. As elsewhere in occupied Europe, the local leaders, in the Polish case personified by Gomułka, took a more expansive view of the new line on the independence of Communist parties while the Muscovites hewed closer to instructions from the center.[61] Fully aware of these tensions and suspicious of the local Communists who were unknown to them, Stalin and Molotov also recognized that in the absence of a Polish government that was both "friendly" and broadly based they faced the prospect of a civil war in the rear of the Red Army.[62] Receiving conflicting reports from different factions and their own agents on the ground, the Soviet authorities scrambled to bring some order out of the confused political situation. As the Red Army reached the boundary of what Moscow considered "indisputable Polish territory," the decision was taken to fuse representatives of the Polish Communist underground, émigrés in the Soviet Union and left-wing sympathizers into a Polish Committee of National Liberation. In an obvious attempt to copy the model of the French Committee of National Liberation as an alternative to the Vichy government, Stalin was ratcheting up the pressure on some of the London Poles and the Western allies to accept the new body as the basis for the future government of Poland. The moderate "democratic" program of the Polish Committee was "designed to attract as many non-Communists as possible."[63]

---

[60] A. I. Khrenov *et al.* (eds.), *Dokumenty i materialy po istorii sovetsko-pol'skikh otnoshenii,* 7 vols. (Moscow: Akademiia Nauk, 1963–86), vol. VII, p. 391.

[61] For the intra-party conflicts see M. K. Dziewanowski, *The Communist Party of Poland: An Outline of History* (Cambridge MA: Harvard University Press, 1959) and Anthony Polonsky and Boleslaw Druker (eds.), *The Beginnings of Communist Rule in Poland* (London: Routledge and Kegan Paul, 1980), pp. 7–10, 12.

[62] As late as June 1944 the Comintern veteran and member of the PPR Central Committee, Bolesław Bierut, appealed to Dimitrov to resolve the deep crisis situation in the party, accusing Gomułka and others of dangerous errors. Gennadiia Bordiugov *et al.* (eds.), *SSSR-Pol'she: Mekhanizmy-Podchineniia 1944–1949. Sbornik dokumentov* (Moscow: Airo-XX, 1995), doc. 17, pp. 47–8. Soviet political officers with the First Polish Army (formerly the Kościuszko Division) harshly denounced the Polish political officers for Trotskyism, Zionism, careerism and speculation, *ibid.*, doc. 18, p. 49. Manuilskii joined the chorus of criticism, *ibid.*, doc 19, p. 60. For his part, Dimitrov was upset by the program of the Union of Polish Patriots which he consider too radical. Molotov agreed, *ibid.*, doc. 12, pp. 40–1.

[63] Dziewanowski, *The Communist Party,* pp. 176–7. There was no mention of socialism or communism, but the manifesto repeated the territorial reconstruction of Poland first outlined by Stalin and incorporated into the program of the Union of Polish Patriots.

Stalin made two attempts – in July, on the eve of the ill-fated Warsaw Uprising, and again in October 1944 – to persuade Mikołajczek to accept the Curzon Line and, together with some of the more moderate London Poles, to join the Polish Committee of National Liberation and turn it into a provisional government. When Mikołajczek failed to persuade the London Poles to accept the Curzon boundary, he resigned from the government-in-exile. Stalin promptly reacted at the end of December by recognizing the National Committee as the provisional government of Poland, even though the internal and international political situation was not propitious. In Poland the National Committee was a weak reed on which to rely. It was unable to subdue the Home Army or to establish administrative order in the countryside. The NKVD had to shoulder these tasks.[64] The Western allies had hoped to postpone decisions on postwar Poland until the Big Three met. But Stalin brushed aside President Roosevelt's appeal by arguing that the Home Army threatened civil war in the rear of the Red Army.[65] At the Yalta Conference, Stalin was still willing to entertain the idea that postwar governments in Eastern Europe did not have to be Communist-dominated at the moment of liberation in order to be considered "friendly." Poland was the exception.

Romania and Hungary

In Romania instructions of the State Defense Committee (GOKO) to the General Staff of the Second Ukrainian Front, dated April 1944 and signed by Stalin, set down the guidelines for the activities of the Red Army. The population was to be informed that the Soviet forces had no intention of acquiring any part of Romanian territory or of changing the social structure of the country. The Soviet offensive into Romania had as its sole aim to destroy the German Army and to end the domination of Hitlerite Germany over the country. Although these assurances may be dismissed as window-dressing, they were reinforced by fifteen specific articles concerning the behavior of the army in maintaining order. The responsibility for the organization and control of civil administration was placed in the hands of General I. Z. Susaikov, a member of the Military

---

[64] VE, vol. I, Serov to Beria, October 16, 1944, doc. 20, pp. 81–4; Beria to Stalin and Molotov, November 14, 1944, doc. 26, pp. 99–100; *SSSR-Pol'she*, docs 26, 27, 28, pp. 74–91.

[65] Ministry of Foreign Affairs of the USSR, *Correspondence*, vol. I, doc. 381, pp. 289–92, Stalin to Roosevelt, December 27, 1944 and January 1, 1945. Without making the Polish connection explicit, Stalin continued to stress in his correspondence with Churchill his willingness to follow the Western line in dealing with de Gaulle and the French Committee of National Liberation as the provisional government. *Ibid.*, vol. I, docs. 364 and 366, pp. 280–1, 282.

Council of the Second Romanian Front and subsequently chairman of the Allied Control Commission (ACC).

Bearing in mind that the entry of the Soviet forces into Romania is dictated exclusively by military necessity and is not in pursuit of any aim other than to smash and liquidate the continuing resistance of the enemy forces; soviets and organs of soviet power will not be created in areas occupied by the Red Army. All the existing Romanian organs of power and the economic and political structure existing in Romania will be maintained without change.

There would be no interference with public or private worship. "The Romanian regime (*poriadok*) will not be destroyed and a Soviet regime will not be introduced." Domestic order in areas not occupied by the Red Army would be carried out by Romanian administration under the supervision of the Red Army represented by local military commandants. They would reassure the Romanian population on the need to continue to operate all social and economic institutions and enterprises in a normal fashion. Garrisons of Red Army or NKVD troops would be stationed in large urban areas. In cases of flight by directors of commercial and industrial enterprises, the military command would appoint temporary replacements from the remaining personnel. Individuals would be removed from their positions only if they opposed the instructions of the army.[66]

Soviet policy continued to maintain these aims throughout the fall and winter of 1944. The armistice agreement of September 1944 specified that the Soviet–Romanian frontier of 1940 would be restored, confirming the cession of Bessarabia and that Transylvania or the greater part of it would be returned from Hungarian occupation to Romania. Reparations to the Soviet Union were set at a modest $300 million in light of the fact that Romania had reversed fronts and joined the Red Army in its military campaign against Hungary and Germany. The Romanian civil administration was restored behind a 150 kilometer front zone, but all communications would be subject to the control of the Allied (Soviet) Control Commission (ACC). At the same time, the official instructions drafted by the Soviet Foreign Ministry to its representatives on the ACC stated that the functions of the ACC were limited to carrying out the armistice agreement and working with the Romanian administration in order to maintain civil order in areas up to 100 kilometers from the front. There was no mention of any other political activity in which the ACC was to engage.[67] It was only when the Soviet authorities believed that

[66] Order of the State Committee of Defense (Stalin), April 10, 1944, VE, vol. I, doc. 4, pp. 53–6.
[67] AVP RF, f. Vyshinskogo, op. 5, p. 47, ll. 8–13.

the Romanians were violating the armistice agreements that they harshly intervened in Romanian politics after the Yalta Conference.[68]

Stalin proceeded cautiously in Romania despite the fact that Churchill had assured him during their famous "percentage agreement" meeting in October 1944 that he was entirely satisfied with the "very moderate" terms of the armistice agreement, making it absolutely clear that the Soviet Union should have the decisive role in Romanian affairs in return for Britain's decisive role in Greece. In accepting Churchill's offer, Stalin explicitly acknowledged Britain's traditional strategic interest protecting its passage through the Mediterranean. "Greece," he told Churchill "was an important point in guaranteeing this passage. England should have the right to have a preponderant voice in Greece." This assurance was given at a time when the Communist-dominated Greek resistance occupied over half the country and was likely to take over the rest when the Germans evacuated. Was Stalin simply recognizing political and strategic realities?[69] This was, at least, the case he subsequently presented to Molotov and Dimitrov. He told them that he thought the Greek Communists had insufficient strength to go it alone. "Evidently, they counted on the Red Army penetrating to the Aegean Sea. We could not do that. We cannot send our troops into Greece."[70] He later gave a similar explanation to the Yugoslavs. The Greek Communists, he stated, had left the coalition government-in-exile "without our advice." This was a mistake. The situation would be different if the Red Army had liberated Greece. He claimed this had surprised the British (!). It was not understood that the Red Army strategy was to operate along "converging lines" (*dvizhenii po skhodiashchimsia liniiam*). The implication was that moving into Greece would have diverted forces from the main thrust into Central Europe. Besides, Stalin added, "in Greece nothing can be done without a fleet."[71] Stalin followed the same strategic line in Finland at the other end of the western borderlands. The Red Army bypassed the country, concentrating along the "converging lines" focused on East Prussia. But even though the Soviet chairman of the ACC was Zhdanov and the Finnish Communists were strong, there was no attempt to organize a seizure of power. The common element in Stalin's wartime policy of liberation was to maintain coalition governments that would represent within each country the spirit of the Grand Alliance, although the presence of the Red

---

[68] Alfred J. Rieber, "The Crack in the Plaster: Crisis in Romania and the Origins of the Cold War," *Journal of Modern History* 76 (March, 2004), pp. 66ff.

[69] This is the view of Roberts, *Stalin's Wars*, pp. 217–22.

[70] Rzheshevskii, *Stalin i Cherchill'*, doc. 161, p. 420 and notes pp. 435–6.

[71] Conversation with Andreas Hebrang, head of Yugoslav mission, January 4, 1945, VE, vol. I, doc. 35, p. 130.

Army would assure and strengthen the political role of the Communists where they were unable to do this by themselves. Hungary is a case in point.

In Hungary, the regent, Admiral Horthy, failed to pull his country out of the war, unlike the young King Michael in Romania, who established a coalition government and declared war against Germany, turning his army against his erstwhile ally. Horthy was overthrown by a fascist coup which opened the gates to the German Army. A small group of Hungarian generals who had been dispatched to Moscow to negotiate Hungary out of the war were overtaken by events. In his meeting with them Molotov had told them that the main Soviet aim was to shorten the war. He proposed that the Hungarian provisional committee be composed of representatives of all the Hungarian democratic parties and political tendencies. Molotov added that there were a few Hungarians in Moscow who might join in, but he added, "we do not have in mind Hungarian Jews, but only Hungarians." It was important to find people who would enjoy authority in Hungary.[72] Despite the willingness of the Soviet government to deal with the Horthy generals, the overthrow of Horthy forced a change of plan. As Stalin remarked, Horthy was finished; he had committed political suicide. It was necessary to bring the Communists into the picture (led by Molotov's Hungarian Jews!). A group led by Ernő Gerő arrived in the liberated town of Szeged to proclaim the reestablishment of the Communist Party and submit an action program to Dimitrov, while in Moscow Mátyás Rákosi maintained contact with the Soviet leaders. The Hungarian Communists then joined the Horthy generals in Moscow where negotiations were held to form a provisional committee, with the early prospects of converting it into to a democratic provisional government. Meeting separately with the Communists in Moscow in December, Stalin advised them to form a government of four parties but insisted that the Hungarian Communist émigrés in the Soviet Union (including Rákosi and Gerő, the first and second men in the party) should not be brought into the government for "they'll be considered Soviet puppets." He urged that pressure be brought on the Horthy generals to participate in the government. He promised the Hungarian Communists far-reaching assistance, concluding emphatically: "But Soviet power cannot do everything for them. Let them do some struggling, let them do some work themselves."[73] Zhdanov

---

[72] Diary of V. M. Molotov, November 13, 1944, VE, vol. I, doc. 25, pp. 94–6, quotation on p. 95.

[73] A composite of Gerő's notes on the conversion and subsequent memoir translated in William O. McCagg, *Stalin Embattled, 1943–1948* (Detroit: Wayne State University Press, 1978), pp. 314–16. Cf. László Borhi, *Hungary in the Cold War, 1945–1956: Between*

was giving similar advice to the Finnish Communists who were complaining that Soviet tanks did not get to Helsinki. "The Soviet Union rejects the idea of achieving success by 'riding through a foreign country.' Every country must win its own victory by its own forces. Every step [forward] of an independent Communist movement is worth more than hundreds of tanks."[74]

Bulgaria and Yugoslavia

Stalin was determined to exercise full control over Bulgaria as well as Romania. In negotiations with Churchill and Eden in October 1944, Stalin and Molotov also demanded 90 percent influence. Eden complained that this would reduce the British and American representatives on the Advisory Council to the role of observers, as in Romania. Molotov resorted to geopolitics to counter Eden's argument that the Soviet Union had been at war with the Bulgarians for only forty-eight hours while Britain had been fighting them for three years. Romania and Bulgaria, he stated, were Black Sea states where Britain had less interest than in the Mediterranean: "For its conduct in the war, Bulgaria will not have access to the Mediterranean." But he was willing to exchange 75–25 percent in Bulgaria for 60–40 percent in Yugoslavia instead of the 50–50 percent that Churchill had proposed. Molotov vaguely assured Eden that "the Soviet Union did not intend to interfere in affairs along the sea coast of Yugoslavia." The attempt to link Soviet influence in the two countries was rejected by Eden who complained about Tito. The British had supplied him, but he rushed off to Moscow in September 1944 without informing them and agreed to leave Bulgarian troops in Yugoslavia. Molotov correctly denied this. But he admitted that Tito had made a mistake in not informing the Western allies about his secret trip to Moscow. He explained this by portraying Tito as someone who considered himself something of a regional (*provintsial'nogo*) political leader. "This shortcoming of Tito we will correct," he concluded. Finally, a marginal increase in British influence in Bulgaria from 10 to 20 percent was agreed upon, not at the expense of reducing British influence in Yugoslavia but in Hungary, where Churchill's proposal for a 50–50 split was drastically changed to 80–20 percent in favor of the Soviet Union.[75] Debate continues over the significance of the "percentages agreement."

---

the United States and the Soviet Union (Budapest: CEU Press, 2004), p. 35, who notes that McCagg omitted the sentence "not to be sparing with words, not to scare anyone. But once you gain strength you may press on . . . move as many people as possible who may be useful."

[74] RGASPI, f. 77, d. 48, l. 44.   [75] Rzheshevskii, *Stalin i Cherchill'*, pp. 423, 431–5.

Throughout the war the Soviet and Comintern leaders had persistently urged Tito to rein in his revolutionary impulses. They only belatedly accepted his denunciations of the rival nationalist resistance, the Četniks of Draža Mihailović. At the same time, they turned aside his appeals for military equipment. Only in February 1944 did Stalin authorize the dispatch of Soviet military advisors to the partisans.[76] In 1945 he warned Andreas Hebrang, the head of a delegation from the National Committee for the Liberation of Yugoslavia, to avoid antagonizing the Western powers. "You've created a situation in which you are at odds with Romania, Hungary, Greece, intending to take on the whole world: don't think of creating such a situation." He added, "It doesn't pay to fight with England." Stalin rejected the idea of proclaiming the Communist-dominated National Committee as a provisional government. "It should be recognized, but the English and Americans will probably not recognize it; the Soviet government could recognize it but now it is still tied up with the Polish question." He advised Hebrang to wait until February, that is until after the meeting of the Big Three, when things would be clearer. Churchill was looking for an excuse to intervene in Yugoslavia as he had done in Greece. The Greek Communists (ELAS) had made a mistake withdrawing from the government. There was no need for the Yugoslavs to make Churchill's task easier by starting a fight. It would be desirable, he added, "to ask our advice before taking important decisions, or else we would end up in a foolish position."[77] In early February the Yugoslavs grudgingly acceded. Kardelj reported that the party had made concessions on the composition of the government and in its relations with the English and Americans on the frontiers of Yugoslavia. Once the Western powers recognized them, they would be in a position to take stronger steps in foreign policy.[78]

Finland

The relative moderation of Soviet policy in defining what was meant in Finland by a "friendly government" was due in large part to the Finnish decision to leave the war before the occupation of its territory by the Red Army or an internal coup. As Zhdanov explained to the Finnish Communists:

The question of war crimes differs from that in Romania and Bulgaria. There the fascist faction did not surrender and had to be crushed with the help of the Red Army. In Finland the fascist faction surrendered and agreed to make peace.

---

[76] For a documentary record see Dallin and Firsov, *Dimitrov and Stalin*, pp. 206–22.
[77] VE, vol. I, doc. 37, pp. 130–2.
[78] Volokitina et al., *Sovetskii factor*, vol. I, doc. 35, pp. 136–7.

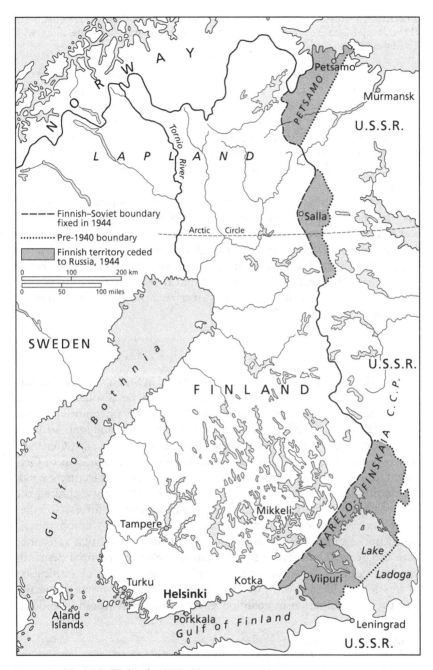

Map 9.2 Finland, 1940–44

The Allied Control Commission has no basis for demanding the resignation of [President] Mannerheim because he surrendered. It was the same thing with Bagdolio in Italy.[79]

According to the armistice, the Finns were put in charge of implementing the political obligations to disband all fascist organizations, arrest and punish war criminals, demobilize the army, free political prisoners, organize the payment of reparations, and permit the creation of democratic organizations, meaning the legalization of the Finnish Communist Party. In contrast to the armistice terms for Hungary, Bulgaria and Romania the ACC had no authority to control public communications and the press.[80]

In assuming his duties as chair of the ACC, Zhdanov privately informed his staff that the Soviet policy stood for "a strict legal point of view." He warned them not to get mixed up in internal Finnish affairs, or to bring pressure on political groups, even to give advice. "We do not have two policies," he stated, but only one policy, a strictly official policy based on the armistice agreements. He admitted that this was due in part to the Finnish government's agile policy of seizing the initiative in "leading movement toward peace."[81]

Conclusion

In sum, the general outlines of what constituted in Stalin's eyes a "friendly government" in the European borderlands can be distilled from the negotiations on armistice agreements or terms of unconditional surrender (Finland, Hungary, Romania, Bulgaria, Germany and Austria). These included: first, vigorous participation in the war against Germany which in the case of Hitler's former allies meant the expulsion of German forces from their territory or a complete reversal of fronts; second, unconditional cooperation with the liberating Red Army including the subordination of all civilian authorities and all armed forces, whether resistance fighters or regular army units to Soviet front commanders; third, the signing of bilateral treaties of alliance and mutual assistance with the Soviet Union; fourth, acceptance of Soviet territorial demands as a prerequisite to the signing of armistice agreements or ratification of treaties of alliance; fifth, the legalization of local Communist parties and their participation in coalition governments that would include all

[79] RGASPI, f. 77, d. 63, l. 11.
[80] Thede Palm, *The Finnish–Soviet Armistice Negotiations* (Stockholm: Almqvist and Wiksell, 1971), p. 60; for the Soviet definition of reparations, RGASPI, f. 77, op. 3, d. 39, ll. 39–40, the meeting of the ACC, October 9, 1944.
[81] RGASPI, f. 77, d. 39, ll. 19, 21, 22.

major "anti-fascist" parties and the elimination of any official opposition; sixth, purges of all collaborationist and anti-Communist elements from the government and armed forces; seventh, recognition of the primacy of Soviet interests in foreign policy and the prohibition of any criticism of the Soviet Union in the press; eighth, reparation payments from former enemies for war damage and/or in allied states economic agreements for the joint exploitation of natural resources in the country as a whole or in frontier provinces adjacent to Soviet territory; ninth, the abolition of "feudal privileges" including the breakup of large landed estates and the redistribution of land to the peasantry. As a corollary, local Communist parties were urged to improve their positions without antagonizing the Western powers or giving them an excuse to intervene.

10 Friendly governments: the outer perimeter

In countries outside the zone of Soviet military operations such as Western Europe and Greece, or in Allied countries like Iran and China, where the Red Army was engaged along with Western forces for limited periods of time, the concept of a friendly government diverged in important ways from the model of the inner periphery. These differences should not obscure Stalin's intentions to forge new political and economic relationships that would enhance the influence of the Soviet Union outside this inner periphery.

Friendly governments in Western Europe

In negotiating with his major and minor allies in Western Europe, Stalin learned important lessons on how he might conduct his pursuit of hegemony in the borderlands of Eastern Europe. The first indications emerged from the political decisions taken by the three powers before the Yalta Conference and the Declaration on Liberated Territories. This chronology is important, for by the time the Red Army crossed the 1941 frontiers of the Soviet Union, Stalin had ample evidence to indicate how far the British and Americans were prepared to go in exercising political control over areas occupied by their military forces. And he could test the effectiveness of his policy of instructing local Communists in the liberated areas to subordinate themselves to the overall strategic and military demands of the Western allies but remain politically active as an example or even a precedent of how non-Communists ought to behave in territories liberated by the Red Army.

One of the most important recommendations of the planning commissions which has been ignored in the literature is contained in a memo of October 13, 1943 from Voroshilov to Molotov addressing the need to provide an alternative to the American military administration (AMGOT) imposed on the liberated territories. In North Africa the American military had experienced frustrations in dealing with conflicting civilian authorities. As a result the War Department began to plan for the creation of American military government for liberated territories. In Italy the Allied commander in chief, General Eisenhower, was determined that "so long as active military operations are being carried on, final authority regarding the political relations between the occupying armies and the local administration should remain with the Allied Commander-in-Chief."[1] The reaction of the Soviet Union helps explain the origins of their alternative model for administering the liberated territories as a key aspect of their political aims.

Voroshilov's memo written during the Moscow Conference of Foreign Ministers laid out the case for Soviet opposition to the imposition by the Americans of a military administration in France and elsewhere on the continent. In his view AMGOT would "replace local democratic forces by previously prepared administrations which are nothing less than police powers and organs of intelligence around which inevitably will be grouped the most reactionary local elements." It would pose a direct threat to the economic interests and national independence of the liberated territories. These fears help to explain the Soviet preference for inter-Allied control commissions which would work closely with "local public figures who sympathize with the victory of the Allies" and assure "the establishment of organ of local power on a democratic basis." These organs would assume all the functions of a civilian government under the control of the Allied military command.[2]

Italy was the first test case of Stalin's policy. The Allied landings in Sicily and the collapse of Mussolini's power in July 1943 led to armistice negotiations with the new government of Marshal Pietro Badoglio. Stalin immediately complained of not being adequately informed by his allies and then being treated "as a passive observer ... I have to tell you," he wrote to Churchill and Roosevelt, "that it is impossible to tolerate such a

[1] FRUS, *Europe* (1943), vol. I, pp. 588–9. For the evolution of American and British policies, see David W. Ellwood, *Italy, 1943–1945* (New York: Holmes and Meier, 1985), pp. 38–44; John Lewis Gaddis, *The United States and the Origins of the Cold War, 1941–1947* (New York: Columbia University Press, 2000), pp. 103–5; and H. L. Coles and A. K. Weinberg, *Civil Affairs: Soldiers Become Governors* (Washington, DC: Office of the Chief of Military History, Department of the Army, 1964), especially pp. 222–6 and 256. In April 1944 the representative of the French mission in Moscow, Roger Garreau, complained to Soviet diplomats about the excessive authority that the Allied military commander would have in organizing the civil administration in France. He contrasted this with what he considered the more democratic basis on which the Czech administration would be based in territory liberated by the Red Army. *Sovetsko-frantszuskie otnosheniia vo vremiia velikoi otechestvennoi voiny, 1941–1945 gg. Dokumenty i materially,* 2 vols. (Moscow: Politizdat, 1983), vol. II, p. 490, note 22.
[2] AVP RF, fond Molotova, op. 6, delo 150, papka 15, ll. 475–7.

situation any longer."[3] Reacting to Stalin's prodding, the United States and Britain reluctantly agreed to establish a Military Political Commission on Italian affairs with purely advisory functions to sit in Algiers. But then the Western allies, partly in response to their military needs, and partly in order to circumscribe Soviet interference, set up a separate Allied Control Commission that excluded the Russians. This deepened Stalin's suspicions of Allied intentions.

By this time Churchill was showing signs of concern over the growth of Soviet and/or Communist influence in the Mediterranean, particularly in Greece, Yugoslavia and Italy. In line with traditional British policy in the region, Churchill saw monarchies as the most reliable defenders of British interests and the staunchest bulwark against the Russians. In Italy, for example, the monarchy, although overshadowed by Mussolini's fascist extravaganza, had survived as an institution with strong ties to the army, church and elements of the civil bureaucracy. After twenty years of a single-party dictatorship no strong center of political authority existed outside the monarchical forces and except for the Communists no well-organized underground. Churchill was fearful that the old-style liberals, whom he despised, and the socialists, whom he considered weak and dispirited, could not stand up to the Communists. He did his best to support the monarchy and keep the Soviet Union out of internal Italian politics where, with the help of Communists, they might make themselves more than a nuisance. For these reasons he abandoned the idea first proposed by Eden and endorsed by his own war cabinet to create tripartite machinery with equal representation by the great powers to administer all the liberated territories of Europe, including Italy.[4]

Stalin and Molotov pressed the Western allies to accept something like Eden's proposals for an inter-Allied political–military commission for Europe based on the principle of unanimity of the Big Three. This was the origin of the European Advisory Commission (EAC) created at the Moscow Conference of Foreign Ministers in October 1943. But Molotov's attempt to turn the commission into a drafting body for all subsequent armistice terms did not win British and American approval.[5] It soon became clear that the American leaders were indifferent to the workings of the EAC, fearing to surrender policy-making to an international body sitting in London. Their attitude diminished the chances that

[3] *Correspondence between the Chairman of the Council of Ministers of the USSR and the Presidents and Prime Ministers of Great Britain during the Great Patriotic War, 1941–1947*, 2 vols. (Moscow: Foreign Languages Publishing House, 1957), vol. II, doc. 104, p. 84.
[4] E. L. Woodward (ed.), *Documents on British Foreign Policy, 1919–1939*, 3rd series, 5 vols. (London: H. M. Stationery Office, 1952), vol. III, pp. 443–4.
[5] FRUS, *Europe* (1943), vol. I, pp. 588, 597–8, 643.

consistent and regular procedures would be established for dealing with Hitler's satellites in Eastern Europe and increased the risk that the negotiation of each armistice agreement would become the occasion for fresh suspicions and disputes to arise.[6] The case of Italy illustrates how the Western allies, in their eagerness to shut out the Soviet Union, handed the Soviet leaders the perfect excuse for returning the favor in Romania and Bulgaria.

Although Andrei Vyshinskii was finally admitted to the Allied Control Commission for Italy, the British and Americans excluded him from the key political decisions. In retaliation the Soviet government took advantage of the growing disillusionment of the Badoglio government with the Anglo-American policy in Italy to step boldly back into the picture. The initiative came from the Italian Foreign Minister, who early in January 1944 proposed to Vyshinskii that the Soviet Union recognize the Badoglio government in a secret bilateral agreement that would outflank the attempt of the Western allies to keep Italy subservient to the ACC, and to reject its claim to become a full-fledged ally in the war against Hitler. At the same time, he insisted that the Italian Communist Party drop its opposition to the existing government and to the monarchy. In return he agreed to the immediate repatriation from Moscow of the Italian Communist leader, Palmiro Togliatti. Careful to avoid the appearance of undercutting the British and Americans, Vyshinskii had by March worked out an agreement with the Italian government to exchange representatives, though not at the ambassadorial level. Within a month, Togliatti, writing in *Pravda*, reversed the stand of the Italian Communists, endorsed the Badoglio government and proposed to postpone a decision on the abolition of the monarchy until after the war. Shortly afterward he showed up in Rome to shoulder the delicate task of mediating between the anti-monarchist parties and the government.

On the eve of his departure from Moscow Togliatti met with Stalin. They agreed on the need to implement a policy of "national unity" in order to avoid civil war and counter British influence. This ended an internal debate within the Soviet hierarchy on the best tactics to promote the influence of the Communist Party in Italy.[7] Once in Italy, Togliatti's intervention led to a compromise and the formation of a broadly based coalition government in which the Communists took part.

[6] William Hardy McNeill, *America, Britain and Russia* (New York: Johnson, 1953), p. 310; Gabriel Kolko, *The Politics of War: The World and United State Foreign Policy, 1943–1945* (New York: Random House, 1970), pp. 50–2, and Gaddis, *The United States and the Origins of the Cold War,* pp. 90–1, 106–9.

[7] Banac, *The Diary of Georgi Dimitrov,* p. 305; Silvio Pons, "Stalin, Togliatti, and the Origins of the Cold War in Europe," *Journal of Cold War Studies* 3:2 (2001), pp. 6–9.

Togliatti rejected the demands of his more radical comrades that the Communists be assigned the Ministry of War. He adopted the position that every political advantage ought to be sacrificed for the war effort. In response to angry Western protests that the Soviet Union had violated the Moscow Conference by unilaterally extending diplomatic recognition to Italy, Vyshinskii replied that the United States and Great Britain acting through the ACC and AMGOT enjoyed close contact with the government "which was denied the Soviet government since these institutions were purely Anglo-American in character."[8]

This shrewd but legitimate Soviet diplomatic maneuver had a peculiar double effect on the stability of the coalition. In practical matters it immeasurably strengthened the Italian government by ending the opposition of the republican parties, leading to the replacement of Badoglio by a civilian government and ensuring that the Italian Communist Party would not go its own way. This meant in turn that the partisan movement in the north of Italy, which had been vigorously fighting the Germans and Mussolini's rump regime, would not attempt to install a revolutionary power in the industrial cities when the Germans finally surrendered. In the same spirit, the leaders of the Committee of National Liberation, with strong Communist representation, signed an agreement in November 1944 placing themselves under the authority of AMGOT. Despite the skepticism of American and British diplomats they adhered strictly to its terms. During the heady days of liberation when the partisan insurrection liberated Milan and other major northern towns before the arrival of the Allied forces, there was widespread fear among British observers and Italian industrialists that the Communists intended to seize power. Togliatti was able to hold the line against more radical elements among the Italian Communists; the partisans agreed to carried out the instructions of the Allied command for "prompt demobilization" of the armed bands.[9] Consequently there was no friction between the Allied military forces and the partisans. This was in sharp contrast to Poland where the Home Army refused steadfastly to place itself under Soviet command even though there were Polish units in the Red Army.[10]

---

[8] FRUS, Europe (1944), vol. III, pp. 1044, 1089, 1103: Mario Toscano, Designs in Diplomacy (Baltimore, MD: Johns Hopkins University Press, 1970), pp. 269–70, 273, 279; G. Warner, "Italy and the Powers, 1943–49," in S. J. Woolf (ed.), The Rebirth of Italy, 1943–1950 (New York: Humanities Press, 1972), pp. 30–40.

[9] G. Quazza, "The Politics of the Italian Resistance," in Woolf, The Rebirth, pp. 15–29; Elwood, Italy, pp. 184–89 and Pons, "Stalin, Togliatti," pp. 10–11.

[10] Stalin made this point forcefully in his conversation with Oscar Lange, adding that the Soviet Union had no intention of "acting like AMGOT in Italy. There must be some kind of Polish organ of power." "Stalin i Pol'sha, 1943–1944 gody. Iz zakrechennykh

The second effect was to increase suspicions of Soviet motives on the part of Western diplomats who interpreted the move as an attempt to get direct access to the Yugoslav partisans from Italian airfields and, more seriously, to challenge Western influence in an area outside the tacitly accepted Soviet sphere. In a characteristic response, Ambassador Harriman denounced "the sharp practice of Soviet diplomacy." He went on to generalize in a remarkably revealing statement how the Soviet recognition of Italy demonstrated that:

we have a long and perhaps difficult road while the Soviet learn how to behave in the civilized world community. Effective results can, I believe, be obtained by taking a firm position when they take improper steps . . . If we don't follow this procedure now in connection with each incident we may well look forward to a Soviet policy of playing the part of a world bully.[11]

In light of future developments his statement might well be considered prescient. It would not raise any eyebrows had it been made a year later. But there was nothing in the Italian governmental crisis that could have given rise to this judgment. Ironically, at this very moment Molotov was giving repeated warnings to the first Italian diplomatic representative in Moscow not to expect any more favors. The Soviet Union, he declared, would support diplomatically all efforts to increase Italian participation in the war, but "in its relations with Italy the Soviet Union was obliged and desired to proceed only in full accord with its allies."[12] Stalin took much the same line in developing his war aims with other political groups within the Anglo-American sphere of military operations.

In dealing with the French, Stalin similarly set his own interpretation on the approach proposed by the Litvinov Commission. He grasped the advantages of encouraging General de Gaulle's aspiration to restore France as a great power, at least to the point of separating him from the British and Americans without permitting him to play off the Soviet Union against the Western allies. As early as January 1942 de Gaulle assured the Soviet ambassador to the governments-in-exile, Alexander Bogomolov, that he desired to establish close, bilateral agreements independent of his relations with Britain and the United States. He stressed the common ties between France and the Soviet Union that were not, he argued, shared by "the Anglo-Saxons" who "wish to preserve a strong

---

dokumentov rossiiskikh arkhivov," ed. A. F. Noskova, *Novaia i noveishaia istoriia* 103 (May–June, 2008), pp. 125 and130.

[11] FRUS, *Europe* (1944), vol. III, p. 1055.

[12] Toscano, *Designs in Diplomacy*, p. 302. The quotations indicate the author's paraphrase of Molotov's remarks.

Germany against the USSR and France." De Gaulle expressed his profound suspicion of Britain and insisted that "the French people now think little of the Americans and English – they look to you, the Soviet Union."[13]

In Stalin's eyes, de Gaulle could be useful in pursuing several important war aims: to defeat Hitler, to prevent the emergence of a Western bloc, and to obtain de facto recognition of the Lublin Poles and the 1941 western frontier of the Soviet Union. France had historically occupied a special place in Polish cultural and military life. He could only have been pleased to obtain de Gaulle's assurance that France would support the establishment of a favorable strategic frontier "in the spirit of the Curzon Line" if he came to power.[14] De Gaulle had also shown himself to be a partisan of unity of action in an all-out war against Hitler. He offered Stalin a squadron of French aircraft with French crews to fight on the eastern front. The Normandie-Nieman squadron was the only Western military unit to serve there. It may have had only symbolic significance, but Soviet propaganda made much of its presence and after the war Moscow ceremoniously organized the return of the much decorated crews and their aircraft to France.[15]

De Gaulle also took seriously the not too subtle suggestions made to him by Soviet representatives in Moscow and London on Molotov's and Vyshinskii's instructions that the support of the Soviet government would depend on the extent to which his National Committee could "rely on all the anti-Hitlerite tendencies in France and if it would become a movement of the entire people."[16] Throughout 1942 de Gaulle and the French Communists warily approached one another like two reluctant dancing partners. In January 1943 two months after de Gaulle declared that he would accept the assistance of French Communists in the struggle against Hitler, Fernand Grenier, a representative of the party showed up in London with a pledge of support for the duration of the war. From that moment the French Communists were politically integrated into the Gaullist-led underground; the Communists had already agreed to incorporate their paramilitary forces into the forces of Fighting France led by de Gaulle. Their energy and tactical skill gradually gained them a commanding position on the National Council of the Resistance in occupied France.[17] De Gaulle appointed two Communists to the French Committee of National Liberation when he created it in the summer of

---

[13] *Sovetsko-frantsuzskie otnosheniia*, vol. II, doc. 28, pp. 67–8.   [14] *Ibid.*, doc. 55, p. 133.
[15] *Ibid.*, appendix, docs. 11, 12, 13, 14, 15, 16, 17, pp. 434–7.
[16] *Ibid.*, docs. 38 and 39, pp. 86, 88 and 75.
[17] Alfred J. Rieber, *Stalin and the French Communist Party, 1941–1947* (New York: Columbia University Press, 1962), pp. 17, 27, 81–98.

1943. They were the only Communists to accept posts in an Allied government-in-exile in London; not even the Czech Communists agreed to serve under Beneš.

However anxious Stalin and Thorez might have been to close down the insurrectionary path, it was difficult to control the enthusiasms or ambitions of party militants during the liberation. In August 1944 in the southwest, and especially in Paris, there were attempts, as in Northern Italy, to liberate areas before the arrival of the Allied troops. But party discipline asserted itself and the resistance closed ranks to greet the liberating forces. The French Communist press then boasted of having behaved responsibly in contrast to the Home Army adventurers who at the very same time were ignoring the balance of forces in the east that determined the right course of political action.[18]

Stalin also backed de Gaulle in his rivalry with General Giraud in North Africa. But he did not break ranks with the Americans and British as he had in Italy by recognizing de Gaulle's French Committee of National Liberation ahead of his allies. He made it clear to de Gaulle, however, that the delay of several months was not due to Soviet objections. He also supported French membership on the European Advisory Commission and on the ACC for Italy. By contrast, the Americans and British were at first reluctant to admit de Gaulle into their inner councils, still regarding him as difficult and unpredictable. Stalin continued to press his allies for more information on their plans for administering French territory, complaining that the Soviet Union was being ignored in violation of the Moscow Foreign Minister agreements.[19] But this was as far as he would go in bringing pressure on his allies on behalf of Fighting France.

Stalin's plans for France in postwar Europe emerged most clearly from his negotiations with de Gaulle in November 1944 over a Franco-Soviet treaty of alliance. His general objective was to cultivate a special relationship with France outside the framework of the coalition with the United States and Britain. Stalin's specific aim was to persuade de Gaulle to endorse Soviet policy in Poland. De Gaulle reiterated his endorsement of the Curzon Line and the shift of Polish frontiers to the west. But Stalin wanted more. He cleverly played on the French desire for a bilateral treaty

---

[18] *Ibid.*, p. 147; Adrian Dansette, *Histoire de la Libération de Paris* (Paris: A. Fayard, 1946). In the streets of Brussels, by contrast, the partisans of the Independence Front dominated by Communists came close to an open clash with British troops and actually clashed with the Belgian police before agreeing to disarm. Henri Bernard, *Histoire de la résistance européen: la "quatrième force" de la guerre 39–45* (Verviers: Gérard, 1968), pp. 130–1.

[19] *Sovetsko-frantsuzskie otnosheniia*, vol. II, docs. 133, 143, 145, 147, 158, pp. 251, 271, 276, 282, 301; note 41, p. 526 and note 46, p. 529.

in contrast to the British preference for a tripartite Anglo-French–Soviet alliance. In a characteristic horse-trading mood, he offered de Gaulle a deal: "Let the French do us a favor and we will do them one," he began. "Poland is a component (element) of our security... Let the French accept the representatives of the Polish Committee of National Liberation in Paris, and we will sign a bilateral treaty. Churchill will be hurt, but it cannot be helped." De Gaulle demurred. Stalin had to be satisfied with something less. De Gaulle agreed to receive members of the Lublin Poles in Moscow but refused to exchange official representatives with them. Nevertheless, Molotov agreed with French Foreign Minister Georges Bidault that this "changes the situation," whereupon the Franco-Soviet treaty was signed.[20]

In the Stalin–de Gaulle negotiations, there was no mention of the role of the French Communists. But a connection, though unstated, was implicit. A few days before the Soviet invitation unexpectedly arrived in Paris, de Gaulle had telegraphed Thorez informing him that he could return to France following the publication of an amnesty of war criminals (Thorez having been condemned as a deserter in 1940). On the eve of de Gaulle's arrival and Thorez's departure for France, Stalin met with the French Communist leader. In a rambling conversation Stalin repeatedly emphasized three points. First, the French Communists should avoid being isolated. This meant forming a leftist bloc; Stalin initially proposed calling it a front then quickly reconsidered, realizing that this word would remind the bourgeoisie of the "popular front" and thus should be avoided. He proposed "a movement for strengthening democracy in France," but finally left it up to the French comrades to decide on the name. The bloc would be the best means of countering the Anglo-American aim of creating a reactionary government in France. Second, the French Communists were to make every effort to restore French industry, above all war industry. This was important for Stalin not only as a means of increasing the French contribution to the defeat of Hitler, but also of opposing the monopolistic tendencies of the Anglo-Americans who wanted "the whole world to buy their goods." An element of their plans, according to Stalin, was the Allied bombing of German industry in order to prevent Germany from paying reparations. He subsequently took the same line when late in the war the Americans bombed the Czech Skoda works and the Romanian oil fields. Third, Stalin insisted that the so-called patriotic militia organized by the Communists should give up their arms. The Soviet Union and its allies had recognized the

[20] *Ibid.*, doc. 207, p. 380. See also Rieber, *Stalin and the French Communist Party*, pp. 119–24.

government of de Gaulle and there was no way that the Communists could defend maintaining their own armed detachments alongside the regular army; "arms should be hidden," he declared. The Communists had to deal with a new situation; they were not strong enough to "knock the government over the head." If the situation improved then "the forces gathered around the party would prove useful for an offensive." As a further reminder that Thorez should keep the aim of winning the war uppermost in his mind, Stalin praised the French pilots of the Normandie-Nieman fighter squadron after Thorez had made some derogatory remarks about the reactionary views of those among them who were "representatives of the aristocratic families." Stalin retorted that the Soviet Union "did not award medals for nothing and decorated those who fought well against the Germans."[21]

Like Togliatti, Thorez returned to dampen the voices of radicalism and guide the party along the parliamentary path to socialism. Soviet policy toward France and Italy eased their way. Of the five problems discussed at Yalta involving a possible French role in postwar Europe, Stalin conceded to the Western allies on three: assigning an occupation zone to France (though only to be carved out of the British and American zones), membership on the Allied Control Commission for Germany, and a place among the sponsoring powers of the San Francisco Conference to found the United Nations. But he blocked their participation on the two most important commissions on reparations and dismemberment which were to decide the future of Germany.[22]

The Soviet leaders had no illusions about de Gaulle. Soviet diplomats, like their American counterparts, detected quasi-fascist tendencies in the French leader's political ideology. They were critical of his close associates for their right-wing beliefs. They suspected him of fostering a Western bloc, planting a suspicion in Stalin's mind to which he gave full expression in his negotiations with de Gaulle.[23] But Stalin was not averse to dealing with right-wing military leaders in pursuing his immediate war aim of defeating his enemies. He made this clear in his dealings not only with de Gaulle but also, at least in the short run, with Marshal Bagdolio, Marshal Antonescu, Admiral Horthy, Marshal Mannerheim, the German generals in captivity and, over a longer period, General Chiang Kai-shek. But Stalin wanted nothing to do with Francisco Franco.

---

[21] "Anglichane i Amerikantsy khotiat vezde sozdat' reaktionnye pravitel'stva," *Istochnik* 3:4 (1995), pp. 152–8. See also Banac, *The Diary of Georgi Dimitrov*, p. 342.

[22] FRUS, *The Conferences at Malta and Yalta, 1945*, pp. 623 and 701.

[23] *Sovetsko-frantszuskie otnosheniia*, vol. II, docs. 18 and 202, pp. 60 and 359; RGASPI, f. 17, op. 128 ed. kh. 14, ll. 11–13.

Franco's wartime policy was one of unrelieved anti-communism at home reenforced by the dispatch of the so-called Blue Division of Falangist volunteers to fight on the eastern front. Although the division was withdrawn in September 1943, the officers and men were allowed to join German units. Despite the blatant antagonism of Franco, Stalin adopted a measured response that contrasted sharply with his policy during the Spanish Civil War. During the liberation of France in October 1944, Spanish republican exiles who had fought in the French resistance, for the most part Communists, invaded Spanish territory in the Pyrenees. The leadership of the Spanish Communist Party in Moscow energetically sought to discourage them. The invaders were repulsed but a minor guerrilla war continued for the next six years.[24] Stalin limited his opposition to Franco to diplomatic initiatives. At the Potsdam Conference he urged his allies to recommend to the United Nations "to break all relations with Franco's government and render aid to the democratic forces of Spain, giving the Spanish people the opportunity to create a regime that corresponds to its will." Great Britain and the United States demurred, fearing to encourage a civil war. With Stalin's consent they substituted a motion opposing the participation of Spain in the United Nations.[25] It was another case of Stalin's reluctance to support insurrectionary Communist movements in the de facto Western sphere of influence.

As early as the Yalta Conference the general outlines of Stalin's war aims in countries within the operational zone of his Western allies had evolved to the point where they can be summarized under three major points. First, by opposing the establishment of a military government, Soviet policy sought to create the broadest possible sphere for civil authority in reconstructing the postwar political, economic and judicial structures. This would enable the Communists, who had taken a major role in the resistance movements and were the best-organized political party to survive the disruption of war and occupation, to play a large, possibly preponderant role in establishing new governments and shaping new societies. Second, at the very least their presence in these governments would assist the Soviet Union in advancing its major territorial and political interests in the inner periphery and preventing the

---

[24] Paul Preston, *Franco: A Biography* (New York: Basic Books 1994), pp. 347–50, 499, 518, 540–2.

[25] Ministerstvo innostranykh del SSSR, *Sovetskii soiuz na mezhdunarodnykh konferentsiiakh perioda Velikoi Otechestvenoi voiny, 1941–1945 gg. Berlinskaia (Potsdamskaia) Konferentsiia rukovoditelei trekh soiuznykh derzhav SSSR, SShA i Velikobritanii (17 iiulia–2 avgusta 1945 g.) Sbornik dokumentov* (Moscow: Izd. politicheskoi literatury, 1980), p. 28 and docs. 40, 158 and 159.

formation of a Western bloc. Third, by stressing the need for unity of action during the war and promoting the continuation of a united front after the war the West European Communists would have a better chance of blocking the revival of the right as a political force within their societies, introducing far-reaching socioeconomic reforms, and promoting the formation of a unified party of the left. When and if conditions changed "for the better," in Stalin's words to Thorez, the Communists could go over to the offensive, in other words take power. The cautious policy he applied to France and Italy broke down in Greece.

Greece

Stalin's policy toward Greece represents the strongest case of his commitment to coalition politics and recognition of Britain's sphere of influence in the outer perimeter by trading in a genuine revolutionary opportunity for an ephemeral friendly government. Once the Soviet Union entered the war, it recognized the royalist Greek government-in- exile sheltering in Cairo under British protection as part of the anti-German coalition. But Moscow did not send agents into Greece and adopted a passive role in the internal conflicts leading to civil war. By contrast, British agents were active in Greece. As in Yugoslavia, they faced a deeply split resistance. In Greece the leftist Communist-dominated movement, EAM-ELAS, lacked both the disciplined unity of the Yugoslav partisans and an acknowledged leader like Tito. Smaller nationalist bands were led by former Greek army officers. From the outset, relations between the two groups, as in Yugoslavia, were hostile. Until February 1943 the resistance was limited to small-scale actions, such as raiding police stations and communication lines. After the Germans imposed a labor draft, young men began escaping into the mountains, fueling a large-scale uprising and sparking armed conflict among the bands. The leadership of the Greek Communist Party was not in full control of the leftist bands. The secretary of the party, Giorgios Siantos, emphasized the importance of political work. He attempted to restrain the more radical leftists from launching major attacks against the Germans and other bands in order to avert reprisals and to avoid alienating the British and the Greek government-in- exile. Unlike the Yugoslav partisans the Greek Communist policy was not to replace but to join the government-in-exile.[26]

For this policy to succeed, EAM had to make good its claim to represent all of mainland Greece. It hastened to absorb the non-party military

---

[26] John L. Hondros, *Occupation and Resistance: The Greek Agony, 1941–1944* (New York: Pella Publishing, 1983), pp. 113–18.

resistance organizations as rapidly as the British Special Operations Executive created them. Eager to end the strife among the bands, the British agents successfully negotiated a National Bands Agreement, signed by the rival resistance groups in the summer of 1943. It committed the political wing of the leftist movement, EAM, to full cooperation with the Allied Mediterranean Command. Its military wing, ELAS, retained a large measure of freedom of action but accepted the creation of a joint headquarters in the mountains for the purpose of coordinating all resistance activity in order to draw off German forces from Italy and facilitate the Allied landings.

The National Bands Agreement inaugurated the most active period of the Greek resistance. But in October 1943 it broke down, touching off the first round of the Greek civil war which lasted until February 1944, when it ended in a stalemate. Four events precipitated the crisis. First, there was the unsuccessful attempt of the British military mission to bring together representatives of EAM, "mountain Greece," and the government-in-exile in Cairo in order to bring about a mutual understanding and an exchange of delegates.[27] The main stumbling block to political unity was the constitutional question. As early as September 1942 EAM had taken a firm stand that a plebiscite on the monarchy should be held before the return of the king. In November 1943, in the interests of accommodating the demands of the left, Churchill and Eden advised George II to accept a regency council and not to return to Greece until the Greek people had been consulted. The king refused after having consulted with Roosevelt. Neither side was willing to compromise on this issue.[28] The EAM representatives returned to Greece embittered and convinced that only a show of force would change the views of the royal government.

Second, after the surrender of Italy, the Italian occupation forces in Greece turned over massive quantities of arms to ELAS, freeing it from dependence on British supplies. Third, Churchill tried to force the pace of liberation in the Balkans by launching an amphibious landing on three Greek islands, but a German counter-attack turned the demonstration into a humiliating setback. Fourth, the Communists' main nationalist

---

[27] E. C. W. Myers, *Greek Entanglement* (London: R. Hart-Davis, 1955), pp. 236–43. Myers was the head of mission who had organized the expedition and was forced to resign when it failed. See also E. C. W. Myers, "The Andarte Delegation to Cairo: August 1943," in Phyllis Auty and Richard Clogg (eds.), *British Policy toward Wartime Resistance in Yugoslavia and Greece* (New York: Barnes and Noble, 1975), pp. 151–2.

[28] Anthony Eden, *The Reckoning: The Eden Memoirs* (London: Cassell, 1965), pp. 498–9. This temporary lapse on Roosevelt's part was due to his personal relationship to the Greek king. He soon reversed his opinion.

rival, the rightist band of Napoleon Zervas, which was receiving the bulk of the British supplies, began to withdraw from the fighting against the occupation forces in order to put an end to reprisals and avoid annihilation by the reenforced German Army. Although there were differences among the leaders of EAM, their general aim was consistent with the established policy of imposing unity, by force if necessary, on the internal resistance.[29] The British attempt to hold down ELAS to 25,000 men and build up Zervas as a counter-weight was not successful; Zervas's forces never numbered more than 5,000.

The relative strength of the left and right in Greece did not deter Churchill from his determination to keep Greece out of Communist hands. He had learned his lesson from the Yugoslav experience. Greece was too important strategically to allow military expediency to take precedence over political considerations. He was sufficiently concerned over the results of the first round of fighting to press for a coalition of Greek political forces in which the resistance would be subordinated to the royal government and not the other way round, as in Yugoslavia.

The end of the first round of fighting signaled a new effort by the Communists to insinuate themselves into a revamped democratic coalition government-in-exile. If they could not fight their way in, then they might negotiate their way in by threatening to create an alternative government in the mountains. In March 1944, shortly after ELAS failed to impose military unity on the resistance, the Communist Party took the initiative in forming the Political Committee of National Liberation (PEEA) to administer the free areas under the control of EAM.[30] There is no question that the Communists dominated the new organization. But their efforts to broaden its base, in accordance with the general Comintern line to give such movements an all-inclusive republican character, complicated their task of giving the committee a clear direction.

The PEEA had a short life, but the mere fact of its creation stirred the British and the government-in-exile to seek a compromise with the mountains. The committee followed the precedent set by Tito's proclamation at Jajce, demanding that the king not return until a plebiscite was held on the mainland. The republican politicians in Cairo seized the

---

[29] Hondros, *Occupation and Resistance*, pp. 180–3; Ole E. Smith, "'The First Round': Civil War in Greece during the Occupation," in David H. Close (ed.), *The Greek Civil War, 1945–1950: Studies of Polarization* (London and New York: Routledge, 1993), pp. 58–71.

[30] According to Woodhouse, it was "a state organized in the mountains," which for the first time in Greek history brought the advantages of civilization and culture to those untamed regions. C. M. Woodhouse, *Apple of Discord: A Survey of Recent Greek Politics in their International Setting* (Reston, VA: W. B. O'Neill, 1985), p. 146.

occasion to put pressure on the king to delay his return, even though they were split over the issue of cooperation with EAM. Their intrigues spread to the Greek troops stationed in Egypt. In February rivalry among monarchist, old republican and leftist elements sparked a mutiny. Then pro-EAM elements among the troops took the lead in making political demands to include the resistance in a government of national unity. The British insisted that the rebels surrender unconditionally; the rebels were equally insistent that a government of national unity be formed before they gave up their arms. The episode was a dress rehearsal for the outbreak of fighting in Athens in December.

The American ambassador, MacVeagh, apportioned the blame among the Greek politicians in Cairo, the king and the British. The Soviet press confined itself to citing critical comments in the Western newspapers. Roosevelt gave his full backing to the repressive British policy. The British and troops loyal to the king crushed the mutiny and politically segregated the demoralized Greek units. The monarchist elements were reorganized into the Third Brigade. Dispatched to the Italian front, they won their combat spurs and the appellation "Rimini Brigade." Subsequently, the British transported them to Greece after the liberation where they played an important role in fighting during the second round of the civil war in December. The remainder of the Greek armed forces, numbering about 10,000 men, were interned in Palestine by the British under harsh conditions.[31]

The British, now faced with the prospects of another setback to their interests in the Balkans, cast about desperately for a respectable man of the center to head the government-in-exile. They found him in George Papandreou, one of the most staunchly anti-Communists of the republican politicians in exile. He won the support of the British ambassador and highly place officials in London by virtue of his memo dividing the world into "pan-Slavist Communism and Anglo-American liberalism." He became Churchill's candidate for premier of the government-in-exile. Once installed in office, he confided to his republican colleagues that he intended to break EAM by force.[32]

The Communist Party, together with EAM, agreed to participate in a conference sponsored by the British in hopes of sorting out the Greek imbroglio. The negotiations revealed that the party leaders themselves

---

[31] Evangelos Spyropoulos, *The Greek Military and the Greek Mutinies in the Middle East (1941–1944)* (Boulder, CO: East European Monographs, 1993), especially ch. 10 for the background and ch. 18 for the mutiny itself. See also John O. Iatrides, *Revolt in Athens: The Greek Communist "Second Round," 1944–45* (Princeton University Press, 1972), pp. 55–6.

[32] Hondros, *Occupation and Resistance*, pp. 215–19.

were not in total agreement. Their control over EAM representatives was by no means complete. In the spring of 1944 in Beirut a delegation of the left, including EAM, the Communist Party and the PEEA, met together with representatives of over two dozen other Greek political groups to hammer out a political settlement. The Lebanon Charter of May 20, 1944 cleared the path for the Communists to enter a coalition government for the first time in Greek history. It provided for a reorganization of the Greek armed forces and unity of the resistance under a government of national unity headed by George Papandreou. EAM was promised five cabinet posts out of fifteen (later twenty). But radical elements in "the mountain" repudiated the signature of their own representative. They demanded amnesty for the mutineers and an assurance that the king would not return before a plebiscite. They launched fresh attacks on Zervas, and the underground press criticized Papandreou.[33] Backed by Churchill, Papandreou stood firm.

The British were upset that the treatment of the mutiny in the Soviet press presaged a more active policy of supporting the EAM. In April, Eden went so far as to suggest to the Soviet ambassador in London, Fedor Gusev, that if the Soviet Union would stay out of Greek affairs, the British would be prepared to reciprocate in Romania, thus anticipating by five months the key provisions of the Churchill–Stalin spheres of influence agreement.[34] But Churchill was in a fighting mood. Ignoring all evidence to the contrary, he wrote Roosevelt on June 23, 1944 that the only way to prevent anarchy in Greece was "by persuading the Russians to quit boosting EAM and ramming it forward with all their forces."[35]

Contrary to Churchill's fears, the Soviet representatives counseled moderation. In Cairo the Soviet ambassador, Nikolai Novikov, advised Alexandros Svolos, the non-Communist left-wing president of PEEA, that EAM should accept terms and join the government. He confided to MacVeagh, the American ambassador: "They are terribly afraid of me here lest I engage in subversive activity. But I intend doing nothing of the sort. I don't have to. Conditions in the country will do all that is necessary."[36] At the same time in Greece, the first Soviet military mission under Colonel Gregori Popov reached ELAS headquarters in Thessaly

[33] Hagen Fleischer, *Kreuzschatten der Mächte: Griechenland 1941–1944* (Frankfurt and New York: P. Lang, 1986), pp. 489–95, 503–10.
[34] Eden's telegram to Clark Kerr, cited in Lars Bærentzen and David H. Close, "The British Defeat of EAM, 1944–45," in David H. Close (ed.), *The Greek Civil War: Studies in Polarization* (London: Routledge, 1993), p. 76 and note 13, p. 93.
[35] FRUS, *Europe* (1944), vol. V, pp. 126–7.
[36] John O. Iatrides (ed.), *Ambassador MacVeagh Reports: Greece, 1933–1947* (Princeton University Press, 1980), p. 627.

from Yugoslavia and held secret talks with the Greek Communists. There is no record of the conversations, but according to an associate of Svolos, the Russians apparently advised accepting the terms without insisting on the replacement of Papandreou. In any case they made it clear that Russia was in no position to intervene and whatever course EAM took, it would have to assume full responsibility for its actions. Colonel Popov confided to the British mission that he was skeptical about the claims of ELAS and had little respect for their military potential. For their part, EAM were disappointed that Popov did not offer to supply them with arms or money.[37]

Stalin was determined to adhere to his informal agreement with Churchill in May that assigned Greece to the British sphere in return for having Romania included in the Soviet sphere of influence. Once Churchill had won Roosevelt's approval for landing a 10,000-man force in Greece to keep order in Athens at liberation, he and the President informed Stalin of the plan. Stalin's laconic but pregnant response was "good and high time."[38] On September 23, 1944 the Soviet Union in an official note recognized the right of the British to send troops to Greece.[39] Three days later the Greek Communist representatives agreed to place their armed guerrilla forces under the authority of the Greek government of national unity, which in turn placed them under the command of the British Lieutenant-General Ronald Scobie.

The Caserta Agreement of September 1944 had no parallel with any other wartime agreements between a domestic resistance and a foreign power. Although the division of authority between the British units in Athens and ELAS was vague, the political implications of the arrangement were clear. It is doubtful that the Greek Communists could have been planning to take power under the terms of the Caserta Agreement.[40] Yet within two months the city of Athens was plunged into a bloody nightmare of fighting between EAM and the government supported by General Scobie's British Army units. The battle of Athens was the opening salvo in the second round of the Greek civil war. Social conflict and international politics met in a fateful encounter.

---

[37] Hondros, *Occupation and Resistance*, p. 225; Peter J. Stavrakis, *Moscow and Greek Communism, 1944–1949* (Ithaca, NY: Cornell University Press, 1989), pp. 32–3; Bærentzen and Close, "The British Defeat of EAM," p. 77; Michael S. Macrakis, "Russian Mission on the Mountains of Greece, Summer 1944 (A View from the Ranks)," *Journal of Contemporary History* 23 (1988), pp. 387–408, based on the diary of one of Svolos's associates who had contact with Popov's group.

[38] W. Averell Harriman and Elie Abel, *Special Envoy to Churchill and Stalin, 1941–1946* (New York: Random House, 1973), p. 350.

[39] Hondros, *Occupation and Resistance*, p. 233, citing Foreign Office documents.

[40] Iatrides, *Revolt in Athens*, p. 116.

When, in October, the government of national unity under George Papandreou with its Communist ministers returned to Athens in the wake of the retreating Germans, the city was a time bomb waiting to explode.[41] After the German evacuation of Athens, but before British troops entered the city, EAM/ELAS organized demonstrations celebrating the liberation. They made no attempt to seize public buildings or give any sign that they intended to take power. For several months an uneasy calm settled over the capital. In their secret party instructions, as well as in the pages of their newspapers, the Greek Communists, just like their comrades elsewhere in liberated Europe, called for order, discipline and reconstruction, but also for the punishment of collaborators.

By early November, Churchill was prepared for the worst. He put the British troops in Greece at the disposal of Papandreou, noting that "I fully expect a clash with EAM and we must not shrink from it provided the ground is well-chosen." As the tension over demobilization and disarmament of the armed bands mounted, Churchill found it necessary to stiffen Papandreou's resolve when the premier tentatively sought a compromise with the Communists. His bellicose messages even shocked high-ranking officials in the Foreign Office.[42]

The Communists remained consistent in their policy of applying limited force. They refused to knuckle under to Papandreou and the British but they also shrank from making a direct bid for power. They were unwilling to precipitate a civil war, although they appeared to anticipate it. Siantos tersely summed up the policy in one of his secret telegrams to the local party cadres in Athens: "Watch and be ready to repulse any danger."[43] The danger came on December 1 when Scobie issued an ultimatum demanding the disarming of ELAS by December 10. The following day the EAM ministers resigned. They issued a conciliatory statement, but the party mobilized ELAS reserves and called for demonstrations. When jittery police fired on the demonstrators, enraged ELAS members stormed police stations, but avoided clashing with British troops; they made no attempt to overthrow the government. Churchill then issued his notorious order to Scobie to treat Athens as a conquered

[41] Mark Mazower, *Inside Hitler's Greece: The Experience of Occupation, 1941–1944* (New Haven, CT: Yale University Press, 1993), pp. 341–9.
[42] Churchill, The Second World War, vol. VI, pp. 286–7; Hondros, *Occupation and Resistance*, pp. 228–30, 239, 244. Ambassador MacVeagh was deeply troubled by Churchill's high-handed methods. The Soviet ambassador also remarked that the British were "trop brut" in Greece even before the fighting began. Iatrides, *Ambassador MacVeagh Reports*, pp. 613, 615.
[43] Stavrakis, *Moscow and Greek Communism*, p. 37.

city and to hold it "with bloodshed if necessary."[44] The second round of the Greek civil war had begun.

Stalin was also eager first to avoid and then to terminate the fighting in Greece.[45] During the second round the Soviet Union maintained scrupulous neutrality. Its attitude toward the Greek civil war was perfectly consistent with its policy in the outer perimeter. A silent Colonel Popov attended the meeting between Churchill and the Greek factions, along with the American ambassador, as if tacitly to acknowledge the British lead in Greece. In January the Soviet Union named an ambassador to Athens for the first time since 1939. To be sure, the Soviet press quoted dispatches from the Western press that sympathized with EAM, but it made no editorial comment. In desperation the Greek Communists attempted without success to get in direct touch with Moscow.

In Greece, neither side had the power to defeat the other. After a month of fighting, a negotiated settlement was concluded at Varkiza. Immediately after ELAS asked for a truce, the Party Central Committee received a note from the Russian Military Mission categorically disapproving of its militant policy.[46] At Yalta, Stalin made it clear that he "had not the slightest intention of criticizing what the British were doing in Greece, but would simply like to have some information." After he received it he told Churchill: "I have every confidence in British policy in Greece."[47]

The return from Dachau to Greece in May 1945 of the long-imprisoned secretary-general of the party, Nikos Zachariades, signaled a new attempt to reconcile the differences within the party and to promote a conciliatory policy. Zachariades roundly denounced the partisan struggle of radical elements in "the mountain." He proposed a dual strategy in foreign and domestic policy that placed him in the same category as Togliatti and Thorez. He proceeded on the assumption that the Grand Alliance would hold together and there would be no division of the world into two camps. In foreign policy Zachariades adopted the so-called theory of the two poles. "Greece is situated at a sensitive and crucial spot in the British Empire's vital communication network," he told his colleagues at the Twelfth Party Plenum in June. "As long as there is a British Empire this artery will exist and Britain will do everything in its power to preserve it. A consistent Greek foreign policy should function between

[44] Churchill, *The Second World War*, vol. VI, p. 289.
[45] For the Soviet policy of restraint, see Roberts, "Moscow's Cold War."
[46] Stavrakis, *Moscow and Greek Communism*, pp. 37–9.
[47] FRUS, *Conferences on Malta and Yalta, 1945*, pp. 781–2. Ambassador Gromyko had recommended that the Soviet Union should not take any initiative in Greece except to signal its sympathy with the progressive elements. Roberts, "Moscow's Cold War," citing AVP RF f. 06, op. 7a, d. 5, ll. 11–12.

two poles: that of the European Balkans, with its center in Soviet Russia and that of the Mediterranean, with Great Britain at its center."[48] In domestic policy he also sought to occupy the middle ground between preparing for civil war and disarming. To put it most simply, it was a policy of self-defense against right-wing terror. The party would continue to work toward a peaceful and parliamentary transition to socialism. But it would prepare to block a fascist coup. Zachariades told MacVeagh that the Communists needed to conduct political work among the peasants; he shunned responsibility for the second round and referred to his party as "the most conservative" in Greece.[49]

By the time of the Potsdam Conference, Stalin's views began to shift as it became clear that right-wing elements in Greece were using the truce to repress the left. This gave him the opportunity to criticize Western policy while seeking to contrast his acceptance of the anti-Communist government in Greece with their refusal to recognize the pro-Communist governments of Bulgaria and Romania.[50]

At the Seventh Congress in October 1945 there was still talk of the peaceful reconstruction of Greece and the formation of a "people's democracy." But Zachariades warned that it might not be possible without a fight. The Communist press avoided linking the party with the resistance in the mountains until early 1946, when the party decided to build up armed resistance where local conditions were favorable and there was no risk of clashing with the British. The party's main efforts were, nonetheless, directed toward building up mass organizations in the cities. It became increasingly difficult for the party to turn the other cheek as the wave of repression mounted. When the government, backed by the British, announced elections for March 1946, the left, including the Communists, cried foul. The country was still in turmoil. There were large numbers of political detainees who had not been tried and the electoral lists had not been revised. The purge of collaborators had turned

[48] Dominique Eudes, *The Kapetanios: Partisans and Civil War in Greece, 1943–1949* (New York: Monthly Review Press, 1973), p. 249, citing Zachariades's speech at the Twelfth Plenum of the Greek Communist Party in June 1945.

[49] The party's policy as defined in the Twelfth Plenum has become a center of controversy. There is no complete published record of the speeches and debates, though Matthias Esche, *Die Kommunistische Partei Griechenlands, 1941–1949* (Munich: Oldenbourg, 1982), p. 229, appears to be quoting directly from the stenographic record in the Greek Communist Party archives. I follow Ole L. Smith, "Self-Defence and Communist Policy, 1945–1947," in Lars Bærentzen *et al.* (eds.), *Studies in the History of the Greek Civil War, 1945–1949* (Copenhagen: Museum Tusculanum, 1987), pp. 159–60, 163, and Ole L. Smith, "The Greek Communist Party, 1945–9," in Close, *The Greek Civil War*, pp. 131–4. For Zachariades's comments to MacVeagh, Iatrides, *Revolt in Athens*, p. 258.

[50] Roberts, "Moscow's Cold War," p 63.

into a farce: instead of being arrested and tried they were hired to staff the security forces.[51]

After an inconclusive consultation with Soviet authorities, the party supported a boycott but the vote was not unanimous. The right won an overwhelming victory at the polls although only 50 percent of the voters bothered to cast ballots. The outcome was due in part to the boycott and in part to the manipulation of the electoral rolls and large-scale intimidation by the right. There is no sure method of calculating the political strength of the left at this time; support had been dwindling since the December events and estimates range from a quarter to a third of the electorate.[52] The forces of the center were driven by fear and pressure to the right. Although Greece was still split into three camps – supporters of monarchy, republic or popular democracy – the real political choice had been narrowed to EAM or the authoritarian monarchists. Stalin's hopes that the Greek Communists would march down the parliamentary path to a popular democracy as in France and Italy were shattered by civil war.

Friendly governments in Asia

Stalin's concept of friendly governments on his Asian borders represents a variation on the European theme. He did not seek to gain hegemony over all of Iran and China as he did in the countries of the inner perimeter in Eastern Europe; but neither was he content to settle for exercising distant influence solely through surrogate Communist parties as in Western Europe. Instead he pursued a two-track policy. He sought to exploit ancient regional traditions of resistance to the centralizing power of the Iranian and Chinese governments in the borderlands across his frontiers; these were Azerbaizhan in Iran, Xinjiang, Outer Mongolia and Manchuria in China. At the same time, he sought to promote the establishment of "friendly" coalition governments which would include pro-Soviet or Communist parties and which would recognize Soviet interests in the borderlands. In pursuing these aims at the end of the war,

[51] In fact the purge laws were applied more strictly against the left than the right and the record of the Greek government in punishing collaborators compares most unfavorably with other West European governments including Norway, Belgium, Netherlands, Denmark and France. Procopis Papastratis, "The Purge of the Greek Civil Service on the Eve of the Civil War," in Bærentzen et al., History of the Greek Civil War, pp. 43–6.

[52] Hagen Fleischer, "The 'Third Factor,'" in Bærentzen et al., History of the Greek Civil War, p. 197; Smith, "The Greek Communist Party, 1945–9," pp. 136–7; Lawrence S. Wittner, American Intervention in Greece, 1943–1949 (New York: Columbia University Press, 1982), pp. 40–1.

he enjoyed the advantage of having Soviet troops on the ground in all these borderlands; but he also faced opposition from both the nationalist forces within those countries and his erstwhile Western allies, Great Britain and, increasingly, the United States. In the Trans Caspian and Inner Asian borderlands the frontier came closest to blurring between the inner periphery of prime political and strategic importance and the outer periphery of shared power with his Western allies.

Iran and Azerbaizhan

The joint occupation of Iran by the Soviet Union and Britain from 1941 to 1946 had been initiated in order to forestall the spread of German influence. But it radically disrupted the political and social life of the country. As a prelude, Moscow had repeatedly warned Reza Shah of German plans to stage a coup; then it invoked article 6 of the treaty of 1921, allowing Soviet troops to enter Iran in order to secure the Soviet frontiers from attack.[53] Although Britain had no similar treaty rights, it justified joining the Soviet Union by invoking the German threat.

In August 1941 Soviet and British forces invaded Iran, overcame light resistance, and replaced Reza Shah with his son. They sponsored the election of a representative government with its own parliament (the Majlis). The occupying powers divided the country into spheres of influence, as they had in 1907, although the Soviet zone in the far north was far smaller than its imperial predecessor. On Stalin's instructions, a delegation of Soviet Azerbaizhani was dispatched to Tabriz, the provincial capital of Iranian Azerbaizhan, with the explicit aim of promoting Soviet interests in the region. From the outset, the Soviet civil and military authorities denied any intention of detaching Azerbaizhan from Iran or instituting Soviet institutions in the province. However, differences soon surfaced among them over the pace and extent of their influence. The most energetic and ambitious of the Soviet proconsuls was Mira Jafar Bagirov (Baqirov), the chairman of the Sovnarkom of the Azerbaizhan SSR and First Secretary of the Azerbaizhan Communist Party of the Soviet Union. A protégé of Beria, he pushed for a greater degree of autonomy in the province.[54]

---

[53] B. Kh. Parvizpur, *Sovetsko-iranskie otnosheniia v gody vtoroi mirovoi voiny (1939–1945)* (Tblisi: Met's'niera, 1978), pp. 20–36 and appendix 1, pp. 92–4, which provides the text of the Soviet note invoking the treaty and outlining the history of Soviet–Iranian relations.

[54] For Bagirov's activities, see especially Jamil Haslani, *At the Dawn of the Cold War: The Soviet–American Crisis over Iranian Azerbaizhan, 1941–1946* (Lanham, MD: Rowan and Littlefield, 2006).

At first, the Red Army in Northern Iran acted with far greater restraint than elsewhere in the Eurasian borderlands. It soon won a modicum of support from the local population including even some elements of the commercial elite.[55] After an initial period of "non-interference," the occupation forces encouraged the development of autonomous movements in Azerbaizhan and Kurdistan, two ethnically distinctive regions with strong traditions of resistance to the centralizing policies of Reza Shah. They took advantage of class tensions between landowners and peasants in the countryside and the embryonic workers' movement to gain sympathy from the reemerging Iranian left. But Stalin opposed the reestablishment of the Iranian Communist Party, which had been decimated by Reza Shah. Instead, the Soviet occupation authorities allowed the formation of the Tudeh (Masses) Party in 1941 by a small group of young intellectuals who had been influenced by Marxist thought while studying in Berlin in the early 1930s as part of Reza Shah's program of sending promising students abroad for training as the future administrative and scientific elite of the country. When several of them had appealed to the Soviet embassy in Teheran for permission to found a Communist Party, they were initially discouraged and then advised to form a different kind of party – radical, democratic and pro-Soviet but without any suggestion of a socialist platform.[56] This was the origin of the Tudeh Party.

According to Soviet instructions, it was to be a legal party that would adhere strictly to the constitutional order. It was not to betray the slightest hint of Marxist inspiration either in thought or in action. Its endorsement of the Grand Alliance was to emphasize the leading role of the Soviet Union but in no way to criticize the British or Americans. It was instructed to recruit prominent figures in the elite, including landlords and capitalists. The party was to refrain from organizing any labor activity that would disrupt the war effort, in particular the pumping of oil and the manufacture of uniforms and equipment.[57] The decision to organize a National Front discouraged a premature revolutionary movement from developing in Iran that would seriously compromise Stalin's relations

[55] Louise Fawcett, *Iran and the Cold War: The Azerbaizhan Crisis of 1946* (Cambridge University Press, 1992), pp. 86–92.
[56] This had been Dimitrov's advice to the Soviet leadership. Banac, The Diary of Georgi Dimitrov, entry for December 9, 1941, p. 205.
[57] Anvar Khamahi, *Fursati Buzurgi Az Dast Raftah* (The Great Opportunity Lost) (Teheran, 1984), pp. 16–20 (I am grateful to Firouzeh Mostashari for her help with Persian sources); I. Eskandari, "Histoire du parti Tudeh," *Moyen Orient*, 6 (December, 1949), pp. 8–9. Cf. Chaqueri, "Sultanzade," for analysis of this and two additional versions by Eskandari of the founding of the Tudeh which emphasized the party's revolutionary outlook and its independence from Moscow.

with the British, with whom he shared occupation of the country. As a mass parliamentary party the Tudeh would be more useful to Stalin in exercising pressure to obtain his aims in Northern Iran than as a conspiratorial party that might set a social revolution in Iran above the interests of Soviet foreign policy.

From the outset, however, the Tudeh Party leadership was committed to a strong nationalist and anti-colonial stance that placed it in a contradictory position. In setting the conditions for cooperation with the occupying powers, they announced grandly: "We base our friendship with Great Britain as well as the Soviet Union on the condition that they limit their interests to our national interests and the advancement and well being of our people; that these governments do not follow reactionary or extremist policies in Iran." A stern warning followed: "If we at any juncture suspect that our northern neighbor, counter to our expectation, is advancing its own colonial interests or intends to impose by force its system upon us, or annex us, we shall steadfastly oppose its policies."[58] Accompanying this text was an unqualified denial that the Tudeh was a Marxist-Leninist Party. Among the parliamentary factions, the Tudeh stood out by virtue of its greater cohesion and its acceptance of mass politics outside the walls of the Majlis. Moreover, it was opposed to the development of regional autonomy elsewhere in Iran, especially in Kurdistan, where in 1944 Kurds had raided Azerbaizhan villages.[59] Like other Iranian parties, it suffered from factionalism that complicated its domestic and foreign policies.

In dealing with the Iranian labor force, the Tudeh remained indifferent to the workers' appeals for help in their conflicts with Anglo-Iranian Oil; unity of the Big Three took precedence over workers' solidarity. From 1941 to 1944 the Tudeh and the Central Council of Trade Unions, which it dominated, adopted the no-strike policy similar to that of all Communist-dominated trade unions elsewhere in Europe during the Second World War.[60] This created strains within the party and between its official policy and the interests of the workers in the oil fields.

The question of granting oil concessions created a more serious dilemma for the Tudeh Party, forcing it to alter its anti-colonial position in order to accommodate Soviet interests. The attempts of British and American oil interests in 1944 to extract extensive concessions for oil exploration from Iran sparked two reactions: one from the nationalist

---

[58] *Rahbar*, no. 280, April 1943 quoted in JAMI, *Guzashtih Chiragh-i Rah-i Ayandih Ast* (The Past is Light) (n. p., 1978), pp. 137–9.

[59] Haslani, *At the Dawn*, pp. 39–40.

[60] Ervand Abrahamian, "Factionalism in Iran: Political Groups in the 14th Parliament (1944–1946)," *Middle Eastern Studies* 14 (January, 1978), 32–5.

elements in the Majlis grouped around the ardent Iranian nationalist, Dr. Muhammed Mossadegh, and the other from the Soviet Union. Mossadegh proposed to nationalize the oil industry by forming an Iranian corporation and to oppose granting oil concessions to any foreign government. The Soviet response was to demand oil concessions in the north in order to balance the possible expansion of Anglo-American economic influence in the south. The Soviet decision to dispatch a high-level mission led by Deputy Commissar Sergei Kavtaradze in September 1944 to secure an oil concession in the north must be viewed primarily as a political gambit. There were no proven sources of oil in the northern provinces, and none has since been discovered there. Imperial Russian and early Soviet policy toward Iran were similar in their opposition to economic concessions to any other foreign government in the politically sensitive northern provinces of Iran. In 1921–2 the Soviet government had vigorously protested against concessions granted to Standard Oil and Sinclair in Iranian Azerbaizhan. Similarly, in the late 1930s, they had vigorously opposed Nazi economic penetration of the northern provinces. In 1940 and again as recently as February 1944 they had claimed prior right to any oil concessions in Northern Iran. Their position was no secret. Kavtaradze's proposals, apparently hastily drawn up, demanded mineral as well as oil concessions and the exclusion of foreigners from the area, but offered no financial terms. The Iranian government was paralyzed with indecision until the Shah ordered the Prime Minister to reject them. Instead Iran proposed to postpone all oil concessions until after the evacuation of the country.[61] The departure of the Soviet delegation was followed by mass demonstrations in Tabriz, which forced the resignation of the Iranian government. But the Majlis retaliated in December 1944 by passing a law attributed to Mossadegh, who helped to draft it, forbidding negotiations on granting oil concessions.

The Tudeh Party came out against Mossadegh. They denounced the prospective owners of a national corporation as "the same people who have sucked the blood of the workers of Isfahan and Kharasan."[62] In a switch the Tudeh rationalized support for the Soviet oil concession by arguing that the Soviet Union was not "an expansionist country" and that its presence was necessary to "balance other influences."[63] The Tudeh Party's opposition to Mossadegh seriously compromised its claim to represent a radical nationalist constituency in Iran.

[61] Haslani, *At the Dawn*, pp. 48–52; see also Mark Lytle, *The Origins of the Iranian American Alliance, 1941–1953* (New York: Homes and Meier, 1987), pp. 73–81.
[62] *Rahbar*, no. 420, November 1944, quoted in JAMI, *Guzashtihi*, p. 181.
[63] *Ibid.*, pp. 197–8, 200–3, 205.

Within the Tudeh, disagreements arose over the attitude to be taken toward the autonomous movements in Kurdistan and Azerbaizhan. Many of its members deeply believed in the national unity of Iran and had little respect for the Turkic elements in Azerbaizhan. The Soviet encouragement of the Kurds and Azerbaizhani raised competing claims for the loyalty of Tudeh members and paralyzed the party on the autonomy question.

In each of these cases the Tudeh revealed its hybrid character. It was quasi-Marxist and strongly pro-Soviet. But it was not yet "a Leninist party of the new style." It had never been a member of the Comintern; its leaders had not been trained in Moscow; it was still an open, mass party, fluid in membership and lax in organization. Although factional strife over the neo-colonialist demands of the Soviet Union did not lead to an open split in the party until 1948, the seeds were planted and watered in 1946.[64]

In many ways the Tudeh, and later its offshoot, the Democratic Party of Azerbaizhan, reflected the nature of Iranian politics that in the end defeated Soviet attempts to establish a solid foundation for constructing a friendly government. In August 1945, the Soviet ambassador, M. Maksimov, clearly outlined the dilemma. In the search to find at least sixty deputies of the Majlis to strengthen Iranian–Soviet relations, he despaired over the "vagueness that obscures internal politics for the broad masses." The political parties had no idea of what to do and were mired in a "state of ideological confusion." The broad masses were dissatisfied with the government, but the progressive circles could not exploit this because of their fear of a complete restoration of the Reza Shah regime. But Maksimov also pointed out that the weakness of the central government, favored by the British, encouraged separatist tendencies among the tribes of the south where the British had oil concessions.[65] Consciously or not, then, he exposed the contradiction in Soviet policy. Support for the Tudeh and other potentially pro-Soviet Iranian groups was a wager on a strong central government; the encouragement of autonomy for Azerbaizhan was a move in the opposite direction.

During the six months following the passage of the law forbidding negotiations on oil concessions, the Soviet Foreign Commissariat

---

[64] Ervand Abrahamian, *Iran: Between Two Revolutions* (Princeton University Press, 1982), pp. 311–12; cf. Sepehr Zabih, *The Communist Movement in Iran* (Berkeley: University of California Press, 1966), pp. 93, 124–36, and Zabih, *The Left in Contemporary Iran: Ideology, Organization and the Soviet Connection* (Stanford: The Hoover Institution, 1986). For a critique and additional insights into the Tudeh factions, see Cosroe Chaqueri, "Iran's Left in Its True Colors," *Central Asian Survey* 6:3 (1987), pp. 118–19.

[65] AVP RF ref. po Iranu, op. 31b, ind. 712, por. 3, p. 357, report of Maksimov, August 23, 1945 inv. 2068, ind. 18, p. 352, ll. 85–6.

Map 10.1 Iran, 1941–6

hammered away at the successive Iranian cabinets, insisting that relations with Iran could only be improved by repealing the Mossadegh law.[66] When the war in Europe ended, the Soviet forces in Northern Iran made no move to leave despite their agreement with the Western allies and the Iranian government. Moreover, they rebuffed requests by Teheran to strengthen Iranian army garrisons in the north in order to maintain order. The official Soviet reply of November 22, 1945 declared: "In view of the necessity to avoid complications, undesirable for Iran and the Soviet government, connected to the introduction of government

[66] *Ibid.*, op. 31, inv. 2056, ind. 6, p. 351a, ll. 12–13, conversation of Kavtaradze with Iranian ambassador M. Akhi, April 1944; *ibid.*, ll. 30–3, conversation of Vyshinskii with Akhi, August 1945.

troops in the northern regions of Iran, the Soviet government considers the carrying out of such measures inexpedient" (*netselesoobraznyi*, a conventional Soviet diplomatic negative). If Iran sent troops then the Soviet Union would have to send additional forces "in order to guarantee the security of the Soviet garrisons and to avoid possible disorders."[67]

The crisis developed further with the Soviet sponsorship of a new party, the Firqeh (Azerbaizhan Democratic Party) in September 1945. Firqeh was founded in Baku following a meeting with Bagirov and a veteran of the prewar Persian Iranian Communist Party, Mir Jafar Pishevari (Javadzade).[68] Pishevari had been born in Iranian Azerbaizhan but taught school in Baku for many years. He had participated in the Jangali movement, had become Commissar of Foreign Affairs and then Interior in the Gilan Republic and was a close collaborator of Sultanzade. After attending the Third Comintern Congress in 1921, he returned to Iran as a working journalist until he was arrested, jailed and sentenced to internal exile. He was freed by the Anglo-Russian occupation. A staunch supporter of Azerbaizhani linguistic and cultural rights, he had a rocky relationship with the Tudeh. Elected a member of the Fourteenth Majlis, his outspoken advocacy of autonomy for Azerbaizhan led to his expulsion from the party. When in August 1944 the Tudeh refused to accept his credentials as a representative of Azerbaizhan to their general conference, Pishevari became the center of the militant movement for autonomy in the province.[69]

The formation of two parties, both claiming to advocate the same democratic ideals, social reform and sympathetic attitude toward the Soviet Union, seems superfluous. But in fact Firqeh represented something distinctive in the eyes of its founders. They found fault with the Tudeh on two counts. First it was "a parliamentary party that is not suitable for conducting revolution and social change, whereas the Democratic Party of Azerbaizhan assumes the duty of carrying the national-democratic revolution to its final victory." Second, the Tudeh "in spite of the heroic struggle against reaction" had not accomplished anything because it was "an exclusively class party." Furthermore, "the supporters of the Tudeh are known as leftists and use leftist slogans. Those who wish

---

[67] *Ibid.*, papka 351, ll. 63–4, conversation of Dekanosov with Akhi, November 23, 1945. The local Soviet representatives considered the Iranian army a bastion of feudal reaction whose leaders controlled the Shah and whose rank and file were completely submissive, immune to Tudeh influence. *Ibid.*, op. 31, inv. 2068, ind. 18, papka 352, ll. 6, 911, 109.

[68] Khamahi, *Fursati*, p. 247.

[69] Fakhreddin Azimi, *The Crisis of Democracy in Iran* (London: I. B. Tauris, 1989), pp. 135–6; Habib Ladjevardi, *Labor Unions and Autocracy in Iran* (New York: Syracuse University Press, 1985), pp. 110–11.

to join the Firqeh must learn to moderate their statements and slogans."
In particular the official organ of the Firqeh criticized the Tudeh for stirring up trouble between peasants and landlords. It placed equal blame on
both sides, the landlords for extracting illegal taxes and the peasants for
refusing to pay rent "which they legally owed to the landlord."[70] Pishevari
was insistent that the Firqeh was a national liberation movement directed
against the oppression of the Fars: that is, Persians.

The Firqeh moved rapidly to wrest control of the province from the
feeble hands of the central government, while Soviet troops prevented
the intervention of the Iranian army. The party convened a National
Congress of Azerbaizhan which proclaimed its autonomy but denied any
desire to separate from Iran. A provincial election returned an overwhelming majority for the Firqeh. A new autonomous government of
Azerbaizhan took office with Pishevari as premier. The sudden and unexpected appearance of the Firqeh and its stunning success embarrassed
and confused the Tudeh leaders in Teheran. The Firqeh had invited
Tudeh members in Azerbaizhan to join its ranks and over 60,000 had
signed up. The entire provincial committee went over to Firqeh without
consulting Tudeh headquarters in Teheran.[71] An open break was avoided
in part with the help of Soviet mediation. Firqeh compromised on disputed ethnic and agrarian issues. The enthusiasm, energy and efficiency
of the new administration impressed even the British consul in Tabriz.[72]

Its considerable accomplishments notwithstanding, the Azerbaizhan
regional movement had little chance of survival once the screen of Soviet
troops was removed. The majority of Iranian opinion ranging from the
Shah and the army to the nationalists rejected in highly emotional terms
the region's turcophone linguistic policy which, they claimed, "recalls
the traces of Ghenghis Khan and Tamerlane." The Soviet Union was
unwilling to furnish the rebels with heavy equipment to match that of
the Iranian army.[73] Still less was Moscow willing to encourage and arm
the Tudeh in the face of impending government repression. A move in
this direction would have spread the regional revolts into the heart of
Iran, disrupted the oil production and directly involved the British and
Americans.

---

[70] Citations from the newspapers *Aras* and *Azerbaizhan* in Khamahi, *Fursati*, pp. 273–4.
[71] Touraj Atabaki, *Azerbaizhan: Ethnicity and the Struggle for Power in Iran* (London: I. B. Tauris, 2000), p. 107.
[72] Abrahamian, *Iran*, pp. 399–409; Parviz Homayounpour, *L'affaire Azerbaïdjan* (Ambilly-Annemasse: Imp. Franco-Suisse, 1966), pp. 123, 143–6; United States National Archives (USNA), RM, box 419, XL 41134.
[73] Homayounpour, *L'affaire*, p. 74.

A similar set of problems complicated Soviet relations with an autonomous Kurdish movement in Northwestern Iran. The Kurdish revolt and the establishment of a Kurdish republic had its immediate causes in the withdrawal and disintegration of the Iranian Army in 1941. A rash of raiding and brigandage directed mainly at the Azerbaizhani population broke out. The Soviet occupation forces at first prevented Iranian units from reentering the area, but at the height of cooperation with the Western allies, they then agreed to permit the American-trained Iranian gendarmerie to restore order. But the Shah and his chief of staff preferred to have the army, which was under their direct control, move in and the plans fell through.[74] Therefore, as soon as the Soviet forces withdrew to the line designated by the Anglo-Soviet treaty one of the smaller tribes seized 10,000 rifles stacked at an Iranian army post, launched a surprise attack and drove out the regular army units. In time-honored fashion, the government in Teheran appointed the rebel leader governor and for two years allowed him to administer the region behind an official facade.

Soviet agents in the area discreetly encouraged the autonomous aspirations of the Kurds. The first of two meetings was arranged in Baku between Kurdish leaders and Bagirov. The exact nature of the assurances made by Bagirov to the Kurds remains in dispute; as an ambitious client of Beria, Bagirov may have expressed greater enthusiasm for the Kurdish cause than Moscow might have wished. Soviet agents in Kurdistan were more cautious, urging the tribesmen to maintain order, respect the government officials and return stolen arms. It was natural that the Kurds preferred to interpret Soviet policies in ways that would promote their long-held aspirations for full autonomy.

In September 1942 the Sunni Kurdish leaders founded the Committee of the Life (Resurrection) of Kurdistan. The organization excluded Azerbaizhani and members of non-Kurdish tribes on a racial basis. Illegal and clandestine, it nonetheless successful spread its message rapidly throughout North Kurdistan, but it had little appeal to the Kermanshah tribes in the south who were Shiites. By 1945 almost all the Kurdish tribal chiefs and many ordinary Kurds had signed up. Contacts with Kurds in Turkey and Iraq led to the conclusion of a Pact of the Three Borders that promised mutual support for the establishment of a greater Kurdistan.[75]

---

[74] Thomas Ricks, "U.S. Military Missions to Iran, 1943–1978: The Politics of Economy of Military Assistance," *Iranian Studies* 12:3–4 (1979), p. 171.

[75] William Eagleton, Jr., *The Kurdish Republic of 1946* (London: Oxford University Press, 1963), pp. 21–4, 33–6.

As the momentum accelerated toward a Kurdish rebellion, the official Soviet position remained ambiguous. In September 1945 a group of prominent Kurdish leaders made a second visit to Baku at the invitation of the Soviet authorities. Bagirov rehearsed the political situation in Iran in the light of Stalin's nationality theory. He defined four "nations": Farsi-speaking Persians, Gilaki-speaking peoples of the South Caspian littoral, Turkic speakers from Azerbaizhan and the Kurds. He foresaw that each would eventually enjoy local autonomy and the first to be favored would be the Azerbaizhani. He advised restraint for the Kurds in Turkey and Iraq. In the meantime he urged the Iranian Kurds to pursue their autonomy within the framework of the Azerbaizhan regional movement. When the Kurds balked, Bagirov exclaimed: "as long as the Soviet Union exists the Kurds will have their independence." In a burst of enthusiasm he then promised them military equipment including tanks and artillery, financial support, a printing press and places reserved for young Kurds in the Baku Military College. Bagirov made good on his promises for a printing press and military training for Kurdish youths. But as for arms the Soviet authorities proved as consistently stingy as they had been in supplying the Communist resistance in Yugoslavia or China. They turned over 1,200 rifles and ammunition confiscated from the gendarmerie and later provided 5,000 more rifles, but no tanks or heavy weapons.[76] Without them there was no chance for the Kurds to withstand an all-out offensive by well-armed units of the Iranian Army retrained and supplied with modern arms and equipment by the United States.

The Kurds have always paid a high price for their unquenchable optimism and misplaced faith in the support of foreign powers for their aspirations of independence. In November 1945, intoxicated by Soviet promises and fortified by the arrival from Iraq of 3,000 fighters led by Mullah Mustafa Barzani, they proclaimed the formation of the Democratic Party of Kurdistan in Mahabad. Without declaring a fully autonomous government, the party program demanded autonomy in local affairs, a provincial council, Kurdish as the official language, Kurdish-speaking officials to be appointed to all functions, and all revenue collected in the region to be spent there. Initially, the Democratic Party declared its fraternity with the emerging autonomous regime in Azerbaizhan.[77]

---

[76] *Ibid.*, pp. 44–6, 55, 74, 83.
[77] Farpideh Koohi-Kamali, *The Political Development of the Kurds in Iran: Pastoral Nationalism* (Basingstoke: Palgrave Macmillan, 2003), pp. 105–6.

Yet, the Mahabad Kurdish regime was different in significant ways from its fraternal counterpart in Azerbaizhan. Its leaders were mainly representatives of the upper class, or at least came from respected families who were conservative in their social outlook. Despite the personal authority and magnetism of the President, Quasi Mohammad, the favorite of the Soviet officials, power was not centralized, but diffused along tribal and personal lines in the traditional pattern of Iranian politics. There were no Marxist-Leninists, no Soviet-trained representatives in the cabinet. The land reform was not on their agenda.[78]

Friction rapidly developed between the two regional movements. In Iranian Azerbaizhan, the proclamation of autonomy in December 1945 included a territorial claim over Kurdistan. It was followed by the formation of a National Assembly which accepted five Kurdish representatives. But the Kurds soon discovered that their Azerbaizhani friends were not even willing to grant them a provincial council. Disillusioned, they returned to their capital of Mahabad and declared autonomy on their own terms. The Soviet agents attempted to mediate between the two groups but failed to budge the Kurds and finally accepted the existence of two autonomous governments. Small-scale clashes had already broken out over disputed boundaries. The Soviet officials applied heavy pressure to obtain a Treaty of Friendship and Alliance between the two hostile groups that attempted to regulate the territorial and minority questions.

The government in Teheran was shocked by the prospect of its citizens signing an agreement that bore all the marks of a treaty between two sovereign states. But the Iranian Army proved incapable of breaking the Kurdish resistance. Its columns were ambushed and driven back, or else it won local skirmishes at a very high cost in men compared to minimal losses for the rebels. The stand-off was only resolved when in 1946 the withdrawal of Soviet troops from Azerbaizhan forced both regional regimes to attempt to negotiate for their survival with a vengeful Teheran.[79] Stalin had ordered the formation of the Firqeh purely in order to engage in the kind of bargaining that was so characteristic of his own and the Iranian style of politics. When it was of no further use to him he was prepared to abandon it, together with the Kurds.[80] Stalin desired

---

[78] Eagleton, *The Kurdish Republic*, pp. 57–60, 70–1.

[79] *Ibid.*, pp. 82–3, 90–3; USNA, RM, box 412, XL 40013; box 433, XL 3775.

[80] Soviet representatives in Iran were not impressed by the political profile of the Democratic Party. They found it riddled with unreliable, downright dishonest and anglophile elements, lacking understanding at the local level of how to carry out propaganda and agitation or draft programmatic statements. "Given the presence of such people, it is difficult to expect any successful progress in the work of the Democratic Party of Kurdistan." AVP RF, ref. po Iranu, op. 31, inv. 2068, ind. 18, p. 325, ll. 30–1.

not to spread a civil war but to control it. What he was aiming for was a
friendly government in Teheran that would recognize the special interests
of the Soviet Union in a sensitive frontier zone. A full-fledged civil war
and confrontation was not what he had in mind.[81]

In February 1946 Stalin and Molotov conducted negotiations on the
conditions for the withdrawal of Soviet troops with Ahmad Qavam, a
wealthy landowner and typical product of the Iranian political system. A
master of the art of bargaining and coalition-building, Qavam's skillful
maneuvering and apparent opportunism had two fixed points. In domestic affairs he worked to limit the power of the monarchy and army and in
foreign affairs he maneuvered to play off Britain against the Soviet Union
with the help, if possible, of the United States.[82]

In his opening gambit, Molotov emphasized that granting the Soviet
Union an oil concession in the north was "the true measure of Iran's
sincerity in her friendship with the Soviet Union just as the southern
oil concessions have been given to Britain for years" in the same spirit.
He maintained that the movement in Azerbaizhan was an internal affair
that must be solved by Tabriz and Teheran. He agreed to withdraw the
Soviet Army from certain areas despite Soviet concern over the internal
situation and international complications. Qavam would have none of
this. The Iranian position was that the Majlis had forbidden by law
not only granting oil concessions to foreign powers but even discussing
the issue with them. Azerbaizhan was an integral part of Iran; Turkic
(Azeri) was a local language and those threatening the independence
and sovereignty of Iran should mend their ways; there would be reforms,
however, and the law on provincial councils would be carried out. He
concluded that there was no justification for the continued presence of
the Soviet troops and they should be evacuated by March 2; the Soviet
Union need have no worries about the friendship with Iran.

The Soviet counter-proposals substituted for an outright concession a joint Soviet–Iranian company for exploration and drilling with a
51 percent Soviet share. Although the Soviet leaders acknowledged that
Azerbaizhan was an internal affair, they pressed for specific changes in
the political life of the region, including the recognition of the provincial council as the Majlis of Azerbaizhan, the acceptance of the Prime
Minister, Pishevari, as governor, and the allocation of a quarter of
the province's tax revenue for local government and the remainder for
social and economic reform. They promised that the partial evacuation
of the Soviet Army would begin on March 2, but that the remainder

---

[81] This is also the view of Fawcett, *Iran and the Cold War*.
[82] Homayounpour, *L'affaire*, pp. 225–7; Ladjevardi, *Labor Unions*, pp. 261–2; USNA,
RM, box 20118.

would be withdrawn only when relations between Moscow and Teheran improved.

The Iranian delegation responded evasively on the joint stock company and refused to treat Azerbaizhan any differently from any other region of Iran, insisting that its culture was Farsi (Persian). The second formal set of Soviet proposals returned to the idea of an outright concession, withdrew all suggestions about the future of Azerbaizhan and justified the continued presence of the Soviet Army by claiming that relations with Iran had not been based on friendship since the October revolution. Complaining that the Soviet Union had been treated unfairly compared to Great Britain, the Soviet draft ended in a veiled threat: "the existence of unfriendly elements and adherence to a discriminatory policy towards the Soviet Union may result in the implementation of point 6 of the 1921 treaty with Iran; that is the right of the Soviet Union to enter Iran and defend itself in the event that foreign forces in Iran hostile to the Soviet Union threaten its security."[83] At this point Qavam decided to return to Iran but without breaking off the negotiations. He was accompanied by a new Soviet ambassador, Ivan Sadchikov, a Middle East expert fresh from a one-year stint as ambassador to Yugoslavia, who was authorized to continue the talks.

The Soviet position, strong on the surface, was eroding. The Western powers and Iran kept up a steady barrage of criticism on the floor of the United Nations, although there is no truth to President Truman's contention that he sent Stalin an ultimatum to leave Iran or face the consequences.[84] But preparations for the Paris Peace Conference with Hitler's satellites were well under way. With the Iranian case hovering over his head in the UN, Stalin could ill afford to defend non-intervention in the internal affairs of the European borderlands slipping under his control. Moreover, Qavam's position had become shaky in Teheran.

Under the circumstances Qavam represented for Stalin the best he could expect from among the old-style politicians who still dominated the Majlis; there was certainly no hope of a Tudeh government. Almost immediately upon his return to Teheran, Qavam gave Stalin a clear signal of his good intentions. He relaxed the restrictions imposed on the Tudeh, lifted martial law in Teheran, permitted the Tudeh to engage in normal political activities, and arrested half a dozen of the most prominent right-wing politicians who had been agitating against autonomy for Azerbaizhan. Shortly thereafter Sadchikov initialed a four-point

---

[83] Khamahi, *Fursati*, pp. 338–41, based on the published account by one of the Iranian delegates in *Daad* (Justice), nos. 713, 714, 717.
[84] Rouhollah K. Ramazani, *Iran's Foreign Policy, 1941–1973: A Study of Foreign Policy in Modernizing Nations* (University of Virginia Press, 1975), pp. 138–9.

agreement, stipulating Soviet evacuation by May 1946, Iranian withdrawal of its protest to the UN, a settlement between Teheran and Tabriz
"in a peaceful manner" that would respect the need for reforms and the
Iranian constitution, and submission to the Majlis by Qavam of a proposal to establish a joint Iranian–Soviet oil company with a fifty-year lease
and an equal division of profits. Qavam followed up with fresh overtures
to the left. Qavam's vigorous actions against the right and his acceptance
of this agreement convinced Stalin that nothing more could be gained.
A month after the Soviet withdrawal was completed Qavam reached an
agreement with the Firqeh.

The negotiations defining autonomy for Azerbaizhan were tough and
prolonged with the Soviet ambassador, Sadchikov, playing a strong mediating role. Pishevari warned his colleagues that Azerbaizhan had to make
concessions "because the Americans and British are using the Azerbaizhan question to play tricks with our big friend, the Soviet Union."
He rejected calls for the defense of Azerbaizhan's frontiers by reminding them that "their frontiers stretched beyond Azerbaizhan."[85] It was a
familiar refrain claiming the priority of Soviet interests in local conflicts.
Recognizing this, Qavam threatened to resign if the talks collapsed. Stalin
knew that this could only lead to a renewal of the civil war and international complications that he sought to avoid. The most intractable issues
were not the provincial councils or the use of Azeri but internal security
and the agrarian question. In June 1946 a compromise was hammered
out between the central Iranian government and the representatives of
Azerbaizhan. But the agreement soon collapsed.

The Shah, backed by the army, forced Qavam to order the repression of
Kurdish and Azerbaizhani autonomy. The Soviet ambassador denounced
Qavam as an agent of the British and issued veiled threats of Soviet
retaliation. At the same time he had been pressing Pishevari to avoid a
clash with Teheran. The Soviet government was caught on the horns of a
dilemma. To have made good its threat would have meant the end of any
chance to obtain ratification of an oil concession by the Majlis and most
probably a British or Anglo-American move in the south to partition
Iran. To stand by while the autonomous movements were crushed might
sound the death knell for Tudeh influence in Iran.[86] Stalin opted for the
latter course.

The closest thing we have to an explanation of Stalin's thinking is
contained in a letter he wrote to Pishevari in May 1946 justifying Soviet

[85] Robert Rossow Jr., "The Battle of Azerbaizhan, 1946," *Middle Eastern Journal* 10
(Winter, 1956), p. 25. Rossow was the American consul in Tabriz, strongly anti-Soviet,
rather alarmist, but a reliable eyewitness of events.
[86] Azimi, *The Crisis of Democracy*, pp. 160–2; Abrahamian, *Iran*, pp. 237–9, 413.

policy in Iran. He reproached the Firqeh leader for having misjudged the situation within and outside Iran. There were numerous conditions, he declared, that precluded an immediate revolutionary solution. First, "there is no profound revolutionary crisis in Iran." There were too few workers and they were poorly organized. The peasantry was passive. In the absence of an external war, there was no chance for the army to be defeated. Second, the Soviet forces in Iran that would have assisted in a revolutionary struggle were obliged to withdraw in order to deny the British and Americans an excuse for keeping their troops in Egypt, Syria, Indonesia, Greece, China, Iceland and Denmark. Given the lost chance "to unfold the struggle in Azerbaizhan and organize a broad democratic movement with far-reaching demands" (an elliptic formulation which suggests the pursuit of a popular democracy rather than a revolutionary seizure of power), the proper tactic was now to support Qavam and isolate the anglophiles, while wrenching concessions from him. To break with Qavam would be "stupidity." Stalin concluded by rejecting Pishevari's complaints about being let down and disgraced. He reassured Pishevari that had he not pressed the government hard he would not have gained a basis for legalizing the autonomy of Azerbaizhan.[87]

It would appear, then, that Stalin had in mind using the autonomous movement in Azerbaizhan and to a lesser extent in Kurdistan as a base or lever to promote a radicalization of Iranian politics throughout the country rather than to detach and annex Iranian territory. If he were running true to form, he probably was willing to let Bagirov and his agents go as far as they could in supporting the autonomous movements without involving the Soviet Army or compromising the main line of his diplomacy. At the very least an autonomous Azerbaizhan within Iran would provide both protection against British and American control of the entire country right up to the Soviet border and a constant pressure point on Iranian domestic politics. When the operation became too risky he abandoned it to twist in the wind. That is what he did in 1920, and he repeated the performance in 1946.

China and its borderlands

In China Stalin's policy of promoting a friendly government was based on three assumptions, none of which were shared by either the Nationalists or the Communists. First, no party would be strong enough to control

---

[87] "Joseph V. Stalin to Ja'afar Pishevari, Leader of the Democratic Party of Azerbaizhan, 8 May, 1946," from AVP RF, f. 06, op. 7, d. 544, ll. 8–9, as cited *in extenso* as Appendix to Natalia I. Yegorova, "The Iran Crisis of 1945–1946: A View from the Russian Archives," Cold War International History Project Working Paper 15 (May, 1996), pp. 23–4.

the entire country after the war; second, civil war should be prevented in the interests of both the Soviet Union and the United States which would inevitably be drawn in on opposite sides if the fighting broke out; and, third, China and the Western powers would have to recognize preeminent Soviet interests in the borderlands of Xinjiang, Outer Mongolia and Manchuria. Toward the end of the war both the Nationalists and the Communists were preparing to take up positions that flatly contradicted Stalin's China policy.

Stalin remained remarkably consistent in his commitment to the idea of cooperation between the Communists and the Nationalists, first against Japan in the 1930s and then after the Japanese surrender, as the only means to avoid a civil war. In August 1945 he urged the Chinese Communists to join in discussions with the Kuomintang to reconstruct the country: "If a civil war were to break out," he informed them, "the Chinese nation itself would face self-destruction."[88] At the same time, during the negotiations in Moscow he assured the Chinese Foreign Minister, T. V. Soong, of his disinterest in the Chinese Communists: "we do not support them and have no intention of supporting them . . . China must have only one government and one armed force."[89] As late as 1948, Stalin was still actively seeking to mediate between the warring sides in China. New evidence shows that even in 1949 he warned Mao against crossing the Yangtze River and urged the establishment of a coalition government. Stalin was gravely concerned that an impending victory of the Chinese Communists would trigger American intervention.[90]

Mongolia

In the latter stages of the war Stalin's main concern in China, after securing the strategic strong points, was to take additional steps to bolster

---

[88] Cited in Jian Chen, *Mao's China and the Cold War* (Chapel Hill: University of North Carolina Press, 2001), pp. 27–8; see also Shuguang Zhang, "'Preparedness Eliminates Mishaps': The CCP's Security Concerns in 1949–1950 and the Origins of Sino-American Confrontation," *Journal of American–East Asian Relations* 1 (Spring, 1992), especially pp. 43–9.

[89] Garver, *Chinese–Soviet Relations*, pp. 220–1.

[90] Donggil Kim, "The Crucial Issues of the Early Cold War: Stalin and the Chinese Civil War," *Cold War History* 10:2 (2010), pp. 185–202, and Odd Arne Westad, *Decisive Encounters: The Chinese Civil War 1946–1950* (Stanford University Press, 2003), pp. 49–50 and 119–20. Throughout the postwar period, Soviet specialists on China were optimistic about the possibility of a coalition despite the fact that they perceived Chiang as an instrument of American foreign policy. See, for example, the reports of the Soviet representative in China on the "Political and Economic Situation in the China for 1946," RGASPI, f. 17, op. 128, d. 180, ll. 7, 8, 14–19, 28, 31–2, 75–6 and appendix (March 12, 1947), l. 90.

the Soviet influence in the borderlands adjacent to China. He was able to pursue his aims in Outer Mongolia and Xinjiang without becoming directly involved in the nascent civil war. The Soviet victories in the unofficial war against Japan in 1938 and again in 1939 had enabled their most loyal supporter in Outer Mongolia, Choibalsang, to eliminate his rivals and consolidate his position as unchallenged leader of the country. Although his rivals had concluded a trade agreement with the USSR in 1934, they apparently did not cut all their ties with the Japanese. They were no doubt attracted by the possibility of unifying all the Mongols in Outer and Inner Mongolia with Japanese support. After purging them, Choibalsang claimed – falsely as it turned out – that he nurtured no such ambitions. During the war he maintained a steady flow of supplies to the Soviet Union and kept his army at full strength facing the Japanese forces in Manchuria and Inner Mongolia despite the risks that this entailed. His dedication to the Soviet Union had never been in doubt since his period of training there in 1923. One test of his loyalty was his unwillingness to be drawn into the Nationalist–Communist conflict in China. In a private conversation with Owen Lattimore in 1944, he spoke openly of the inability of "the Chinese," without making a distinction between the parties, to pull together in the war against Japan. In other words, he endorsed the Soviet version of the incipient civil war in China.[91] When the Soviet forces launched their attack on Manchuria in 1945, Choibalsang fully committed his small army to the campaign. Stalin treated his modest but not insignificant contribution as worthy of a brother in arms. Another test was his willingness, however reluctant, to give up his long-concealed aspirations to become the unifier of the Mongol people. These became clear briefly in the course of the tense negotiations in Moscow during the summer of 1945 over the provisions of the Soviet–Chinese Friendship Pact.

Stalin was adamant in insisting that the Yalta agreement on maintaining the "status quo" in Outer Mongolia amounted to recognizing its independence.[92] Stressing its strategic importance, he believed that in the hands of a hostile power like Japan, Outer Mongolia would make the defense of the Soviet Far East virtually impossible. In a private conversation with Chiang's son, Jiang Jingguo, he pointed out that under Japanese influence Outer Mongolia would serve as the jump-off point to cut the Trans-Siberian Railroad. Japan could easily recover its strength in five years, he stated, especially "if its defeat is administered by the United

---

[91] Owen Lattimore, *Nationalism and Revolution in Mongolia* (New York: Oxford University Press, 1955), p. 65.
[92] Garver, *Chinese–Soviet Relations*, pp. 214–30, on which the following relies heavily.

States." Nor was there any guarantee that at some point in the future the US might not use it as a base. As for China, Stalin admitted it was weak, but "once China is united it will make progress faster than any other country," and one could not predict its politics.[93]

In the face of Chinese reluctance to recognize the independence of Outer Mongolia, Stalin resorted to another form of pressure. In his talks with Soong he raised the specter of Mongolian nationalism, hinting that unless China concluded an agreement with the Soviet Union it would face a surge of nationalist feeling in both Outer and Inner Mongolia.[94] There was some substance behind the implied threat. The development of strong sentiments for the autonomy of Inner Mongolia dated from the late 1920s when numbers of younger Mongol aristocrats had supported the Kuomintang in the belief that it took seriously Sun Yat-sen's principles of racial equality and regional autonomy. In return they expected concessions that would preserve their traditional way of life in Inner Mongolia. But Chiang's government intensified the colonization and drafted plans to ring the tribal lands with administrative units under the control of the central bureaucracy. Moreover, the Mongol republicans who favored autonomy were undercut by some of their own princes who aided and abetted the process of sinicization in order to preserve their political influence.[95] In desperation, the autonomists, led by De Wang (Prince Demchugdongrob) of the West Sunid Banner and other veterans of the abortive pro-Kuomintang movement among the Mongols, turned to the Japanese who equipped them with arms and supplies. But they still found themselves too weak to overcome the power of the local warlords who remained loyal to Chiang.

New opportunities opened up with the Japanese invasion in 1937. The Kwantung Army rapidly occupied Inner Mongolia but then committed a series of political blunders. They created a Federated Autonomous

---

[93] Chiang Ching-kuo, "My Encounter with Stalin," in Dun J. Li, *Modern China: From Mandarin to Commissar* (New York: Scribner's, 1978), pp. 300–1. This is the translation of excerpts from Chiang's long article, "My Father," originally published in the 1950s and reprinted in the *Central Daily News*, Taiwan, April 15–16, 1975. Although occasionally journalistic, even melodramatic, in tone, the account appears to be factually accurate in its main outlines. Stalin justified Soviet control over the Chinese Eastern Railroad in similar terms. According to the Chinese ambassador in Moscow, he stated that "the USSR need the use of the CER during the 30 years required to make the Soviet Far East impregnable against an attack by Japan." FRUS (1946), vol. X, p. 569.

[94] Odd Arne Westad, *Cold War and Revolution: Soviet American Rivalry and the Origins of the Chinese Civil War* (New York: Columbia University Press, 1993), p. 37.

[95] Owen Lattimore, "On The Wickedness of Being Nomad," reprinted in Lattimore, *Studies in Frontier History: Collected Papers, 1928–1958* (The Hague: Mouton, 1967), pp. 416–19.

Government of Mongolia but then ignored the advice of their Mongol experts. In Lattimore's telling judgment they "killed what Japanese statesmanship might have accomplished." The Mongol appointees were mere figureheads; Japanese bureaucrats ran the administrative offices; and exploitation of the Mongol herds disrupted the region's natural pastoral economy. The possibility was lost of creating a Mengkukuo or Independent Mongol Nation modeled on Manchukuo.[96]

On the eve of the Soviet attack on Japan, the fate of Inner Mongolia once again hung in the balance. At a critical moment in the Soviet–Chinese negotiations in Moscow in August 1945, Chiang Kai-shek insisted that recognition of Outer Mongolian independence would depend on a preliminary delimitation of the disputed region of Altai on the boundary with Xinjiang. Stalin had no intention of claiming the Altai for Outer Mongolia, but he was concerned that Chiang was using the issue of boundary delimitation as an excuse to avoid recognition of Outer Mongolian independence. Therefore, he "upped the ante" by invoking for the second time and more strongly the threat of Mongolian nationalism and gave some encouragement to Choibalsang's aspirations to unify the Mongol people.[97] Joining the Soviet forces in attacking Japan, the troops of the Mongolian People's Republic were assigned the liberation of the entire area of Prince De's Autonomous Mongolian State but not the territories east of the Khinggan range of mountains which were, according to Christopher Atwood, "the heartland of the educational and nationalist renaissance that had occurred in Inner Mongolia under Japanese patronage." These were to be occupied by Soviet forces. Organizers and propagandists of the Mongolian People's Republic and public statements by Choibalsang extolled the cause of Mongolian unity, but these voices fell silent once the Chinese government had ratified the Soviet–Chinese Treaty of Friendship. Choibalsang had fallen into line again. The Chinese Communists then brought the autonomous movement under their control.[98] For Stalin the cause of Mongol unity was merely a pawn in his broader policy of keeping to the letter of the Yalta agreements, reaching an accommodation with the Chinese Nationalist government while taking no action to oppose the activities of the Chinese Communists who also opposed the unity of the Mongols.

[96] Lattimore, "The Phantom of Mengkukuo," *Pacific Affairs* 10:4 (December, 1937), reprinted *ibid.*, p. 404.

[97] Garver, *Chinese–Soviet Relations*, p. 227, and Christopher Atwood, "Sino-Soviet Diplomacy and the Second Partition of Mongolia, 1945–1946," in Stephen Kotkin and Bruce A. Elleman (eds.), *Mongolia in the Twentieth Century: Landlocked Cosmopolitan* (Armonk, NY: M. E. Sharpe, 1999), pp. 137–48.

[98] Atwood, "Sino-Soviet Diplomacy," pp. 152–3, 157.

Xinjiang

In the latter stages of the war, the Stalin exploited his military successes in the west to recover and expand his influence in Xinjiang. By the time of the Soviet–Japanese Neutrality Treaty, the British consul in Kashgar was able to report on the complete recovery of Russian influence from the imperial days. Four objectives guided Soviet policy: to exclude Nanking's influence, to prevent a return of the Gansu Muslim forces; to prevent further rebellions of the indigenous Muslims; and to block a possible Japanese thrust from their bases in Inner Mongolia.[99] But the instrument of his policy, Sheng Shicai, proved to be a typical borderland opportunist. When the Germans stood at the gates of Moscow, he began to shift his allegiance to the Kuomintang. He resisted Soviet proposals to form a joint stock company for the exploitation of the Dushanze oil fields which were supplying the Red Army. When Moscow attempted to blackmail him by turning over incriminating evidence of his pro-Soviet activities to Chiang Kai-shek, he renounced his former patrons, appealing to Chiang and accusing the Soviet Union of seeking to establish a soviet regime in Xinjiang. As the German summer offensive of 1942 approached the Volga, he abandoned his tolerant nationality policy, arrested Communist advisors and Uighur nationalists, executed Mao Zemin, the brother of Mao Zedong, and restored his strained personal relations with Chiang.[100] Brusquely, he demanded the withdrawal of all Soviet military and civilian personnel.

Stalin retaliated. He pulled out not only the Soviet regiment stationed at Hami and civilian personnel but all the equipment and material for the operation of the tin and wolfram mines and the oil fields as well as the aircraft factory and other installations.[101] The Soviet withdrawal precipitated a major crisis in the province. Ninety percent of the region's

---

[99] Forbes, Warlords, pp. 141–8, 155; Whiting and Sheng Shih-ts'ai, Sinkiang, pp. 269–84, reproduces the text of the tin agreement. Forbes challenges the views of Lattimore, Whiting and Jack Chen in The Sinkiang Story (New York: Macmillan, 1977), on the progressive nature of Sheng's cultural and educational reforms. James A. Millward, Eurasian Crossroads: A History of Xinjiang (New York: Columbia University Press, 2007), pp. 224–30, reviews the contradictory evidence on the Soviet role in the East Turkestan Republic.

[100] Lattimore, Pivot of Asia, pp. 74–8; Forbes, Warlords, pp. 157–62. Writing to Chiang Kai-shek, Molotov and Stalin denied that the Soviet Union intended to annex or sovietize Xinjiang. Chiang accepted the denial but insisted that henceforth all Soviet contacts with the province should be made through his office. P. A. Mirovitskaia, Kitaiskaia gosudarstvennost' i sovetskaia politika v Kitae. Gody Tikhookeanskoi voiny: 1941–1945 (Moscow: Pamiatniki istoricheskoi mysli, 1999), pp. 90–2.

[101] Garver, Chinese–Soviet Relations, pp. 166–77. Provincial authorities hampered and harassed the withdrawal. Mirovitskaia, Kitaiskaia gosudarstvennost', pp. 122–3.

exports had gone to the Soviet Union when trade was abruptly interrupted. Inflation, held down with the help of Soviet advisors, began to catch up with the rest of China. The loss of foreign aid was also keenly felt in the two major sectors of the economy, agriculture and animal husbandry, where Soviet technical experts had checked the long decline in productivity going back to the 1920s. Sheng Shicai shattered the ethnic peace in order to placate Chungking. Over ten thousand Chinese officials flooded the province, expelling the Uighurs and Kazakhs who had occupied important posts in Sheng's provincial government.

The sudden loss of markets for the Kazakh herdsmen, combined with the restoration of Sheng's neo-colonial administration, touched off a revolt. It began in the winter of 1943–4 in the Altai region where the economic slump and influx of bureaucratic carpetbaggers had aroused a bitter reaction. The fighting spread rapidly to other ethnic groups, including the local Mongols, Uighurs and Turkic tribes, until it enveloped the whole of the Altai, Ili and Chuguchak regions and threatened the capital of Urumchi. The rebels buried their differences in a common front against the Chinese. They proclaimed an East Turkestan Republic in imitation of the insurrectionary movement of the 1930s but broadened its appeal by dropping the word "Muslim" from their banners.[102]

By this time the Red Army had recovered. Bolstered by the victories at Stalingrad and Kursk, it was poised to deliver a devastating blow to the German central front, opening the way to an invasion of Central Europe. At the same time, the Japanese Ichigo offensive had delivered an almost fatal blow to the Chinese Nationalist armies. Sheng reversed his opinion again and appealed for Soviet assistance – in vain, as it turned out. His maladroit maneuvering had intensified domestic opposition and further complicated the international position of Xinjiang.

Stalin not only rejected Sheng's overtures but stepped up Soviet support for the rebellion, despite the fact that it represented "a nomadic reaction to agricultural encroachment and centralized authority [lacked] a coherent political philosophy and remained essentially anarchic in character."[103] The Soviet Union provided military advisors, training and weapons to an Ili National Army and to Kazakh guerrillas. In the tradition of frontier zones, the nomadic Kazakh tribesmen ignored the state boundary lines, crossing into the sanctuary of Soviet Kazakhstan when necessary, only to reappear later at another border point. Outer

---

[102] Whiting and Sheng Shih-ts'ai, *Sinkiang*, pp. 99–101; N. G. Mingulov, "Natsional'no-osvobozhditel'noe dvizhenie v Sindzhange," in *Voprosy istorii Kazakhstana i vostochnogo Turkestana* (Alma Ata: Tarik, 1962).
[103] Forbes, *Warlords*, 170–2, quotation on p. 172.

Mongolian troops also became involved in assisting the rebels. The Soviet position was sufficiently strong to have detached the province from China in the same way as it had promoted independence for Outer Mongolia. But this would have violated the Yalta agreements and alienated the Nationalist Chinese and the Americans at a time when he was seeking to consolidate his influence in the Eurasian borderlands.

Abandoned by Stalin, Sheng was removed by Chiang who sought to reimpose Chinese control over the rebellious province. Pressed by T. V. Soong, Molotov appended a note to the Treaty of Alliance and Friendship stating, "as for the recent developments in Xinjiang, the Soviet government confirms that . . . it has no intention of interfering in the internal affairs of China." But Kuomintang officials in Urumchi were not so easily satisfied. They threatened to make an international issue out of the alleged Soviet intervention unless Moscow agreed to mediate between the rebels and the provincial government. Stalin could not have planned it better himself. The "ultimatum" perfectly suited his interests in the region.

It hardly mattered to Stalin that there was no Communist Party in Xinjiang. The Turkic rebels would serve his purposes just as well. The Soviet consul-general in Urumchi made it perfectly clear to them that his government would not recognize the independence of the East Turkestan Republic or accept their demands that all Nationalist officials and troops evacuate Xinjiang. He sponsored a compromise agreement in January 1946 that led to the formation of a coalition provincial government with several important posts going to the rebels, including the vice-chairman and the heads of the education and welfare departments. The Kuomintang representatives also accepted the rebel demand that national languages be introduced into the local schools and Muslim army units.[104] Soviet mediation in Xinjiang ran parallel to similar initiatives in Northern Iran and Manchuria: an Asian variation of the East European borderlands strategy was taking shape. The Soviet position remained dominant until the arrival of the Chinese Communists in 1949.

Manchuria

From the Yalta Conference until the end of the Chinese civil war, Stalin conspired to make certain that no matter who ruled in China Soviet influence would be paramount in the borderlands. Although Stalin's

---

[104] Whiting and Sheng Shih-ts'ai, *Sinkiang*, pp. 110–11; Lattimore, *Pivot of Asia*, pp. 88–90; O. E. Clubb, *China and Russia* (New York: Columbia University Press), p. 367; Herbert Feis, *The China Tangle* (Princeton University Press, 1953), pp. 318–19, 378–9.

objectives were similar to those of his tsarist and early Soviet predecessors, the big difference in 1945 was the military capability of the colossus of the north. Once assured of victory over Nazi Germany, the Soviet forces would be free to settle old scores with the Kwantung Army from a position of overwhelming military superiority. In Manchuria, strategically the most important of the three border regions, the massive attack against the Japanese in August 1945 plunged Soviet troops into the thick of the Nationalist–Communist scramble for control over the province. In a whirlwind campaign the Soviet Far Eastern Command shattered the Kwantung Army, the only Japanese force in mainland China to be defeated in the field. For an entire week after the Japanese unconditional surrender, the Soviet Army continued to advance until it had occupied the entire region and parts of Jehol and Chahar provinces as well. Its commander, General Rodion Malinovskii, had the political experience of having liberated Romania, and he proceeded to treat Manchuria in a similar fashion. His relations with the official representatives of the Nationalist government were correct, for the most part, but not very helpful. At the same time, he permitted the indigenous anti-Japanese forces to take over the local administration and help the Soviet forces maintain order.

The Chinese negotiators insisted on holding the Soviet Union to the three-month schedule for the withdrawal of its troops from Manchuria. Stalin and Molotov did not argue but admitted to being puzzled as to why there was no similar time limit imposed on the American withdrawal from China. Disagreement of a different sort flared over the status of the Changchun branch of the Southern Manchurian Railroad. The Soviet side resisted Chinese efforts to secure exclusive rights to move troops along this line, a setback to the Nationalists that cost them dearly in the early stages of their race with the Communists to get back to Manchuria.[105] The Chinese further demanded assurances that the Soviet Union would not assist the Chinese Communists in any way and would only cooperate with the central government. The official Soviet response was limited to the declaration that it would help China against the Japanese and that it viewed the Communist–Nationalist rivalry as a domestic problem in which the Soviet Union would not interfere. When pressed, Stalin allegedly put it more bluntly: "What do you want me to do? To fight against Mao?"[106] The final version of the treaty of alliance,

[105] A. M. Ledovskii, *SSSR, SShA i narodnaia revoliutsiia v Kitae* (Moscow: Nauka, 1979), pp. 53–8.
[106] *Ibid.*, p. 82; Brian Crozier, *The Man Who Lost China: The First Full Biography of Chiang Kai-shek* (New York: Scribner's, 1976), p. 273.

signed in August 1945, left much unresolved, in particular concerning Sino-Soviet economic relations. In light of what was already known by that time about Soviet economic policies in Romania and the eastern zone of Germany, this was from the point of view of the Nationalist government a fateful omission.

In the northeast border areas, Stalin was able to use the strong regional Communist armed forces to put pressure on the Nationalists in order to obtain his strategic aims. But the Soviet Army did not turn Manchuria over to the Communists. On the contrary, at the time the chances were probably even that Stalin would allow the Nationalists to take it back, under certain conditions. But in the end they did not meet his price and they were left to fight it out with the Communists.

Stalin had not concealed from the Nationalists his main interests in the borderlands. In the negotiations over the Treaty of Friendship, he had sought to impress upon Chiang that the prospects of the Nationalists recovering Manchuria, and Xinjiang as well, depended upon their recognizing the paramount Soviet interests in these regions. He strongly opposed American attempts, in cooperation with the Nationalists, to secure a military or economic foothold in the region. The civil war in the northeast became a testing ground of Soviet and American influence in China. When the Americans agreed to Chiang's request to use warships of the Seventh Amphibious Force to ferry Nationalist troops to Dairen, Moscow's reaction was swift and uncompromising. Stalin refused permission for the Americans to land on the grounds that this would violate Dairen's status as a "commercial port" defined in the Sino-Soviet Treaty of Friendship. Stalin was resorting to a technicality. The terms of the treaty described Port Arthur as "an exclusive naval base [to] be used only by Chinese and Soviet military and commercial vessels." There were no such restrictions imposed on the use of Dairen during peacetime, but the treaty specified that the port "shall be subject to the military supervision or control established in this zone only in case of war against Japan." Malinovskii claimed that in so far as a state of war with Japan still existed, the port must be "considered subject to Soviet military regulations."[107]

In his talks with T. V. Soong in August 1945 Stalin had pressed the Chinese for a Soviet lease over the entire Liaotung peninsula that would have placed Dairen under the same restrictions as Port Arthur. He had not won his point because the US had intervened in the negotiations to

---

[107] For separate notes on the administration of Port Arthur and Dairen, see Aitchen Wu, *China and the Soviet Union* (New York: J. Day, 1950), pp. 407–11; for the controversy over Dairen, FRUS, *China* (1946), vol. X, pp. 1167–74.

stiffen Soong's resistance. By blocking US access to Dairen, Stalin was stretching the letter of the treaty while remaining true to his interpretation of its spirit: the Americans were to be kept out of Manchuria. The same attitude underlay Stalin's and Molotov's refusal to put in writing their grudging verbal assurance to Harriman and Byrnes that the doctrine of the open door would be applied to Dairen.[108]

From Stalin's perspective Chiang had violated the spirit of the treaty by relying on American naval power to get him back into Manchuria. After the American ships retired from Dairen, they attempted to disembark Nationalist troops at the two smaller Manchurian ports of Hukutao and Yankow, but found them already in the hands of the Chinese Communists. Malinovskii rejected Chiang's request to cover the landing of the Nationalist forces from the American vessels. The Soviet commander claimed that his army had already evacuated the area and could not intervene in the relations between governmental and "non-government" forces in Manchuria on the grounds that this was purely an internal affair. The American ships backed off again, fearing a clash. Shortly thereafter, Malinovskii informed the Nationalist representatives that he had no objection "in principle" to American transport planes ferrying Nationalist troops to Manchurian airfields. But he insisted that the flights could only begin on the eve of Soviet withdrawals and rejected requests to accept advanced parties of American technicians in order to secure and prepare the landing sites.[109] Within days of this announcement, Chinese Communist troops occupied the main airfield at Ch'angch'un. Stalin was not closing the door on Manchuria to Chiang; he was merely reminding him who the doorman was.

The subsequent activity of the Soviet army in Manchuria has sparked historical controversy among Soviet, Chinese and Western historians over Soviet motives. The reason for the confusion is not hard to find. Stalin was playing his habitually devious game which allows for divergent interpretations. For all his tactical flexibility his actions reveal a consistent purpose: to secure Soviet hegemony in the Chinese borderlands; to exclude American influence from these regions; to ensure the establishment in China of a friendly legally constituted government in which the Communists would play a prominent but not dominant role.

The timing and conditions of Soviet withdrawal from Manchuria were a crucial component of Stalin's policy. Despite treaty obligations, the

---

[108] Feis, *The China Tangle*, pp. 328, 345.
[109] Ledovskii, *SSSR, SShA*, pp. 125–7. Ledovskii was a high-ranking specialist in Chinese affairs from 1942 to 1952 and though he does not explicitly cite Soviet archives, it is clear that he has relied upon them as well as his own personal diary to describe the events he witnessed.

Soviet forces postponed their evacuation until May 1946. On two occasions they induced the Nationalist government itself to request a delay, and on the third occasion they unilaterally declared their intention of remaining beyond the deadline that had been jointly agreed upon. The parallel with Azerbaizhan is obvious, if not exact. In the two cases, the pattern of Soviet relations with the regional and central authorities was roughly similar. Only the outcome was radically different. What made the difference in Manchuria was not the level of Soviet aid but the strength of the local Communist forces.

By the terms of the Yalta Conference and the Treaty of Friendship, the Soviet Union had already obtained a strong economic foothold in the northeast. It either controlled directly or shared jointly with the Chinese the administration of the major ports of Port Arthur and Dairen and the Chinese Eastern and Southern Manchurian Railroads. The next step was to integrate the transportation system with the large industrial complex built by the Japanese over the previous fifteen years. Manchurian industry had survived the war almost unscathed. American air raids had damaged only a few large plants. In a war-ravaged world Manchurian industrial production ranked fourth after the three surviving giants, the US, the USSR and Great Britain. But the Chinese negotiators in Moscow in the summer of 1945 had failed to pin down the Russians on the disposal of this extraordinary resource. Stalin immediately exploited the opening.

The civilian representatives of the Chinese Nationalist government negotiating with the Soviet military and economic personnel in Southern Manchuria understood fully the price for Soviet support for a Nationalist recovery of Manchuria. It was no less than a Sino-Soviet economic condominium in the region. In Manchuria, as in Azerbaizhan, the overriding Soviet aim was to make certain that no matter who ended up in nominal control of the border region, Soviet economic and political interests would be recognized as paramount.[110] The postwar negotiations dragged on. In December 1945 the Nationalists took a series of decisions that spelled their doom in Manchuria. Chiang and his top associates refused to budge on their demands that the Soviet forces withdraw before any

[110] Donald G. Gillin and Raymond H. Myers (eds.), *Last Chance in Manchuria: The Diary of Chang Kia-gnau* (Stanford University Press, 1989). A perspicacious member of the political science clique, Chang accurately summed up the Soviet strategy: "the Soviets have a regional strategy for the northeast that will not be altered by any change in the international situation." *Ibid.*, p. 188. He had taken the measure of Soviet policy when, as Minister of Transportation in the Nationalist government, he had worked closely with Soviet military advisors in the late 1930s. Kaliagin, *Po neznakomym dorogam*, p. 219.

economic agreement could be signed. He turned a deaf ear to his two best-informed advisors on the ground in Manchuria: the chief negotiator Chang and his own son Chiang Ching-kuo. It was then that Chiang Kai-shek lost his best chance of reaching a compromise with Stalin along the lines of the Azerbaizhan settlement.

Conclusion: A transient hegemony

In the closing months of the war, Stalin was forced to recognize that his policy of maintaining the wartime coalition into the postwar period, and at the same time tightening his grip on the Eurasian borderlands, was coming apart. Although the show of unity among the Big Three at Potsdam appeared to paste over the growing divergence, it was increasingly evident that the British, and especially the Americans, were no longer prepared to accept the Soviet interpretation of the Declaration on Liberated Territories or what constituted the essential elements in Stalin's view of a "friendly country."[1] Moreover, the anti-Communist elements abroad and in the territories liberated, or, as they insisted, "occupied" by the Red Army, took encouragement from the public disagreements among the erstwhile allies. They hoped for a breakup of the wartime alliance and even anticipated an armed conflict between the Western powers and the Soviet Union.[2] From Stalin's point of view these hopes and expectations resembled those expressed by Hitler and Goebbels during the last stages of the war, and confirmed his already deeply held suspicions that

---

[1] In the fall of 1945, Stalin showed signs of growing impatience and irritability in reaction to the American and British resistance to his policies in the Balkans and demands for an increased role in the Advisory Commission for Japan. This showed up most strikingly in the tone and brusque language of his instructions to Molotov, which had no precedence in their long relationship. See Vladimir O. Pechatnov, "'The Allies Are Pressing on You to Break Your Will...': Foreign Policy Correspondence Between Stalin and Molotov and Other Politburo Members, September 1945–December 1946," Working Paper no. 26, Cold War International History Project (Washington, DC: Woodrow Wilson International Center for Scholars, September 1999).

[2] See, for example, the remarks of General Władysław Anders to Mikołajczek in August 1944, and to a member of the American embassy in Paris in May 1945, about the necessity and inevitability of war between the United States and the Soviet Union. Keith Sword et al., The Formation of the Polish Community in Great Britain, 1939–1950 (London: School of Slavonic and East European Studies, University of London, 1989), p. 196, and Tyler Thompson to State, US Department of State, Central Files, 1945–1949 The Soviet Union, reel one, May 13, 1945. Maiskii reported from London in the summer of 1944 that members of the Polish government-in-exile also anticipated an American–Soviet war, which would then bring them to power in Warsaw. AVP f. referentura po Pol'she, op. 26i, pap. 308, delo 031, ll. 12–16.

resistance of any kind to the Soviet definition of a "friendly government" was "objectively" speaking tantamount to fascism.

Consequently, Stalin began to withdraw to his traditional borderland thesis, conceiving the Soviet Union as an embattled fortress but now buttressed by defensive outworks that could at some future, more auspicious time become the launching pads for a renewed political offensive. This shift meant that the consolidation of the inner periphery assumed greater importance, evolving into a series of concentric security zones. In the first zone, the re-sovietization of the liberated regions of the USSR within its 1940 borders accelerated as hostilities came to an end in Europe. At the same time, within the Soviet core Stalin dashed wartime hopes for a relaxation of controls and an end to repressive measures. The restoration of the collective farm system and the suppression of anti-Soviet guerrilla bands in the forests of Belorussia and West Ukraine, and the deportations of national minorities from frontier areas, alternated with amnesties and hard-driving political work.

A second zone was made up of advanced military bases and annexed territories: strategic "strong points," as Stalin once called them. Facing Finland these included the far northern point of Petsamo, the naval base at Hängo in the vicinity of Helsinki, and a defensive glacis for Leningrad in Ingria. To strengthen Soviet and diminish German presence on the Baltic the city of Königsberg and its environs in East Prussia were annexed. On the edges of the Pontic steppe, the formerly Czech territory of Sub-Carpatho Ukraine, with its predominantly Ukrainian population, was annexed, giving the Soviet Union a common frontier with Czechoslovakia for the first time; such a frontier in 1938 during the pre-Munich crisis would have made an enormous difference in the Soviet strategic situation vis-à-vis its treaty obligations to assist the Czechs against Hitler's threats. Further south the reoccupation of Bessarabia restored the Soviet position as a riparian power on the Danube. Stalin's failure to acquire bases in the Straits and the return of the provinces of Kars and Ardahan in the South Caucasus was the sole glaring gap in this section of the second zone.

In Asia, the second security zone was formed by the annexation of Tanu Tuva in 1944, the Soviet-sponsored independence of Outer Mongolia, the reacquisition of the Chinese Eastern Railroad in Manchuria and Port Arthur, the recognition of Dairen as a "free port," the restoration of Southern Sakhalin lost to Japan in 1905, and the acquisition of the northern Kurile Islands, providing an exit point for the Soviet Far Eastern Fleet into the open Pacific. Finally, the occupation of Korea north of the thirty-eighth parallel fulfilled part of the dream of the tsarist admirals and provided a buffer for the Soviet Maritime Provinces.

A third zone comprising "friendly governments" began to take shape by the end of the war. In keeping with Stalin's idea of different roads to socialism, inaugurated by his abolition of the Comintern, "friendly governments" exhibited both similar general characteristics in line with Soviet security concerns and specific features that reflected local socioeconomic conditions and the strength of local Communist parties. In Europe Soviet authorities used the term "popular democracies," although Stalin preferred "democracies of a new type." He employed neither of these terms in referring to postwar Iran or China. In dealing with these two countries, his main concern was to obtain economic concessions in Azerbaizhan, Xinjiang and Manchuria, both to strengthen the Soviet economy and to prevent the penetration of Western capital into borderlands adjacent to Soviet territory. His reluctance to endorse a more ambitious political program derived from his stated opinion that neither the Tudeh nor the Chinese Communist Party were sufficiently proletarian to carry out a socialist transformation. In any case, Stalin had no timetable for the transition of a "friendly government" into a popular democracy or some other kind of intermediate phase. The pace and extent of the change would depend on a number of factors which he was not willing to predict.

A more faintly drawn fourth zone lay outside the Eurasian borderlands and beyond the reach of the Red Army. These were countries Stalin had tacitly recognized within the British or American spheres of influence. But they had Communist parties which had played a leading role in the resistance, as in Belgium, France, Italy and Greece, or else, as in the case of Japan, had reemerged from a lengthy period of repression with the potential to occupy an important place in postwar politics. They were encouraged to operate within a legal, constitutional framework along the lines of the so-called "parliamentary road" to socialism. This option was, apparently, also open to Finland and Czechoslovakia, where free postwar elections returned large Communist representations at the national level. The primary function of the Communist parties in the fourth zone was to oppose the formation of anti-Soviet governments and political alignments with Great Britain and the United States in a new version of capitalist encirclement.[3]

---

[3] Stalin showed little interest in promoting Communist parties outside these perimeters, despite the prospects for revolution which were considerable in the colonial areas. In addition to his disdainful attitude toward peasant-based movements, he deferred to metropolitan Communist parties, like the French, which saw their own success as the prerequisite and best guarantee of anti-colonial revolutions. Indo-China was a striking example. See the essays in Christopher E. Goscha and Christian F. Osterman (eds.),

This analysis is not to suggest that the appearance of these zones was in any way predetermined, or even that they were envisaged in this way by Stalin or the local Communist parties. Rather it represents a conceptual scheme that reflects real power relationships on the ground within the context of Stalin's general thinking about the role of borderlands and the outer world, which may be traced back to his early revolutionary career and experiences in the civil war. Nor is there any intention here of drawing static, clear-cut lines separating these zones or of predicting changes within them.

Even several years after the end of the war, the question of how Soviet hegemony in Eurasia would be theoretically conceptualized in Marxist-Leninist discourse and politically consolidated remained unanswered by Stalin or his trusted associates.[4] Postwar discussions of how to define the great transformation brought about by the Soviet victory and the transition to socialism had their roots in Lenin's embryonic idea of the "democratic dictatorship of the proletariat and peasantry." His ideas were subsequently embellished by Dimitrov in the late 1930s and revived in the debates over the so-called Varga thesis. Out of this amalgam the concept of popular democracy emerged full-blown by 1949, although even then Stalin declined to include the People's Republic of China within its precincts. From the outset, however, the attempt to consolidate hegemony was deeply flawed.

Within three years of the war Finland remained "friendly" but resisted the transition to a popular democracy. Yugoslavia ceased to remain "friendly," yet retained all the attributes of a popular democracy. Czechoslovakia followed the parliamentary path (according to Stalin's definition) to popular democracy, France and Italy fell short of making the transition. China followed its own direct path to socialism, skipping an intermediate stage and regaining control over the Inner Asian borderlands of Xinjiang and Manchuria. Analyzing the variety of these and other outcomes in the postwar period goes beyond the limits of this book.

At the end of World War II, the Soviet Union under Stalin's leadership had achieved apparent hegemony over the Eurasian borderlands. Beyond that his armies had played a major role in eliminating his only two continental rivals. But the cost had been enormous in material and human losses. In his brusque way of calculating, he acknowledged the war had cost two Five-Year Plans. He never admitted the loss of life, and the full

---

Connecting Histories: Decolonization and the Cold War in Southeast Asia, 1945–1962 (Woodrow Wilson Center, Washington, DC, and Stanford University Press, 2009).

[4] Alfred J. Rieber, "Popular Democracy: An Illusion?," in Vladimir Tismaneanu (ed.), *Stalinism Revisited: The Establishment of Communist Regimes in East-Central Europe* (Budapest: CEU Press 2009), pp. 103–30.

accounting had to wait until *perestroika* when a figure of 27 million dead was officially announced. The number of shattered lives, severely damaged physically or psychologically, is impossible to estimate. So, as always, is the loss of talent. It remains debatable whether the Soviet Union ever fully recovered economically or demographically.[5] The ostensible repair of the wartime destruction and the rise to superpower status was due primarily to the pouring of resources into nuclear and missile hardware. Calculating the cost of applying Stalin's borderland thesis, World War II rightly deserves the appellation of a Pyrrhic victory.

The system survived for another forty-five years, but the end came very suddenly. Like imperial rule in 1917, the will to sustain it no longer existed, and the borderlands exacted their revenge. Soviet hegemony was already beginning to show cracks in 1948 in Yugoslavia, and further weakness showed up in East Germany (1953), Hungary (1956), China (1960s), Czechoslovakia (1968), Romania (late 1960s) Albania (1961 and 1968) and Poland (1980s). By the end, the only countries that had not attempted to break away or had not succeeded in doing so were Bulgaria, which had the oldest and deepest attachment to Russia, and the German Democratic Republic, where a breakaway meant not independence but dissolution. Only part of the erosion can be attributed to the effects of the Cold War with the West. The foundations of hegemony were never strong. Once the defenses of the inner perimeter gave way, the citadel of Russia stood alone.

[5] Mark Harrison, *Accounting for War: Soviet Production, Employment, and the Defence Burden, 1940–1945* (Cambridge University Press, 1996), pp. 164–9.

Index

Aaland Islands, 192
Abkhaziia, 127
Action AB, 204
Adalat (Justice Party), 62
Adamov, E. A., 298
Adzharian Autonomous Republic, 280
Afghanistan, Afghans, 43, 104, 127–8,
   153, 175, 218
Ahmad Qavam, 388–91
All-Union Communist Party (CPSU), 3,
   12, 33, 42, 43, 47, 60, 67, 115, 122,
   146, 148, 154, 177, 182, 241, 320
   Eighteenth Party Congress (1930), 183,
      193
   Eighth Party Congress (1919), 49,
      107
   Fifteenth Party Congress (1927), 95,
      148
   Fourteenth Party Congress (1925), 104
   Fourth Party Conference, 76
   Seventeenth Party Congress (1929),
      154
   Tenth Party Congress (1921), 65, 69,
      74
   Twelfth Party Congress (1923), 65, 68,
      70, 75–9, 119, 122
All-Union Communist University of the
   Toilers of the East, 145
Allied Control Commission (ACC),
   348–9, 354, 357–60, 363, 365
Allied Mediterranean Command, 368
Amanullah, King, 127
American Military Government
   (AMGOT), 320, 360
Anders, General Władysław, 344
Andreev, A. A., 176, 182, 212
Anglo-Russian agreement (1907), 224
Anglo-Soviet Treaty of Alliance (1941),
   224, 322, 328–9, 336, 342, 385
Anti-Comintern Pact (1936), 174, 186,
   188
anti-fascist Committees (Antifas), 308

anti-Semitism, 256, 264. *See also* Jews
   Ukraine, 265
Antonescu, Ion, 365
Antonov-Ovseenko, V. A., 52, 124
Anvelt, Jan, 211
Apresov, G. A., 141
Ardahan, 2, 61, 338–9, 405
Armand, Inessa, 38
Armenia, Armenians, 2, 4, 33–4, 44, 59,
   60–1, 65, 88, 93, 127, 175, 180–1,
   220, 338–9
Armstrong, John, 275
Astakov, Georgii, 195
Atlantic Charter, 284, 329, 330, 342
Atwood, Christopher, 395
Augustinas, Voldemar, 188
Austria, Austrians, 49, 183, 310–16, 354
Austria-Hungary, 2, 49
Austro-Marxism, 36, 37, 40
Azerbaizhan, Azerbaizhani, 19, 28–33, 59,
   60, 61–2, 64, 65, 127, 175, 181, 217,
   220, 284, 376, 377–91, 402, 406

Badoglio, Pietro, 304, 357, 359, 365
Bagirov (Baqirov), Mir Jafar, 181, 377,
   383, 385–6, 391
Balkaria, 274
Bandera, Stepan, 263. *See also* OUN
Barzani, Mulla Mustafa, 386
Bashkirs, 58, 66, 69, 71, 77
Basmachis, 60, 75, 77, 128, 140, 182
Belgium, Belgians, 188, 325, 340, 406
Belorussia, Belorussians, 44–5, 54, 57, 61,
   110, 113, 116, 121, 198, 199, 200–4,
   252, 260–1, 268–71, 276–7, 331, 405
Beneš, Edvard, 213, 286, 302, 327, 332–5,
   363
Beria, Lavrentii, 179–81, 194, 202–4, 246,
   247, 258, 267, 269–71, 273, 276,
   277–9, 305, 339, 377
Bermondt-Avalov, Pavel, 187
Berne incident, 290

Bessarabia, 2, 110, 154, 198, 213–16, 226, 233, 254, 325, 330, 348, 405
Bidault, Georges, 364
Blue Division (Spain), 366
Bogdo Khan, 143–4
Bogomolov, Alexander, 361
Bolsheviks, 5–8
Bolshevism, Bolsheviks, 2–3, 5–6, 11–12, 27, 34–5, 41, 61, 62, 90
  in Azerbaizhan, 62
  in Georgia, 18–19
  in South Caucasus, 25, 31, 32–4
  in Ukraine, 48–9, 53
borderland thesis (defined), 34–5
Borovets, Taras (Taras Bulba), 264, 271
British Special Operations Executive, 368
Brotherhoods of Ukrainian Nationalists (DUN), 264
Budenny, Semeon, 56, 266
Bukharin, N. I., 42, 55, 66, 68, 71, 93, 101, 154, 156–7, 178, 180, 182, 235–7
Bukovina, 116, 178, 212–13, 263, 325
Bulgaria, Bulgarians, 2, 90, 175, 224, 225, 240, 327, 336–7, 338, 351, 354, 375
Bund, 34–5
Buryats, 84, 144–6
Byrnes, James, 401

Caballero, Largo, 162, 166
Carol, King of Romania, 212
Carr, E. H., 177
Casablanca Conference (1943), 289
Caserta Agreement, 372
Caucasian Bureau (Kavbiuro), 60, 64–5, 179
Central Bureau of the Communist Organizations of the Peoples of the East (Musbiuro), 45, 74
Central Council (Rada) (Belorussia), 268
Central Council of Trade Unions (Iran), 379
Četniks (Yugoslavia), 352
Ch'angch'un, 401
Chahar, 399
Chamberlain, Neville, 185, 197
Chechen-Ingush Autonomous Republic, 179, 273
Chiang Ching-kuo, 403
Chiang Kai-shek, 97, 100, 135, 169–73, 226–7, 235, 286, 340, 365, 394–6, 398, 400–3
Chicherin, Georgii, 58–9, 60–1, 65, 71, 83, 104–5, 153–4

China, Chinese, 2, 17, 70, 80–4, 90, 100–1, 104, 129–44, 161, 169–73, 175, 199, 222, 226–31, 234–5, 284, 330, 340, 376, 386, 391–403, 406, 407, 408
Chinese Revolution (1911), 134, 143
Chinese Revolution (1927), 144
Chinese–Soviet Treaty of Friendship, 400–2
Chitadze, Gola, 25
Chkheidze, Nikolai, 27
Cho Man-sik, 318
Choibalsang, Khorloogin, 83, 143, 393, 395
Chou En-lai, 171
Chubar, Vlas, 115, 117, 120, 177
Chuikov, V. I., 226–7
Churchill, Winston, 57, 61, 232, 287–9, 300, 304, 313, 324, 328, 330–2, 337–9, 349, 352, 357–8, 364, 368–9, 374
collectivization, 92, 100, 102, 151, 163, 175, 243, 273, 281, 325
  in Belorussia, 122
  in Central Asia, 140
  in Kazakhstan, 141
  in Mongolia, 148
  in North Caucasus, 179
  in South Caucasus, 126–8
  in Ukraine, 53, 105–9, 112–13, 116–23
colonization
  Chinese in Manchuria, 133–4
  German, 250–1, 252, 253, 256, 326
  Germans in Romania, 214
  Japanese in Manchuria, 131–2, 135
  of kresy, 113–14
  of Russian Empire, 4
  of Ukraine, 7
  Polish, 332
  Russian, 256
  Russians in Mongolia, 82
Comintern (Third International), 6, 12, 43, 45, 55, 58, 62, 72, 73, 88, 90, 91, 99, 103, 110, 111, 115, 123, 139, 144, 145, 150, 157, 158, 160, 161, 169, 210–11, 235–42, 243, 284, 306, 320, 334, 344, 383, 406
Commission on Armistice Problems, 299, 302, 306–7, 324
Commission on Dismemberment, 301
Commission on Questions of the Peace Treaties and Postwar Construction, 298–301
Commission on Reparations, 294–7

Committee for the Freedom of the People of Russia (KONR), 275
Committee for the Preparation of Korean Independence, 318
Committee of National Liberation (Italy), 360
Committee of the Life (Resurrection) of Kurdistan, 385
Communism, Communist parties
  Armenian Communist Party, 180–1
  Azerbaizhani Communist Party, 32–3, 62, 181, 377
  Belgian Communist Party, 239
  Belorussian Communist Party, 261, 277
  Bessarabian Communist Party, 215
  British Communist Party, 240
  Chinese Communist Party, 97, 100, 129, 130, 138–9, 142–3, 144, 169–73, 226–7, 235, 240, 319, 391–2, 395, 401–3, 406
  Communist Party of Eastern Galicia, 110
  Communist Party of South Korea, 320
  Communist Party of West Ukraine, 110, 114–16
  Czechoslovak Communist Party, 116, 236, 334
  Estonian Communist Party, 210–11
  Finnish Communist Party, 208, 316, 354
  French Communist Party, 104, 239, 240
  Georgian Communist Party, 64, 180
  German Communist Party, 104, 236, 240, 303, 306, 307–10, 311
  Greek Communist Party (ELAS), 284, 349, 352, 367–9, 370–4
  Greek Communists (EAM), 367–74
  in Austria, 312–16
  in Czechoslovakia, 363
  in Finland, 349, 351, 352–4
  in Hungary, 350–1
  in South Caucasus, 65–6
  Inner Mongolian Communist Party, 146
  Iranian Communist Party, 62–4, 217, 284, 378
  Italian Communist Party, 359–60
  Korean Communist Party, 319, 320–1
  Latvian Communist Party, 210–11
  Lithuanian Communist Party, 211–12
  Mongolian People's Revolutionary Party, 143, 145
  North Korean Communist Party, 320
  Persian Communist Party, 383
  Polish Communist Party, 110–11, 114, 116, 236–7, 345

  Popular Revolutionary Party of Tuva, 147
  Romanian Communist Party, 116, 237
  Spanish Communist Party, 161, 163–9, 366
  Transcarpathian Communist Party, 334
  Turkmen Communist Party, 182
  Ukrainian Communist Party, 47, 53, 111, 114, 115, 116, 119, 120, 215, 262
  Ukrainian Socialist Revolutionary Party (Borobitsy), 112
  West Belorussian Communist Party, 110, 175
  West Ukrainian Communist Party, 175, 236
  Yugoslavian Communist Party, 237
Communist University of the Toilers of the East, 238
Cossacks, 49, 51, 60, 84–5, 144, 265–6, 272–3
Council of the Confederation of the Caucasus, 180
Crimea, 51, 263, 265–6, 280
Curzon, George, 55, 56–7, 331
Curzon Line, 54, 323, 331–2, 341, 347, 362, 363
Czechoslovak government-in-exile, 327, 332–6
Czechoslovakia, Czechs, 44, 55, 61, 157, 185, 186, 189, 322, 323, 325, 326, 327–8, 330, 332–6, 405, 406, 407, 408

Dairen, 136, 340, 400–2, 405
Danzig, 186–7, 188, 195, 346
Dashnaks, 111
De Gaulle, Charles, 342–4, 361–5
De Wang (Prince Demchugdongrob), 394–5
Declaration on Liberated Territories, 284, 330, 356, 404. See also Yalta Conference
Dekanozov, Vladimir, 209
Denikin, Anton, 54, 60
Department of Foreign Affairs of the Central Committee, 298
deportations. See forced population transfers
Diaz, José, 163, 165–6, 168
Dimenshtein, S., 110
Dimitrov, Georgi, 158, 160–1, 163–4, 172, 175, 198, 205, 237, 238–9, 241, 305, 307, 334, 344, 349, 350, 407
Djilas, Milovan, 285

Dmowski, Roman, 54, 113
Donbas, 328
Donetsk, 254
Droz, Humbert, 235
Dzerzhinskii, F. E., 101
Dzhibladze, Silvester, 25

East Prussia, 299–301, 323, 328, 331, 332, 346, 349, 405
Eden, Anthony, 222, 287, 299, 322–4, 326, 328–9, 332, 351, 358, 368, 371
Egypt, 370, 391
Ejtima-i-Amiyyun (Social Democracy), 31–2
Enver Pasha, 337
Estonia, Estonians, 2, 45, 123, 125, 174, 175, 193, 204, 205, 208–9, 252, 257, 259–60, 268, 277, 285, 324, 330
European Advisory Commission (EAC), 295, 301, 306, 358, 363
Extraordinary Law on Crimes against the Republic (China), 170
Ezhov, N. I., 176, 237

Far East region, 137
Far Eastern Republic, 2, 86–8
Federation of Foreign Communists, 45
Fierlinger, Zdeněk, 327
Finland, Finns, 4, 45, 88, 104, 123, 125, 174, 175, 191–2, 200, 204–8, 216, 223–4, 233, 257, 268, 310, 322, 323, 324, 325, 326, 329, 349, 352–4, 405, 406, 407
Firqeh (Azerbaizhan Democratic Party), 383–4, 387, 390
First All-Russian Congress of Communist Organizations of the Eastern Peoples, 72
First Cavalry Army, 332
Fisher, Louis, 153
Five-Year Plans, 92, 105, 163
First Five-Year Plan, 92, 103, 122, 148–9
Second Five-Year Plan, 122
forced population transfers, 248, 276
"social undesireables" from Romania, 214
Crimean Tatars, 280
Germans, 322, 326–8
Hungarians from Czechoslovakia, 327
in Soviet frontier zones, 125
Irans from Azerbaizhani frontier, 220
Kalmyks, 273
North Caucasus, 267
Poles, 325

Transcaucasia, 280
Ukrainians, 253
Volga Germans, 258
Fourth Lend-Lease Protocol. *See*
Lend-Lease agreements
France, French, 2, 58, 100, 124–5, 154, 156, 157, 178, 181, 185, 189, 193, 196–7, 200, 212, 221, 225–6, 282, 289, 300, 330, 340, 361–5, 367, 406, 407
Franco, Francisco, 161, 365–6
Franco-Soviet Treaty, 364
Fuhrnberg, Friedel, 315–16

Galaktinov, M. P., 299
Galicia, 51, 54, 55, 56, 190, 254, 262, 271, 279, 325
Galician Division (Waffen SS), 264, 271
Gansu, 139, 140, 141, 170, 396
General Government (German-occupied Poland), 262
Georgia, Georgians, 5, 11, 12–27, 34, 44, 52, 59, 64–6, 74, 76, 88, 93, 109, 127, 280, 285
German Democratic Republic (GDR), 238, 303, 408
German–Soviet Boundary Treaty (1939), 201
German–Turkish Treaty of Friendship, 336
Germany, Germans, 1, 2, 10, 36, 49–51, 53, 90, 104–5, 121, 124–5, 129, 148, 151, 153, 154, 155–6, 159, 178, 180, 185–99, 201, 204–5, 208, 209, 212–17, 218–24, 226, 230–2, 233–4, 240, 246–7, 254, 282, 284, 287, 295, 297–316, 323, 326, 330, 333, 342, 354
Gerö, Ernö, 350
Gilan Republic, 181, 383
Goebbels, Joseph, 253, 290, 404
Goldman, Wendy Z., 164
Goltz, Colmar Freiherr von der, 187
Gomułka, Władysław, 346
Göring, Herman, 186
GPU, 79–80
Great Britain, British, 58, 60, 100, 103–4, 127, 153, 155, 156, 181, 185, 186–7, 189, 193, 196–7, 200, 221–6, 247, 277, 282, 284, 286, 299, 304, 311, 322–4, 327, 330, 373, 406
Greater East Asian Co-Prosperity Sphere, 132, 223
Greece, Greeks, 175, 226, 240, 244, 340, 349–50, 352, 358, 367–76, 391, 406
Greek Civil War, 367–76

Greek government-in-exile, 349, 367, 368, 370
Grenier, Fernand, 362
Grin'ko, Grigorii, 177
Gromyko, Andrei, 294
Guria, 17
Gusev, F. T., 301, 371

Harriman, W. Averell, 295, 296, 339, 361, 401
Harris, James, 100
Hebrang, Andreas, 352
Himmat (Endeavor) Party, 16, 30–1
Himmler, Heinrich, 253, 274
Hindenberg, Paul von, 187
Hitler, Adolf, 10, 57, 88, 125, 148, 156, 185–6, 187, 191, 194, 196–7, 201, 217, 218, 221, 223–4, 246, 247, 249, 250, 251, 252, 253, 255, 256, 262, 263, 266, 274, 288, 304, 308, 336, 354, 359, 362, 364, 404
Holloway, David, 247
Holocaust, 248, 250–1, 253, 256
    Austria, 312
    Belorussia, 261
    Latvia, 260
    Lithuania, 258–9
    Ukraine, 265
Home Guard (Belorussian), 260
Home Guard (*Omakaitse*) (Estonia), 260
Hopkins, Harry, 296, 318
Horthy, Admiral Miklós, 350, 365
Hungary, Hungarians, 2, 55, 58, 90, 93, 189–90, 238, 240, 295, 310, 327, 328, 335, 350–1, 352, 354, 408

Ibárruri, Dolores, 163
Ibrahim Beg, 128
Igna'ev, A. A., 299
Ikramov, Akmal, 182
Ili, 397
India, Indians, 43
Indonesia, 391
Ingria, 233
Ingush, 273
inner periphery (defined), 283–4
Inonu, Ismet, 336–7
Ioffe, Adolph, 143
Iran, Iranians, 2, 9, 29, 31, 32, 44, 59, 61–4, 104, 175, 217–22, 224, 284, 315, 345, 376, 377–91, 406
Iriye, Akira, 136
Isakov, Admiral I. S., 299, 306
Italy, Italians, 93, 189, 198, 213–14, 223, 224, 225, 230, 240, 290, 304, 306,

323, 326, 330, 337, 357–61, 363, 367, 368, 370, 406, 407
Ivanov-Rinov, General Pavel, 84

Japan, Japanese, 1, 2, 10, 80–8, 100, 121, 129–40, 148–50, 151, 153, 154, 155, 156, 161, 169–74, 176, 198, 199, 222–3, 224, 226–32, 283, 284, 287, 316, 330–1, 394–5, 406
Jehol, 399
Jews, 243, 253, 256, 257
    Austria, 312
    Belorussia, 260
    Bukovina, 325
    German occupation, 250–1
    in Baltic littoral, 204
    in Romania, 214
    in Soviet-occupied Poland, 201–2
    in Ukraine, 113
    Latvia, 260
    Lithuania, 258–9
    pogroms, 257
    resistance, 269
    Ukraine, 265, 271
Jiang Jingguo, 393
Jibladze, Sylvester, 17
Johnston, Eric, 293
Jones, S. F., 17
Judeo-Bolshevism, 250, 264–5. *See also* anti-Semitism, Holocaust, Jews

Kabardino-Balkarian Autonomous Republic, 274
Kaganovich, Lazar, 112, 114–15, 117, 119, 124
Kaledin, Ataman Aleksei, 49
Kalinin, Mikhail, 26, 70
Kalmykov, B. E., 179
Kalmykov, Ivan, 84
Kalmyks, 70, 84, 146, 273
Kamenev, Sergei, 56–7, 64, 101, 158, 164
Kaminsky Brigade, 269
Kandelaki, David, 159
Karachaev, 273–4
Karakhan, Lev, 124, 143
Kardelj, Edvard, 352
Karelia, 192, 207, 324
Kars, 2, 51, 61, 338–9, 405
Katyn massacre, 332, 345
Kautsky, Karl, 36
Kavtaradze, Sergei, 380
Kazakhstan, Kazakhs, 71–2, 77, 121, 140, 141, 151, 182, 397
Kellogg–Briand Pact, 105, 153–4
Kemal, Mustafa ("Ataturk"), 60, 61, 286

Kesselring, Albert, 290
Khadzhaev, Faisullah, 182
Khandzhian, A., 181
Kholm, 272
Khomeriki, Noe, 17
Kim Il-sung, 319, 320
Kirchenstein, A., 210
Kirghiz, 45, 66, 121, 139, 141
Kirov, Sergei, 56, 60, 62–3, 125, 159, 236
Kleist, Field Marshal von, 253
Koch, Erich, 253
Kolchak, Alexander, 82, 85–6, 146
Komsomol, 127, 182, 212, 257, 274, 279
Königsberg, 300, 323, 331, 405
Konovalets, Evhen, 263
Koplenig, Johann, 315–16
Korea, Koreans, 131, 132, 173, 316–21, 405
Korneichuk, O., 345
Kornilov, General Lavr, 49
Kościuszko Division, 345
Kosior, S. V., 117
kresy, 55, 88, 110, 116, 201, 202, 325, 326, 328, 332, 341, 345
Krupskaya, N., 39
Krylov, S. B., 299
Kuban, 110, 120, 272–3
Kuchuk Khan, 61, 62–3
Kuibyshev, Valerian, 77
Kuomintang (Chinese Nationalist Party), 97, 129, 134, 135–6, 139, 141, 144, 169–73, 226–7, 240, 315, 391–2, 395–6, 398, 399–403
Kurdistan, Kurds, 110, 378, 379, 381, 385–8, 391
Kurile Islands, 86–8, 230, 231, 339–40, 405
Kursk, 256, 292, 303, 397
Kuusinen, Otto, 206
Kwantung Army, 80, 130, 131, 135, 136–7, 173, 227, 317, 394, 399

Lange, Oscar, 298
Lattimore, Owen, 84, 139, 393, 395
Latvia, Latvians, 2, 44, 45, 53, 58, 105, 123, 175, 193, 204, 205, 208–9, 252, 257, 259–60, 268, 278, 285, 324, 330
League of Nations, 124, 157
Lebanon Charter, 371
Lend-Lease agreements, 287, 288, 291–4, 296
Lenin, V. I., 3, 9, 33–4, 35, 36–42, 44, 45–7, 49–66, 69–71, 72–3, 75–9, 90–1, 93–5, 97, 99, 118–20, 161, 163–4, 179, 205, 206, 286, 307, 331, 407

Leninism, 45, 91, 94, 119, 150
Lentsman, Jan, 211
Li Li-san, 138–9
Lithuania, Lithuanians, 2, 45, 53, 105, 123, 125, 187–8, 201, 205, 208–9, 223, 252, 257, 258–9, 278–9, 285, 324, 329–30
Litvinov, Maksim, 123, 124, 153–4, 157, 158–60, 183–5, 191–4, 220–1, 233–4, 284, 298, 299, 301
Litvinov Commission, 302, 361
Loly, O. N., 38
London Protocol (1933), 123
Lozovskii, S. A., 157, 298, 300–1
Luxemburg, Rosa, 36–7, 45, 111

Macedonia, Macedonians, 175
MacVeagh, Lincoln, 370, 371, 375
Maiskii, Ivan, 185, 193, 222, 294–5, 299, 301, 306, 307, 332
Makharadze, Pilipe, 18, 20–1, 25, 33
Makhnovites, 120
Maksimov, M., 381
Malenkov, Georgii, 194, 276
Malinovskii, General Rodion, 399, 400–1
Manchuria (Manchukuo), 2, 80–4, 129–39, 150, 151, 173, 227, 231, 284, 295, 316–19, 322, 330, 337, 340, 376, 393, 395, 398–403, 405, 406, 407
Mannerheim, Karl, 354, 365
Manstein, Field Marshal von, 253
Manuilskii, D. Z., 53, 77–8, 157, 198, 298, 300, 306
Mao Zedong, 17, 97, 142, 171, 235, 319, 392, 399
Mao Zemin, 396
Maritime Provinces, 80, 88, 131, 137, 155, 173, 174, 405
Marshall, George C., 296, 297
Martikian, S. N., 181
Martin, Terry, 122
Marxism in South Caucasus, 18–21
Marxism-Leninism, 100, 129, 151, 285–6, 379, 381, 387, 407
Matsuoka Yōsuke, 134–5, 230–2
Mdivani, Budu, 179
Medvedev, Roy, 121
Mekhlis, Lev, 270
Mel'nyk, Andrei, 263. *See also* OUN
Menemenciolğlo, Numan, 225
Mengkukuo, 395
Menshevism, Mensheviks, 11, 86, 164
    in Georgia, 16–19, 25, 27, 30, 33–5, 37, 65, 180
Menzhinskii, V. R., 80, 102–3
Meretskov, General K. A., 206

Merkulov, Colonel, 314
mesame-dasi, 25–6, 27
Michael, King of Romania, 350
Mihailović, Draža, 352
Mikoian, A. I., 59, 292–3, 313
Mikołajczek, Stanisław, 341, 347
Milli Farka Party, 266
Millspaugh, Arthur, 218
Millward, James, 139
Ministry of Power and Electricity (Austria), 315
Moldavia, Moldavians, 110, 117, 214, 215, 330
Moldova, Moldovans, 4
Molotov, V. M., 124, 130, 153, 158–9, 162, 164, 193–9, 205, 212–13, 222–4, 225–33, 285, 287–8, 291, 293, 301, 302, 304, 324, 328, 329–30, 331, 335–6, 340, 346, 349, 350, 351, 361, 362, 388, 398, 399, 401
Mongolia, Mongolians, 2, 80–4, 129, 132, 143–6, 148, 173, 231, 392–5
Inner Mongolia, 82, 129, 139, 144, 145, 394–5
Outer Mongolia, 2, 82, 83–4, 85, 143, 145, 174, 227–30, 234, 340, 376, 395, 405
Montreux Convention (1924), 223, 337–9
Morgenthau, Henry, 294
Moscow Conference of Foreign Ministers, 297, 321, 357, 358, 360, 363
Mossadegh, Dr. Muhammed, 380
Munich Conference (1938), 185, 189, 332, 335
Mussavetists, 111, 180
Mussolini, Benito, 189, 304, 357, 358

Nadir Shah, 127
Nagorno-Karabakh, 28, 33
Narimanov, Nariman, 31–3, 61
Narkomindel, 12
National Committee for a Free Germany, 303–5
National Committee for the Liberation of Yugoslavia, 352
national committees
Czechoslovakia, 334
Poland, 345
Transcarpathian (*Zakarpatskaia*) Ukraine, 333
National Congress of Azerbaizhan, 383
National Council of the Resistance, 362
National Socialism (ideology), 249–51
Nationalist Military Detachments (VVN), 264

nationality policy, 4–5, 44–7, 66–71, 106–9
in Ukraine, 105–25
korenezatsiia (indigenization), 66–7, 107, 126, 141, 146
Nazi–Soviet non-aggression pact (1939), 173, 180, 181, 194, 198, 199, 200, 221, 223, 225, 227, 239, 323, 341
Negrin, Juan, 166–7, 169
Nelson, Donald, 302
Nemets, F., 333, 334
Netherlands, Dutch, 188, 325
New Democracy, 319
New Economic Policy (NEP), 92
Ninoshvili, E. F., 25
NKGB, 270
NKVD, 122, 143, 176, 194, 211, 221, 236, 238, 245, 258, 263, 268, 269–71, 273–4, 276, 277, 278–80, 281, 295, 310, 317, 332, 334, 347, 348
Normandie-Nieman squadron, 362, 365
North Caucasian mountain peoples, 180
Northern Bukovina, 325
Novikov, Nikolai, 371
Nuri Pasha, 336

OGPU, 102–3, 112–13, 116, 126–8, 140–1. *See also* NKVD, GPU
oil industry, 9, 16, 19, 27–8, 29–30, 60, 61, 64, 86, 141, 142, 170, 181, 192, 221–2, 224, 230, 244, 295, 315, 331, 364, 378, 379–82, 384, 388–90, 396
Operation Barbarossa, 197, 224, 227, 243, 251, 257, 283
Operation Burza (Tempest), 269
Ordzhonikidze, Sergo, 32, 33, 56, 59–60, 62–5, 124
Organization of Ukrainian Nationalists (OUN), 114, 178, 201, 264, 265
OUN-B, 263–4, 271
OUN-M, 263
Ottoman Empire, 2, 50, 242
outer periphery (defined), 283–4

pan-Asianism, 132
pan-Islamism, 18, 29, 111, 140
pan-Mongolism, 82–3, 145, 147
pan-Turkism, 18, 29, 60, 111, 128, 140, 280, 336–7
Papandreou, George, 370–3
Paris Peace Conference (1919), 83, 132, 187
Paris Peace Conference (World War II), 389
partisans (Yugoslavia), 352, 367. *See also* Tito, Josip Broz

Pauker, Ana, 237
Pauker, Marcel, 237
Paulus, Field Marshal Edwin von, 304
Payne, Stanley, 167, 168
People's Party (*Volkspartei*) (Austria),
    312–14
Persian Soviet Republic, 62
Pestkowski, Stanislas, 45
Petliura, Simeon, 48, 51, 55, 117, 120,
    262, 264
Petrov, General, I. E., 334–5
Piatakov, Grigory, 52–3
Piatnitskii, Osip, 38
Pieck, Wilhelm, 307–8
Piłsudski, Józef, 54–5, 115, 117, 286, 342
Pipes, Richard, 39
Pishevari, Mir Jafar, 62, 383–4, 388, 390–1
Plekhanov, Georgii, 25, 35
Pokrovskii, M. N., 298
Poland, Poles, 2, 4, 18, 37, 44, 45, 53–7,
    61, 88, 93, 96, 103, 104, 105–6,
    112–14, 123, 124–5, 150, 154, 174,
    186–7, 188–9, 196–9, 200–4, 213,
    223, 242, 243, 250, 252, 254, 256,
    284, 288, 322, 323, 324–5, 326–7,
    329, 330, 331–2, 340–7, 352, 362,
    363–4
Poletskice, Justas, 210
Polish Committee of National Liberation,
    331, 341, 346–7, 364
Polish Defense Corps, 178
Polish government-in-exile (London
    Poles), 61, 202, 282, 321, 329, 332,
    341–5, 347
Polish Home Army, 114, 267, 268, 272,
    277, 279, 332, 345, 347, 360, 363
Polish Military Organization, 236
Polish Workers Party (PPR), 344–5
Political Committee of National Liberation
    (PEEA), 369
Pomerania, 301, 332
Ponomarenko, Panteleimon, 176, 261,
    269–71
Pons, Silvio, 100
Popov, Colonel Gregori, 371, 372, 374
Poqelman, Hans, 211
Porrkala-Ud, 324
Port Arthur, 340, 400, 402, 405
Portsmouth Treaty (1905), 230
Postyshev, P. P., 120, 177
Potemkin, V. P., 299
Potsdam Conference, 287, 296, 318, 338,
    366, 375, 404
    Austria, 313–14
Pravda, 47, 48, 57, 66, 100

Prieto, Indalecio, 166
prisoners of war, 45, 250, 256, 259, 274,
    303, 305, 341
Profintern, 157
Promethean League, 174
propaganda, 27, 31, 62
    Comintern, 161, 240
    German, 156, 158, 253, 262, 287, 289,
        290. *See also* Goebbels, Joseph
    Japanese, 132
    National Committee for a Free
        Germany, 304
    pan-Islamist, 140
    Soviet, 5, 74, 101, 111, 114, 129, 256,
        290, 302, 303, 326–7, 328, 339
purges, 121, 175–83, 243, 246, 270, 298
    anti-Soviet purge in Iran, 220
    of Afghans, 175
    of Armenian Communist Party, 180–1
    of Azerbaizhani Communist Party, 181
    of Belorussian Communist Party, 178
    of Belorussian Party, 176
    of Bulgarians, 175
    of Chinese, 175
    of Comintern, 235–42
    of Estonian Communist Party, 210–11
    of Estonians, 175
    of Finns, 175
    of Georgian Communist Party, 179–80
    of Germans, 175, 176
    of Greeks, 175
    of Iranians, 175
    of Kazakh parties, 182
    of "Kharbintsy," 176
    of Kurds, 175
    of Latvian Communist Party, 210–11
    of Latvians, 175
    of Lithuanian Communist Party, 211–12
    of Macedonians, 175
    of national deviationists, 122, 175
    of Ossetian obkom bureau, 179
    of Poles, 175, 176
    of Polish Communist Party, 88
    of "Polish operation," 237
    of Polish prisoners of war, 202–4
    of Romanians, 175
    of Tadjikistan Party, 182
    of Tatar Bolsheviks, 126
    of Uzbeks, 182
    of West Belorussian Communist Party,
        175
    of West Ukrainian Party, 175
    in North Caucasus, 179
    in Ukraine, 177–9
    Iranians, 175

Quasi Mohammad, 387

Radek, Karl, 124
railroads
  Chinese Eastern Railroad, 129–30, 134,
    137–8, 144, 176, 183, 340, 402, 405
  Southern Manchurian Railroad, 131,
    134, 136, 340, 399, 402
  Trans-Siberian Railroad, 146, 393
  Turkistan–Siberian (Turksib) Railroad,
    140
Rákosi, Mátyás, 350
Rakovski, Khristian, 53, 71, 76, 177
Ramashvili, Isidor, 17, 25, 27
Ramzin, L. K., 102–3
Rasulzade, M. E., 30–1, 63–4
Reichstag Fire Trials, 160
religion
  Buddhism, 4
  conversion, 178
  Greek Catholic Church, 262, 281
  Islam, 4
  Judaism, 4
  Latvian Lutheran Church, 278
  Lutheran Church (Finland), 207
  Protestant, 4
  Roman Catholicism, 4
  Russian Orthodox Church, 4, 215, 262,
    281
  Ukrainian Autocephalous Church, 113,
    252
Renner, Karl, 313–14
reparations, 298, 309, 310, 348
Revolutionary Socialist Party (Austria),
  312
Reza Shah, 222, 377–8, 380, 385
Ribbentrop, Joachim von, 187–8, 194–5,
  198, 204, 223, 230
Rinchino, El'bekdorzhi, 144, 145–6
Roma, 253
Romania, Romanians, 2, 55, 61, 93, 96,
  103, 104, 110, 123, 125, 154, 175,
  192, 196, 202, 212–17, 223–4, 226,
  233, 244, 254, 263, 295, 310, 322,
  323, 325, 327, 328, 330, 338,
  347–50, 354, 372, 375, 399, 408
Romer, Tadeus, 266–7
Roosevelt, Franklin D., 57, 61, 232,
  287–9, 295, 296, 304, 324, 330–2,
  339, 341, 347, 357, 368, 370, 371,
  372
Rosenberg, Alfred, 252–3
Rotshtein, F. A., 63
Roy, M. N., 73
Ruhr, 297, 301–2, 310–11

Ruppen, Robert, 145
Russian Civil War (1918–22), 2, 5, 7, 44,
  47, 143, 157, 175, 183, 187, 242,
  255, 259, 266, 272, 275, 281, 342
Russian Liberation Movement, 275. See
  also Vlasov, Major-General Andrei
  Andreevich
Russian Revolution (1905), 14, 16, 28, 30,
  34, 163
Russian Revolution (1917), 32, 210
  February Revolution, 12, 164, 205–6
  October Revolution, 41–2
Russian Soviet Federated Socialist
  Republic (RSFSR), 69, 109, 121
russification, 11, 17, 108–9
Russo-Japanese War (1904–5), 231
Rykov, A. I., 104
Rykov–Iagoda Commission, 117

Sadchikov, Ivan, 390
Sakhalin, 86–8, 224, 230–1, 339, 340, 405
San Francisco Conference, 365
Sapir, Jacques, 291–2
Saraçoğlu, Şükrü, 225–6
Schulenburg, F. W., 194, 196, 209, 212
Scobie, Lieutenant-General Ronald, 372–4
Second Socialist International, 35, 93
Seidlitz, General Walter von, 304
Semenov, Ataman Grigorii, 82
Semenov, Iu. I., 39
Seton-Watson, Hugh, 215
Shaposhnikov, B. M., 244, 299, 324
shatter zones (definition), 4–5
Shaumian, Stepan, 33, 38–9
Shcherbatov, Alexander, 303
Sheng Shicai, 140–3, 396–8
Sheptyts'kyi, Andrei, 190, 262, 271–2
Shtein, Boris, 298
Shumskyi, O. I., 112, 114–16
Siantos, Giorgios, 367, 373
Siare, Karl, 257
Siberia, 2, 11, 80, 86, 130, 143, 174
Sikorski, General Władysław, 341–4
Silesia, 300–1, 332, 346
Skoropads'kyi, Hetman Pavlo, 51, 262,
  263
Skrypnik, Mykola, 49, 93, 111, 118–20
Smolensk, 261
Snyder, Timothy, 255
Social Democracy
  German Social Democratic Party, 36,
    157, 310
  Hnchak (Armenian Social Democratic
    Party), 32
  Latvian Social Democracy, 37

Social Democracy (*cont.*)
  Russian Social Democratic Labor Party,
    26, 29, 31, 33, 34–5, 37
  Social Democratic Party (Austria),
    312–14
  Spilka (Ukrainian Social Democratic
    Union), 34
Soong, T. V., 392, 394, 398, 400–1
Sorge, Victor, 247
South Caucasian Federation, 69
Soviet Far Eastern Command, 399
Soviet–Chinese Treaty of Friendship, 393,
  395
Soviet–Finnish War (1939–40), 191, 208,
  260, 324
Soviet–Japanese Neutrality Treaty, 396
Soviet–Polish War (1920), 106, 202, 332
Soviet–Turkish Treaty of Non-Aggression,
  338
Sovnarkom, 274
Spain, Spanish, 161–9, 199, 238, 331,
  366
  Spanish Civil War (1936–9), 161–9,
    237, 249, 366
Spandarian, Suren, 33
Stalin (Dzhugashvili, Koba)
  as Commissar of Nationalities, 43–7
  at wartime conferences, 61, 254, 289,
    296, 318, 327, 331, 332, 338, 339,
    365, 374, 378
  borderland thesis, 34–5
  in 1917 Revolution, 42
  in Civil War and Intervention, 43–7
  in Civil War and Intervention in
    Ukraine, 47–58
  in struggle for power, 65–71
  "man of the borderlands," 9–10
  on "socialism in one country," 92–6
  on British and American alliance,
    286–92
  on civil war in South Caucasus, 58–71
  on collectivization, 53, 92, 100, 102,
    105, 106
  on Comintern, 235–42
  on industrialization, 92, 100, 102–3,
    107–9, 122. *See also* Five-Year Plans
  on intermediate stages of socialism, 96–7
  on intervention in Poland, 53–8
  on intervention in Spain, 161–9
  on relations with foreign communist
    parties. *See* individual parties
  on relations with foreign countries. *See*
    individual countries
  on relations with Muslim communists,
    71–80
  on relationship with Lenin, 38–41, 56–8
  on relationship with Trotsky, 51–2, 79,
    92–5
  on war aims, 253–5, 285–6. *See also*
    Chapters 8–10
  on war scares, 100–5
  youth in Georgia, 21–7
Stalingrad, 256, 267, 271, 273, 302–3, 397
State Committee of Defense (GOKO),
  258, 280, 347
Stepanian, Nersik, 180
Stettinius, Edward, 296
Stockholm Congress (1906), 11
Stomoniakov, B. S., 218–20
Straits Convention, 339
Stuchka, P. I., 38, 211
Sub-Carpatho Ukraine, 116, 178, 189–91,
  213, 263, 325, 332–6, 405. *See also*
  Czechoslovakia
Sudetenland, 189, 328
Sukhe Bator, 83, 143
Sultan-Galiev, Mirza, 45, 72–4, 76–80, 92,
  126
Sultan-Girei Klych, 180
Sultanzade (Mikhailian), 62–3, 73, 383
Sun Yat-sen, 394
Surits, Jacob, 160, 185, 298
Susaikov, General I. Z., 347
Svolos, Alexandros, 371
Sweden, Swedish, 192, 242, 268
Syria, 391

Tadjikistan, Tadjiks, 128, 182–3
Tanu Tuva, Tuvans, 144, 146–50, 405
Tarim Basin, 139–40
Tarle, Evgenii, 298
Tatars, 44, 58, 66, 69, 71–3, 121, 126,
  174, 265–6, 280
Teheran Conference, 254, 287, 289, 297,
  299, 305, 322, 330–1, 337
terrorism, 14
Third International. *See* Comintern (Third
  International)
Thorez, Maurice, 239, 241, 363, 364–5,
  367, 374
Tibet, 70, 82
Timoshenko, S. K., 226, 244, 246, 247
Tito, Josip Broz, 17, 237, 351–2, 369
Togliatti, Palmiro, 158, 164–6, 241,
  359–60, 365, 374
Tōgō, Shigenori, 227
Toka, Salčak, 147
Tokushiro, Ohata, 174
Transcaucasia, 122, 127, 280
Transylvania, 240, 348

Treaty of Alliance and Friendship (Xinjiang), 398
Treaty of Brest-Litovsk (1918), 2, 42, 49–53, 93, 175, 180
Treaty of Friendship and Alliance (Iran), 387
Treaty of Locarno (1924), 104
Treaty of Neutrality (1941), 135, 199
Treaty of Versailles, 299
Tripartite Pact, 230, 240
Trotsky, Leonid, 37, 42, 43, 46, 47, 51–2, 56, 62, 64, 66, 68, 72, 73, 75–9, 92, 93–100, 101–2, 154, 156, 180
Troyanovskii, Alexander, 38
Truman, Harry S., 296, 313, 339, 389
Tserendorzh, B., 144
Tsereteli, Grigori, 25
Tskhakaia, Mikha, 25
Tucker, Robert C., 91
Tudeh Party, 378–84, 389–90, 406
Tukhachevskii, M. N., 56, 149–50, 245
Tuominen, Arvo, 206
Turkestan, 2, 44, 60, 62, 69, 74, 140, 141, 252, 397–8
Turkey, Turks, 2, 29, 31, 43, 50, 59, 60–1, 76, 104, 125, 127, 175, 223–6, 336–9
Turkish–Soviet Pact of Mutual Assistance, 225
Turkmenistan, 140

Uighurs, 139–41, 397
Ukraine, Ukrainians, 4, 44, 45, 47–58, 61, 75, 76, 105–6, 112–22, 151, 154, 198, 199, 200–4, 213, 244–5, 247, 251–2, 253, 257, 261–5, 271–2, 279–80, 285, 324–5, 332, 335–6
Ukrainian Central Rada, 48–9, 50–1
Ukrainian Insurgent Army (UPA), 264–5, 271–2, 279, 336
Ukrainian Liberation Army (UVV), 264
Ukrainian National Army (UNA), 264
Ukrainian Revolutionary Council, 52
Ukrainian Revolutionary War, 1918–20, 264
Ukrainian Soviet Socialist Republic (SSR), 69, 110, 111, 213, 236, 263, 333, 345
Ukrainian Union Republic, 215
Ulbricht, Walter, 240, 308
Ungern-Sternberg, Baron Roman, 83
Union for the Liberation of Ukraine, 117
Union of German Officers, 304, 305
Union of Polish Patriots, 345–6
United Nations, 284, 365–6, 389

United States, 86, 104, 137, 154, 157, 158, 277, 282, 284, 286, 299, 304, 311, 328, 330–2, 399, 406
University for the National Minorities of the West, 238
Uzbeks, 128, 182

Validov, Akhmed-Zaki Akhmetovich, 79
Vares, Johannes, 210
Varga, Evgenii, 238
Vatican, 262, 271
Vatutin, General N. F., 244
Vienna Award (1938), 240
Vienna Award (1940), 190
Vlasov Major-General Andrei Andreevich, 274–5
Voevodina, 328
Volga Germans, 66, 121, 258
Volhynia, 55, 113, 114, 116, 178, 179, 213, 263, 271–2, 325
Volksdeutsche, 185, 191, 213, 252
Voroshilov, Kliment, 52, 56, 70, 137, 162, 196, 206, 298, 306–7, 356–7
Voznesenskii, N. A., 292–3
Vyshinskii, Andrei, 30, 202, 209, 310, 359–60, 362

Wang Jingwei, 172
Wang Ming, 171
Wasilewska, Wanda, 345
Weimar Republic, 306, 310
West Belorussia, 54, 88, 111, 200, 285, 324–5, 329, 345
West Ukraine, 54, 88, 111, 178, 200, 214, 285, 324–5, 329, 331, 332, 336, 345, 405
Wrangel, P. N., 55–6

Xinjiang, 2, 129, 139–43, 148, 174, 230, 234, 284, 340, 376, 396–8, 406, 407
Xu Shucheng, 82

Yagoda, Genrikh, 126
Yalta Agreement. *See* Yalta Conference
Yalta Conference, 172, 287, 293, 295, 296, 298, 299, 301, 305, 308, 318, 321, 330–2, 338, 339, 347, 349, 356, 365, 366, 374, 393, 395, 398, 402
Yenan faction, 319
Young Turk revolution (1908), 31
Yugoslavia, 17, 240, 244, 289, 323, 326, 327, 328, 351–2, 358, 367, 369, 386, 389, 407–8

Zachariades, Nikos, 374–5
Zervas, Napoleon, 369
Zhang Xueliang, 135–6
Zhang Zuolin, 86, 129–30, 134–5
Zhdanov, Andrei, 108, 153, 159, 193–4,
    198, 205, 209, 234, 241, 315–16,
    349–51, 352–4

Zhongying, Ma, 141
Zhordania, Noe, 17–18, 25, 27, 33–4,
    180
Zhukov, G. K., 173, 244, 247,
    309–10
Zinoviev, Grigorii, 55, 62, 92, 94–5,
    97–9, 101, 164, 180